A GUIDE TO REINSURANCE LAW

Related titles

Insurance Law: An Introduction
by Robert Merkin
(2007)

Directors' and Officers' Liability
by Adolfo Paolini and Deepak Nambisan
(2007)

Private International Law of Reinsurance and Insurance
by Raymond Cox QC, Louise Merrett and Marcus Smith
(2006)

The Law of Insurance Contracts, 5th Edition
by Professor Malcolm A. Clarke
(2006)

Insurance Disputes, 2nd Edition
by Rt. Hon Lord Justice Mance, Iain Goldrein QC and Robert Merkin
(2004)

Good Faith and Insurance Contracts, 2nd Edition
by Peter MacDonald Eggers, Patrick Foss and Simon Picken
(2004)

A GUIDE TO REINSURANCE LAW

EDITED BY

PROFESSOR ROBERT MERKIN

informa
LONDON
2007

Informa Law
Mortimer House
37–41 Mortimer Street
London W1T 3JH
law.enquiries@informa.com

an Informa business

First published 2007

A catalogue record for this book is available from the British Library

ISBN 978-1-84311-678-3

Typeset by
Interactive Sciences Ltd, Gloucester
Printed in Great Britain by
MPG Books
Bodmin, Cornwall

GENERAL EDITOR'S PREFACE

This book is intended to be a practical guide for lawyers and professionals working in and with the reinsurance market. The publishers have assembled a distinguished team of lawyers and reinsurance practitioners, each of whom has been asked to prepare a practical yet comprehensive guide to the most significant issues affecting reinsurance law and practice. Fully up to date, each chapter sets out the framework of the law, and incorporates commentary on the most important and recent judicial decisions. It is hoped that the structure that has been adopted highlights the key matters which typically arise in reinsurance disputes, and does so in a manner more readily accessible than is often the case where the material is presented in traditional textbook form.

Rob Merkin
Sidmouth
July 2007

AUTHORS' BIOGRAPHIES

Professor Robert Merkin

Professor Robert Merkin is professor of Commercial Law at Southampton University. He is the author of a number of texts on insurance, reinsurance and arbitration law and edits *Lloyd's Law Reports: Insurance and Reinsurance*, and *Insurance Law Monthly*. His works have been cited in several High Court decisions in England together with a number of other jurisdictions including the High Court of Australia and the U.S. Supreme Court. Professor Merkin is a member of the Presidential Council of AIDA, secretary to the AIDA Reinsurance Working Party, a member of the Law Society's Insurance Law Sub-Committee and a past member of the executive committee of the British Insurance Law Association.

Peter Cave

Peter Cave (B.A. Hons) FCII, has worked in the reinsurance and insurance industry for approximately 40 years and has extensive international experience at the highest levels. He has been actively involved in various London Market committees, including both Broker and Market Legal Groups. Before setting up his own training consultancy he was a director of a leading international reinsurance broker with specific territorial production and placing responsibilities—in addition he was actively involved in training. He has been a senior tutor for the CII for many years, chairing an Advanced Study Group on Proportional Treaty Reinsurance. For City University he prepared and delivers the Reinsurance Course within the M.Sc. Banking and Finance Programme. Papers presented include those for Tulane University (U.S.), Moscow Finance Academy and the Insurance Regulatory Authority of Jordan.

Christopher Henley

Christopher Henley, a Fellow of the Chartered Insurance Institute, is a counsel specialising in insurance and reinsurance at the London office of Debevoise & Plimpton LLP. His publications include *The Law of Insurance Broking* and *All Risks Property Insurance* (co-author, which won the British Insurance Law Association prize in 1996). He is a contributing editor of *The Encyclopedia of Insurance Law* and *Astor's Law of Lloyd's*, and has contributed chapters to *Reinsurance Practice and the Law*, *Insurance Disputes* and *Privity of Contract*. He is a member of the Accident Committee and the Advanced Study Groups Committee of the Insurance Institute of London, and a British Insurance Law Association committee on Insurance Contract Law Reform. He has also been elected a vice president of the Insurance Institute of London.

Dexter Morse

Dr. Dexter Morse is CEO of Dexter Morse International Ltd, a Swiss-based company specialising in training, coaching and consulting in the areas of insurance/reinsurance, fraud, legal, claims, workplace and related intercultural issues. Dexter has over 15 years' experience in these fields and works with major international companies and organisations such as the United Nations Agencies. He holds a Master of Laws degree in insurance and reinsurance law from Cardiff University, UK and a Doctor of Laws degree from the University of Zurich, Switzerland. He is currently Professor of International Business Law at a leading Swiss business university. Dexter is an active member of a number of legal and insurance bodies. In 2004, he co-authored the book *Tackling Insurance Fraud: Law and Practice* published by LLP. A prolific writer, he also regularly contributes articles to leading publications.

Angus Rodger

Angus Rodger moved from Clifford Chance to become the Head of Insurance in the London office of U.S. law firm Steptoe & Johnson in January 2004. Angus has 14 years' experience of insurance and reinsurance law. His practice covers dispute resolution and non-contentious insurance matters, including policy drafting and regulatory advice. He is the author of a book on EC Insurance Law, a contributing author to a book on reinsurance claims handling, and a frequent contributor to industry journals and conferences.

Raj Parker

Raj is a dispute resolution partner and co-head of Freshfields Bruckhaus Deringer's financial institutions disputes group practice based in London. He specialises in general commercial dispute resolution, with particular experience of the insurance and reinsurance, public and administrative areas. Raj joined the firm in 1986 and became a partner in 1993. He is Centre for Dispute Resolution (CEDR) accredited and a solicitor-advocate, as well as a recorder for the Crown Court. He has also contributed to LLP's *Insurance Disputes* (first published 1999) and LLP's *Professional Negligence and Liability* (first published 2001).

Michelle Bramley

Michelle Bramley is a senior lawyer in Freshfields Bruckhaus Deringer's financial institution's dispute group based in London. Her main area of practice is insurance and reinsurance work, although she also has broad experience of general civil and commercial dispute resolution. She has written on a wide range of insurance and reinsurance related issues and is co-author of the chapter on "Insurance Litigation" in *Insurance Disputes* (published by LLP). She is also co-author of the *Woolf Reforms In Practice* and *The Civil Justice Reforms One Year On* (both published by Butterworths).

CONTENTS

Preface v
Authors' Biographies vii
Table of Cases xiii
Table of Legislation, Conventions and Rules xxv

1. THE NATURE OF REINSURANCE 1
— Peter Cave
Introduction 1
What is reinsurance? 4
Facultative 10
Proportional treaty 14
Non-proportional 41
Alternative risk transfer 68
Test Your Understanding 76

2. FORMATION OF REINSURANCE AGREEMENTS 79
— Professor Robert Merkin
Authorisation of reinsurers 79
Placing procedures in the London market 83
The use of agency agreements in the London market 95
Reinsurance pools and underwriting agencies 104
Insurable Interest 115
Text Your Understanding 122

3. UTMOST GOOD FAITH IN REINSURANCE AGREEMENTS 125
— Professor Robert Merkin
The elements of the duty of utmost good faith 125
Materiality and inducement 135
Material facts in reinsurance agreements 140
Post-contractual utmost good faith 151
Remedies for breach of duty 156
Reinsurance placed by brokers 162
The reinsurers' duty of utmost good faith 166
Test Your Understanding 166

4. TERMS OF REINSURANCE AGREEMENTS 171
— Professor Robert Merkin
Express and implied terms in reinsurance agreements 171

Incorporation and the "full reinsurance" clause 174
Incorporation of dispute resolution provisions 188
Back to back cover 195
Test Your Understanding 199

5. RIGHTS AND OBLIGATIONS OF THE PARTIES 201
— *Professor Robert Merkin*
The construction of reinsurance agreements 201
Reinsurance conditions 203
Reinsurance warranties 215
The premium 225
Inspection clauses 230
Test Your Understanding 234

6. FOLLOW THE SETTLEMENTS AND FOLLOW THE FORTUNES 237
— *Christopher Henley*
Introduction 237
The unqualified follow the settlements position 238
The qualified follow the settlements position 242
Can the reinsured decide what will be binding on reinsurers? 244
Follow the fortunes 250
Why not characterise the obligation as a debt rather than a contractual obligation? 251
Extra-contractual liability 252
Costs 253
Commutations: is a reinsurer legally obliged to pay the commuted sum to the reinsured? 257
Can the insured claim against the reinsurer if the reinsured fails to pay his claim, or becomes insolvent? 259
Can the reinsured obtain interest from the reinsurer? 261
When does the reinsured's cause of action accrue? 262
Test Your Understanding 264

7. CLAIMS 267
— *Dexter Morse*
Introduction 267
The notification and payment of claims 267
Claims cooperation and claims control clauses 272
The costs of litigation 277
Ex-gratia payments 279
The liability of the reinsurer 280
Interpretation—events, causes and occurrences 281
Reinsurance contracts—governing law and jurisdiction 283

The limitation issue 286
The rights of the reinsurer 288
Grounds for denying liability 292
Discharging the reinsurance contract 295
The leading underwriter and the follow market 300
Issues relating to run-off 302
Dispute resolution 307
Conclusions 309
Test Your Understanding 313

8. INTERMEDIARIES 315
— *Christopher Henley*
Intermediary, broker or agent? 315
Obligations 330
Liabilities of brokers 337
Rights of brokers 348
Limitation issues 351
Regulation 353
Test Your Understanding 356

9. JURISDICTION AND APPLICABLE LAW 359
— *Angus Rodger*
Introduction 359
Jurisdiction 359
Concurrent proceedings 374
Applicable law 380
Test Your Understanding 387

10. ARBITRATION 391
— *Michelle Bramley and Raj Parker*
Introduction 391
The use of arbitration in reinsurance disputes 392
What are the advantages and disadvantages of using arbitration to resolve reinsurance disputes? 397
The arbitration agreement 406
Scope of the arbitration clause 408
Incorporation of arbitration clauses 414
Jurisdiction of arbitrators 416
Conduct of arbitration 417
Judicial control of arbitration 422
Enforcement of arbitration awards 428
Test Your Understanding 431

Appendix 1: LMP Schedule 435
Appendix 2: Subjectivities 439
Appendix 3: The provisions of the Marine Insurance Act 1906 443
Appendix 4: Comparison of LCIA and ARIAS Arbitration Rules 445
Appendix 5: Resolution of jurisdictional disputes under the Arbitration Act 1996 449

Bibliography 451

Answers to Test Your Understanding Questions 453

TABLE OF CASES

ACE Insurance SA-NV (formerly Cigna Insurance Co. of Europe SA NV) *v.* Zurich Insurance Co. [2000] 2 Lloyd's Rep. 423; affirmed [2001] Lloyd's Rep. I.R. 504; [2001] 1 Lloyd's Rep. 618 (C.A.) ... 186, 197
AIG Europe (Ireland) Ltd *v.* Faraday Capital Ltd [2007] Lloyd's Rep. I.R. 1 ... 248
AIG Europe SA *v.* QBE International Insurance Ltd [2002] Lloyd's Rep. I.R. 22 ... 193
AIG Europe (UK) Ltd *v.* Ethniki [2000] Lloyd's Rep. I.R. 343 (C.A.) ... 20, 193, 365
AT&T Corp and Lucent Technologies Inc *v.* Saudi Cable Co. [2000] 2 Lloyd's Rep. 127 (C.A.) ... 424
AXA Reinsurance (UK) Ltd *v.* Field [1996] 1 Lloyd's Rep. 26 (C.A.); reversed [1996] 2 Lloyd's Rep. 233 (H.L.) ... 51, 197, 198, 282
Aetna Reinsurance Co. (UK) Ltd *v.* Central Reinsurance Corp Ltd [1996] L.R.L.R. 165 ... 232
Agapitos *v.* Agnew, The Aegeon [2002] Lloyd's Rep. I.R. 473; [2002] 3 W.L.R. 616 ... 153, 293
Agapitos *v.* Agnew (No. 3) [2003] Lloyd's Rep. I.R. 54 ... 222
Agnew, Ian Charles *v.* Lansforsakringsbolagens AB [1996] L.R.L.R. 392 ... 371
Aiken *v.* Stewart Wrightson Members Agency Ltd [1995] 2 Lloyd's Rep. 618 ... 147
Akai Pty Ltd *v.* People's Insurance Co. Ltd [1998] 1 Lloyd's Rep. 90 ... 387
Alfia Worldwide Insurance *v.* Deutsche Ruckversicherungs AG (1983) N.L.J. 621 ... 366
Alfred McAlpinep plc *v.* BAI (Run-Off) Ltd [2000] Lloyd's Rep. I.R. 352 (C.A.) ... 211, 212
Ali Shipping Corp *v.* Shipyard Trogir [1998] 2 All E.R. 136; [1998] 1 Lloyd's Rep. 643 (C.A.) ... 401, 403
Allianz Assurance *v.* Marchant, 1997, unreported ... 131
American Insurance Co. *v.* North American Co. for Property and Casualty Insurance, 697 F 2d 79 (1982) ... 251
American International Marine Agency of New York Inc *v.* Dandridge [2005] EWHC 829 (Comm) ... 181, 182
American International Speciality Lines Insurance Co. *v.* Abbott Laboratories [2004] Lloyd's Rep. I.R. 815 ... 175, 191
Amin Rasheed Shipping Corp *v.* Kuwait Insurance Co., The Al Wahab [1983] 2 Lloyd's Rep. 365 (H.L.) ... 383
Aneco Reinsurance Underwriting Ltd *v.* Johnson & Higgs Ltd [1998] 1 Lloyd's Rep. 565 (Q.B.D.); reversed in part on other grounds [2002] Lloyd's Rep. I.R. 93 (H.L.) ... 91, 144, 154, 346
Anglo African Merchants Ltd *v.* Bayley [1970] 1 Q.B. 311; [1969] 1 Lloyd's Rep. 268 ... 319
Arab Bank plc *v.* Zurich Insurance Co. [1999] 1 Lloyd's Rep. 262 ... 329
Arbory Group Ltd *v.* West Craven Insurance Services Ltd, QBD, 13 March 2007 ... 347
Arig Insurance Co. Ltd *v.* Sasa Assicurazione Riassicurazione SpA, 1998, unreported ... 192
Assicurazioni Generali SpA *v.* Arab Insurance Group (BSC) [2003] Lloyd's Rep. I.R 3; [2003] Lloyd's Rep. I.R. 131 (C.A.) ... 85, 125, 131, 133, 137, 138, 145, 218
Assicurazioni Generali SpA *v.* CGU International Insurance plc [2003] EWHC 1073; [2004] Lloyd's Rep. I.R. 457 ... 271, 272 245, 271
Assicurazioni Generali SpA *v.* Ege Sigorta AS [2002] Lloyd's Rep. I.R. 480 ... 92
Associated Electric Gas Insurance Services Ltd *v.* European Reinsurance Co. of Zurich [2003] UKPC 11 (P.C.) ... 404
Assunzione, The (No. 1) [1953] 2 Lloyd's Rep. 716 (C.A.) ... 383

Australia & New Zealand Bank Ltd *v.* Colonial & Eagle Wharves Ltd [1960] 2 Lloyd's Rep. 241 ..... 128, 268
Australian Widows Fund Life Assurance Society Ltd *v.* National Mutual Life Association of Australasia Ltd [1914] A.C. 634 (P.C.) 132
AXA Reinsurance (UK) Ltd *v.* Field [1996] 2 Lloyd's Rep. 233 (H.L.) 245

BAS Capital Funding Corp Ltd *v.* Medfinco Ltd [2003] EWHC (Ch) 1798 367
Baker, Colin *v.* Black Sea & Baltic General Insurance Co. Ltd [1995] L.R.L.R. 261 (Q.B.D.); [1998] Lloyd's Rep. I.R. 327 (H.L.) ... 171, 172, 198, 230, 231, 253, 254, 278, 310
Balfour *v.* Beaumont [1982] 2 Lloyd's Rep. 493; affirmed [1984] 1 Lloyd's Rep. 272 (C.A.) ... 12, 95, 96
Bancroft *v.* Heath (1901) 17 T.L.R. 425 174
Bank Leumi le Israel BM *v.* British National Insurance Co. Ltd [1988] 1 Lloyd's Rep. 71 ..... 89, 90
Bank of Nova Scotia *v.* Hellenic Mutual War Risk Association (Bermuda) Ltd, The Good Luck (No. 2) [1991] 2 Lloyd's Rep. 191 (H.L.) 220
Bankers Insurance Co. Ltd *v.* South [2003] EWHC 380; [2004] Lloyd's Rep. I.R. 1 205
Banque Financiere de la Cite SA (formerly Banque Keyser Ullmann SA) *v.* Westgate Insurance Co. (formerly Hodge General & Mercantile Co Ltd) [1989] 2 All E.R. 952; [1988] 2 Lloyd's Rep. 513 (C.A.) 299
Banque Keyser Ullmann SA *v.* Skandia (UK) Insurance Co. [1987] 1 Lloyd's Rep. 69; reversed [1988] 2 Lloyd's Rep. 513 (C.A.); affirmed [1990] 2 Lloyd's Rep. 377 (H.L.) 298, 299
Barlee Marine Corp *v.* Trevor Rex Mountain, The Leegas [1987] 1 Lloyd's Rep. 471 .. 97, 98, 301
Barnard *v.* Faber [1893] 1 Q.B. 340 (C.A.) 174
Barrett Bros (Taxis) Ltd *v.* Davies; *sub nom.* Lickliss *v.* Milestone Motor Policies at Lloyd's, Third Parties [1966] 2 All E.R. 972; [1966] 2 Lloyd's Rep. 1 (C.A.) 268
Bates *v.* Robert Barrow Ltd [1995] 1 Lloyd's Rep. 680 81
Bennett *v.* Axa Insurance plc [2004] Lloyd's Rep. I.R. 615 221
Berriman *v.* Rose Thomson Young (Underwriting) Ltd [1996] L.R.L.R. 426 ..... 343, 344
Black King Shipping Corp *v.* Massie, The Litsion Pride [1985] 1 Lloyd's Rep. 437 ... 153, 296
Blackburn Low & Co. *v.* Haslam (1888) L.R. 21 Q.B.D. 144 ..... 128, 324
Blackburn Low & Co. *v.* Vigors (1887) L.R. 12 App. Cas. 531 (H.L.) 128, 324, 326, 327
Bonner *v.* Cox Dedicated Corporate Member Inc [2006] Lloyd's Rep I.R. 385; affirmed [2005] EWCA Civ 1512 (C.A.) 86, 139, 152, 173
Bonner-Williams *v.* Peter Lindsay Leisure Ltd [2001] 1 All E.R. (Comm) 1140 205
Bradley and Essex and Suffolk Accident Indemnity Society, Re [1912] 1 K.B. 415 (C.A.) 205
Bristol and West plc *v.* Bahdresa [1999] 1 Lloyd's Rep. I.R. 138 257
British Dominions General Insurance Co. Ltd *v.* Duder [1915] 2 K.B. 394 (C.A.) 253, 278
British Eagle International Airlines Ltd *v.* Compagnie Nationale Air France [1975] 1 W.L.R. 758; [1975] 2 Lloyd's Rep. 43 (H.L.) 112, 260
British and Foreign Marine Insurance Co. Ltd *v.* Sturge (1897) 2 Com. Cas. 244 149
Brotherton *v.* Aseguradora Colseguros (No. 2) [2003] EWCA Civ 705; [2003] Lloyd's Rep. I.R. 758 ..... 141, 160, 166, 294
Brotherton *v.* Aseguradora Colseguros (No. 3) [2003] EWHC 1741 (Comm); [2003] Lloyd's Rep. I.R. 774 ..... 91, 142, 149, 150, 154, 160
Brown (R E) *v.* GIO Insurance Ltd [1998] Lloyd's Rep. I.R. 201 (C.A.) 245

CGU International Insurance plc *v.* Szabo [2002] Lloyd's Rep. I.R. 196 386
CNA International Reinsurance Co. Ltd *v.* Companhia de Seguros Tranquilidade SA [1999] Lloyd's Rep. I.R. 289 ..... 183, 184, 268
Cantieri Navali Riuniti SpA *v.* Omne Justitia NV, The Stolt Marmaro [1985] 2 Lloyd's Rep. 428 (C.A.) 383
Cape plc *v.* Iron Trades Employers Insurance Association Ltd [2004] Lloyd's Rep I.R. 75 138
Carradine Properties Ltd *v.* DJ Freeman & Co. [1999] Lloyd's Rep. P.N. 483 (C.A.) 340
Carter *v.* Boehm (1776) 3 Burr 1905 292

Carvill America Inc. *v.* Camperdown UK Ltd [2004] EWHC 2221; [2005] Lloyd's Rep. I.R. 55 (Comm Ct); [2005] EWCA Civ 645; [2005] 1 C.L.C. 845 (C.A.) 348, 349
Caudle *v.* Sharp [1995] L.R.L.R. 433 (C.A.) 197, 245, 281, 282, 310
Charlesworth *v.* Faber (1900) 5 Com. Cas. 408 ....144, 178
Charman *v.* Guardian Royal Exchange Assurance; *sub nom.* GRE *v.* Charman [1992] 2 Lloyd's Rep. 607 ....239, 244, 273, 334, 335
Charman *v.* New Cap Reinsurance Corp Ltd [2003] EWCA Civ 1372; [2004] Lloyd's Rep. I.R. 373 (C.A.) 225
Charter Reinsurance Co. Ltd (In Liquidation) *v.* Fagan [1996] 2 Lloyd's Rep. 113; [1997] A.C. 313 (H.L.) 206, 281, 310
Cigna Life Insurance Co. of Europe SA NV *v.* Intercaser SA de Seguros y Reaseguros [2001] Lloyd's Rep. I.R. 821; [2002] 1 All E.R. (Comm) 235 .... 175, 191, 415
Citadel Insurance Co. *v.* Atlantic Union Insurance Co. SA [1982] 2 Lloyd's Rep. 543 (C.A.) 383
Citibank NA *v.* Excess Insurance Co. Ltd (t/a ITT London and Edinburgh) [1999] Lloyd's Rep. I.R. 122 257
Citi-March Ltd *v.* Neptune Orient Lines Ltd [1997] 1 Lloyd's Rep. 72 368
Clarke *v.* Earl of Dunraven, The Satanita [1897] A.C. 59 (H.L.) 104
Clark Boyce *v.* Moyatt [1994] 1 A.C. 428; [1993] 3 W.L.R. 1021 (P.C.) 340
Collen *v.* Wright (1857) E.L. & B.L. 622 320
Commercial Union Assurance Co. plc *v.* Mander [1996] 2 Lloyd's Rep. 640 334
Commercial Union Assurance Co. plc *v.* NRG Victory Reinsurance Ltd [1998] 2 Lloyd's Rep. 600; [1998] Lloyd's Rep. I.R. 439 (C.A.) 241, 276, 277
Commercial Union Assurance Co. plc *v.* Sun Alliance Insurance Group plc [1992] 1 Lloyd's Rep. 475 196
Compagnia Tirrena Di Assicurazioni SpA *v.* Grand Union Insurance Co. Ltd [1991] 2 Lloyd's Rep. 143 289
Companhia de Seguros Imperio *v.* Heath (REBX) Ltd [1999] Lloyd's Rep. I.R. 571; affirmed [2001] Lloyd's Rep. I.R. 109 (C.A.) 108, 287, 353
Company (No. 013734 of 1991), Re [1992] 2 Lloyd's Rep. 415 258
Company (No. 008725 of 1991 and No.008727 of 1991), Re, ex parte Pritchard [1992] B.C.L.C. 633 231
Container Transport International Inc (CTI) *v.* Oceanus Mutual Underwriting Association (Bermuda) Ltd (No. 1) [1984] 1 Lloyd's Rep. 476 (C.A.) 136, 292, 299
Continental Bank NA *v.* Aeakos Compania Naviera SA [1994] 1 Lloyd's Rep. 505 (C.A.) 368
Continental Illinois National Bank & Trust Co. of Chicago and Xenofon Maritime SA *v.* Alliance Assurance Co. Ltd, The Captain Panagos DP [1986] 2 Lloyd's Rep. 470 ... 296, 297
Cormack & Cormack *v.* Excess Insurance Co. Ltd [2002] Lloyd's Rep. I.R. 938 257
Cox *v.* Bankside Members Agency Ltd [1995] 2 Lloyd's Rep. 437 (C.A.) 197, 206, 282
Credit Lyonnais *v.* Russell Jones & Walker [2002] Lloyd's Rep. P.N. 7 340

Decorum Investments Ltd *v.* Atkin, The Elena G [2002] Lloyd's Rep. I.R. 450 149
Deepak Fertilisers & Petrochemicals Cor. *v.* ICI Chemicals and Polymers Ltd [1999] 1 Lloyd's Rep. 387 (C.A.) 119
Denby *v.* English & Scottish Maritime Insurance Co. Ltd, *The Times*, 16 March 1998; [1998] Lloyd's Rep. I.R. 343 (C.A.) 14, 86, 96, 97
Department of Economic Policy & Development, City of Moscow *v.* (1) Bankers Trust Co. & (2) International Industrial Bank [2003] EWHC 1377 (Comm); affirmed in part [2004] EWCA Civ 314 (C.A.) 402
Derry *v.* Peek (1889) L.R. 14 App. Cas. 33 (H.L.) 161, 164
Deutsche Ruckversichering AG *v.* Walbrook Insurance Co. Ltd [1995] 1 Lloyd's Rep. 153; [1994] 4 All E.R. 181; affirmed on appeal Group Josi Re Co. SA *v.* Walbrook Insurance Co. Ltd [1996] 1 Lloyd's Rep. 345 (C.A.) 113, 146, 325, 326, 328
Deutsche Ruckversicherung *v.* Zion Insurance Co Ltd, March 2001, unreported 108
Direct Line Insurance plc *v.* Khan [202] Lloyd's Rep. I.R. 634 .... 293, 297
Doheny *v.* New India Assurance Co. [2005] Lloyd's Rep. I.R. 251 151
Dolling-Baker *v.* Merrett [1990] 1 W.L.R. 1205; [1991] 2 All E.R. 890 (C.A.) 401
Donohue *v.* Armco Inc [2000] 1 Lloyd's Rep. 579 (C.A.); reversed [2002] 1 Lloyd's Rep. 425 (H.L.) 376

Drake Insurance plc *v.* Provident Insurance plc [2003] Lloyd's Rep. I.R. 793; [2004] Lloyd's Rep I.R. 277 (C.A.) 136, 138, 139, 158, 160, 161, 166
Dresser UK *v.* Falcongate Freight Management, The Duke of Yare [1991] 2 Lloyd's Rep. 557 (C.A.) 378

ERC Frankona Reinsurance *v.* American National Insurance Co. [2006] Lloyd's Rep. I.R. 157 .... 86, 129, 130, 163
Eagle Star Insurance Co. Ltd *v.* Cresswell [2003] EWHC 2224 (Comm); [2004] Lloyd's Rep. I.R. 437; [2004] EWCA Civ 602 (C.A.) 206, 207, 208, 250, 273
Eagle Star Insurance Co. Ltd *v.* Spratt [1971] 2 Lloyd's Rep. 116 (C.A.) 86
Economides *v.* Commercial Union Assurance Co. plc [1998] Lloyd's Rep. I.R. 9 (C.A.) .. 126, 135
Eide UK Ltd *v.* Lowndes Lambert Group Ltd, The Sun Tender [1998] 1 Lloyd's Rep. 389 (C.A.) 228, 352
Empress Assurance Corporation Ltd *v.* Bowring & Co. Ltd (1905) 11 Com. Cas. 107 ... 101, 102
English and American Insurance Co. Ltd *v.* Axa Re SA [2007] Lloyd's Rep. I.R. 14 249
Eras EIL Actions, Re; *sub nom.* Societe Commerciale de Reassurance *v.* Eras International Ltd (formerly Eras (UK)) [1992] 1 Lloyd's Rep. 570 (C.A.) 372
Esso/BHP *v.* Plowman [1995] 128 A.L.R. 391 401
Euro-Diam Ltd *v.* Bathurst [1988] 1 Lloyd's Rep. 228 (C.A.) 215
Evialis SA *v.* Siat [2003] EWHC 863 (Comm) 192
Excess Insurance Co. Ltd *v.* Mander [1997] 2 Lloyd's Rep. 119; [1995] L.R.L.R. 358 ... 175, 190

Faraday Capital Ltd *v.* Copenhagen Reinsurance [2007] Lloyd's Rep. I.R. 23 247
Feasey *v.* Sun Life Assurance Co. of Canada [2002] Lloyd's Rep. I.R. 835; [2003] Lloyd's Rep. I.R. 637 (C.A.) 117, 118, 119, 120, 121, 132
Fenton Insurance Co. *v.* Gothaer Versicherungsbank VVaG [1991] 1 Lloyd's Rep. 171 ..... 226, 288, 296
Figre Ltd *v.* Mander [1999] Lloyd's Rep. I.R. 193 227
Fiona Trust & Holding Corporation & 20 Ors *v.* Yuri Privalov & 17 Ors [2007] EWCA Civ 20 (C.A.) 408, 414
Fireman's Fund Insurance Co. Ltd *v.* Western Australian Insurance Co Ltd (1927) 28 Ll. L. Rep. 243 279
First National Commercial Bank plc *v.* Barnet Devanney (Harrow) Ltd (formerly Barnet Devanney & Co Ltd) [1999] 2 All E.R. (Comm) 233; [1999] Lloyd's Rep. P.N. 908 (C.A.) 339, 340
Fisher *v.* Unione Italiana de Riassicurazione SPA [1999] Lloyd's Rep. I.R. 215 371
Fitzherbert *v.* Mather (1785) 14 East 494 328
Formica Ltd *v.* Export Credits Guarantee Department [1995] 1 Lloyd's Rep. 692 333
Forsikringsaktieselskapet Vesta *v.* Butcher [1989] 1 A.C. 852; [1989] 1 Lloyd's Rep. 331 (H.L.) 174, 180, 185, 186, 187, 195, 196, 218, 219, 220, 221, 250, 275
Franco-Hungarian Insurance Co. *v.* Merchants Marine Insurance Co., *Shipping Gazette*, 7 June 1888 178
Frans Maas (UK) Ltd *v.* Sun Alliance and London Insurance plc [2004] Lloyd's Rep. I.R. 649 205
Friends Provident Life Office, Re [1999] Lloyd's Rep. I.R. 547 (C.A.) 80
Friends Provident Life and Pensions Ltd *v.* Sirius International Insurance Corp [2005] EWCA Civ 601; [2006] Lloyd's Rep. I.R. 45 (C.A.) 211, 212, 213, 214

GE Reinsurance Corporation *v.* New Hampshire Insurance Co. [2004] Lloyd's Rep. I.R. 404 .... 173, 187, 198, 217
Gan Insurance Co. Ltd *v.* Tai Ping Insurance Co. Ltd (No. 1); Royal Reinsurance Co. Ltd *v.* Central Insurance Co. Ltd [1999] Lloyd's Rep. I.R. 229; affirmed [1999] Lloyd's Rep. I.R. 472 (C.A.) 194, 195, 198, 284, 385
Gan Insurance Co. Ltd *v.* Tai Ping Insurance Co. Ltd (No. 2) [2001] Lloyd's Rep. I.R. 291; reversed on other grounds [2001] Lloyd's Rep. I.R. 667 (C.A.) 133, 134, 151, 166, 209, 210, 252, 254, 255, 256, 257
General Accident Fire & Life Assurance Corp Ltd *v.* J H Minet & Co. Ltd (1942) 72 Ll. L. Rep. 48 344

General Accident Fire and Life Assurance Corp Ltd *v.* Peter William Tanter, The Zephyr [1984] 1 Lloyd's Rep. 58; reversed [1985] 2 Lloyd's Rep. 529 (C.A.) 88, 89, 90, 93, 94, 317, 342
General Accident Fire & Life Assurance Corp. Ltd *v.* Campbell (1925) 21 Ll. L. Rep. 151 ... 146
General Insurance Co. of Trieste Ltd *v.* Corporation of the Royal Exchange (1897) 2 Com. Cas. 144 .... 177, 178
General Reinsurance Corporation *v.* Forsakringsaktiebolaget Fennia Patria [1983] 2 Lloyd's Rep. 287 (C.A.) 87, 88
George Hunt Cranes Ltd *v.* Scottish Boiler & General Insurance Co. Ltd [2002] Lloyd's Rep. I.R. 178; [2002] 1 All E.R. (Comm) 366 (C.A.) 205
Gerling-Konzern General Insurance Co. *v.* Polygram Holdings Inc [1998] 2 Lloyd's Rep. 544 220
Glacier Bay, The [1998] Lloyd's Rep. I.R. 201 245
Glasgow Assurance Corporation *v.* William Symondson & Co. (1911) 27 T.L.R. 245 156
Glencore International AG *v.* Ryan, The Beursgracht (No. 1) [2002] 1 Lloyd's Rep. 574; [2002] Lloyd's Rep. I.R. 335 (C.A.) 156, 204, 212, 213, 227
Gloucestershire Health Authority *v.* MA Torpy & Partners Ltd (t/a Torpy & Partners) (No. 2) [1999] Lloyd's Rep. I.R. 203 257
Goshawk Dedicated Ltd *v.* Tyser Co. Ltd [2005] Lloyd's Rep. I.R. 379; [2006] 2 All E.R. (Comm) 115 .... 228, 331
Goshawk Syndicate Management Ltd and others *v.* XL Specialty Insurance Co. [2004] Lloyd's Rep. I.R. 683 196
Great Atlantic Insurance Co. *v.* Home Insurance Co [1981] 2 Lloyd's Rep. 219 ....20, 147, 322
Great Western Assurance Co. SA, Re [1999] Lloyd's Rep. I.R. 377 (C.A.) 80
Group Josi Reinsurance Co. SA *v.* Universal General Insurance Co. (UGIC) (Case C–412/98) [2000] 2 All E.R. (Comm) 467 (E.C.J.) 364
Group Josi Re Co. SA *v.* Walbrook Insurance Co. Ltd [1996] 1 Lloyd's Rep. 345 (C.A.) 163, 328, 329
Groupama Insurance Co. Ltd *v.* Overseas Partners Ltd [2003] EWHC 34 (Comm) .. 134, 155
Groupama Navigation et Transports *v.* Catatumbo CA Seguros [2000] 2 Lloyd's Rep. 350 (C.A.) 180, 186, 187, 195, 196, 221

HIH Casualty & General Insurance Ltd *v.* Axa Corporate Solutions [2003] Lloyd's Rep. I.R. 1 24
HIH Casualty & General Insurance Ltd *v.* Chase Manhattan Bank [2001] Lloyd's Rep. I.R. 191; [2003] UKHL 6; [2003] Lloyd's Rep. I.R. 230 (H.L.) 13, 125, 150, 162, 165, 166, 324
HIH Casualty & General Insurance Ltd *v.* JLT Risk Solutions Ltd [2006] EWHC 485 (Comm) 336
HIH Casualty & General Insurance Ltd *v.* New Hampshire Insurance Co [2001] Lloyd's Rep. I.R. 244; affirmed [2001] Lloyd's Rep. I.R. 596 (C.A.) ... 10, 92, 93, 175, 176, 179, 181, 202, 216, 217, 218, 223, 24
Hadenfayre *v.* British National Insurance Society [1984] 2 Lloyd's Rep. 393 152
Halbot *v.* Lens [1901] 1 Ch. 344 321
Halvanon Insurance Co. Ltd *v.* Companhia de Seguros do Estado de Sao Paulo [1995] L.R.L.R. 303 (C.A.) 263, 286
Hampshire Land Co. (No. 1), Re [1894] 2 Ch. 632 .... 325, 329
Hampshire Land Co. (No. 2), Re [1896] 2 Ch. 743 .... 129, 328, 329
Handelswekerij G.J. Bier BV and Stichtung Reinwater (The Reinwater Foundation) *v.* Mines de Potasse D'Alsace SA (Case C–21/76) [1976] E.C.R. 1735 (E.C.J.) 372
Harbour Assurance Co. (UK) Ltd *v.* Kansa General International Assurance Co. Ltd [1993] 1 Lloyd's Rep. 455 (C.A.) 409, 414, 416
Harrods (Buenos Aires) Ltd (No. 2), Re [1992] Ch. 72; [1991] 3 W.L.R. 397 (C.A.) 374
Hassneh Insurance Co. of Israel *v.* Stuart J Mew [1993] 2 Lloyd's Rep. 243 .... 402, 403
Hayter *v.* Nelson Home Insurance [1990] 2 Lloyd's Rep. 265 309
Heath Lambert Ltd *v.* Sociedad de Coretaje de Seguros [2004] Lloyd's Rep. I.R. 905 ... 228, 229, 230
Hedley Byrne & Co Ltd *v.* Heller & Partners Ltd [1964] A.C. 465; [1963] 1 Lloyd's Rep. 485 (H.L.) 161, 164, 323

Hewitt *v.* London General Insurance Co Ltd (1925) 23 Ll. L. Rep. 243 122
Heyman *v.* Darwins Ltd [1942] A.C. 356; (1942) 72 Ll. L. Rep. 65 (H.L.) 414
Highlands Insurance Co. *v.* Continental Insurance Co. [1987] 1 Lloyd's Rep. 109 (Note) 131, 132, 133, 157, 162
Hill and Berry *v.* Mercantile & General Reinsurance Co. plc [1996] 1 W.L.R. 1239; [1996] L.R.L.R. 341 (H.L.) 241, 242, 243, 245, 271
Hill *v.* Citadel Insurance Co. Ltd [1997] L.R.L.R. 167 (C.A.) 148
Hiscox *v.* Outhwaite (No. 3) [1991] 2 Lloyd's Rep. 524 ....240, 241, 244, 245, 246, 247
Hoffmann *v.* Economic Insurance Co. (1956) 4 SA 380(W) 319
Hogg Insurance Brokers (HIB) Ltd *v.* Guardian Insurance Co. Inc [1997] 1 Lloyd's Rep. 412 375
Home Insurance Co. Ltd and St Paul Fire and Marine Insurance Co. *v.* Administratia Asigurarilor de Stat [1983] 2 Lloyd's Rep. 674 308
Home Insurance Co. of New York *v.* Victoria Montreal Fire Insurance Co. [1907] A.C. 59 (P.C.) 182, 183
Home & Overseas Insurance Co. *v.* Mentor Insurance Co. (UK) [1989] 1 Lloyd's Rep. 473; [1990] 1 W.L.R. 153 (C.A.) 308, 393

Imperio Reinsurance Co. (UK) Ltd *v.* Iron Trades Mutual Insurance Co. Ltd (1991) 1 Re. L.R. 213 .... 155, 158
Insurance Co. *v.* Lloyd's Syndicate [1995] 1 Lloyd's Rep. 272 403
Insurance Co. of Africa *v.* SCOR (UK) Reinsurance Co. Ltd [1985] 1 Lloyd's Rep. 312 (C.A.) 209, 238, 240, 241, 243, 244, 245, 246, 250, 251, 252, 253, 254, 255, 256, 270, 278, 310
Insurance Corp. of the Channel Islands *v.* McHugh and Royal Hotel Ltd (No. 2) [1997] L.R.L.R. 94 .... 141, 297
International Lottery Management Ltd *v.* Dumas [2002] Lloyd's Rep. I.R. 237 ......91, 127, 133, 154
International Management Group (UK) Ltd *v.* Simmonds [2003] EWHC 177 (Comm); [2004] Lloyd's Rep. I.R. 247 .... 91, 137, 142, 154
Inversiones Manria SA *v.* Sphere Drake Insurance Co, Malvern Insurance Co. and Niagara Fire Insurance Co., The Dora [1989] 1 Lloyd's Rep. 69 (C.A.) 101
Investors Compensation Scheme Ltd *v.* West Bromwich Building Society (No. 1) [1998] 1 All E.R. 98 (H.L.) 201
Iowa Mutual Tornado Association *v.* Timmons, 105b N.W.2d 209 (Iowa, 1960) 4
Iron Trades Mutual Insurance Co. Ltd *v.* Companhia de Seguros Imperio [1992] Re L.R. 213 .... 233, 290, 300
Iron Trades Mutual Insurance Co. Ltd *v.* J K Buckenham Ltd [1989] 2 Lloyd's Rep. 85 ....352, 353
Islander Trucking Ltd (In Liquidation) Ltd *v.* Hogg Robinson & Gardner Mountain (Marine) Ltd [1990] 1 All E.R. 826 353

J A Chapman & Co. Ltd (In Liquidation) *v.* Kadirga Denizcilik ve Ticaret AS [1998] Lloyd's Rep. I.R. 377 (C.A.) 220, 226, 319
J Kirkaldy & Sons Ltd *v.* Walker [1999] Lloyd's Rep. I.R. 410 223
Jaglom *v.* Excess Insurance Co. Ltd [1971] 2 Lloyd's Rep. 171 ....84, 88
James *v.* CGU Insurance plc [2002] Lloyd's Rep. I.R. 206 141
Johnston *v.* Leslie & Godwin Financial Services Ltd [1995] L.R.L.R. 472 .... 335, 348
Joyce *v.* Realm Marine Insurance Co. (1872) L.R. 7 Q.B. 580 .... 177, 195

K/S Merc-Scandia XXXXII *v.* Lloyd's Underwriters, The Mercandian Continent [2000] Lloyd's Rep. I.R. 694; affirmed [2001] Lloyd's Rep. I.R. 802; [2001] 2 Lloyd's Rep. 563 (C.A.) 153, 155, 166, 212, 213
King *v.* Brandywine Co. (UK) Ltd [2004] EWHC 1033 (Comm); [2004] 2 All E.R. (Comm) 443 .... 277, 285
Kingscroft Insurance Co. *v.* H. S. Weavers (Underwriting) Agencies [1993] 1 Lloyd's Rep. 187 105
Kingscroft Insurance Co. Ltd *v.* Nissan Fire & Marine Insurance Co. Ltd (No. 1) [1999] Lloyd's Rep. I.R. 371 (C.A.) 329

Kingscroft Insurance Co. Ltd *v.* Nissan Fire & Marine Insurance Co. Ltd (No. 2) [1999] Lloyd's Rep. I.R. 603 .... 94, 112, 114, 131, 138, 148, 202
Kleinwort Benson Ltd *v.* Glasgow City Council (No. 2) [1997] 4 All E.R. 641; [1998] Lloyd's Rep. Bank 10 (H.L.) 371
Kler Knitwear Ltd *v.* Lombard General Insurance Co. Ltd [2000] Lloyd's Rep. I.R. 47 ... 222
Knapp *v.* Ecclesiastical Insurance Group plc [1998] Lloyd's Rep. I.R. 390; [1997] All E.R. (Comm) 44 (C.A.) 352
Kumar *v.* AGF Insurance Ltd [1999] Lloyd's Rep. I.R. 147 23
Kurz *v.* Stella Musical Veranstaltungs GmbH [1992] Ch. 196; [1991] 3 W.L.R. 1046 368
Kuwait Airways Corp *v.* Kuwait Insurance Co. SAK (No. 1) [1996] 1 Lloyd's Rep. 664 .. 51, 283, 310
Kuwait Airways Corp *v.* Kuwait Insurance Co. SAK (No. 2) [2001] 1 All E.R. (Comm) 972 (C.A.) 262

LG Caltex Gas Co. Ltd *v.* China National Petroleum Corp; Contigroup Companies Inc (formerly Continental Grain Co.) *v.* China Petroleum Technology & Development Corp [2001] EWCA Civ 788; [2001] 1 W.L.R. 1892 (C.A.) 417
La Banque Financiere de la Cite SA (formerly Banque Keyser Ullmann SA) *v.* Westgate Insurance Co. (formerly Hodge General & Mercantile Co Ltd) [1988] 2 Lloyd's Rep. 513 (C.A.) 164, 166
Lake *v.* Reinsurance Corp Ltd, 1967 (3) SA 124 (W) 226
Lancashire County Council *v.* Municipal Mutual Insurance Ltd [1995] L.R.L.R. 293 252
Law Guarantee Trust & Accident Society *v.* Munich Reinsurance Co. [1912] 1 Ch. 138; (1915) 31 T.L.R. 572 .... 152, 156
Layher Ltd *v.* Loi [2000] Lloyd's Rep. I.R. 510 (C.A.) 60
Leicestershire CC *v.* Michael Faraday and Partners, Ltd [1941] 2 K.B. 205 (C.A.) 333
Lewis *v.* Nicholson (1852) 18 Q.B. 503 320
Lewis *v.* Tressider Andrews Associates [1987] 2 Qd. R. 533 342
Lincoln National Life Insurance Co. *v.* Employers Reinsurance Corp [2002] Lloyd's Rep. I.R. 853 386
Locabail (UK) Ltd *v.* Bayfield Properties Ltd (Leave to Appeal) [2000] Q.B. 451; [2000] 2 W.L.R. 870 (C.A.) 424
London County Commercial Reinsurance Office Ltd, Re [1922] 2 Ch. 67; (1922) 10 Ll. L. Rep. 370 .... 121, 270
London General Insurance Co. Ltd *v.* General Marine Underwriters Association Ltd [1921] 1 K.B. 104; (1920) 4 Ll. L. Rep. 382 (C.A.) 127, 150
London and Leeds Estates Ltd *v.* Paribas Ltd (No. 2) [1995] 1 E.G.L.R. 102 402
Lower Rhine and Wurtemberg Insurance Association *v.* Sedgwick [1899] 1 Q.B. 179 (C.A.) 180
Lucena *v.* Crauford (1806) 2 Bos. & P.N.R. 269 117
Lumbermen's Mutual Casualty Co. *v.* Bovis Lend Lease Ltd [2005] 1 Lloyd's Rep 494 249
Lynch *v.* Dunsford (1811) 14 East 494 142

Maciej Rataj, The. Owners of Cargo Lately Laden on Board the Tatry *v.* Owners of the Maciej Rataj (Case C–406/92) [1991] 2 Lloyd's Rep. 458 (Q.B.D.); affirmed [1992] 2 Lloyd's Rep. 552 (C.A.); [1995] 1 Lloyd's Rep. 302; [1995] I.L.Pr. 81 (E.C.J.) 379
Mahli *v.* Abbey Life Assurance Co. [1996] L.R.L.R. 237 (C.A.) 299
Mander *v.* Commercial Union Assurance Co. plc [1998] Lloyd's Rep. I.R. 93 .... 99, 301
Marc Rich & Co. AG *v.* Portman [1996] 1 Lloyd's Rep. 430 138
Marc Rich & Co. AG *v.* Societa Italiana Impianti pA (Case C–190/89) [1992] 1 Lloyd's Rep. 342; [1991] E.C.R. I–3855 (E.C.J.) 363
Manifest Shipping Co. Ltd *v.* Uni-Polaris Insurance Co. Ltd, The Star Sea [1995] 1 Lloyd's Rep. 651 (Q.B.D.); affirmed [1997] 1 Lloyd's Rep. 360 (C.A.); affirmed [2001] Lloyd's Rep. I.R. 247 (H.L.) 153, 295, 297
Mann *v.* Lexington Insurance Co. [2001] Lloyd's Rep. I.R. 179 (C.A.) 196
Maritime Insurance Co. *v.* Stearns [1901] 2 K.B. 912 .... 178, 179
Mark Rowlands Ltd *v.* Berni Inns Ltd [1985] 3 All E.R. 473; [1985] 2 Lloyd's Rep. 437 (C.A.) 116

Markel International Insurance Co. Ltd *v.* La Republica Argentina de Suguros Generales SA [2004] EWHC 1826 (Comm); [2005] Lloyd's Rep. I.R. 90 .... 146, 285
Marten *v.* Nippon Sea and Land Insurance Co. Ltd (1898) 3 Com. Cas. 164 178
May & Butcher Ltd *v.* King, The [1934] 2 K.B. 17; [1929] All E.R. Rep. 679 (H.L.) 409
Meridian Global Funds Management Asia Ltd *v.* Securities Commission [1995] 2 A.C. 500; [1995] 3 W.L.R. 413 (P.C.) 128
Midland Bank Trust Co. Ltd *v.* Hett Stubbs & Kemp [1979] Ch. 384; [1978] 3 W.L.R. 167 340
Mitsubishi Corp *v.* Castletown Navigation, The Castle Alpha [1989] 2 Lloyd's Rep. 383 383
Monkton Court Ltd (t/a CATS) *v.* Perry Prowse (Insurance Services) Ltd [2002] Lloyd's Rep. I.R. 408 257
Moore Large & Co. Ltd *v.* Hermes Credit & Guarantee plc [2003] Lloyd's Rep. I.R. 315 158
Morrison *v.* Universal Marine Insurance Co. (1873) L.R. 8 Ex. 197 299
Municipal Mutual Insurance Ltd *v.* Sea Insurance Co. Ltd [1996] L.R.L.R. 265; reversed in part [1998] Lloyd's Rep. I.R. 421 (C.A.) 183, 279, 281, 310
Murphy *v.* Young & Co's Brewery plc [1996] L.R.L.R. 60 257
Mutter *v.* Eastern and Midlands Railway Co. (1888) L.R. 38 Ch. D. 92 (C.A.) 290

NRG Victory Reinsurance Ltd, Re [1995] 1 All E.R. 533 ....4, 79
NRG *v.* Bacon & Woodrow [1997] L.R.L.R 744 330
National Fire and Marine Insurance Co. of New Zealand *v.* Australian Mercantile Union Insurance Co. (1887) 6 N.Z.L.R. 144 273
National Insurance Company for Co-operative Reinsurance *v.* St Paul Reinsurance Co. Ltd, April 1998, unreported 278, 279
National Insurance and Guarantee Corp *v.* Imperio Reinsurance Co. (UK) Ltd and Russell Tudor-Price & Co. Ltd [1999] Lloyd's Rep. I.R. 249 ....322, 339
National Oilwell (UK) Ltd *v.* Davy Offshore Ltd [1993] 2 Lloyd's Rep. 582 119
Nemgia *v.* AGF Holdings [1997] 2 B.C.L.C.C. 191 260
New Hampshire Insurance Co. Ltd *v.* MGN Ltd (1996) [1997] L.R.L.R. 24 (C.A.) 340
New Hampshire Insurance Co. Ltd *v.* Philips Electronics North America Corp (No. 1) [1999] Lloyd's Rep. I.R. 58 (C.A.) 375
New Hampshire Insurance Co. Ltd *v.* Strabag Bau AG [1990] 2 Lloyd's Rep. 61; affirmed [1992] 1 Lloyd's Rep. 361 (C.A.) 364, 373, 409
North Atlantic Insurance Co. Ltd *v.* Nationwide General Insurance Co. [2004] Lloyd's Rep. I.R. 466; [2004] Lloyd's Rep. I.R. 774 (C.A.) 104, 111
North British Fishing Boat Insurance Co. Ltd *v.* Starr (1922) 13 Ll. L. Rep. 206 149
North & South Trust Co. *v.* Berkeley [1970] 2 Lloyd's Rep. 467; [1971] 1 W.L.R. 470 .... 66, 320
Norwich Union Fire Insurance Society Ltd *v.* Colonial Mutual Fire Insurance Co. Ltd [1922] 2 K.B. 461; (1922) 12 Ll. L. Rep. 215 ....180, 181

O'Brien *v.* Donoghue [1995] L.R.L.R. 90 342
O'Brien *v.* Hughes-Gibb & Co. (No. 2) [1995] L.R.L.R. 90 339
O'Kane *v.* Jones [2004] Lloyd's Rep. I.R. 389 ....141, 159
Odyssey Re (London) Ltd *v.* Reinsurance Australia Corp Ltd, 12 April 2001, S.C. N.S.W. 251
Orakpo *v.* Barclays Insurance Services Ltd [1995] L.R.L.R. 443 (C.A.) 293, 297
Orion Compania Espanola de Seguros *v.* Belfort Maatschappij voor Algemene Verzekgringeen [1962] 2 Lloyd's Rep. 257 ....287, 308
Osman *v.* Moss (J Ralph) Ltd [1970] 1 Lloyd's Rep. 313 (C.A.) 341
Overseas Marine Insurance Co Ltd, Re (1930) 36 Ll. L. Rep. 183 (C.A.) 121, 122
Overseas Union Insurance Ltd *v.* AA Mutual International Insurance [1988] 2 Lloyd's Rep. 63 409
Overseas Union Insurance Ltd *v.* New Hampshire Insurance Co. (Case C–351/89) [1992] 1 Lloyd's Rep. 204; [1991] E.C.R. I–3317 (E.C.J.) 364
Owusu *v.* Jackson [2002] EWCA Civ 877 (C.A.) 374

PCW Syndicates *v.* PCW Reinsurers [1996] 1 Lloyd's Rep. 241; [1996] 1 W.L.R. 1136 (C.A.) 130, 163, 326, 328, 329

Pacific & General Insurance Co. Ltd (In Liquidation) *v.* Baltica Insurance Co (UK) Ltd [1996] L.R.L.R. 8 233
Pacific & General Insurance Co. Ltd *v.* Hazell [1997] L.R.L.R. 65 .... 227, 319, 321
Pan Atlantic Insurance Co. Ltd *v.* Pine Top Insurance Co. Ltd [1989] 1 Lloyd's Rep. 568 (C.A.) 110, 111
Pan Atlantic Insurance Co. Ltd *v.* Pine Top Insurance Co. Ltd [1992] 1 Lloyd's Rep. 101; affirmed [1993] 1 Lloyd's Rep. 496 (C.A.); affirmed [1994] 2 Lloyd's Rep. 427; [1995] 1 A.C. 501 (H.L.) 26, 126, 135, 136, 137, 150, 157, 300
Paragon Finance plc (formerly National Home Loans Corp) *v.* Nash [2001] EWCA Civ 1466; [2002] 1 W.L.R. 685 (C.A.) 256
Pendennis Shipyard Ltd *v.* Magrathea (Pendennis) Ltd [1998] 1 Lloyd's Rep. 315 257
Phoenix General Insurance Co. of Greece SA *v.* Administratia Asigurarilor de Stat; Phoenix General Insurance Co. of Greece SA *v.* Halvanon Insurance Co. Ltd [1985] 2 Lloyd's Rep. 599; reversed [1986] 2 Lloyd's Rep. 552; [1988] Q.B. 216 (C.A.) 39, 172, 173, 230, 290, 334
Pilkington United Kingdom Ltd *v.* CGU Insurance plc [2004] Lloyd's Rep. I.R. 891 205
Pine Top Insurance Co. *v.* Unione Italiana Anglo Saxon Reinsurance Co. [1987] 1 Lloyd's Rep. 476 .... 189, 190, 415
Prentis Donegan & Partners Ltd *v.* Leeds & Leeds Co. Inc [1998] 2 Lloyd's Rep. 326 .... 229, 319
Prifti *v.* Musini Sociedad Anonima De Seguros y Reaseguros [2004] Lloyd's Rep I.R. 528 .... 175, 193, 194, 219
Printpak *v.* AGF Insurance Ltd [1999] Lloyd's Rep. I.R. 542 216
Property Insurance Co. Ltd *v.* National Protector Insurance Co. Ltd (1913) 108 L.T. 104 ... 144
Provincial Insurance Co. Ltd *v.* Morgan & Foxon [1933] A.C. 240; (1932) 44 Ll. L. Rep. 275 (H.L.) 222
Pryke (John W.) *v.* Gibbs Hartley Cooper Ltd [1991] 1 Lloyd's Rep. 602 .. 101, 102, 323, 348
Punjab National Bank *v.* De Boinville [1992] 1 Lloyd's Rep. 7 (C.A.) 92

Quorum A/S *v.* Schramm (No. 2) [2002] Lloyd's Rep. I.R. 315 263

R *v.* Gough (Robert) [1993] A.C. 646; [1993] 2 W.L.R. 883 (H.L.) 424
R+V Versicherung AG *v.* Risk Insurance and Reinsurance Solutions SA, November 2004, unreported 106
Ramco (UK) Ltd *v.* International Insurance Co. of Hannover Ltd [2004] Lloyd's Rep. I.R. 606 (C.A.) 118
Revell *v.* London General Insurance Co Ltd (1934) 50 Ll. L. Rep. 114 151
Road Management Services (A13) plc *v.* Power Networks plc [2003] B.L.R. 303 417
Roadworks (1952) Ltd *v.* Charman [1994] 2 Lloyd's Rep. 99 .... 98, 99
Roar Marine Ltd *v.* Bimeh Iran Insurance Co., The Daylam [1998] 1 Lloyd's Rep. 423 ... 98, 301
Rosseel NV *v.* Oriental Commercial & Shipping Co. (UK) Ltd [1991] 2 Lloyd's Rep. 625 431
Royal & Sun Alliance Insurance plc *v.* Dornoch Ltd [2004] Lloyd's Rep. I.R. 544; [2004] EWHC 803 (Comm) 208, 248, 275
Royal & Sun Alliance Insurance plc *v.* Retail Brand Alliance Inc [2004] EWHC 2139 375

SAIL *v.* Farex; *sub nom* Societe Anonyme d'Intermediaries Luxembourgeois *v.* Farex Gie [1995] L.R.L.R. 116 (C.A.) ...39, 128, 147, 148, 156, 163, 231, 232, 290, 325, 326, 329
SDL International Ltd *v.* Centre de Cooperation Internationale en Recherche Agronomique pour le Developpement [2001] C.L.C. 903 378
St Paul Fire & Marine Insurance Co. (UK) Ltd *v.* McConnell Dowell Constructors Ltd [1995] 2 Lloyd's Rep. 116 (C.A.) 136, 137
Salton *v.* New Beeston Cycle Co. [1900] 1 Ch. 43 321
Scott *v.* Copenhagen Re [2003] EWCA Civ 688; [2003] Lloyd's Rep. I.R. 696 (C.A.) 243
Scottish Metropolitan Assurance Co. Ltd *v.* Groom (1924) 20 Ll. L. Rep. 44 (C.A.) 253
Sedgwick Tomenson Inc *v.* PT Reasuransi Uman Indonesia [1990] 2 Lloyd's Rep. 334 ... 101
Shinedean Ltd *v.* Alldown Demolition (London) Ltd and Axa Insurance UK plc [2006] Lloyd's Rep. I.R. 846 210
Siboti K/S *v.* BP France SA, May 2003, unreported 188, 189
Simner *v.* New India Assurance Co. Ltd [1995] L.R.L.R. 240 .... 128, 326, 327, 329

Sirius International Insurance Corp. *v.* Oriental Assurance Corp. [1999] Lloyd's Rep. I.R. 345 .... 131, 132, 133, 135, 152, 300
Slater *v.* Buckinghamshire County Council [2004] Lloyd's Rep. I.R. 432 205
Smout *v.* Ilbey (1842) 10 M. & W. 321
South Australia Asset Management Corp *v.* York Montague Ltd [1997] A.C. 191; [1996] 3 W.L.R. 87 (H.L.) 346
Sphere Drake Insurance Ltd *v.* Euro International Underwriters Ltd [2003] EWHC 1636 (Comm); [2003] Lloyd's Rep. I.R. 525 .... 102, 103, 105
Sphere Drake Insurance plc *v.* Basler Versicherungs-Gesellschaft [1998] Lloyd's Rep. I.R. 35 .... 107, 241
Spiliada Maritime Corp *v.* Cansulex Ltd, The Spiliada [1987] 1 Lloyd's Rep. 1; A.C. 460 (H.L.) 367, 375
Star Sea, The. *See* Manifest Shipping Co. Ltd *v.* Uni-Polaris Insurance Co. Ltd
Strive Shipping Corp. *v.* Hellenic Mutual War Risks Association (Bermuda) Ltd, The Grecia Express [2002] 2 Lloyd's Rep. 88; [2002] Lloyd's Rep. I.R. 669 .... 158, 159, 160, 234, 334
Sumitomo Heavy Industries *v.* Oil and Natural Gas Commission [1994] 1 Lloyd's Rep. 45 410
Sun Life Assurance Co. of Canada, American Phoenix Life and Phoenix Home Life *v.* Lincoln National Life Insurance Co. [2004] EWCA Civ 1660 (C.A.) 84
Sun Life Assurance Co. of Canada *v.* CX Reinsurance Co. Ltd [2003] EWCA Civ 283 ... 406
Suncorp Insurance and Finance *v.* Milano Assicurazioni SpA [1993] 2 Lloyd's Rep. 225 .... 108, 322
Svenska Kreditfursakrings AB *v.* Munchener Ruckversicheruns-Gesselschaft, Schweizeriche Ruckversicherungs-Gesellschaft and other Reinsurers, Swedish Arbitration, Stockholm, 11 November 1998 .... 293, 294, 311
Syndicate 1242 at Lloyd's *v.* Morgan Read & Sharman [2003] Lloyd's Rep. I.R. 412 ..... 103, 104

TGA Chapman Ltd *v.* Christopher [1998] 2 All E.R. 873; [1998] Lloyd's Rep. I.R. 1 (C.A.) 257
Taylor *v.* Eagle Star Insurance Co. Ltd (1940) 67 Ll. L. Rep. 136 151
Taylor *v.* Yorkshire Insurance Co. Ltd (1913) 2 I.R. 1 329
Tiernan *v.* Magen Insurance Co. Ltd [2000] I.L.Pr. 5178 383
Tonicstar Ltd (t/a Lloyd's Syndicate 1861) *v.* American Home Assurance Co. [2004] 1234 (Comm) 285
Toomey *v.* Banco Vitalicio de Espana SA de Seguros y Reaseguros [2003] EWHC 1102 (Comm) (Q.B.D.); [2004] Lloyd's Rep. I.R. 354; [2004] EWCA Civ 622 (C.A.) 92, 143, 147, 174, 175, 218, 219, 250, 297
Toomey *v.* Eagle Star Insurance Co. Ltd [1993] 1 Lloyd's Rep. 429; reversed [1994] 1 Lloyd's Rep. 516 (C.A.) 4, 280
Touche Ross & Co *v.* Baker (Colin) [1992] 2 Lloyd's Rep. 207 (H.L.) 89, 95
Trade Indemnity plc *v.* Forsakringsaktiebolaget Njord [1995] L.R.L.R. 367 367
Traill *v.* Baring (1864) De G.J. & S.M. 318 147
Transcontinental Underwriting Agency *v.* Grand Union Insurance Co. [1987] 2 Lloyd's Rep. 409 110
Travelers Casualty and Surety *v.* Sun Life assurance Co. of Canada (UK) Ltd [2004] EWHC 1704 (Comm) 285
Trinity Insurance Co. Ltd *v.* Overseas Union Insurance Ltd [1996] L.R.L.R. 156 232
Tryg Baltica International (UK) Ltd *v.* Boston Compania de Seguros SA [2005] Lloyd's Rep. I.R. 40 94
Trygg Hansa Insurance Co. Ltd *v.* Equitas Ltd [1998] 2 Lloyd's Rep. 439 .... 191, 309, 415

Universal Cargo Carriers Corp *v.* Citati (No. 1) [1957] 1 Lloyd's Rep. 174 295
Unum Life Insurance Co of America *v.* Israel Phoenix Assurance Co Ltd [2002] Lloyd's Rep. I.R. 374 .... 99, 100, 415

Versicherungs und Transport A/G Daugava *v.* Henderson [1934] All E.R. Rep. 626; (1934) 49 Ll. L. Rep. 252 (C.A.) 262, 263, 286
Vita Food Products Inc *v.* Unus Shipping Co. Ltd (In Liquidation) [1939] A.C. 277; (1939) 63 Ll. L. Rep. 21 (P.C.) 386

WISE Underwriting Agency Ltd *v.* Grupo Nacional Provincial SA [2003] EWHC 1706 (Comm); [2004] Lloyd's Rep. I.R. 764 .... 127, 131, 143, 150, 159
Wace *v.* Pan Atlantic Group Inc [1981] 2 Lloyd's Rep. 339 317
Walker *v.* Pennine Insurance Co. [1980] 2 Lloyd's Rep. 156 (C.A.) 286
Walker & Sons *v.* Uzielli (1896) 1 Com. Cas. 492 174
Walkinshaw *v.* Diniz (Stay of Proceedings) [2000] 2 All E.R. (Comm) 237 408
Walkinshaw *v.* Diniz (Amendment to Particulars of Claim) [2001] 1 Lloyd's Rep. 632; affirmed [2002] EWCA Civ 180 (C.A.) 408
Wasa International Insurance Co. Ltd and AGF Insurance Co. Ltd *v.* Lexington Insurance Co. [2007] EWHC 896 (Comm) 172, 179, 180, 196
Waterkeyn, The *v.* Eagle Star & British Dominions Insurance Co. Ltd (1920) 4 Ll. L. Rep. 178; (1920) 5 Ll. L. Rep. 42 338
Wilkinson *v.* General Accident Fire and Life Assurance Corp [1967] 2 Lloyd's Rep. 182 329
Winterthur Swiss Insurance Co. *v.* The Insurance Corp of Ireland plc [1989] I.L.R.M. 13 ... 290
Wise *v.* Grupo Nacional Provincial SA [2004] 2 Lloyd's Rep. 483 298
Woolfall & Rimmer Ltd *v.* Moyle [1942] 1 K.B. 66; (1941) 71 Ll. L. Rep. 15 (C.A.) 222
Wurttembergische AG Versicherungs Beteiligungsgesellschaft *v.* Home Insurance Co [1993] 2 Re L.R. 253 242
Wurttembergische AG Versicherungs Beteiligungsgesellschaft *v.* Home Insurance Co (No. 2) [1997] L.R.L.R. 86 114
Wurttembergische AG Versicherungs Beteiligungsgesellschaft *v.* Home Insurance Co (No. 3) [1999] Lloyd's Rep. I.R. 397 (C.A.) 114, 115

XL Insurance Ltd *v.* Owens Corning [2001] 1 All E.R. (Comm) 530; [2000] 2 Lloyd's Rep. 500 414

Yasuda Fire & Marine Insurance Co of Europe Ltd *v.* Orion Marine Insurance Underwriting Agency [1995] 1 Lloyd's Rep. 525 .... 105, 291, 333
Yona International Ltd *v.* La Reunion Francaise SA D'Assurances et de Reassurances [1996] 2 Lloyd's Rep. 84 109
Yonge *v.* Toynbee [1910] 1 K.B. 215 (C.A.) 321
Yorkshire Insurance Co. Ltd *v.* Campbell [1917] A.C. 218 (P.C.) 219
Youell *v.* Bland Welch & Co Ltd (No. 1) (Superhulls case) [1992] 2 Lloyd's Rep. 127 (C.A.) ... 92, 94, 198, 203, 205, 344
Youell *v.* Bland Welch & Co Ltd (No. 2) (Superhulls case) [1990] 2 Lloyd's Rep. 431 ..... 94, 330, 344
Yukos Oil Co. *v.* Dardana Ltd; *sub nom.* Dardana Ltd *v.* Yukos Oil Co. (No. 1) [2002] EWCA Civ 543 (C.A.) 431

Zelger *v.* Salinitri (129/83) [1985] 3 C.M.L.R. 366 (E.C.J.) 378
Zephyr, The. *See* General Accident Fire and Life Assurance Corp Ltd *v.* Peter William Tanter
Zeus Tradition Marine Ltd *v.* Bell, The Zeus V [2000] 2 Lloyd's Rep. 587 (C.A.) 204

TABLE OF LEGISLATION, CONVENTIONS AND RULES

Arbitration Act 1950 .... 391, 424
Pt II 429
ss. 35–42 429
s. 35 429
s. 37 429
(1) 430
(2) 429
s. 38 429
Arbitration Acts 1975, 1979 391
Arbitration Act 1996 .... 190, 391 *et seq.*
Pt III 428, 429
s. 1 .... 392, 424
(b) 399
s. 2 423
s. 3 391
s. 4(3) 422
s. 5 190
(1), (4) 407
s. 6 406
(1) 407
(2) 191, 414, 415
s. 7 414
s. 9 .... 415, 423
s. 13 423
ss. 15–18 423
ss. 15–29 423
s. 15(3) 410
ss. 17–19 443
s. 18 410
(3) 412
(a)–(d) 410
s. 20 444
s. 24 .... 412, 422, 423, 424
s. 29 425
ss. 30–32 425
s. 30 416
(1) 416
s. 31 416
(1), (2) 416
(4) 417
s. 32(1) 417
ss. 33–41 .... 418, 421
s. 34 421
s. 35 .... 405, 413
(2) 405

Arbitration Act 1950—*cont.*
s. 38 421
(1) 411
(3)–(6) 411
(3) 426
s. 39 411
s. 41 .... 398, 406
s. 42 398
s. 43(1) 425
s. 45 425
s. 46(1)(b) 393
s. 48 422
s. 49 .... 261, 426
s. 52 422
s. 54 422
s. 58 404
ss. 59–65 425
s. 60 425
s. 66 428
ss. 67–69 .... 426, 427
s. 67 399
(1)(a) 417
s. 68 .... 400, 402
s. 69 .... 393, 400
s. 81 407
s. 82(1) 428
ss. 99–104 428
s. 99 429
s. 101 430
s. 102 430
s. 103 431
Sch. 1 422
Brussels Convention 1968 ... 192, 361 *et seq.*, 431
Art. 1 431
Art. 17 .... 192, 193
Art. 21 377
Art. 22 379
Art. 23 377
Art. 25 431
Civil Jurisdiction and Judgments Act 1982 361
Civil Jurisdiction and Judgments Act 1991 361

Civil Procedure Rules 1998, S.I. 1998 No. 3132 .... 393, 399
r. 19.6(1) 110
Consumer Arbitration Agreements Act 1988 391
Contracts (Applicable Law) Act 1990 .... 283, 381
Contracts (Applicable Law) Act 1995 ... 194
Contracts (Rights of Third Parties) Act 1999 .... 259, 261
Council Directive 2205/68/EC Reinsurance Directive 80
Council Regulation 44/2001/EC of 22 December 2000 .... 361 *et seq.*
Art. 23 .... 192, 194
Art. 27 377
Art. 28 379
Art. 29 378
Art. 30 378
Financial Services Act 1986 355
s. 1342 81
Financial Services and Markets Act 2000 ... 80, 353
ss. 19, 20 79
s. 22 79
s. 26 82
s. 27 .... 82, 83
ss. 26–28 .... 81, 340
ss. 104–117 80
sch. 3 79
Financial Services and Markets Act 2000 (EEA Passport Rights) Regulations 2001, S.I. 2001 No. 2511 79
Financial Services and Markets Act 2000 (Regulated Activities) Order 2001, S.I. 2000 No. 544 79
Gambling Act 2005—
s. 335 117
Gaming Act 1845—
s. 18 117
Geneva Convention on the Execution of Foreign Abitral Awards 1927 429
ICC Rules 1988 424
Insurance Brokers (Registration) Act 1977 .... 315, 355
Insurance Companies Act 1973—
s. 50 116
Insurance Companies Act 1984 (Australia) 387
Insurance Companies Act 1982 .. 80, 81, 355
Judgments Act 1838 261
Life Assurance Act 1774 .... 116, 120
s. 1 .... 116, 121
s. 2 116
s. 3 .... 116, 120
s. 4 116
Limitation Act 1980 423
s. 5 .... 229, 286
Limitation Act 1980—*cont.*
s. 32(1)(b) 353
(2) 353
Lugano Convention 1989 ..... 361 *et seq.*, 431
Art. 1 431
Art. 17 192
Art. 21 377
Art. 22 379
Art. 23 377
Ar. 25 431
Marine Insurance Act 1745 115
Marine Insurance Act 1906 .... 66, 135
s. 1 121
s. 4 .... 116, 122
(1), (2) 216
s. 5(2) 117
s. 6 .... 116, 117
s. 9(1) 119
s. 17 .... 153, 292, 297
s. 18 .... 130, 326
(2) 126, 129, 130, 135
(3) 132, 148
(a) 148
(4), (5) 133
(7) 134
s. 19 .... 127, 128, 130, 164, 323–327, 329
(a) 113, 162, 163, 164, 329
(b) 162
s. 20(2) 135
(6) 125
s. 23 85
s. 33(1) 215, 216
(2) 215
s. 34(1) 223
(2) 222
(3) 223
s. 36 215
s. 39(1), (5) 215
s. 41 215
s. 53 229
(1) 227
(2) 228, 351, 352
s. 55(2)(a) 173
s. 84 .... 130, 156
Misrepresentation Act 1967—
s. 2(1) 164, 299
(2) 161, 162
New York Convention on the Recognition and Enforcement of Foreign Arbitral Awards 1958 .... 400 *et seq.*
Prevention of Corruption Act 1986 331
Rome Convention (on the Law Applicable to Contractual Obligations) 1980 .... 380 *et seq.*
Art. 1 382
Art. 2 384
Art. 3 283
Art. 3.1 194
Art. 16 386

Rules of the Supreme Court 1968, S.I 1976 No. 1776—
Ord. 14 243
Ord. 15, r. 2 110
Supply of Goods and Services Act 1982—
s. 13 330
Supreme Court Act 1981—
s. 35A 261
s. 51 253
Theft Act 1968 331
UNCITRAL Arbitration Rules—
Art. 21.2 414

CHAPTER 1

THE NATURE OF REINSURANCE

A list of potentially interesting web sites of relevance to this book

IRMI.com (International Risk Management Institute—U.S.)
BILA.org.uk (British Insurance Law Association—U.K.)
BRMA.org (Broker Reinsurance Market Association—U.S.)
Law.cornell.edu (Cornell University—U.S.)
Llgm.com (Le Boef Lamb—U.S.)
Ealaw.com (Edwards and Angell—U.S.)
DAC.co.uk (Davies Arnold Cooper)
BLG.co.uk (Barlow, Lyde & Gilbert)
law-now@cmck.com
Insurancereinsurance@bplaw.com (Berwin Leighton Paisner)
Onlinedmc.co.uk
legal-definitions.com
marketreform.co.uk (London Market Slips, Contract Certainty . . .)

INTRODUCTION

The aim of this book is not to teach the principles of reinsurance as such but to try to explain and encourage thought on the legal principles applying to reinsurance.

However, as we progress through this chapter we hope to explain the basic purposes of the different types/styles of Reinsurance albeit it at a basic level —the detail will become more apparent as one reviews words used to express intent within differing styles of reinsurance contract.

This chapter provides an introduction to the text by:

- explaining (or confirming) the basic concepts of Reinsurance
- encouraging lateral thinking re the meaning of words in Slips and Wordings
- touching on some of the core legal principles that will be explained in more detail later in the course
- encouraging further research into some of the issues raised

Within this chapter differing examples of clauses used will be included—in no case are they being put forward as the "correct" version. They are being provided as examples of words that are used, and are included to help explain the concepts and core legal principles from an English law perspective.

With regard to legal principles, except where specifically mentioned these are based on the Common Law of England and Wales. It could be dangerous to assume that the principles that are outlined necessarily apply elsewhere.

However, it is important to realise that English legal decisions will be "highly persuasive" in situations within Common Law based countries, particularly where there is little local legal discussion on matters such as Reinsurance. Certainly judges in Common Law jurisdictions do review decisions in other jurisdictions, e.g. England, Australia, Ireland, Singapore, many US states . . . sometimes agreeing and other times not!

Arbitration

This will be dealt with in Chapter 10 but in reading this and other chapters it is important to remember that many issues are decided by arbitration. Such decisions do not create legal precedent and are often never reported because of confidentiality clauses. The growing trend towards ADR (alternative dispute resolution) via mediation . . . should also be borne in mind.

You will see this symbol in this book encouraging you to take a "legal" time out. Consider the question or case asked using your own logic, perhaps a little research?—then review the answer or opinion given. Please remember you are entitled to your views as much as anyone else. The important point of these "breaks" is to encourage you to think laterally through the logic and the reasons for the decisions made.

On other occasions you will see the coffee cup symbol. Questions here are more to do with reinsurance issues—again step back and think through the question and then work through the answer. Even on a law course you might need a calculator.

What follows is based on the author's extensive experience in reinsurance and except where specifically indicated, opinions expressed reflect his own personal views, not a specific legal opinion.

Legal views come from a range of sources—particularly including:

> *Reinsurance Practice and the Law*—published by LLP (Informa), prepared by Barlow Lyde & Gilbert;
> *The Law of Reinsurance*—published by Sweet and Maxwell; CMSCameron McKenna and various notes issued by lawyers such as:
>> Davies Arnold & Cooper, Barlow Lyde and Gilbert, Berwin Leighton Paisner, Kendal Freeman.

Where appropriate, a full reference has been made to relevant court cases. Cases reported in *Lloyd's Insurance and Reinsurance Law Reports* can be viewed online at *www.insurancelawreports.com.* Look for this symbol:

Whether one operates mainly in Common Law jurisdictions or not, the knowledge gained in this and other Modules will still be invaluable. They should encourage thought on how different people can write the same thing, view the same thing and come to different interpretations of the meaning, and how other "forums" and legal bases, e.g. civil law, might view the same things differently.

Common law—civil law

A simple review of the core differences "as a place to start". In my opinion some of the core differences between common law and civil law legal systems are:

Common law	**Civil law**
Concept from England 12th century – creating "standard law"	Concept from Rome 1st–2nd century
Based on the concept of: – interpretation of the law as written – precedent – decisions of higher courts to be followed by lower court	Based on the concept of interpretation of the Aims of Codes – no basic concept of precedent
Meaning of the words used in contracts VERY IMPORTANT	Today's view of the objective of the Code is VERY IMPORTANT
Aims of the parties of lesser importance	Meaning of the individual word used of lesser importance
Decisions tend to be long and full of legal reasoning	Decisions tend to be short—NOT trying to create precedent
Past court cases very important	Past court cases not normally important
Most countries where "England" was "involved" tend to have a common law structure – e.g. US (most states), Ireland, Singapore, Australia, NZ, Caribbean	Most of Europe, Asia, Latin America, including "newly created countries", will create a legal system based around codes and their constitution.

WHAT IS REINSURANCE?

Reinsurance is the transfer of risk from an insurer to another party (reinsurer).

In law?

Basically reinsurance and retrocession (reinsurance of reinsurance) are seen to be insurance contracts.

- "insurance of insurers" (*Reinsurance in Practice*, Kiln).
- "the insurance of contractual liabilities to pay claims incurred under contracts of direct insurance or reinsurance" (*Reinsurance*, Carter).
- "any contract which is placed by or for the benefit of an insurer". This seems a simple statement but there has been some debate whether in law some forms of stop loss are reinsurance (*Toomey* v. *Eagle Star* [1994] 1 Lloyd's Rep. 516).
- In *NRG Victory Insurance* [1995] 1 All E.R. 533—both reinsurance and retro treated as insurance.

What is a reinsurer in law?

- "A reinsurer is an insurer which deals with other insurers as its policy holders." Supporting the concept of reinsurance being insurance (*Iowa Mutual Tornado Association* v. *Timmons*, 105b N.W.2d 209 (Iowa, 1960)).

Why is it legally important and helpful that reinsurance be seen as insurance?

The fact that Reinsurance is basically seen in common law as insurance helps in many legal scenarios—one can revert back to basic insurance legal principles as a starting point, e.g. utmost good faith. However it is also important to remember that different jurisdictions may come to different interpretations.

The placing process and clarity of contract

The placing process

Many of the disagreements in reinsurance stem from the placing process:

- what was or was not said at the time of placing
- the words used on the offer (the "slip")
- the words used in the Policy or Treaty Wording

Before discussing the differing types of reinsurance the placing process would seem to be a logical place to start from—it will be covered in more detail in Chapter 2.

In the scenario that follows it is assumed that the risk is placed in the London Market by a broker:

- Information provided by client to broker
- Placing slip prepared by broker—together with supporting information
- Leader (the person chosen to set the terms and conditions) is offered the risk
  - perhaps more than one potential leader is approached to ensure that the best possible terms are achieved
- "Firm order" is given by the client (reinsured)
- Broker proceeds to endeavour to complete the placement
- Broker keeps client fully advised of progress
- If "over" placed—the reinsurer's acceptances (written lines) are converted into "signed lines"
- An appropriate evidence of cover confirming what has been placed and with whom is prepared and sent to the reinsured by the broker. An "appropriate evidence of cover" as per the guidance notes can include;
  - Policy
  - Copy of complete slip
  - Certificate of Insurance
  - Brokers Insurance Document
- A Policy—Treaty Wording is prepared for signature by the reinsured and the reinsurers

In a growing number of scenarios it is possible that the slip itself will formally be converted into the policy—the concept of the "slip policy". In 2005 and 2006 various initiatives were undertaken to ensure contract certainty at placement time—see *marketreform.co.uk* (documents). These include the issuing of:

- Code of Practice for Contract Certainty, check list and guidance notes
- Late placement guidance
- Signed line guidance
- An augmented slip (now called MRSlip (Market Reform Slip))
- A market note regarding preparation of subjectivities

What legal issues do the above steps of the placing process raise?—At least 10!

Contract certainty

Given that a high percentage of reinsurance is placed using a slip—irrespective of what form of reinsurance is being placed it should be obvious that a well-drafted slip will lead to much less argument in the future re the intention of the parties. In addition it ought to lead to the production of a more accurate wording (where necessary), with its production being prompt! This unfortunately has not been the case in many instances in the past.

In the context of contract certainty and slip preparation two very important trends should be highlighted; the MR (Market Reform) slip and the Code of Practice for Contract Certainty (see Appendix?).

Contract certainty—Code of Practice check list

In October 2005 a contract certainty Code of Practice and supporting documentation was issued with the aim that this be signed up to at board level by all members of LMBC, IUA and LMA. The market target was to achieve 85% contract certain placements for 31 December 2006

- estimated 90% was achieved for 31 December 2005
- for full documentation see *marketreform.co.uk*

NB: Contract certainty is defined as "Contract certainty is achieved by the complete and final agreement of all terms (including signed down the lines) between the (Re)insured and the (Re)insurers before inception"

From a legal perspective a slip complying with this definition may still not be legally certain—this will depend on the drafting of the document itself. Certainly looking to the future the target should be contract quality at placement time.

LMP

The LMP concept formed part of an overall aim to make the London Market more efficient and professional with one of its core aims being "to create contract clarity at placement time". In 2005 this target was changed to read contract certainty. Although the whole market reform concept is much wider than just the slip structure the information given by the market reform programme office on how a MR slip should be presented and what it should contain should be of interest to anyone studying reinsurance and reinsurance law as it provides a template for a clearer and hopefully legally stronger placement slip.

Contract certainty will only come about by clearer, fuller and more professionally prepared slips at the outset.

For full information on market reform see *marketreform.com*. For background, the headings of a MR slip are shown in Appendix 1.

NB: The use of the LMP slip was "mandated" by Lloyd's from 2 January 2004 (with certain specific exceptions) with its use also being actively encouraged by the IUA (International Underwriting Association of London).

One specific legal issue is with regard to an optional heading: recording transmitting and storing information (and the specific text). It is recommended that this field be used to allow brokers the right to digitally store files and destroy the paper version without passing the paper file over to their client.

Personally I would include this on my slips if I was the placing broker BUT discuss the situation with my legal advisor before actually destroying files.

Amongst others:
Responsibilities

- client responsibilities

- intermediary responsibilities
  - utmost good faith
  - material fact
- law of agency

When is there a contract in place?
The power of the slip v. the wording
The responsibilities of the leader
Signing down

- legally acceptable?
- to what amount?
- disproportionate signing
- advising signed lines . . .

When might the broker's cover note have a legal role?
What is the broker's responsibility if reinsurers they have chosen fail?
What if the wording has not been signed?
Do the words on the slip, policy or treaty wording convey in law what they were intended to?

Another area that is potentially going to cause some interesting legal issues in the future is that the LMA formally confirmed in February 2007 that a Lloyd's slip no longer has to be signed by the LPSO (Lloyd's Policy Signing Office). A full slip, stamped and signed by the underwriters, can be forwarded to the client as the total and full legal confirmation of cover—assuming that this documentation is acceptable to the client and in the country concerned.

All will be dealt with as you work through the book, e.g.:

Utmost good faith, material fact (see Chapter 3).
The role and responsibilities of the leader (see Chapter 2).
The role and responsibilities of the broker (see Chapter 8).
Written lines—signed lines (see Chapter 2).
The cover note—what is its legal value? (see Chapter 2).
The power of the slip v. the contract wording (see Chapter 2).

The basic forms of reinsurance

To save a great deal of repetition a few of the core terms used in reinsurance are explained immediately. Firstly three words used regularly in proportional treaty reinsurance in particular:

Cede—to give
Cedant—the giver of reinsurance
Cession—what is given

"cedant cedes a cession" or "a reinsured gives a reinsurance"

The term "cedant" in many cases is replaced by the term Reinsured or Reassured. Both Reinsured and Reassured are seen as being interchangeable (not in the same contract) although perhaps Reassured is used more in Marine and Life.

Retrocession—reinsurance of reinsurance . . . (normally referred to as "Retro").

Retrocedant (often referred to as the "Reinsured"!)—the buyer of "Retro".

Retrocessionaire—the acceptor of "Retro".

Bordereaux—(Premium—Loss)

- a detailed breakdown, risk by risk of premium or loss supporting the entries within a Quarterly Account under a Pro-Rata Treaty.

Facultative v. treaty

Facultative—optional reinsurance normally on a policy by policy basis ("facultative" derives from "facultativo"—meaning "optional").

- the reinsured does not have to reinsure the risk (it is not "obligatory reinsurance") and the reinsurer(s) has the right to decline or offer alternative terms.

Treaty—a "deal", which once agreed gives cover for a range of risks in a particular way, over a period of time.

- once the terms of the treaty are agreed between the parties the reinsured has automatic cover for all risks as specified for a pre-agreed period—normally 12 months.

NB: There is a school of thought that will argue that the word "treaty" infers proportional and that non-proportional arrangements should be termed contracts.

In general today the word treaty is used for both proportional and non-proportional (*Reinsurance Principles and Practice*, Gerathewohl, Vol. 1, p. 374).

In this chapter at least the term treaty is used to differentiate from facultative reinsurance.

Proportional (also called pro-rata) v. non-proportional

(a) *Proportional*—the sharing of risk, premium, acquisition costs and losses based on the amount of risk retained and reinsured

e.g. Factory—sum insured	1,000,000
Retention	100,000
Reinsurance	900,000

Retention	**Reinsurance**
100,000	**900,000**
1,000,000	
10%	**90%**

Premium will be allocated based on the allocation of the risk (10%–90%)

- with the reinsured being allowed to deduct a pre-agreed amount of commission to cover their acquisition costs.

Losses will be allocated based on the allocation of the risk (10%–90%).

(b) *Non-proportional* (Also known as excess of loss or X/L)

The buying of an amount of cover in excess of a chosen deductible (often referred to as the retention or perhaps even primary—U.S.).

The premium charged by reinsurers for giving the cover will be based on their perception of the chance of a loss or losses to the particular reinsurance being considered

- there will normally be no deduction of commission to cover acquisition costs.

Losses will be collectable only for the amount "in excess of" the deductible.

e.g. Factory—sum insured	1,000,000
Retention	100,000
Reinsurance	900,000

Cover	**900,000**
	xs
Deductible	**100,000**

Re

How would the following loss be allocated over the two different variations?

(i) Loss 50,000 on original policy

(ii) Loss 400,000 on original policy

(a) Proportional	**(i)**	**(ii)**
(b) Non-proportional	**(i)**	**(ii)**

(a) Both losses will be split 10%–90% based on the allocation of the risk

(i) 5,000	45,000	(ii) 40,000	360,000
10%	90%	10%	90%

(b) (i) No claim to the reinsurers (below the deductible)
(ii) Claim 300,000 on reinsurers (400,000–100,000 deductible)

Reinsurance types—in summary

Proportional

Facultative
Treaty—differing types (see later)

Non-proportional

Facultative
Treaty—differing types (see later)

FACULTATIVE

Facultative is the earliest form of reinsurance with apparent references back to the 14th century. As already explained facultative is reinsurance based on individual offers where both parties reinsured and reinsurers have options

- do not have to reinsure
- do not have to accept
- terms are fully negotiable

Facultative can be placed both proportionally or non-proportionally (often called Fac X/L).

Some of the core issues from a legal perspective include:

Full RI clause—Chapter 4
Claim cooperation clause—Chapter 7
Claims control clause—Chapter 7
"Back to back" cover—Chapter 4

- and/or as original . . .

Many facultatives are placed as slip policies with the intention and expectation that the reinsurance will follow the original insurance—"back to back". terms such as:

"and/or as original"
"all terms clauses and conditions as original"

might be used.

Although it will be dealt with later in Chapter 4 the issue of using terms such as those above in facultative reinsurances should be touched on now.

There is an arbitration clause in the original insurance. The facultative R/I states "all terms clauses and conditions as original".

The reinsurers want to go to arbitration, the reinsured does not. Is the arbitration clause "incorporated" into the facultative by the use of these words?

Almost certainly not! (*HIH Casualty and Gen* v. *New Hampshire and others* [2001] Lloyd's Rep. I.R. 244). Incorporation *will* only be achieved IF

- the term is germane to the R/I
- the term makes sense
- the term is consistent with the express terms of the R/I
- the term is apposite for inclusion in the R/I.

This is supported by various other court decisions. NB: Such a phrase would almost certainly not incorporate law or jurisdiction into the R/I either.

Why facultative?

Reasons for use of facultative might include:

- to obtain cover for risks which are larger than the reinsured would normally accept
- to obtain cover for a risk in a class of insurance where the reinsured is not normally involved
- enabling an insurer to obtain cover on a risk where, perhaps for commercial reasons, they have had to accept the whole or a very large share
- where the reinsured does not wish to pass its normal share to Treaty reinsurer(s) (perhaps the risk is very hazardous)
- the reinsured's normal Treaty protections are not large enough to deal with a particular risk
- the risk is excluded from the reinsured's Treaty protections
- the risk is one for which the reinsured has no Treaty protection

Open covers—binding authorities—line slips (sometimes referred to as "facilities")

By its very nature (individual offers, accounts, etc.) facultative is expensive to administer for all parties and therefore various time and cost saving methods of handling facultative have evolved, all requiring TRUST in varying degrees:

- open cover—the "underwriting pen" to the reinsured
- binding authority—the "underwriting pen" to the broker or other party (the cover holder)
- line slip—the "underwriting pen" to the leading underwriter(s) of the facility

Although mentioned under the heading of facultative reinsurance all of these types of arrangement could and do equally apply to direct insurance.

Open covers

An agreement by the (re)insurer to accept risks, within the terms of the open cover, if the (re)insured decides to cede. In reinsurance this would often be called a facultative obligatory contract or treaty ("Fac Oblig"). What can be ceded should be specified by firmly laid down guidelines.

The important difference between this and proportional treaties such as quota share and surplus (see later) is that risks do not have to be ceded under an open cover or Fac Oblig but have to be ceded (normally) to quota share and surplus subject to treaty terms—thus an open cover is a "half-way house" between facultative and treaty.

Binding authority "binder"

The underwriting pen to accept certain types of risk (as specified) is passed from the (re)insurers to another party (called the "cover holder"), e.g. a producing broker. The (re)insurers are automatically bound when the cover holder accepts a risk on their behalf.

Such facilities can be very cost effective for the cover holder. They save time, administration and therefore money. Perhaps they can also offer too much temptation?

Binding authority placements into the Lloyd's Market were mandated to fall within the overall LMP (now MRSlip) structure for all binders with an inception date of 1/1/2005 and later. There are very strict rules re the structure and operating procedures of Binders particularly in the Lloyd's Market.

Do both open covers and broker's binders create an agency agreement between the "giver" of the risk and the (re)insurer?

No.

- The open cover is an agreement by the (re)insurer(s) to accept any risks, within the terms of the arrangement, IF they are ceded.
- The binding authority delegates power to the broker or other party to accept risks on behalf of the (re)insurer—thus the "broker" will be operating as an agent of the (re)insurer.

Lastly:

Line slip

Here it is necessary to remember the placing process mentioned above—the broker obtaining a quotation from a recognised "leader" (a specialist who is likely to be followed by others) who then, having received a firm order from the client, proceeds to visit other reinsurers to complete the placement. In many situations the same or similar reinsurers will be seen on a regular basis for a particular class or group of territories by a particular broker.

To save time and administration costs the broker might put together a line slip.

"A line slip is an authority (known in the London Market as a facility) given in writing by a number of underwriters which enable the leading underwriter(s) to agree to proposals for (re)insurance of risks within a prescribed class on behalf of all underwriters subscribing to the line slip provided that the proposed (re)insurance is within the scope of the terms of the authority" (*Balfour* v. *Beaumont* (1982) 2 Lloyd's Rep. 493).

The base line slip contract would state that subject to the agreement of the leader (or maybe joint leaders) to accept an offered risk (on a separate slip called an "off slip") the following market would automatically be bound for pre-agreed shares.

Words such as the following might be used:

> This Line Slip authorises the leading underwriter Mx xxx of ABC Insurances (and . . .) to bind (re)insurances emanating from xxxxxxxx Brokers Ltd of xxx,xxx, xxx.in respect of the following classes of business:
>
> xxxx
> xxxx
> Excluding;
> xxxx
> xxxx
> xxxx
>
> which shall be binding on all other underwriters hereon following the agreement of the leading underwriter.

In this version of a "facility" following (re)insurers are relying on the expertise of the leader(s). The following market would normally receive a schedule of the risks accepted, on a regular basis. Line slips and the declarations under them were brought within the LMP mandate in summer 2005.

Three specific legal points need to be considered with regard to contracts such as line slips:

What is the legal relationship between the leader and the following market?

Is the line slip a contract of (re)insurance?

When are the (re)insurers on risk—from date of acceptance of the line slip or the date of acceptance of the "off-slip"?

The leader and a line slip?

A line slip is seen as the following market delegating authority to the leader, creating an agency relationship.

Contract of (re)insurance?

A line slip is seen to be a contract *for* (re)insurance (IF risks are accepted by the leader they are automatically covered) NOT a contract of (Re)insurance. This subtle difference means that it probably becomes an ordinary contract in law ("buyer beware") and not a contract of "utmost good faith" (*HIH Casualty and General Ltd* v. *Chase Manhattan Bank and others* [2001] Lloyd's Rep. I.R. 191).

The rules of UGF . . . would apply to the offering of the individual risks to the leader(s) but not (in general) to the original line slip when it was being placed, although there would still be a common law need to disclose "unusual features of the transaction".

When are the "reinsurers" on risk?

When the "off-slip" is signed by the leading underwriter(s) not when the line slip is accepted (*Denby* v. *English and Scottish Maritime Ins*, *The Times*, 16 March 1998).

Underwriting agencies/pools

These arrangements which grant power to underwriters to put down their lines on behalf of other (re)insurers should not be confused with line slips. Here an underwriter makes acceptances on behalf of pool or underwriting agency members. Under a line slip, the leader or leaders are taking shares for themselves and for other participants on the line slip.

Facultative—what is wrong with it?

Facultative has the advantage for both parties of being optional, but also some very major disadvantages

- very high administration—particularly proportional
- placement not certain (no automatic cover)

In the mid 1800s the concept for the proportional treaty was developed to overcome these problems.

PROPORTIONAL TREATY

There are three differing types of contract, each with their own peculiarities and purposes:

- Quota share
- Surplus
- Facultative obligatory

The first two could be described as "obligatory contracts"—the reinsured must (within the terms of the treaty) reinsure applicable risks, and the reinsurer(s) must (within the terms of the treaty) accept them.

The third—the facultative obligatory treaty—is a different variation. The reinsured does not have to reinsure any risk but the reinsurer(s) must (within the terms of the contract/treaty) accept them if they are ceded (see the comments above regarding the "open cover"). This variation will be looked at last.

Although "anything is possible!", proportional treaties tend to protect specific classes or departments of business, e.g.

"in respect of all risks allocated to the reinsured's xxx and yyy accounts, excluding zzz"

Quota share treaty

A fixed percentage of each risk (subject to a maximum monetary amount per risk) is automatically reinsured as soon as the insurer accepts the insurance or part of it.

e.g. "Retention" 70% "Reinsuring" 30%

This would be called a 30% Quota Share Treaty.

The percentage being reinsured is *always* the amount used to describe the treaty.

i.e. Retain 10% = Cede 90% = a 90% Quota Share Treaty
Retain 60% = Cede 40% = a 40% Quota Share Treaty

Fairly obviously reinsurers are not going to take X% of every risk without some form of overall monetary limit per risk.

An example

The reinsured has decided it wants to retain 70% of every risk (within a particular class) but NOT more than 175,000 per risk

Reinsurers have agreed to take a maximum of 30% of every risk but NOT exceeding (for their share) 75,000 per risk.

This produces what would be described as a 30% Quota Share Treaty.

Maximum Limit for 100% Q/S 250,000 per risk

- Maximum Limit for Q/S reinsurers 75,000 per risk (30% of 250,000)
- Maximum Limit for the reinsured 175,000 per risk (70% of 250,000)

How did the reinsured come to decide on this structure?

Firstly by deciding on a retention per risk of a maximum of 175,000 and then reviewing their risk profile to ascertain how much automatic reinsurance per risk is needed in addition—assuming it was practical to place the amount sought.

Retention

The decision on the retention per risk is one of the core decisions in reinsurance. Until the reinsured knows what it can afford to keep on a risk it cannot decide on its reinsurance needs or design its reinsurance programme.

What factors might have been taken into account in coming to the decision to retain 175,000 per risk?

The calculation of a retention is not a precise science, numerous factors can be taken into account. It usually ends up as a compromise between;

- Total capital and free reserves
- Premium volume in the class/classes being considered
- Management attitude towards risk
- Reinsurer's attitude (whether within a hard market, softening market)
- Territory/location
- Class/quality
- Regulation
- Price—terms of reinsurance

It is possible that price, management attitude and reinsurer's attitude would be at the forefront of any decision.

For a more detailed view, see *swissre.com: Designing a Reinsurance Programme—a practical approach.*

Graded retentions

Although it is quite common in some markets for insurers to keep a fixed retention on every risk within a class, in many cases reinsureds vary their retention. This decision might in property for example be based on:

- Type of risk within the class
- The quality of the risk itself
  - whether the risk itself is good, average, poor . . .
- The location of the risk
  - inner city . . .

The ability to change retention depending on varying factors such as the above will help further smooth and balance the retained portfolio and hopefully the retained results of insurers. The stronger and more diversified the business of the insurer, the less the need for grading.

From a reinsurer's perspective they ought to have a wider spread of risks than many insureds and assuming the base premiums being charged by insurers are adequate, they can support the concept of graded retentions, *if they wish to.*

Premium and claim calculations under a quota share treaty

If you understood the allocation of risk and premium for facultative proportional the Q/S is based on exactly the same set of concepts—everything is based on the allocation of the risk between the parties

An example

Assuming a 30% Q/S
Maximum cession for 100% Q/S 100,000

Risk sum insured	Cession (amount given) to treaty
100,000	30,000 (30% of 100,000)
50,000	15,000
40,000	12,000
20,000	6,000

How is the premium going to be split?

30% of the risk to reinsurers, 30% of the premiums to reinsurers

		Premium (100%)	To quota share
SI 100,000	Cession 30,000	500	150
SI 50,000	Cession 15,000	300	90
SI 40,000	Cession 12,000	400	120
SI 20,000	Cession 6,000	200	60

Reinsurers are getting 30% of each risk and therefore 30% of the premium

BUT

Commission

Although premium is paid "pro-rata" to the amount of risk being reinsured, the reinsurers agree to commission being deducted by the reinsured before passing the premiums onto the reinsurers to help cover acquisition costs of the reinsured.

It is the reinsured who has the production and servicing costs of the original insurances NOT the reinsurers.
e.g. Commission 40%

30% quota share, commission—40%

		Premium (100%)	To quota share	Less commission 40%
SI 100,000	Cession 30,000	500	150	(60)
SI 50,000	Cession 15,000	300	90	(36)
SI 40,000	Cession 12,000	400	120	(48)
SI 20,000	Cession 6,000	200	60	(24)
			420	**168**

Thus if quarterly account	Premium	**420**
	Less commission	**168**
		252

In these examples reinsurers receive 30% of each risk, 30% of the premium for each risk—less 40% commission and will pay 30% of any loss under the policies ceded.

Although it may seem simple to many of you—if proportional is not totally clear to you take "time out" and work through the example below based on a different set ot terms and sums insured.

60% Quota share, commission—30%

		Premium (100%)	To Quota Share	Less Commission 30%
SI 90,000	Cession	300		
SI 40,000	Cession	100		
SI 20,000	Cession	50		
SI 10,000	Cession	30		
			–	–
Thus if quarterly account	Premium			
	Less commission		–	

60% Quota share, commission—30%

			Premium (100%)	To quota share	Less commission 30%
SI 90,000	Cession	54,000	300	180	(54)
SI 40,000	Cession	24,000	100	60	(18)
SI 20,000	Cession	12,000	50	30	(9)
SI 10,000	Cession	6,000	30	18	(5.4)
				288	86.4
Thus if quarterly account	Premium			288	
	Less commission			(86.4)	
				201.6	

To summarise: premium and claims allocations under all forms of proportional reinsurance are based around the size of the risk and how it is allocated between reinsured and reinsurers not the size of the premium or any losses.

Quota share—the contract

To understand the workings of a quota share treaty and to a great extent any of the types of pro-rata treaty a review of *some of the typical clauses* making up a typical treaty wording follow.

Is there a particular order in drafting a contract wording?

No, different people will prepare wordings in a different order but the core content stays similar.

Should there be?

From a clarity viewpoint—yes. I would recommend a consistent "house style" whenever this is practical.

PREAMBLE

PURPOSE: To establish without any doubt the identities of the parties between whom the Agreement is made and in this example emphasise the fact that all reinsurers have several (separate) liability

> *QUOTA SHARE REINSURANCE AGREEMENT between*
> *ABC INSURANCE COMPANY LIMITED of London, England*
> *(hereinafter called the "Reinsured")*
> *and*
> *The Reinsurers whose names and proportions appear on the attached signing schedules each for its own part and not one for the other (hereinafter called the "Reinsurer").*

It is important to remember that unless very specifically stated all participants have a separate (several) liability and that the individual acceptances are all separate legal contracts with the reinsured even if all contained within one overall document. The words of this preamble just emphasise this. See also the several liability clause in the signing schedule.

INTEREST CLAUSE

PURPOSE: To establish:

(1) the partnership basis of the Agreement by *"The Reinsured agrees to cede and reinsurer agrees to accept . . . "*
(2) the percentage of each risk being ceded
(3) cover is for insurance risks only (not reinsurances) in this example
(4) cover is for all business written in the Fire Department—subject to exclusions
(5) the territorial scope is "Ruritania" only
(6) what perils are covered
(7) the limit of liability under this Agreement per "risk"
(8) the retention of the reinsured
(9) what constitutes "any one risk"

The Reinsured agrees to cede and the Reinsurer agrees to accept by way of reinsurance a fixed proportion of 50% of all insurances accepted or renewed by the Reinsured in its Fire Department on risks situated in Ruritania against direct and/or indirect and/or consequential loss by Fire and/or any other peril covered by the Reinsured —subject to any specific exclusions in Article XX—up to a limit of x,xxx,xxx per insurance for the 50% ceded.

The Reinsured agrees to retain for its own account the balance of 50%.

The Reinsured shall be the sole judge as to what constitutes any one risk.

"The reinsured agrees to retain for its own account the balance of 50% of all business." Can they buy any other reinsurances?

Almost certainly they can NOT reduce their share down by further proportional reinsurance but would be able to place Risk X/L protecting the retention against unexpected larger individual losses and protect the accumulation of losses by Catastrophe X/L. If the reinsurer wants this retention to be totally unreinsured they should make this very clear (*Great Atlantic* v. *Home* (1981) 2 L.R. 219).

FOLLOW THE FORTUNES

PURPOSE: To establish:

(1) that once the reinsured has written a risk they have the protection of this agreement
(2) a maximum policy period any cession
(3) the partnership basis of this Agreement by stating this agreement shall follow the same terms and conditions as are set on the original insurance

This does not incorporate things that are not "germain" to the reinsurance (*AIG* v. *The Ethneki* (2000) L.R. 243), e.g. Law, Jurisdiction, Arbitration—see Chapters 9 and 10

(4) reinsurers will follow the settlements provided they are within the terms of this reinsurance—This probably does not cover ex-gratia settlements unless specifically mentioned in the clause—see Chapter 7.

The liability of the Reinsurer shall commence simultaneously with that of the Reinsured.

Each cession will be of no longer duration than 12 months plus odd time, not exceeding 18 months in all.

This Agreement shall be on the same terms, clauses and conditions as original and shall follow the settlements and/or agreements of the Reinsured in all respects provided they are within the terms and conditions of this Agreement.

PERIOD

PURPOSE: To:

(1) confirm the continuous nature of this agreement
(2) establish the period of the agreement
(3) set out the notice period required for cancellation

(4) set out what action should be taken in the event of notice being given
(5) make clear under what circumstances either of the parties can terminate this agreement, and IF special notice is invoked what happens to the risks already written.

This agreement comes into force 1 January xxxx, at 00.00am local standard time and applies to all business attaching on or after that date. It is concluded for an indefinite period but either party may terminate it by giving 3 months notice in writing to the other party at each anniversary date; the anniversary date shall be regarded as 31 December of any year.

During the term of a notice to terminate, and until its expiry the Reinsured shall renew existing cessions and take new risks in the same manner and in all respect as if no such notice has been given.

Special cancellation

Either party shall have the right to terminate this Agreement immediately if:

(a) the performance of the whole or any part of this Agreement be prohibited or rendered impossible de jure or de facto

In particular and without prejudice to the generality of the preceding words in consequence of any law or regulation which is or shall be in force in any country or territory or if any law or regulation shall prevent directly or indirectly the remittance of any or all of any part of the balance or payments due to or from either party

(b) the other party has become insolvent or unable to pay its debts or has lost the whole or any part of its paid up capital

(c) there is any material change in ownership or control of the other party

(d) the country or territory in which the other party resides or has its head office or is incorporated shall be involved in armed hostilities with any other country whether war be declared or not or is partly or wholly occupied by another power

(e) the other party shall have failed to comply with any of the terms and conditions of this Agreement.

All notice of termination in accordance with any of the provisions of this Article shall be deemed to be served upon despatch or, where communications between the parties are interrupted, upon attempted despatch.

In the event of this Agreement being terminated in accordance with this Article the liability of the Reinsurer under current cessions at the date of termination shall continue in full force until their natural expiry.

SECURITY DOWNGRADE CLAUSE

A comparatively new and topical addition to many contracts. What follows is one of a number of variations of this clause that have appeared recently. It would normally appear as part of the cancellation clause above within the special cancellation section.

If, in respect of any reinsurer hereon:

- *(i) the reinsurer ceases underwriting operations completely or withdraws from underwriting the class of business to which it has designated this reinsurance; or*
- *(ii) the reinsurer's security rating from Standard & Poor's (or any future agency employed by the reinsured for the purpose of reinsurance security rating) is downgraded to BBB+ or below (or equivalent from any future agency, as determined by the Reinsured)*

the reinsured shall have sole option to cancel this agreement immediately by giving notice in respect of the participation of such reinsurer.

In the event of this agreement being terminated in accordance with this Article the liability of the reinsurer under current cessions at the date of termination shall continue in full force until their natural expiry.

It is agreed that the reinsured shall have sole discretion in assessing the above and in invoking the provisions of this clause.

Whether this clause or variations of it are legally strong or clear is a different issue—it is possible the answer is no.

EXCLUSIONS

PURPOSE: To establish what is not covered by this agreement remembering this is proportional reinsurance and meant to be a contract based on sharing risks, acquisition costs, premiums, losses, etc.

Core exclusions are likely to fall into three broad categories:

- (1) Those relating to *territory*
- (2) Those relating to *peril*
- (3) Those relating to *class*

and then detailed specifics within some, e.g. those relating to war, terrorism, nuclear, etc.

Will include a variation of the following:

Notwithstanding anything contained herein to the contrary, this Agreement excludes:

- *(A) War, invasion, act of foreign enemy, hostilities or warlike operations (whether war be declared or not), civil war*
- *(B) Mutiny, civil commotion assuming the proportions of or amounting to popular rising, insurrection, rebellion, military or usurped power, or any act of any person or persons acting on behalf of or in connection with any organisation the object of which are to include the overthrowing or influencing of any de jure or de facto Government by terrorism or by any violent means.*

(C) Nuclear Energy Risks Exclusion Clause (Reinsurance) (1994)

(WORLDWIDE EXCLUDING USA & CANADA)

This Agreement shall exclude Nuclear Energy Risks whether such risks are written directly and/or by way of reinsurance and/or via Pools and/or Associations

For the purpose of this Agreement Nuclear Energy Risks shall mean all first party and/or third party insurances or reinsurances (other than Workers' Compensation and Employers' Liability) in respect of:

- *(I) All Property on the site of a nuclear power station. Nuclear Reactors, reactor buildings and plant and equipment therein on any site other than a nuclear power station.*
- *(II) All Property, on any site (including but not limited to the sites referred to in (I) above) used or having been used for*
  - *(a) The generation of nuclear energy, or*
  - *(b) The Production, Use or Storage of Nuclear Material*
- *(III) Any other Property eligible for insurance by the relevant local Nuclear Insurance Pool and/or Association but only to the extent of the requirements of that local Pool and/or Association*
- *(IV) The supply of goods and services to any of the sites, described in (I) to (II) above, unless such insurances or reinsurances shall exclude the perils of irradiation and contamination by Nuclear Material.*

Except as undernoted, Nuclear Energy Risks shall not include:

- *(i) Any insurance or reinsurance in respect of the construction or erection or installation or replacement or repair or maintenance or decommissioning of Property as described in (I) to (III) above (including contractors' plans and equipment).*
- *(ii) Any Machinery Breakdown or other Engineering insurance or reinsurance not coming within the scope of (i) above.*

Provided always that such insurance or reinsurance shall exclude the perils of irradiation and contamination by Nuclear Material.

However, the above exemptions shall not extend to:

- *(1) The provision of any insurance or reinsurance whatsoever in respect of:—*
  - *(a) Nuclear Material*
  - *(b) Any Property in the High Radioactivity Zone or Area of any Nuclear Installation as from the introduction of Nuclear Material or—reactor installations—as from fuel loading or first criticality where so agreed with the relevant local Nuclear Insurance Pool and/or Association.*
- *(2) The provision of any insurance or reinsurance for the undernoted perils:*

- *Fire, lightning, explosion;*
- *Earthquake;*
- *Aircraft and other aerial devices or articles dropped therefrom;*
- *Irradiation and radioactive contamination;*
- *Any other peril insured by the relevant local Nuclear Insurance Pool and/or Association;*

in respect of any other Property not specified in (I) above which directly involves the Production, Use or Storage of Nuclear Material as from the introduction of Nuclear Material into such Property.

Definitions

"Nuclear Material" means:

(i) Nuclear fuel, other than natural uranium and depleted uranium, capable of producing energy by a self-sustaining chain process of nuclear fission outside a Nuclear Reactor, either alone or in combination with some other material,

and

(ii) Radioactive Products or Waste

"Radioactive Products or Waste" means any radioactive material produced in, or any material made radioactive by exposure to the radiation incidental to the production or utilisation of nuclear fuel, but does not include radioisotopes which have reached the final stage of fabrication so as to be usable for any scientific, medical, agricultural, commercial or industrial purpose.

"Nuclear Installation" means:

(i) Any Nuclear Reactor;
(ii) Any factory using nuclear fuel for the production of Nuclear Material, or any factory for the processing of Nuclear Material, including any factory for the reprocessing of irradiated nuclear fuel; and
(iii) Any facility where Nuclear Material is stored, other than storage incidental to the carriage of such material.

"Nuclear Reactor" means any structure containing nuclear fuel in such an arrangement that a self-sustaining chain process of nuclear fission can occur therein without an additional source of neutrons.

"Production, Use or Storage of Nuclear Material" means the production, manufacture, enrichment, conditioning, processing, reprocessing, use, storage, handling and disposal of Nuclear Material.

"Property" shall mean all land, buildings, structures, plant, equipment, vehicles, contents (including but not limited to liquids and gases) and all material of whatever description whether fixed or not.

"High Radioactivity Zone or Area" means:

(i) or nuclear power stations and Nuclear Reactors, the vessel or structure which immediately contains the core (including its supports and shrouding) and all the contents thereof, the fuel elements, the control rods and irradiated fuel store;

and

(ii) or non-reactor Nuclear Installations, any area where the level of radioactivity requires the provision of a biological shield. Also likely to have exclusions for Terrorism, Electronic Date Recognition.

UNDERWRITING POLICY

PURPOSE:
Having established a partnership with the reinsured, to make sure that the philosophy of the reinsured does not alter, e.g. Graded Retention tables.

The Reinsured undertakes not to introduce, without the prior approval of the Reinsurer, any change in its established acceptance and underwriting policy of those insurances to which this Agreement relates.

ERRORS AND OMISSIONS

Paragraph 1

PURPOSE: To ensure; that neither party is disadvantaged by an inadvertent error or omission of the other party (i.e. forget to cede a risk) providing that no greater liability shall be imposed on the Reinsurer and that the clause shall not override any specific terms and conditions contained in the Agreement.

Any delay error or omission on the part of the Reinsured in rendering any account or furnishing any advices or making any entry in the Reinsurance Memoranda or notifying any claim or giving any information which ought under the provisions of this Agreement to be given to the Reinsurer shall not invalidate any reinsurance hereunder or release the Reinsurer from any obligation hereby imposed on it. It is however understood that any delay error or omission shall be corrected immediately upon discovery.

Paragraph 2

PURPOSE: To re-emphasise the partnership which exists between the parties.

It is agreed that for all things coming within the scope of this Agreement the Reinsurer shall follow, to the extent of its interest, the fortunes of the Reinsured.

Do you think this clause allows the core purpose of the contract to be changed because of a "*mistake*"?

In law it is very clear that this clause is seen to be in place to deal with minor matters and NOT to allow the core purpose of the contract to be changed because of a "mistake" (*Pan Atlantic Insurance* v. *Pine Top Insurance* [1993] 1 Lloyd's Rep. 496 (C.A.); 2 Lloyd's Rep. 427 (H.L.)).

PREMIUM AND COMMISSION

PURPOSE: To establish:

- how the "consideration" for the contract (premium) shall be calculated.
- what is the basis of the premium (in this case Original Net Premium —ONP)
- on what the commission is based.

To confirm:

- the proportional nature of the contract

OGP–ONP

Whether reinsurers are to receive their proportionate share of the original insurance premium (OGP—original gross premium) or after someone has deducted something e.g. local agency commission (ONP—original net premium), this must be made clear. It is a very important part of any proportional Treaty.

The Company shall pay to the Reinsurer the latter's proportion of the Original Net Premium which shall be defined as Gross Premiums received less local brokerage—not exceeding 10%—received by the Reinsured in respect of all cessions made under this Agreement.

The Reinsurer shall allow to the Reinsured a further commission of xx% computed on the Reinsured's share of the Original Net Premium (sometimes referred to as Over-riding Commission).

ACCOUNTS

PURPOSE: To establish:

- when the accounts are to be rendered
- when balances due are to be paid
- how often the accounts are to be prepared

The Reinsured shall render accounts quarterly as at 31 March,
30 June, 30 September and 31 December in each year,
within 45 days after the close of each quarter.

What do you think of this clause?

A very bad example?

Perhaps should be tighter?

No references to when balances to be paid by either party

- with the accounts (balances due to reinsurers)?
- within X days of receipt (where balances due from reinsurers)

No reference to penalties if not complied with? (NB: Normally there are none.)

A better version perhaps:

(a) The accounts between the Reinsured and the Reinsurer in respect of the business under this Agreement shall be closed as stated in the Schedule and rendered by the Reinsured as soon as possible thereafter but in any event not later than two months after the end of the stated period.

(b) Accounts shall be confirmed by the Reinsurer within one month of receipt but inadvertent errors and/or omissions in the accounts shall not delay the payment of any balance due hereunder unless such errors and/or omissions have a major effect on the remittable balance. Any necessary correction shall be made in the next account rendered hereunder except in those cases where the error and/or omission has a major effect on the remittable balance necessitating an immediate adjustment.

(c) Balances due to the Reinsurer shall be paid by the Reinsured at the same time as the accounts are rendered and balances due by the Reinsurer shall be paid at the time of confirmation by the Reinsurer.

Perhaps also adding in the following

OVERDUE BALANCES

Any amounts outstanding after the date on which settlement is due should be subject to the payment of interest by the debtor. Interest shall be calculated at the rate stated in the Schedule and remain payable until the date upon which payment is received by the creditor.

RATES OF EXCHANGE CLAUSE

(sometimes called Currency Conversion Clause)

PURPOSE: To specify:

If risks are from various countries and premiums/claims in differing currencies —how to account to reinsurers.

For the purpose of this Agreement currencies other than the currency in which this Agreement is written shall be converted into such currency at the rates of exchange used in the Reinsured's books or where there is a specific remittance for a loss settlement at the rates of exchange used in making such remittance.

NB: When considering non-proportional later do not confuse the purpose of this clause with the currency fluctuation clause

PROFIT COMMISSION

In many cases, if the treaty has made a profit "*as far as reinsurers are concerned*", reinsurers are willing to allow the reinsured further commission to encourage good results—this clause explains the basis of calculation.

As this is to calculate whether reinsurers have made a profit, an item called reinsurers' expenses or management expenses is specified to be included in the debit side of the calculation. Its purpose, to ensure that reinsurers only pay a profit commission after a deduction has been made to help cover their own acquisition costs.

PURPOSE: To establish:

- on what basis a profit commission is payable by reinsurers
- when any profit commission is payable
- what items are to be taken into account
- the amount of reinsurers' management expenses provision
- the deficit carry forward provision

This clause explains in detail the calculations of additional commission that reinsurers are willing to give after taking into account 3 negotiable factors.

(a) The amount of profit commission payable
(b) The amount of reinsurers' expenses

- in this case 5% of written premium is added to the OUTGO to cover some of the costs of the reinsurer in accepting the business (it is an accounts function—no one receives it!).

(c) The "deficit" if any from previous years calculations—in this case any deficit shall not be carried forward for more than three years

In this particular contract the Treaty is on a "clean cut" basis meaning that each year can be closed off at the end of the year—therefore the reference to "portfolios" (see the next clause).

In addition to the Commission provided for in this agreement the Reinsurer shall allow the Reinsured a Profit Commission of 20% on the actual net profit for each year. Such Profit Commission shall be calculated as at the 31 December in accordance with the following formula:

INCOME

(a) Original Net Premiums ceded to the treaty
(b) Credit of an amount equivalent to the Premium and Loss Portfolios as specified in this wording

OUTGO

(a) Debit of an amount equivalent to the Premium and Loss Portfolios as specified in this wording
(b) X% Commission calculated on item (a) of INCOME
(c) Losses paid and expenses incurred less salvages and recoveries received
(d) 5% for Reinsurers' Management Expenses calculated on item (a) of INCOME
(e) Deficit, if any, brought forward from the previous year or years

The balance of the statement shall be the profit on which the Profit Commission is calculated.

Any Profit Commission due to the Reinsured shall be taken into account in the settlement of the next Quarterly balances rendered.

In the event of the Profit Commission statement showing a deficit to the Reinsurer by reason of the "OUTGO" exceeding the "INCOME" then the total of such deficit shall be added to the "OUTGO" of the Profit Commission statement for the ensuing Year or Years (as the case may be) and no Profit Commission shall become payable to the Reinsured in respect of such ensuing year or years unless and until the previous deficit has been recovered and a net profit re-established provided however, that the deficit of any one year shall not be carried forward into the Profit Commission statement of more than three subsequent years.

In the event of termination of this Agreement the final Profit Commission statement shall be rendered after all liability has elapsed.

PORTFOLIO CLAUSE

Premium and loss portfolios

A method of transferring un-expired liability (premium portfolio) and outstanding losses (loss portfolio) from one year to the next thereby alleviating large administration costs.

If left on an "underwriting year" basis (e.g. marine cargo) where all premiums and all claims on policies issued during the treaty year go back to the reinsurers of that year there is substantially higher administration and the higher possibility of Security Failures.

For example marine cargo—on an "underwriting year" basis:

Year 1 4 quarterly accounts—Year 1
Year 2 4 a/cs—Year 1 + 4 a/cs Year 2
Year 3 4 a/cs—Year 1 + 4 a/cs Year 2 + 4 /cs Year 3

Then an ever-growing number of accounts for perhaps up to 6 years or more.

PURPOSE:

- making provision for portfolios
- confirming method and amount
- what action to take if materially unfair (in the opinion of the reinsured).

As soon as practical, but not later than 3 months after the start of the year Reinsurers will be credited with a Premium and Loss portfolio as herein provided

> ***Credit*** *50% of the Net Premiums ceded, less Treaty Commission to cover the unexpired risk still current at 31st December of the preceding year*
> ***Credit*** *90% of the Reinsurer's share of all outstanding losses as at 31st December of the preceding year*

Each Year will be closed at the end of the year and the portfolio transferred to the next year as herein provided.

As soon as practicable, but not later than 3 months after the end of the year, a portfolio account for the year in question shall be drawn up and certified by the Reinsured and a copy thereof sent to the Reinsurer constituted in accordance with the following formula:

> ***Debit*** *50% of the Net Premiums ceded, less Treaty Commission to cover the unexpired risk still current at 31st December*
> ***Debit*** *90% of the Reinsurer's share of all outstanding losses as at 31st December.*

In the event of any material alteration which in the opinion of the Reinsured renders any transfer in accordance with this ARTICLE inequitable between one year and another, the Reinsured will effect an appropriate adjustment.

CLAIMS SETTLEMENT CLAUSE—CASH LOSS—PLA

PURPOSE: To establish:

- how losses will be handled by the reinsured
- what involvement or not reinsurers have in loss settlement decisions
- size of cash loss limit
- size of preliminary loss advice limit

Claims settlement clause

The Reinsured at its sole discretion and without any right on the part of the Reinsurer to interfere, shall adjust, settle or compromise all claims and losses. Every such adjustment, settlement and compromise, including "ex gratia" with reinsurer's prior consent, shall be binding on the Reinsurer. The Reinsured shall likewise, at its sole discretion, commence, continue, defend, compromise, settle or withdraw from actions, suits or prosecutions, and generally do all such matters and things relating to any claims or losses as in its judgement may be beneficial or expedient, and all payments made and costs and expenses incurred in connection therewith shall be shared by the Reinsurer in proportion to its liability for the claim or loss. Any share of expenses in connection with the settlement of claims shall not include expenses and salaries of employees or office/expenses of the company.

The reinsurer on the other hand shall be entitled to share in all recoveries of salvage or otherwise.

If, however, there was no loss in the end at all, just costs, possibly another sentence could be added:

In the event of there only being costs in respect of the investigation and/or defence of a claim that would have fallen under the reinsurance, reinsurers agree to pay their proportionate share based on the cession of the original risk to the Treaty.

Cash loss provision

It is quite possible that there can be a long delay between the occurrence of a major loss to the reinsured—perhaps at the start of the quarter and rendition of the accounts and receipt of funds from reinsurers well after the end of the quarter—this clause is intended to help speed up the process—whether it is strong enough and actually has the necessary effect is a different topic and outside the scope of this course.

All loss settlements shall be debited in account but where a loss falling under this Agreement attains or exceeds the sum of xxx,xxx in respect of any one loss, the Reinsurer shall pay its share to the Reinsured within 14 days of application.

Preliminary loss advice—(PLA)

If reinsurers are accepting this treaty without bordereaux they will not be aware of any larger losses within the quarterly accounts, unless requested under a cash loss.

This clause ensures that reinsurers are aware of major losses.

The Reinsured shall advise the Reinsurer as soon as possible after receiving notice thereof of any claim which is estimated to attain or exceed xxx,xxx to the Treaty.

RESERVE DEPOSITS

Premium Reserve Deposits—the reinsured retaining a % of premiums from the quarterly A/C and releasing this amount at a later date plus a pre-agreed amount of interest.

Loss Reserve Deposits—the reinsurers funding the reinsured's outstanding losses.

Both may be sought by a reinsured as a "security reserve"—in most cases they are only likely to be given where it is a legal requirement in the reinsured's country of domicile

NB: In the US, for example, an irrevocable letter of credit might replace the loss reserve deposit.

OFFSET CLAUSE

PURPOSE: To establish the right to deduct from any payment due to the other party any amounts owed to them by the other party.

A difficult clause to implement if it includes the words underlined as it can be very hard to implement on other agreements which may be direct (not through a broker) or through another broker and are definitely separate legal contracts.

Either party may at its discretion offset against any amounts advised to and due from the other party hereunder any amounts which have been previously advised and are due at that time under this or other Agreements.

Clauses common to both proportional and non-proportional

The following clauses or variations of them are going to be found in all the variations of treaty reinsurance—whether proportional or non-proportional so they will only be presented once unless there are specific reasons for including elsewhere.

INSPECTION OF RECORDS CLAUSE

PURPOSE: To make clear:

- the reinsurer's rights to investigate the business being ceded under this agreement
- when the rights can be taken
- what can they see
- for how long they have the rights
- who will pay for the copying

The Reinsurer or their representatives may at any time during normal office hours, inspect and take copies of the Reinsured's records and documents which relate to business covered under this Agreement. It is agreed that the Reinsurers' right of inspection shall continue as long as either party has a claim against the other arising out of this Agreement.

Many versions of this clause also deal with the issue of costs involved in such situations . . . *and the said representatives may arrange for copies to be made at the Reinsurers' expense of any of the records containing such information as they may require and be entitled to.*

AMENDMENTS AND ALTERATIONS

PURPOSE: To create the means whereby any amendment to the Agreement may be made without having to cancel and replace the entire wording.

The terms of this Agreement may at any time be altered by mutual consent of the parties hereto and evidenced by Addendum signed by a responsible official of each of the parties hereto or by correspondence between responsible officials of the parties hereto. Such Addendum or correspondence shall be deemed to be an integral part of this Agreement.

NB: Would recommend that one should always use addenda (and perhaps reflect this in the wording)—letters get lost and are not numbered!

INTERMEDIARY

PURPOSE: To define the role of the broker where there is one despite the broker not being party to the contract.

Although the broker is not a party to the contract the broker will be mentioned in the contract to clarify their responsibilities.

Getaline Insurance Brokers Limited of . . . are hereby recognised as the intermediary negotiating this Agreement for all business hereunder. All communications (including but not limited to notices, statements, premiums, return premiums, commissions, taxes, losses, loss adjustments, expenses, salvages and loss settlements) relating thereto shall be transmitted to the Reinsured or the Reinsurer through Getaline Insurance Brokers Limited.

Certain intermediary clauses—particularly those involving U.S. domiciled brokers—are likely to have the following paragraph inserted:

Payment by the Reinsured to the intermediary shall be deemed to constitute payment to the Reinsurer. Payment by the Reinsurer to the intermediary shall be deemed only to constitute payment to the Reinsured to the extent that such payments are actually received by the Reinsured.

This section of the clause was introduced following a major collapse of a broker in the 1970s (Pritchard and Baird) and the requirements of NAIC (National Association of Insurance Commissioners) to seek protection for domestic insurers.

LAW AND JURISDICTION

This very important area has been overlooked particularly in facultative and is now a specific field in the LMP slip.

PURPOSE: To establish the laws under which any disagreement about the functioning of this agreement should be conducted and what jurisdiction can hear the case

The original policies underwritten by the Reinsured shall be based on English Law and Jurisdiction.

A clause that the author finds is misunderstood surprisingly regularly. The clause in this section is to do wth interpretation and disagreements over the contract between the (re)insured and (re)insurers. It has nothing to do with coverage given under the cover as such. Lloyd's Memos Y3327 and Y3406 specifically refer to this area.

What do you think of the above clause? Does it protect all the parties?

It only deals with a specific insurance issue. It makes no reference to the basis of law and jurisdiction in the reinsurance! (It is a "local" jurisdiction clause.)

A more comprehensive clause might be along the following lines;

This Agreement shall be subject to the jurisdiction of the High Court of Justice or its equivalent in the country specified in Item xx of the Schedule which shall apply the laws of the country specified in Item xx of the Schedule as the proper law of this Agreement.

The issues of law and jurisdiction will be dealt with in Chapter 9—for now it should be noted that unless a clause is (a) included (b) included in a strong and clear specific manner it is not certain that the law and jurisdiction wanted by one party or the other will necessarily be achieved.

Perhaps a better version of the clause clarifying how both the reinsurance contract and the underlying risks are to be handled with regard to proper law might read like this—if this is what is wanted by the parties.

This reinsurance shall be governed by and construed according to English law. Any arbitration tribunal or other Forum, however, shall construe any terms and conditions of the original insurance and any obligations deriving therefrom which are or become governed by some other law, rule, practice or jurisdiction as having the same meaning and/or effect as has or would be given to them under such law, rule, practice or jurisdiction.

The inclusion of a "proper law and jurisdiction" clause may also influence how the following clause can be interpreted and implemented in different jurisdictions.

ARBITRATION

PURPOSE: To determine:

- how any disputes between the parties should be handled
- the methodology for the Arbitration
- the location of the Arbitration
- the proper law of the Arbitration

All matters in difference between the parties arising under, out of or in connection with this Agreement, including formation and validity, whether arising during or after the period of this Agreement, shall be referred to an arbitration tribunal in the manner hereinafter set out.

Unless the parties appoint a sole arbitrator within 14 days of one receiving a written request from the other for arbitration, the claimant (the party requesting arbitration) shall appoint his arbitrator and give written notice thereof to the respondent.

Within 30 days of receiving such notice the respondent shall appoint his arbitrator and give written notice thereof to the claimant, failing which the claimant may apply to the appointer hereinafter named to nominate an arbitrator on behalf of the respondent.

Before they enter upon arbitration the two arbitrators shall appoint a third arbitrator. Should they fail to appoint a third arbitrator within 30 days of the appointment of the respondent's arbitrator then either of them or either of the parties may apply to the appointer for the appointment of the third arbitrator.

The three arbitrators shall decide by majority. If no majority can be reached the verdict of the third arbitrator shall prevail.

The third arbitrator shall also act as Chairman of the Tribunal.

Unless the parties otherwise agree the arbitration tribunal shall consist of persons (including those who have retired) with not less than ten years' experience of insurance or reinsurance as persons engaged in the industry itself or as lawyers or other professional advisers.

The arbitration tribunal shall, so far as is permissible under the law and practice of the place of arbitration, have power to fix all procedural rules for the holding of the arbitration including discretionary power to make orders as to any matters which it may consider proper in the circumstances of the case with regard to pleadings, discovery, inspection of the documents, examination of witnesses and any other matter whatsoever relating to the conduct of the arbitration and may receive and act upon such evidence whether oral or written strictly admissible or not as it shall in its discretion think fit.

The appointer shall be the Chairman for the time being of ARIAS (UK) or if he is unavailable or it is inappropriate for him to act for any reason, such person as may be nominated by the Committee of that ARIAS (UK). If for any reason such persons decline or are unable to act, then the appointer shall be the judge of the appropriate Courts having jurisdiction at the place of arbitration.

All costs of the arbitration shall be determined by the arbitration tribunal who may, taking into account the law and practice of the place of arbitration, direct to and by whom and in what manner they shall be paid.

The place of arbitration shall be xxxxxx, xxxxxxx.

The proper law of this Agreement shall be the law of xxxxxxxx.

The award of the arbitration tribunal shall be in writing and binding upon the parties who covenant to carry out the same.

SIGNING SCHEDULE

This wording will then be followed by a Signing Schedule. It is very common for the Signing Schedule to be headed with a *Several Liability Clause*.

SEVERAL LIABILITY

PURPOSE: To (re)confirm: Each reinsurer is only liable for their proportion of any obligations under the contract NOT that of any other reinsurer.

The subscribing Reinsurers' obligations under contracts of reinsurance to which they subscribe are several and not joint and are limited solely to their individual subscriptions.

The subscribing Reinsurers are not responsible for the subscription of any co-subscribing reinsurer who for any reason does not satisfy all or part of its obligations.

One of the compulsory fields in the LMP slip is reference to several liability.

Surplus treaty

The next form of proportional treaty reinsurance—how does it operate?

Whilst the Q/S treaty means giving away a share of every risk within the rules of the treaty, the surplus has a different purpose and method of operation.

The surplus is providing automatic reinsurance for any risk that is surplus to the reinsured's retention. All smaller risks remain retained 100%.

Here again the core decision is how much the reinsured can afford to keep on one risk—based on capital, management attitude, reinsurers' attitude, territory, location, price, etc.

Once this decision is made, a decision on the automatic capacity needed under the surplus can be made.

Treaty limit

Reinsurers limit the amount of capacity that they are willing to give to a multiple of what is retained and ensure there is a proportional relationship between what is retained and ceded.

An example

Retention per risk 175,000
Seeking automatic capacity per risk up to a further 1,750,000
The treaty would be described as a 10 line surplus treaty ("line" means retention)

Retention	**10 Line Surplus**	**Automatically issue a policy for**
175,000	Max limit 1,750,000	1,925,000 (10 × 175,000 + 175,000)

A further decision would have to be made by the reinsured as to whether to seek reinsurers' agreement to introducing graded retentions as mentioned earlier (as the risk is seen to get worse by the underwriter as the retention decreases). By decreasing the retention on a specific risk the amount of automatic reinsurance available under the surplus treaty decreases.

Retention	**10 Line Surplus**	**Automatically issue a policy for**
A 175,000	Max limit 1,750,000	1,925,000
B 100,000	1,000,000	1,100,000
F 25,000	250,000	275,000

How would you allocate the following risks?
Three risks – Category B
Sum insured
(a) 100,000
(b) 800,000
(c) 2,000,000

Category B risk = Retention of 100,000

Retention	**10 Line Surplus**	**The balance?**
(a) 100,000 *100%*	0	0
(b) 100,000 *12.5%*	700,000 *87.5%*	0
(c) 100,000 *5%*	1,000,000 *50%*	900,000 *45%*

As it is proportional reinsurance the allocation of the premium and any losses are based on the allocation of the risk itself as shown in the percentages in italics above. In example (c) the reinsured has not got enough automatic treaty capacity. The reinsured is likely to endeavour to try to place the balance as facultative—in this example proportionally.

It is possible that if there are enough risks above the capacity of the first surplus to justify it that the reinsured might seek to place another Treaty—a second surplus. If this was the case the picture would look slightly different.

Retention	10 Line Surplus	15 Line Second Surplus
100,000	0	0
100%		
100,000	700,000	0
12.5%	*87.5%*	
100,000	1,000,000	900,000
5%	*50%*	*45%*

The second surplus normally only picks up risks after a share has been placed with the first surplus as shown above.

In the example above a 10 line first surplus and a 15 line second has been used. Whether the reinsured can place a second surplus and, if so, for how many "lines", will be based on negotiations between reinsurers and reinsured.

Facultative obligatory

Before looking at any specific clauses applicable to a surplus we will finish looking at Proportional treaty by considering the facultative obligatory treaty ("Fac Oblig").

The way to understand this arrangement is to see its title as separate statements:

Facultative—optional for reinsured
Obligatory—for the reinsurer
Treaty—a contract for a period of time

The "Fac Oblig" normally sits after other proportional treaties. The main difference between the "Fac Oblig" and surplus is that under the surplus the reinsured normally must cede (give) a cession to surplus reinsurers (as in both examples above) if the risk is large enough. Under the "Fac Oblig" the reinsured can decide whether to cede nothing, something or a full amount. If a cession is made, it must be accepted by reinsurers.

How might it work?

Sum insured 4,100,000

Retention	10 Line 1st S	20L 2nd S	10L Fac Oblig	Fac
100,000	1,000,000	2,000,000	1,000,000	0

or

Retention	10 Line 1st S	20L 2nd S	10L Fac Oblig	Fac
100,000	1,000,000	2,000,000	0	1,000,000

The reinsured could in fact cede any amount between 0 and 1,000,000 to Fac Oblig.

Can be "unlined"!

Under exceptional circumstances (a very soft treaty market) it might be possible to find "Fac Obligs" without mention of line—just a treaty Limit—In this situation there is no relationship between the retention and how much can be reinsured under the contract, just a maximum cession per risk.
For example, sum insured 1,155,000

Retention	10 Line 1st S	20L 2nd S	Fac Oblig	Fac
5,000	50,000	100,000	1,000,000 (Treaty limit)	0

Do you have to have a retention to make cessions to the above treaties?

A retention is not inferred into a Fac Oblig (*Phoenix General Ins Co. of Greece SA* v. *Halvanon Ins Co. Ltd* [1985] 2 Lloyd's Rep. 599) or any other proportional treaty. If the reinsurer expects there to be one, this should be made very clear at the time of placement. In another case (*Sail* v. *Farex* (1995) L.R.L.R. 116) the Court of Appeal commented that if the reinsured's presentation is not clear it is up to the reinsurer to ask whether a retention applies. However, where there is reference to "line" it is inferred that there is a retention. Line = retention.

How would any premium or loss be allocated in the example immediately above?

Sum insured 1,155,000

Based on the allocation of the sum insured

Sum insured 1,155,000

Retention	10 Line 1st S	20 Line 2nd S	Fac Oblig
5,000	50,000	100,000	1,000,000 (Treaty Limit)
0.43%	4.33%	8.66%	86.58%

CONTRACT DOCUMENTATION, FOR THE SURPLUS AND THE FACULTATIVE OBLIGATORY TREATY

All the clauses reviewed above under the Q/S would be found in a treaty wording for either surplus or Fac Oblig. The only clause that would be different would be the reinsuring clause—explaining how the treaty operates.

OTHER PROPORTIONAL ISSUES

Quota share as well as surplus?

Whilst it is common to have only a quota share or only surplus(es), it is possible to have a proportional treaty programme with both quota share and surplus(es) in conjunction.

PML and pro-rata treaties?

Although the examples given above have been based on the sum insured (SI) of each risk—if the reinsured operates on a PML (probable maximum loss) or equivalent basis and reinsurers will agree, the treaties could be placed based on the reinsured's PML assessments.

An example

Retention	5 "Line" Surplus
1,000,000 PML	5,000,000 PML

Risk SI 12,000,000
PML 25%

How would the risk, premium and any losses be allocated in this example?

First, reduce the SI down by the PML 12,000,000 × 25% = 3,000,000
Then, think proportional allocation of the risk
PML = 3,000,000

Retention	5 "Line" Surplus
1,000,000 PML	2,000,000 PML
33.33%	66.67%

Premium and claims would be allocated 33.33%/66.67%.

But what if the PML is wrong?
Loss of 6,000,000

How is the loss allocated?

33.33%	66.67%
2,000,000	4,000,000

The loss would still be allocated based on the split of cession 33.33%–66.67%—the fact that the PML is wrong is just unfortunate—the treaty was offered to reinsurers on a PML basis and they accepted it, knowing there could be PML failure.

Some treaties now include specific clauses limiting reinsurer's exposure if the PML failure is too great.

PML clause

(Limitation of liability where an estimated PML is exceeded)

(1) The reinsurance is based on the Probable Maximum Loss (PML). When fixing the PML of any risk the ceding company shall act as prudently and carefully as possible.

(2) If in the case of a loss occurrence the PML forming the reinsurance basis for a specific risk proves to be too low, the additional liability of the reinsurers shall be limited to a further 50% of the amount of the PML.

This provision shall not apply;

- *to losses caused by crashing aircraft*
- *in case of concurrent arson in several, spatially separated areas within one risk*
  - *these are to be treated as separate loss occurrences under the clause*
- *in cases where the PML is exceeded as a result of the estimate not having taken into account "disaster-like events related neither directly nor indirectly to the risk insured".*

This provision shall override any other clause or condition of the treaty and, in particular, the errors and omissions clause.

AGGREGATE LIMITS UNDER PROPORTIONAL TREATIES

Another issue particularly in a hard market is where reinsurers impose overall limits in the event of a catastrophe. If no aggregate limit is imposed:

- Reinsurers receive a proportionate share of the premium of every risk
- Reinsurers receive a share of every risk
- Reinsurers would have to pay their share of any claim under policies ceded
  - giving a potential for unlimited liability any one event!

This has become a very topical issue again, since the 2004 Caribbean Hurricanes, Charley, Frances, Ivan and Jeanne.

An example of a clause showing how it might work is as follows:

IF THE TOTAL of the Earthquake Sums Insured ceded, as per the latest accumulation report due or as per the date of the loss if lower exceeds the overall cession limit as specified in the Schedule then in the event of a loss all claims recoverable from the reinsurers shall be reduced in the relation which the cession limit bears to the total of the earthquake sums insured ceded.

A variation just imposes a maximum limit for any one event on the treaty.

NON-PROPORTIONAL

The products we are going to review in this section are:

Facultative
"Treaty"

Risk X/L
Catastrophe X/L—Event X/L
Stop loss
Aggregate X/L

How do they work ?

The core issue to understand is how all of these differ from proportional, whether treaty or facultative.

Proportional is based on the concept of sharing: risk, premium, claims and acquisition costs (commission)

Non-proportional or X/L is based on buying an amount of cover for a price for a period of time—normally 12 months.

Facultative X/L

As a refresher the following has been taken from the opening section. Take a few moments out—if it is necessary—and ensure you are happy with the different concepts.

(a) *Proportional*—the sharing of risk, premium, losses based on the amount of risk retained and reinsured.

For example, Factory sum insured 1,000,000—Retention 100,000; Reinsurance 900,000

Retention		**Reinsurance**
100,000		900,000
	1,000,000	
10%		90%

Premium will be allocated based on the amount at risk (10%/90%).
Losses will be allocated based on the amount at risk (10%/90%).
NB: Commission will be deducted from the premiums due to reinsurers to cover acquisition costs of the reinsured.

(b) *Non-Proportional*
The buying of an amount of Cover in excess of a chosen Deductible.
Premium charged by reinsurers for giving the Cover will be based on their perception of the chance of a loss or losses to the particular reinsurance being considered.
Losses will be collectable only for the amount "*in excess of*" the deductible.

Cover	900,000
	xs
Deductible	100,000

i.e.—loss 50,000 on original policy

(a) Will be split 10%/90%
(b) No claim to the reinsurers (below the deductible)

Loss 400,000 on original policy

(a) Will be split 10%/90%
(b) Claim to the reinsurers of 300,000 (400,000 less 100,000 deductible)

Whether a reinsured decides to place any Facultative on a Proportional or Non-Proportional basis will come down to such things as:

- availability of cover on either basis
- perceived "cost" of such reinsurance
- risk aversion of the reinsured
- possibility of increased retained premiums

There is a strong impetus in many scenarios from international reinsurers to encourage facultative X/L (and per risk X/L):

- simpler administration
- less involvement in small losses
- less concern about base prices—can charge the "correct price for the cover given".

There is an issue with regard to the way in which Facultative X/L should be handled in conjunction with Pro-Rata Treaties which really does not form part of this course.

However, to summarise: any cession should be made to Proportional Treaties first based on the allocation of the risk in the normal way. (Retention, X Lines, X Lines, etc.). What is left after cession to Treaty(ies) can be added back to the standard retention and then Fac X/L placed on the sum of the 2 retentions.

COSTS AND EXPENSES CLAUSE

There is an issue that should be dealt with very clearly on Facultative X/L placements—how loss adjustments should be allocated over the various layers.

A clause seen recently that is trying to deal with the issue of adjustment expenses and how they should be allocated over the various layers of a Fac X/L follows:

Reinsurers agree to pay their proportion of expenses, charges, adjusters fees, legal and other costs incurred in connection with the adjustment, investigation and settlement of any original policy claim (but excluding office expenses and salaries of the Reinsured) in addition to the Limit as stated under the Limit of Liability and in the ratio that the Reinsurers loss payment bears to the 100% original policy loss payment which shall exclude the amount of any excess or deductible payable by the Insured.

Not every one agrees with this methodology.

Per risk X/L

PURPOSE: To protect a class of business (as defined) by trying to take out individual losses that are larger than normal, which could unbalance the results of the reinsured.

An example

Retention in 2004 100,000 per risk
4 line surplus = Capacity 400,000

For 2005:

- reinsurers insist the retention per risk is increased to 150,000 or they will not continue to give the same amount of pro-rata treaty capacity

or

- the reinsured decides to increase its retention per risk to 150,000
  - potential for more retained premium

Although both these scenarios are different, the potential impact is the same. IF individual losses on the retention are larger than 100,000 the reinsured will be totally responsible for the increased loss.

For peace of mind they might consider buying per risk X/L reinsurance for 50,000 xs 100,000 to take out any loss amount in excess of 100,000.

NB: Although they will be liable for 100% of all losses on their retention up to 100,000 they are protected against the unexpected large individual loss.

Two other scenarios where a per risk X/L might be considered are:

- the reinsured decides or is actively encouraged by reinsurers to drop its proportional treaty and replace fully by X/L—the current trend;
- the reinsured decides to change its retention per risk from being based on the sum insured of the risk to the PML (probable maximum loss).

PML

PML retention based on maximum SI of 150,000
Subject to a minimum PML 66.67%

If the PML is never wrong the reinsured can only lose a maximum of 100,000 of the same figure as they were retaining "last year" BUT if the PML fails they could be liable for up to 150,000.

A possible solution—buy reinsurance for 50,000 xs 100,000 for peace of mind.

Replacing proportional with risk X/L

The current trend?—replace pro-rata treaty with risk X/L.

Why?

- Easy to administer
  - Four quarterly accounts for the same figure (plus an adjustment)
- Easy to explain
  - either a claim or not
- Dramatic increase in retained premium
- Reinsurers less involved in pricing of the original policies
- Reinsurers less involved in the original results
- Low administration as compared to pro-rata

The downside for the reinsured?

- Solvency ratio—may be substantially worsened
  - increased retained premium
- Exposure to catastrophe perils may be dramatically increased
  - more Cat X/L required
- Risks X/L's will normally have event and annual aggregate limits

NB: Reading through the core risk X/L clauses and their purposes as presented below will give a more detailed view of how this cover operates.

Risk X/S of loss

Advantages for a reinsured (compared to pro-rata)

- reduces cost of catastrophe reinsurance (reduces net/net aggregate exposures)
- easy to administer compared to surplus
- depending on state of Reinsurance Market, can be cheap

Disadvantages for a reinsured (compared to pro-rata)

- reinsured pays all individual losses below the deductible (no sharing)
- reinsured cannot limit exposure by retention selection very easily
- no contribution to acquisition costs—no commission

- market very volatile—price and capacity
- no retention of premium/loss reserves
- limitation on aggregate of losses claimable (per event or per year)
- if on a "losses occurring" basis no guaranteed cover after year end if cancelled.

This last point means that normally there would NOT be cover for risks still running at the end of the risk X/L period, whilst under a pro-rata protection, either because on an underwriting year or clean cut basis such "ongoing" protection exists. How to solve the problem? Place the reinsurance on a "risks attaching" (during the period basis).

What is one risk?

"at the option of the reinsured"

Important for all parties to be clear as to the definition of one risk, as differing organisations have different views.

An office complex
One building
Every five floors of a building occupied by a particular insured

The wording might read as follows:

Definition of "Loss Any One Risk"

The words "loss any one risk" shall mean each and every loss affecting any one risk and each being considered as an individual claim hereunder irrespective of the number of risks affected in the same event.

As regards the word "risk", the Reassured shall be the sole judge as to what constitutes one risk; it being understood and agreed that one risk shall mean all property or interest at any one location and designated by the Reassured in its records as subject to one risk retention.

Risk X/L—the contract

To understand the workings of a risk X/L and to a great extent any of the types of non-proportional treaty a review of *some of the typical clauses* making up a typical treaty wording follow.

Not unsurprisingly many of the clauses under a pro-rata treaty will be found under non-proportional and vice versa—only where there are core difference will the clause be referred to again. The relevant headings of each clause and a reminder of their purpose, however, have been included to help get a feeling of the whole contract.

PREAMBLE

Who is reinsuring who and on what basis?

NB: Likely to include reference to "in consideration of premium being paid" as in these products Cover is being bought for a price.

INTEREST CLAUSE

Core Coverage—Classes

PERIOD

PURPOSE: To establish:

(1) The period for the agreement
(2) What losses are covered during the period

Cover in non-proportional reinsurance is normally placed on one of the following bases:

- Losses occurring during the period
- Claims made during the period
- Losses discovered during the period
- Risks attaching or policies issued during the period

The period of cover is an essential part of the insurance and reinsurance buying and underwriting process. The buyer and/or advisor needs to be very clear as to the period and "trigger" of coverage being given under any insurances and their reinsurances.

Losses occurring during (LOD)

The most common overall is "losses occurring during" which in many scenarios will be clearly ascertainable. Problems do arise (particularly in some liability classes) as to when a loss occurred e.g. industrial disease (employers' liability), environmental pollution (public liability).

There has been much legal debate on the meaning of specific words such as "occurring" and "cause".

LOD is in many cases not used for professional indemnity, directors and officers (D&O) and perhaps product liability—which are often on a claims made basis.

What is your view of this clause? Is it clear to you what losses can fall under this contract?

This Agreement is in respect of losses occurring during the period from 1 January xxxx and ending 31 December xxxx Local Standard Time, both days inclusive where loss occurs.

In respect of Policies that are in force as of the effective date of this Agreement, or that are written or renewed with effective dates during the term of this Agreement.

Many reinsurance offers do refer to local standard time, but fail to make it clear what LST actually refers to e.g. place of loss, head office of reinsured. Wherever possible an actual local standard time would be clearer.

Claims made during—the retroactive date

Particularly common in professional indemnity, product liability and directors and officers liability, reinsurers have no peace of mind regarding losses occurring on policies issued in the past unless the wording is suitably clear.

This Agreement is amended in that it shall not apply to:

- *(a) all claims already made against the Reinsured arising directly or indirectly from loss(es) that took place prior to the inception date of this Agreement;*
- *(b) all claims made against the reinsured during the period of this Agreement attributable directly or indirectly to loss(es) that took place prior to the inception date of this Agreement of which the reinsured had knowledge or should reasonably have foreseen might result in a claim or suit against the Reinsured.*

Extended loss reporting clause

Under a claims made reinsurance problems can occur when a reinsurance is cancelled and not replaced with further cover. Losses may be reported later but there is no reinsurance cover available unless an extended loss reporting clause is included.

This clause does NOT extend the period of the reinsurance only the time in which a claim can be made.

The term of this Agreement shall begin as of x/x/xxxx and continue for 12 months.

In the event of termination and non replacement of this Agreement, the Reinsurer shall remain liable for losses emanating from Claims first reported under Policies in force as of the date of termination until the date of expiration or cancellation of such Policies in the ordinary course of business, or until twelve months following the termination date of this Agreement, whichever date first occurs.

Losses discovered during

This is particularly used in fidelity, and possibly credit, political risks, e.g. accountant discovers that the company secretary has been stealing money from the company for the past five years. The total claim would fall on the reinsurance in the year this was discovered.

This Agreement shall apply for 12 months to losses discovered on and after 1/1/2004 . . . and shall apply to all new and renewal policies effective on or after . . . 1/1/2004.

Risks attaching during (policies issued during)

In reality this provides cover for risks incepting during the period of the reinsurance.

Major advantages for the reinsured—peace of mind that whatever happens at the renewal of the reinsurance programme the reinsured has cover for all policies issued.

Major disadvantage for reinsurers—have to keep their books open for longer —they are on risk for as long as it is possible a claim might materialise under an original policy.

This Agreement is effective from 00.00 am Local Standard Time, 1/1/2006 in respect of policies incepting or having an anniversary date on and after such date, and shall remain in effect until 24.00 Local Standard Time, 31/12/2006.

EXCLUSIONS

An ongoing ever changing list—particularly in the area of terrorism

REINSURING CLAUSE

PURPOSE: To establish:

(1) The monetary amount of the deductible under the layer
(2) The monetary amount that can be claimed "each and every loss"
(3) That "each and every loss" refers to "each and every risk" separately

   – cover is per risk

(4) An "event" limit—any one occurrence
(5) An overall limit as per the reinstatement provisions.

This Agreement is only to pay the excess of an ultimate net loss to the Reinsured of the amount x,xxx,xxx each and every loss each and every risk, up to a further amount x,xxx,xxx ultimate net loss each and every loss each and every risk, subject however, to an Occurrence Limit in respect of losses arising out of one event of xx,xxx,xxx and subject to the provisions of the Reinstatement Clause.

Occurrence limit

As there is an "occurrence limit" in this reinsurance certain clauses that would appear in a catastrophe X/L would also appear in this wording, e.g. extended expiration clause, "hours clause".

EXTENDED EXPIRATION CLAUSE

PURPOSE: To confirm that if a loss covered by the treaty is in progress at its expiry, (particularly applicable to an "event") the whole of the "event" is covered whether individual losses occur before or after expiry, provided, no claim in respect of the same occurrence is made against any renewal or replacement of the treaty.

Reinsurers agree that if this Agreement should expire whilst a loss is in progress, it is agreed that subject to the other conditions of this Agreement, the Reinsurers shall pay their proportion of the entire loss or damage, provided that the loss had occurred during the currency of this Agreement.

No such loss may be used for the purposes of calculating both the Reinsured's Ultimate Net Loss under this Agreement and that for any renewal of this Agreement.

DEFINITIONS

PURPOSE: To establish (in this particular example):

(1) What constitutes any one risk
(2) What constitutes any one event—there in an occurrence limit
(3) What the reinsured may do to calculate the period of one event *Loss occurrence*

The word "loss occurrence" shall mean all individual losses arising out of and directly occasioned by one catastrophe.

However, the duration and extent of any "loss occurrence" so defined shall be limited to:

(a) 72 consecutive hours as regards hurricane, typhoon windstorm, rainstorm, hailstorm and/or tornado
(b) 72 consecutive hours as regards earthquake, seaquake, tidal wave and/or volcanic eruption
(c) 72 consecutive hours and within the limits of one city, Town or Village as regards riots, civil commotions and malicious damage
(d) 72 consecutive hours as regards any "loss occurrence" which includes individual loss or losses from any of the perils mentioned in a), b), and c) above
(e) 168 consecutive hours for any "event" of whatsoever nature which does not include individual loss or losses from any of the perils mentioned in a), b) and c) above and no individual loss from whatever Insured peril, which occurs outside these period or areas, shall be included in that "loss occurrence".

The Reinsured may choose the date and time when any such period of consecutive hours commences
and

if any catastrophe is of greater duration than the above periods, the Reinsured may divide that catastrophe into two or more "occurrences", provided no two periods overlap and provided no period commences earlier than the date and time of the happening of the first recorded individual loss to the Reinsured in that catastrophe.

Depending on the territory being covered the coverage might go on to include a variation of this definition.

Notwithstanding the above, as regards loss or losses from collapse caused by weight of snow and water damage from burst pipes and/or melting snow, the Reinsured shall have the option to deem any one "event" to be the aggregate of all individual losses which occur during a period of 168 consecutive hours within one continent. No period may commence earlier than the date and time of the happening of the first recorded individual loss to the Reinsured in that "event" and the period of two or more "events" may not overlap.

Definition of event

Obviously, the definition of what constitutes one loss for the purpose of an excess of loss reinsurance will vary considerably according to the type of reinsurance and the nature of the original business reinsured.

The "hours clause", of which there are numerous variations, was originally introduced in the 1940s–50s. It endeavours to determine what constitutes an event or occurrence. For example in the case of property covers, it imposes time and/or geographical limits on the event or occurrence. It also makes clear what happens if the "event" continues for longer than the specified number of hours.

For a totally different view of how to view an "event" loss" see Swiss Re web-site *swissre.com* and their clause SE 460 (Booklet: *Event Definition, Swiss Re's new event clause* (2000)). Under this clause the "hours" limitation only comes into play IF one event cannot be clearly proved.

There have been various very important legal decisions regarding the meanings of words such as, event, occurrence, cause . . . in the meantime, what is your opinion on the following?

Do the words event and occurrence have similar or different meanings?

The word "cause" is similar in meaning to the above words?

In various court cases (e.g., *KAC* v. *KIC* (1996) ILR 664) it has been decided that unless specifically shown to have a different meaning the two words event and occurrence have basically similar meanings.

However, cause is seen to have a totally different meaning (*AXA RI (UK) Plc* v. *Field* [1986] 1 Lloyd's Rep. 26).

"in my opinion these expressions are not at all the same . . . in ordinary speech, an event is something which happens at a particular time at a particular place in a particular way . . .

A cause is to my mind something altogether less constricted. It can be a continuing state of affairs; it can be the absence of a happening."

Event, occurrence or claim describes what happened; cause describes why it happened.

TERRITORIAL SCOPE

Self explanatory

ULTIMATE NET LOSS CLAUSE

PURPOSE: To establish:

(1) what can be included in a claim
(2) all collections from "inuring reinsurances" must be taken into account in calculating the loss "whether collected or not".

See reference to the purpose of the Liquidation Clause, particularly with regard to the meaning of the word "actually".

The term "Ultimate Net Loss" shall mean the sum actually paid by the Reinsured in settlement of losses or liability after making deductions for all recoveries, all salvages and all claims upon other reinsurances, whether collected or not, and shall include all costs and adjustment expenses arising from the settlement of claims other than the salaries of employees and the office expenses of the Reinsured.

All salvages, recoveries or payments recovered or received subsequent to a loss settlement under this Agreement shall be applied as if recovered or received prior to the aforesaid settlement and all necessary adjustments shall be made by the parties hereto. Nothing in this clause shall be construed to mean that a recovery cannot be made hereunder until the Reinsured's Ultimate Net Loss has been ascertained.

Recoveries under any underlying Excess of Loss Reinsurance Agreements (as far as applicable) are for the sole benefit of the Reinsured and shall not be taken into account in computing the Ultimate Net Loss or Losses in excess of which this Agreement attaches, nor in any way prejudice the Reinsured's right of recovery hereunder.

If the Excess of loss was protecting not just the reinsured's retained account but perhaps pro-rata treaty reinsurers as well it would have to be amended —perhaps along the following lines.

Notwithstanding the foregoing, Reinsurances effected by any Proportional Treaty Reinsurers protected hereunder, if described in this Agreement as being reinsured hereunder shall not be taken into account in computing the Ultimate Net Loss or Losses in excess of which this Agreement attaches, nor in any way affect the amount recoverable hereunder.

In summary:

- take the total of all losses involved in the "event", under policies covered by the reinsurance
- subtract the total of all losses covered under "inuring" reinsurances

  e.g. quota share, surplus, fac—"whether collected or not"
  – see net retained lines clause below.

The figure left is the reinsured's "ultimate net loss" (unl) which can now be applied to the risk X/L deductible to see if there is a claim or not. The initial collection may need to be adjusted when all the final figures are known.

NET RETAINED LINES CLAUSE

PURPOSE: To establish:

(1) That the reinsurance applies only to that portion of any business which the reinsured retains net for its own account.
(2) Reinsurers are NOT liable for increases in liability caused by errors and omissions
(3) This reinsurance is not giving protection for non-paying reinsurers under "inuring programmes".

This Agreement shall only protect that portion of any business the subject matter of this Agreement which the Reinsured, acting in accordance with their established practices, retain net for their own account.

Reinsurers' liability hereunder shall not be increased due to an error or omission which results in an increase in the Reinsured's normal net retention nor by the Reinsured's failure to reinsure in accordance with their normal practice, nor by the inability of the Reinsured to collect from any other reinsurer any amounts which may have become due from them whether such inability arises from the insolvency of such other reinsurer or otherwise.

PREMIUM CLAUSE

PURPOSE: To establish:

(1) The deposit premium due and when it is to be paid
(2) The minimum premium being charged
(3) How any adjustment shall be calculated and when it should be done
(4) To define the adjustable base (e.g. GNWPI).

The Reinsured shall pay to the Reinsurers a Deposit Premium of 20,000 payable 25% on 1st January, 1st April, 1st July, 1st October xxxx.

Whether quarterly, half yearly . . . will depend on negotiations with reinsurers and the state of the reinsurance market (the norm is quarterly in advance).

As soon as possible after the expiry of this Agreement the above Deposit Premium shall be adjusted to an amount equal to the rate of x.xx% of the Reinsured's Gross Net Written Premium Income as defined hereunder.

Nevertheless, the final adjusted premium for this Agreement shall not be less than a Minimum Premium of x,xxx,xxx. The payment of any adjustment due between the parties shall become payable forthwith.

The term "Gross Net Written Premium Income" shall mean the gross premium written by the Reinsured during the period of this Agreement on business protected hereunder less only returned premiums and premiums paid for reinsurances, recoveries under which inure to the benefit hereof.

What happens if the premium is NOT paid on time? Can the cover be cancelled?

As you will see in Chapter 5, unless the payment of premium has been made an express part of the contract, making it very clear what will happen if there is non payment, it is very unlikely the courts will allow a contract to be cancelled following non-payment.

"Except as provided for in the Marine Insurance Act 1906 (MIA 1906) in the absence of an express provision in the contract, the payment of premium is NOT a condition precedent to liability of the reinsurer" (*The Law of Reinsurance,* Sweet & Maxwell 5–79).

Here it might be appropriate just to touch on Warranties (see also Chapter 5).

Even if the words premium payment warranty are used it is not guaranteed that the court will view the term as a warranty—it will be the intent not the description that will help the final decision. For a warranty to be seen as a warranty it must be seen to "go to the root of the contract".

CURRENCY FLUCTUATION CLAUSE

In situations where cover and deductible are in currency A but it is possible that claims may arise in currency B a pre-agreed rate of exchange might be agreed or a variation of this clause introduced.

PURPOSE: To explain how any claims in currencies other than that of the cover and deductible are to be dealt with.

This clause covers a situation where the reinsurance expresses the limit and deductible in one currency but the business covered is underwritten by the reinsured in another currency or a number of currencies.

The clause is designed to preserve the equivalent value of the limit and deductible in other currencies against a variation in the exchange rate between such other currency and the named currency.

For example:

This reinsurance is agreed for £1,000,000 excess of £100,000 but for business written by the Reinsured in Ruritanian Crowns, for which the exchange rates at inception of the reinsurance is 10 Crowns to £1, this gives an equivalent protection of Crowns 10,000,000 excess of Crowns 1,000,000.

In the event of a loss in Ruritanian Crowns this protection is maintained, the balance of any loss payment in excess of the deductible of Crowns 1,000,000 being converted into Sterling at the rate ruling at the date of settlement of the loss by the reinsured.

Summary

Any loss in "Crowns" is applied to the cover and deductible as specified in crowns that would have been appropriate when the cover was priced (at inception).

Any loss paid by reinsurers will be settled by them at the ROE applicable when the loss was settled by the reinsured.

A variation of this clause might be based on the ROE at inception and not specify a specific figure.

The above should not be confused with the

CURRENCY CONVERSION CLAUSE

If original risks and losses are from various countries possibly in a Catastrophe for example and premiums are received in differing currencies—how to account to reinsurers?

For the purposes of this agreement currencies other than the currency in which this agreement is written shall be converted into such currency at the rates of exchange used in the Reinsured's books or where there is a specific remittance for a loss settlement at the rates of exchange used in making such remittance.

RUN OFF

PURPOSE: To establish:

(1) What cover is available in the event of the reinsurance (on a losses occurring during basis) not being renewed
(2) At what terms "run off" cover is available
(3) When the reinsured must elect to take the "run off", cover.

In the event of this Agreement not being renewed or replaced, it is agreed to indemnify the Reinsured for losses occurring during the period of twelve months from the expiry date hereof in respect of policies and/or contracts written on or prior to such expiry date at terms to be agreed.

It is understood and agreed that the Reinsured must elect to accept the "run-off" provision before the effective date if such "run-off" is required, each annual period being deemed a separate Agreement.

SELF INSURANCE

PURPOSE: To confirm:

That "self insured" risks can be included in any claim by the reinsured.

This clause establishes the right of the reinsured to receive the benefit of a reinsurance recovery even though there is no third party claimant as such—the reinsured would be the insured in respect of their own buildings, i.e. an insurance company may insure its own buildings under one of its own policies and include them within the ultimate net loss (UNL).

In the absence of such a clause it could be argued that there can be no liability at law to pay such a claim, as no entity can be legally liable to itself, therefore there can be no right of recovery under a reinsurance agreement.

It is understood and agreed that an insurance or a reinsurance issued by any Reinsured protected hereby wherein that Reinsured is named as the Insured, either alone or jointly with another party or other parties, shall be deemed to be an insurance or a reinsurance coming within the scope of this Agreement notwithstanding that no Legal Liability may arise in respect thereof by reason of the fact that the Reinsured in question is named as the Insured or one of the Insured.

REINSTATEMENT

(The re-buying of cover that has been used up after a claim)

A very important part of the overall X/L programme design and processing process.

Reinsurers have in many cases to buy their own retrocession and would be loath to give the equivalent of "unlimited cover in a year" when they could not buy suitable retrocession themselves. Reinstatement provisions provide a limitation and additional premium for granting further automatic cover. How many reinstatements and at what terms will always be negotiable.

PURPOSE: To establish:

(1) That reinstatement premium is payable
(2) How they shall be calculated
(3) When the reinstatements are to be paid

(4) The maximum amount of reinsurers' liability
(5) The order in which losses are taken into account
(6) That an adjustment shall be done if a premium adjustment is done

e.g., if limit of cover per risk 5,000,000

In the event of loss or losses occurring under this Agreement it is hereby mutually agreed to reinstate this Agreement to its full amount of 5,000,000 from the time of the occurrence of such loss or losses to the expiry of this Agreement subject to Additional Premium as follows;

(a) In respect of the first full reinstatement of the indemnity there shall be no payment of additional premium.
(b) The premium payable hereunder in respect of the second full reinstatement of the indemnity will be calculated pro-rata of 50% of the premium hereon.
(c) The premium payable hereunder in respect of the third full reinstatement of the indemnity will be calculated at pro-rata of 100% of the premium hereon.

For the purposes of the foregoing:

(i) The term pro-rata shall mean pro-rata only as to the fraction of the limit of indemnity reinstated.
(ii) The additional premium shall be paid by the Reinsured when any loss or losses arising hereunder are settled but nevertheless the Reinsurers shall never be liable for more than 5,000,000 in respect of each and every loss, each and every risk nor for more than the 20,000,000 in all hereunder.
(iii) Losses shall be considered in date order of their occurrence but this shall not preclude the Reinsured from making provisional collections in respect of claims which may ultimately not be recoverable hereon, provided at no time shall the Reinsurers have paid more than 20,000,000

Summary

Reinsurers have agreed to give a total of three reinstatements under this cover meaning total amount claimable in the year = 20,000,000

Premium for	5,000,000	of Cover
3 Reinstatements	15,000,000	of Cover
	20,000,000	

The price of the reinstatements has been agreed as follows:

First "Free"

Second "50%"
Third "100%"

How much would be due to reinsurers as reinstatement premium for the following losses—assuming a minimum and deposit premium of 20,000?

Losses *to the Layer*

3,000,000—January

2,000,000—March

Step 1: *pro-rata shall mean pro-rata only as to the fraction of the limit of indemnity reinstated* (often referred to as "Pro-rata for amount").

$$\frac{3{,}000{,}000}{5{,}000{,}000} = \text{Free}$$

$$\frac{2{,}000{,}000}{5{,}000{,}000} = \text{Free}$$

Thus collected 5,000,000 in losses; reinstated 5,000,000 of cover for "free".

But what happens if there is a further loss of 2,500,000 to the layer in May?

$$\frac{2{,}500{,}000}{5{,}000{,}000} \times 50\% \times 20{,}000 = 5{,}000$$

Thus collected a further 2,500,000 in losses; reinstated a further 2,500,000 of cover.

The calculations have not changed, but the numbers have. Now the reinstatement is based on 50% of the M and D (often referred to as 50% for time), and will be adjusted when the final premium for the cover is known.

How much cover can be reinstated for the rest of the year?

2,500,000 for 2nd reinstatement
5,000,000 for 3rd reinstatement

What happens if there is no reference to reinstatements on the reinsurance slip?

What do you think might happen?

It will depend on the words of the slip and wording but if no obvious reference such as "in all" or an overall aggregate limit it is highly arguable that the contract pays out on each and every loss and is, in effect, probably subject to unlimited reinstatements.

UNDERWRITING POLICY

It is a condition precedent to the Reinsurers' liability hereunder that the Reinsured shall not introduce at any time after the Reinsured enters into this Agreement any change in its established acceptance and underwriting policy which may increase or extend the liability or exposure of the Reinsurers hereunder in respect of the class(es) of business to which this Agreement applies without prior written approval of the Reinsurers.

CLAIMS NOTIFICATION AND SETTLEMENTS CLAUSE

Will be slightly different from proportional

PURPOSE: To establish:

(1) By when claims (or possible claims) must be advised
(2) That reinsurers must be kept fully informed of development of losses
(3) What original loss settlements are covered.

A liability reinsurance might include words such as the following to ensure any losses of likely relevance are drawn to the attention of Reinsurers who in many cases have greater expertise in Liability claims and reserving.

"In addition to the provisions of paragraph . . . above, the Reinsured shall immediately report to the Reinsurer all losses where the Company's reserve is 50 % or more of the Company's retention herein."

In addition, the following categories of claims shall be reported to the Reinsurer —immediately, regardless of any questions of liability of the insured or coverage under the policy:

1. *Death*
2. *Serious Brain damage resulting in physical or intellectual impairment*
3. *Paraplegia/Quadriplegia*
4. *Serious sensory impairment (sight or hearing)*
5. *Loss of or loss of function of major limb(s) including multi finger or toe*
6. *Loss of or loss of function of vital organ*
7. *Severe burns causing serious disfigurement or constrictive scarring and any third degree burns involving 25% or more of the body*
8. *Multiple fractures*
9. *Severe internal injuries which are life threatening or may result in long term impairment*
10. *Cosmetic deformities*
11. *Sexual abuse*
12. *Multiple claims/claimants arising from one occurrence.*

The importance of words

What do you think these words mean—will they produce the same result as the above?

"the assured shall give immediate notice in writing with full particulars of a happening of any occurrence likely to give rise to a claim under this . . . "

In *Layher Ltd* v. *Loi and Others* (1996) (Court of Appeal), it was held that the clause not breached as "likely" means "at least a 50% chance that such a claim would arise"—in practical terms it is very hard for an insurer or reinsurer to establish if there was "at least a 50% chance".

TERMINATION CLAUSE

The words of this for Non-Proportional Treaty might be slightly different from Proportional but the overall aims are similar and may include the reference to possible cancellation following a Security Downgrading (see earlier).

PURPOSE: To establish:

(1) Situations under which either party can terminate the contract immediately
(2) What happens after such termination.

e.g., in this example the liability of reinsurers ceases except for losses that occurred before termination.

Either party shall have the right to terminate this agreement immediately by giving the other party notice:

A. If the performance of the whole or any part of this Agreement be prohibited or rendered impossible de jure or de facto in particular and without prejudice to the generality of the preceding words in consequence of any law or regulation which is or shall be in force in any country or territory or if any law or regulation shall prevent directly or indirectly the remittance of any or all or any part of the balance of payments due to or from either party.
B. If the other party has become insolvent or unable to pay its debts or has lost the whole or any part of its paid up capital.
C. If there is any material change in the ownership or control of the other party.
D. If the country or territory in which the other party resides or has its head office or is incorporated shall be involved in armed hostilities with any other country whether war be declared or not or is partly or wholly occupied by another power.
E. If the other party shall have failed to comply with any of the terms and conditions of this Agreement.

After the date of any such termination the liability of the Reinsurers hereunder shall cease outright other than in respect of individual insured losses which occurred prior thereto.

All notices of termination served in accordance with any of the provisions of this Article shall be addressed to the party concerned at its head office or at any other address previously designated by that party.

All notices of termination in accordance with any of the provisions of this paragraph shall be by any permanent means of instantaneous communication, and shall be deemed to be served upon despatch or where communications between the parties are interrupted upon attempted despatch.

In the event of this Agreement being terminated at any date other than (the normal expiry date) then the premium due to the Reinsurers shall be calculated upon the Premium Income of the Reinsured up to date of termination or pro rata temporis of the annual Minimum Premium, whichever is the greater.

The rights and obligations of both parties to this Agreement shall remain in full force until the effective date of termination.

Words in most wordings

Whether Non-Proportional or Proportional

All of the following have been reviewed in Section 3—Proportional.

INSPECTION OF RECORDS CLAUSE

AMENDMENTS OR ALTERATION OF RECORDS CLAUSE

ERRORS AND OMISSIONS CLAUSE

ARBITRATION CLAUSE

APPLICABLE LAW & JURISDICTION CLAUSE

INTERMEDIARY CLAUSE

LIQUIDATION CLAUSE

PURPOSE: To confirm that irrespective of the words "actually paid" in the UNL clause reinsurers will pay on the basis of "assumed to have been paid" if a reinsured is in liquidation.

As mentioned earlier, the issues surrounding the meaning of the words "sums actually paid" in the UNL clause will be discussed in greater detail in a separate chapter. The "liquidation clause" was introduced initially in 1992 to clarify the intent of the reinsurance. Even with the words "actually paid" in the UNL clause, reinsurers will still pay valid claims to reinsureds who are in liquidation.

(A) This clause shall only apply in the event of the insolvency of the Reinsured and it entering into liquidation or its affairs being subject to any scheme of administration

or receivership approved by a court, excluding any voluntary arrangements of the Reinsured with its creditors.

Notwithstanding that this Agreement constitutes an indemnity in respect of amounts actually paid by the Reinsured it is agreed that in the circumstances specified in para (A) above the liability of the Reinsurer shall be determined as if the Reinsured had not gone into liquidation, administration or receivership to the extent that amounts payable by the Reinsurer shall not be reduced nor the time of their payment be delayed merely by reason of such liquidation, administration or receivership, subject always to any rights of set-off both legal and contractual which the Reinsurer may have.

Lastly:

SIGNING SCHEDULE

which is likely to include the

SEVERAL LIABILITY CLAUSE

A reminder:

How would the risk X/L operate in this scenario?
Sum insured 200,000
Retention 100,000
Risk X/L 60,000 xs 40,000
Loss 90,000

Who would pay how much?
– assume there is some proportional facultative
Would it make a difference if the Facultative Reinsurer went bankrupt?

Step 1: Back to proportional initially

Retention	**Facultative**
100,000	100,000
50%	50%

Step 2: What is the UNL (Ultimate Net Loss)?

Total Loss 90,000	
Retained 50%	Reinsured 50%
Retained 45,000	Facultative 45,000

Step 3: Apply the deductible to the UNL

UNL	45,000
Deductible	40,000
	5,000 collectable from Risk X/L reinsurers

Would it make a difference if the Facultative Reinsurer went bankrupt?
No! (read the UNL clause "whether collected or not").

Catastrophe X/L

PURPOSE: To protect the reinsurer against an accumulation of losses following a catastrophe or event. As, for example:

- accumulation of retentions following a flood
- accumulation of retentions on PA following an avalanche in a ski resort.

What clauses in the risk X/L wording discussed above would you expect to be different because it is now called catastrophe X/L?

Whilst the terms might be different, with regard to the clauses, there would be basically only one particular change—the reinsuring clause. This time it would refer to A xs B any one event (not any one risk).

The rest of the wording would basically follow the risk X/L already discussed—including clauses such as *Extended Expiration* and "*Hours Clause*".

The reinsurance might include a two risk warranty to ensure that it is not going to operate as a per risk X/L.

STOP LOSS

Excess of loss ratio—Aggregate X/L

(The last of the three main types of X/L contracts?)

Different people view the above words differently. For this short explanation I will use the words "stop loss" as a generic phrase to describe a branch of reinsurance with a particular purpose—to deal with overall results or losses over a period of time.

Where does the "stop loss" fit?

- Risk X/L takes out individual losses larger than "normal"
- Catastrophe X/L (or event X/L) takes out an accumulation of losses from one "event" bigger than normal
- Stop loss—protects what is left after all other reinsurances have been utilised (where appropriate) from overall poor results over a period of time, e.g. a very poor hail season

Excess of loss ratio

In general most people would describe this product as a stop loss—although its older name is a more accurate description of how it works.

This product seems for many people the hardest to understand perhaps because the words of the *Reinsuring Clause* seem more complicated.

In reality it is still only a contract that pays a certain amount in excess of a certain amount like any other non-proportional arrangement.

An example might look like:

The Reinsurers hereby agree for the consideration paid or to be paid and subject to the terms, clauses and conditions hereinafter set forth ***to pay the aggregate net loss in excess of*** *an amount equal to* ***122.50% of the Reinsured's Net Premium Income*** *(hereinafter defined) for the period stated in Article (?)* ***or £4,287,500 whichever be the greater up to*** *a further amount equal to* ***20% (twenty per cent) of the Reinsured's Net Premium Income*** *for the period with a* ***maximum limit hereon not exceeding £1,540,000.***

In other words, cover is:
20% of net premium income but not exceeding £1,540,000
in excess of a loss greater than
122.5% of net premium income or £4,287,500 whichever is the greater

- specific monetary limits to ensure that a dramatic increase in premium does not totally change the monetary basis of the reinsurance

Would there be a claim under this reinsurance if the figures at the end of the year were as follows?

Aggregate new loss 11,000,000

Net premium income 8,000,000

If so—how much would it be?

Loss Ratio 137.5% (11,000,000/8,000,000 × 100/1) of Net Premium
Deductible 122.5% of Net Premium
Claim 15.00% of Net Premium

and in monetary terms:

Losses	11,000,000	
Deductible	9,800,000	(122.5% × 8,000,000) "or *4,287,500* whichever is the greater"
Claim	1,200,000	

Aggregate X/L *(a simpler variation of the Excess of Loss Ratio Cover)*

- Cover and deductible are expressed in monetary amounts
- To pay x,xxx,xxx in the aggregate in the year in excess of x,xxx,xxx in the aggregate in the year
- Not based on percentages but actual monetary amounts

NB: Both are likely to have co-reinsurance factor—"To pay 90% of . . . "

The component parts of the wordings for both of these are likely to be very similar in general to other non-proportional contracts.

Other clauses of interest

In a generic overview of reinsurance it is not possible to cover all the different clauses used—nor is this the purpose of this module—but a few other clauses and their purposes should be highlighted.

Index clause or severe inflation clause (SIC)

PURPOSE: To ensure in liability covers that the deductible of the reinsured and (usually) the maximum liability of the reinsurers retain the same relative monetary values as existed when the treaty commenced.

Its purpose; to avoid placing the effect of inflation solely onto the reinsurance contract.

The opening part of the clause might read as follows:

"It is the intention of this agreement that the retention of the reinsured and the maximum liability of the re-insurer as set out in the schedule shall retain the relative values which exist at the x/xx/xxxx

Any change in relative monetary value shall be ascertained from the latest available index of basic hourly wage rates of all workers in manufacturing industries issued by Department of . . . " The clause would then show the specific methodology for working out the revised cover and deductible.

To avoid carrying out quite a complex calculation for every loss it is now common to see a *severe inflation clause (SIC)*. This ensures that the index clause only applies after a pre-agreed amount of inflation.

Change of law

A fairly self explanatory clause

"In the event of any change in the law by which Reinsurers' liability hereunder is materially increased or extended, the parties hereto agree to take up for immediate discussion a suitable revision in the terms of this Agreement

If the parties fail to agree a suitable revision, this Agreement shall operate from the effective date of the change of law as if the change had not occurred or upon its termination the Reinsurers' liability will not be increased or extended by any change of law affecting this Agreement which has not been agreed to by the Reinsurers."

An example where this situation could arise would be if cover is being given for workers' compensation and the local government increased the payments due to injured workers during the currency of the reinsurance.

Leading underwriter clause

A topical issue in the context of the LMP slip and general underwriting agreements (GUA). A very specific example follows that was held by the courts to bind all the followers to the decision of the leader.

"All alterations, additions, deletions, extensions, agreement, rates and changes and conditions to be agreed by the leading Lloyd's underwriter . . . only. Such agreements to be binding on all underwriters subscribing hereon . . . "

Four clauses to finish with—both requiring your "legal" opinion!

The following clauses can be seen around the international reinsurance market

They probably have not been put to the legal test so your view is as valid as anyone else's

What do you think of these from a legal perspective?

BROKER'S NOTICE OF CANCELLATION CLAUSE
A clause that appears in various contracts in London including energy and aviation.
"the broker reserves the right to give notice of cancellation on behalf of reinsurers in the event of non-payment of premium"

"It is agreed between the Underwriters and the Assured that in the event of the Assured and/or the Assured's Agent failing to pay ABC Broker Limited the premium or any instalment thereof on the due dates, this policy may be forthwith cancelled by ABC Broker Limited, giving to the Assured notice in writing and the Underwriters will thereupon return to ABC Broker Limited through whom this policy is effected pro rata premium from the date of notice or from such later cancellation dates as may be stated in said notice.

Written notice sent by or through ABC Broker Limited or their correspondents who negotiated the Insurance to said Assured at his last known address, shall constitute a complete notice as required under this clause. Such cancellation shall be without prejudice to the premiums earned and due for the period the policy is in force, and to any losses pending on the date of cancellation."

My personal view is that although under the MIA (1906) a broker can possibly be held liable for non-paid premium any court ought to be concerned that the Broker who is the agent of the reinsured, should be seen to be specifically acting as agent of the reinsurer (*North & South Trust* v. *Berkeley* (1970) 2 L.R. 467).

"INFORMATION NOT WARRANTED OR LIMITED" (NWOL Clause)
Different people again see these letters or words from different viewpoints—what is your opinion?

Again a personal view. The information is "not warranted".
So what?
Information is Information—it is not warranted.
The information is "not limited". "Not limited" to what?

It seems to infer to me that the broker has more information. If the information is material do not believe that this clause would be strong enough as a defence if it was not presented to underwriters.

What do you feel is the purpose behind the following clause?

"any such information provided by or non-disclosure by the insured and its agent to insure shall not be grounds for avoidance of the insurers' obligations under the policy or cancellation thereof".

Waiver clauses

This particular clause was used in an attempt to make a contract placed with insurers (subject to utmost good faith . . .) as "watertight" as a policy placed with a specialist financial guarantee Insurer (*HIH Casualty and General* v. *Chase Manhattan Bank* (H.L.) (2003) UKHL—"Phoenix"). Under financial guarantee contracts with U.S. "monoline" insurers in the event of a credit default, they will pay out irrespective of circumstances seeking recoveries where appropriate after payment.

This clause and variations of it are attempting to:

- limit or even exclude entirely the (re)insured's duty of utmost good faith
- exclude the remedies available to a (re)insurer for breach of utmost good faith

The House of Lords held that a clause of this type was sufficient to exclude the (re)insurer's right of avoidance for innocent and negligent misrepresentation/non-disclosures, although for specific reasons not the broker's non-disclosure or if the non-disclosure was fraudulent.

The two variations of this theme that follow have been seen on standard facultative reinsurances recently—both it seems attempting to waive the impact of the principles of utmost good faith:

The insured, and his agent to insure, will have no obligation to make any representation, warranty or disclosure express or implied to the insurer.

The reinsured will have discharged its duties of disclosure of all material facts by providing the reinsurer with copies of a completed proposal form and reinsurers further acknowledge that they have made an independent investigation of the subject matter reinsured in assessing the risks of underwriting this policy.

What is your view of the legal impact of this clause?

For the avoidance of doubt, any agreement from the slip leader which is in accordance with the above shall not be deemed an amendment, special agreement or similar as incorporated within underwriter's stamps or otherwise (even when the words notwithstanding internal slip conditions or similar are used) unless it is specifically stated by the subscribing underwriter (within the stamp or otherwise) that such amendments are to be agreed as leading underwriter or as slip leader. In such circumstances, the requirement shall apply to the specific subscribing underwriter's participation only.

This clause can be found on some placement slips. It seems to be saying—if an underwriter imposes a line condition (a condition applicable to their share only) that this is over-ridden by the words of this clause.

Currently no official legal answer—a conundrum.

- written would normally over-ride "typed" but underwriter put his stamp on a slip with these words on it.

Subjectivities

London market has traditionally used initials and short forms of text to express complex things. Under new contract certainty rules this should not now be the case. Words such as "Sub satis survey" or initials such as VRI (very rough indication) should become history. See copy of the Market note on this subject in the Appendix.

ALTERNATIVE RISK TRANSFER

Other legal forms of Reinsurance including Alternative Risk Transfer and Securitisation

A very complex subject that cannot be dealt with in any detail at all in a short section of one chapter—regrettably but understandably there is substantial intellectual property rights within these products so discussion on the actual terms used is not possible.

There are a wide range of "products" under various names and guises in this area—for this chapter we will only be looking briefly at four. These are:

Contingent capital
Catastrophe bonds
Swaps
Finite risk

A core issue to keep in mind at all times, whichever product is being discussed and from whatever position you are viewing the products, whether as:

- buyer
- seller (provider)
- advisor or intermediary
- regulator
- tax authority

Is there risk transfer? Is it insurance or reinsurance? Is it an indemnity contract?

This in turn will influence how the following questions can be answered/ dealt with:

Are the payments for the cover being bought—premiums?
How can any income or outgo be treated in the balance sheet?
Will the product impact on solvency or not?

For all of the so called ART (alternate risk transfer) or ARF (alternate risk financing) or . . . products one of the core issues is going to be whether the regulator and the fiscal authorities view them as being (re)insurance contracts or just "banking arrangements".

This whole issue became very topical following the investigations by E. Spitzer in 2004/5—see finite risk.

Unfortunately the definitions available to help decide this issue are not specific but rely on subjective words such as significant, reasonably possible, etc.

The examples below showing part of the words on which U.K. and U.S. GAAP (generally accepted accounting practices) is based highlight the problem.

U.S. GAAP

The (re)insurer must assume "significant insurance risk" under the (re)insured portions of the underlying contracts . . . (SFAS 113: *Statement of Financial Accounting Standards*).

It must be "reasonably possible for the (re)insurer to realise a significant loss from the transaction, based on a comparison of expected cash flows and present value of premiums paid to reinsurers, assuming under reasonably possible outcomes".

U.K. GAAP is very similar

It is necessary to assess whether there has been transfer of significant (re)insurance risk (U.K. FRAG 35/94 (1999))—any decision should take into account whether:

- it is reasonably possible that the (Re)insurer may realise a significant loss from the contract;
- there is a reasonable possibility of a significant range of outcomes under the contract;
- there is a significant degree of uncertainty in respect of the timing of claim payments.

NB: "Significant" must be assessed in the context of the commercial substance of the contract being evaluated as a whole.

Timing risk alone may be sufficient to constitute a transfer of risk.

UK GAAP apparently differs from US GAAP (where both timing and underwriting risk need to be present).

Three key legal issues often emerge when the (re)insurance and capital markets converge (*Reinsurance Risk Financing—Service Providers Guide to ART*—Review).

1. Determination of whether a particular transaction is a (re)insurance product or other type of financial transaction.
2. The application of legal peculiarities to a particular ART transaction.
3. Issues relating to the documentation of the ART product.

Are ART contracts legal?

It is essential to be clear whether the contract being proposed is a (re)insurance or some other financial style contract as in many countries, as in the U.K. "an insurer must not carry on any commercial business in the U.K. or elsewhere other than insurance business activities directly arising from that business" (FSA: *Integrated Prudential Sourcebook*). Care must be taken to ensure that the reinsurance part of any transaction can be properly shown as being a contract of reinsurance.

The starting point for the English courts when considering whether a financial transaction is a contract of (re)insurance in law is the substance of the contract rather than its form (*Reinsurance Risk Financing—Service Providers Guide to ART*—Review). They will consider the contract as a whole, taking into account its commercial context.

If it is seen to be (a) a pure banking arrangement, or (b) an arrangement dressed up to look like a reinsurance contract, then it is likely to be considered as a non-insurance contract.

What is a "contract of insurance"? The closest to a definition in the English courts comes from *Prudential Insurance Company* v. *Inland Revenue Commissioners* (1904) where it was stated that a contract of insurance normally had three characteristics:

1. There was entitlement to a benefit on the happening of an event (including there being consideration);
2. There must be some uncertainty as to whether the event would occur or when it would occur; and
3. The event must be adverse to the interest of the assured; this characteristic is generally satisfied if there is an insurable interest.

NB: Under a banking contract there is no need for insurable interest which explains why some of the products are placed in the money markets and not (re)insurance markets.

Contingent capital

Not a reinsurance product as such. It is securing access to funds in advance which are available after the happening of a pre-agreed significant event when refinancing might be very costly (a variation of a credit line).

Paying a "premium" to have the *right to raise equity or loan capital*—subject to certain conditions:

- via a "CSN" (contingent surplus note)
- terms agreed in advance
- "triggered" IF a contractually defined event occurs.

The (re)insured has the option to issue capital within predetermined limits after a pre-specified event or combination of events occurs, e.g., earthquake above X.X on Richter Scale, or stock market drops by X points.

Insurer purchases the *right to issue* in the future to investors pre-agreed paper at pre-set terms, e.g., September 2002 Horace Mann (U.S.)—three year deal—if major U.S. catastrophe as defined happens they have the right to issue up to $75m of convertible securities which must be taken up.

The deal can be based on any style of capital, in many cases preference shares or subordinate debt. The aim of the product, if designed correctly, is to achieve access to capital without diluting shareholders' interests.

It is highly recommended by the specialists in this area that such a product be discussed with regulators, rating agencies, etc.

Why might this path be considered?

Possibly:

- Cheaper and more efficient than buying conventional forms of R/I
- Requires less detailed information re specific business
- Can be put in place quicker than placing Cat X/L
- Does not require proof of specific loss amount—not indemnity

Catastrophe bonds

(Corporate bonds with special language)

Funds are provided (in advance) to pay for a catastrophe (as defined) IF it occurs (this is different from contingent capital—the funds are "received" in advance).

IF the event happens (the trigger) bondholders "forgive" or defer:
coupon (interest) **or** loan (principal) **or** a combination of both.

Firstly back to basics. What is a bond?

A wants to borrow money. **B** is willing to lend the money at certain terms. **A** issues a bond to **B** that states **B** will lend $xx,xxx,xxx to **A**, *subject to*:

- the loan (principal) being repaid on xx/xx/xxxx
- interest (coupon) being paid at x% payable monthly, quarterly, etc.

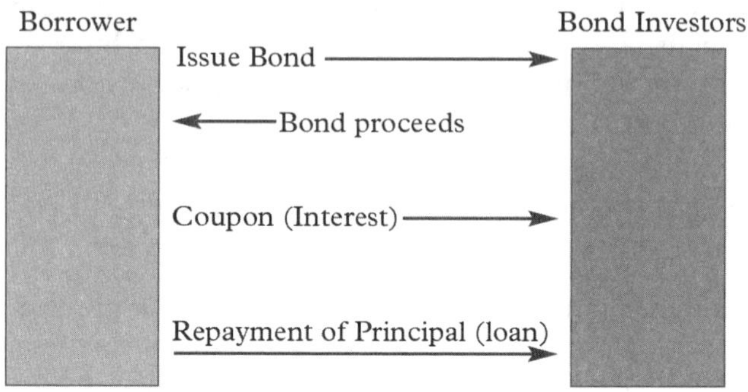

As an example:

Tokio Marine wanted a further $100,000,000 of catastrophe X/L to augment their existing X/L programme particularly with regard to the Kanto region of Japan.

What is the process?

Want "reinsurance" for $100,000,000.
Issues a bond to borrow $100,000,000.
Investor(s) lends $100,000,000, subject to:

- pre-agreed interest
- repayment at a fixed date
- some form of collateral

Loss happens—funds from the bond are used to pay the claims.

At this point it seems just like any other bond with no particular relationship to reinsurance. The money lent under the bond will have to be re-paid. So how does it become "reinsurance"?—through the terms of the bond.

IF "trigger" occurs (e.g. earthquake above 7.1 on the Japanese Scale) there will be loss of principal for the investors in the bond (or, in the Tokio Marine example, partial loss of principal).

Now the product is in basic terms operating like catastrophe reinsurance. Premium has been paid for cover (interest). Funds (which do not have to be repaid) are used to pay losses following a pre-specified catastrophe.

Although supposedly "non-traditional", there is a standard way of putting these products together using a SPV (special purpose vehicle).

Reinsured buys "R/I protection" from a SPV.

SPV issues a "cat bond" to investors.

Why the SPV?

To convert reinsurance risk into a "securitisable asset" by converting the reinsurance risk into a form the capital market can understand and legally accept.

What are the specifics of an SPV?

- probably very low capital
- normally registered "offshore"

How does it all work?

(a) the SPV issues traditional cover to the reinsured;
(b) the SPV issues a bond(s) to the traditional bond market to obtain the capital to cover their liabilities under the "reinsurance";
(c) the bond as with any other bond will be fully rated by the major rating agencies and will probably require some form of collateral or "credit wrap".

Giving an overall picture looking something like this:

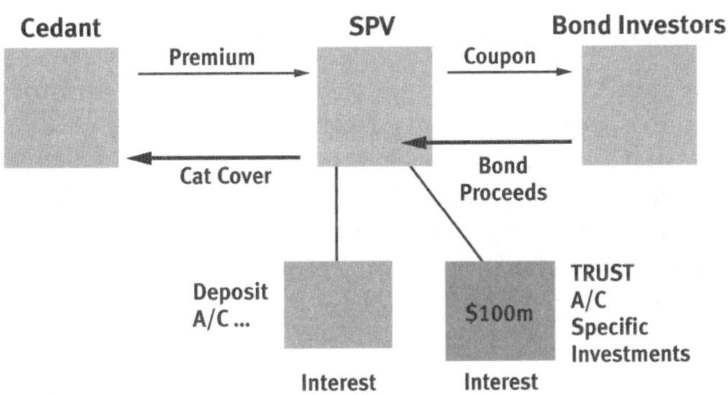

These products should be seen as an important adjunct to traditional reinsurance. Although the actual volume in terms of numbers of contracts purchased is still low—perhaps 10 +/–5 per year, total protection being bought is in the vicinity of $1bn–$1.5bn per year—with particular interest being shown by major reinsurers, e.g., Swiss Re, Hannover Re, Munich Re, covering a range of differing perils and areas.

In the opinion of Standard & Poor's, for financial strength rating purposes, a properly structured catastrophe bond serves the same function as a program of reinsurance even if it is not structured as such.

Following the major losses of 2005 (Katrina, Rita, Wilma . . .) there has been renewed interest in cat bonds and other variations of securitisation. Some analysts believe that over $4bn of such deals were put together in 2006 even though it is very likely that a 2005 issuance will be a total loss. Zurich–KampRe

Swaps

What is a swap?

"Privately negotiated financial contracts in which two parties agree to exchange or swap specific price-risk exposures over a pre-determined period of time (*wrma.org*).

There is no "cost" for a "swap". Most deals involve the payment of periodic payments between the parties—one side paying a fixed price and the other a variable price keeping the deal in balance.

The concept in reinsurance is basically two parties agreeing to pass to the other a pre-agreed monetary amount of exposure for specified perils in a pre-determined area thus reducing down the need for catastrophe X/L and diversifying the portfolios of both parties.

The concept is probably best explained by using a specific real example:

In June 2003 Swiss Re and Mitsui agreed two swaps;
Swiss Re swapping $50m of exposure to loss from North Atlantic Storm for $50m of exposure to loss from Japanese Typhoon;

and under a separate contract

Swiss Re swapping $50m of exposure to loss from European storm for $50m of exposure to loss from Japanese typhoon.

Both parties have passed out peak exposures for them and taken in exposures from other areas with which they feel more comfortable.

The swap has basically only become possible because of the major advances in weather and catastrophe simulation, "proving" that the chance of loss in a given scenario is similar for both sides.

Finite risk

A very complex area where the issue of risk transfer has to be considered very carefully.

What does it mean?

A *long term strategy of risk sharing* between the (re)insured and the (re)insurer which is generally based on a multi year arrangement with an overall aggregate limit.

Losses or expenses or profits are spread over a number of years, with the maximum profit/loss for both parties reasonably clear.

The overall basis of the "premium" formula is likely to create similar income and outgo on both sides over the period of the contract.

May not be to do with specific perils and is more likely to be concerned with the impact on the overall financial position.

As an example—a new life insurer with very poor cash flow in the early years (very high expenses) might place a finite risk quota share treaty. The reinsurer would agree to "fund" the Treaty commission to the reinsured in advance at the start of the contract (subject to an agreed formula for interest). The commission (and interest) would be being paid back out of any profits from Q/S

- the arrangement would be subject to a maximum limit of loss or profit with one party or the other having to "top up" the overall fund if it ends up too far into deficit or profit.

In summary: finite risk deals in many cases are "smoothing covers" the purpose of which is not necessarily to transfer risk as such.

Following problems with HIH in Australia among others, regulators worldwide became very concerned that such deals are correctly structured and documented.

The Royal Commission into the collapse of HIH made it very clear that in their view it is the responsibility of the reinsurer to ensure that the documentation of such deals as presented in annual reports must reflect the WHOLE DEAL, not just selective parts of the deal. Surely this also puts responsibility onto the brokers involved in such deals to ensure clarity of documentation in its entirety?

If HIH drew attention to some of the problems inherent in some finite risk deals, the risk deals between AIG and General Cologne Re uncovered by E. Spitzer highlighted the need for transparency, no side deals and an acceptable level of risk transfer.

Lastly, two specific developments which may cause some legal debates in the future.

Sidecars

Sidecars came into being to support the newly formed reinsurers particularly in Bermuda at the end of 2005. In most cases they offer a Quota Share of a specific class of business to a specific insurer. The investors in the so-called "sidecars" tend to be Hedge Funds seeking short term investment at a time when prices are high. They are set up as a Special Purpose Vehicle (SPV). The deals enable reinsurers to accept more risk, greater premium without the need to seek a further injection of capital. Although these deals have been done with major "money market" investors the contracts themselves have apparently been drafted as ordinary proportional reinsurance treaties.

ILWs (Industry Loss Warranties)

ILWs have been around in various guises for many years. They are currently becoming a major "alternative" market for catastrophe style reinsurance. The products pay out a *predetermined amount* IF there is a loss to the reinsured of *$X,000,000* AND a loss of to the whole market of *$Y,000,000,000*. For this product to be deemed to be reinsurance it cannot just payout if there is a market loss from to this particular catastrophe of *$Y,000,000,000*. The reinsured has to have an insurable interest. The issue will be the size of the involvement—in many cases very small.

TEST YOUR UNDERSTANDING

1. Is the following statement true or false?: "Insurance and reinsurance are fundamentally different in legal terms."

2. Which of the following most accurately describes Facultative Reinsurance?

(a) Facultative reinsurance is reinsurance that the reinsured can offer to reinsurers but which reinsurers must accept
(b) Facultative reinsurance is reinsurance that the reinsured must offer to reinsurers and which reinsurers must accept
(c) Facultative reinsurance is reinsurance that the reinsured can offer to reinsurers and reinsurers can accept

3. Which of the following could be described as proportional RI and which non-proportional?

(a) Quota share
(b) Facultative obligatory
(c) Stop loss
(d) Facultative

4. Which of the following is likely to be described as obligatory reinsurance?

(a) Surplus
(b) Risk X/L
(c) Stop loss
(d) Facultative obligatory

5. Under proportional reinsurance which reflects the correct method of calculating a loss?

(a) Allocation of losses between reinsured and reinsurers is based on the aggregate total of all losses at the end of the year
(b) Allocation of losses between reinsured and reinsurers is based on the premium paid to reinsurers on the specific risk

(c) Allocation of losses between reinsured and reinsurers depends if the loss is large or small
(d) Allocation of losses between reinsured and reinsurers is based on the allocation of the original risk

6. Which of the following explains the correct workings of a second surplus treaty?

(a) Reinsurers will receive a share of all risks
(b) Reinsurers will receive a share of all risks except those that fall into the retention
(c) Reinsurers will receive a share of risks which are larger than the retention
(d) Reinsurers will receive a share of risks that are larger than the retention and cession to 1st Surplus

7. Reinstatements—Which of the following are true?

(a) Reinstatements are common in all types of reinsurance
(b) The term "1 reinstatement at 100%" means:

  (i) The reinsured can put in 1 claim in the year
  (ii) The reinstatement premium will be 100% of what the reinsured paid for 12 months cover

8. Which is the true explanation of the extended expiration clause?

(a) At the end of the year if the contract is not renewed reinsurers agree to give cover for the run off of ongoing risks at a pre-agreed price
(b) If a peril covered has started causing damage at the end of the contract period this clause explains how the loss will be allocated over the two years
(c) If a peril covered has started causing damage at the end of the contract period this clause confirms that the whole loss falls on the second year
(d) If a peril covered has started causing damage at the end of the contract period this clause confirms that the whole loss falls on the year the loss started in.

9. Based on "market terminology" which of the following best reflects the term "stop loss"?

(a) A facultative reinsurance that will pay if an individual loss is larger than $?
(b) A reinsurance protecting a portfolio of business that will pay if a loss in the year for all risks covered exceeds $?

(c) A reinsurance protecting a portfolio of business that will pay if a loss in the year for all risks covered a loss ratio of X%
(d) A reinsurance protecting a portfolio of business that will pay if a loss from a catastrophe exceeds $X

10. Do the words "Terms; As original, and to follow settlements in all respects" mean that the following terms are likely to be automatically incorporated into a reinsurance?

(a) Original premium (Y/N)
(b) Original deductions (Y/N)
(c) Arbitration (Y/N)
(d) Local law (Y/N)
(e) Local jurisdiction (Y/N)

CHAPTER 2

FORMATION OF REINSURANCE AGREEMENTS

AUTHORISATION OF REINSURERS

The authorisation requirement

The Financial Services and Markets Act 2000 regulates the supply of financial services in the UK market. Any person who wishes to carry on a regulated activity in the UK as a principal must be authorised to do so by the Financial Services Authority (section 19), and an authorised person may only carry on a regulated activity in respect of which the authorisation applies (section 20). Contravention of the "general prohibition" in section 19 is a criminal offence, although contravention of section 20 does not attract criminal sanctions. An insurer which is established and authorised elsewhere in the EEA does not require authorisation by the Financial Services Authority and may take advantage of EEA passport rights by either forming an establishment in the UK or supplying insurance directly to customers in the UK from establishments elsewhere in the EEA. Equally, an insurer which is authorised and established in the UK has equivalent passport rights to establish, or to sell insurance directly, in any other EEA country, without having to seek authorisation from that country's regulatory authorities (Financial Services and Markets Act 2000, schedule 3, and the Financial Services and Markets Act 2000 (EEA Passport Rights) Regulations 2001, S.I. 2001 No. 2511).

Insurance is designated as a regulated activity for the purposes of the 2000 Act by the Financial Services and Markets Act 2000 (Regulated Activities) Order 2000 (S.I. 2000 No. 544, made under s. 22 of the 2000 Act), so that authorisation is required for "effecting and carrying out contracts of insurance". Insurance business is divided into 10 classes of long term (life and related) business and 18 classes of general (property, liability, guarantee, etc.) business, and authorisation is to be obtained for each individual class. As a result of EU rules, it is no longer possible for a new insurer to be authorised to carry on both long term and general business. Reinsurance is treated as insurance for the purposes of the Financial Services and Markets Act 2000, so that reinsurers are similarly required to be authorised to carry on insurance business in the U.K. on a class-by-class basis.

***Re NRG Victory Insurance* [1995] 1 All E.R. 533**
The company petitioned the court for its approval of a scheme of arrangement under which the long term (life and related) reinsurance and retrocession business would be transferred to another insurer, ERL. Questions arose as to whether these forms of business were insurance business and thus subject to regulatory provisions.

The case was decided under the Insurance Companies Act 1982, the predecessor of the Financial Services and Markets Act 2000.

Held (Lindsay J.): (1) reinsurance business was to be treated as insurance business for regulatory purposes; (2) reinsurance business fell into the class of direct business to which it related, so that reinsurance of long term risks was itself to be treated as long term business; (3) retrocession was also to be treated as insurance business.

***Re Friends Provident Life Office* [1999] Lloyd's Rep. IR 547**

In 1983 FPLO, a life insurer, reinsured its long term business with FPLAA, a wholly-owned subsidiary formed for the purpose. The transaction was put in place for tax reasons. FPLAA had no employees of its own and its functions were carried out by other members of the corporate group. Following changes to the tax regime in 1990, the parties proposed to bring the transaction to an end by transferring FPLAA's reinsurance business to FPLO, and an application was made to the court for the approval of the transfer under the Insurance Companies Act 1982, which required approval of transfers of insurance business (see now, Financial Services and Markets Act 2000, ss. 104 to 117).

Held (Neuberger J. and C.A.): (1) references to insurance in the legislation included reinsurance, so that the consent of the court was required for the transfer of reinsurance business; (2) the scheme qualified as a transfer of business, as it involved the transfer of functions as well as the transfer of a contract; (3) the transfer should be approved as it was a genuine transaction and did not affect the rights of policy holders.

Business is carried on in the U.K. if risks are accepted or claims are paid in the U.K., and it is immaterial that the risks in question are located in some other jurisdiction or that the contracts are governed by a law other than English law.

***Re Great Western Insurance Co. SA* [1999] Lloyd's Rep. IR 377**

The case concerned four insurance companies—Offshore 1 (incorporated in Barbados), Offshore 2 (incorporated in Belgium) and Cyprus 1 and 2 (incorporated in Cyprus)—none of which was authorised to carry on insurance business in the UK. Business was obtained in the UK by two sets of brokers, and this was directed to Offshore 1 and 2 through Cyprus 1 and 2. Underwriting decisions were made offshore by Cyprus 1 and 2. The Secretary of State sought winding up orders against all six companies on the basis that they were carrying on unauthorised insurance business in the UK.

Held (C.A.): (1) Offshore 1 and 2 were carrying on insurance business in the UK. The mere fact that underwriting decisions were made offshore did not prevent the operation of the UK legislation, as the activity regulated was the "effecting and carrying out" of insurance contracts, and this included negotiation of such contracts; (2) the brokers operating in the UK were in practice performing functions on behalf of Offshore 1 and 2, including applying underwriting criteria, advising premium rates and terms, receiving notification of claims and settling claims within agreed financial limits—these activities constituted the carrying on of insurance business by Offshore 1 and 2 through the brokers, although the brokers themselves were not carrying on insurance business as they were merely agents; (3) it was not appropriate to wind up the companies, as Offshore 1 and 2 were acting lawfully as regards non-UK business and there was no evidence that UK policy holders had been harmed by the carrying on of unauthorised UK business.

Regulation of "pure" reinsurers, i.e., companies which do not carry on direct business, will be required throughout the EU by the Reinsurance Directive, European Parliament and Council Directive 2205/68/EC, which is to be implemented by Member States by 10 December 2007. The Directive provides for: authorisation of reinsurers, which requires the submission of a satisfactory scheme of operations to the home state regulator; the principle of home state control, which allows a reinsurer authorised in its home state to establish branches or to sell reinsurance directly elsewhere in the EU with minimal intervention by the host state regulator; compliance with rules on technical reserves and the maintenance of a solvency margin; restrictions on the persons who may be shareholders in and controllers of reinsurance undertakings; and limited regulation of certain forms of Alternative Risk Transfer arrangements, specifically financial reinsurance and special purpose vehicles used for raising funds in the capital markets.

Contracts made by unauthorised insurers and reinsurers

The Court of Appeal, in *Phoenix General Assurance of Greece* v. *Administratia Asigurarilor de Stat* [1986] 2 Lloyd's Rep. 552, inclined to the view that contracts made by an insurer who failed to obtain the authorisation required by the Insurance Companies Act 1982 were illegal and that no claim could be made by the assured for any loss. It followed that an unauthorised insurer who had reinsured its liability was unable to recover from its reinsurers in the event that payment was made under an unauthorised insurance contract, as (a) the insurer's payment would have been *ex gratia* and did not give rise to a legal liability within the meaning of the reinsurance; and (b) a claim against reinsurers would be in reliance on the insurer's own illegal act. This decision was reversed by section 132 of the Financial Services Act 1986, which removed the illegality from contracts made by unauthorised insurers and allowed direct policy holders to recover under their contracts, although authorised insurers were entitled to enforce their contracts only with a court order. The section also provided that an unauthorised insurer could recover under its reinsurances where it was required to pay a claim to a direct policy holder. Section 132 of the 1986 Act was held to be retroactive by the Court of Appeal in *Bates* v. *Robert Barrow Ltd* [1995] 1 Lloyd's Rep. 680.

Section 132 was superseded by sections 26 to 28 of the Financial Services and Markets Act 2000, which reproduce that section in an amplified form. The broad effects of the sections are that: (a) an unauthorised insurer cannot enforce its insurance contracts against policy holders, who are able to recover payments made by them and compensation; (b) the court may make an order permitting enforcement by the insurer; and (c) the policy holder may enforce the contract against the unauthorised insurer. There is no mention of the enforceability of an unauthorised insurer's reinsurance contracts, although it is thought that such contracts are enforceable as any payment by the insurer cannot be regarded as *ex gratia* and there is no illegality involved in making payments under direct policies so that the insurer does not have to plead its own illegality to claim against its reinsurers.

It should be noted that a person who is authorised to carry on regulated activities, but who carries on activities beyond the scope of the authorisation contrary to section 20 of the 2000 Act, suffers no civil consequences as regards its contracts. Thus an authorised insurer who carries on insurance business of a class for which it is not authorised is entitled to enforce its contracts. The statutory rules on the enforcement of contracts applies only to persons carrying on insurance business who have no authorisation at all, in contravention of the "general prohibition" in section 19 of the 2000 Act.

Extracts from the Financial Services and Markets Act 2000

Agreements made by unauthorised persons

26.—(1) An agreement made by a person in the course of carrying on a regulated activity in contravention of the general prohibition is unenforceable against the other party.

(2) The other party is entitled to recover—

(a) any money or other property paid or transferred by him under the agreement; and

(b) compensation for any loss sustained by him as a result of him having parted with it.

Agreements made unenforceable by section 26

27.—(1) This section applies to an agreement which is unenforceable because of section 26 . . .

(2) The amount of compensation recoverable as a result of that section is—

(a) the amount agreed by the parties; or

(b) on the application of either party, the amount determined by the court.

(3) If the court is satisfied that it is just and equitable in the circumstances of the case it may allow—

(a) the agreement to be enforced; or

(b) money and property paid or transferred under the agreement to be retained.

(4) In considering whether to allow the agreement to be enforced or (as the case may be) the money or property paid or transferred under the agreement to be retained the court must—

(a) if the case arises as a result of section 26, have regard to the issue mentioned in subsection (5) . . .

(5) The issue is whether the person carrying on the regulated activity concerned reasonably believed that he was not contravening the general prohibition by making the agreement.

. . .

(7) If the person against whom the agreement is unenforceable—

(a) elects not to perform the agreement; or

(b) as a result of this section, recovers money paid or other property transferred by him under the agreement he must repay any money and return any other property received by him under the agreement.

. . .

(9) The commission of an authorisation offence does not make the agreement concerned illegal or invalid to any greater extent than is provided by section 26 . . .

Summary

- Insurers and reinsurers must be authorised to carry on insurance business in the United Kingdom unless they are authorised elsewhere in the EEA. Criminal sanctions may be imposed upon unauthorised persons.
- The definition of "carrying on insurance business" is a wide one, and business may be carried on in the United Kingdom by insurers who are situated abroad but who use United Kingdom agents.
- The policy holders of unauthorised insurers are able to enforce their policies, but unauthorised insurers do not have the right to enforce policies against their policy holders.
- The reinsurers of unauthorised insurers are unlikely to be able to avoid making payment.

PLACING PROCEDURES IN THE LONDON MARKET

The slip subscription procedure

The usual method of placing reinsurance business in the London market is by means of subscription to the slip. The broker appointed by the reinsured will prepare a slip which summarises the risk, and then presents the slip to individual Lloyd's syndicates or insurance companies operating in the market. The broker will initially approach a Syndicate or Lloyd's underwriter who is well regarded in the market, and will make a presentation to him which will be partly oral and backed up by documentation. If the reinsurer is satisfied that the risk is acceptable, he will attach his Syndicate or company stamp to the slip and sign the slip, a process known as scratching. The reinsurer is unlikely to accept 100% of the risk, and will almost certainly scratch the slip for a far smaller amount, say between 10 and 25%. The broker, armed with the slip and the initial scratching, must then take the slip round the market to achieve further subscriptions. In the reinsurance market it is increasingly common for there to be a relatively small number of subscribers.

Once the process has been completed, the broker may issue a cover note to the reinsured, setting out the terms upon which subscription has been achieved and the identity of the reinsurers. The cover note is not, however, a contractual document, but is merely a notification by the broker to the reinsured as to what has been done, and the reinsurers are not party to the cover note. Accordingly, should a dispute between reinsurers and reinsured arise, the cover note cannot be relied upon as evidence of the terms of the reinsurance agreement. In due course the slip may be replaced by a formal policy wording, although it is the practice of the London market in the placing of facultative reinsurance for the slip—with the policy being reinsured attached to it—to be used as the only contractual document: facultative reinsurance slips are thus often described as "slip policies" and it is stated on the slip that no formal policy wording is to be issued.

The making of the contract

Making a contract without scratching a slip

After a period of some doubt (mainly as a result of the decision in *Jaglom* v. *Excess Insurance Co.* [1971] 2 Lloyd's Rep. 171), it is now settled law that a binding contract of insurance comes into existence as soon as a slip is scratched by an underwriter. The slip is regarded as the offer, and the scratching by the underwriter is regarded as the acceptance. Although this is not the only mechanism by which a contract of reinsurance may be effected, it is certainly the most important. In principle it is possible for a contract to come into existence as soon as the reinsurer and the reinsured have reached agreement, and this may be in advance of the slip being scratched, although a court is unlikely to find that a contract has been brought into existence at some point in a chain of negotiation leading to the scratching of a slip.

Sun Life Assurance Co. of Canada* v. *CX Reinsurance Co. Ltd
[2003] EWCA Civ 283, [2004] Lloyd's Rep. IR 86

Sun Life had in 1988 joined a US-based reinsurance pool which was managed by IOA Re. Another of the pool's members was CCC, the parent of CNA. The pool specialised in underwriting accident and health reinsurance. Sun Life had delegated underwriting authority to IOA Re and had also authorised IOA Re to settle claims on its behalf. The pool prospered, and in 1996 it began to carry on reinsurance business in London. An individual, N, had at one time been employed by Sun Life and then IOA Re, transferred to London in 1998 and began working for IOA Global. At this time, CNA were parties to a Management and Administration Agreement under which CNA had delegated the underwriting of their UK accident and health reinsurance to another insurer, IGI, under the supervision of IOA Global. N contacted B, who was employed by Sun Life, and offered her a 40% line in a new medical account which IOA Global was developing, and also a 10% line on a personal accident quota share agreement from CNA. On 20 July 1998 N sent B a slip for medical reinsurance: this specifically stated that it was governed by the terms of the Management and Administration Agreement between IGI, IOA and CNA. B signed the slip for the medical reinsurance business on 29 October 1998. At this time no slip had been prepared for the personal accident cover, as the relevant treaty wording had not yet been drafted. On 22 March 1999 a copy of a treaty for personal accident cover signed by CNA was sent to Sun Life for its approval and signature. That wording included an arbitration clause. B raised two queries on the wording. The first was the date of the cancellation clause in the treaty. The second related to the fact that the draft wording did not contain an "access to records" clause, so that Sun Life would have no access to CNA's records. N discussed each of these points with Sun Life's medical and accident business underwriter, O, at a meeting on 7 April 1999, and N agreed to modify the treaty wording by changing the cancellation date and inserting an access to records clause. At that point no new wording was prepared, and the matter was left that wording would follow. On 16 June 1999 N duly sent to B an addendum to the treaty wording incorporating the changes to the wording which had been requested by O. Sun Life expressed its approval to the new wording. However, neither the treaty nor the addendum was ever signed by Sun Life. On 27 September 1999 O sent two faxes to N, one referring to the personal accident treaty and the other to the medical quota share treaty. Those faxes purported to give 90 days' notice of cancellation of each of the treaties. At that point it became apparent that no slip for the treaty had ever been signed, and that the treaty and addendum had themselves never been formally executed by Sun Life. The present action was brought by Sun Life, presumably for declaratory relief in relation to the personal accident treaty. CNA sought a stay of the proceedings under section 9 of the Arbitration Act 1996 on the strength of the arbitration clause in the draft treaty wording. If the treaty wording was binding, plainly CNA were entitled to their stay. However, if the entire relationship between the parties was governed by the Management and Administration Agreement there was no obligation to go to arbitration and the judicial proceedings could continue.

Held (C.A.): that the treaty wording was not binding on Sun Life. The case was recognised to be an unusual one, as there was no dispute as to the existence of a treaty: the problem was its content. The Court of Appeal, following the reasoning of the trial judge, held that the key question was not the authority of M and O to bind Sun Life (as it was clear that they had the relevant authority to sign a slip or treaty wording on behalf of Sun Life) but rather whether the discussions between them and N had proceeded on the basis that the treaty wording would not be binding unless it was formally executed by Sun Life's signature. The Court of Appeal held that this was the case. CNA's argument was that the absence of a formal contract was irrelevant, as the parties had reached consensus. The Court of Appeal accepted that it was perfectly possible for there to be a binding oral contract of insurance (except, of course, in the case of a marine policy, where a policy is required by section 23 of the Marine Insurance Act 1906) although this would be unusual. What would normally be expected was a signed slip followed by an agreed treaty wording: this procedure meant that, while in the case of an ordinary commercial contract the court would be content to find that negotiations were not subject to formal confirmation, that finding would be relatively unusual in an insurance or reinsurance case given that there was an accepted method of doing business. In the absence of a slip, the parties had chosen to regulate their relationship on the terms of the incorporated Management and Administration Agreement. That being the case, the Management and Administration Agreement was the governing document unless and until there had been an agreed modification of it. The evidence was that the only acceptable agreed modification was a signed treaty, but in the absence of an executed formal document the Management and Administration Agreement remained in place. The Court of Appeal emphasised the distinction between assent to terms being included in a contract, and assent to the contract itself.

CNA sought to overcome this ruling by arguing that Sun Life was estopped from denying the validity of the treaty terms, in that O had been held out by Sun Life to have the authority to bind Sun Life without the need for any formal signature on their part. The Court of Appeal regarded this argument as unsustainable. O's authority was not the point. What was in issue was whether O could be taken to have intended to bind Sun Life to the wording submitted to her without a formal treaty wording being signed, and that question had been answered in the negative.

Assicurazioni Generali SpA v. *Arab Insurance Group* (BSC) [2003] Lloyd's Rep. IR 131

The claimant was the reinsurer of a U.S. insurer, UIG. The claimant's brokers sought retrocession cover from the defendant, and faxed an invitation to the defendant to participate in the retrocession. The defendant replied by fax, stating its willingness to accept a 7.5% line as long as various conditions were met and requesting the submission of final slips for its signature. Slips were duly faxed to, and scratched by, the defendant. The issue was whether a contract had been made by the exchange of faxes or whether the contract had been made at the date of the scratching of the slips.

Held (C.A.): that the contract had been made when the slips were scratched. Even if the brokers' fax had been an offer (which was unlikely as it was not sufficiently specific) the defendant's fax had not been an acceptance as conditions upon final acceptance had been imposed. The Court of Appeal recognised that the usual method of contracting was by the scratching of a slip, but held that this was not the only method by which a binding contract could be reached.

Not every scratched slip is a binding contract. The broker may put forward a slip purely for a quotation, and the scratching of a quotation slip is simply a statement by the underwriter of the terms upon which he would be willing to do business in the event that a proposal was to be put to him. Whether a slip is a final slip or a quotation slip is not always apparent from the face of the document, and it is to be assumed that the slip is a full offer unless it specifically states otherwise. Even where the slip does constitute an offer, the underwriter's scratch may be conditional, e.g., subject to approval by a third party.

***Eagle Star Insurance* v. *Spratt* [1971] 2 Lloyd's Rep. 116**

A slip for an aviation risk was presented to an underwriter for his signature. The slip was scratched by him, but he underlined the signature in an attempt to indicate to subsequent underwriters that he had reservations as to the risk. The question was whether this amounted to a qualification on the underwriter's scratch or whether the contract was binding at that point.

Held (C.A.): that there was a binding contract. Looking at the matter objectively, there was nothing to indicate that the underwriter's acceptance had been anything other than unconditional. While the underlining might have meant something to other underwriters within the same syndicate, it could not be regarded as having any contractual effect.

There has to be an actual scratching or signature: the mere affixing of a stamp is not enough.

***Denby* v. *English and Scottish Maritime Insurance Co. Ltd* [1999] Lloyd's Rep. IR 343**

A Lloyd's underwriter was granted authority by two other syndicates to accept risks on their behalves. A slip was submitted to the underwriter, and he affixed the stamps of both syndicates to the slip but only appended his signature to one of the stamps. The issue was whether both syndicates were bound to the slip, or only the syndicate whose stamp had been signed by the underwriter.

Held (C.A.): that the syndicate whose stamp had not been signed was not bound by the slip. A contract will be made only where the slip is actually scratched by the underwriter, and it is not enough that it has been stamped without signature. It could not be held on the facts that the underwriter's signature was intended to extend to both stampings.

In Bonner v. *Cox Dedicated Corporate Member Inc* [2006] Lloyd's Rep. IR 385 Morison J. held that a scratching in pencil was as binding as a scratching in ink. There was no appeal against this aspect of the decision, [2005] EWCA Civ 1512. *In ERC Frankona Reinsurance* v. *American National Insurance Co.* [2006] Lloyd's Rep IR 157 it was held that the addition of the letters "TBE" (to be entered) to a scratching did not signify that the scratching was conditional in any way but simply operated as a reminder to the underwriter himself that the subscription was to be entered into his own records.

Effect of scratching a slip

Once an unconditional reinsurance slip has been scratched, a contract arises as between the reinsurers and the reinsured for the proportion of the risk accepted by the subscribing underwriter. The binding contract between the parties is unaffected by later developments in the placement process. The fact that the slip has been subscribed by an underwriter does not mean that the underwriter becomes immediately liable for losses, as the risk itself will generally be stated to incept from a given date rather than from the date of scratching: there is a distinction to be drawn between the making of the contract and the commencement of the risk. The making of the contract does, however, determine the reinsured's duty of utmost good faith, so that disclosure of material facts which have arisen after the scratching is not required.

The principles that the scratching of a slip creates a contract of reinsurance, and that each subsequent scratching will bring a fresh contract of reinsurance into effect as from the date of a scratching so that there are as many contracts as there are participating subscribers and made at different times, gives rise to the following propositions:

- Neither party may unilaterally withdraw from the slip after it has been scratched even if the broker is unable to obtain sufficient subsequent subscriptions to cover 100 per cent of the risk.
- The reinsured's duty of good faith is owed to each underwriter in turn, and each may separately rely upon misrepresentations or failures to disclose in the negotiations with him.
- If changes are made to the slip by subsequent underwriters those changes cannot be relied upon by underwriters who have earlier subscribed to the slip unless the consent of the assured to a variation in their terms can be obtained.

***General Reinsurance Corporation* v. *Forsikringsaktiebolaget Fennia Patria* [1983] 1 Lloyd's Rep. 287**

FP, a Finnish insurer, had agreed to insure a cargo of paper and board under an open cover, and reinsured with the claimant and other reinsurers under two separate policies: a whole account cover offering all risks protection; and a specific risks cover which confined liability to loss by fire and flood. The whole account cover was for FM12 million, with a deductible of FM3 million. The specific risks cover, which had been subscribed to by 27 reinsurers, was an excess of loss contract, and provided for cover of FM15 million in excess of FM15 million. After inception of these policies, FP obtained an increase in the financial limits of the whole account cover, increasing the sum insured to FM20 million in excess of FM5 million. As a result of this amendment there was an overlap in coverage where the loss was caused by fire or flood. Accordingly, on 14 February 1977 FP's brokers prepared an amendment slip for the specific risks cover which was designed to remove the overlap: the specific risks cover was to become one for FM15 million in excess of FM25 million (the sum insured plus deductible under the whole account cover). An amendment slip was prepared, and this was scratched by the claimant and one other reinsurer, but not by any other of the remaining 25 subscribers to the specific risks cover. However, at this point it became apparent that a loss had occurred, amounting to some FM27 million. It was agreed by the parties that, without the amendment to the specific risks cover, the loss would have been borne in the sum of FM15 million by the whole account reinsurers and FM10 million by the specific risks reinsurers. However, had the amendment taken effect, the whole account reinsurers would have borne FM20 million of the loss and the specific risks insurers only FM2 million.

FP sought to withdraw the amendment slip, arguing that as it had not been fully subscribed it was not binding. The claimant refused to agree to the withdrawal, and argued that the amendment slip was binding upon those reinsurers who had scratched it. Accordingly, the claimant's share of the loss under the specific risks cover could only be its proportion of the insured sum of FM2 million.

Held (C.A.): that the amendment slip could not be withdrawn and that it was binding on those reinsurers who had signed it but was not binding on the rest of the market who had not signed it.

(1) The presentation of the slip by the broker constituted the offer and the writing of each line constituted an acceptance of this offer by the underwriter. Neither party could unilaterally withdraw from the slip or vary its terms.

(2) The evidence did not support the assertion that there was a binding market custom entitling a reinsured unilaterally to withdraw from a slip which had been partially subscribed: the law was that a subscription created a binding contract. In the absence of any custom, FP had no right to cancel the amendment slip and the defendant was entitled to rely upon that slip.

(3) There was no basis for implying a term which permitted the reinsured to withdraw from a partly subscribed slip. The Court of Appeal in *Fennia Patria* apparently recognised that the law might be inconvenient, in that it gave rise to the possibility that the reinsured might be bound by an undersubscribed slip, or that reinsurers might be bound on different terms if there were variations during the placement process, but this did not make the implication of a right of withdrawal necessary to give business efficacy to the contract.

(4) The reasoning of Donaldson J. in *Jaglom* v. *Excess Insurance Co.* [1971] 2 Lloyd's Rep. 171, that the submission of a slip by the broker to the underwriter was an invitation to treat, that the scratching of the slip was an offer by the underwriter and that the offer was accepted by the assured once the slip was fully subscribed, would not be followed.

Signing down

There is one exception to the rule that a scratched slip is a binding contract which cannot be unilaterally varied. This arises where the slip has been oversubscribed. It is a custom of Lloyd's that if a slip has been signed for more than 100% the broker is entitled to reduce the liabilities of the subscribers proportionately to the point at which the subscription has been reduced to 100%. This exception was recognised by the Court of Appeal in *General Reinsurance Corporation* v. *Forsikringsaktiebolaget Fennia Patria* [1983] 1 Lloyd's Rep. 287 and was confirmed by the Court of Appeal in *General Accident Fire and Life*

Assurance Corporation v. *Tanter, The Zephyr* [1985] 2 Lloyd's Rep. 529. The facts of this case are given below.

The rights of reinsurers under a multiple subscription

A typical slip will have multiple subscribers, each of whom has a separate contract with the reinsured. The rights and liabilities of the subscribing reinsurers are, therefore, quite distinct (although, as will be seen below, there may be an exception in the case of misrepresentation to the leading underwriter).

***Touche Ross & Co.* v. *Baker* [1992] 2 Lloyd's Rep. 207**

The claimants, a firm of accountants, took out professional indemnity insurance which consisted of a primary layer of cover and several excess layers. The defendant, who represented Syndicate 126 at Lloyd's, participated in the primary cover and in a number of the layers. The policy contained a "discovery extension clause" which stated that if the underwriters refused to renew the cover beyond its expiry date, the claimants would have the right, upon payment of an additional premium, to obtain an extension of cover in respect of any claims made against them during the succeeding period of 36 months in respect of acts committed before the termination date. Most of the underwriters agreed to renew the cover, but the defendant's syndicate refused to do so. The claimants sought a declaration that they were entitled to avail themselves of the discovery extension clause. The defendant asserted that the clause was a collective clause, which could be operated only if all of the subscribing underwriters refused to renew the policy: as most of the underwriters had agreed to renew, the clause was inoperative.

Held (H.L.): that the argument by the defendant that the discovery extension clause could be exercised either against all of the underwriters where there was a collective refusal to renew the insurance, or none of them if they all renewed, was incorrect. The liability of a subscribing underwriter was divisible from that of the other underwriters, and was not joint. This was in any event confirmed by the express wording of the covers which stated that "We, the Underwriters . . . hereby bind ourselves each for his own part and not one for another . . . in respect of his due proportion only . . . "

The duty of disclosure in a market placement

Each placement is a separate contract and therefore the duty of utmost good faith is owed to each individual subscribing underwriter. The mere fact that there has been a failure to disclose material facts to the leading underwriter does not permit the following market to avoid the policy as well, as it remains necessary for them to prove that the same facts were also withheld from them.

***Bank Leumi Le Israel BM* v. *British National Insurance Co. Ltd* [1988] 1 Lloyd's Rep. 71**

The claimant bank agreed to lend US$5.5 million to Sagittarius Films to finance the production of a film. The loan was secured by a letter of credit in favour of the borrowers and assigned to the bank, payment to be made on the production of four specified documents. The bank stated that it was only prepared to advance the money if it was also secured against the risk that three out of the four necessary documents would not be forthcoming. The bank obtained contingency insurance with the defendant insurers. The loan was not repaid and a claim was made against the insurers, who purported to avoid the policy on the ground that the bank had failed to disclose that the film was no longer to be produced by Sagittarius Films and that Sagittarius had ceased to be the owner of rights in the film.

Held (Saville J.): that the allegations of misrepresentation and non-disclosure would be dismissed on the facts. In the course of his judgment Saville J. discussed an argument put forward by the brokers (who had been joined to the proceedings), to the effect that there had been no evidence by certain members of the following market to support their assertions of non-disclosure.

"It is no doubt the position (at least in some insurance markets) that following underwriters often do subscribe simply or largely on the basis of trusting the skill and judgement of the leading underwriter and upon the assumption that the leading underwriter has subscribed only after considering full and accurate information about the risk. Thus it might be that, in any case where this is established, the supposed rule could perhaps be supported by proving a custom or usage in the particular market, or by importing an implied term into the contracts of the following underwriters, or even perhaps by treating the rule as resting upon some implied representation made to following underwriters that all material circumstances have been accurately provided to the leading underwriter. Even then the supposed rule could cause difficulties: for example, would it apply when the following underwriters (but not the leading underwriter) have been given full and accurate details of the risk? It must always be remembered that each subscribing underwriter makes a separate contract for himself (or for those he represents) so that it is difficult to accept the proposition that the mere fact that the leading underwriter may be able to avoid his contract should allow the others, contracting separately with the assured, also to do so."

A slightly different situation arises where a material false statement has been made to the leading underwriter, but no equivalent false statement has been made to the following market. There is a division of opinion in the cases as to whether the following market are entitled to rely upon the false statement. One view is that there is no such right: this was the conclusion of the Court of Appeal in *General Accident Fire and Life Assurance Corporation* v. *Tanter, The Zephyr* [1985] 2 Lloyd's Rep. 529. The alternative view, taken at first instance in a succession of subsequent cases, is that the following market can rely upon the false statement to the leading underwriter either because: (a) the fact that a false statement has been made to the leading underwriter is of itself a material fact, and this has to be disclosed to the following market; or (b) if the cover is specialised, it is to be assumed that the following market have relied upon the presentation to the leading underwriter and the underwriting judgement exercised by him in the consideration of the risk.

General Accident Fire and Life Assurance Corporation v. _Tanter, The Zephyr_ [1985] 2 Lloyd's Rep. 529

A broker was instructed to place direct insurance on a vessel. Instead of approaching insurers directly, the broker chose to seek reinsurance first so that he would be able to offer direct insurers both the risk and also security for coverage in the form of reinsurance. The broker presented the risk to the defendant, the underwriter for a Lloyd's syndicate. The broker was asked whether he intended to seek to have the slip oversubscribed, and the broker informed the defendant that it was his intention to do so and that subscribing reinsurers would be signed down to one-third of their original subscription. In reliance on this signing indication, the defendant subscribed to the slip. The broker then presented the slip to two further reinsurance underwriters: no signing indication was made to them, but they subscribed to the slip on the assumption that a signing indication had been given to the leading underwriter. The broker was thereafter able to place the insurance risk with other underwriters. In the event, the broker was not able to obtain the anticipated level of subscription for the reinsurance, and the final written down proportion of the subscription was 88.48 per cent rather than the promised one-third. The defendant and the two other members of the following market, having been held liable to indemnify the reinsureds (see below), sought damages against the broker.

Held (C.A.): that the broker was liable to the leading reinsurance underwriter for breach of contract, but that there was no liability to the following market.

(1) The broker, in giving the signing indication, undertook a collateral contractual obligation to the effect that he would use his best endeavours to obtain the level of oversubscription which he had indicated would be obtained. There was no need to imply a duty of care in tort given that there was contractual liability.

(2) The following market were unable to rely upon the representation made to the leading underwriter but not to them. The following market had no idea of exactly what statement had been made to the leading underwriter, so there could not be reliance. Further, if by the time that the broker had approached the following market it had become clear that the signing indication given to the leading underwriter was unrealistic, it could not be right that the following market could purport to claim damages for a statement made to the leading underwriter at the very start of the process.

Aneco Reinsurance Underwriting Ltd **v.** ***Johnson & Higgins*** **[1998] 1 Lloyd's Rep. 565**

The defendant brokers placed retrocession cover for retrocedants who had subscribed to a reinsurance treaty. The presentation made to the leading retrocessionaire underwriter was false, as it indicated that the liability faced by the retrocedant was under an obligatory treaty whereas the treaty was in fact a facultative obligatory treaty under which the retrocedant was required to accept such risks as its policy holders chose to cede. This was a material fact and the leading underwriter had the right to avoid. The further question was whether the following market of retrocessionaires had the right to avoid as well even though no material misstatement had been made to them.

Held (Cresswell J.): that the following market had the same right to avoid as the leading underwriter. The false statement made to the leading underwriter was of itself a material fact which ought to have been disclosed. The following market thus had the right to avoid for non-disclosure.

The *Aneco* case was followed in *International Lottery Management Ltd* v. *Dumas* [2002] Lloyd's Rep. IR 237, where H.H.J. Dean QC emphasised the specialised nature of the cover in this case—political risks insurance against the possible nationalisation of a private lottery operated by the assured—and held that it was inherent in a placement of this type that the following market would rely upon the judgement of the leading underwriter. Accordingly, if a false statement was made to the leading underwriter and that false statement affected his judgement, the following market could themselves be regarded as having received a false presentation. The same reasoning has since been adopted in: *International Management Group (UK) Ltd* v. *Simmonds* [2003] EWHC 177 (Comm), [2004] Lloyd's Rep. IR 247; *Brotherton* v. *Aseguradora Colseguros (No. 3)* [2003] EWHC 1741 (Comm), [2003] Lloyd's Rep. IR 774 and *Toomey* v. *Banco Vitalicio de Espana SA de Seguros y Reaseguros* [2004] Lloyd's Rep. IR 354.

Relationship between slip and policy

The slip is a binding contract in its own right, and there is no formal need for a policy.

Marine Insurance Act 1906, extracts

21.—A contract of marine insurance is deemed to be concluded when the proposal of the assured is accepted by the insurer, whether the policy be then issued or not: and for the purpose of showing when the proposal was accepted, reference may be made to the slip or covering note or other customary memorandum of the contract.

89.—Where there is a duly stamped policy, reference made as before to the slip or covering note, in any legal proceedings.

Where a policy is subsequently issued, it ought to be consistent with the slip, and it is the practice of the market to refer to the policy as governing the relationship between the parties. However, if the policy is ambiguous it may be permissible to refer to the slip to resolve any ambiguity, and if the policy does not comply with the slip then it may be permissible for the policy to be rectified so as to conform to the slip. These propositions have only been recently established. Until the decision of the Court of Appeal in *HIH Casualty and General Insurance Ltd* v. *New Hampshire Insurance Co.* [2001] Lloyd's Rep. IR 596, the courts had come to accept that the slip was a mere provisional contract which was superseded by the policy so that rectification was not possible and at the very most the slip might be relevant as an aid to the construction of the policy where the policy terms were ambiguous (see *Youell* v. *Bland Welch & Co. (No. 1)* [1992] 2 Lloyd's Rep. 127 and *Punjab National Bank* v. *De Boinville* [1992] 1 Lloyd's Rep. 7). However, after *HIH* it has become clear that the slip is the governing document and that the issue of the policy is "a purely ministerial exercise" (*per* Colman J. in *Assicurazioni Generali* v. *Ege Sigorta AS* [2002] Lloyd's Rep. IR 480).

***HIH Casualty and General Insurance Ltd* v. *New Hampshire Insurance Co.* [2001] Lloyd's Rep. IR 596**

The claimant entered into two contracts of insurance with investors in film production companies. Under those policies, the claimant was obliged to make payment to the investors if, on a given day, the revenues from the films fell short of the insured sum. The contracts were contained in slips, and the slips referred to the number of films to be made (six in one case, and 10 in the other). The claimant subsequently issued policies, although the policies made no reference to the number of films to be made. In the event, the number of films made by the production companies fell short of the numbers identified in the slips. The underlying wording was incorporated into reinsurance agreements issued by the defendants, and one of the questions was whether the statements as to the number of films in the direct slips formed a part of the direct contracts and (by means of incorporation) of the reinsurance.

Held (C.A.): that the terms of the slips governed the position, and that the statements as to the number of films constituted contractual warranties both in the direct insurance and in the reinsurance. It was perfectly possible for the parties to intend the policy to supersede the slip, and where such an intention was found then the slip had no part to play in the contractual relationship between the parties and could not be used either to rectify the policy or as an aid to its interpretation. However, there was no rule of law which provided that the policy superseded the slip, and it would generally be permissible to have regard to the slip for the purposes of rectifying the policy or as an aid to the construction of the policy because: (a) the slip formed part of the factual matrix surrounding the policy; and (b) it was not to be assumed that the parties intended the slip to be superseded by the policy. If there was a dispute as to the significance of the slip, then the court was required to admit the slip as evidence so that the court itself could determine the relationship between the two contracts. It thus followed that it was only where the parties agreed that the slip had been superseded that the slip became inadmissible.

The placement of reinsurance in advance of insurance

It will be appreciated from the discussion of *General Accident Fire and Life Assurance Corporation* v. *Tanter, The Zephyr* [1985] 2 Lloyd's Rep. 529, above, that it is not uncommon in the London market for reinsurance to be arranged in advance of the insurance to which it relates. This may occur when the broker appreciates that it may be difficult to place the risk unless insurers are guaranteed protection in the form of reinsurance and thus chooses to approach reinsurers first, or where he attempts to place insurance directly and is informed by the underwriters that they are only prepared to act as reinsurers for any direct underwriters that the broker is able to find. It is also a common practice for insurance and reinsurance to be negotiated at the same time, with the same presentation being used for both the insurance and reinsurance and with the contracts being signed at the same time. The practice of obtaining reinsurance in advance of insurance gives rise to legal complexities.

***General Accident Fire and Life Assurance Corporation* v. *Tanter, The Zephyr* [1985] 2 Lloyd's Rep. 529**

(See also above.) A broker, having been instructed to place insurance on a vessel, sought to obtain the subscription of reinsurers first. In obtaining the subscription of the leading reinsuring underwriter, the broker gave a signing indication of one-third, leaving the leading underwriter with the belief that his agreed subscription would be reduced to one-third of the stated sum. However, the broker failed to obtain the relevant level of oversubscription, and the leading underwriter was instead signed down to 88.48% of the sum agreed. The leading underwriter sought to avoid the reinsurance agreement against the insurers who had subsequently subscribed to the direct risk or, in the alternative, to claim damages from the broker. As was seen above, the leading underwriter was held to be entitled to claim damages from the broker. The aspect of the Court of Appeal's decision considered here is the claim for the right to avoid against the insurers.

Held (Hobhouse J. and C.A.): that there was no right to avoid the reinsurance agreement.

(1) The general rule was that the broker was the agent of the person who appointed him to obtain reinsurance. The broker was not, therefore, the agent of the reinsurers, and accordingly it could not be argued that the signing indication was a limitation on

the broker's authority to act for the reinsurers, restricting the broker to binding them to one-third of the risk.

(2) In presenting the risk to reinsurers, the broker was to be regarded as the agent of the reinsureds (who had not yet come into existence). However, the reinsurance could not be avoided for misrepresentation as the broker had merely given a statement of his intention and belief rather than a misrepresentation of fact, and in any event the signing indication did not form a part of the presentation for reinsurance. On the agency issue, Hobhouse J. noted that:

> "[A] broker who approaches an insurer with an offer of reinsurance is offering to act as the agent of the insurer. If the insurer accepts the reinsurance offered he thereby constitutes the broker his agent to obtain the cover offered."

(3) Once the reinsurance had been agreed, then pending the making of the direct insurance contracts to which it was designed to relate the reinsurers were not permitted to withdraw the offer of reinsurance as the consideration for their promise to provide reinsurance was a corresponding implied promise on the part of the broker not to place the reinsurance with other reinsurers.

In later cases Hobhouse J.'s point (2) has been approved (see *Youell* v. *Bland Welch & Co. (No. 2)* [1990] 2 Lloyd's Rep. 431 and *Kingscroft Insurance Co. Ltd* v. *Nissan Fire & Marine Insurance Co. Ltd (No. 2)* [1999] Lloyd's Rep. IR 603) but his reasoning on point (3) has been modified. The view which has now come into favour is that the reinsurer, by agreeing to provide reinsurance for direct insurers who chose to accept the risk, had entered into a unilateral contract whereby an offer was made to the world and could crystallise into a binding contract by any person who met its conditions. The offer could not be withdrawn once it had been accepted by an insurer who had chosen to write the direct risk. This approach was adopted by Moore-Bick J. in *Kingscroft Insurance Co. Ltd* v. *Nissan Fire & Marine Insurance Co. Ltd (No. 2)* [1999] Lloyd's Rep. IR 603. See also *Bonner* v. *Cox Dedicated Corporate Member Inc* [2006] Lloyd's Rep. IR 385, affirmed [2005] EWCA Civ 1512, where reinsurers had scratched a reinsurance slip and subsequently claimed the right to avoid it for non-disclosure of a direct loss. Morison J. held that the reinsureds had accepted the reinsurers' standing offer before the loss had become known to their broker, so that there was no breach of the duty of utmost good faith. The theoretical problem of the incidence of agency of a broker who has been appointed to obtain insurance but who first applies for reinsurance has not been treated by the courts as a major issue. In *Tryg Baltica International (UK) Ltd* v. *Boston Compania de Seguros SA* [2005] Lloyd's Rep IR 40 the issue was whether the English court had jurisdiction to hear an action by English reinsurers against Argentinian insurance companies. The reinsurance had been placed in London by London market brokers acting on instructions from the insurance companies and from brokers in Argentina. The head of jurisdiction relied upon was that the reinsurance had been placed in England by an agent residing in England and acting for the insurers. Cooke J., without any analysis of the point, relied on *The Zephyr* to hold that the London placing brokers met this description even though at the time the reinsurance was placed there was no direct insurance in existence.

Summary

- Reinsurance is generally placed in the London market on a subscription basis involving the use of a slip, although other methods may be used.
- There is no need for a policy to be issued, as the slip is a binding contract, although if there is a policy then the slip and policy must be read together.
- Each subscription to a slip is a binding contract in its own right, and each underwriter has its own defences against the assured.
- A false statement made to the leading underwriter may generally be relied upon by members of the following market.
- Once a slip has been scratched, neither the reinsured nor the subscribing underwriter can alter the terms of the subscription unilaterally: the consent of both parties is needed.
- The only exception to this principle arises where a slip has been oversubscribed, in which case the broker may sign down proportionately the subscriptions of each reinsurer.
- If reinsurance is placed in advance of insurance, the reinsurers are treated as having made a standing offer to all potential insurers, and the contract of reinsurance is completed when an insurer agrees to accept the direct risk.

THE USE OF AGENCY AGREEMENTS IN THE LONDON MARKET

Line slips

The time-consuming nature of a typical market placement, and the legal complexities which arise from such placements, may in practice be avoided by the use of agency agreements, one type of which is the line slip. A line slip is in essence an agreement which authorises one underwriter to accept business on behalf of other underwriters. Accordingly when a broker approaches a particular underwriter to subscribe to a risk, that underwriter may well be authorised to accept subscriptions on behalf of other underwriters. The procedure in reinsurance cases is that the line slip constitutes the agency relationship between the underwriters, and that when a risk is accepted an off slip is issued: this evidences the contract of insurance and confirms that the risk is reinsured. A line slip is thus not a contract of reinsurance but rather is an agreement between reinsurers, and it follows that the reinsured cannot rely upon it as evidence of the terms upon which reinsurance has been provided to him (see *Touche Ross & Co.* v. *Baker* [1992] 2 Lloyd's Rep. 207).

***Balfour* v. *Beaumont* [1984] 1 Lloyd's Rep. 272**
McDonnell Douglas Corporation, aircraft manufacturers, was insured against product liability under four policies arranged in layers. The claimant, Syndicate 619 at

Lloyd's, was a participant in the three excess layer policies. Following the crash of an aircraft near to Paris in March 1974, Syndicate 619 indemnified McDonnell against third party claims. The defendants, two Lloyd's syndicates and an insurance company, were subscribers to an excess of loss reinsurance policy which reinsured Syndicate 619. The reinsurance was in force for the period for 12 months at 1 December 1972. A claim was made under the reinsurance agreement but the Court of Appeal held that the reinsurers were not liable as the policy had been written on a losses occurring basis which meant that the reinsurers were liable only for losses which occurred during the 12 months after 1 December 1972; the policy had not been written on a "risks attaching basis" whereby the reinsurance applied to direct policies in force during the 12 months after 1 December 1972. In the course of his judgment, Lord Donaldson MR described the line slip process as follows:

"The reinsurance policy itself took the form of what is called a 'slip policy'. This, as its name implies, is a slip which has been converted into a policy by the addition of a standard wording signed by Lloyd's Policy Signing Office. Nothing turns on this standard wording and the slip is to be construed and takes effect as a policy of reinsurance.

The reinsurance policy refers, under the heading of 'interest', to a 'line slip'. This calls for a word of explanation. It is a curious document, but one which serves in the present context a commercial purpose in addition to its main function as an authority enabling leading underwriters to buy-in foreign underwriters. Suppose that a broker approaches an underwriter asking him to write a risk. The underwriter may be unwilling to do so unless he is certain that he can reinsure part of that risk. However, if he does not accept the risk, he has nothing to reinsure and if he does accept it he may find that he cannot effect reinsurance. The line slip and associated reinsurance policy provide an escape from this dilemma. The reinsurance policy evidences the agreement of the reinsurer to reinsure original risks accepted by underwriters in accordance with the line slip. Where risks are so insured, the contract between the assured and the original primary underwriter is contained in a separate contract called an 'off slip', indicating that it is concluded under the auspices of the line slip and is reinsured under the reinsurance policy. A lawyer would rightly say that any loss suffered by the primary underwriter was suffered under the 'off slip' contract and not under the line slip, but in the market such losses are referred to as occurring under the line slip."

WWW ***Denby* v. *English and Scottish Maritime Insurance Co. Ltd* [1999] Lloyd's Rep. IR 343**

Two Syndicates at Lloyd's had written professional indemnity cover under line slips, and had reinsured their liability with the defendant reinsurers. The reinsurance provided that it was to apply to "risks written prior to 22 October 1992." The line slips were in force before this date, but no risks were accepted by the Syndicates under the line slips until after that date. The issue was whether the date of 22 October 1992 referred to the line slips themselves, so that all risks whenever written were subject to the reinsurance, or whether the date referred to risks accepted under the line slips. The Syndicates argued for the former construction, whereas the reinsurers argued for the latter construction.

Held (C.A.): that the defendants' construction was correct. A line slip was simply the first stage in the making of a reinsurance contract, and was not a contract of reinsurance in its own right. The line slip itself simply created the machinery whereby contracts of reinsurance could be effected, by means of declarations in the form of off slips. Accordingly, the contracts of reinsurance which were covered by the reinsurance agreements were those which had come into force before 22 October 1992 by means of declaration to the line slip. As there were no such declarations, the reinsurers were under no liability.

Leading underwriter clauses

Scope of authority of leading underwriter

The common law rules on the placement procedure adopted in the London market, and in particular the principle that a slip or policy evidences a series of parallel bilateral contracts between the reinsured and each participating reinsurer, mean that the administration of the reinsurance agreement is potentially unwieldy as every reinsurer must agree to every decision which is taken or request which is made. To overcome this problem, it is very common in the London market for reinsurance slips to include "leading underwriter" clauses, which authorise the broker to approach the nominated leading underwriter on behalf of the market as a whole. Such clauses are not in standard form, and may cover matters such as amendments or extensions to the insured peril, receiving notice from the assured where this is required by the policy and, in some cases, settlements. The use of leading underwriter clauses is generally encouraged by the London market under the London Market Principles 2001 Initiative, and the most recent direct marine hulls and machinery clauses published in October 2002 delegate a range of additional functions to the leading underwriter.

Leading underwriter clauses are typically included in the slip which is presented to the market for subscription. The clause takes effect as a contract between the reinsured and each of the reinsurers that the reinsurers will be bound by the decisions of the leading underwriter in the circumstances provided for by the clause. Thus, if the clause requires the following market to follow the settlements of the leading underwriter, the reinsured has the right to insist that all reinsurers do just that, as long as the settlement falls within the scope of the leading underwriter's authority.

***Barlee Marine Corporation* v. *Mountain, The Leegas* [1987] 1 Lloyd's Rep. 471**

The claimants were the owners of the vessel *Leegas*, which was insured for a period of four months from 9 February 1985 under a war risks policy. The insurance covered hull and machinery, loss of earnings and expenses for voyages to the Persian Gulf. The slip contained a leading underwriter clause which provided that the leading underwriter could bind the following market in respect of "Any amendments additions deletions including new and or managed and or chartered notice of assignment ratings and alterations of any description". The leading underwriter, but not the following market, scratched an endorsement under which the period of insurance was extended until 31 May 1986. The vessel was lost under fire in April 1986, and the following market denied liability on the basis that they had not agreed to the extension of cover.

Held (Hirst J.): that the claimants were entitled to summary judgment against the following market. The case turned on the construction of the leading underwriter clause, and it was clear from the wording of the clause that it embraced all of the classes of risk insured and that there was no limitation on the phrases "amendments, additions and deletions" or "alterations of any descriptions". Accordingly, the following market was bound by the leading underwriter's decision to extend time.

***Roadworks (1952) Ltd* v. *Charman* [1994] 2 Lloyd's Rep. 99**

The claimants were the charterers of a barge which was to be used to transport granite. The barge was to be beached, and the assured obtained a survey of the proposed beaching area. The assured then instructed the broker to obtain insurance against the possible liability of the assured to the owners of the barge in the event of damage caused by the beaching. The slip stated that towing arrangements were subject to London Salvage Association approval. The slip also contained a leading underwriter clause which provided that "All alterations, additions, deletions, extensions, agreements, rates and changes in conditions to be agreed by the leading Lloyd's underwriter", and in due course this became fully subscribed. The broker then sought to arrange a survey by the LSA, but that body refused to approve the beaching operations. Faced with this refusal, the broker took the slip back to the leading underwriter and secured his scratching on an endorsement which removed the requirement for LSA approval. Thereafter the barge was damaged in the course of beaching operations. Members of the following market argued that they were not bound by the second slip.

Held (H.H.J. Kershaw QC): that the new agreement bound both the leading underwriter and the following market.

(1) The leading underwriter clause took effect as a contract between the assured and the subscribing underwriters.

(2) The leading underwriter was the agent of the following market, and was authorised by the leading underwriter clause to waive the inspection condition.

(3) The leading underwriter's amendment was not intended to be binding only on his syndicate: the leading underwriter had intended to exercise the powers under the leading underwriter clause and to bind the entire market. Thus, the certification condition was to be taken to have been waived.

***Roar Marine Ltd* v. *Bimeh Iran Insurance Co.* [1998] 1 Lloyd's Rep. 423**

The claimants held various interests in the vessel *Daylam* and their interests were insured under a hull and machinery policy issued by a number of underwriters from the London, French and Belgian markets as well as an insurer situated in Abu Dhabi, the defendant. The risk was led by the London market, and the terms upon which the insurance was placed included the statement: "It is agreed with or without previous notice to follow leading British underwriters in regard to . . . settlements in respect of claims . . . " The vessel suffered an engine breakdown, and the claim was settled by the London market on the basis that the loss had been caused by crew negligence. The defendant refused to pay.

Held (Mance J.): that the defendants were liable and the claimants were entitled to summary judgment.

(1) The wording of the leading underwriter clause was clear that settlements agreed by the leading underwriter were binding on the following market.

(2) There was no custom in the London market which confined the obligation to follow settlements to cases in which the claim was proved to be legitimate.

(3) The obligation to follow settlements was not subject to an implied limitation that the settlement reached by the leading underwriters had to be concluded in a bona fide and businesslike fashion. Unlike the position under a follow the settlements clause contained in a reinsurance agreement where the reinsurers agreed the follow the settlements of the reinsured, the insurers in the present case had a mutuality of interest, and accordingly there was no implied limitation on the discretion of the leading

underwriters. Even if this was wrong and there was an implied limitation to this effect, on the facts the leading underwriters had acted properly in investigating the claim and settling with the claimants.

The effect of the leading underwriter clause as between the underwriters themselves is a matter of some debate. In *Roadworks (1952) Ltd* v. *Charman* (see above) H.H.J. Kershaw QC expressed the view that

"a leading underwriter is the agent of the following underwriters. By taking a leading line he knows that there will be following underwriters and he sees the terms of any L/U clause on the slip. He may require the L/U clause to be altered if he is to take a line. The following underwriters see from the slip the identity of the leader or leaders. They see the terms of the L/U clause. By taking a line they not only make a contract with the insured but also make those leader or leaders their agent or agents for the purpose shown in the L/U clause."

However, this reasoning was rejected by Rix J. in *Mander* v. *Commercial Union Assurance Co. plc* [1998] Lloyd's Rep. IR 93, who sought to deny that the following market would have any cause of action against the leading underwriter if his actions bound them in a manner which they did not anticipate and who also denied that the reinsured could bring an action against the leading underwriter for breach of warranty of authority in the event that his actions on behalf of the following market were outside the scope of his authority.

***Mander* v. *Commercial Union Assurance Co. plc* [1998] Lloyd's Rep. IR 93**

The claimant, a representative of a Lloyd's syndicate, had acted as reinsurer in respect of marine liability policies. The Syndicate in turn entered into a retrocession agreement under an open cover subscribed to by a number of underwriters. Those underwriters refused to indemnify the claimant, asserting that the leading underwriter had not been authorised to bind them to accepting the risk presented by the claimant or, alternatively, that the declaration to the open cover could be avoided. The present action was against brokers who had purported to place the cover, and also against the leading underwriter on the basis that he was in breach of his warranty of authority in indicating that he was authorised by the other underwriters to write the risk on their behalves.

Held (Rix J.): that judgment would be given against the brokers but not against the leading underwriter. While it was the case that the leading underwriter had not been authorised to bind the following market, the leading underwriter did not act as agent of the following market but rather operated as the "trigger" by which the following market would become bound.

The conflict between the agency and trigger theories was referred to, but not resolved, by the Court of Appeal in *Unum Life Insurance Co. of America* v. *Israel Phoenix Assurance Co. Ltd* [2002] Lloyd's Rep. IR 374 (see below).

Appointment and removal of leading underwriter

The leading underwriter may be designated by the slip, although if this is not the case then the leading underwriter is normally the first underwriter to subscribe to the slip. There is no need for the leading underwriter to have the largest subscription. Once the leading underwriter has been identified, the fact that the clause is a contract between the assured and the following market means that the following market cannot unilaterally terminate the authority of the leading underwriter, and that authority will survive the termination of the policy insofar as there are outstanding questions as to claims and dispute resolution processes. However, if the policy is avoided *ab initio* for non-disclosure or misrepresentation, the authority of the leading underwriter will similarly be revoked as there is no basis upon which such authority can exist.

***Unum Life Insurance Co. of America* v. *Israel Phoenix Assurance Co. Ltd* [2002] Lloyd's Rep. IR 374**

The claimants were the reinsurers of the defendants under quota share reinsurance treaties in respect of personal accident business. The cover had been placed by slip in 1995, the slip stating that the wording was to be agreed by the leading underwriter only. The first underwriter to scratch the slip was Liberty, which took a subscription of 5%. The slip was completed by subscriptions from the following market. In July 2000 the claimants avoided the reinsurance treaties, alleging that material facts relating to the scope of the cover provided by the underlying policies had not been disclosed and that there had been misstatements about previous losses. In December 2000 Liberty agreed with the defendants that the matter should go to arbitration The claimants in the present action sought a declaration that they had validly avoided the treaties and that the agreement for arbitration had been made by the leading underwriter without the authorisation of the following market and was thus void.

Held (Andrew Smith J. and C.A.): that the arbitration provision was not binding on the following market.

(1) The C.A. held that once the treaties had been avoided, the leading underwriter no longer possessed any authority to act on behalf of the following market, and accordingly the arbitration agreement had been reached without authorisation. It was not necessary to decide whether the ability of the leading underwriter to bind the following market was based on agency or the "trigger" theory.

(2) Andrew Smith J. made various comments on the nature of the leading underwriter clause, to which the Court of Appeal found it unnecessary to make reference:

(a) on the balance of probabilities, Liberty were the leading underwriters even though Liberty had subscribed to only 5% of the risk;
(b) the slip contemplated that there would be a leading underwriter, and there was nothing in the slip which prevented the appointment of a leading underwriter after the slip had been fully subscribed;
(c) there was no implied term in the agreement that the leading underwriter clause could lapse even though it was not implemented, and it was not usually the case that a leading underwriter provision would be revocable;
(d) the commencement of litigation did not of itself affect the operation of the leading underwriter clause.

Binding authorities

A binding authority is an agency agreement between an insurer or reinsurer and an intermediary whereby the intermediary is authorised to accept risks on behalf of the underwriter: the intermediary is often stated to "hold the pen" for the underwriter. In some cases the intermediary may act for a number of underwriters who have formed a reinsurance pool (see Reinsurance Pools and Underwriting Agencies, below). A binding authority, or binder, is typically issued to a broker by a reinsurer, and authorises the broker to accept business of particular classes up to given financial limits. The usual contractual structure is for the broker to be authorised to accept risks, and then to declare them to the reinsurer, the reinsurer becoming automatically bound by the broker's acceptances.

The use of binding authorities between reinsurers and brokers gives rise to a number of issues. First, what is the scope of the broker's right to accept risks on behalf of the reinsurer? This will depend upon the proper construction of the binding authority. By way of illustration of the limits which may be imposed, in *Inversiones Manria SA* v. *Sphere Drake Insurance Co. plc, The Dora* [1989] 1 Lloyd's Rep. 69, a binding authority conferred upon the broker the right only to accept yacht insurance risks placed by Italian insurers.

***Sedgwick Tomenson Inc* v. *PT Reasransi Unum Indonesia*, 1990, unreported**

The first and second defendants agreed that they would jointly authorise a broker, under a binding authority, to accept risks. The first defendant imposed a maximum financial limit of US$50,000 per risk, but this limitation was not communicated to the broker by the second defendant, with the result that the broker accepted a number of risks in excess of US$50,000.

Held (Evans J.): that the second defendant had exceeded its authority from the first defendant, and accordingly that risks accepted by the broker which were in excess of US$50,000 were not binding on the first defendant. However, as each declaration to the open cover by the broker took effect as a separate contract, there was basis upon which the first defendant could refuse to make payment in respect of declarations of risk for US$50,000 or less.

The second issue concerns the capacity in which the broker acts when accepting declarations under a binding authority. The established agency rule in English law is that the broker is assumed to be the agent of the person seeking insurance or reinsurance, as the case may be, whereas under a binding authority the broker is authorised by the reinsurer to underwrite risks on behalf of the reinsurer. The English courts have yet to ascertain, in a modern context, whose agent the broker may be in such circumstances, although it would seem that as a matter of strict law the broker continues to act as the agent of the assured and does not owe the reinsurer any duty of care in the consideration and acceptance of risks as any such duty of care would give rise to a conflict of interest (*Empress Assurance Corporation Ltd* v. *Bowring & Co. Ltd* (1905) 11 Com. Cas. 107). There may nevertheless be a duty of care imposed in respect of a binding authority where no conflict of interest is involved.

***Pryke* v. *Gibbs Hartley Cooper* [1991] 1 Lloyd's Rep. 602**

An underwriting agent, Atlas, had been authorised under binding authorities to accept risks on behalf of underwriters. Atlas accepted certain U.S. risks—financial guarantee insurance—which were outside the scope of its authority, and were asked by the underwriters to cancel the policies. In fact, Atlas failed to do so despite having informed the underwriters that cancellation had been effected. The underwriters appointed the defendant brokers to investigate the situation in the US, but the defendants failed to inform the underwriters that the policies remained in place. Claims were eventually made against the underwriters, and indemnity was sought by the underwriters from the defendants on the basis that the brokers had failed to disclose the true position in the U.S. and thus had caused the underwriters not to take further action of their own. The grounds on which the indemnity was sought were that (1) the brokers had taken over the administration of the binding authority from Atlas and were thus the agents of the underwriters or, in the alternative, (2) the brokers owed the underwriters a duty of care in respect of their assumption of responsibility to check the position in the US.

Held (Waller J.): that the brokers were liable.

(1) There was no agreement between the brokers and the underwriters whereby the brokers had assumed responsibility to administer the open cover. The general position, as expressed in *Empress Assurance* v. *Bowring*, was that there was no agency relationship between a broker acting under a binding authority and the underwriters. As there was no contract imposing a duty of care, it followed that there could be no tortious duty of care in the acceptance of risks under the binding authority.

(2) As a binding authority was not a contract of insurance, it was not a contract of utmost good faith. Accordingly, there was no duty on a broker to disclose material facts to an underwriter when the agreement was being negotiated.

(3) There was, however, a duty of care owed by the brokers as regard the provision of information. The brokers had undertaken personal responsibility to provide information to the underwriters on the operations of Atlas, and there was no reason why the brokers should not be under a duty to exercise reasonable care in supplying that information.

Thirdly, in the case of a binding authority issued to a person who is not a broker and thus who does not face conflict of interest problems, there are questions as to the scope of the agent's responsibilities to the underwriters. It is now settled that the agent owes duties in contract, tort and in equity to the reinsurer.

***Sphere Drake Insurance Ltd* v. *Euro International Underwriting Ltd* [2003] EWHC 1636 (Comm), [2003] Lloyd's Rep. IR 525**

SD employed EIU as its underwriting agent under a binding authority. EIU agreed to accept reinsurance of U.S. workers' compensation "carveout" business, which was being offered by brokers SCB. Under the scheme devised by SCB and EIU, the premium which was paid to SD was far less than the likely amount of claims, and accordingly the reinsurance was deliberately written at a loss. This was disguised by outwards retrocession: most of the business accepted by SD was then retroceded to other insurers in the market, and there were further levels of reinsurance and retrocession cover, leading to the creation of a spiral. It was anticipated by EIU and SCB that SD would make a small profit on the difference between losses which had to be paid plus outward retrocession premiums, and the sums received from retrocessionaires. EIU made substantial profits by way of commission received from SD, and SCB itself made substantial profits in the form of brokerage by placing risks at various levels in the spiral which had been established at taking up to 15% of the premium at each stage. Thomas J. was satisfied that the scheme had been devised to profit EIU and SCB. SD was not informed that the business was not genuine reinsurance, and that any profits would not be derived from underwriting but from "making a turn". There were substantial claims faced by SD from the US, and in the present proceedings SD sought to recover those sums from EIU.

Held: (1) While it was in principle unobjectionable for reinsurance to be written at a loss for competitive reasons, it was to be expected that the amount of business would be small.

(2) EIU's fiduciary duties to SD were: to act in good faith and in the interests of SD, and not to have regard to the interests of any person other than SD; and to disclose and to report to SD all material information in relation to the business written under it.

(3) EIU was in breach of fiduciary duty in the present case, in that:

(i) EIU operated the binder in deliberate disregard of the interests of SD and subordinated SD's interests those of EIU (in their remuneration) and to those of SCB so that the binder was operated as a facility for their benefit;
(ii) EIU made no genuine assessment of the programmes presented but accepted them without regard to their commercial viability as viewed from SD's standpoint;
(iii) EIU accepted numerous programmes which no honest or faithful agent would have accepted;
(iv) EIU exposed SD to a high degree of accumulation;
(v) EIU exposed SD to the risks inherent in contrived reinsurance and in spirals;
(vi) EIU misrepresented and concealed the true nature of the business written;
(vii) EIU exceeded the premium income limits under the binder. This conduct had been fraudulent; and
(viii) SCB were liable for knowing assistance of EIU in breach of EIU's fiduciary duties. Further, there was an unlawful conspiracy between EIU and SCB.

(4) There had been deceit by both EIU and SCB.

(5) While SD had itself been negligent in failing to monitor the activities of EIU, and in particular had signed documents without seeking explanations of them, there was no defence of contributory negligence to an intentional tort or to breach of fiduciary duty, and damages—to be assessed—would be awarded for the full amount of SD's loss.

Whether an agreement for a binding authority has been concluded is a matter to be determined by the objective intentions of the parties.

***Syndicate 1242 at Lloyd's* v. *Morgan Read & Sharman* [2003] Lloyd's Rep. IR 412**

Syndicate 1242 was formed in 1998, with A as its active underwriter and N as the class underwriter for personal accident business. In 1999, on the advice of N, the Syndicate withdrew from providing travel insurance business, on the basis of poor results. Brokers, represented by E, operated a binding authority for the provision of travel business, and E sought to persuade N to allow Syndicate 1242 to subscribe to the business. N refused, and in the summer of 1999 E contacted A directly. As a result of that meeting, E again approached N, with draft wordings for the binding authority. N continued to refuse participation. In February 2000 E had a further meeting with A and presented him with draft wording. A initialled the wording in pencil, but added "N requirements met". The brokers asserted that this signature amounted to an agreement to participate in the binding authority.

Held (Thomas J.): that there was no agreement under which Syndicate 1242 had become a party to the binding authority. The evidence showed that A was prepared to agree to participate only with the approval of N, and the qualification "N requirements met" was a condition which had to be satisfied before there was cover: it was not a statement to the effect that N's requirements were deemed to have been met.

Summary

- The subscription process may be replaced by agency agreements.
- One underwriter may authorise another to bind him, by the use of line slips.
- An underwriter may authorise a coverholder or broker to bind him, by the use of binding authorities (binders).
- Where there is a market placement involving a number of reinsurers, they may bind themselves, by means of a leading underwriter clause, to amendments, modifications, waivers and even settlements agreed with the leading underwriter alone.

REINSURANCE POOLS AND UNDERWRITING AGENCIES

Legal structures

An underwriting agent is an agent authorised by a number of insurers or reinsurers to accept risks on their behalves: the group is generally referred to as a "pool". A number of separate legal relationships are created where a reinsurance pool has been established, and these will be considered in more detail in later parts of this chapter:

- a series of parallel bilateral contracts between the underwriting agent (pool manager) and each member of the pool, setting out the scope of the underwriting agent's authority to bind the pool member and the general powers, duties and rights of the underwriting agent;
- a multilateral agreement between pool members whereby they all agree to adhere to their individual agreements with the underwriting agent—if there is no express agreement to this effect, such an agreement will be implied by the courts by analogy with the well known authority *Clarke* v. *Dunraven, The Satanita* [1896] A.C. 59 which holds that entrants into a competition impliedly agree with each to obey the rules of that competition (see, e.g., *North Atlantic Insurance Co. Ltd* v. *Nationwide General Insurance Co.* [2004] Lloyd's Rep. IR 774);
- supplementary agreements between pool members, regulating matters such as the insolvency of a pool member or the underwriting agent;
- reinsurance of the liabilities of the pool as a whole, normally to be arranged by the underwriting agent;
- internal reinsurance arrangements between pool members, which will be used where one or more members of the pool accept risks as "fronts" for other pool members.

The role of the underwriting agent

Duties and rights of underwriting agents

The primary duty of an underwriting agent is to write business on behalf of the pool, and to place external reinsurance to cover the pool's liabilities. The agent is remunerated by commission on the transactions. The agent will be required to administer the pool by: allocating liabilities as between pool members; receiving inward premiums and paying outward reinsurance premiums; paying losses to policy holders and recovering sums from external reinsurers; and maintaining records for inspection by the pool members. The obligation to maintain records continues after the expiry of the underwriting agency agreements.

***Yasuda Fire and Marine Insurance Co. of Europe Ltd* v. *Orion Marine Insurance Underwriting Agency Ltd* [1995] 1 Lloyd's Rep. 525**

Two marine underwriting agency agreements provided that the defendant underwriting agency would maintain all necessary books, accounts, records and other documentation appertaining to the business underwritten by the agency for the members of the pool. The books were the property of the defendants, and could be inspected by the claimant pool member at any reasonable time. The agreements came to an end, and the pool went into run-off. The claimant sought to inspect the defendant's books and records, but access to particular records was denied by the defendant. The claimant accordingly terminated the run-off agreement on the basis that the defendant was in repudiatory breach. Thereafter the claimant sought to inspect the defendant's books and records, but the defendant argued that the termination of the agreement brought an end to its obligation to allow inspection.

Held (Colman J.): even though the agency agreement had been terminated, the obligation to permit inspection remained in place, as that obligation was a continuing one which survived the termination of the agency relationship. However, the claimant was not entitled to delivery up of the books and records, as these had remained the property of the defendant.

***Kingscroft Insurance Co.* v. *H. S. Weavers (Underwriting) Agencies Ltd* [1993] 1 Lloyd's Rep. 187**

The defendant carried on business as the underwriting agent for five insurance companies, the KWELM companies. Weavers received premiums and paid claims, and in so doing held sums received on deposit in its own name. The KWELM companies became insolvent, and issues arose as to the ownership of the funds held by Weavers.

Held (Harman J.): that the funds held by Weavers by way of premiums received were not held on trust for the KWELM companies, and Weavers was entitled to discharge the obligations of the KWELM companies as it thought fit.

The law requires the agent's obligations to be exercised with reasonable care and skill, and an underwriting agent owes parallel duties in contract and in tort in this regard. In addition to express and implied contractual duties, underwriting agents are bound by fiduciary duties by reason of their control over the financial affairs of the pool. The fiduciary relationship requires the underwriting agent to act in the best interests of the pool member rather than in its own interests. These points are illustrated by *Sphere Drake Insurance Ltd* v. *Euro International Underwriting Ltd* [2003] Lloyd's Rep. IR 535. More recently, in *R+V Versicherung AG* v. *Risk Insurance and Reinsurance Solutions SA*, November 2004, unreported, RVV was a German insurance company and also a holding company for a group of other insurers, including RIRS. The group was controlled by C from the Paris office. In 2001 and 2002 G, a senior underwriter for RVV, agreed with C that two binding authorities would be granted to RIRS to write reinsurance for RVV on the London market. Commission was payable to RIRS at rates slightly more favourable than market rates. The binders were supplemented by an addendum under which RIRS was to receive an additional commission of 49% of gross premium, and RVV was to receive 30% of the share capital of an underwriting agency formed by RIRS. In 2003 RVV gave notice to terminate the binding authorities: RVV argued that the addendum had not been disclosed to it, and that the arrangement constituted a fraudulent conspiracy between C and G to obtain commission for themselves. RVV claimed in the alternative that RIRS as an underwriting agent owed fiduciary duties to RVV, and that these had been broken. In what was essentially a judgment on the facts, Moore-Bick J. found that there had been a conspiracy to defraud between C and G and that RVV was entitled to terminate the binding authorities immediately as well as any other binding authorities, and to seek damages.

An underwriting agent is not an insurer in its own right and does not face liability on contracts made by it for members of the pool. Accordingly, the agent does not have to be authorised to act as insurer, although members of the pool do require such authorisation insofar as risks are accepted and losses are paid. However, an underwriting agent does have to be authorised to carry on its activities as an intermediary.

Authority to write business

The classes of risks which may be accepted by the underwriting agent will be set out in the management agreement. The usual rules on the authority of agents apply here. Thus, the underwriting agent will bind the members of the pool if: (a) he is acting within the terms of his actual authority; or (b) he is acting outside his actual authority but within the scope of the authority that an underwriting agent would normally have, in the situation where the restrictions on that authority which have not been disclosed to third parties; or (c) he is acting outside the scope of both his actual and usual authority, but the reinsurers have held expressly or impliedly led the third party to believe that the agent has the necessary authority (apparent authority, or agency by estoppel). Classes (b) and (c) are collectively referred to as "ostensible authority". Whether there is actual or ostensible authority is a matter of fact in every case.

Feasey v. _Sun Life Insurance of Canada_ [2003] Lloyd's Rep. IR 637

Two companies, Sun Life and Phoenix, appointed an underwriting agent, Centaur, to write risks on their behalves. Centaur, acting for Sun Life and Phoenix, in May 1997 agreed to reinsure Syndicate 957 at Lloyd's in respect of the Syndicate's liabilities to a P&I Club, the companies sharing the risk equally between them. In March 1998 it was agreed that Centaur would have no authority to write business for Phoenix with effect from September 1998, and the Syndicate was duly informed. In October 1998 Centaur nevertheless agreed, by endorsement, to extend the reinsurance for a further year. Disputes arose under the reinsurance, and both Sun Life and Phoenix denied liability to the Syndicate on the basis that there had been misrepresentations made as to the nature of the Syndicate's business and also that Steamship Mutual had no insurable interest to reinsure: these arguments were rejected by Langley J. and by the Court of Appeal. The remaining issues turned on the authority of Centaur.

Held: (1) At first instance Langley J. held that Phoenix was not bound by the October 1998 endorsement, as Centaur no longer had authority to act on behalf of Phoenix and there was no ostensible authority which could be relied upon by the Syndicate.

(2) The 1998 endorsement did bind Sun Life, but Sun Life remained liable only for 50% of the sum reinsured and not the full amount of the risk following the withdrawal of Phoenix. Centaur had no actual authority to bind Sun Life to accept 100% of the risk, and Centaur had not intended to extend Sun Life's subscription. Had there been an intention to replace Phoenix's subscription with 100% subscription by Sun Life the documentation would have been differently worded and Sun Life would have been identified as the sole reinsurer. While Centaur might have had the requisite authority, that authority had not been exercised.

Settlements and run-off

An underwriting agent will generally have the power to negotiate settlements on behalf of the pool where claims are made against it, and there is often a provision in the management agreement that if the pool ceases writing new business and goes into run-off that the underwriting agent will administer the run-off for the pool's members if requested to do so by the pool members.

***Sphere Drake Insurance plc* v. *Basler Versicherungs AG* [1998] Lloyd's Rep. IR 35**

The claimant was the member of a pool, and had been reinsured by the defendant in relation to losses incurred from risks accepted by the pool. The pool went into run-off, and the run-off was administered by the original underwriting agent. The underwriting agent, acting for the pool, subsequently became a party to the "Wellington Agreement" under which a number of insurers and reinsurers reached a settlement in respect of claims originating from the U.S. in respect of liabilities incurred as a result of the use of asbestos. The issue was whether the members of the pool were bound by the settlement reached by the underwriting agent.

Held (Moore-Bick J.): that the settlement was binding on the pool members.

(1) The fact that the pool had gone into run-off did not affect the authority of the underwriting agent, as the management agreement provided that the underwriting agent was required to undertake all necessary work in connection with the final liquidation of the pool's business, and this plainly contemplated that the underwriting agent was being given authority to conduct the run-off and to reach settlements with policy holders.

(2) Although the Wellington Agreement was not a settlement of any individual claim, by its nature it did constitute a compromise of present and future disputes. It was not possible to divorce sums payable under the Wellington Agreement from claims under policies, and accordingly the underwriting agent had been authorised to enter into the Wellington Agreement.

Fronting within the pool

The use of pool members as fronting companies

One of the advantages of a reinsurance pool is the ability of the pool to write business in several different jurisdictions. The regulatory and licensing rules which apply to insurance and business in almost all countries make it difficult and expensive for a reinsurer to carry on business in numerous jurisdictions. A pool may consist of reinsurers who are authorised in different jurisdictions; if so, it becomes possible for the pool to accept risks from various jurisdictions by using authorised pool members as fronts. In essence, an authorised pool member accepts 100% of a risk and then retrocedes his liability to the remaining pool members. Thus if a pool has four members who have agreed to share risks equally between them, one reinsurer may accept 100% of the risk as a front and then retrocede 75% of the risk to the remaining pool members: by this means each pool member is liable for 25% of the risk, albeit indirectly.

Fronting is potentially a risky business for the fronting company, as it runs the risk that other companies within the pool may become insolvent and be unable to meet their obligations under the retrocession agreements. Accordingly, an underwriting agent will not be permitted to use members of the pool as fronting companies unless they have agreed to such exposure for inward risks. Where fronting is permitted by the arrangements which govern the pool, then it would seem that the underwriting agent is under an implied duty not to use any one member as a front so as to expose that member to a disproportionate amount of inward liability (this was assumed to be the case in *Compania de Seguros Imperio* v. *Heath (REBX) Ltd* [1999] Lloyd's Rep. IR 571).

***Deutsche Ruckversicherung* v. *Zion Insurance Company Ltd*, March 2001, unreported**

The parties participated in the ICRA reinsurance pool in 1975 and 1976. The management agreements between the underwriting agents and the individual members of the pool authorised the underwriting agents to use members as fronts for the rest of the pool. The claimants were used as a front, and sought to recover from the defendants under retrocession agreements operating within the pool covering the liability of the claimants on inwards business.

Held (Andrew Smith J.): that there was a good arguable case that there was a contract between the parties as it was the intention of the parties to create contracts of retrocession between the fronting company and the rest of the pool. This could be inferred from the statement in the management agreements that "Each subscriber shall be indemnified by others to the extent of its proportion."

***Suncorp Insurance and Finance* v. *Milano Assicurazioni SpA* [1993] 2 Lloyd's Rep. 225**

The defendant joined the ICRA reinsurance pool in 1976 and under its arrangement with the underwriting agent the latter was authorised to accept 20 per cent of any risk on behalf of the defendant, subject to a financial limit of £10,000 per risk. ICRA acting for the pool accepted risks placed by the claimants, the defendant's subscription being stated as 32.52%. The defendant had in fact been used as a fronting company on this risk. Following losses, the defendant asserted that ICRA had no authority to bind the defendant to any proportion in excess of 20%.

Held (Waller J.): that the defendant was bound to a subscription of 32.52%.

(1) ICRA had not been expressly authorised to bind the defendant to more than 20% of any risk accepted for the pool, and that the £10,000 figure was not an alternative to 20% but rather operated as a cap on any liability accepted which did not exceed 20%.

(2) The defendant had done nothing to indicate to the claimants that ICRA had authority to use the defendant as a fronting company for any proportion of the risk greater than 20%, and accordingly there was no apparent authority.

(3) There was no universal rule in the London market that an underwriting agent had the authority to use a member of a reinsurance pool as a front for the other members of the pool, so that any person dealing with an underwriting agent was not entitled to assume that such authorisation existed. Accordingly, there was no usual authority.

(4) However, on the facts of the case, the defendant had ratified the contracts with the claimants even though they had been made without authority. The defendant had, with knowledge of the fact that ICRA had on previous occasions and on this occasion exceeded its authority in relation to contracts made on behalf of the defendant, adopted the contracts with the claimants and thus the defendant was bound by them.

***Yona International Ltd* v. *La Reunion Francaise SA d'Assurances et de Reassurances* [1996] 2 Lloyd's Rep. 84**

The defendant was a participant in the "Paris Pool", a pool of insurance companies which had appointed Parissa as their underwriting agent. Each member had a contract with Parissa setting out its own contribution towards any risks accepted by the pool, and Parissa was authorised to accept all risks on goods or merchandises. Other risks could be accepted on behalf of the pool only with the authorisation of the Acceptance Committee operated by the pool members. The claimants placed political risks insurance with the pool through a sub-agent, UIC. Losses occurred, and the defendant argued that Parissa and UIC had not been authorised to accept political risks insurance and accordingly that the defendant was not bound.

Held (Moore-Bick J.): that Parissa had exceeded its authority and that the defendant was not bound to provide an indemnity under political risks covers. Parissa had not at any time been authorised to delegate underwriting decisions to UIC.

(1) On the evidence neither Parissa nor the pool had at any time authorised UIC to write political risks cover on behalf of the pool.

(2) Parissa itself had no authority to write political risks without the consent of the Acceptance Committee, but such consent had not been obtained.

(3) There had been no holding out by the pool members that Parissa or UIC had been authorised to write political risks insurance for the pool, and such authorisation was in any event inconsistent with the published material issued by the pool.

(4) Parissa had not ratified the policy, as it had not been aware of UIC's attempts to bind the pool and in any event Parissa had taken no positive steps to affirm the policy: a failure to act on the part of Parissa could not amount to a ratification.

The pool's external reinsurance

Placing the cover and dealing with the proceeds

It is generally a part of the function of an underwriting agent, under the individual management agreements, to arrange reinsurance on behalf of the pool. The reinsurance is commonly taken out in the name of the underwriting agent, although it is clear that the underwriting agent is not a reinsured party in its own right—as it has no insurable interest to support a reinsurance—but rather is the agent of the pool as a whole. The underwriting agent will nevertheless be able to maintain an action under the reinsurance on behalf of the pool, although the proceeds will fall to be allocated amongst the pool members in the manner agreed within the pool. It is open to the pool members to agree how the proceeds are to be allocated, subject, in the event of the insolvency of a pool member, to the overriding insolvency principle of equality of treatment of unsecured creditors.

The pool arrangements may be silent on the persons by whom claims may be made against external reinsurers in the event of losses suffered by the pool. The general principle here is that each member of the pool is reinsured separately for its own loss, so that the reinsurance is some form of composite policy which embodies a series of separate obligations as between the reinsurers and each pool member. Accordingly, each pool member may bring an action against the reinsurers for its own loss, but it may also be the case (particularly where a fronting arrangement is involved) that a pool member can claim the entirety of the pool's losses from the reinsurers and account to other members of the pool for the surplus. However, the pool arrangements may expressly or implicitly preclude any individual member from bringing an action against external reinsurers for his own loss or for the loss of the pool as a whole, although these arrangements will come to an end if a pool member has become insolvent.

***Transcontinental Underwriting Agency* v. *Grand Union Insurance Co. Ltd* [1987] 2 Lloyd's Rep. 409**

TU was the underwriting agent for a reinsurance pool. The pool's liabilities had been reinsured by the defendants as retrocessionaires, and TU itself was named as the retrocedant. Disputes arose under the retrocessions, and TU sought to bring an action in its own name against the defendants.

Held (Hirst J.): that TU was entitled to sue in its own name. TU was a party to the retrocession agreement as it had been described as a party, even though it had acted as agent for the pool members. The usual rule of agency, that an agent could sue or be sued on a contract made in his own name, was applicable.

***Pan Atlantic Insurance Co. Ltd* v. *Pine Top Insurance Co. Ltd* [1989] 1 Lloyd's Rep. 568**

The three claimant reinsurers had retroceded some 90 per cent of their liability to a pool consisting of 35 members (one of the claimants also being a member of the pool). The remaining 10 per cent of the risk had been ceded by way of retrocession to the defendant. The pool itself had also reinsured with the defendant. Losses occurred and claims were made by the claimants and the pool, which the defendant refused to pay. The claimants commenced proceedings against the defendant on behalf of themselves and also the pool, and the defendant contested the action on the procedural ground that the claimants had no right to bring such an action.

Held (C.A.): that the claim could be brought as a representative action under rule 19.6(1) of the Civil Procedure Rules (at the time, Order 15, rule 2, of the Rules of the Supreme Court), which provides that where one or more persons has the same interest in a claim then that claim may be brought by any one or more of those persons as representatives of the others. The Court of Appeal rejected the argument that the interests of the claimants and the pool were different, and held that the reality of the position was that each of the parties had retroceded their liabilities to the defendant. The Court of Appeal also held that it was immaterial that there were disputes between the members of the pool, as those disputes had no impact upon the liability of the defendant.

At first instance Hirst J. had additionally held that the action by the claimants could have been maintained by reason of: (1) fiduciary trusteeship on the part of the claimants, which Hirst J. held to arise whenever a person with an insurable interest in the insured subject matter brings an action against insurers on his own behalf and on behalf of co-assureds; and (2) assignment of the cause of action to the pool prior to the issue of the claim form. These points did not arise in the Court of Appeal.

***North Atlantic Insurance Co. Ltd* v. *Nationwide General Insurance Co.* [2004] Lloyd's Rep. IR 466**

A reinsurance pool was operated by Rutty between 1962 and 1967. Each pool member had a separate contract with Rutty on the same terms. These contracts authorised Rutty to underwrite risks on the member's behalf up to given financial limits, and to settle inward claims. Rutty was also empowered to procure external reinsurance for the pool member, and the member was required to pay its proportion of the outward premium. Inward premium received by Rutty for the pool was to be paid into a Premium Reserve Fund: the Fund was to be used to discharge inward claims and other costs and expenses (including outward reinsurance premiums). Any balance was payable to the member one month after the expiry of the third year after making provision for outstanding losses. In the event of a member's insolvency, no further payments were to be made to it until all of its liabilities had been discharged, and an agreement between the members themselves supplemented this provision. As a result of these arrangements, in the event of a member's insolvency recoveries from the pool's external reinsurers were to be used to pay off the liabilities of the pool as a whole and could not be allocated to that member until the pool's liabilities had been discharged. The agreements also authorised Rutty to bring proceedings against external reinsurers in Rutty's own name. The outward reinsurances obtained by Rutty were in different forms, some identifying Rutty as the reinsured and some referring to individual members of the pool. The background to the dispute in the present case was that two members of the pool had been used as fronting companies by Rutty, and external reinsurances had been taken out in their names. However, two other members of the pool, who had under the usual arrangements acted as reinsurers of the fronting company with regard to the liability undertaken by the pool, had become insolvent. The external reinsurers paid the pool, and the question arose as to who within the pool could claim the reinsurance moneys. The fronting companies, in whose name the external reinsurances had been taken out, claimed that the proceeds of the reinsurance belonged to them. The liquidators of the insolvent pool members argued that the outwards reinsurance proceeds belonged to each pool member in accordance with their agreed proportions, so that the fronting companies ranked alongside the other pool members' other unsecured creditors for a share of the outwards reinsurance proceeds.

The Court of Appeal agreed with the liquidators' arguments, and held that the reinsurances were composite contracts under which each individual pool member had a claim against the external reinsurers. The question had to be approached by construing the agreements themselves. Even though the fronting company was named as the reinsured, the reinsurances were based on pool liabilities and not on the fronting company's liabilities. This could be seen from the external reinsurance agreements themselves, which referred to pool retentions, pool aggregates in the ultimate net loss clauses and aggregate minimum and deposit premium.

Given, therefore, that the sums were payable to individual pool members, a second issue was whether the fronting companies had any secured claim against the sums due to them under the internal reinsurance arrangements supporting the fronting. The Court of Appeal held that this was not the case. The clause in each contract between the pool members and Rutty, whereby in the event of the insolvency of a pool member it was not entitled to any payments until the fronting companies had been indemnified, was void under the insolvency *pari passu* rule in *British Eagle Air Lines Ltd* v. *Compagnie Internationale Air France* [1975] 1 W.L.R. 758. Further, there was nothing in the arrangements within the pool which created an express trust of sums received by Rutty from the external reinsurers in favour of the fronting companies: the only agreed trust was over premium income. It was assumed, however, that a trust arrangement could have been adopted had the correct words been used.

Disclosure of material facts to reinsurers

As noted above, a key responsibility of an underwriting agent responsible for a reinsurance pool is to place reinsurance for the pool members. Two questions arise here. First, what facts are material to reinsurers who are insuring a pool? Secondly, to what extend does the underwriting agent have to disclose the nature of its own activities to the reinsurers?

The classes of fact which are regarded as material for reinsurance purposes and which have to be disclosed to reinsurers will be considered in detail in a later chapter. It suffices to say here that the most important information as far as reinsurers are concerned is the performance and profitability of the pool. The internal arrangement of the pool, and in particular the use of fronting within the pool, are unlikely to be material facts, as are the existence of other forms of reinsurance which protect the pool.

***Kingscroft Insurance Co. Ltd* v. *Nissan Fire & Marine Insurance Co. Ltd (No. 2)* [1999] Lloyd's Rep. IR 603**

The pool in this case consisted of two classes of member: stamp companies, who were authorised to write direct risks as fronting companies; and whole account quota share reinsurers, who reinsured the fronting companies. The stamp companies and the whole account quota share reinsurers were treated in the same way within the pool, and the effect of the internal arrangements was to ensure that each pool member bore ultimate responsibility for its agreed proportion of losses whether it acted as a fronting company or a reinsurer of a fronting company. The underwriting agent took out, with the defendants, treaty reinsurance for the pool as a whole, and the reinsurance agreement provided that the pool agreed to cede 50% quota share of the pool's share of liability and that the pool "will retain 50%" of that liability. In fact, the pool had taken out separate excess of loss reinsurance on the amount retained. The defendants sought to avoid the treaty for non-disclosure of the existence of the pool's internal reinsurance arrangements and for misrepresentation by the pool of its statement that 50% of the risk would be retained by the pool and not reinsured elsewhere.

Held (Moore-Bick J.): that neither fact was material.

(1) As to the quota share reinsurance arrangements of fronting companies within the pool, the defendant reinsurers ought to have known that such arrangements were likely to exist within a pool, so that the fact could not be material. Further, the internal arrangements had not increased the potential liability of the pool as a whole, but was

simply a mechanism for allocating liability within the pool: the external treaty reinsurers were concerned only with the liability of the pool as a whole rather than that of its individual members.

(2) There had been no misrepresentation as to retention. At best there had been a statement of present intention rather than a promise as to the future. Further, the fact was not material as it was common practice for insurers to reinsure their retentions, and there was no inducement as the external treaty reinsurers would have subscribed to the treaty in any event.

The second question relates to the conduct of the underwriting agent. The question which has arisen is whether the manner in which the underwriting agent has managed the pool is a material fact which has to be disclosed to external reinsurers. The point is likely to be significant only where the underwriting agent has acted fraudulently. The cases indicate that the conduct of the underwriting agent does not have to be disclosed, but the reason for this is unclear.

***Deutsche Ruckversicherung Aktiengesellschaft* v. *Walbrook Insurance Co. Ltd* [1995] 1 Lloyd's Rep. 153, on appeal *Group Josi Reinsurance Co. SA* v. *Walbrook Insurance Co. Ltd* [1996] 1 Lloyd's Rep. 345**

The defendant was one of the five KWELM companies in a reinsurance pool managed by the underwriting agents, Weavers. Reinsurance of the pool had been arranged by Weavers, which had appointed brokers to place the reinsurance for the pool. The reinsurers alleged that Weavers had defrauded members of the pool by withholding sums from them, and asserted that this was a material fact which ought to have been disclosed. Under section 19(a) of the Marine Insurance Act 1906 an "agent to insure" is required to disclose to underwriters all material facts which are or ought to be known to him.

Held (Phillips J.): that the mere fact that an underwriting agent had been guilty of fraud against pool members was not of itself material. It was only where the fraud related to a material fact that disclosure was required.

Held (C.A.): that whether or not the fact in question was material, there was no obligation for it to be disclosed.

(1) (*per* Saville and Rose L.JJ.): The phrase "agent to insure" in section 19(a) of the Marine Insurance Act 1906 applied only to a placing broker and not to an intermediate agent. Thus, only the brokers who had been instructed by Weavers to place the risk were subject to the statutory duty, and not Weavers itself.

(2) (*per* Staughton and Rose L.JJ.): A person who was defrauding his principal could not be expected to disclose that fact to underwriters. Accordingly, on the assumption that Weavers was under a duty to disclose material facts under section 19(a), the fact of its own fraud was not one which had to be disclosed even if it was otherwise material.

Scope of the pool's reinsurance

Reinsurance cover procured by an underwriting agent for the pool extends to all members of the pool. Reinsurances are generally written in a fashion which extends the cover to all pool members who were on risk during the currency of the reinsurance, so that pool members who have left, and pool members who have joined, in the period covered by the reinsurance are nevertheless protected. External reinsurance will normally be restricted to the liability of pool members to meet claims by persons who have placed business with the pool. However, there is no reason in principle why pool members cannot insure other forms of risk which they may face arising from the operation of the pool, e.g., risks flowing from the incompetence, fraud or insolvency of the underwriting agent or from the insolvency of other pool members. Specific wording will be required to extend the reinsurance to such risks, and it will be appreciated that the pool is in these respects a direct assured for first party losses rather than an insurer or reinsurer reinsuring its own actual liability to policy holders. However, it is perfectly possible for a pool member to reinsure on the basis that the reinsurer assumes all the risks that had been accepted by the pool member flowing from the membership of the pool.

***Kingscroft Insurance Co. Ltd* v. *Nissan Fire & Marine Insurance Co. Ltd (No. 2)* [1999] Lloyd's Rep. IR 603**

The reinsurance obtained by the underwriting agent, Weavers, for the pool extended to a named pool member "and other Companies underwritten by . . . Weavers" and came into force on 1 April 1986. A number of companies, which had not even been incorporated at that time, joined the pool in 1987. The reinsurers asserted that these companies were not protected by the reinsurance.

Held (Moore-Bick J.): that the new members were entitled to the benefit of the reinsurance. The effect of the reinsurance treaty was that it constituted a standing offer of reinsurance to any company which joined the pool, and that the offer was accepted as soon as Weavers started underwriting for that company.

***Wurttenbergische Akteingesellschaft Versicherungs-Beteiligungsgesellschaft* v. *Home Insurance (No. 2)* [1997] L.R.L.R. 86**

This case arose out of the operations of the Rutty pool, which had ceased writing new business in 1967 and which had then gone into run-off. Under the management agreement, Rutty was to administer the run-off without further remuneration. The claimant had been a member of that pool, and some time after the run-off had commenced the claimant had entered into a reinsurance agreement with the defendant under which the defendant agreed to indemnify the claimant in respect of "all losses which [the claimant] may be or may become liable to pay, arising out of risks written by [Rutty]" as long as they were within the terms and conditions of the policies issued by Rutty. In return, the defendant was entitled to receive income which would otherwise have been payable to the claimant by Rutty. In the present case the issue was whether the risk that the run-off might be managed negligently by Rutty, or that Rutty might become insolvent, was covered by the reinsurance.

Held (CA, and remission to Waller J.): The effect of the reinsurance agreement was to substitute the defendant for the claimant as the party to whom Rutty owed duties during the run-off, and the claimant dropped out of the picture. Accordingly, if Rutty was negligent or became insolvent, the risk was borne by the defendant without recourse to the claimant as the original principal of Rutty.

***Wurttenbergische Akteingesellschaft Versicherungs-Beteiligungsgesellschaft* v. *Home Insurance (No. 3)* [1999] Lloyd's Rep. IR 397**

This was a further dispute arising out of the claimant's membership of the Rutty pool and the run-off of the pool's liabilities. The management agreement between the claimant and Rutty authorised Rutty to use any member of the pool as a fronting company, and in a separate agreement between pool members it was agreed that in the event of the insolvency of any one member the others would accept liability in their agreed proportions for unpaid losses. As seen above, the claimant subsequently reinsured its liabilities, and the defendant agreed to assume the risk of "all losses which [the claimant] may be or may become liable to pay, arising out of risks written by [Rutty]" as long as they were within the terms and conditions of the policies issued by Rutty. There were in due course insolvencies within the pool, and the claimant sought to recover from the defendant not only the amounts which the claimant owed to policy holders but also sums for which the claimant had become liable under the separate agreement between pool members providing for additional payments in the event of an insolvency.

Held (C.A.): The reinsuring words in the contract between the claimant and the defendant were not sufficiently wide to encompass the additional liability assumed by the claimant: that liability was entirely separate from the claimant's liabilities as a pool member for risks accepted by Rutty, and was not within the scope of the reinsurance. The Court of Appeal also noted that settlements reached by Rutty which were *ex gratia* would not have been covered by the reinsurance, as the reinsurance was—by the express wording of the reinsuring clause—confined to cases in which the settlement reached by Rutty was within the terms of the cover issued by the pool.

Summary

- A reinsurance pool is an agreement between reinsurers establishing a mechanism for the underwriting of reinsurance business.
- The pool will be managed by an underwriting agent/pool manager who has a contract with each participating reinsurer.
- The underwriting agent may be authorised to use individual members as "fronts" so as to overcome authorisation problems in different jurisdictions.
- Fronting entails the use of internal reinsurance within the pool.
- The pool may itself obtain external retrocession cover, although this will not necessarily cover anything other than reinsurance liabilities incurred by pool members and may not extend to losses incurred following the insolvency of a pool member.

INSURABLE INTEREST

Insurable interest in general

The requirement for insurable interest

The requirement for a contract of insurance to be supported by insurable interest has been a feature of English law since the eighteenth century, and was originally devised primarily to limit the use of insurance policies as a form of wagering on property or lives and to remove the danger that persons holding policies would attempt the deliberate destruction of the insured subject-matter. The earliest legislation was the Marine Insurance Act 1745 which banned the making of marine insurance policies unless the assured had an interest in the subject-matter, and the prohibition was extended to life and related policies by the Life Assurance Act 1774.

Life Assurance Act 1774, section 1

> **1.** No insurance shall be made by any person or persons, bodies politic or corporate, on the life or lives of any person or persons, or on any other event or events whatsoever, wherein the person or persons, for whose use, benefit, or on whose account such policy or policies shall be made, shall have no interest, or by way of gaming or wagering: and that every assurance made, contrary to the true intent and meaning hereof, shall be null and void, to all intents and purposes whatsoever.

Section 4 excludes policies on "ships goods and merchandises", although the modern view of the legislation is that it is confined to non-indemnity contracts and excludes all forms of property and liability covers (*Mark Rowlands Ltd* v. *Berni Inns Ltd* [1985] 3 All E.R. 473).

The modern law on insurable interest is found in a complex combination of common law and statutory principles, which may be outlined in the following way.

Life policies are governed by the Life Assurance Act 1774. This legislation, as construed by the courts, provides that:

(a) the assured must have an insurable interest in the life of the insured person at the date the policy is taken out, failing which the policy is illegal (section 1), although there is no need for the assured to possess an insurable interest at the date of the death of the insured person as the contract is not one of indemnity but rather is in the form of an investment;
(b) the assured can recover under the policy only the amount of his interest as measured at the inception of the policy (section 3);
(c) the names of all persons interested in the policy must be inserted at the outset (section 2), although this requirement was relaxed by section 50 of the Insurance Companies Act 1973, which deems this requirement to be satisfied where a beneficiary belongs to a class of persons identified in the policy.

Marine policies are governed by the Marine Insurance Act 1906. This provides that:

(a) the assured must have either an actual insurable interest, or the reasonable expectation of obtaining an insurable interest, when the policy is taken out, failing which the policy is deemed to be made by way of gaming or wagering and is void (section 4);
(b) the assured must be interested in the subject-matter insured at the time of the occurrence of the insured peril (section 6)—if he has no

interest at the date of the loss, then the common law principle of indemnity reflected in section 6 means that he has no right of recovery.

Other policies, including property and liability covers are not governed by any specific statute, but the principles are much as for marine insurance:

(a) section 18 of the Gaming Act 1845 renders unenforceable contracts made by way of gaming or wagering, and an insurance policy taken out by a person who has no actual insurable interest and no reasonable expectation of obtaining such an interest will contravene this legislation. However, section 18 is to be repealed and replaced by section 335 of the Gambling Act 2005 from a date to be announced, so that it may be that it will no longer be necessary for the assured to show any actual or anticipated insurable interest at the outset—it is not clear whether the 2005 Act affects insurable interest rules;

(b) the assured must be interest in the subject-matter insured at the time of the occurrence of the insured peril, as the common law principle of indemnity permits the assured to recover only the amount of his actual loss.

Definition of insurable interest

Section 5(2) of the Marine Insurance Act 1906, which is based on the judgment of Lawrence J. in *Lucena* v. *Craufurd* (1806) 2 Bos. & P.N.R. 269, defines insurable interest as

> "any legal or equitable relation to . . . any insurable property at risk . . . in consequence of which [the assured] may benefit by the safety or due arrival of the insurable property, or may be prejudiced by its loss, or by damage thereto, or by the detention thereof, or may incur liability in respect thereof."

The most recent authorities have recognised that modern market developments in the forms of insurance agreements have required a wider approach to the definition of insurable interest than was at one time thought necessary. The modern approach is set out by the Court of Appeal in *Feasey* v. *Sun Life Insurance of Canada* [2003] Lloyd's Rep. IR 637, where it was emphasised that if the parties have entered into a commercial arrangement there is every reason to seek to support that arrangement and not to strike it down on technical grounds. The judgment of Waller L.J. in *Feasey* indicates that three questions have to be asked where an insurable interest issue is raised:

(1) What is the subject-matter of the insurance policy? This question involves interpreting the policy to see exactly what has been insured.

(2) What is the interest of the assured in the subject-matter of the policy? This question is a matter of law, and involves the court considering the range of possible interests that the assured may have in the insured subject-matter.

(3) Does the policy encompass the assured's insurable interest? This question again involves the proper construction of the policy, the issue being whether the policy by its terms actually covers the insurable interest of the assured in the insured subject-matter or whether it refers to some other interest.

There are numerous illustrations of insurable interest in the cases. The mere fact that the assured is not wagering is not determinative of the question, although it is an important consideration in determining the existence of insurable interest.

As far as property is concerned, any interest in that property will give rise to an insurable interest. Such interests may include ownership, possession or security. Whether a person in possession of property (e.g., a warehouseman) has insured the property itself, holding the proceeds for the true owner, or whether he has insured his liability to the true owner in the event that the property is damaged, is a question of the proper construction of the policy (see the recent discussion by the Court of Appeal in *Ramco (UK) Ltd* v. *International Insurance Co. of Hannover Ltd* [2004] Lloyd's Rep IR 606). A person who has agreed to purchase property also has an insurable interest in that property. It follows, therefore, that a limited interest is insurable, and that there may be a variety of different interests in the same property. *Feasey* itself recognised that a person may have insurable interest in property if he stands to suffer a loss in the event that the property is destroyed (e.g., where the assured is a contractor who has been engaged to carry out work on that property). A person who faces liability in the event that that property is lost or damaged as a result of his negligence plainly has an insurable interest for the purposes of a liability policy, and he may also have sufficient insurable interest to support a policy on the property itself, although under the third principle in *Feasey* it is a matter of a construction of the policy to determine whether it covers liability for property.

As far as lives are concerned, it is presumed that a person has an unlimited insurable interest in his or her own life and that of his or her spouse, although other family relationships and friendships do not give rise to an insurable interest unless the policy holder can demonstrate some actual financial interest in the life of the person insured. Commercial relationships can give rise to insurable interest in lives, e.g., a creditor has an insurable interest in the life of his debtor, an employee has an interest in the life of his employer and an employer has an insurable interest in the life of his employee. A person who faces liability for the death or personal injury of an individual can insure his liability under an ordinary liability policy, but in some circumstances it may be possible for that person to insure the life of the individual in question: this matter was considered in the *Feasey* case, discussed in detail in the next section.

Where different interests are insured under a single policy, that policy is regarded as composite with the result that each assured has a separate contract with the insurers in respect of his own interest. The separability of interests means that in the event of a loss, each assured has a separate claim against the insurers. The separability principle means that insurers may have defences against some assureds (e.g., for breach of policy terms) but not others.

Insurable interest under reinsurance contracts

The reinsured's insurable interest

Reinsurance agreements are contracts of indemnity, and it follows that the reinsured must have an insurable interest to support the reinsurance. In the vast majority of cases the reinsured's insurable interest will be in the liability which the reinsured faces to its direct assureds under the contracts issued to them. This appears to be the effect of section 9(1) of the Marine Insurance Act 1906:

"The insurer under a contract of marine insurance has an insurable interest in his risk, and may reinsure in respect of it."

Reinsurance contracts are, therefore, typically drafted in terms of cover in respect of the liability of the reinsured. Some reinsurance agreements require the reinsured to have made payment to the assured before any claim can be made against the reinsurers, but even where this is the case the essential point remains that it is the potential liability of the reinsured to make payment in the event of a claim by the assured which gives the reinsured its insurable interest.

Although it is usual for reinsurance agreements to be expressed in terms of liability to pay, there is in principle no reason why a reinsurance agreement should not be framed as a contract for payment on the occurrence of an event which causes the loss of or damage to the subject-matter insured under the direct policy. This proposition has indirect support from the construction cases in which the courts have held that a contractor has, under a property policy on the building works, an insurable interest in the works by reason of his potential liability for the works in the event that his negligence causes loss or alternatively, an insurable interest in his own personal loss in the event that he is no longer able to perform his contract following loss of or damage to the works (*National Oilwell (UK) Ltd* v. *Davy Offshore Ltd* [1993] 2 Lloyd's Rep. 582; *Deepak Fertilisers* v. *ICI Chemicals* [1999] 1 Lloyd's Rep. 387). The Court of Appeal confirmed this analysis in the *Feasey* case.

***Feasey* v. *Sun Life Insurance of Canada* [2003] Lloyd's Rep. IR 637**

In 1994 Syndicate 957 at Lloyd's had reinsured a P&I Club, Steamship Mutual, against exposure to its shipowner members for their liability for personal injury or death in relation to vessels entered with Steamship. In September 1994 Lloyd's announced changes to its risk codes for the 1995 year of account, the effect of which was that, for the purposes of reinsurance, bodily injury and illness-related elements in liability policies could no longer be classified as personal accident insurance but were classified as long-tail liability cover for which substantial reserves were to be held. Personal accident cover was to be treated as short-tail only if payments were on a fixed benefit basis, the amount payable was dependent only upon the degree of injury or illness sustained and the amount could be assessed within a reasonable time. This change in the risk codes prompted Syndicate 957 and brokers acting for Steamship to devise a personal accident reinsurance scheme, under which Syndicate would pay fixed benefits within 30 days of Steamship producing documentary evidence of the death of, or injury to, any employee or person on board a shipowner's vessel: proof of Steamship's liability to indemnify the shipowner was not required. This structure enabled the business to be classified as personal accident cover for the purposes of Lloyd's risk codes. Although the reinsurance was not expressed to be in terms of Steamship's liability to its members, the payments were calculated in a manner which meant that, over a period of time the sums paid out by Steamship would be more or less equal to the sums received by Steamship from the Syndicate. In the event, there was a shortfall and Steamship obtained top-up reinsurance from another source. The Syndicate retroceded its liability to the defendant insurers. Disputes arose, and the defendants denied liability to the Syndicate. One of the arguments raised by the defendants was that the reinsurance issued by the Syndicate to the Steamship was a personal accident policy on the life or lives of employees of Steamship's members, and thus caught by the Life Assurance Act 1774, but that Steamship had no insurable interest in the lives of those individuals. It was not disputed that, had the reinsurance been in traditional liability form, Steamship would clearly have had an insurable interest in its own liability.

Held (by the Court of Appeal, Waller and Dyson L.JJ., Ward L.J. dissenting): that the Syndicate had the necessary insurable interest and that the insurable interest was covered by the reinsurance.

(1) It was unattractive for a court to refuse to give effect to a commercial contract.

(2) The policy fell within the Life Assurance Act 1774 as it was a policy whose subject-matter was lives. While it was clear that Steamship was not wagering, that was not of itself enough to satisfy the Life Assurance Act 1774: it remained necessary to show that Steamship possessed an insurable interest.

(3) Steamship had an insurable interest in its liability to its members. However, the existence of that class of insurable interest did not preclude other forms of insurable interest. While it was arguably the case that an insurer might not for reinsurance purposes have insurable interest in the life of a specific individual insured by the insurer, the position was different where the policy dealt with many lives and over a substantial period, and this was a pecuniary interest in lives which satisfied the 1774 Act. The necessary insurable interest to support the reinsurance was thus in place independently of any insurable interest that Steamship had in its own liability.

(4) The fact that Steamship might have reinsured under an ordinary liability policy did not mean that reinsurance in a different form was not legitimate. The object of the policy was to cover Steamship for the losses it would suffer as insurer of its members under its rules, and it could not be said that the subject-matter of the reinsurance was so specific as to preclude Steamship from reinsuring its pecuniary interest in lives.

(5) The reinsurance was not defeated by section 3 of the 1774 Act, which holds an assured to recovering the amount of its interest measured at the date of the policy. It was clear that the sums which Steamship might have to pay were in excess of the amount of the reinsurance, and thus it could not be said that Steamship was seeking to recover an amount in excess of its own actual payments to its members.

[*Note*: The *Feasey* case is to be appealed to the House of Lords in the second half of 2004.]

Application of insurable interest legislation to reinsurance

The *Feasey* case shows that, while the insurable interest of a reinsured is generally to be regarded as its potential liability to its direct policy holders, it is perfectly possible to draft a reinsurance as a further policy on the original subject-matter. If this is the case, the reinsured must possess an insurable interest which complies with the rules applicable to the insured subject-matter.

***Re London County Commercial Reinsurance Office* [1922] 2 Ch. 67**
This case concerned the admissibility of claims in the winding up of a reinsurance company. The reinsurer had, to match the direct cover, issued a reinsurance contract on a marine insurance form to provide payment to the reinsured "in the event of peace not being declared between Great Britain and Germany on or before 31 March 1918". The policy was stated to be an honour policy and that the insurers would pay on the basis of policy proof of interest (ppi), so that payment was to be made interest or no interest. The issue was whether the reinsurance was valid under the insurable interest rules.

Held (by Lawrence J.): that the reinsurance was unlawful and that proof of a claim under it was not to be admitted.

(1) Although the direct policy was stated to be a marine policy, it was not an insurance on a marine adventure as required by section 1 of the Marine Insurance Act 1906 and thus was not governed by that legislation.

(2) The direct policy was one on events and thus fell within section 1 of the Life Assurance Act 1774.

(3) The direct policy was illegal under the 1774 Act as the original assured had no insurable interest in a declaration of peace. The fact that the policy was an honour policy did not affect the position under the 1774 Act, as the assured either had an interest or he did not have an interest.

(4) As it had been established that the original insurance was illegal, it followed that the reinsurance was tainted with the same illegality and was itself illegal and void.

Absence of insurable interest on the part of the assured

If the assured has no insurable interest under the direct policy but the insurer nevertheless makes payment to the assured, the reinsurers are not liable to indemnify the reinsured. As was seen in *Re London County Commercial Reinsurance Office* [1922] 2 Ch. 67, the reinsurance itself may be illegal or void for want of insurable interest if it is made on the same terms as the direct policy. However, even if the reinsurance is expressed to be a cover against the reinsured's liability, then while the reinsurance agreement is not of itself rendered void or illegal the reinsured will simply be unable to show that its payment to the assured was based on legal liability but rather was an *ex gratia* payment. This was an alternative ground for the decision in *Re London County Commercial Reinsurance Office*.

***Re Overseas Marine Insurance Co. Ltd* (1930) 36 Ll. L. Rep. 183**
A direct marine policy was taken out by Ruby Steamship Co. on their vessel *Hurona*, covering loss of disbursements and anticipated earnings. Part of the risk had been insured with the Insurance Office of Australia, and IOA had reinsured with

Overseas Marine. Losses occurred under the direct policy, but before the claim could be resolved Overseas Marine went into liquidation: IOA sought to prove in liquidation in respect of Overseas Marine's contingent liability to IOA. The direct policy had been written on a ppi basis and was thus void under section 4 of the Marine Insurance Act 1906.

Held, by the Court of Appeal: that IOA could not be liable under the direct policy, and accordingly that Overseas Marine was under no obligation to provide an indemnity under the reinsurance.

***Hewitt* v. *London General Insurance Co. Ltd* (1925) 23 Ll. L. Rep. 243** A cargo of nitrate was insured under a marine policy, for carriage from Tocopilla to France via the Panama Canal. The insurers reinsured their liability under a contract which was written on the same terms and conditions as the original. The cargo had been purchased by AG & Sons from the French Government. There was a deviation, and the reinsurers refused to provide an indemnity to the reinsured on that basis, and also on the basis that the real assured were the French Government and not AG & Sons, and accordingly that AG & Sons had not borne any risk of loss during the course of the voyage. The reinsurers argued that in the absence of any insurable interest on behalf of AG & Sons, the insurers were not liable to provide an indemnity and accordingly they had no claim against the reinsurers.

Held, by Branson J.: that the reinsurers were liable. The direct policy, on its proper construction, insured AG & Sons for the duration of the voyage and that they had not acted merely as agents for the French Government.

Summary

- An insurer must have insurable interest to support a reinsurance agreement.
- Such insurable interest will generally be found in the insurer's liability to make payment to the assured in the event of the occurrence of an insured peril.
- It may be possible to draft a reinsurance agreement in terms of the direct policy, so that the reinsurer is liable to pay on the occurrence of an insured peril rather than on the basis of the insurer establishing and quantifying its liability to the assured.

TEST YOUR UNDERSTANDING

1. Which of the following elements determine whether a reinsurance company is carrying on business in the United Kingdom?

(a) the place where the agreement is negotiated and made,
(b) the place where the underwriting decision is taken,
(c) the law governing the agreement,
(d) the place where losses are paid.

2. **Which of the following statements are true in relation to the authorisation requirement?**

(a) a reinsurer must be authorised to carry on insurance business in the UK,
(b) a reinsurer must be authorised to carry on reinsurance business in the UK,
(c) UK authorisation confers the right to establish branches elsewhere in the EEA,
(d) UK authorisation confers the right of direct sales elsewhere in the EEA.

3. **Which of the following statements are correct?**

(a) an unauthorised insurer is always liable to its policy holders,
(b) an unauthorised insurer is always able to enforce its contracts with policy holders,
(c) an unauthorised insurer who has to pay its policy holders is able to recover from its reinsurers only with a court order,
(d) an unauthorised insurer who has to pay its policy holders is able to recover from its reinsurers in all circumstances.

4. **Which of the following statements are correct?**

(a) a slip is an invitation to treat,
(b) a subscription to a reinsurance slip is a contract of reinsurance,
(c) the law requires a policy document to be issued,
(d) a cover note issued by a broker is a binding contract of reinsurance.

5. **Which of the following statements are correct?**

(a) a slip is not binding until it is fully subscribed,
(b) a subscribing underwriter can never alter the terms of his subscription to a slip,
(c) the broker can withdraw an undersubscribed slip,
(d) the broker can vary the subscribed percentages to an oversubscribed slip.

6. **Which of the following statements are correct?**

(a) a contract of reinsurance cannot be made in advance of a contract of insurance,
(b) a contract of reinsurance made in advance of a contract of insurance is a unilateral contract,
(c) a broker who attempts to place reinsurance in advance of insurance is the agent of the reinsured,

(d) a broker can face personal liability to reinsurers when placing reinsurance in advance of insurance.

7. Which of the following statements are correct?

(a) a slip is a temporary contract,
(b) policy wording is subject to the wording in the slip,
(c) the following market can always avoid a subscription where false statements have been made to the leading underwriter,
(d) the following market can always avoid a subscription for material non-disclosure to the leading underwriter.

8. Which of the following statements are correct?

(a) a line slip constitutes an agency agreement between underwriters,
(b) a leading underwriter clause constitutes an agency agreement between underwriters,
(c) a leading underwriter under a leading underwriter clause owes a duty of care to the following market,
(d) a leading underwriter clause is irrevocable.

9. In the *Sphere Drake* case, which of the following heads of liability were faced by the underwriting agent?

(a) breach of contract,
(b) breach of duty of care,
(c) breach of fiduciary duty,
(d) conspiracy to injure.

10. Which of the following risks does the external reinsurance of the members of a reinsurance pool cover?

(a) underwriting losses incurred by the pool's members,
(b) extended liability in the event of the insolvency of a pool member,
(c) breach of duty on the part of the underwriting agent,
(d) losses suffered by a fronting company when other pool members refuse to pay.

11. Which of the following statements concerning the insurable interest of a reinsurer are true?

(a) the reinsured's insurable interest is always in its liability,
(b) the reinsured's insurable interest is always in the subject-matter insured under the direct policy,
(c) the rules relating to insurable interest under the direct policy apply to reinsurance,
(d) the reinsurer is liable to indemnify the reinsured if the reinsured has paid a direct policy holder who has no insurable interest.

CHAPTER 3

UTMOST GOOD FAITH

THE ELEMENTS OF THE DUTY OF UTMOST GOOD FAITH

Nature of the duty

The duty of utmost good faith is a doctrine which is in English law unique to insurance and reinsurance contracts. The usual obligation of a contracting party to avoid misrepresentation is supplemented by the additional obligation on a party to an insurance or reinsurance agreement to disclose all material facts to the other party prior to the making of the contract.

The distinction between non-disclosure and misrepresentation is sometimes difficult to draw. A failure by the reinsured to respond to a specific question is deemed to amount to a negative answer, so that this may amount to a positive misrepresentation. A reinsured who reveals some but not all of the truth may also be regarded as having misrepresented the unstated facts insofar as what is withheld detracts from the reliability of what has been said. This point was emphasised by the House of Lords in *HIH Casualty and General Insurance Co.* v. *Chase Manhattan Bank* [2003] Lloyd's Rep. IR 230, where it was noted that "pure" non-disclosure is relatively rare. Finally, where the reinsured makes accurate statements but, prior to the making of the contract circumstances have changed and the statements have become untrue, failure by the reinsured to correct the statement will amount to misrepresentation even though nothing has actually been said (see s. 20(6) of the Marine Insurance Act 1906), which recognises the ability of the reinsured to withdraw or correct a statement before the contract is concluded, and also *Assicurazioni Generali* v. *Arab Insurance Group* [2003] Lloyd's Rep. IR 131 where Clarke L.J. pointed out that it was incumbent on the reinsured to correct a false statement in a manner such that the true picture was fairly presented to the reinsurers.

Non-disclosure

What amounts to non-disclosure

The obligation on the reinsured is to make a fair presentation of the risk by making all material facts available to the reinsurers. It is not the task of the reinsured or his broker to draw attention to the significance of particular matters or to advise the reinsurers how to underwrite the risk. Whether all material facts have been made available to the reinsurers is a matter of fact.

***Pan Atlantic Insurance Co. Ltd* v. *Pine Top Insurance Co. Ltd* [1995] 1 A.C. 501**

Between 1977 and 1982 the claimants were insurers under a number of US liability risks. The defendants became the claimant's reinsurers in 1980, and the reinsurance was renewed in 1981. In making the presentation for the 1982 renewal the claimant's broker prepared a long record and a short record. The short record contained details of losses for the 1980 and 1981 years, and the long record contained details of losses between 1977 and 1979. Both documents were taken by the broker to his meeting with the reinsurers' underwriter, although the broker presented the risk in a fashion which focused on the more favourable short record and which discouraged inspection of the less favourable long record. In the event the reinsurers' underwriter had the long record made available to him but he did not actually look at it as he was persuaded by the broker's presentation of the risk. The trial judge found that the documents had not been prepared to assist the underwriter but rather "in the hope that the underwriter would concentrate on one record rather than the other."

Held (H.L.) (Lord Mustill dissenting): that there had not been a failure to disclose in the circumstances and (*per* Lord Mustill) that in any event the reinsurers' underwriter had waived the information in the long record by not examining it.

The most important comments were made by Waller J. at first instance ([1992] 1 Lloyd's Rep. 101), who found that there had been full disclosure or, if that was wrong, then there was waiver:

"This was, as I have already stressed, a reinsurance and a rating of that contract was for the underwriter. An underwriter knows as well as anybody, or should know, that the earlier years are the only real guide to assessing a rate. The broker has brought along for the underwriter the history in relation to the earlier years and that history, if the underwriter had bothered to study it, was a perfectly fair presentation of those earlier years. As I see it the negotiation is a commercial one, the broker does not have an obligation to tell the underwriter how to do his job. It might have been wiser in this instance to show the underwriter the full record and to encourage him to re-rate the risk having regard to the poor rating from the previous years. I say that because the result of the exercise has been, as was always likely, that terrible losses have been suffered, which have led to a very detailed investigation of the way in which this contract was placed."

Reinsured must know of facts

In order for there to be actionable non-disclosure, the reinsured must be aware of the facts which he has failed to disclose: to this extent an innocent reinsured cannot be guilty of non-disclosure. The reinsured is, however, under section 18(2) of the Marine Insurance Act 1906, "deemed to know every circumstances which, in the ordinary course of business, ought to be known to him." Whether a circumstance ought to have been known to the reinsured in the ordinary course of business is itself a question of fact, and the courts have held that if there is no reason for the reinsured to believe that a fact exists and it is not one which ought to be known to him in the ordinary course of events then he is under no duty to make inquiries to see whether there are any material facts in existence (see, for the general principle, *Economides* v. *Commercial Union Insurance plc* [1998] Lloyd's Rep. IR 9).

***London General Insurance Co. Ltd* v. *General Marine Underwriters Association Ltd* [1921] 1 K.B. 104**

On the morning of 25 September 1918 the claimant insurers instructed their brokers to procure a policy of reinsurance in respect of the cargo on board a vessel, the *Vigo* which had been insured by the claimants. It was known in the Lloyd's market the previous evening that part of the cargo had been destroyed by fire. This information was posted on the Lloyd's casualty board on the morning of 25 September and a casualty slip was sent to the claimants at the same time. The claimants did not, however, read the casualty slip and were unaware of the casualty when the brokers were instructed. The defendants, who were also ignorant of the loss, agreed to write the risk later the same day

Held (Q.B.D.): that the defendants were entitled to avoid the reinsurance for non-disclosure of the fire. The claimants ought to have known in the ordinary course of business that there had been a casualty and ought to have recalled their instructions to the brokers. By contrast, the defendants were not to be taken to have known of the existence of the casualty on board the *Vigo* as at the time the risk was presented to them they had no interest in the vessel.

More recently, in *WISE Underwriting Agency Ltd* v. *Grupo Nacional Provincial SA* [2004] Lloyd's Rep. IR 764 (reversed by the Court of Appeal on other grounds), Simon J. held that the reinsured had not failed to disclose certain facts relating to the operation of the direct assured's business as those facts were unknown to the reinsured.

However, if the reinsured is aware of the facts but takes the view that they are not material then non-disclosure is not excused. The test of materiality is not that of the prudent reinsured but rather that of the prudent underwriter.

Some reinsurance agreements provide that the reinsured is required to make disclosure only to the best of its knowledge and belief. As it is the case that the reinsured is not under any obligation to disclose what it did not know and had no reason to believe, on the face of things this type of clause has no real impact. However, it was decided by H.H.J. Dean QC in *International Lottery Management Ltd* v. *Dumas* [2002] Lloyd's Rep. IR 237 that the clause could not be disregarded, and that to give it some meaning it was necessary to construe it as excusing the reinsured from disclosing facts which he knew but which he did not believe were material. That defence is only available where the reinsured has addressed his mind to the materiality issue and has concluded reasonably, albeit wrongly, that the fact is not material.

Facts known to reinsured's agent

The use by the reinsured of agents is significant in two respects. First, in determining what the reinsured knows or ought to know, it is necessary to take account of the knowledge of the reinsured's agents and to ascertain the extent to which the reinsured is deemed to know what is known by his agents. Secondly, where the reinsured uses a broker to place the risk, section 19 of the Marine Insurance Act 1906 imposes upon the broker an independent duty to disclose to the reinsurers facts which are known by the reinsured and also facts which are known to the broker whether or not known by the reinsured. The second situation, that of disclosure by a placing broker, is discussed below. Here, the matter under consideration is the extent to which a reinsured is deemed to know what is known to his agents.

There is no general rule that information known to an agent is deemed to be known by his principal by means of imputation.

***Blackburn, Low & Co.* v. *Vigors* (1877) 12 App. Cas. 531**
The claimants had insured a vessel which had sailed from New York to Glasgow. The claimants instructed Glasgow brokers RMT to effect reinsurance. It was known to RMT that the vessel had suffered a casualty, but this fact was not passed on to the claimants. A reinsurance policy was then negotiated by RMT's London agents and was placed in the London market. A second policy was placed with the defendant by another firm of brokers independent of RMT: the brokers were unaware of the casualty. The defendant sought to avoid the second reinsurance agreement on the basis that the knowledge of RMT was imputed to the claimants.

Held (H.L.): that the defendant was liable. Lords Halsbury, Watson and Fitzgerald decided the case on the basis that there was no imputation of RMT's knowledge to the claimants. Lord Macnaghten held that it was the duty of a placing broker to make full disclosure to reinsurers, but that as RMT were not placing brokers their knowledge was not relevant to the placement.

The latter view has subsequently been accepted as the correct explanation of the *Vigors* case: see the decision of the Court of Appeal in *Société Anonyme d'Intermediares Luxembourgeois* v. *Farex Gie* [1995] L.R.L.R. 116 (discussed below). In a sequel to the *Vigors* case, *Blackburn, Low & Co.* v. *Haslam* (1888) 21 Q.B.D. 144, it was held that the first policy was voidable as it had been negotiated by RMT's own agents, and accordingly RMT owed a separate duty of disclosure to the reinsurer (the situation now governed by section 19 of the Marine Insurance Act 1906). The effect of these decisions is that the knowledge of an agent is only to be treated as the knowledge of the reinsured himself if the agent was employed to know or acquire that information or if the agent was in practice in control of the reinsured's affairs. Thus the knowledge of a junior employee is not deemed to be known to the employer (*Australia and New Zealand Bank Ltd* v. *Eagle and Colonial Wharves Ltd* [1960] 2 Lloyd's Rep. 241) although within a corporate structure the knowledge of an agent with authority to act on behalf of the company for a particular matter is to be imputed to the company (see the general principles of corporate attribution laid down in *Meridian Global Funds Management Asia Ltd* v. *Securities Commission* [1995] 2 A.C. 500, where it was held that there is no fixed rule of attribution and that in every case the relevant attribution rule will depend upon the context in which the question of attribution arises).

***Simner* v. *New India Assurance Co. Ltd* [1995] L.R.L.R. 240**
The claimant, representing a Lloyd's Syndicate, was a subscriber to a binding authority held by a broker under which the risk of local authorities suffering loss by reason of illness of or injury to their employees could be declared. The business had a

poor claims experience, but this was not known by the claimant. Subsequently the claimant reinsured with the defendant reinsurers, but did not disclose—because he was not aware—of the poor claims experience. The reinsurers purported to avoid the reinsurance.

Held (H.H.J. Anthony Diamond QC): that the policy could not be avoided.

(1) The claimant was unaware of the poor loss experience and thus could not have disclosed it to the reinsurers. The claimant was not under any duty to make inquiries of the broker on this matter, as the risk was one to be assessed by the reinsurers by making their own assessment.

(2) The knowledge of the broker was not the knowledge of the claimant. There was no duty owed by the broker to communicate loss experience to the claimant.

(3) The broker had not acted as the agent of the claimant in the administration of the binding authority. The broker had a limited authority to write business on behalf of the claimant, but was not in such a predominant position with regard to the claimant that the broker's knowledge was to be deemed to be that of the claimant.

ERC Frankona Reinsurance v. *American National Insurance Co.* [2006] Lloyd's Rep IR 157

ESR were the quota share reinsurers of Anico in respect of Anico's participation in an American individual and group accident and health insurance pool (NAIG) managed by NAIU. The pool began business in 1997, and ESR acted as reinsurers for one of its members, Philadelphia Life. The risk was presented to ESR (and its underwriting agent IGI) in January 1997 by placing brokers Bradstock. In 1998 Philadelphia Life became the sole underwriter, although Anico subsequently took over from Philadelphia Life. Anico wished to have 90% quota share reinsurance, and placing brokers Kininmonth (who had taken over from Bradstock) made a presentation to ESR in September 1998: this included a three-page placing document which stated that "NAIU operates as a full service MGU [managing general underwriter] providing all the necessary services including marketing, underwriting, claims and compliance" and that NAIU's "expertise and creativity" enabled it to price all forms of accidental death and disablement insurance. In September 1998 ESR took a 35% line in what became the 1998/99 quota share. In April 1999 ESR was asked to increase its line to 50%, and on 29 April 1999 ESR scratched a slip but added the letters "TBE" ("to be entered"). The slip was again scratched on 4 June 1999, with the letters "TBE" deleted. Substantial claims were made by Anico, and ESR raised a number of defences based on utmost good faith and breach of warranty. The issues and the outcome were as follows.

(1) ESR claimed that it was entitled to avoid the agreement to increase the line to 50%, made in 1999, by reason of Anico's failure to disclose that losses under the Reliance Policy were substantial: when the original slip, annotated with "TBE" had been scratched in April 1999 the losses had reached nearly US$5.2 million; and when the slip was scratched again with the letters "TBE" removed in June 1999 the losses had reached some US$7.9 million. These facts were known to NAIU, and give that NAIU was under a contractual duty to make monthly declarations of losses to Anico it followed that the information ought to have been known to Anico in the ordinary course of its business, so that disclosure was required by Anico under section 18(2) of the Marine Insurance Act 1906. In so deciding Andrew Smith J. rejected the argument that the principle in *Re Hampshire Land* [1896] 2 Ch. 743 prevented the imputation of knowledge to Anico. That case established a fraud exception for imputation of knowledge from agent to principal, based on the notion that a principal is not deemed to have knowledge of his agent's fraud for the obvious reason that an agent cannot be expected to disclose his own fraud. Andrew Smith J. held that the losses incurred by Reliance were embarrassing and might show incompetence but the information was not of a type which an agent could not be expected to disclose.

One preliminary issue in respect of this point was whether the contract to increase the line to 50% had been concluded in April 1999 or in June 1999, as clearly it became easier to prove materiality at the later date. Andrew Smith J. held on this point that the contract was to be treated as having been made on the earlier date, and that the letters "TBE" taken alone did not prevent the scratching of the slip from taking effect as a binding contract.

(2) ESR relied upon the statements in the three-page placing document presented to them in September 1998, asserting that they amounted to implied representations which were false. Andrew Smith J. disagreed. The statement that NAIU were "providing" services including underwriting and claims handling did not imply that NAIU would themselves underwrite and administer the programme and not engage others to do so, and the reference in the document to NAIU having the "expertise and creativity" to put forward competitive pricing for specified classes of business was not a representation that NAIU were not writing workers' compensation or workers' compensation carveout cover.

(3) ESR finally relied upon the fact that the chief executive of NAIU, Mr Drobny, a lawyer, had in September 1983 faced two charges of fraud (and served a four year sentence in respect of one of them) and had been disbarred in December 1983. This was plainly material and had an inducing effect. The defence raised by Anico was that neither it nor any of its relevant agents were aware of these facts and therefore could not have disclosed them. Andrew Smith J. disagreed, and found on the facts that Anico (through a senior employee) either actually knew the facts, or had deliberately shut his eyes to them, or at the very least ought to have been aware of them in the ordinary course of business (the test for disclosure laid down in section 18(2) of the 1906 Act). Had that been wrong and had Anico not itself had the necessary knowledge, then disclosure would not have been required. The person with the relevant knowledge would have been NAIU, but NAIU was not Anico's agent for the purpose of obtaining knowledge so that its knowledge could not be that of Anico for the purposes of disclosure under section 18 of the 1906 Act, and was not Anico's placing broker and so did not owe a duty of disclosure under section 19 of the 1906 Act (on the latter point, following the decision of the majority of the Court of Appeal in *PCW Syndicates* v. *PCW Reinsurers* [1996] 1 Lloyd's Rep. 241, discussed below).

Misrepresentation

There is misrepresentation for insurance purposes if a series of conditions are satisfied. In each case the state of the assured's mind is irrelevant, as misrepresentation is made out whether the reinsured has acted fraudulently, negligently or innocently, as in each case the reinsurers will not have received the information appropriate to the assessment of the risk. State of mind might be significant for other purposes, eg, because the contract provides that the reinsured is only required to make statements to the best of its knowledge and belief. Further, if a policy is avoided for misrepresentation the premium is not recoverable by the reinsured if it has acted fraudulently (Marine Insurance Act 1906, section 84). A false statement does not become an actionable misrepresentation simply because it has been made fraudulently: it remains necessary for the reinsurers to show that all of the requirements for misrepresentation have been made out.

The elements of misrepresentation are as follows.

Representation

There must be a statement which is capable of being referred to as a representation. A number of separate points may be made here.

(a) A general statement which, viewed objectively, is not one which was reasonably designed to be relied upon is not a representation but a mere "puff": see *Allianz Assurance* v. *Marchant,* 1997, unreported, where this lesser status was afforded to statements by the reinsured's broker that the business was profitable and prestigious. See also *Assicurazioni Generali SpA* v. *Arab Insurance Group (BSC)* [2003] Lloyd's Rep. IR 131, discussed below, where the Court of Appeal was divided as to whether a representation had been made by the reinsured by fax as to the participation of other co-insurers. Further, if there is no record of a conversation between the parties then it might be difficult to ascertain whether anything sufficiently specific was said to the reinsurers.

(b) In the same way, statements which appear in draft wordings which are then withdrawn cannot be regarded as representations (*Kingscroft Insurance Co. Ltd* v. *Nissan Fire and Marine Insurance Co. Ltd (No. 2)* [1999] Lloyd's Rep. IR 603).

(c) If a reinsured merely repeats or forwards information which it has received from the direct assured, then in the appropriate circumstances it may be possible to argue that no representation is being made at all and that the facts disclosed by the assured are being put forward either by way of information or by way of an untested opinion on the part of the reinsured. The latter was held to be the case in *WISE Underwriting Agency Ltd* v. *Grupo Nacional Provincial SA* [2003] EWHC 1706 (Comm) (see below). All depends upon the proper construction of the statement.

***Highlands Insurance Co.* v. *Continental Insurance Co.* [1987] 1 Lloyd's Rep. 109**

Insurance on buildings in Israel was issued by local companies under a fronting arrangement, and they were reinsured by Continental which took a 21% line. Highland (along with eight other companies) was the retrocessionaire of Continental, having taken a line of just under 5%. The buildings were damaged by fire. Highland sought to avoid the retrocession on the ground that there had been a false statement as to the sprinkler arrangements in the buildings. The slip stated "Top location Hollon with non-combustible construction and sprinklered . . . "

Held (Steyn J.): that the words amounted to a representation of fact, and that the appropriate test was to ask what the words would have conveyed to prudent underwriter in the position of Highland. They were not merely a statement that Continental had been informed that there were sprinklers.

***Sirius International Insurance Corporation* v. *Oriental Assurance Corporation* [1999] Lloyd's Rep. IR 345**

The direct policy in this case was on the contents of a building. A fax was sent by the reinsured's producing brokers to the reinsured's placing brokers, stating that "we have been informed" by the assured's brokers that there were fire hydrants in the insured premises. The producing brokers did not attempt to verify this information, which proved to be false, as the building was equipped only with dry risers which had not been connected to the mains water supply. The reinsurers sought to avoid the reinsurance.

Held (Longmore J.): that there had been a misrepresentation. The correct test to apply was that laid down by Steyn J. in *Highlands Insurance* v. *Continental Insurance* [1987] 1 Lloyd's Rep. 109 (above), namely the meaning that would have been conveyed to a reasonable underwriter. The words used here indicated that a statement of fact was being made and that this was not simply a matter of a third party's statement being passed on.

It may also be the case that the assured's presentation of the risk has been expressly incorporated into the reinsurance agreement, in which case the reinsured cannot deny that the statements in the original presentation form a part of the presentation to the reinsurers.

***Australian Widows Fund Life Assurance Society Ltd* v. *National Mutual Life Association of Australia Ltd* [1914] A.C. 634**

A life policy was issued by the reinsured on the life of one Moran. The proposal for that policy contained a basis clause rendering all of the assured's answers warranties. The reinsured obtained a facultative reinsurance policy which was stated to be written on the same terms and conditions as the original. The assured had made false statements which rendered him in breach of warranty, and the reinsurers asserted that the reinsured was itself in breach of warranty by reason of the incorporated clause.

Held (Privy Council): that the proposal form was incorporated into the reinsurance agreement, so that false statements made by the assured were to be regarded as a part of the presentation of the risk to the reinsurers, and accordingly that the reinsurance could be avoided for misrepresentation.

(d) A representation may be either a representation as to a matter of fact, or as to a matter of expectation or belief (Marine Insurance Act 1906, s. 18(3)). The statement may also be of the reinsured's intentions.

(e) There must have been a specific statement and not merely the suggestion that something can be implied from the presentation made by the reinsured.

***Feasey* v. *Sun Life Assurance of Canada* [2002] Lloyd's Rep. IR 835**

A P&I Club insured its member shipowners against their liabilities to employees and others offering injury on board the shipowners' vessels. The club reinsured with the claimant's syndicate under a reinsurance agreement which took the form of a life cover rather than a traditional liability cover, so that in the event that an injury occurred the syndicate would pay a predetermined fixed benefit to the syndicate. The syndicate reinsured its liabilities under this contract with the defendant retrocessionaires. The retrocessionaires sought to avoid the retrocession by asserting that there had been implicit misrepresentations as to two matters: (1) the fixed benefits payable to the club were based upon a proper calculation of the actual liabilities faced by the club to its members; and (2) there had been a professional appraisal of the risk run by the club.

Held (Langley J.): there was no misrepresentation. The syndicate had not made any express statement to either of these effects, and it was not possible to extract implicit statements from the overall presentation of the risk by the syndicate. In the absence of express statements, reliance on misrepresentation of sufficient clarity to justify avoidance was "unpromising".

Representation made by reinsured or broker

The representation must have been made by the reinsured or his broker. The reinsurer may, for example, commission an independent expert to report on a particular matter relating to the risk. Error by the expert which results in him making false statements to the reinsurer is not to be regarded as misrepresentation on the part of the reinsured or his broker even if the broker has been authorised by the reinsurer to commission the report. This was the position in *International Lottery Management Ltd* v. *Dumas* [2002] Lloyd's Rep. IR 237, where insurers were held to be unable to avoid a policy by relying on errors contained in the report of an independent lawyer who had been asked to report on the validity of a foreign-owned lottery in Azerbaijan.

Falsity

The representation must be false. Falsity depends upon the nature of the representation. A representation as to a matter of fact to be true must be substantially correct, in that the difference between what was said and what was actually correct would not be considered material by a prudent underwriter (Marine Insurance Act 1906, s. 18(4)). In *Assicurazioni Generali SpA* v. *Arab Insurance Group (BSC)* [2003] Lloyd's Rep. IR 131 the statement by the reinsured to the reinsurers that it had the "support" of a named co-insurer on the risk was held by a majority of the Court of Appeal (Ward L.J. and Sir Christopher Staughton) to be false, as the named co-insurer was only participating in one part of that risk, whereas Clarke L.J. felt that the statement was true as the word "support" did not imply 100% support. By contrast in *Sirius International Insurance Corporation* v. *Oriental Assurance Corporation* [1999] Lloyd's Rep. IR 345 the court found that a statement that a building was equipped with a sprinkler system would be false if the system did not work: in the case itself the statement was made after the contract had been concluded and thus was immaterial on that basis (see below). A representation as to a matter of expectation of belief is true if it is made in good faith (Marine Insurance Act 1906, s. 18(5), in that the reinsured must have genuinely held the stated belief at the time that the representation was made) (see *Highlands Insurance Co.* v. *Continental Insurance Co.* [1987] 1 Lloyd's Rep. 109). It is important to distinguish between fact and opinion, as a statement which proves to be false on an objective basis will not amount to misrepresentation if the statement was merely a genuinely-held opinion.

***Gan Insurance Co. Ltd* v. *Tai Ping Insurance Co. Ltd (No. 2)* [2001] Lloyd's Rep. IR 291 (reversed on other grounds, [2002] Lloyd's Rep. IR 667)**

The direct policy was on a computer wafer factory in the course of construction in Taiwan, and the risk was reinsured. The reinsurers alleged that they were shown architects' drawings of the building, and these illustrated that there were to be extensive fire precaution mechanisms in the building. There was subsequently a fire which severely damaged the building under construction, and the reinsurers claimed the right to avoid the reinsurance agreement on the basis that the drawings had amounted to a representation that the fire precautions had been installed in the building.

Held (Longmore J.): that the reinsurers had no right to avoid the policy. The reinsurers had not demonstrated that they had been shown the drawings, but even if that was wrong then they did not amount to a representation that the fire precautions had been installed in the building under construction but rather that the assured intended to install such protection in the finished building. That intention had been honestly stated.

Response to unambiguous question

Where the representation is in response to a question, the question must have been unambiguous. If there is doubt as to what is being asked by the reinsurers then the reinsured is entitled to be regarded as having answered truthfully if the construction put upon the question was a reasonable one.

***Groupama Insurance Co. Ltd* v. *Overseas Partners Re Ltd* [2003] EWHC 34 (Comm)**

US shipping companies were insured in London by insurers led by Syndicate 724 at Lloyd's against liability to their employees for causing death and bodily injury. The risk had been offered by Texas producing brokers and placed in London by placing brokers JLT. The insurers appointed A as their broker to place reinsurance, and A obtained the subscription of the claimants. The reinsurance was for 100% of the underlying risk. The claimants themselves appointed A to place retrocession, and the defendants agreed to subscribe to 50% of a quota share retrocession treaty. The defendants subsequently agreed to increase their subscription to 75%, having asked by fax whether there were any "losses incurred on the program to date". A replied for the claimants, confirming that there had been no losses advised that would affect any of the declarations to the treaty. This was a true statement insofar as the claimants themselves and their brokers had not been advised of any losses, although there had been losses at the direct level which were unknown to the claimants and to A: that information could easily have been ascertained by a simple telephone call. The defendants argued that there had been misrepresentation.

Held (Morison J.): that the retrocession agreement could not be set aside. The question asked by the defendants in their fax referred only to the book of business written by the claimants, and did not request information as to losses at the direct level which had yet to crystallise into claims against the claimants. The market evidence showed that it was general practice to treat a question by reinsurers or retrocessionaires requiring losses to be identified as confined to actual losses suffered by the reinsured or retrocedant and not potential future losses. Further, the statement that claimants and A could confirm that there were no losses was confined to matters actually known by them.

Materiality and inducement

The false statement must be material to the risk. This is an objective test, which is considered below. Whether a particular representation be material or not is, in each case, a question of fact (Marine Insurance Act 1906, s. 18(7)). Further, the false statement must have induced the reinsurer to enter into the contract. This is a subjective test, based on the effect that the statement had on the reinsurers' decision to enter into the contract. The question of inducement is also discussed below.

Obligation to state facts to best of knowledge and belief

It is open to the reinsurers to modify the rules on misrepresentation by simply requiring the reinsured to answer questions to the best of his knowledge and belief. Where this form of wording is used, a false statement made by the reinsured will not give rise to the right to avoid unless the reinsurers can show that the reinsured did not believe his statement or that the reinsured was aware of circumstances which rendered his statement untrue but chose not to investigate them (blind eye knowledge). See *Economides* v. *Commercial Union Insurance* [1998] Lloyd's Rep. IR 9, a domestic property insurance case where the assured innocently misstated the value of the property in his flat. It would also seem that a reinsured who expresses an opinion without having any ground for believing what he has said has not acted to the best of his knowledge and belief. This was so held in *Sirius International Insurance Corporation* v. *Oriental Assurance Corporation* [1999] Lloyd's Rep. IR 345, the facts of which were given above. Longmore J. held that if he had been wrong in his view that the phrase "we have been informed" made in the broker's presentation amounted to a statement of fact, and instead that it was to be regarded as merely expressing an opinion, then the reinsured was not saved by a best of knowledge and belief clause as the brokers had not attempted to verify the truth of what they had been told.

MATERIALITY AND INDUCEMENT

Materiality

A reinsurer can avoid a reinsurance agreement for breach of the duty of utmost good faith if two conditions are satisfied: the fact withheld or misstated was material; and the reinsurer was induced by the reinsured's presentation of the risk to enter into the agreement. The Marine Insurance Act 1906 refers only to the materiality test; the inducement test was superimposed by the House of Lords in the landmark decision *Pan Atlantic Insurance Co.* v. *Pine Top Insurance Co.* [1994] 2 Lloyd's Rep. 527. English law does not impose any requirement for a causal connection between the fact withheld or misrepresented and the loss suffered by the reinsured: if a fact is material and there has been inducement then the reinsurers have the right to avoid the reinsurance agreement irrespective of the possibility that the loss may have arisen from an entirely separate set of circumstances.

Materiality is defined by section 18(2) (non-disclosure) and section 20(2) (misrepresentation) of the Marine Insurance Act 1906. A fact is material if it is one "which would influence the judgment of a prudent insurer in fixing the premium, or determining whether he will take the risk." This is an objective test, which can be satisfied by the production of evidence by the insurer to show that the market would have regarded the fact as material. A "prudent insurer" is one who was in the market at the relevant time. It was commented by Clarke L.J. in *Drake Insurance plc* v. *Provident Insurance plc* [2004] Lloyd's Rep. IR 277 that materiality cannot be wholly objective, as it is necessary to take into account the characteristics of the underwriter in question in order to determine how a prudent underwriter operating in the same fashion would have responded to the information in question.

The key matter is that the fact must be one which was premium-sensitive in that it would have influenced the judgement of the prudent underwriter. In *Pan Atlantic* v. *Pine Top* there was some dispute as to the meaning of the phrase "influence the judgement": Lord Mustill was of the view that it was enough for the reinsurers to show that a prudent reinsurer in the market at the time would have wanted to know the information in question even though he would ultimately have written the risk on the same terms, whereas Lord Lloyd was of the view that a fact could be regarded as objectively material unless it would have had a "decisive influence" on the judgement of a prudent underwriter. The broader approach adopted by Lord Mustill was approved by the Court of Appeal soon afterwards, in *St Paul Fire & Marine Insurance Co. (UK) Ltd* v. *McConnell Dowell Constructors Ltd* [1995] 2 Lloyd's Rep. 116. The market materiality test is, therefore, one which can be satisfied relatively easily by reinsurers, as it is necessary to show only that a prudent underwriter would have been interested in the fact withheld or misstated, and not that a prudent underwriter would have taken a different view of the risk. The phrase "judgement of a prudent insurer" thus refers to his thought processes and not to his ultimate decision.

Inducement

As noted above, in *Pan Atlantic Insurance Co.* v. *Pine Top Insurance Co.* [1994] 2 Lloyd's Rep. 527 the House of Lords laid down the principle that objective materiality alone is not enough, and that a reinsurer has to show that he was actually induced by the reinsured's presentation of the risk to enter into the agreement. In so holding the House of Lords overruled the earlier decision of the Court of Appeal in *Container Transport International* v. *Oceanus Mutual Underwriting Association* [1984] 1 Lloyd's Rep. 476, where it had been decided that the only issue was one of objective materiality.

Presumption of inducement

In *Pan Atlantic* diverging views were expressed on the independent significance of inducement. Lord Mustill felt that there was a "presumption of inducement", whereby a reinsurer who was able to demonstrate objective materiality would have the benefit of a presumption that, being a prudent person, he was himself induced by the presentation. Lord Lloyd vigorously rejected this notion. In a series of cases since *Pan Atlantic* it has become clear that there is no generalised presumption of inducement, and that the issues of materiality and inducement are quite separate. The point was discussed by the Court of Appeal in *Assicurazioni Generali* v. *Arab Insurance Group* [2003] Lloyd's Rep. IR 131. The Court of Appeal here confirmed earlier decisions to the effect that it is the duty of the reinsurer to give evidence as to his own state of mind, so that the reinsured is able to cross-examine the reinsured and is thereby given the opportunity to demonstrate that the reinsurer would have entered into the agreement on the same terms and conditions even if there had been full disclosure or material facts had not been misstated. The leading judgment of Clarke L.J. laid down the following principles on the relationship between materiality and inducement, and these also set out what has to be proved by a reinsurer who asserts that he was induced to enter into the contract by the reinsured's presentation of the risk.

> "(1) In order to be entitled to avoid a contract of insurance or reinsurance, an insurer or reinsurer must prove on the balance of probabilities that he was induced to enter into the contract by a material non-disclosure or by a material misrepresentation.
> (2) There is no presumption of law that an insurer or reinsurer is induced to enter in the contract by a material non-disclosure or misrepresentation.
> (3) The facts may, however, be such that it is to be inferred that the particular insurer or reinsurer was so induced even in the absence from evidence from him.
> (4) In order to prove inducement the insurer or reinsurer must show that the non-disclosure or misrepresentation was an effective cause of his entering into the contract on the terms on which he did. He must therefore show at least that, but for the relevant non-disclosure or misrepresentation, he would not have entered into the contract on those terms. On the other hand, he does not have to show that it was the sole effective cause of his doing so."

A finding that a statement was objectively material is not, therefore, inconsistent with a finding that the statement did not subjectively induce the reinsurers to enter into the agreement. The only situation in which a reinsurer is entitled to rely upon the presumption of inducement is that in which the individuals responsible for writing the risk are unable for good reason to give evidence as to what occurred and their response to the presentation. To date the presumption of inducement has only been successfully relied upon in cases in which a single underwriter in a subscription placement involving other underwriters was unable to give evidence: see *St Paul Fire and Marine Insurance Co. UK Ltd* v. *McConnell Dowell Constructors Ltd* [1995] 2 Lloyd's Rep. 116 (direct insurance), *International Management Group (UK) Ltd* v. *Simmonds* [2004] Lloyd's Rep. IR 247 (reinsurance) and *Toomey* v. *Banco Vitalicio de Espana SA de Seguros y Reaseguros* [2004] Lloyd's Rep. IR 354.

Proof of inducement

In all other situations, the reinsurer must prove, as was stated by Clarke L.J. in the *Assicurazioni Generali* case, that the presentation of the risk was an effective cause—although not necessarily the only effective cause—of his decision to underwrite the risk on the terms ultimately agreed. This is not always an easy question.

***Assicurazioni Generali SpA* v. *Arab Insurance Group (BSC)* [2003] Lloyd's Rep. IR 131**

The trial judge in this case ruled that the reinsurers had not been induced by the reinsured's statement that there was to be a named co-insurer supporting the reinsured. Clarke L.J. and Sir Christopher Staughton accepted the views of the trial judge: because the reinsurers had not been able to show that they would have refused to accept the risk on the agreed terms had they been aware that the co-insurer's support was to be limited to one part of the cover. Ward L.J., dissenting, held that it was open to the Court of Appeal to review the inferences drawn by the judge from the evidence put to him even though the facts as found by the trial judge could not be challenged, and that the trial judge had drawn the incorrect inference on the inducement issue.

Inducement is a question of fact in every case. An underwriter will not be able to establish inducement if he paid no heed to the risk being presented to him (see *Marc Rich & Co. AG* v. *Portman* [1996] 1 Lloyd's Rep. 430, although the underwriter ultimately succeeded in establishing that there was inducement on one key matter), if he relied upon other information in his decision to write the risk (*Cape plc* v. *Iron Trades Employers Insurance Association Ltd* [2004] Lloyd's Rep. IR (forthcoming)), or if the risk would have been written with or without such disclosure (*Kingscroft Insurance Co. Ltd* v. *Nissan Fire & Marine Insurance Co. Ltd (No. 2)* [1999] Lloyd's Rep. IR 603).

In *Drake Insurance plc* v. *Provident Insurance plc* [2004] Lloyd's Rep. IR 277 a majority of the Court of Appeal, Rix and Clarke L.JJ., held that in determining whether there has been inducement it is necessary to consider exactly what would have been likely to happen had full disclosure been made: it is not enough to show that the fact withheld or misstated would have induced the insurer to enter into the contract if full disclosure would have led to other matters coming to light which would have left the decision unchanged. In *Drake* v. *Provident* itself the assured failed to disclose a driving conviction, and the insurer sought to avoid the policy by showing that the combination of an earlier accident (which had been disclosed) and the conviction would have led to a higher premium under its underwriting criteria. The majority held that if the conviction had been disclosed and the insurer had attempted to charge a higher premium, it would have come to light that the accident had not been the fault of the assured and thus would have been disregarded, thereby reducing the premium to the normal level. Pill L.J., dissenting, held that it was not open to the court to speculate on what might have occurred had full disclosure been made.

The significance of the ruling in *Drake* v. *Provident* in requiring the court to undertake an assessment of exactly what would have occurred with full disclosure is illustrated in a reinsurance context by *Bonner* v. *Cox Dedicated Corporate Member Ltd* [2006] Lloyd's Rep. IR 385. In this case reinsurers subscribed to a reinsurance slip which operated as a standing offer to provide reinsurance to any underwriters who agreed to insure a direct energy risk. A number of underwriters accepted the energy risk, and thereby the reinsurance, but a loss occurred—in the form of an oil well blow-out—during the direct placement process. The reinsurers were not informed of the loss. A number of underwriters subsequently agreed to take the direct risk, and the reinsurers sought to avoid the reinsurance against them for non-disclosure of the loss. The reinsurers' argument was that if they had been informed of the loss they would have withdrawn the reinsurance slip so as to prevent further acceptances of it. Morison J. held that it was likely that the reinsurers would not have acted differently had the direct loss been disclosed to them, as by the time of the loss the broking process was well under way and the reinsurers would have been most unlikely to withdraw the slip at that late stage. The Court of Appeal on appeal, [2005] EWCA Civ 1512 upheld the reasoning of the trial judge.

Date of materiality and inducement

The materiality of a fact, and the issue of whether or not it induced the reinsurers to enter into the agreement, have to be assessed at the date the agreement was made. Thus, if there is intelligence known to the reinsured which suggests that there is an increased risk of loss, or if there are outstanding circumstances which indicate that the risk is greater than it appears (e.g., a criminal charge against the direct assured) then the mere existence of the intelligence or the outstanding circumstances is of itself a material fact. In the event that the intelligence is shown to have been flawed, or if the criminal charge is dismissed, materiality and inducement are not retrospectively removed and the policy remains voidable. However, in such circumstances the court may regard an attempt by the reinsurers to avoid the policy as one which contravenes their own duty of utmost good faith it may thus be denied to them (see below).

This situation should be distinguished from that in which the reinsured withheld a fact which he believed existed but which on objective grounds did not. In *Drake Insurance plc* v. *Provident Insurance plc* [2004] Lloyd's Rep. IR 277 Rix and Clarke L.JJ. (Pill L.J. dissenting) were cautiously of the view that a fact should not be regarded as material if at the time of the making of the contract, and contrary to the views of the parties, the fact did not exist or was untrue. Pill L.J. preferred the "state of mind" test whereby a fact was to be regarded as material if it would have influenced the judgement of a prudent underwriter, even though objectively speaking the fact did not exist.

MATERIAL FACTS IN REINSURANCE AGREEMENTS

Significance of the duty of utmost good faith

Non-disclosure and misrepresentation is significant for a number of reasons. First, if the direct policy has been obtained by non-disclosure or misrepresentation on the part of the assured, then the policy is voidable and the reinsurers cannot be liable to indemnify the reinsured should they choose to make payment to the reinsured as reinsurance covers only legal liability. Secondly, the presentation of the risk may be made simultaneously to the reinsured and to the reinsurers, as is often the case where the reinsured is fronting for the reinsurers and intends to cede most or all of the risk: in these circumstances, any misrepresentation or non-disclosure will render both contracts voidable and the reinsurers will be able to avoid their own contract. Thirdly, the presentation made to the reinsured may have been perfectly proper but the presentation made by the reinsured to the reinsurers may have been tainted by material non-disclosure or misrepresentation. In such a case the reinsurers are able to avoid the reinsurance agreement even though the reinsured remains liable to the direct assured. Accordingly, in assessing the liability of reinsurers it is necessary to consider facts which are material at the direct level and also facts which are material at the reinsurance level.

Facts material to direct policies

Physical hazard

There are numerous authorities on the physical hazard in direct insurance. It suffices to say here that the physical hazard is simply any fact which increases the risk of loss of the insured subject matter. The physical hazard varies as between the various forms of underlying cover. In relation to property insurance, material facts include the age and description of the insured subject matter, the uses to which it is put, its location and security arrangements protecting it from loss. In relation to life insurance, material facts include the age, health, occupation and hobbies of the assured. Liability insurers are concerned with the nature of the risk being run by the reinsured and previous claims experience. Insurers of ships, aircraft and goods in transit will wish to know the nature of what is being carried, the route and any particular risks which may be faced. It is material for credit insurers to know the value of outstanding debts and of particular problems with individual customers. In all cases insurers will have to be informed of measures taken by the assured to protect against loss, and whether the insured subject matter has been substantially over-insured.

Moral hazard

The moral hazard relates to facts concerning the assured himself which indicate that the assured is not a person with whom the insurers would want to do business. There are numerous illustrations of moral hazard in the cases.

(1) The financial position of the assured may be a material fact. There are numerous cases where it has been shown that an assured who has destroyed his own property in order to make a fraudulent insurance claim was impecunious. However, it was held in *O'Kane* v. *Jones* [2004] Lloyd's Rep. IR 389 that the mere fact that the assured was in arrears with his premiums on some other existing policy was not a material fact as there could have been a number of reasons for late payment and was not sufficient to justify an allegation that the assured might not be able to afford to maintain the insured subject matter (here, a vessel) in a satisfactory condition.

(2) Outstanding criminal charges are material facts if the charges would, if proved, themselves be material. The conflicting authorities on the point were reviewed by Mance L.J. in *Brotherton* v. *Aseguradora Colseguros SA (No. 2)* [2003] EWCA Civ 705, [2003] Lloyd's Rep. IR 758, and his Lordship concluded as follows:

(a) If at the time of the placement the assured was facing a criminal charge which he knew he had not committed, then he was bound to disclose the charge but he was also entitled to present evidence showing his innocence.
(b) If at the time of the placement the assured had been charged with and acquitted of a criminal offence, but he was in reality guilty, that guilt remained a material fact.
(c) If at the time of the placement the assured had been charged with and convicted of a criminal offence, but was in reality innocent, it remained necessary for the assured to disclose the conviction although he could temper this by attempting to show the insurers that the conviction was an error.

(3) The general dishonesty of the assured may be a material fact. It was held in *Insurance Corporation of the Channel Islands* v. *Royal Hotel (No. 2)* [1997] L.R.L.R. 94 that the intention of the assured hotel to defraud its bankers by obtaining a loan with the use of false information was a material fact which had to be disclosed to the hotel's material damage insurers. Again, in *James* v. *CGU General Insurance plc* [2002] Lloyd's Rep. IR 206 it was held to be material to a policy on a garage that the garage owner had defrauded customers and was in dispute with the Inland Revenue and the Customs and Excise Commissioners.

(4) The claims history of the assured is a material fact.

Rumours and intelligence

An assured is required to disclose to his insurers any information which is in his possession which leads him to believe that the subject matter of the policy is at risk or indeed that it has actually been lost. It is irrelevant in determining whether or not the assured has broken his duty that the information proves at a later date to be false or unreliable, as the questions of materiality and inducement have to be assessed at the date of the placement (although there may be situations in which the insurers are unable to rely upon their right to avoid—see the discussion of "Remedies" in section below).

There is, however, a distinction between mere rumour, which is not material, and hard intelligence, which is material. The following cases illustrate the position:

- The policy covers a cargo and there is solid intelligence that the cargo was on board an unseaworthy vessel (*Lynch* v. *Dunsford* (1811) 14 East 494).
- The policy covers possible financial loss in the event of the cancellation of a sporting event. Information received from a reliable government source that the government intends to prevent its team from participating in the event is a material fact (*International Management Group (UK) Ltd* v. *Simmonds* [2004] Lloyd's Rep. IR 247—cricket match between India and Pakistan from which the Pakistani government subsequently withdrew its team).
- The policy is a bankers' blanket bond insurance which covers loss due to the fraud of employees, and there are media reports that a senior employee of the assured Bank has been accused by the Bank and by government authorities of the misuse and misappropriation of the Bank's assets (*Brotherton* v. *Aseguradora Colseguros (No. 3)* [2003] Lloyd's Rep. IR 774).

Facts material to reinsurance contracts

Facts are material to a reinsurer if they relate to the risk run by the reinsured under the direct policy or if they relate to the reinsured's underwriting practices and claims experience.

The risk run by the reinsured

The following cases illustrate the importance of the need for the reinsured to disclose and not to misrepresent the potential liabilities which have been undertaken under the direct policy.

The fact that *the risk posed by the direct assured* is greater than that indicated is a material fact.

***Brotherton* v. *Aseguradora Colseguros (No. 3)* [2003] EWHC 1741 (Comm), [2003] Lloyd's Rep. IR 774**

In this case there was a misrepresentation to the reinsurers of a bankers' blanket bond policy as to the nature of allegations of fraud made against the President of the Bank and as to the reasons for his absence from a meeting in London to discuss the various placements.

***WISE Underwriting Agency Ltd* v. *Grupo Nacional Provincial SA* [2004] Lloyd's Rep. IR 764**

Goods insured by the defendant, a Mexican insurer, were insured from a container parked outside the assured's warehouse in Cancun, Mexico. The goods included a quantity of Rolex watches and spare parts to a value in excess of US$700,000. The risk had been reinsured in London with the claimant reinsurers. The reinsurers were informed that the insured subject matter consisted of jewellery, perfumes and clocks, but there was no mention of watches. The reinsurers asserted that they had been induced by misrepresentation and non-disclosure to subscribe to the risk.

Held (C.A.): that the reinsurance agreement could be avoided by the claimants. There was non-disclosure of the fact that the goods to be shipped included Rolex watches. The reference to clocks did not amount to a disclosure of the true nature of the cargo. Rolex watches were uniquely attractive to thieves. The reinsurers were able to show that they had been induced by the presentation of the risk to enter into the contract.

The amount of reinsured's potential exposure is a material fact.

***Toomey* v. *Banco Vitalicio de Espana SA de Seguros y Reaseguros* [2004] Lloyd's Rep. IR 354**

In 1996 the Spanish first division club Atletico de Madrid agreed with a broadcaster, Audiovisual, that for a seven year period Audiovisual would have exclusive broadcasting rights in the Club's home matches. The Club was to be paid a minimum of Pts 3 billion, topped up by other payments. Failure by the Club to qualify for either of the two major European club football competitions, the Champions League and the UEFA cup, imposed an obligation on the Club to repay Pts 500 million to Audiovisual. The sums payable by Audiovisual were in the form of promissory notes. In September 1998 Audiovisual lodged with the Club's bank promissory notes to the value of Pts 3.48 billion for the forthcoming season, and it was agreed that the Club would insure against the risk of relegation. The policy, issued by a Spanish insurer, Vitalicio, was issued to the Club but was stated to indemnify Audiovisual for economic loss suffered in the event of the Club's relegation. The sum insured was Pts 2,900,000,000. Vitalicio reinsured with the claimants on the same terms as original. In the event the Club was relegated at the end of the 1999/2000 season. The claimants asserted that there had been non-disclosure of two material facts: the fact that the policy was valued; and the fact that the true assured was Audiovisual rather than the Club.

It was held by Andrew Smith J. and the Court of Appeal that the policy was voidable. It was common ground between the parties that the false statement as to the nature of the direct policy could only be a material fact if the amount recoverable was greater under a valued policy than under an unvalued policy, i.e. that the Club's loss on relegation could be less than Pts 2.9 billion. The judges agreed with the reinsurers that a smaller loss had been possible and that the fact was material. When the Club was relegated it lost Pts 2.639 billion by way of television rights and it also had to repay Pts 500 million for not qualifying for Europe, a total of Pts 3.169 billion. However, the Pts 500 million had to be disregarded as it had nothing to do with relegation: that sum would have been repayable without relegation but on failure to qualify for Europe.

Andrew Smith J. rejected the utmost good faith defence based on the identity of the assured, as he was satisfied that the Club and not Audiovisual was the insured person. There was no appeal against this aspect of the decision.

Andrew Smith J. went on to find that, had the utmost good faith defence not been made out, Vitalicio had been guilty of a breach of an express warranty that the direct policy was an indemnity rather than a valued policy. The Court of Appeal upheld the judge's ruling on this point as well.

The terms of the direct policy may be material insofar as they are unusual. This is of particular significance as regards facultative policies, as the usual practice is for the terms of that policy to be incorporated into the reinsurance agreement by means of the "full reinsurance clause" ("all terms and conditions as original") although in many cases the reinsurers may not have had sight of the direct policy at the time the reinsurance was agreed. The terms must, however, be unusual.

***Charlesworth* v. *Faber* (1900) 5 Com. Cas. 408**

The claimant was the insurer of the hull and machinery of the steamship *Merrimac* under a marine time policy for a period of 12 months. The policy contained a "held covered" clause whereby in the event that the vessel was still at sea on the expiry of the policy, the assured would be held covered at a pro rata daily premium. The claimant was reinsured with the defendant. The *Merrimac* became a total loss and the defendant sought to avoid the policy on the ground that the held covered clause had not been disclosed to him.

Held (Bigham J.): that the held covered clause was in common use and the defendant ought to have known that the policy would probably have contained such a clause.

***Property Insurance Co. Ltd* v. *National Protector Insurance Co. Ltd* (1913) 108 L.T. 104**

The reinsured issued a marine policy insuring the hull of a vessel. The premium was 6% of the sum insured. The policy conferred upon the assured the option to extend the cover for navigation on the Great Lakes, for an additional premium of 3% of the sum insured. The reinsurers were not informed of the option, and received a share of the basic premium only.

Held (Scrutton J.): that the extension of cover to navigation of the Great Lakes was an extraordinary risk which ought to have been disclosed by the reinsured, and accordingly the reinsurance was voidable.

***Aneco Reinsurance Underwriting Ltd* v. *Johnson & Higgins* [1998] 1 Lloyd's Rep. 565 (reversed in part on other grounds, [2002] Lloyd's Rep. IR 93)**

Direct marine business had been written by certain Lloyd's Syndicates. The defendant brokers were instructed by the Syndicates to place treaty reinsurance cover (the Bullen Treaty). The defendants obtained the agreement of the claimant to participate in the Bullen Treaty, but only on condition that the brokers arranged retrocession for a substantial part of the claimant's exposure. The defendant arranged retrocession cover with excess of loss retrocessionaires, but informed the retrocessionaires that the Bullen Treaty had been written on a quota share basis, so that any risks which were underwritten by the Lloyd's Syndicates were automatically to be ceded to the Bullen Treaty. In fact, the Bullen Treaty was a facultative/obligatory arrangement under which the Lloyd's Syndicates were permitted to decide which risks were to be ceded to the Bullen Treaty, but the claimant had no right to reject the risks. The excess of loss retrocessionaires avoided their contracts on the basis of misrepresentation as to the nature of the Bullen Treaty, obtaining an arbitration award to that effect, and in the present proceedings the claimant sought to recover damages from the defendant. In order to recover damages it was necessary for the claimant to show that the excess of loss retrocessionaires had been entitled to avoid their contracts.

Held (Cresswell J.): that the claimant was entitled to damages. The nature of the Bullen Treaty was a material fact as far as the retrocessionaires were concerned, as they believed that they were providing cover for liability for all of the risks written by the Lloyd's Syndicates whereas in fact the risks to be ceded were selective. Market evidence showed that it was almost impossible to obtain retrocession cover for a facultative/obligatory reinsurance treaty.

The assessment of the risk by other reinsureds might be material in appropriate circumstances, particularly where the reinsured itself has drawn attention to this fact.

***Assicurazioni Generali* v. *Arab Insurance Group* [2003] Lloyd's Rep. IR 131**

The reinsured, in placing the risk for reinsurance, stated that it was being supported by two other insurers. This statement was partly true, as the co-insurance related only to one section of the risk. The Court of Appeal unanimously held that this information was material as otherwise there would have been no point in disclosing it. However, on the facts the reinsurers had not been induced by the information and could not avoid the cover.

The reinsured's practices and claims experience

Reinsurers are keenly interested in the manner in which the reinsured conducts its business, as this will have a major impact on the quality of the reinsured's underwriting and also on the amounts of loss suffered by the reinsured. Further, if the reinsured's accounting and reserving principles are out of line with market practice then the amount of potential liabilities faced by the reinsured might be understated. These points may be illustrated by the following.

Reserving policy is material to the extent that it is unusual or unexpected.

***Assicurazioni Generali* v. *Arab Insurance Group* [2003] Lloyd's Rep. IR 13**

The claimant was the reinsurer of US contractors' risks policies, having earlier been the direct insurer on those risks. At the end of 1991, while acting as insurer for the programme, the claimant had appointed loss adjusters, G&T, to assist it in the processing and evaluation of claims. G&T's functions included giving advice on the establishment of reserves for potential or outstanding claims. The claimant reinsured its liabilities with the defendant. Following substantial losses the defendant asserted that the reserving policy adopted by G&T was imprudent in that a reserve was recommended only where a loss was almost certain to occur, and that this policy was so unusual that it ought to have been disclosed to the defendant.

Held (C.A.): the defence failed. There was no material fact as market evidence showed that G&T's reserving policy was not so unusual as to require disclosure, and in particular did not constitute "stair stepping" once losses became certain. Clarke L.J. summarised the requirements for reserving thus:

"Generali was bound to make every effort to establish the full circumstances surrounding an event that had given rise to a claim. Having done so, it was incumbent on the Generali to set a reserve that properly represented its most likely financial exposure in the context of coverage provided by the policy(ies) and for that reserve to be fixed as soon as was reasonably practicable, including reserving for legal and associated expenses. The reserves were to be reviewed on a regular basis (including liaison with and obtaining regular updates from external advisers, such as loss adjusters and/or lawyers involved in actual or potential claims)."

Claims experience is perhaps the most important fact.

The amount of brokerage taken by the brokers from the direct premium may itself be material because non-disclosure or misrepresentation of an unusually high brokerage rate may give the impression that the direct risk is greater than the reinsurers have been led to believe. In *Markel International Insurance Company Ltd and another* v. *La Republica Compania Argentina de Seguros Generales SA* [2004] EWHC 1826 (Comm) the claimants were the reinsurers of Argentinian insurance companies in respect of medical malpractice risks written for an Argentinian association of doctors. The reinsurers alleged that they had been informed that the premium payable by the association would be approximately US$4.3 million per annum with a brokerage level of 27.5%. The premium paid by each doctor was on this basis stated to be US$4.30. In fact, the actual commission taken by the direct brokers was far greater so that the actual premium paid by doctors was US$9 per month. David Steel J. held that it was arguable that this was a material fact: had the reinsurers appreciated that doctors were willing to pay US$9 per month rather than the stated US$4.30, they might well have taken an entirely different approach to the rating of the risk.

Matters relating to the reinsured's broker may also be material. Phillips J. in *Deutsche Ruck* v. *Walbrook* [1995] 1 Lloyd's Rep. 153 was of the view that the fraud of the broker is not of itself a material fact simply because it goes to moral hazard. However, in *Markel International Insurance Company Ltd and another* v. *La Republica Compania Argentina de Seguros Generales SA* [2005] Lloyd's Rep. IR 90 David Steel J. held that the contrary proposition was arguable. In this case the reinsured's placing brokers informed the reinsurers that a key employee of the Argentinian placing brokers had had some minor problems in the London Market. In fact he had been required to leave the market following suspicions of fraud against him. David Steel J. held that the allegation of material misrepresentation in this regard was not one which should be regarded as unarguable by the reinsurers for the purpose of the grant of permission for service abroad, and that "as a matter of common sense, a dishonest broker, anxious to place a risk and thus earn his commission, may perhaps more readily misrepresent facts or suppress information".

***General Fire and Life Assurance Corporation* v. *Campbell* (1925) 21 Ll. L. Rep. 151**

The claimant was the underwriter of an accident insurance scheme operated by a national newspaper. Reinsurance was placed in layers. The first two layers covered the claimant's liability up to £50,000 and the defendant agreed to act as reinsurer for the third layer of £50,000 to £100,000 at a premium of £500. The claimant failed to disclose that the newspaper's losses were running in excess of £10,000 per month, so that the third layer would inevitably be penetrated.

Held (Branson J.): that the defendant was fully entitled to avoid the reinsurance for non-disclosure, and that had the true position been disclosed the reinsurer would have rejected the risk without a second thought.

***Aiken* v. *Stewart Wrightson Members Agency Ltd* [1995] 2 Lloyd's Rep. 618**

The claimants were members of Lloyd's Syndicates which had issued cover against asbestos liability in the United States. The claimants authorised their Lloyd's agents to obtain reinsurance cover for the years up to 1975 and this was obtained from a reinsuring Syndicate at Lloyd's. The reinsurers successfully avoided the reinsurance for non-disclosure of material facts, and the present action was brought by the claimants against their agents for negligence in placing the risk. A range of preliminary issues were considered by the court.

Held (Potter J.): that the defendants owed duties of care to the claimants in contract and in tort, and were in breach of that duty in that their presentation had justified the avoidance of the reinsurance on three separate grounds: the business was falsely described as short-tail when in fact it was long-tail cover for asbestos-related injuries; the number of lines to which the claimants' Syndicates had subscribed to was greater than had been stated; and the reinsured Syndicates had established block reserves for certain forms of liabilities, the existence of those reserves not being disclosed to the reinsurers so that the Syndicates' view of their own potential liabilities had been understated.

Immaterial facts

The cases have shown that a number of facts are immaterial to the risk run by the reinsurers and do not require to be disclosed in the absence of an express question.

(1) The identity of the direct assured is not material for reinsurance purposes if the risk is no different: see *Toomey* v. *Banco Vitalicio de Espana SA de Seguros y Reaseguros* [2004] Lloyd's Rep. IR 354, discussed above.

(2) It has also been held that the amount of the reinsured's retention is not a material fact. The retention serves the twin functions of eliminating the reinsurers' liability for small claims and providing a guarantee of the quality of the business underwritten. The view taken by the courts is that the former is more significant, and that the reinsured is free to seek separate reinsurance of its retention unless the policy otherwise expressly provides.

***Société Anonyme d'Intermediares Luxembourgeois* v. *Farex Gie* [1995] L.R.L.R. 116**

The reinsured chose to seek reinsurance for part of its retention without informing the primary reinsurers. The contract was silent on the point. The question was whether this was a material fact.

Held (Gatehouse J.): that the fact was not material and there was no obligation on the reinsured to disclose this fact unless it was expressly asked. Failure to ask a question of this type amounted to implicit waiver of the information.

There is earlier contrary authority (*Traill* v. *Baring* (1864) De G.J. & S.M. 318) although this case appears to have turned on a positive misstatement. The principle in *SAIL* v. *Farex* appears to be established. In *Great Atlantic Insurance Co.* v. *Home Insurance Co.* [1981] 2 Lloyd's Rep. 219 it was held that the statement that the reinsured would hold 10% of the risk "for its own account" did not amount to a promise that this would be retained by the reinsured, but meant simply that it was not for the account of the reinsurers. In *Kingscroft Insurance Co. Ltd* v. *Nissan Fire & Marine Insurance Co. Ltd (No. 2)* [1999] Lloyd's Rep. IR 603 the reinsured stated that it would retain 50 per cent of the risk: Moore-Bick J. held that this was not a promise and that it merely amounted to a statement of intention.

(3) If the reinsurer has sought retrocession cover, then any information which the reinsured has about the security of that cover is not a material fact, as it is for the reinsurer to determine this matter for itself and in any event the information possessed by the reinsured will be purely coincidental. This was so held by the Court of Appeal in *Société Anonyme d'Intermediares Luxembourgeois* v. *Farex Gie* [1995] L.R.L.R. 116. The position may be different if the contracts are interlinked and the reinsurers' subscription to the reinsurance agreement is conditional on the existence of valid retrocession.

***Hill* v. *Citadel Insurance Co. Ltd* [1997] L.R.L.R. 167**
The claimant syndicates were excess of loss reinsurers, and retroceded their liabilities to the two defendant companies. Both defendants were informed that there was excess of loss protection in place for them, the first defendant being told that the cost of protection was about 20% of the premium and the second defendant being told that the cost was very reasonable. In fact the cost of the excess of loss cover had risen to 40%, and the protection was less than had been indicated by reason of the fact that there were different inception dates.

Held (C.A.): that both defendants were entitled to avoid their subscriptions. The defendants had relied upon the statements concerning the excess of loss cover in agreeing to participate as retrocessionaires, and the facts misstated or withheld were material.

Facts which need not be disclosed

Section 18(3) of the Marine Insurance Act 1906 states that, in the absence of any express question posed by the insurers, four types of fact need not be disclosed:

(a) any circumstance which diminishes the risk;
(b) any circumstance which is known or presumed to be known to the insurer.
   The insurer is presumed to know matters of common notoriety or knowledge, and matters which an insurer in the ordinary course of his business, as such, ought to know;
(c) any circumstance as to which information is waived by the insurer;
(d) any circumstance which it is superfluous to disclose by reason of any express or implied warranty.

Any circumstance which diminishes the risk

Section 18(3)(a) of the 1906 Act removes the need for the assured to disclose facts which diminish the risk: but for this subsection such facts would be material as they are premium-sensitive. Thus if the insurers have agreed to underwrite a risk for a given premium, the assured does not have to disclose that he has installed extensive security measures to protect the insured subject matter. In *Decorum Investments Ltd* v. *Atkin, The Elena G* [2002] Lloyd's Rep. IR 450 David Steel J. rejected the insurers' argument that this fact was material as it demonstrated that the assured believed the insured vessel to be at risk.

Facts within the actual or presumed knowledge of the reinsurers

The duty of utmost good faith is not designed as a trap or test for the reinsured, but is concerned to ensure that the reinsurers have all material facts at their disposal. Thus, if the reinsurers are aware of facts then they cannot avoid the policy for their non-disclosure: see *Kingscroft Insurance Co.* v. *Nissan Fire & Marine Insurance Co. Ltd (No. 2)* [1999] Lloyd's Rep. IR 603 where reinsurers were held not to be able to rely upon non-disclosure of the fact that the reinsured had sought separate reinsurance cover for its retention, as they were subscribers to that separate cover and accordingly were aware of the fact. Equally if reinsurers ought to know of a fact—either because it is a matter of general knowledge or because it is a fact which would have come to them in the ordinary course of business—then disclosure is not required.

***British and Foreign Marine Insurance Co. Ltd* v. *Sturge* (1897) 2 Com. Cas. 244**

The claimant insurers insured a cargo of cotton to be carried from the USA to Liverpool, and reinsured their liability with the defendant reinsurer. In the reinsurance slip the cargo was described as being "on deck". The cargo had been damaged by exposure to sea water, and the reinsurer claimed the right to avoid the policy on the basis that it was a material fact that the cargo was damaged when the risk was placed.

Held (Mathew J.): that the reinsurer was liable. The reinsurer ought to have appreciated that the phrase "on deck" meant that the cotton would have been exposed to sea water and would have been damaged.

***North British Fishing Boat Insurance Co. Ltd* v. *Starr* (1922) 12 Ll. L. Rep. 206**

The claimant was the insurer of a motor vessel which had become a constructive total loss, and the defendant had reinsured the claimant's liability. The defendant argued that he had the right to avoid the policy for non-disclosure of the facts that: (a) there had been an unusually high number of losses of such boats in the previous year; (b) the previous reinsurer had refused to renew its coverage; and (c) the reinsured's premium rate for vessels of this type was higher than that charged by the reinsurer.

Held (Rowlatt J.): that the reinsurer did not have the right to avoid the policy. Points (b) and (c) were not material facts, as it was for the reinsurer to assess the risk for himself. As to point (a), the reinsurer as an underwriter of such risks ought to have been aware of the fact that the number of losses had increased, and it was not for the reinsured to investigate the matter and to provide that information to the reinsurer.

***Brotherton* v. *Aseguradora Colseguros (No. 3)* [2003] EWHC 1741 (Comm), [2003] Lloyd's Rep. IR 774**

The reinsurers of a bankers' blanket bond cover issued to a Colombian Bank, which included fidelity insurance, were not informed by the reinsured's brokers of reports circulating in the Colombian media that the President of the Bank was under suspicion of fraud and had been suspended from office. The reinsured argued that the reinsurers ought to have been aware of the media reports because the underwriter for the reinsurers regularly wrote business in the South American market, and also because the underwriter had used a Colombian company to carry out audits of the Bank.

Held (Morison J.): that the underwriter did not know and could not be expected to have known the facts in question.

(1) A London market underwriter was not in the same position as an underwriter operating in the Colombian market, even though the Colombian policy was simply a front for the reinsurance, and occasional visits were not enough to fix the London underwriter with the requisite knowledge.

(2) The audit firm used by the underwriter had not been employed to investigate the possibility of fraud in the Bank, and even if such fraud had been discovered by the firm then its discovery and disclosure would not have formed of its duties to the underwriter.

See also *London General Insurance Co. Ltd* v. *General Marine Underwriters Association Ltd* [1921] 1 K.B. 104, the facts of which were given above: it was here held that information as to a direct loss was not deemed to be known to reinsurers because, prior to their writing of the reinsurance risk, such information would have been of no interest to them.

Any circumstance the disclosure of which is waived by the reinsurers

Reinsurers can waive disclosure in a number of ways.

(1) By express policy term which relieves the reinsured of any duty of disclosure, either generally or in relation to particular information (see the "Truth of Statement" clause used in *HIH Casualty and General Insurance Ltd* v. *Chase Manhattan Bank* [2003] Lloyd's Rep. IR 230, discussed below, in the context of brokers).

(2) By failing to read documents presented by the reinsured or his brokers. In *Pan Atlantic Insurance Co.* v. *Pine Top Insurance Co.* [1994] 2 Lloyd's Rep. 527, the facts of which were given above, Lord Mustill held that the broker had, by deflecting the reinsurers' attention from the full details of the risk, failed to disclose material facts, but that the reinsurers had waived the information by failing to avail themselves of the opportunity to read the documents.

(3) By failing to ask further questions when they have been alerted by the reinsured's presentation that further material facts might exist. This principle cannot operate if the reinsurers could not reasonably have been alerted to this possibility by what has been said by the reinsured, and in particular there cannot be waiver if the reinsured's presentation appears on the face of things to be complete.

***WISE Underwriting Agency Ltd* v. *Grupo Nacional Provincial SA* [2004] Lloyd's Rep. IR 764**

The reinsurers were informed that goods which were the subject matter of the direct policy included jewellery, perfume and clocks. The reinsurers were also aware that the goods were to be sold by the assured in Cancun, Mexico, which was a high class tourist resort. The reinsurers were not, however, informed that the goods included Rolex watches, this being a material fact by reason of the value of such watches. The reinsured claimed that the reinsurers had waived disclosure by reason of being alerted to the possibility that the goods insured were valuable but failing to make further inquiries, given the nature of Cancun and the disclosure of the fact that the goods included clocks

Held (C.A., Rix L.J. dissenting): that the points alleged were insufficient to give rise to waiver. The majority view of Longmore and Peter Gibson L.JJ. was that it is necessary first to consider whether the presentation was unfair and then to ask the question whether there was waiver. Rix L.J. preferred an integrated approach under which the possibility of waiver itself formed a part of the wider question of whether the presentation was unfair.

(4) By asking limited questions. It may be assumed that if the reinsurer asks a question which is limited to specific matters, then they have waived disclosure of related matters. Authority for this proposition is found in direct motor cases where questions limited to specific motoring convictions were held to waive disclosure of other convictions (*Revell* v. *London General Insurance Co. Ltd* (1934) 50 Ll. L. Rep. 114; *Taylor* v. *Eagle Star Insurance Co. Ltd* (1940) 67 Ll. L. Rep. 136; *Doheny* v. *New India Assurance Co.* [2005] Lloyd's Rep. IR 251).

Circumstances covered by an express warranty

Where the reinsurers are discharged from liability in given circumstances, the existence of those circumstances need not be disclosed. In *Gan Insurance Co. Ltd* v. *Tai Ping Insurance Co. (No. 2)* [2001] Lloyd's Rep. IR 291 (reversed on other grounds [2001] I.R. 667) the assured had warranted the existence of fire precautions, and it was thus unnecessary for the assured to disclose that those precautions had not been put into place.

POST-CONTRACTUAL UTMOST GOOD FAITH

Duty of utmost good faith terminates when contract made

The general rule is that the reinsured's duty of utmost good faith comes to an end once the contract has been made. The materiality test refers to facts which are premium sensitive, so that once the contract has been made and the premium has been fixed there is no obligation on the reinsured to disclose any further information. On the same principle, a post-contractual misrepresentation does not give any right to avoid, although if it is made fraudulently or negligently the insurers may have a right to damages at common law in the unlikely event that loss can be shown to have flowed from the false statement.

***Sirius International Insurance Corporation* v. *Oriental Assurance Corporation* [1999] Lloyd's Rep. IR 345**

A reinsurance agreement covering the insurers of a building's contents was entered into. After the contract had been made, the reinsurers were shown a document which indicated that the building was protected by a sprinkler system. The statement was untrue as the sprinkler system did not work.

Held (Longmore J.): that as the false statement was made after the reinsurance agreement had been entered into, the duty of utmost good faith had ceased to operate and the reinsurers could not avoid the reinsurance.

***Bonner* v. *Cox Dedicated Corporate Member Ltd* [2006] Lloyd's Rep IR 385**

Reinsurers scratched a reinsurance slip in November 1998, in respect of a reinsurance to come into effect when accepted by underwriters who subscribed to a direct open cover in respect of energy risks. A material loss occurred in December 1998, and the reinsurers purported to avoid the reinsurance for non-disclosure of the loss.

Held (C.A.): that the duty of disclosure came to an end when the offer of reinsurance was accepted by the direct underwriters, and that this had occurred before the brokers had become aware of the loss and were able to disclose it.

Should the risk increase after the contract has been made, the reinsurers' protection is not the right to be informed of that fact (unless of course the contract so provides) but rather the common law principle that the contract is discharged if the risk agreed to be run becomes something quite different. Whether this is the case depends upon the proper interpretation of the reinsurance, and if the court finds that the risk has increased but in a fashion contemplated by the contract then its validity is unaffected.

***Law Guarantee Trust and Accident Society* v. *Munich Reinsurance Co.* [1912] 1 Ch. 138**

The claimant reinsured's business consisted of guaranteeing debts secured by charges or debentures. Its liabilities under the guarantees were reinsured with the defendant reinsurers. The claimant insured a debt secured by debentures issued by a company, R, and the risk was declared to the reinsurers. Subsequently R hit financial difficulties and entered into a scheme of arrangement under which the rate of interest on the debentures was reduced from 4.5% to 3%. The reinsurers argued that the risk had been discharged as the reduction in the rate of interest amounted to a material alteration in the risk.

Held (Warrington J.): that the reinsurers were not discharged from liability. The reinsurance treaty on its true interpretation anticipated that the risk might increase in this way and accordingly the reinsurers were not discharged when this occurred.

This case was followed by Lloyd J. in *Hadenfayre Ltd* v. *British National Insurance Ltd* [1984] 2 Lloyd's Rep. 393, a direct insurance case involving a floating policy.

Duty of utmost good faith in performance of contract

It was at one time believed that the assured/reinsured owed a generalised continuing duty of utmost good faith to the insurers/reinsurers. This belief arose primarily from the decision of Hirst J. in *Black King Shipping Ltd* v. *Massie, The Litsion Pride* [1985] 1 Lloyd's Rep. 437, where it was held that an assured was under a contractual obligation to provide information to the insurers then he was under a duty to disclose all material facts, i.e., facts which would affect the insurers' decision-making process in the administration of the policy. In that case Hirst J. ruled that an assured who made a claim for the loss of a vessel in a war zone was in breach of his continuing duty of utmost good faith in suppressing the fact that proper notice of the entry of the vessel into the war zone had not been given so that additional premium payable had been withheld, and that as a consequence the insurers had the option either of avoiding the policy *ab initio* or of rejecting the claim itself. The foundation of the decision was section 17 of the Marine Insurance Act 1906, which states in general terms that a contract of insurance is one of utmost good faith and does not purport to limit the duty to the pre-contractual position.

The scope of the continuing duty of utmost good faith has been restricted by a trio of subsequent decisions. In *The Star Sea* [2001] Lloyd's Rep. IR 247 insurers purported to avoid a marine policy by arguing that the assured had, in legal proceedings on the policy, failed to disclose documents which related to the pre-loss condition of the vessel. The House of Lords treated the case as one involving an alleged fraudulent claim, and held that the defence failed because it had not been shown that the assured had acted fraudulently and also because questions of disclosure during a trial were a matter for the court and not for the insurers. However, their Lordships considered the continuing duty of good faith and each of their Lordships expressed a view (albeit differently formed in each speech) deprecating the notion of a generalised post-contractual duty which could potentially result in avoidance *ab initio.* Lord Hobhouse overruled *The Litsion Pride* insofar as the decision was based on the notion of a fraudulent claim.

Matters were clarified by the Court of Appeal in two later cases, *K/S Merc-Skandia XXXXII* v. *Certain Lloyd's Underwriters, The Mercandian Continent* [2001] Lloyd's Rep. IR 802 and *Agapitos* v. *Agnew* [2002] Lloyd's Rep. IR 473. In *The Mercandian Continent* the assured had submitted a forged document to his liability insurers in an attempt to assist them in defending a claim brought against him by a third party. The Court of Appeal held that the insurers could not rely upon this fraud to defeat the claim or to avoid the policy. Longmore L.J., speaking for the Court of Appeal, held that the continuing duty of utmost good faith did not apply to fraudulent claims (as these were governed by the common law principle that an assured cannot benefit from his own wrong) at all, and extended only to those situations in which the assured was required to provide information to insurers. However, to ensure that the right to avoid a policy *ab initio*—the only remedy available for breach of the duty of good faith—was not available in circumstances where the lesser remedy of treating a policy as terminated for breach could not be relied upon, there would only be a breach of the continuing duty of utmost good faith where the assured's failure to disclose material facts amounted also to a repudiation of the insurance policy as a whole. Put another way, the right to avoid *ab initio* arises only as an alternative to the right to treat the policy as terminated for breach. In fact, as will be seen in a later Module, there are very few circumstances in which breach of an information provision amounts to repudiation, so it would seem that the continuing duty of utmost good faith has a very limited role to play.

In the last case in the series, *Agapitos* v. *Agnew*, the Court of Appeal confirmed that the continuing duty of utmost good faith did not apply to fraudulent claims, and that a policy could not be avoided *ab initio* in the event of a fraudulent claim by the assured.

Subscription placements

It was noted in the introductory chapter of this book that facultative reinsurance contracts are normally placed in the London market by use of the slip procedure. This entails the broker submitting the slip to a succession of underwriters for their subscription. In such a case the slip operates as an offer and every subscription to the slip operates as an acceptance in its own right, so that the slip will take effect as a series of parallel bilateral contracts between the reinsured and each subscribing reinsurer. As each contract is separate, a duty of utmost good faith is owed each time the slip is presented to a potential subscriber. A practical problem has arisen in that in many situations the risk is assessed by the leading (normally the first) underwriter, and the remaining underwriters are generally content to add their own names to the slip in reliance on the leading underwriter's judgment. Although the matter is not entirely free from doubt, the modern view is that the "following market" are entitled to rely upon the presentation made to the leading underwriter, so that if false statements have been made, or facts have not been disclosed, to him then the entire market can avoid the policy even though any falsities were confined to the presentation to the leading underwriter. The cases also make it clear that the reliance requirement is satisfied, as the following market is to be taken to have relied both on the presentation to the leading underwriter and the exercise of judgement by the leading underwriter (see *Aneco* v. *Johnson & Higgins* [1998] 1 Lloyd's Rep. 565; *International Lottery Management* v. *Dumas* [2001] Lloyd's Rep. IR 237; *International Management Group (UK) Ltd* v. *Simmonds* [2004] Lloyd's Rep. IR 247; *Brotherton* v. *Aseguradora Colseguros (No. 3)* [2003] Lloyd's Rep. IR 774).

Renewal

The renewal of a reinsurance agreement creates an entirely fresh contract to which the duty of utmost good faith is applicable. Thus, on an application for renewal, the reinsured must disclose to the reinsurers all material facts which have arisen during the currency of the earlier policy. Reinsurance treaties may be written on a long-term basis, e.g., for a period of three years, but subject to "Notice of Cancellation at Anniversary Date" (NCAD), and it is generally thought that this wording operates to confer upon the reinsurers the right to bring the cover to an end on each anniversary date. The reinsured will, therefore, be required to make a presentation of the risk to the reinsurers prior to the anniversary date, and although it is uncertain whether there is a duty to disclose material facts at that point it is clearly the case that if the reinsured makes any deliberate or negligent false statements the reinsurers would have an action in damages if avoidance is not legally permissible. In *Imperio Reinsurance Co. (UK) Ltd* v. *Iron Trades Mutual Insurance* (1991) 1 Re. L.R. 213, Hobhouse J. stated that a reinsured faced with a notice of cancellation under a continuing treaty was not obliged to say anything, but was merely required to avoid any misrepresentation.

Amendment of reinsurance agreement

Where the risks covered by a reinsurance agreement have been extended during the currency of the policy, the variation takes effect as a fresh contract in its own right. Thus, if the application for variation was accompanied by a material false statement or failure to disclose a material fact, the reinsurers have the right to avoid the extension to the cover but remain bound by the reinsurance agreement in its unamended form. This outcome follows from two principles: an endorsement takes effect as a fresh agreement; and there is no duty of utmost good faith during the currency of a policy, so that any misrepresentation or non-disclosure which relates to a renewal or to an extension does not affect existing cover: *K/S Merc-Skandia XXXXII* v. *Lloyd's Underwriters* [2001] 1 Lloyd's Rep. 563; *Groupama Insurance Co. Ltd* v. *Overseas Partners Re Ltd* [2003] EWHC 34 (Comm).

Treaties

The application of the doctrine of utmost good faith to reinsurance treaties is problematic. Reinsurance is effected under a treaty in two stages: the making of the treaty; and the making of declarations to the treaty. The treaty itself is not a contract of reinsurance, as it simply provides the framework for the making of declarations to the treaty, and accordingly it is a contract for reinsurance. If this is right it would appear that as a matter of strict law there is no duty of utmost good faith in relation to a treaty and the only obligation on the reinsured is not to misrepresent material facts in accordance with the general law on misrepresentation. It may be, however, that the distinction between contracts of reinsurance and contracts for reinsurance is unjustifiable. The argument that a treaty may be set aside for material non-disclosure is particularly powerful argument where the treaty is obligatory, i.e., the reinsurers must accept any risk which is accepted or declared by the reinsured, as in such a case the reinsurers plainly have no right to assess the premium in respect of any individual risk accepted by the reinsured. The decision of Scrutton J. in *Glasgow Assurance Corporation* v. *William Symondson & Co.* (1911) 27 T.L.R. 245 proceeded on the assumption that an obligatory open cover was subject to the duty of utmost good faith: the point did not, however, arise, as the fact withheld—that the cover holder was an insurer and not a broker so that the open cover provided reinsurance rather than insurance —was held not to be material.

Declarations or cessions to a reinsurance treaty take effect as contracts of reinsurance in their own right. If the treaty is obligatory there cannot in principle be any duty of utmost good faith in relation to any one declaration or cession, as reinsurers cannot refuse it and will simply receive the agreed proportion of premium. This approach was adopted by Eve J. in *Law Guarantee Trust and Accident Society Ltd* v. *Munich Reinsurance Co.* (1915) 31 T.L.R. 572 in relation to declarations to an obligatory treaty. The protection to reinsurers in such a case is conferred by the treaty itself, as any risk falling outside its terms will by definition fall outside the scope of the cover. In *Glencore International AG* v. *Ryan, The Beursgracht* [2002] 1 Lloyd's Rep. 574 it was held that the risk under an obligatory contract attached automatically as soon as the assured itself became bound, so that there was no need for any declaration to be made to the insurers even though the contract itself demanded notification of new risks. It follows from this analysis that there could not have been any duty of disclosure in respect of new risks.

By contrast, if the treaty is non-obligatory, so that the reinsurers can refuse individual declarations or cessions, then it is plainly the case that each declaration or cession is a contract of reinsurance to which the duty of utmost good faith applies. In *Société Anonyme d'Intermediares Luxembourgeois* v. *Farex Gie* [1995] L.R.L.R. 116 Gatehouse J. held that each declaration under a non-obligatory treaty was a distinct contract of reinsurance, so that if there was misrepresentation or non-disclosure in relation to a particular declaration then that declaration could be avoided but the treaty itself and other declarations made under it were unaffected and remained valid.

REMEDIES FOR BREACH OF DUTY

Avoidance

The only remedy for breach of the duty of utmost good faith is avoidance of the reinsurance agreement *ab initio*. The agreement is treated as if it had never existed, so that all outstanding losses are no longer payable, and any premium is returnable to the reinsured (other than in cases of fraudulent breach of duty—Marine Insurance Act 1906, s. 84). English law does not recognise any concept of proportionality, whereby the reinsured is able to recover that part of the loss represented by the premium actually paid, neither does English law permit the reinsured to tender the shortfall in premium and to recover the full amount of any loss.

Waiver of the right to avoid

Waiver by contract term

The right of reinsurers to avoid a contract of reinsurance for breach of the duty of utmost good faith may be waived by them. The reinsurers may state in the contract that they waive the right to avoid where there is a breach of duty: this form of waiver is discussed below in the context of brokers, where it is pointed out that it is not permissible for insurers to waive their rights in the event of fraud by the reinsured.

It was held by Steyn J. in *Highlands Insurance Co.* v. *Continental Insurance Co.* [1987] 1 Lloyd's Rep. 109 that an "errors and omissions" clause in a reinsurance agreement did not amount to a promise by the reinsurers to waive its rights of avoidance. The clause in that case provided that:

> *The insured hereunder is not to be prejudiced by an unintentional and/or inadvertent omission error incorrect valuation or incorrect description of the interest, risk or property, provided that notice is given to the Company as soon as practicable upon the discovery of any such error or omission.*

Steyn J. held that the language did not refer to a pre-contractual material misrepresentation, which otherwise would have entitled the reinsurers to avoid on the grounds of misrepresentation. The approach was followed by Waller J. in *Pan Atlantic* v. *Pine Top* [1992] 1 Lloyd's Rep. 101.

Waiver by representation or conduct

If the contract is silent on waiver then reinsurers can nevertheless lose their right to avoid by reason of their conduct after the loss has occurred.

Two forms of waiver are possible. The first is waiver by affirmation, where the reinsurers in full knowledge of material non-disclosure or misrepresentation make it clear to the reinsured by word or deed that they do not intend to rely upon their right to avoid. The second is waiver by estoppel, where the conduct of the reinsurers has induced the reinsured to believe that they do not intend to avoid the contract and the reinsured has acted accordingly. In practice there is very little difference between the requirements for waiver by affirmation and for waiver by estoppel. The reinsured has to show in every case that:

(a) the reinsurers knew that there had been a breach of the duty of utmost good faith and also of their right to avoid; and
(b) the reinsurers had by their statements or conduct led the reinsured to believe that they were aware of their legal rights but had no intention to rely upon them.

There are numerous cases on the acts by insurers and reinsurers which are sufficient to convey to the policy holder the belief that the right to avoid is not to be exercised.

First, the reinsurers may have defended legal proceedings by reference to a defence based on the coverage or terms of the policy in the knowledge that an utmost good faith defence might exist, and have attempted to rely upon utmost good faith at a late stage in the proceedings (*Moore Large & Co. Ltd* v. *Hermes Credit & Guarantee plc* [2003] Lloyd's Rep. IR 315). This case makes it clear that reinsurers cannot argue that they are not bound by the tactical decisions of their legal advisers.

Secondly, the reinsurers may have purported to exercise contractual rights. This is on the face of things inconsistent with the right to avoid, as avoidance denies that a contract ever existed. Thus a claim for unpaid premiums or for instalments of premiums would on the face of things appear to be a waiver of rights. The general principle is illustrated by *Drake Insurance plc* v. *Provident Insurance plc* [2004] Lloyd's Rep. IR 277, where the insurer, having purported to avoid a motor policy, failed to cancel a direct debit for premiums and generally acted inconsistently with the idea that the relationship had been terminated: there were indeed internal memoranda showing that a final decision had not been taken. The Court of Appeal held that this was more than administrative inefficiency, and that there had been a waiver of the right to avoid.

Imperio Reinsurance Co. (UK) Ltd **v.** ***Iron Trades Mutual Insurance*** **(1991) 1 Re. L.R. 213**

The claimant was the reinsured under two marine quota share reinsurances issued by the defendant. The defendant purported to avoid the treaties for non-disclosure and misrepresentation. After learning of the right to avoid, the defendant purported to exercise rights of inspection.

Held (Hobhouse J.): that there had not been any unfair presentation, but even if that was wrong then the right to avoid had been lost:

> "The insurer is under no obligation to elect to treat the contract as at an end within any particular length of time and accordingly delay, without more, does not deprive him of his right to do so. However, if he does some act in affirmation of the contract, that is to say, some act which is only consistent with an intention not to treat the contract as at an end, he will thereafter have lost his right to do so provided that he had actual knowledge of the facts which gave rise to that right . . . Invoking or asserting a contractual right is a clear example of electing not to treat the contract as at an end."

The learned judge emphasised that in such a case it is necessary for the reinsurer to reserve its rights while purporting to take advantage of contractual provisions.

In *Strive Shipping Corporation* v. *Hellenic Mutual War Risks Association, The Grecia Express* [2002] 2 Lloyd's Rep. 88 Colman J. distinguished *Imperio*, and held that if the insurers were simply trying to obtain information to determine whether or not to avoid then they should not be treated as having affirmed the policy.

Cancellation of the policy by agreement or under a contract term is not inconsistent with a later right to rely upon non-disclosure or misrepresentation, as it cannot be assumed that a decision to cancel amounted to a statement that if the cancellation was for some reason ineffective the insurers had waived other defences (*O'Kane* v. *Jones* [2004] 1 Lloyd's Rep. IR 389; *WISE Underwriting Agency Ltd* v. *Grupo Nacional Provincial SA* [2004] Lloyd's Rep. IR 764). In the *WISE* case the Court of Appeal held by a majority (Rix and Peter Gibson L.JJ., Longmore L.J. dissenting) that the reinsurers had given an oral notice of cancellation, thereby waiving the right to avoid: the existence of the notice was evidenced by e-mails subsequently sent by the reinsured to its brokers informing them of the position.

Restrictions on the right to avoid

A contract of reinsurance may be avoided in one of two ways: by the unilateral decision of the reinsurers which is notified to the reinsured; and by means of an application to the court for a declaration of the right to avoid. Each approach has the effect of avoiding the policy *ab initio*, although the latter is the more secure option for the reinsurers in that if the reinsurers simply inform the reinsured that they have avoided they be found to have repudiated the contract should a court rule in subsequent proceedings between the parties that the fact relied upon was not material or that there had been no inducement.

As noted earlier in this module, if it is the case that the reinsured has failed to disclose or has misstated a material fact and the reinsurers were thereby induced to enter into the agreement, then the right to avoid accrues at the date of the making of the contract. Unless the reinsurers have waived their rights by their actions, subsequent events cannot affect the reinsurers' accrued rights. The fact that the right accrues on placement is of some significance in the situation where the material fact withheld or misstated is one which has not been definitely established at that date, as is the case with intelligence which has not been substantiated or an accusation made against the assured the truth of which has yet to be established. In *Strive Shipping Corporation* v. *Hellenic Mutual War Risks Association, The Grecia Express* [2002] 2 Lloyd's Rep. 88, Colman J. suggested that the right to avoid might be lost if the facts, although material at the date of the contract, had in the light of subsequent events, shown not to have any foundation. In *Strive Shipping* the assured's vessel became a total loss in suspicious circumstances. The insurers asserted that she had been scuttled, and also purported to avoid the policy for the assured's failure to disclose that he had been interested in four other vessels each of which had been lost in circumstances which objectively raised doubts as to the assured's probity. At the trial Colman J. dismissed the scuttling accusation in respect of the insured vessel itself, and held that although the earlier losses were material facts the assured had the right at trial to adduce evidence to show each of those losses had a wholly innocent explanation. Such evidence was indeed adduced, and the assured was shown to have had no involvement in the losses. Colman J. held that in those circumstances the equitable principles which underlay the duty of utmost good faith permitted the court in its discretion to refuse to allow avoidance (even though the insurers had at an earlier stage validly avoided the policy). Colman J. also laid down the further principle (which was inapplicable on the facts) that if insurers were aware at the time of their purported avoidance that the material facts relied on by them had been undermined by subsequent events or information, then it would be a breach of the insurers' own duty of good faith to attempt to avoid.

The equitable argument was rejected by the Court of Appeal in a reinsurance case, *Brotherton* v. *Aseguradora Colseguros SA (No. 2)* [2003] Lloyd's Rep. IR 758. The President of the direct assured, a Colombian Bank, had in a series of media reports circulating in Colombia been accused of misappropriation of the assured's funds. The Colombian insurers of the Bank, who had issued a bankers' blanket bond cover which included fidelity insurance, failed to disclose the existence of the media reports to London market reinsurers, who avoided the reinsurance for non-disclosure. The reinsurers then sought a declaration that their avoidance had been proper. An application was made by the defendant insurers to admit evidence to show that the media reports had been unjustified and that the President of the assured Bank had been cleared of all serious charges. The Court of Appeal held that such evidence was not admissible. Avoidance was a self-help remedy which did not require either a court order or a court confirmation, and accordingly it was not open for the defendant insurers to bring evidence to the court to attempt to show that the underlying facts had after the avoidance been shown to be false. The Court of Appeal pointed out that the effect of *Strive Shipping* was to create a trial within a trial, where what was at stake was the truth of facts which had nothing to do with the insured risk itself but rather related to other matters: it was difficult to see why, if the assured was able to establish that the material facts had been undermined, the insurers should pay the costs of that process.

In *Brotherton (No. 3)* the second of Colman J.'s grounds in *Strive Shipping*—the insurers' own duty of utmost good faith—did not arise, as at the time of avoidance the reinsurers had not been aware of any suggestion that the media reports were untrue. However, the Court of Appeal doubted that Colman J. had been right on this point either. The only available remedy for breach of the duty of utmost good faith is avoidance, and it was difficult to see how avoidance could be of any assistance to the assured or reinsured. Further, as the courts had all but eliminated the post-contractual continuing duty of good faith imposed on the assured (see below), it would be incongruous to impose such a duty on insurers or reinsurers.

Colman J.'s continuing utmost good faith argument was, however, accepted by the Court of Appeal in *Drake Insurance plc* v. *Provident Insurance plc* [2004] Lloyd's Rep. IR 277, implicitly rejecting the contrary opinion expressed in *Brotherton (No. 2)*. *Drake* v. *Provident* was a road traffic case in which insurers purported to avoid a motor policy by relying on non-disclosure of a speeding conviction. The conviction, taken with an earlier accident involving the vehicle, would have triggered a premium increase under the insurers' underwriting criteria. Prior to avoidance the insurers became aware that the earlier accident had not been the fault of the assured, and accordingly that it should have been disregarded: on that basis, the speeding conviction would not have affected the writing of the risk as taken alone it would not have triggered a premium increase. At first instance ([2003] Lloyd's Rep. IR 793) Moore-Bick J. held that the insurers were nevertheless entitled to maintain their avoidance. The Court of Appeal disagreed. Its view was that insurers were subject to a good faith restriction on avoidance. The Court of Appeal was unanimous that it would be a breach of the duty of good faith for an insurer to avoid a policy when it actually knew that the facts relied upon—although material at the time—had been undermined. There was also unanimity that if the insurer had "blind eye" knowledge that this was the case, i.e., if the insurer deliberately shut its eyes to the true position and simply proceeded to avoid, then there would similarly be a breach of the continuing duty. However, Pill L.J. alone was prepared to go further and to say that "a failure to make any enquiry of the insured before taking the drastic step of avoiding the policy was . . . a breach by the insurer of the duty of good faith," and that on the facts that duty had been broken. Rix L.J. confined his support to the situation in which the insurer was on notice of a problem, whereas Clarke L.J. commented that at the present time there is "no authority for the proposition that an insurer owes the insured a duty to take reasonable care to make appropriate enquiries before avoiding the policy".

Damages

Breach of the duty of utmost good faith does not give rise to an action for damages: the only remedy is avoidance of the policy. Any right to damages rests upon ordinary principles of law. As the law does not recognise a duty of disclosure outside the insurance context, there can never be damages for a pure failure to disclose. However, damages are awardable against an assured who has deliberately misrepresented the position (in the tort of deceit—see *Derry* v. *Peek* (1889) 14 App. Cas. 337) or who has negligently misrepresented the position (either at common law under *Hedley Byrne & Co.* v. *Heller & Partners* [1964] A.C. 465 or by virtue of the Misrepresentation Act 1967). In either case damages would normally be awardable only where the reinsurers chose not to avoid the policy or were debarred from doing so.

Section 2(2) of the Misrepresentation Act 1967 provides a further possibility for damages. The section reads as follows:

> Where a person has entered into a contract after a misrepresentation has been made to him otherwise than fraudulently, and he would be entitled, by reason of the misrepresentation, to rescind the contract, then, if it is claimed, in any proceedings arising out of the contract, that the contract ought to be or has been rescinded, the court or arbitrator may declare the contract subsisting and award damages in lieu of rescission, if of opinion that it would be equitable to do so, having regard to the nature of the misrepresentation and the loss that would be caused by it if the contract

were upheld, as well as to the loss that rescission would cause to the other party.

In *Highlands Insurance Co.* v. *Continental Insurance Co.* [1987] 1 Lloyd's Rep. 109 Steyn J. held that it was inappropriate for a court to overturn an avoidance of a contract by declaring that the contract remained in existence and that the reinsurers were merely entitled to damages under section 2(2) of the 1967 Act. Steyn J. said that:

"Where a contract of reinsurance has been validly avoided on the grounds of a material misrepresentation, it is difficult to conceive of circumstances in which it would be equitable within the meaning of s. 2(2) to grant relief from such avoidance. Avoidance is the appropriate remedy for material misrepresentation in relation to marine and non-marine contracts of insurance . . . The rules governing material misrepresentation fulfil an important 'policing' function in ensuring that the brokers make a fair representation to underwriters. If s.2(2) were to be regarded as conferring a discretion to grant relief from avoidance on the grounds of material misrepresentation the efficacy of those rules will be eroded. This policy consideration must militate against granting relief under s.2(2) from an avoidance on the grounds of material misrepresentation in the case of commercial contracts of insurance."

REINSURANCE PLACED BY BROKERS

The broker's duty of utmost good faith

Disclosure by broker

Reinsurance contracts are in practice placed by brokers. It has been settled law for many years that the broker is, in the absence of special circumstances, to be regarded as the agent of the reinsured in the placement process. The duty of utmost good faith applies to a placement by a broker just as if the risk was placed directly by the reinsured, albeit in a slightly different way. First, section 19(b) of the Marine Insurance Act 1906 requires the broker to disclose "every material circumstance which the assured is bound to disclose, unless it came to his knowledge too late to communicate it to the agent", so that material facts known to the reinsured himself have to be disclosed by the broker. Therefore, if the reinsured has failed to disclose the relevant information to the broker, or if the broker has failed to pass it on to the reinsurer, the reinsurance agreement is voidable.

Secondly, section 19(a) of the Marine Insurance Act 1906 requires the broker to disclose "every material circumstance which is known to himself, and an agent to insure is deemed to know every circumstance which in the ordinary course of business ought to be known by, or to have been communicated to, him". This provision is independent of section 19(b) and creates a personal obligation on the broker to disclose material facts known to him, whether or not they were known to the reinsured. The duty is independent of that owed by the assured himself (see *HIH Casualty and General Insurance Ltd* v. *Chase Manhattan Bank* [2003] Lloyd's Rep. IR 230, below).

The nature of the broker's duty to disclose facts known to him is subject to two major uncertainties. The first is the meaning of the phrase "agent to insure" in section 19(a): there is some dispute as to whether this phrase applies only to the placing broker, or whether it applies also to an intermediate agent of the reinsured, including an underwriting agent or a producing broker. The second issue is the scope of the broker's duty to disclose: it is now settled that the reinsurer cannot avoid the policy simply because the broker has failed to disclose the fact (assuming this to be material) that he has defrauded the reinsured, although it is less certain whether the broker must disclose facts which have come to his knowledge other than in his capacity as a broker for the reinsured, e.g., from general market knowledge or indeed from private knowledge entirely divorced from his activities as a broker.

***PCW Syndicates* v. *PCW Reinsurers* [1996] 1 Lloyd's Rep. 241**

The claimants were members of Lloyd's syndicates which had reinsured their liabilities under Lloyd's policies with the defendant reinsurers. The reinsurance contracts were placed by brokers acting on the instructions of the claimant's underwriting agent for the Lloyd's Syndicates to which the claimants belonged. The reinsurers sought to avoid the reinsurance on the strength of allegations that the underwriting agent had defrauded the claimants and that this was a material fact which ought to have been disclosed by the underwriting agents.

Held (C.A.): that, on the assumption that the fraud was a material fact. The reinsurers had no right to avoid the policy.

(1) *Per* Saville L.J., Rose L.J. concurring: the duty to disclose under section 19(a) applied only to an "agent to insure", but that phrase applied only to the placing broker and not to any intermediate agent appointed by the reinsured. The reinsured's underwriting agent was not a person from whom the section required disclosure.

(2) *Per* Staughton L.J., Rose L.J. concurring: it was fanciful to believe that an agent would disclose his own fraud, and accordingly a reinsurer could not avoid a reinsurance agreement if an agent to insure (assuming that this phrase encompassed an intermediate agent such as an underwriting agent) failed to disclose that he had acted fraudulently towards the reinsured.

See also *Group Josi Re* v. *Walbrook Insurance Co. Ltd* [1996] 1 Lloyd's Rep. 345, which was argued at the same time as the *PCW* case. In *Group Josi* the reinsureds were members of a reinsurance pool the underwriting agent for which had allegedly defrauded the pool's members. The Court of Appeal more or less repeated the divergent reasoning adopted in *PCW*. See also *ERC Frankona* v. *American National Insurance Co.* [2006] Lloyd's Rep IR 157 discussed earlier.

***Société Anonyme d'Intermediares Luxembourgeois* v. *Farex Gie* [1995] L.R.L.R. 116**

The claimant SAIL wished to reinsure its liabilities, and appointed brokers HF to place cover for them. HF were able to obtain the agreement of SP to act as retrocessionaires if a reinsurer could be found, and HF in due course were able to place the reinsurance risk with the defendants, FG. The retrocession agreement entered into by SP proved to be void, as it had been agreed to by an unauthorised agent, and FG (which as a result had no retrocession cover) purported to avoid the reinsurance on the ground that HF should have disclosed to FG the fact that the retrocession was of no effect.

Held (C.A.): There had been no failure to disclose on the part of HF, as they had not been aware of the fact that entry into the retrocession agreement had not been authorised by SP and thus could not have disclosed it. However, even if HF had been aware of that fact, the information would not have fallen to be disclosed within section 19(a) of the Marine Insurance Act 1906 because: (a) there would have been fraud by HF, which was not on general principle something which a reinsurer could expect to be disclosed to him; and (b) the fact was not material either because as it was one which FG ought to have ascertained for itself or because the fact related to an entirely different contract which had nothing to do with the placing of the reinsurance.

Failure by the broker to comply with the duty of utmost good faith imposed upon him by section 19 of the 1906 Act entitles the reinsurer to avoid the policy in the usual way. The reinsurer may, however, choose not to avoid the policy, or may be precluded by a waiver clause from doing so. In that situation the broker cannot be sued for damages, as the duty of utmost good faith itself does not give a cause of action in damages (*La Banque Financiere de la Cite SA* v. *Westgate Insurance Co. Ltd* [1988] 2 Lloyd's Rep. 513).

Misrepresentation by broker

Where a broker makes a false statement to reinsurers—irrespective of whether the statement was innocently made, or made negligently or fraudulently—then the policy is voidable at the instance of the reinsurers. However, if the reinsurers are unable to avoid or choose not to do so, then the broker faces potential liability in damages. The common law rules on damages are the same as in respect of misrepresentation by the reinsured:

- There is no liability in damages at common law for innocent misrepresentation.
- If the broker's misrepresentation has been negligent, then there will be a cause of action for damages under section 2(1) of the Misrepresentation Act 1967 or under the ordinary negligence principle in *Hedley Byrne & Co.* v. *Heller & Partners* [1964] A.C. 465.
- If the broker has fraudulently misstated a material fact then he will face liability in the tort of deceit, under the ordinary rule in *Derry* v. *Peek* (1889) 14 App. Cas. 337.

Exclusion of liability in respect of broker's presentation of risk

In some circumstances it may be appropriate for reinsurance agreements to modify the reinsured's strict duty of utmost good faith. This is in recognition of the fact that the risk is commonly placed by a broker who may have been responsible for the organisation of the entire chain of placements from direct policy up to the highest level of reinsurance or retrocession. Further, the business itself may have been devised by the broker, or the reinsured may be little more than a fronting company for reinsurers. In these circumstances the reinsurance agreement may attempt to reassign to the reinsurers in full or in part the risk of non-disclosure or misrepresentation on the part of the broker.

This may be done by deeming the broker to be the agent of the reinsurers or removing from the broker the authority to speak on behalf of the reinsured. The term in question may be more limited, and may restrict any disclosure obligation to the broker, so that the reinsured is under no personal duty of disclosure, or eliminate the reinsurers' right to avoid the policy following non-disclosure or misrepresentation by the reinsured or the broker. The most important case to consider an exclusion clause is that of the House of Lords in the *HIH* case.

***HIH Casualty and General Insurance Ltd* v. *Chase Manhattan Bank* [2003] Lloyd's Rep. IR 230**

The case concerned a direct insurance policy—time variable cover—issued to the Bank by HIH. The Bank had financed a film production company and had insured against the inability of the company to repay the loans on a given day. TVC insurance had been developed and sold by London brokers Heaths since 1992 and enabled the financing arrangements in question to proceed. The risk was negotiated and presented to HIH by Heaths, and the Bank had no part to play at all. Substantial losses arose, and HIH purported to avoid the policy on the ground of a series of misrepresentations and non-disclosures concerning the nature and extent of the risk. The preliminary issues before the House of Lords concerned the correct interepretation of a "Truth of Statement" Clause which provided that:

> *6. . . . [the Insured] will not have any duty or obligation to make any representation, warranty or disclosure of any nature, express or implied (such duty and obligation being expressly waived by the insurers), and . . .*
> *7. . . . [the Insured] shall have no liability of any nature to the insurers for any information provided by any other parties and any such information provided by or non-disclosure by other parties including, but not limited to [Heaths] (other than Section I of the Questionnaire) . . .*
> *8. . . . and any such information provided by or non-disclosure by other parties including, but not limited to [Heaths] (other than Section 1 of the Questionnaire) shall not be a ground or grounds for avoidance of the insurers' obligations under the Policy or the cancellation thereof.*

Held (H.L.) that:

(1) Heaths' duty of disclosure under section 19 of the Marine Insurance Act 1906 was wholly independent from that imposed upon the Bank. Accordingly, where the Truth of Statement clause sought to relieve "the Insured" from its obligations the clause did not extend to Heaths' own duty of disclosure.

(2) The Truth of Statement clause did not operate to remove from Heaths the authority to speak on behalf of the Bank.

(3) Paragraph 6 of the Clause merely recognised that Heaths alone would be negotiating with HIH, and purported to relieve the Bank from its own obligation to make disclosure. It did not relieve Heaths from its independent obligation to disclose material facts.

(4) Paragraph 7 of the Clause relieved the Bank from any claim for damages as a consequence of negligent non-disclosure and misrepresentation by itself or by Heaths, and this was so even though the word "negligence" had not been used in the clause. It was not possible as a matter of public policy for the Clause to entitle the Bank to be granted relief from the consequences of its own fraud. Their Lordships were divided as to whether the Clause could as a matter of law protect the Bank against the fraud of

Heaths: Lord Hobhouse thought that this was not possible; Lord Scott thought that it was possible and that the words used were sufficient to achieve that objective; the remainder of their Lordships simply held that even if it was possible to exclude liability for the fraud of a broker the Clause in question had not done so.

(5) Paragraph 8 of the Clause prevented the insurers from avoiding the contract in the case of misrepresentation or non-disclosure by the Bank itself or by Heaths, whether innocent or negligent. As per point (4) their Lordships were divided on the fraud issue.

THE REINSURERS' DUTY OF UTMOST GOOD FAITH

The duty of utmost good faith as expressed in section 17 of the Marine Insurance Act 1906 is a mutual one, so that the reinsurers owe a duty of good faith to the reinsured. The duty is of limited value, however, as the only remedy for breach is avoidance *ab initio*. Accordingly, it can only be in the very rare situation in which the reinsured wishes to avoid the policy because it is unnecessary or because it does not meet his needs that the duty will become relevant: once a loss has occurred, the last thing that the reinsured will want to do is to avoid the policy. In *La Banque Financiere de la Cite SA* v. *Westgate Insurance Co. Ltd* [1990] 2 Lloyd's Rep. 377 the House of Lords recognised that insurers did owe a duty of utmost good faith to the assured, and that this extended to disclosing facts material to the recovery of a claim, but that the only remedy was avoidance.

It has also been recognised that there may be a post-contractual duty of utmost good faith owed by reinsurers. Although the duty has yet to be properly formulated, it may be that it consists of an obligation to act fairly in handling claims and in particular not to avoid the policy where it would be inequitable to do so. There are comments of Longmore L.J. supporting the former proposition in *K/S Merc-Skandia XXXXII* v. *Certain Lloyd's Underwriters* [2001] Lloyd's Rep. IR 802 (although these were implicitly doubted by Mance L.J. in *Gan Insurance Co.* v. *Tai Ping Insurance Co. (No. 2)* [2001] Lloyd's Rep. IR 667) and the latter proposition is supported by *Drake Insurance* v. *Provident Insurance* [2004] Lloyd's Rep. IR 277 (not following the views of the Court of Appeal expressed shortly beforehand in *Brotherton* v. *Aseguradora Colseguros (No. 2)* [2003] Lloyd's Rep. IR 758). If these views are correct, the remedy is not avoidance but rather a restriction on the reinsurers exercising their ordinary rights.

TEST YOUR UNDERSTANDING

1. Which of the following statements are correct?

(a) the reinsured must disclose all material facts whether or not he is aware of them,

(b) the reinsured must disclose all material facts which he ought to have discovered by making inquiries,
(c) the reinsured must disclose all material facts which he knew or which he turned a blind eye to,
(d) the reinsured must disclose all material facts known to his agents.

2. Which of the following statements are correct?

(a) any material false statement made by the reinsured is a breach of the duty of utmost good faith,
(b) a material false statement made by the reinsured is a breach of the duty of utmost good faith only if the reinsured acted fraudulently or negligently in misstating the fact,
(c) a material false statement made by the reinsured is a breach of the duty of utmost good faith only if the reinsured was aware that the fact was material,
(d) non-disclosure of a material fact by the reinsured is a breach of the duty of utmost good faith only if the reinsured was aware that the fact withheld was material.

3. In which of the following circumstances is a fact material?

(a) it was regarded as material by the reinsurers involved,
(b) it would have been regarded as material by a prudent reinsurer,
(c) it was regarded as material by the reinsured involved,
(d) it would have been regarded as material by a prudent reinsured.

4. Which of the following must be shown to give rise to inducement?

(a) the reinsurers must show that they would have wanted further information before writing the risk,
(b) the reinsurers must show that the risk would on the balance of probabilities have been written on different terms, or not at all, had full disclosure been made,
(c) the reinsurers are, by reason of a presumption of inducement, always entitled to rely upon proof of materiality as evidencing inducement,
(c) the reinsurers can rely upon the presumption of inducement only if they are unable to give their own evidence on inducement.

5. Which of the following facts are material for reinsurance purposes?

(a) the amount of retention held by the reinsured,
(b) the reinsured's claims experience,

(c) rumours that events giving rise to possible losses have occurred,
(d) the dishonesty of the assured.

6. Which of the following statements are true?

(a) a fact need not be disclosed if it was known to the reinsurers,
(b) a fact need not be disclosed if it ought to have been known to the reinsurers in the ordinary course of their business,
(c) a fact need not be disclosed if the reinsurers could have discovered it on making reasonable inquiries,
(d) a fact need not be disclosed if the reinsurers have failed to ask any questions relating to it.

7. Which of the following statements describes the reinsured's post-contractual duty of utmost good faith?

(a) the reinsured is never required to disclose facts after the contract has been entered into,
(b) the reinsured is required to disclose facts after the contract has been entered into only if there is a contractual obligation to provide information,
(c) the reinsurers may avoid the policy if there is a breach of the continuing duty,
(d) the obligation not to make fraudulent claims forms a part of the continuing duty.

8. Which of the following statements concerning the reinsurers' remedies for breach of the duty of utmost good faith are correct?

(a) the reinsurers can avoid the policy,
(b) the reinsurers can claim damages,
(c) the reinsurers are entitled to rely upon breach of duty even though at the time of avoidance they are aware that the facts have proved to be immaterial,
(d) the right to avoid will be lost if the reinsurers insist upon the reinsured adhering to the claims procedure without reserving their rights.

9. The reinsurers are entitled to avoid the contract for non-disclosure by the reinsured's brokers in which of the following circumstances?

(a) the facts were not known to the broker but were known to the reinsured,
(b) the facts were known to the reinsured's producing broker but not to the reinsured's placing broker,

(c) the facts were known to the reinsured's placing broker and were derived from his relationship with the reinsured,
(d) the facts were known to the reinsured's placing broker but were derived from general market knowledge.

10. The reinsurers are free by contract term to waive their rights under the duty of utmost good faith in which of the following circumstances?

(a) innocent or negligent failure by the reinsured to disclose material facts,
(b) innocent or negligent failure by the reinsured's broker to disclose material facts,
(c) fraudulent failure by the reinsured to disclose material facts,
(d) fraudulent failure by the reinsured's broker to disclose material facts.

CHAPTER 4

TERMS OF REINSURANCE AGREEMENTS

EXPRESS AND IMPLIED TERMS IN REINSURANCE AGREEMENTS

Express terms

The terms of a reinsurance agreement depend upon its nature. A reinsurance treaty may be a lengthy and complex document or it may be relatively short. It is to a large extent administrative, setting out the method of calculating losses and premiums and the information to be provided by the reinsured to the reinsurers at various times. It will also usually contain some provision authorising the reinsurers to inspect the reinsured's books and records. A facultative reinsurance agreement made in the London market is likely to be a very short document—often expressed as a "slip policy" (see Chapter 2)—which incorporates at least some of the terms of the direct policy by means of the "full reinsurance" clause (one version of which is "warranted same gross rate, terms and conditions as original and to follow the settlements"), and which lays down terms for the regulation of claims.

Implied terms

The position here is much the same as in the general law. A term will be implied into a reinsurance agreement only where such implication is necessary to give business efficacy to the agreement or where there is established custom and practice known to and accepted by the market as a whole. There have been numerous attempts to argue for the implication of terms into reinsurance agreements, but on the whole such attempts have been unsuccessful as it has not been shown either that the term was necessary to make sense of the contract, or that the market assumed that the relevant clause would be incorporated. The courts have regularly pointed out that they will not imply a term which could readily have been expressly agreed to by the parties without judicial assistance.

***Baker* v. *Black Sea and Baltic General Insurance Co. Ltd* [1998] Lloyd's Rep. IR 327**

The defendant was the reinsurer of Lloyd's underwriters represented by the claimant, under a policy of reinsurance covering the claimant's liability for, amongst other things, US asbestos claims. The reinsurance was in the form of a surplus treaty which contained an obligation on the defendant to "follow the settlements and agreements" of the claimant. A dispute arose as to whether the defendant was liable to indemnify the claimant for costs incurred by the claimant in investigating or defending claims by policy holders. In the lower courts the claimant argued that the defendant was liable for such costs by reason of: (1) the operation of the follow the settlements clause; (2) an implied term based on business efficacy; and (3) an implied term based on the custom of the market. In the House of Lords ground (1) was abandoned and the case proceeded purely on the implied terms.

Held (H.L.): (1) There was no implied term based on business efficacy, as the weight of authority was against the implication of such a term.

(2) As to the implied term based on custom, it was necessary to remit the case to the High Court so that market evidence could be adduced as to the possible existence of the alleged term. [*Note*: No such application was ever made because of the supervening provisional liquidation of Black Sea & Baltic. This case was followed in *Wasa International Insurance Co. Ltd and AGF Insurance Co. Ltd* v. *Lexington Insurance Co.* [2007] EWHC 896 (Comm).]

***Phoenix General Insurance Co. of Greece* v. *Halvanon Insurance* [1985] 2 Lloyd's Rep. 599**

The reinsurance agreement in this case was a facultative obligatory treaty. The reinsured was required to retain a proportion of the risk for its own account, although no figure had been agreed. The reinsured in the event did not retain any of the risk, and the reinsurers asserted that the reinsured was in breach of an implied obligation to retain a reasonable proportion of the risk. Hobhouse J. held that there was no implied term to this effect, as there was nothing inconsistent with a contract of reinsurance for the reinsured to reinsure 100% of its liability. The business efficacy test did not, therefore, operate to imply a term into the agreement. In so deciding Hobhouse J. set out his views of the terms which were to be implied into a facultative obligatory agreement for the protection of the reinsurers. The generally accepted view of both those in the market and lawyers is that the terms set out by Hobhouse J. are to be implied into all obligatory treaties:

"It was a term of the . . . contracts implied . . . so as to give the same commercial effect that the plaintiffs would conduct their business in accordance with the ordinary practice of the market and exercise due care and skill in the conduct of all business carried on under the . . . contracts or alternatively that the plaintiffs would act as prudent reinsureds for this purpose. Those duties require the plaintiffs inter alia to:

(a) keep full and proper records and accounts of all risks accepted or premiums received and receivable and all claims made or notified;
(b) investigate all claims and confirm that they fell within the terms of the contract and were properly payable before accepting them;
(c) properly investigate risks offered to them before acceptance and closings relating thereto subsequently;
(d) keep full and proper accurate accounts showing at all times the amounts due and payable by the plaintiffs to the defendants and by the defendants to the plaintiffs under the contracts;
(e) ensure that all amounts owing to them were collected promptly when due and entered forthwith in their accounts, and all balances owing to the defendants were likewise paid promptly when due;
(f) obtain, file or otherwise keep in a proper manner, all accounting claims and other documents and records and make these reasonably available to the defendants."

This decision was at one time widely accepted as applying to obligatory contracts as well as to facultative obligatory contracts. *Phoenix* v. *Halvanon* has, however, recently been doubted by Morison J. and the Court of Appeal in *Bonner* v. *Cox Dedicated Corporate Member Ltd* [2006] Lloyd's Rep IR 385.

***Bonner* v. *Cox Dedicated Corporate Member Ltd* [2006] Lloyd's Rep IR 385**

The claimants were Lloyd's Syndicates whose business included writing risks in the energy market. They subscribed to an Open Cover for the 1999 year, operated by Aon. Under the Cover the subscribers agreed to be bound by risks accepted by the leading underwriter. The 1999 year was reinsured by two reinsurers. A number of disputes arose between the reinsureds and the reinsurers. The relevant issue for present purposes was the assertion of the reinsurers that the subscribers to the Cover had engaged in "writing against" the reinsurance, ie, they had written on the basis that reinsurance was in existence so that there was no need to observe prudent standards of underwriting. Morison J. in an important passage in his judgment rejected the notion that the reinsured under an excess of loss contract owes any duty of care or continuing duty of good faith to the reinsurers, and that the obligations of the reinsured were limited to implied terms in respect of: (a) exercising some judgment in the acceptance of risks (even if that judgment was misconceived); (b) acting honestly; and (c) accepting risks which were not intended to fall within the terms of the reinsurance (although this matter was often one of pre-contract disclosure). There were no further obligations, and the notion that "writing against" reinsurance was a breach of duty was misconceived as the very essence of reinsurance was that this would occur. In so deciding, Morison J. distinguished proportional from non-proportional reinsurance, although he did cast some doubt on the notion that even a reinsured under a proportional contract might owe various implied duties to the reinsurers (as held in by Hobhouse J. in *Phoenix* v. *Halvanon* [1985] 2 Lloyd's Rep. 599). The Court of Appeal agreed with Morison J. on this matter. The Court of Appeal was of the view that *Phoenix* was concerned with a facultative obligatory quota share agreement, a contract which contemplated a sharing of risk. The present case, by contrast, was excess of loss which did not involve any sharing and no payment to the reinsured for writing it. The Court of Appeal held that the implied terms in *Halvanon* did not operate in respect of excess of loss reinsurance, and that any such implication was inconsistent with section 55(2)(a) of the Marine Insurance Act 1906 under which a policyholder can recover even though he has been negligent: the touchstone of any possible defence would have to be recklessness. The Court of Appeal went on to reject Morison J.'s more limited implied terms. The Court of Appeal further noted that if there were implied terms binding the reinsured then the reinsurers might be subject to similar terms in respect of any retrocession, and that point aside there would be complex issues in deciding how damages might be assessed for the breach of the duties. Its conclusion was that there were no implied terms in non-proportional reinsurance, although the Court of Appeal did not take the further step of overruling *Phoenix* because that case was concerned with proportional reinsurance. At present, therefore, the law is different as between proportional and non-proportional reinsurance. The Court of Appeal added that on the facts there was no breach of any implied duty in any event.

A term may not be implied if it runs contrary to what has actually been agreed by the parties. It was thus held in *GE Reinsurance Corporation* v. *New Hampshire Insurance Co.* [2004] Lloyd's Rep. IR 404 (see the full discussion below) that there was no implied term in a reinsurance agreement that the reinsurers would not rely upon a defence set out in the reinsurance agreement which was unavailable to the reinsured as against the direct policy holder.

INCORPORATION AND THE "FULL REINSURANCE" CLAUSE

The concept of incorporation

Wordings

The modern wording, the "full reinsurance" clause, is typically in the following form:

> *Being a reinsurance of and warranted same gross rate, terms and conditions as and to follow the settlements of the company . . . and to follow the settlements*

This replaced the earlier formulation:

> *Subject to the same terms and conditions as the original and to pay as may be paid thereon.*

Although there is much authority, in the context of the incorporation of the terms of first layer direct policies into excess layer direct policies, that the phrase "warranted same gross rate, terms and conditions" created a warranty that the terms of the first layer policy were consistent with the assured's representations (*Barnard* v. *Faber* [1893] 1 Q.B. 340; *Walker & Sons* v. *Uzielli* (1896) 1 Com. Cas. 492; *Bancroft* v. *Heath* (1901) 17 T.L.R. 425), the view now accepted is that the word "warranted" does not have the effect of creating a warranty of any kind. Instead, the words simply incorporate the terms of one policy into the other.

The leading authority on this point is *Forsakrings Vesta* v. *Butcher* [1989] 1 A.C. 852, the facts of which are given below. Here, the House of Lords held by a 4:1 majority that the full reinsurance clause operated to incorporate into the reinsurance agreement the terms of the direct policy. Only Lord Griffiths objected to this interpretation, reverting to the original meaning of the phrase as giving rise to a warranty that the terms of the direct policy were as represented to the reinsurers. The conflict of opinion was considered by Andrew Smith J. in *Toomey* v. *Banco Vitalicio de Espana SA de Seguros y Reaseguros* [2004] Lloyd's Rep. IR 354, where reinsurers argued that the reinsured had warranted that the direct policy issued by them in the sum of 2.9 billion pesetas was an unvalued policy with the sum insured fixing the maximum amount recoverable by the policyholder (a Spanish football club, which had insured against the risk of relegation from the Spanish First Division). In fact the policy was a valued policy so that the sum insured was payable whether or not the actual loss had reached that figure. Andrew Smith J. adopted the majority approach in *Vesta* and rejected that of Lord Griffiths, and held that the "as original" wording did not create a warranty to the effect that the terms of the direct policy conformed to what the reinsurers had been told. Andrew Smith J. nevertheless found that there had been an express warranty on this point as well as a material misrepresentation. On appeal to the Court of

Appeal, [2004] EWCA Civ 622, the trial judge's rulings on utmost good faith and the express warranty were upheld, but Thomas L.J., speaking for the Court of Appeal on this point, specifically refused to consider the effect of the "as original" wording and ruled that the matter should not be resolved without full argument. This case is considered in more detail in Chapter 5. In *Prifti* v. *Musini Sociedad Anonima De Seguros y Reaseguros*, [2004] Lloyd's Rep. IR 528, decided before the *Toomey* case had gone to the Court of Appeal, Andrew Smith J. repeated his view that the "as original" wording did not create any warranties. This case is discussed below.

Conditions for successful incorporation

Although the full reinsurance clause is general in its phraseology, it is apparent that not every provision of the direct policy can be incorporated into the reinsurance agreement. There may be issues of inconsistency, repugnancy and inappropriateness when a term from the direct policy is transported to the reinsurance agreement. The conditions which have to be satisfied before a term may be regarded as successfully incorporated were laid down by David Steel J. in *HIH Casualty and General Insurance Ltd* v. *New Hampshire Insurance Co.* [2001] Lloyd's Rep. IR 224 and adopted without comment by the Court of Appeal in the same case, [2001] Lloyd's Rep. IR 596. The conditions are that:

(i) The term is germane to the reinsurance.
(ii) The term makes sense, subject to permissible "manipulation", in the context of reinsurance.
(iii) The term is consistent with the express terms of the reinsurance.
(iv) The term is apposite for inclusion in the reinsurance.

Point (iii) recognises the fact that a term contained in a direct policy may refer to the "insurers" and the "assured", whereas if the term is to make sense in the reinsurance contract the words will have to be manipulated gently to read "reinsurers" and "reinsured".

One further point should be noted. If there is to be successful incorporation, it has to be shown that the clause which is allegedly incorporated formed a part of the underlying contract at the time the subsequent contract was entered into. The courts will not presume an intention on the parties to a reinsurance agreement that they have agreed to accept terms which are inserted into the underlying insurance at a later date unless there is some form of statement to that effect. This may cause difficulties in practice, as it is often the case that the underlying wording has not been agreed at the outset and is to be agreed at some later point by the leading direct underwriter. For a case of this type see *Excess Insurance Co. Ltd* v. *Mander* [1995] L.R.L.R. 359, *Cigna Life Insurance Co. of Europe SA-NV & Others* v. *Intercaser SA de Seguros y Reaseguros* [2001] Lloyd's Rep. IR 821 and *American International Speciality Lines Insurance Co.*

v. *Abbott Laboratories,* [2004] Lloyd's Rep. IR 815, discussed below in the context of arbitration.

Consequences of incorporation

Assuming that a term is incorporated from a direct policy into the reinsurance, there are two possible consequences of such incorporation.

(1) The terms of the direct policy are included in the reinsurance agreement and take effect as a part of the reinsurance agreement itself. The relationship between the reinsured and the reinsurers is thus governed by the incorporated terms. In such a case, the "manipulation" of language referred to in the previous paragraph may be necessary to make the incorporated term fit its context.

(2) The terms of the direct policy do not form a part of the reinsurance agreement so as to change the relationship between the reinsured and the reinsurers. Instead, the incorporated terms operate as a statement of the circumstances in which the reinsured will face liability, i.e., they delimit the risk accepted by the reinsured. By incorporating the terms into the reinsurance agreement, the reinsurers thereby acknowledge that they will indemnify the reinsured if the reinsured faces liability to the assured. Where this type of incorporation is at stake, there is no need to manipulate the wording of the incorporated clause as it makes perfect sense as it stands.

This distinction was drawn for the first time by Rix L.J. in *HIH* v. *New Hampshire*.

***HIH Casualty and General Insurance Ltd* v. *New Hampshire Insurance Co.* [2001] Lloyd's Rep. IR 596**

The direct policies were issued to financial institutions who had invested in film production companies. Under the policies, in the event that the production companies were unable to repay the loans from the financial institutions on a given day, the insurer was to make good the shortfall. The direct policies contained a waiver of rights clause which stated that the insurer would not avoid or rescind the policy or reject any claim on the ground of misrepresentation or non-disclosure by the assureds' named brokers. The insurer reinsured with reinsurers under an agreement stated to be "as original". It was alleged by the reinsurers that false statements had been made to them by the reinsured's brokers and the reinsurers purported to avoid the policy. The reinsured argued that the waiver of rights clause had been incorporated into the reinsurance, and took effect as a waiver of rights between the reinsurers and the reinsured after its wording had been manipulated to fit the reinsurance context.

Held (C.A.): that the waiver of rights clause did not protect the reinsured.

(1) It was the case that the waiver of rights clause had been incorporated into the reinsurance: it was germane to reinsurance; it could be given meaningful content at the reinsurance level; there was nothing inconsistent with the clause in the reinsurance agreement itself; and the clause was apposite at the reinsurance level.

(2) The fact that the waiver of rights clause was unusual in its ambit did not preclude incorporation. The clause was not so extensive as to be unknown or unconscionable.

(3) The waiver of rights clause was to be regarded as incorporated in its unmanipulated form. At the direct level the clause precluded the reinsured from avoiding the insurance for non-disclosure or misrepresentation by the assureds, and the incorporation of the clause into the reinsurance served to inform the reinsurers that the reinsured had not utmost good faith defence against the assureds. The reinsurers were, therefore, agreeing to indemnify the reinsured in the event that the reinsured had to make payment to the assureds even though there had been breach of the duty of utmost good faith by the assureds.

(4) The waiver of rights clause was not incorporated in its manipulated form. It did not affect the relationship between the reinsured and the reinsurers, so the reinsurers were not precluded from avoiding the policy in the event of breach of the duty of utmost good faith on the part of the reinsured. This was so for two reasons:

(a) the waiver of rights clause identified by name the assureds' brokers—it was not possible on linguistic grounds to manipulate a clause which actually identified the persons whose breaches of duty were waived;

(b) if the waiver of rights clause had been incorporated in manipulated form it would have prevented avoidance by the reinsurers for breaches of the duty of utmost good faith entirely unconnected with the direct risk, and thus would not have allowed the insurance and reinsurance to operate on a back to back basis.

Incorporation of coverage

The primary purpose of the full reinsurance clause, as that purpose is now understood, is to incorporate into the reinsurance the cover provided by the direct policy. It is unclear from the early decisions on coverage whether they were based on incorporation or the overlapping notion of providing back to back coverage, but it is clear that today they would be rationalised on the ground of incorporation. The point to be taken from the cases on coverage is that the courts will, wherever possible, seek to ensure that the cover provided by the reinsurance and the insurance are back to back.

***Joyce* v. *Realm Marine Insurance Co. Ltd* (1872) L.R. 7 Q.B. 580**
The insurance was on a marine cargo to be transported to Africa and then to the United Kingdom. The policy stated that cargo on board the vessel when it reached the first part of discharge in Africa was for the first 24 hours deemed to be on its homeward voyage. The reinsurance, which was "subject to all clauses and conditions of the original policy" was on the homeward voyage only. The cargo was damaged within 24 hours of its arrival in Africa.

Held: that the reinsurers were liable. The terms of the direct policy defining the homeward voyage bound the reinsurers.

***General Insurance Co. of Trieste Ltd* v. *Corporation of the Royal Exchange* (1897) 2 Com. Cas. 144**

The direct policy covered cargo during the course of loading and on its subsequent voyage. The policy defined cargo on each lighter for loading to be a separate risk. The insurers reinsured and the reinsurers entered into a retrocession agreement. The retrocession was against total loss only although was otherwise "subject to the terms, clauses and conditions of the original policy". A fire took place on the vessel, destroying the cargo then on board. However, cargo which had yet to be loaded and which was still on lighters was unaffected. The retrocessionaires refused to make payment as there had been only a partial loss of the cargo as a whole.

Held: that the retrocessionaires were liable. The terms of the direct policy—including the provision that cargo on lighters was a separate risk—took effect in the retrocession. It was therefore necessary to disregard the cargo on lighters, and there had accordingly been a total loss of the remaining cargo.

***Marten* v. *Nippon Sea and Land Insurance Co. Ltd* (1898) 3 Com. Cas. 164**

The direct policy was a warehouse to warehouse insurance on a cargo to be transported from Liverpool to Guayaquil. The policy covered the cargo after it had been discharged and during its period of inland transit to the consignee. The reinsurance, which was "subject to the same terms and conditions" referred to the coverage lasting until the cargo was discharged and safely landed. The cargo was lost while in a customs warehouse.

Held (Bigham J.): that once the goods had reached the customs warehouse they had been delivered to the consignee, and accordingly the direct policy no longer applied. It followed that there was no liability under the reinsurance. However, the warehouse to warehouse clause had been incorporated into the reinsurance and, had the loss occurred at an earlier stage, both the insurers and the reinsurers would have faced liability (on the latter point, see *Charlesworth* v. *Faber* (1900) 5 Com. Cas. 408, also a decision of Bigham J.).

If incorporation is not possible, e.g., because the terms of the reinsurance are self-contained and are expressed differently to those in the direct policy, then it follows that the coverage of the direct policy will not be incorporated into the reinsurance. Further, if the wording of the direct policy is so unusual that the reinsurers could not have anticipated that the direct risk would have been written in that way, then there is authority for the proposition that incorporation is not possible. That said, it is not always easy to reconcile the early authorities and it may be that a more liberal view of incorporation would be taken today.

***Franco-Hungarian Insurance Co.* v. *Merchants Marine Insurance Co., Shipping Gazette*, 7 June 1888**

The insurance was a time policy on a vessel. The policy contained a held covered clause under which the insured vessel remained covered for the remainder of her voyage to Marseilles in the event that the period insured expired before the voyage was completed. The risk was reinsured and then retroceded. The retrocession was "subject to the terms and conditions of the original policy". The vessel was lost after the expiry of the time policy and during the held covered period.

Held: that the retrocessionaires were not liable. The retrocession was itself a self-contained time policy which made no provision for any extension of cover, and it was not possible to undermine the express terms of the retrocession by incorporating additional provisions from the direct policy.

[*Note*: This case is poorly reported, and seems to be out of line with contemporary authorities such as *Joyce*, discussed above.]

***Maritime Insurance Co.* v. *Stearns* [1901] 2 K.B. 912**

The direct insurance covered a cargo of coal to be transported from Newcastle to ports in Scandinavia. The policy contained a held covered clause which provided that, in the event of deviation during the course of voyage the risk was not discharged and the assured was held covered on payment of additional premium. The reinsurance was stated to be "subject to the same terms and conditions as the original policy". The reinsurers denied that they were bound by the held covered clause.

Held (Mathew J.): that the reinsurers were not liable. It had not been shown that the held covered clause was commonplace in cargo policies at the time, and thus it had not been incorporated into the reinsurance.

[*Note*: This case would not today be followed on its facts, as held covered clauses have become standard. The more difficult question whether unusual terms could be incorporated was discussed by David Steel J. and the Court of Appeal in *HIH* v. *New Hampshire*, above. In that case the courts were satisfied that the clause was not sufficiently unusual to preclude incorporation. If the coverage of the direct policy is unusually wide, then either the offending provision is not incorporated at all or, if it is, then the reinsurance is voidable for non-disclosure. It is uncertain which of these approaches is correct. The point is of significance where the loss is caused by a "usual" peril, as reinsurers would still have the right to avoid.]

A further restriction on the operation of the full reinsurance clause in coverage issues relates to the situation where the reinsured has agreed to extend the coverage granted to the assured under the direct policy. As a matter of general principle, the reinsurers cannot be bound by this extension as they are to be taken to have agreed to reinsure the risk as originally presented to them, and not as varied. Clearly reinsurers can agree from the outset to be bound by changes in coverage, although it would seem that the full reinsurance clause does not fulfil this purpose as it is concerned only with indemnifying the reinsured in respect of the risk as originally accepted by the reinsured.

***Wasa International Insurance Co. Ltd and AGF Insurance Co. Ltd* v. *Lexington Insurance Co.* [2007] EWHC 896**

In August 1977 insured Alcoa from 1 July 1977 until 1 July 1980 against loss of or damage to property and business interruption risks, with a limit of liability of "US$20,000,000 loss or damage arising from an one occurrence" and a per occurrence deductible for property damage of US$250,000. Lexington agreed to submit to the jurisdiction of the court of any competent jurisdiction within the United States at the request of Alcoa. Lexington obtained facultative reinsurance cover from the London market on more or less the same terms, in the usual form of a slip policy which covered all risks of physical loss (excluding fire) "as original", the amount reinsured was US$20,000,000 each occurrence and in the annual aggregate, and the period of the cover was stated to be "36 months 1.7.77 L/U &/or pro rata to expiry of original". The slip policy referred to a "full reinsurance clause", which provided "warranted same . . . terms and conditions and to follow the settlements", and the slip stated that the reinsurers would "pay . . . all such loss as may happen to the subject matter . . . during the currency of the policy" and that the reinsurers agreed to indemnify the reinsured in respect of loss to the insured subject matter "during the continuation of this Policy". Wasa subscribed to a 1% line and AFG subscribed to a 1.5% line. It was not disputed that the reinsurance was governed by English law. In the early 1990's Alcoa was required by various US Federal and State environmental regulators to clean up pollution at some thirty-five sites used by Alcoa for some fifty years. In turn Alcoa commenced proceedings in Washington against its property and liability insurers on risk in the period from 1965 to 1985, seeking a declaration of their liability. The trial judge held that there had been two occurrences, wastage from manufacturing units and wastage from other sources, and that the appropriate apportionment was to divide the total repair costs for each site by the number of years in which damage occurred and then to allocate the appropriate proportion to each year. The evidence showed that the damage had occurred over many years up to the date of the inception of the insurance in 1977 and for some years thereafter, so that by using the allocation forumla Lexington was liable only for relatively small percentages of the total loss. The losses at some sites were below Aloca's deductible. However, this decision was reversed on appeal, the Supreme Court of Washington holding that the insurers—including Lexington—were jointly and severally liable to Alcoa for all property damage, including damage which occurred before the 1977 cover incepted. Lexington thereafter settled with Alcoa on 24 November 2003, agreeing to pay $US103,140,500 over a two year period. Wasa and AFG commenced in London seeking negative declaratory relief. Lexington cross claimed for sums which it alleged were due under the reinsurance: as against Wasa that sum was US$1,031,405 plus defence costs of US$283,747.53 (1%) and against AGF that sum was US$1,547,107.50 plus defence costs of US$452,621.30 (1.5%).

Simon J held that the resinsurers were not bound by the settlement. Although Simon J accepted that the two policies were back to back, he rejected the argument that the duration clauses were to be construed in the same way in the two documents. The learned judge distinguished both *Forsakrings Vesta* v. *Butcher* [1989] A.C. 852 and *Groupama Navigation et Transports* v. *Catatumbo CA Seguros* [2000] 2 Lloyd's Rep. 350 (both discussed below) on the ground that in each of those cases the meaning of the term in the direct policy was clear or at least readily ascertainable under the law applicable to the direct policy, so that the same meaning could be ascribed to that term as incorporated into the reinsurance even though a different law governed the reinsurance. In the present case, by contrast, there was no certainty as to how the duration provision in the direct policy would be interpreted, as there was no common view in the US on the matter and the outcome depended upon the court in which the claim under the direct policy was resolved. For that reason, the express wording of the duration clause in the reinsurance prevailed, and the reinsurers were not liable for losses occurring before the reinsurance incepted. Simon J also rejected an alternative argument that a decision by a court on the meaning of a direct policy bound the English court in its interpretation of the same words in the reinsurance agreement. Simon J found no authority for that proposition.

***Lower Rhine and Wurttemburg Insurance Association* v. *Sedgwick* [1899] 1 Q.B. 179**

The defendant underwriters issued two time policies insuring hull and cargo. The claimants were the reinsurers under a reinsurance agreement stated to be on the same terms and conditions as the original. The reinsurance agreement required the underlying policies to be identified in a space provided. The blank space was not completed at the outset. Subsequently the two time policies were cancelled and replaced by two further policies on much the same terms but with a higher premium. Losses occurred, and the reinsurers refused to make payment, arguing that the reinsurance applied only to policies in force at the date the reinsurance was made and did not extend to replacement policies.

Held (C.A.): that the reinsurers were not liable. The incorporation clause did not have the effect of binding the reinsurers to indemnify the reinsured for new risks accepted during the currency of the reinsurance, but applied only to the risks which were in place when the reinsurance was taken out.

***Norwich Union Fire Insurance Society Ltd* v. *Colonial Mutual Fire Insurance Co. Ltd* [1922] 2 K.B. 461**

The direct insurance was a hull and machinery policy under which the agreed value of the insured vessel was £313,000. The risk was reinsured under a reinsurance agreement against total loss only, and subject to the same terms and conditions as the original. During the currency of these policies, following a revaluation, the agreed value of the hull was reduced to £225,000. A total loss occurred, and the reinsurers refused to pay on the ground that the reduction in the agreed value of the vessel made it far more likely that a loss would fall to be treated as a constructive total loss (as the cost of repairs would exceed the agreed value of the vessel).

Held (McCardie J.): that the reinsurers were discharged. Once the risk had altered in this significant fashion, the reinsurers could no longer be bound. The incorporating words did not affect the position as they did not operate to bring into the reinsurance agreement the revised terms agreed by the reinsured.

The modern practice is to give contractual effect to these decisions by a provision whereby in the event of any proposed change which is material to the direct risk the reinsured is required to consult the reinsurers and to obtain their agreement to the amendment. A clause of this type was considered by David Steel J. and the Court of Appeal in *HIH Casualty and General Insurance Ltd* v. *New Hampshire Insurance Co.*, above, and was held to amount to a warranty that the risk would not be varied.

An attempt was made in *American International Marine Agency of New York Inc* v. *Dandridge* [2005] EWHC 829 (Comm) to overcome the rule that reinsurers are not bound by underlying change in coverage, by arguing that a leading underwriter clause in the direct policy had been incorporated into the reinsurance, thereby binding the reinsurers to modifications agreed to at the direct level by the leading underwriter.

***American International Marine Agency of New York Inc* v. *Dandridge* [2005] EWHC 829 (Comm)**

This case concerned the insurance of a vessel by the claimants, who subscribed to 15% of the risk as part of the following market. The leading underwriter was Axa. The insurance was evidenced by a French Market Slip which incorporated ITC 1983 (including an automatic termination clause on change of class, plus a classification warranty), and reinsured under a later binder which set out the claimants' participation and which contained a leading underwriter clause under which the claimants agreed to follow Axa "in all respects, including rates and claims but excluding ex gratia". The claimants were reinsured by reinsurers under a slip which contained the full reinsurance clause stating that the reinsurance was "subject to the same clauses and conditions and against the same perils as in the original policy" against Total Loss Only, and to follow settlements. The vessel was originally classed with DNV, but the class expired on 31 August 2000. The vessel was reclassed with INSB as from 6 September 2000. Axa agreed orally to the change of class, and the value of the vessel was reduced from US$2.5 million to US$1.5 million: these changes were subsequently endorsed onto the insurance by Axa and also by the claimants. The reinsurers subsequently contended that they had been automatically discharged from liability on the change of class. The claimants' argument was that they were by reason of the leading underwriter clause bound by Axa's variation of the direct policy, and that the clause was incorporated into the reinsurance so that reinsurers were similarly bound by the variation. The reinsurers' response was that: (a) the incorporating words in the reinsurance applied only to the French Market Slip and not to the later binder, so that the leading underwriter clause was not incorporated into the reinsurance; (b) if that was wrong and the binder was incorporated, the incorporating words did not extend to the leading underwriter clause; and (c) if that was wrong and the leading underwriter clause was incorporated, then it made no sense in the reinsurance.

Held (Deputy High Court Judge Richard Siberry QC): that "the original policy or policies" in the full reinsurance clause applied only to the French Market Slip and not to the binder (which had been published and signed into after the date of the reinsurance), so that the leading underwriter clause was not incorporated. If that was wrong, then the leading underwriter clause was not incorporated into the reinsurance because it was not germane or apposite, it made no sense in the context of reinsurance and it was inconsistent with the express terms of the reinsurance. Assuming that the clause had been incorporated in an unmanipulated form, it plainly could not require the reinsurers to follow Axa's settlements, neither could it operate to remove from the reinsurers the right to take a defence under the reinsurance which had been removed from the claimants by reason of some variation by Axa.

Incorporation of claims conditions

Given that the purpose of incorporation is to ensure that the coverage granted by the direct policy is matched by the reinsurance agreement, there is some logic behind the incorporation of insuring and exceptions clauses. There is less logic in permitting the incorporation of claims conditions. This is so for three reasons:

- Facultative reinsurance agreements have their own express clauses which govern claims, notably claims co-operation clauses and claims control clauses. Insofar as the reinsurance contains these provisions, incorporation of those in the direct policy is superfluous.
- Direct policy claims provisions may be inappropriate in the reinsurance context. Reinsurance in most cases resembles liability cover, in that the reinsurers are required to pay where the reinsured has proved that it faces liability to indemnify its policy holders. However, the claims conditions in the direct policy will be pertinent to the class of policy to which they relate, e.g., life, motor, etc.
- The conditions in the direct policy are almost certain to use the language of direct insurance rather than reinsurance, so that if incorporation is to be effected some degree of linguistic "manipulation" may be required.

The cases are inconsistent on the incorporation issue, and each turns on its individual facts.

Home Insurance Co. of New York **v.** ***Victoria-Montreal Fire Insurance Co.*** **[1907] A.C. 59**

Property belonging to the Canadian Pacific Railway was insured by Western, a Canadian company under a fire policy. The policy stated that no suit could be brought on the policy "unless commenced within twelve months after the fire". Western reinsured 20% of their liability with Home in the US and Home entered into a retrocession agreement with Victoria-Montreal. Both the reinsurance and the retrocession agreements incorporated the terms of the direct policy, by adding the prefix "re" to the word "insurance". The issue was whether the service of suit clause was operative in the retrocession, it being common ground that virtually all of the remainder of the direct policy was of no relevance in the context of retrocession.

Held (Privy Council): that the service of suit had not been incorporated into the retrocession.

(1) The slip for the retrocession was complete in itself.

(2) Further, it could not have been the intention of the parties to incorporate just one term from the direct policy into the retrocession while leaving the others behind.

(3) The service of suit clause operated unreasonably in the retrocession as Home had no control over when a claim would be made against it and thus might be defeated by dilatory conduct on the part of the direct assured or Western.

The case is of interest for Lord Macnaghten's comments on the notion of incorporation:

"It is no doubt possible to read the sentence prescribing suits and actions, divorced from its immediate context, into the contract of [retrocession] . . . It is difficult to suppose that the contract of [retrocession] was engrafted on an ordinary printed form of policy for any purpose beyond the purpose of indicating the origin of the direct liability on which the indirect liability, the subject of the [retrocession] would depend, and setting forth the conditions attached to it . . . [A]ccording to the true construction of the instrument, so awkwardly patched and so carelessly put together the condition in question is not to be regarded as applying to the contract of reinsurance. To hold otherwise would . . . be to adhere to the letter without paying due attention to the spirit and intention of the contract.

***Municipal Mutual Insurance Ltd* v. *Sea Insurance Ltd* [1996] L.R.L.R. 265, reversed in part on other grounds [1998] Lloyd's Rep. IR 421**

The claimants were the liability insurers of the Port of Sunderland Authority, the policy covering the Authority's liability to third parties for damage caused to property belonging to third parties. The policy required all accidents and claims to be reported to the claimants immediately and confirmed in writing. Once a third party had commenced proceedings against the Authority, the claimant insurers had the right to take over the conduct of those proceedings and also of any negotiations. The defendants were the facultative reinsurers of the claimants under a policy which provided "follow their settlement. Conditions as underlying". The issue was whether the notice condition had been incorporated into the reinsurance by the words "as underlying", as the claimants had failed to give the defendants due notice of claims.

Held (Waller J.): the phrase "as underlying" did not operate to import all of the terms of the direct policy into the reinsurance. The notice and claims control terms were designed to deal with third party claims under a liability policy, and not with reinsurance disputes. Further, the fact that the reinsurance had been arranged in a series of excess layers rendered notification and claims control problematic.

***CNA International Reinsurance Co.* v. *Companhia de Seguros Tranquilidade SA* [1999] Lloyd's Rep. IR 289**

The promoters of a series of concerts to be given by Placido Domingo took out cover with a Portuguese insurer against loss caused by the cancellation of the concerts. The policy was in Portuguese, and consisted of Portuguese insuring provisions (which were in fact appropriate to civil liability and not to cancellation) and incorporated Lloyd's contingency and non-appearance wordings. Some 90% of the risk was reinsured in London, and it appears that the Portuguese insurers were a front for the London market. The wording of the reinsurance was stated to be "as per Lloyd's Contingency Policy". In the event the concerts were cancelled due to the illness of Placido Domingo's mother. The insurers settled the claim and sought indemnification from the reinsurers. Issues arose as to whether there had been compliance by the reinsured with the claims provisions set out in the direct policy and incorporated into the reinsurance, and declarations as to the position were sought.

Held (Clarke J.):

(1) The direct insurance and the reinsurance were to be construed as providing back to back cover, and accordingly the claims conditions in the direct policy were incorporated into the reinsurance even though some manipulation of the terms was required.

(2) The claims conditions imposed on the assured, setting out the procedure for claims to be made, were incorporated into the reinsurance, by the device of substituting "reinsured" for "assured". The obligations imposed were not onerous, nor were they repugnant to a reinsurance contract.

(3) A condition precedent in the direct policy which required notice of loss to be given to persons designated the schedule to that policy had no application to reinsurance, as there was no reinsurance policy and no schedule.

(4) A condition precedent in the direct policy which prevented the assured from admitting liability was neither inappropriate nor repugnant to the reinsurance agreement, and took effect by allowing the reinsurers to control the negotiations between the reinsured and the assured. Clarke J. did accept that any admission of liability by the reinsured would not have been binding on the reinsurers in any event, given the absence of a follow settlements clause in the reinsurance, but nevertheless felt that meaning could be given to the clause as a whole at the reinsurance level.

Incorporation of warranties

Significance of warranties in the direct policy

A warranty is a promise made on the part of the assured as to an existing fact or a future state of affairs. As will be seen in Chapter 5 the effect of a breach of warranty is automatically to discharge the insurers from any liability under the policy as of the date of the breach. Thus if the assured promises that something will or will not be done, and the promise is broken during the currency of the policy, the insurers cannot face liability other than for previous claims. There has been a series of cases in which reinsurers have sought to rely upon the terms of a reinsurance warranty incorporated from the direct policy in circumstances where the warranty had no application at the direct level and thus which afforded the reinsured no defence against its own policy holders. The attitude of the courts has, wherever possible, been that the reinsurers should not be able to rely upon the concept of incorporation in order to rely upon a defence which would not have been open to the reinsured. To achieve this result the courts have relied upon the principle that the coverage of insurance and reinsurance agreements is intended to be "back to back", so that where the terms of the direct policy have been incorporated into the reinsurance the terms have the same effect in both contracts.

Before the authorities are considered, it is necessary to distinguish them from the situation in which the assured had himself been in breach of a warranty in the direct policy in a manner which afforded the insurers a defence against the reinsured. In such a case, any payment by the reinsured is purely voluntary and will not fall within the scope of the reinsurance. If the reinsured was unaware of its right to refuse payment, and entered into a settlement in error, then the ability of the reinsurers to refuse payment depends upon whether there is a follow the settlements clause in the reinsurance (in which case the reinsurers are obliged to pay as long as the settlement was bona fide and reached in a businesslike fashion—see Chapter 6) or whether the contract is silent (in which case the reinsured has to prove its liability).

Incorporation of direct warranties into reinsurance

The position reached by the English courts is that if the reinsured is not relieved from its obligation to pay the assured despite a breach of warranty on the assured's part, then the reinsurers are not themselves able to rely upon the breach of the same warranty as incorporated into the reinsurance.

***Forsakrings Vesta* v. *Butcher* [1989] 1 A.C. 852**

The notion of aquacultural insurance was developed in London by brokers. London market underwriters agreed to act as reinsurers for foreign risks of this type. Wording was developed by the brokers, and translated for use in other jurisdictions. Aquacultural insurance was obtained by a Norwegian fish farm from the claimants, Norwegian insurers, who had used the brokers' wording translated into Norwegian. The direct policy was governed by the law of Norway. The direct policy contained a number of warranties, including a "twenty-four hour watch" warranty, under which the assured warranted that continuous surveillance of the fish farm would be maintained, and there were also stock control obligations in the form of a warranty. The claimants reinsured with the defendant underwriters in London by way of a facultative policy which contained the full reinsurance clause, "being a reinsurance of and warranted same gross rate and terms and conditions and to follow the settlements of the insurer". The reinsurance contract was governed by English law. It was not disputed that all of the parties had intended the insurance and reinsurance to operate on a back to back basis. As a result of a storm the defences of the fish farm were damaged, and many of the fish were lost. The assured was in breach of the surveillance warranty, as the weather had been too bad to maintain the necessary surveillance, and the stock control warranty had also been broken. The claimants were nevertheless required to indemnify the assured: the policy was governed by Norwegian law, and that law provided that a breach of warranty did not provide a defence unless it was causative of the loss. The defendant reinsurers refused to indemnify the claimants, and placed reliance on the full reinsurance clause which, it was argued, had the effect of incorporating the warranties into the reinsurance. As those warranties were broken, and as the reinsurance was governed by English law, the reinsurers were not liable.

Held (H.L.): that the reinsurers were liable.

(1) The terms of the direct policy were incorporated into the reinsurance by means of the full reinsurance clause. This had been conceded by the reinsurers prior to the trial, and the trial judge, Hobhouse J., had refused to allow a late application for the proceedings to be amended so that the idea of incorporation could be challenged. In the House of Lords Lord Griffiths alone doubted the correctness of the incorporation concession, and held that the full reinsurance clause amounted only to a warranty by the reinsured that the terms of the direct policy corresponded to the presentation of those terms made by the reinsured to the reinsurers.

(2) The two contracts were designed to be back to back. It followed that the reinsurers should not be able to rely upon a defence not open to the reinsured. The necessary congruity could be achieved by holding that the reinsurance agreement, even though governed by English law, was to be construed in the same manner as would have been the case in Norway. By this means the warranties bore the same meaning in both the insurance and reinsurance contracts, and the reinsurers had no defence.

See also *Ace Insurance SA-NV* v. *Zurich Insurance Co.* [2001] Lloyd's Rep. IR 504, discussed below in the context of back to back cover. Minor variations in the wording between the direct insurance warranty and the reinsurance warranty will not produce a result different to that in *Vesta* v. *Butcher* if the court is satisfied that those variations were not intended to be of significance.

***Groupama Navigation et Transports Continent SA* v. *Catatumbo Ca Seguros* [2000] 2 Lloyd's Rep. 350**

The defendants, a Venezuelan insurance company, were the hull and machinery insurers of a Venezuelan shipping company under a policy governed by the law of Venezuela. The policy incorporated US classification provisions, the effect of which was to guarantee the stated classification of the vessel and to bring the policy to an end in the event of a change of class. The claimants were reinsurers who had reinsured 50% of the defendants' liability under a facultative slip policy governed by English law. The slip policy contained a version of the full reinsurance clause, in the form "all terms, conditions, warranties, additional premiums, return premium as original". There was in addition a specific warranty providing "Warranted existing class maintained". Two vessels belonging to the assured were damaged in a storm, and it was later discovered that neither of the vessels had been entered into a classification society. The breach of warranty did not, however, discharge the defendants from liability under Venezuelan law, as there was no causative link between the breach of warranty and the losses. The claimants denied liability, relying on the "existing class maintained" warranty contained in the reinsurance itself, and argued that as this was a specifically agreed term in an English law policy they were discharged from liability by reason of its breach. The claimants did not rely upon the incorporated classification warranty in the direct policy, and it is clear that had they done so they would have been defeated by the decision in *Vesta* v. *Butcher*. Instead, the claimants sought to distinguish *Vesta* v. *Butcher* by arguing that in *Vesta* the reinsurers had relied upon an incorporated term whereas in the present case the term relied upon was a reinsurance term. The defendants for their part argued that the full reinsurance clause had incorporated the US warranty into the reinsurance contract, and this had displaced the express reinsurance warranty.

Held (C.A.): that the defendants' argument succeeded.

(1) The parties' intentions had been to make the insurance and reinsurance back to back in terms of coverage.

(2) The terms of the direct policy, including the classification warranties, were incorporated into the reinsurance. The classification warranties thus took effect as reinsurance terms.

(3) In order to give effect to the back to back cover principle, it was necessary to construe the warranties in the direct policy and in the reinsurance in the same way. The correct approach was to treat the reinsurance warranty as overridden by the incorporated direct warranty. This did not mean that the reinsurance warranty was devoid of effect, as the reinsurers' purpose was to make sure that there was a classification warranty in the reinsurance so that their own warranty was designed as a fallback in the event that the direct policy was silent on the matter.

[*Note*: The Court of Appeal indicated that a different result would have been reached had the wording of the direct and reinsurance warranties been entirely different, as in such circumstances it could not be assumed that the reinsurers intended to provide back to back cover.]

The *Groupama* decision is not free from criticism, as it would seem curious that reinsurers were precluded from relying upon their own express wording.

The Court of Appeal's view was nevertheless that the presumption of back to back cover had to be given primacy. That said, it has not always proved possible for the courts to rescue the reinsured in this way. Thus, if the reinsurance agreement is entirely different in its terms from those of the direct policy then there is no basis for the operation of the presumption of back to back cover, and the reinsurance warranty has to prevail.

***GE Reinsurance Corporation* v. *New Hampshire Insurance Co.*, [2004] Lloyd's Rep. IR 404**

US$100 million had been loaned by investors to a film distribution and production company, Destination, and had been secured by the issue of notes to trustees acting for the noteholders. The key employee of Destination was one Steve Stabler, the director of *Dumb and Dumber* and who was described in the proceedings as Destination's "creative mind". Mr Stabler was to be in charge of the production of films by Destination. Brokers were engaged by the noteholders to place insurance, and initially the brokers obtained 40% subscription from Axa, 20% subscription from New Hampshire and 40% subscription from various other insurers. Subsequently Destination informed the brokers that it wished to have only Axa and New Hampshire as insurers, and the brokers accordingly arranged for Axa to take 40% of the risk with the remaining 60% being taken by New Hampshire. One third of New Hampshire's subscription was taken for itself, and the remaining two-thirds was accepted by New Hampshire as a fronting company for the other insurers, who became New Hampshire's reinsurers for that purpose. The direct policy subscribed to by Axa and New Hampshire was silent on the position of Mr Stabler within Destination, but New Hampshire's outwards reinsurance stated, in addition to the terms being "as original" that a contract in respect of Steve Stabler "to be maintained for the duration of the policy". Soon after the insurance and reinsurance risks incepted, Mr Stabler departed from Destination. In due course Destination became insolvent and defaulted on its payments to the noteholders. The reinsurers refused to make payment, arguing that the "Stabler" term was a warranty which had been broken and which discharged them from liability as of the date of the breach. New Hampshire argued, relying on *Vesta* v. *Butcher* and *Groupama* v. *Catatumbo,* that the insurance and reinsurance agreements should be construed back to back, and accordingly that when the terms of the direct policy were incorporated into the reinsurance agreement the absence of any "Stabler warranty" in the direct policy negatived the express "Stabler warranty" in the reinsurance agreement.

Held (Langley J.): that the reinsurers were not liable. The term relating to Mr Stabler's continuing employment was a warranty (see Chapter 5), and the warranty was not affected by the absence of any equivalent provision in the underlying policy even though it was clear that the reinsurance had been put into place only as a fronting operation and there had never been any intention to render the terms of the insurance and reinsurance at variance. Langley J. distinguished *Vesta* and *Groupama* on the ground that in each of those cases there were warranties in both the insurance and the reinsurance, and the intention of the parties had been that the warranties should have the same effect in each of those contracts. By contrast, in *GE* v. *New Hampshire* there was no warranty in the direct policy and it was impossible to construe the terms of an express reinsurance warranty as matching the terms of a direct policy which made no reference to the warranty at all. The "Stabler Warranty" could not simply be disregarded.

INCORPORATION OF DISPUTE RESOLUTION PROVISIONS

General principles of law

Incorporation is not a device confined to reinsurance agreements. Incorporation is widely used in other forms of commercial contract. There are at least three other illustrations of the use of incorporation:

- *Shipping.* It is standard practice for the terms of the charterparty, as agreed between the shipowner and the charterer, to be incorporated into bills of lading issued by the shipowner to third party purchasers of the cargo.
- *Construction.* The terms of head contracts are frequently incorporated by reference into sub-contracts entered into by the head contractor.
- *Insurance.* Where insurance is arranged in layers, the usual practice is for the terms of the first layer policy to be incorporated into the excess layer policies.

Since the end of the nineteenth century the courts have struggled with the question of whether dispute resolution provisions contained in the head contract have been incorporated into the subsidiary contracts by virtue of words of incorporation in the subsidiary contract. Dispute resolution provisions—arbitration clauses, jurisdiction clauses and choice of law clauses—are treated differently from other contract terms: it is one thing for contractual conditions to be incorporated, but it is quite another to deprive a party of his right to bring proceedings in a court of his own choice by reason of an incorporated dispute resolution provision which forms part of a quite separate contract. The majority of the cases have involved the incorporation of arbitration clauses from charterparties into bills of lading. The law is still in some respects uncertain, although the principles which may be derived from the cases were recently restated by Gross J. in *Siboti K/S* v. *BP France SA*, May 2003, unreported (references to the numerous charterparty authorities omitted):

(1) "The starting point is the contract contained in or evidenced by the bill of lading; it is that contract which the Court must construe."

(2) "The incorporation of terms is to be distinguished from mere notice of terms; the fact that the holder of a bill of lading has notice of terms in a charterparty does not mean that those terms are incorporated in the bill of lading . . . Further, it is terms not intentions which are incorporated. The purpose of referential incorporation is not—or at least not generally—to incorporate the intentions of the parties to the contract whose clauses are incorporated but to incorporate the clauses themselves in order to avoid the necessity of writing them out verbatim."

(3) "General words of incorporation will incorporate into the bill of lading only those provisions of the charterparty which are directly germane to the shipment, carriage and delivery of the goods. Provisions of the charterparty which are ancillary rather than directly germane to the subject matter of the bill of lading as aforesaid, will not be incorporated by general words of incorporation in the bill of lading. By way of amplification:

(a) 'General words of incorporation' are to be distinguished from wording making a specific reference to a particular charterparty provision (for example, a charterparty arbitration clause). Accordingly, even comparatively wide wording such as 'all terms, conditions and exceptions as per charterparty' constitute 'general words of incorporation' for these purposes.
(b) Arbitration clauses are ancillary in this sense."

(4) "Even when the wording of a bill of lading is prima facie of sufficient width to incorporate the charterparty clause in question, such incorporation may be defeated if undue manipulation is required. That said, in this regard the intention of the parties is paramount. Accordingly, while the purported incorporation of certain charterparty clauses may prove ineffective on the ground of linguistic inapplicability alone (for example, charterparty arbitration clause wordings such as 'any disputes arising out of . . . this charter' . . . where the intention to incorporate a particular charterparty clause is clear, difficulties of manipulation may be overcome . . . It may well be that the true intentions of the parties serve to define the ambit of permissible manipulation."

The effect of all of this is that general words of incorporation in the charterparty will not operate to incorporate an arbitration clause, on the narrow grounds that an arbitration clause is not a "term or condition" for the purposes of the incorporation wording and that an arbitration clause is an ancillary and independent contract, and on the broader ground that a person is not to be deprived of access to the courts without his express consent. There must, therefore, be a specific reference to the arbitration clause in the words of incorporation in the bill of lading. The point which remains undecided is whether the wording of the charterparty is of any significance, and in particular whether the absence of clear references to the arbitration clause in the bill of lading can be compensated for by a charterparty provision which states that, e.g., any dispute arising out of the charterparty or any bill of lading is to be referred to arbitration. In *Siboti* Gross J. held that the weight of authority supported the proposition that incorporation was to be determined by the terms of the bill of lading alone.

Arbitration clauses

Arbitration is discussed in Chapter 10. The present discussion is concerned only with the effect of the full reinsurance clause on arbitration. An arbitration clause contained in a direct policy is not incorporated into a reinsurance agreement which purports to carry across the terms of the direct policy by use of the full reinsurance clause. The full reinsurance clause, which refers to "term and conditions" does not extend to arbitration as there is no specific reference to the ancillary obligation to go to arbitration.

***Pine Top Insurance Co. Ltd* v. *Unione Italiana Anglo Saxon Reinsurance Co. Ltd* [1987] 1 Lloyd's Rep. 476**

The insurer issued a number of travel insurance policies providing cover for medical expenses incurred abroad. Each of the policies contained arbitration clauses whereby disputes arising between the assured and the insurer were to be referred to arbitration.

The arbitration procedure was a simple one, reflecting the sums at stake. The insurer reinsured its liabilities with the defendants. The reinsurance slip stated "all terms and conditions as original". The slip also contained its own arbitration clause, and this was far more elaborate than that which applied to disputes under the travel policies themselves. The defendants retroceded their liabilities to the claimant retrocessionaires. The retrocession slip itself stated "all terms and conditions as original", although this time there was no separate arbitration clause. Disputes arose between the claimants and the defendants, and the issue for the court was whether the disputes were to be referred to arbitration.

Held (Gatehouse J.): that there was no arbitration clause incorporated into the retrocession agreement.

(1) The phrase "all terms and conditions as original" was appropriate to incorporate insuring and related provisions from a direct policy into a reinsurance or retrocession agreement, but probably had no other effect.

(2) If it was the case that the incorporation wording could extend to arbitration, it was necessary initially to determine whether the "original" referred to in the retrocession was the underlying travel policies or the reinsurance agreement. The better view was that "original" meant original direct policy and not reinsurance. Accordingly, if an arbitration clause was incorporated, it would be the clause found in the travel policies.

(3) On the basis that the travel insurance arbitration clause had been incorporated into the retrocession, that clause was inappropriate to a dispute arising at the level of retrocession.

***Excess Insurance Co.* v. *Mander* [1995] L.R.L.R. 358**

Two US insurance companies provided cover to US financial institutions against loss caused by the defaults of their directors and officers. The insurers reinsured in London with a number of Lloyd's syndicates and companies. Certain of the reinsurers retroceded their liability to the claimants under an excess of loss treaty, and the claimants in turn retroceded their liability to the defendants. The retrocession slip which governed the relationship between the claimants and the defendants contained the full reinsurance clause which provided that "all terms, clauses, conditions and warranties as original . . . INF original slip [for the excess of loss treaty] attached and noted by reinsurers hereon". The INF original slip itself provided that wording would be agreed by the leading underwriter on the slip. In due course that wording, which included an arbitration clause, was agreed. The arbitration clause became a part of the treaty some four months after the defendants had scratched the slip for the retrocession of that treaty. The claimants sought indemnification under the retrocession, and the defendant sought a stay of proceedings on the ground that the retrocession incorporated the arbitration clause from the excess of loss treaty.

Held (Colman J.): that there was no incorporation.

(1) At the time the retrocession agreement was entered into the excess of loss treaty had not contained an arbitration clause and there was no reference to arbitration in the INF slip. It could not be assumed that the parties intended the retrocession to be varied in accordance with the direct policy.

(2) General words of incorporation were in any event not enough to bring an arbitration clause from one agreement into another. An arbitration clause was an ancillary provision which was collateral to the main subject matter of a contract and express wording was needed to effect incorporation of this type of clause.

These cases were decided before the passing of the Arbitration Act 1996. This Act for the first time set out the requirements for a valid arbitration clause (or, at least, one governed by the 1996 Act). Section 5 provides that an arbitration clause must be in writing, although it need not be signed by the parties, and section 6(2) provides that "The reference in an agreement to a written form of arbitration clause or to a document containing an arbitration clause constitutes an arbitration agreement if the reference is such to make that clause part of the agreement". The question whether this section altered the earlier law by relaxing the rules on incorporation was considered, and rejected, by H.H.J. Jack QC in the following case.

***Trygg Hansa Insurance Co. Ltd* v. *Equitas Ltd* [1998] 2 Lloyd's Rep. 439**

The defendant was the representative of a Lloyd's syndicate which had been reinsured by the claimant under various excess of loss reinsurance contracts. The underlying policy subscribed to by the syndicate provided for arbitration in London. The terms of that policy were incorporated into the reinsurance by the words: "Except as otherwise provided herein this policy is to follow the same terms, exclusions, conditions, definitions and settlements as the Policy of the Primary Insurers." The claimants purported to avoid the reinsurance, and in response to the defendants' action sought an order from the court staying the proceedings so that the dispute could be referred to arbitration.

Held (H.H.J. Jack QC) that there was no agreement to go to arbitration.

(1) The cases decided before the implementation of section 6(2) of the Arbitration Act 1996 made it clear that general words of incorporation were not enough, and the wording in the present case was not to be construed as indicating an intention to incorporate the arbitration clause.

(2) It had not been the intention of the Arbitration Act 1996 to change the law. Accordingly, section 6(2) did not have the effect of allowing incorporation where this would not have been possible at common law.

***Cigna Life Insurance Co. of Europe SA-NV & Ors* v. *Intercaser SA de Seguros y Reaseguros* [2001] Lloyd's Rep. IR 821**

The claimants were the reinsurers of the defendants in respect of certain life and personal accident perils. The reinsurance conditions stated that they were "To follow all terms, clauses, conditions and articles of the Original Policy and/or Underlying Policy as far as applicable . . . " There was a reference here to the "Intercaser Reinsurance Contract", although this did not exist and instead the relevant underlying document was a "Life Reinsurance Contract". A dispute arose as to the duration of the reinsurance, and the defendants relied upon an arbitration clause which was contained in the direct policy.

Held (Morison J.): that the clause had not been incorporated. General words of incorporation were not sufficient, but that point aside there was no such document as the "Intercaser Reinsurance Contract". It could not be assumed that the parties intended to incorporate the arbitration provisions of the Life Reinsurance Contract which was not mentioned in the reinsurance conditions. Further, the relevant terms of the Life Reinsurance Contract had not been agreed to until after the claimants and the defendants had become bound.

See also the decision of Cresswell J. in *American International Speciality Lines Insurance Co.* v. *Abbott Laboratories* [2004] Lloyd's Rep. IR 815, where the terms of a first layer insurance policy were incorporated into an excess layer policy, and the issue was whether an arbitration clause was carried across by general words of incorporation. Cresswell J. held that there was no incorporation: (1) at the time the excess layer contract was entered into there was no arbitration clause in the primary layer policy; (2) there was no express reference in the excess layer policy to the incorporation of an arbitration clause; and (3) the excess layer policy contained its own separate dispute resolution provision which was inconsistent with the incorporation of an arbitration clause.

Jurisdiction agreements

Jurisdiction agreements may be exclusive or non-exclusive. An exclusive jurisdiction agreement binds the parties to bring proceedings in a stated place. A non-exclusive jurisdiction agreement confers the right, but not the obligation, on the parties to sue in a particular place. A non-exclusive jurisdiction clause has two main effects: it operates to confer jurisdiction on the courts of a country which without that agreement might not otherwise have possessed jurisdiction under domestic law rules; and if one party does seek to take advantage of the clause then the other is unable to contest jurisdiction and seek to sue elsewhere. Jurisdiction clauses are considered in more detail in Chapter 9.

The validity and binding effect of jurisdiction clauses has to be considered under two separate regimes. If the defendant is domiciled within the EC or EFTA the requirements for a valid jurisdiction clause are set out (for the EC) in Article 23 of European Council Regulation 44/2001, replacing the Brussels Convention 1968, or (for EFTA) in Article 17 of the Lugano Convention 1989. The Regulation and the Convention are differently worded but are for the most part identical. A jurisdiction agreement is binding under the Regulation and the Convention if it is:

> "(a) in writing or evidenced in writing [. . . any communication by electronic means which provides a durable record of the agreement shall be equivalent to writing];
> (b) in a form which accords with practices which the parties have established between themselves;
> (c) in international trade or commerce, in a form which accords with a usage of which the parties are or ought to have been aware and which in such trade or commerce is widely known to, and regularly observed by parties to contracts of the type involved in the particular trade or commerce concerned."

English cases which have discussed this provision have concluded that the requirements of English law for the incorporation of a jurisdiction clause are indistinguishable from those set out in the Regulation and the Convention (see, e.g., *Evialis SA* v. *Siat* [2003] EWHC 863 (Comm)).

***Arig Insurance Company Ltd* v. *Sasa Assicurazione Riassicurazione SpA*, 1998, unreported**

A contract of reinsurance stated "Policy wording as original". The question was whether this wording operated to incorporate into the reinsurance contract a term in the direct policy which stated that the courts of the "place of the residence or office of the Contracting Party"—in this case, Italy—had exclusive jurisdiction.

Held (Tuckey J.): The requirements of Article 17 of the Brussels Convention 1968 (now Article 23 of the 2001 Regulation) had not been satisfied and there was no valid exclusive jurisdiction agreement. It was necessary to demonstrate consensus, but this had not been shown on the facts.

AIG Group (UK) Ltd v. *The Ethniki* [2000] Lloyd's Rep. IR 343

Hellenic Arms Industry took out insurance with local insurers (the defendants) on their factory in Athens. The policy stated that the parties submitted to the exclusive jurisdiction of the courts of Athens. The defendants reinsured on the London market with the claimants on the usual "as original" terms. Following serious damage to the factory by an earthquake, the claimants applied to the English court for a declaration that they did not face liability under the reinsurance. The defendants argued that the English court had no jurisdiction and that the reinsurance incorporated the exclusive jurisdiction clause in favour of Athens as contained in the direct policy.

Held (C.A.): that the reinsurance was not subject to any exclusive jurisdiction agreement and that the requirements of Article 17 of the Brussels Convention 1968 had not been satisfied. General words of incorporation did not meet the requirements for consensus demanded by either English law or the Convention. Exclusive jurisdiction clauses were not appropriately incorporated, as they were (in the words of Evans L.J.) "wholly inappropriate to disputes arising between insurers and reinsurers under the reinsurance contract".

AIG Europe SA v. *QBE International Insurance Ltd* [2002] Lloyd's Rep. IR 22

AIG were the direct insurers of Aerospatiale in respect of material damage and consequential loss. The policy contained an exclusive jurisdiction clause nominating the French courts. AIG reinsured with the French branch of QBE, using brokers based in Luxembourg. The reinsurance made no reference to jurisdiction but contained the full reinsurance clause, "All terms, clauses and conditions as original and to follow the original in all respects including settlements". AIG commenced proceedings in London to resolve a dispute as to the cancellation of the agreement, and QBE argued that the courts of France had exclusive jurisdiction by virtue of the incorporated clause.

Held (Moore-Bick J.): that the exclusive jurisdiction clause had not been incorporated into the reinsurance agreement. The requirement for consensus imposed by Article 17 of the Brussels Convention 1968 had not been satisfied, and it was settled law that the full reinsurance clause did not operate to incorporate exclusive jurisdiction clauses in the absence of any additional wording in the reinsurance referring to the clause. Even if it had been the case that the clause had been incorporated, the clause would have required considerable linguistic "manipulation" to make it fit in the reinsurance context, and that of itself showed that the parties could not have intended the clause to be incorporated.

Prifti v. *Musini Sociedad Anonima De Seguros y Reaseguros*, [2004] Lloyd's Rep. IR 528

Musini, a Spanish company, were the insurers of a Spanish football club, Real Sociedad. The policy covered Real Sociedad against loss resulting from the personal accident and sickness of its players for a period from 5 December 2000 to 4 December 2001. Musini were reinsured in London to the extent of 98% by the claimant (representing Lloyd's syndicates) for the same period. The policy contained an exclusive jurisdiction clause nominating the courts of the domicile of the assured, ie, the Spanish courts. The reinsurance contained the full reinsurance clause, "Being a reinsurance of and warranted subject to the same terms and conditions (excluding limits and rates) as and to follow the settlements of the Reassured". Real Sociedad brought a claim against Musini in respect of an injury to a player, Frederic Peiremans, whose career was ended following an injury suffered in April 2001. Musini denied liability on the grounds that

Real Sociedad had failed to disclose a pre-existing condition affecting the player, and also that the injury was the result of that pre-existing condition. Pending the determination of the claim, the issue arose as to whether the exclusive jurisdiction clause in the direct policy had been incorporated into the reinsurance agreement and had become binding on the reinsurers (thereby conferring exclusive jurisdiction on the Spanish courts under Article 23 of Regulation 44/2001).

Held (Andrew Smith J.): that there was no jurisdiction agreement. Article 23, like the English common law, treated an exclusive jurisdiction clause as ancillary to the main agreement and for there to be incorporation there had to be express reference to the jurisdiction clause in the reinsurance slip. There was no reference to jurisdiction in the full reinsurance clause, and the express exclusion of "limits and rates" did not imply that everything other than limits and rates was intended to be incorporated.

Choice of law clauses

Under English law the parties to a reinsurance agreement are free to agree the law applicable to the contract. That right is set out in Article 3.1 of the Rome Convention 1980, which became a part of English law by the Contracts (Applicable Law) Act 1995 (for further discussion, see Chapter 9):

> ***Rome Convention, Article 3.1***
> *A contract shall be governed by the law chosen by the parties. The choice must be expressed or demonstrated with reasonable certainty by the terms of the contract or the circumstances of the case. By their choice, the parties can select the law applicable to the whole or a part only of the contract.*

This provision reflects the pre-existing common law. The courts have held, consistently with their rulings on jurisdiction and choice of law, that a choice of law clause will not be incorporated by general incorporation wording.

***GAN Insurance Co. Ltd* v. *Tai Ping Insurance Co. Ltd* [1999] Lloyd's Rep. IR 472**

A building under construction in Taiwan was insured by the defendant insurers, under a contract which was stated to be governed by the law of Taiwan. The insurers reinsured on the London market under a facultative slip policy which at a number of different points was stated to be "as original", "original wording" and "per local standard . . . policy wording". There was no express choice of law provision in the reinsurance agreement, although there was a claims co-operation clause under which the reinsurers were obliged to follow the reinsured's settlements. A fire occurred at the building. The insurers accepted liability, but the reinsurers refused to do so and commenced an action in England for negative declaratory relief seeking orders that they were entitled to avoid the policy for misrepresentation or non-disclosure or that they were not liable by reason of breaches of the claims co-operation clause. The question for the court was whether the English court possessed jurisdiction, which would be the case if the reinsurance was governed by English law. The reinsured argued that the reinsurance was governed by the law of Taiwan, by reason of the incorporation of the choice of law clause in the direct policy.

Held (C.A.): that the reinsurance agreement was governed by English law and that the English court possessed jurisdiction. The choice of law clause in the direct policy had not been incorporated into the reinsurance. It would not be appropriate for London market reinsurers to lose the protection of English law relating to disclosure simply because the direct policy contained a choice of law clause in favour of some other jurisdiction and the reinsurance purported to incorporate the terms of the direct policy.

[*Note*: For later proceedings in the English courts, see Chapters 6 and 7].

BACK TO BACK COVER

The meaning of "back to back" cover

Definition

The notion of back to back cover is in essence a principle of construction of reinsurance agreements, which dictates that in appropriate circumstances the wording of the reinsurance agreement is to be construed in the same way as the wording of the underlying direct policy. In the case of facultative reinsurance agreements, the wording of the direct policy is incorporated into the reinsurance by means of the full reinsurance clause, and it is to be assumed that the meaning of the wording in the reinsurance agreement is to be construed in precisely the same way as in the direct policy. In this sense, back to back cover adds very little to the idea of incorporation, as back to back cover is achieved automatically by incorporation. This was seen above, in the discussion of the decisions in *Forsakrings Vesta* v. *Butcher* [1989] 1 A.C. 852 and *Groupama* v. *Catatumbo* [2000] 2 Lloyd's Rep. 350. There are indeed early decisions in which the full reinsurance clause did not have an incorporating effect but rather simply rendered back to back the terms of the direct policy and the reinsurance (*Joyce* v. *Realm Marine Insurance Co. Ltd* (1872) L.R. 7 Q.B. 580), although the modern view exemplified by *Vesta* and *Groupama* is that those terms are actually incorporated.

Leaving aside the situation where there has been incorporation of the terms of the direct policy into the reinsurance, there will be cases in which the notion of back to back cover may be of independent significance. These will arise where the wording of the direct policy has not been incorporated into the reinsurance agreement, as will typically be the position under reinsurance treaties.

***Forsakrings Vesta* v. *Butcher* [1989] 1 A.C. 852**
Per Lord Griffiths:

"In the ordinary course of business reinsurance is referred to as "back to back" with the insurance, which means that the reinsurer agrees that if the insurer is liable under the policy the reinsurer will accept liability to pay whatever percentage of the claim he has agreed to reinsure. A reinsurer could, of course, make a special contract with an insurer and agree to reinsure only some of the risks covered by the policy of insurance, leaving the insurer to bar the full cost of the other risks. Such a contract would, I believe, be wholly exceptional, a departure from the normal understanding of the back-to-back nature of reinsurance and would require to be spelt out in clear terms. I doubt if there is any market for such reinsurance."

Application

The principle of back to back cover has been applied in a variety of situations, including:

(1) *The coverage of the two agreements*. For a recent illustration, see *Mann* v. *Lexington Insurance Co.* [2001] Lloyd's Rep. IR 179, where the construction of an aggregation clause as meaning that individual instances of rioting were each to be treated as a separate "event" rather than as a composite event was influenced by the consideration that this produced consistency up the reinsurance chain. See also *Goshawk Syndicate Management Ltd and others* v. *XL Speciality Insurance Co.* [2004] Lloyd's Rep. IR 683, in which Morison held that the phrase "this policy to respond only for losses in excess of original annual aggregate deductible of US$5,000,000 and original underlying deductibles" incorporated the entire financial coverage of the direct policy, including a provision under which the insurers were liable for individual losses in excess of US$1,000,000 even though the annual aggregate deductible had not at that point been exceeded. Morison J. held that this provision was to be regarded as an "original underlying deductible" even though it did not operate as a deductible, and justified his decision by the principle that the contracts were written on a back to back basis and that the reinsurers had taken a two-thirds share of the premium so ought to face an equivalent risk. The court recognised that the point was a difficult one, and permission to appeal was given.

(2) *Duration*. This was the issue in *Commercial Union Assurance Co. plc* v. *Sun Alliance Insurance Group plc* [1992] 1 Lloyd's Rep. 475, where the direct policy written in Holland contained a "tacit renewal" clause under which it was to continue unless cancelled by three months' notice. The reinsurance, governed by English law, was stated to be "for 12 months . . . with 120 days NCAD". The phrase—an acronym for Notice of Cancellation at Anniversary Date—was held by Steyn J. to mean much the same as the tacit renewal clause in the underlying policy and accordingly that the reinsurance continued in force unless cancelled by three months' notice. But contrast *Wasa International Insurance Co. Ltd and AGF Insurance Co. Ltd* v. *Lexington Insurance Co.* [2007] EWHC 896 (Comm), discussed above, where it was held that duration provisions were not back to back.

(3) *The scope of warranties or exclusions in the two agreements*. This was the key issue in both *Forsakrings Vesta* v. *Butcher* [1989] 1 AC 852 and *Groupama* v. *Catatumbo* [2000] 2 Lloyd's Rep. 350.

(4) *The interpretation of the agreement*. This point is illustrated by *Forsakrings Vesta* v. *Butcher* [1989] 1 AC 852 and *Groupama* v. *Catatumbo* [2000] 2 Lloyd's Rep. 350 and also by the following case:

***Ace Insurance SA-NV* v. *Zurich Insurance Co.* [2001] Lloyd's Rep. IR 504**

Nabors, a company based in Texas, was insured against material damage to its Saudi Arabian installations by Sol. The policy imposed various warranties on Nabors relating to the company's operations. Sol acted as a front for Zurich, and Zurich reinsured Sol. The reinsurance contract provided that all disputes were to be submitted to the exclusive jurisdiction of the Courts of Texas. Zurich reinsured with Ace, and was stated to be "As original and/or as original following the original in all respects including claims settlements". There was in addition an express service of suit clause which stated that the reinsurers would submit to the court of a competent jurisdiction within the United States. The reinsurance was governed by English law. Following a loss in Saudi Arabia, Ace commenced proceedings in England for a declaration that there was no liability to Zurich by reason of a breach of warranties in the direct policy which had been incorporated into the reinsurance. Zurich subsequently commenced proceedings in Texas. The issue was whether the English proceedings should be stayed on the ground that Texas was a more convenient forum.

Held (C.A.): that the English proceedings should be stayed, and that the service of suit clause was conclusive in conferring jurisdiction upon the courts of Texas. In so deciding, the Court of Appeal commented that the fact that the reinsurance was governed by English law was of no significance in ascertaining whether England was the more appropriate jurisdiction as, even if it was the case that the various warranties in the direct policy had been incorporated into the reinsurance, the English court would have construed the warranties consistently with the law of Texas in order to ensure back to back cover. Thus, the fact that English law governed the reinsurance agreement was of no weight.

Limits

There are three main situations in which the presumption of back to back cover will be inapplicable.

First, the presumption is limited to proportional reinsurances, namely facultative contracts and quota share or surplus treaties. In each of these cases the reinsurers and the reinsured to some extent share the premiums and the risk. By contrast, where the reinsurance is non-proportional—the most important class being excess of loss reinsurance—the insurer and the reinsurer each independently assess the risk to be run and the premium to be charged.

***Axa Reinsurance (UK) plc* v. *Field* [1996] 2 Lloyd's Rep. 233**

The contracts under consideration in this case were excess of loss reinsurances of direct policies which covered underwriting agents at Lloyd's against professional negligence. The direct policies provided that all losses arising from one "originating cause" were to be regarded as a single loss. In *Cox* v. *Bankside Members Agency Ltd* [1995] 2 Lloyd's Rep. 437 Phillips J. held that the relevant event was the "blind spot" of each agent, so that all of the negligent acts of one agent were to be aggregated and treated as a single loss. The reinsurances also provided for aggregation of losses, but on the rather different basis that all losses arising out of one "event" were to be regarded as a single loss. The word "event" as construed in earlier authorities (notably *Caudle* v. *Sharp* [1995] L.R.L.R. 433) referred not to the underlying "originating cause" of a claim but rather the circumstances which led directly to the claim. The issue was, therefore, whether the normal meaning of the word "event" should be altered in the present context in order to mean "originating cause" so as to produce consistency between the insurance and the reinsurance. The point came before the House of Lords on the preliminary issue of whether the two clauses were to be construed consistently.

Held (H.L.): that the two clauses ought not automatically to be construed in the same manner. The phrase "originating cause" was a wide one and looked to background causes, whereas the phrase "event" was a narrow one and looked to something which happened at a particular time, at a particular place and in a particular way. Lord Mustill expressed the point as follows:

"I see nothing surprising in a decision to choose a narrower basis of aggregation: for, as I have suggested, the commercial considerations which determine how the cover of a whole "casualty" account will be framed and rated are not the same as those which shape the individual items comprising that account. If the syndicate had wished to secure identical measures of loss for its inward and outward contracts it could have negotiated with the reinsurers to that end, and taken the obvious course of using the same words in each. They chose not to do so, and thereby accepted the possibility that although in some combinations of facts the outcomes might be the same, in others they might not. What reasons there might be for choosing this course I cannot speculate, in the abstract, but reasons there might certainly be. At all events, I believe that the only safe course is to fall back on the words actually used, and to read them as they stand."

Secondly, if it is clear that different words have been used in the two contracts then the presumption of back to back cover, even in proportional reinsurances, may be ousted. In *GE Reinsurance Corporation* v. *New Hampshire Insurance Co.* [2004] Lloyd's Rep. IR 404 Langley J. found that it was impossible to use the back to back cover rule of construction to disregard terms in the reinsurance agreement simply because there was no equivalent provision in the direct policy. Equally, the financial limits of a reinsurance agreement are not overridden on the basis that cover is intended to be back to back: in *Baker* v. *Black Sea and Baltic General Insurance Co. Ltd* [1998] Lloyd's Rep. IR 327, the facts of which were given above, it was held that the maximum sum reinsured was not to be increased so that the reinsurance covered the reinsured's defence costs as well as the reinsured's direct liability for claims.

Thirdly, as was commented by Langley J. in *GE Reinsurance Corporation*, where (as in the case before him) the underlying insurance and the reinsurance have been separately negotiated, then there is less justification for applying the principle of back to back cover. The point was also made in *Youell* v. *Bland Welch & Co. (No. 1)* [1992] 2 Lloyd's Rep. 127, where it was decided by Phillips J. that a reinsurance agreement which had been taken out for 48 months to cover direct insurance which had been taken out on an indefinite basis was not to be construed back to back in the light of the express words of the two agreements. See also *GAN Insurance Co. Ltd* v. *Tai Ping Insurance Co. Ltd* [1999] Lloyd's Rep. IR 472, the facts of which were given above: the Court of Appeal was doubtful whether the two contracts were back to back by reason of the fact that they had been separately negotiated.

TEST YOUR UNDERSTANDING

1. **Which of the following statements is true?**
   (a) A term may be implied into a reinsurance agreement if the term is necessary to give business efficacy to the agreement.
   (b) A term may be implied into a reinsurance agreement if it would be reasonable to do so.
   (c) A term may be implied into a reinsurance agreement if there is market evidence of a custom.
   (d) A term may be implied into a reinsurance agreement even if it modifies an express term of the agreement.

2. **Which of the following statements is true in relation to the "full reinsurance clause"?**
   (a) The clause creates a warranty by the reinsured that the terms of the direct policy are as presented to the reinsurers.
   (b) The clause incorporates all of the terms of the direct policy.
   (c) The clause incorporates those terms of the direct policy which are germane to reinsurance.
   (d) The clause cannot incorporate terms which are inconsistent with those in the reinsurance agreement.

3. **Which of the following terms will generally be incorporated by a full reinsurance clause?**
   (a) Coverage clauses.
   (b) Claims provisions.
   (c) Warranties.
   (d) Dispute resolution clauses.

4. **Where a term has been incorporated by a full reinsurance clause, which of the following effects may the term have in the reinsurance agreement?**
   (a) The incorporated term may operate as a provision which governs the contractual relationship between reinsured and reinsurer.
   (b) The incorporated term may operate as a statement of the contractual position as between the reinsured and the direct assured.

5. **Which of the following conditions are necessary for the incorporation of an arbitration (or exclusive jurisdiction) clause into a reinsurance agreement?**
   (a) The arbitration clause must state that it applies to reinsurance disputes as well as to insurance disputes.

(b) The arbitration clause must be capable of "manipulation" so that it can be extended to reinsurance disputes.
(c) There must be an express reference to the arbitration clause in the incorporating words in the reinsurance agreement.

6. **Where a warranty has been incorporated from a direct policy governed by a foreign law into a reinsurance agreement governed by English law, which of the following statements is true?**

(a) The reinsurance agreement is to be regarded as governed by the foreign law.
(b) The construction of the warranty is to be regarded as governed by the foreign law.
(c) The warranty is to be construed in accordance with English law.

7. **Which of the following statements relating to the principle of back to back cover are correct?**

(a) The principle of back to back cover applies to all reinsurance agreements.
(b) The principle of back to back cover applies only to proportional reinsurances.
(c) The principle of back to back cover is capable of overriding the express terms of the reinsurance agreement.
(d) The principle of back to back cover is a rebuttable rule of construction only.

CHAPTER 5

RIGHTS AND OBLIGATIONS OF THE PARTIES

THE CONSTRUCTION OF REINSURANCE AGREEMENTS

The guiding principles which govern the construction of commercial contracts, as derived from the leading authorities, were laid down by Lord Hoffmann in *Investors Compensation Scheme* v. *West Bromwich Building Society* [1998] 1 All E.R. 98, as follows (citations omitted):

(1) Interpretation is the ascertainment of the meaning which the document would convey to a reasonable person having all the background knowledge which would reasonably have been available to the parties in the situation in which they were at the time of the contract.

(2) The background was famously referred to by Lord Wilberforce as the "matrix of fact", but this phrase is, if anything, an understated description of what the background may include. Subject to the requirement that it should have been reasonably available to the parties and to the exception to be mentioned next, it includes absolutely anything which would have affected the way in which the language of the document would have been understood by a reasonable man.

(3) The law excludes from the admissible background the previous negotiations of the parties and their declarations of subjective intent. They are admissible only in an action for rectification. The law makes this distinction for reasons of practical policy and, in this respect only, legal interpretation differs from the way we would interpret utterances in ordinary life. The boundaries of this exception are in some respects unclear.

(4) The meaning which a document (or any other utterance) would convey to a reasonable man is not the same thing as the meaning of its words. The meaning of words is a matter of dictionaries and grammar; the meaning of the document is what the parties using those words against the relevant background would reasonably have understood them to mean. The background may not merely enable the reasonable man to choose between the possible meanings of words which are ambiguous but even (as occasionally happens in ordinary life) to conclude that the parties must, for whatever reason, have used the wrong words or syntax.

(5) The "rule" that words should be given their "natural and ordinary meaning" reflects the commonsense proposition that we do not easily accept that people have made linguistic mistakes, particularly in formal documents. On the other hand, if one would nevertheless conclude from the background that something must have gone wrong with the language, the law does not require judges to attribute to the parties an intention which they plainly could not have had.

A number of separate points relevant to reinsurance agreements may be made here.

Firstly, as far as the overall meaning of the document is concerned, the factual matrix is the key consideration. As was seen in Chapter 2, it was held by the Court of Appeal in *HIH Casualty and General Insurance Co.* v. *New Hampshire Insurance Co.* [2001] Lloyd's Rep. IR 596 the factual matrix of a policy includes the slip which preceded it. The factual matrix will also include the market in which the parties were operating (e.g., the forms of cover which were and were not commercially available at the relevant time), but it will exclude previous negotiations between the parties and in particular earlier drafts of the proposed wording which were subsequently abandoned prior to the making the contract.

Secondly, the presumption of back to back cover, which applies to proportional reinsurance agreements (see Chapter 4), may require a particular word or phrase to be construed against its usual meaning and in a manner consistent with the underlying direct policy.

Thirdly, subjective intentions are excluded. This is of particular importance in reinsurance, as it is usually the case that a policy will have a number of subscribing underwriters. While it is the case that each subscription is a separate parallel contract, each contract is to be construed in the same fashion and accordingly the intentions or beliefs of individual subscribing underwriters can have no part to play in the overall interpretation of what has been agreed. This point was made by Moore-Bick J. in *Kingscroft Insurance Co. Ltd* v. *Nissan Fire & Marine Insurance Co. Ltd (No. 2)* [1999] Lloyd's Rep. IR 603.

Fourthly, words used in legal documents are presumed to bear the meaning that the law has placed upon them. Words such as "theft" and "riot", which are specifically defined by statute, are thus treated as having that meaning unless this would produce an absurdity in the relevant context.

Finally, the principle of *contra proferentem*—that ambiguous words are to be construed against the person who drafted them—has relatively little application to reinsurance. This device has typically been used in consumer contracts so as to benefit the weaker party, but that consideration is largely irrelevant in reinsurance. Further, the practice of the London market is for proposed wording to be put forward by the broker acting for the reinsured. That wording may have been specially drafted by the broker and subsequently negotiated with the reinsurers or it may have been adopted from the various standard clauses available on the London market prepared by market committees consisting underwriters, brokers and legal advisers. In these circumstances it is difficult to say which of the parties has drafted the wording. In *Youell* v. *Bland Welch (No. 1)* [1992] 2 Lloyd's Rep. 127 the Court of Appeal held that an ambiguous duration provision in a reinsurance agreement was not to be construed *contra proferentem*: the presumption that words of limitation should be given a restricted meaning was offset by the consideration that they had been drafted by the reinsured's broker.

REINSURANCE CONDITIONS

The classes of insurance and reinsurance conditions

The terms of a reinsurance are in outline:

(1) insuring and reinsuring provisions;
(2) conditions;
(3) warranties;
(4) ancillary matters (e.g., arbitration and other dispute resolution provisions).

Conditions and warranties both impose obligations upon the reinsured, but their legal significance differs. A warranty (unlike a warranty in any other form of contract) is an unconditional promise made by the reinsured as to existing facts or future conduct, breach of which automatically brings the risk to an end. Warranties are considered below. Conditions, by contrast, are potentially more benign terms whose breach is not necessarily fatal to coverage under the agreement. Conditions in reinsurance agreements fall into three categories:

- the condition may be a condition precedent to the making of the policy or to the attachment of the risk—if it is not complied with, the reinsurers cannot face liability for any claim;
- the condition may be a condition precedent to the liability of the reinsurers—if it is not complied with, the reinsurers cannot be liable for the claim to which the condition relates;
- the condition may be a "bare" condition—if it is not complied with, the consequences of the breach will depend upon the importance of the condition and the seriousness of the breach.

Conditions precedent to policy or risk

This type of condition prevents the risk from ever attaching. This may be because the reinsurers have insisted upon a particular course of events before the contract is treated as binding, or because there is a binding contract but the risk itself has not incepted. Reinsurance contracts do not generally contain conditions of this type, although they are fairly common in direct policies and relate to matters such as payment of the premium and—in the case of marine insurance—inspection and classification of the insured vessel. An illustration of the latter is *Zeus Tradition Marine Ltd* v. *Bell, The Zeus V* [2000] 2 Lloyd's Rep. 587, where a condition in a marine policy that the cover was "subject to survey and valuation prior to navigation" meant that the risk could not attach until the survey and valuation had been carried out.

Reinsurance treaties may require the reinsured to submit documents (often called "bordereaux") to the reinsurers, setting out the risks accepted by the reinsured. If the treaty is non-obligatory in the sense that risks accepted by the reinsured are not automatically ceded to the treaty and have to be considered by the reinsurers, then a failure by the reinsured to submit the relevant documents will necessarily prevent the risk from attaching. By contrast, if the treaty is obligatory and a risk accepted by the reinsured is automatically ceded to the reinsurance treaty, then failure by the reinsured to submit the necessary bordereaux to the reinsurers will not prevent the risk from attaching unless the obligation to submit a bordereau is expressly stated to be a condition precedent to the attachment of the reinsurers' liability (see *Glencore AG* v. *Ryan, The Beursgracht* [2002] Lloyd's Rep. IR 335, discussed below).

Conditions precedent to liability

The principle

A condition precedent to liability is a term which, unless complied with, prevents the reinsured from making any claim against the reinsurers. The reinsured is technically not in breach of contract, as there is no liability for failing to comply with a condition precedent: it is simply the case that the reinsurers do not face any liability to meet the claim. A condition precedent is automatic in its effects: there is no need for the reinsurers to prove that the reinsured's failure to comply with the condition precedent in any way contributed to the loss or prejudiced the reinsurers' ability to investigate the circumstances and to negotiate a settlement with the direct assured.

Whether a condition precedent has been created is a matter to be determined by the proper construction of the contract. The same obligation may be framed as a bare condition (where the reinsurers' rights depend upon the seriousness of the breach) or as a condition precedent (where mere proof of breach is enough to prevent liability from attaching to the reinsurers). Thus if the reinsured's obligation to notify potential claims as soon as practicable is a condition precedent then the right to indemnity will be lost if the clause is a condition precedent, whereas it will only be lost if the breach is a serious one if the clause is a bare condition. Accordingly, the courts will not construe a term as a condition precedent unless the wording is clear, and even if the clause does constitute a condition precedent the courts will attempt to construe the obligations imposed by it in a narrow fashion.

Insurance illustrations

Conditions precedent are regarded as draconian provisions in that they automatically bring an end to the insurers' liability whether or not the breach was of any significance to the insurers in terms of contributing to the loss or in terms of allowing the insurers to investigate the circumstances of the loss, and there is a strong presumption that a condition is not to be construed as a condition precedent. It was said by Phillips J. in *Youell* v. *Bland Welch* [1992] 2 Lloyd's Rep. 127 that the court should strive to construe a contract in a way which allows the obligations under it to be enforced rather than evaded. One particular context in which this approach may be illustrated arises where the policy contains a list of provisions, all of which are labelled as conditions precedent: it was decided in *Re Bradley and Essex and Suffolk Accident Indemnity Society* [1912] 1 K.B. 415 that the court was entitled to examine each item in the list to determine whether it could appropriately be treated as a condition precedent, a principle accepted as binding in the modern context in *Bonner-Williams* v. *Peter Lindsay Leisure Ltd* [2001] 1 All E.R. (Comm) 1140. However, in recent cases it has been held that a general clause which deems all conditions to be conditions precedent will be effective provided that the terms in question are not ambiguous and can appropriately be regarded as conditions precedent: *Pilkington United Kingdom Ltd* v. *CGU Insurance plc* [2004] Lloyd's Rep. IR 891; *Slater* v. *Buckinghamshire County Council* [2004] Lloyd's Rep. IR 432.

There are numerous direct insurance decisions in which the courts have refused to construe policy conditions as conditions precedent to liability. See, e.g., *Frans Maas (UK) Ltd* v. *Sun Alliance and London Insurance plc* [2004] Lloyd's Rep. IR 649 (obligation on assured warehouse to trade only on its standard conditions). These decisions may be contrasted with: *George Hunt Cranes Ltd* v. *Scottish Boiler and General Insurance Co. Ltd* [2002] Lloyd's Rep. IR 178 (obligation to take safety precautions in construction work); *Bonner-Williams* v. *Peter Lindsay Leisure Ltd* [2001] 1 All E.R. (Comm) 1140 (obligation to take safety precautions in construction work); *Bankers Insurance Company Ltd* v. *South* [2003] EWHC 380, [2004] Lloyd's Rep. IR 1 (obligation to report claims and to forward legal proceedings when issued).

Even if it is the case that a clause is to be construed as a condition precedent, the obligations imposed by the clause will in the event of ambiguity be construed in favour of the reinsured.

Reinsurance illustrations

The most important condition for the protection of facultative reinsurers is that which regulates claims-handing by the reinsured. The two types of clause used most widely are claims co-operation clauses and claims control clauses (for detailed discussion, see Chapter 7). A claims co-operation clause generally requires the reinsured to notify all losses as soon as the reinsured becomes aware of them, to allow the reinsurers to participate in any negotiations between the reinsured and the direct policy holder, and to preclude any settlement or admission of liability by the reinsured without the consent of the reinsurers. A claims control clause goes further, and requires the reinsured to hand over to the reinsurers all negotiations with the direct policy holder in respect of the direct loss. The courts have refused to construe such provisions as conditions precedent to the reinsurers' liability unless there is express wording to that effect and, where they have been required to do so, they have construed the term in a narrow fashion. See the following:

***Cox* v. *Bankside Members Agency* [1995] 2 Lloyd's Rep. 437**
A general condition in a policy required the assured to give to the Underwriters immediate written notice of any claim made against the assured, any loss discovered by the assured or the discovery by the assured of reasonable cause for suspicion of dishonesty or fraud or negligence such as might give rise to a claim under the policy. The issue was whether compliance was a condition precedent to recovery under the policy.

Held (Phillips J., the point not being appealed): that the condition was not a condition precedent. The provision was not described as a condition precedent, and there was no reason based on commercial efficacy why the provision should be construed in that way as in the majority of cases a limited delay in notifying a claim would not have any adverse effect on underwriters. Treating the provision as a condition precedent would be harsh.

***Charter Reinsurance* v. *Fagan* [1996] 2 Lloyd's Rep. 113**
The reinsured in this case became insolvent and was unable to make payments to its policy holders. The reinsured was covered by an excess of loss reinsurance treaty which defined the sum payable—the "Net Loss" as "the sum actually paid by the Reinsured in settlement of losses or liability after making deductions for all recoveries". The reinsurers argued that they were not liable to make any payment to the reinsured until there had been actual payment by the reinsured to its policy holders.

Held (H.L.): that the reinsured was able to recover. The words viewed in their context did not impose a condition precedent requiring prepayment by the reinsured as a condition of recovery from the reinsurers. The policy construed as a whole showed that the cover was against liability which had been incurred by the reinsured, whether or not any payment had been made to policy holders.

***Eagle Star Insurance Co. Ltd* v. *Cresswell* [2004] Lloyd's Rep. IR 437**
The terms of a reinsurance agreement provided that the reinsurers would follow the settlements of the reinsured, but that it was a condition precedent to any liability under the policy that the claimant would (a) give notice to the reinsurers within seven days of the occurrence of any loss, and (b) co-operate with the reinsurers in the adjustment and settlement of claims. Subsequently the printed form was amended: the claims co-operation clause was struck out, and was replaced with a series of typed clauses. Those clauses stated that the consent of the reinsurers was required before any settlement was binding on them. There was also a claims control clause in the following words:

(a) *To notify all claims or occurrences likely to involve the Underwriters within 7 days from the time that such claims or occurrences become known to them.*
(b) *The Underwriters hereon shall control the negotiations and settlements of any claims under this Policy. In this event the Underwriters hereon will not be liable to pay any claim not controlled as set out above.*

The issue was whether (b) was a condition precedent to the reinsurers' liability, the argument being that if the reinsurers chose not to exercise their rights of control then they were not liable to pay. It was common ground that (a) was not a condition precedent, and Morison J. held at first instance [2003] EWHC 2224 (Comm) that (b) was not a condition precedent either, for a number of reasons: (1) there was no reason to suppose that the parties intended that the two limbs of the same clause would operate differently; (2) clear wording was needed; (3) the deleted insolvency clause made the position clear, but the parties had moved away from that; (4) no obligations were actually imposed on the reinsured, so that if the reinsurers were right it gave them a discretion not to pay by not exercising control rights—the only sensible way of reading the clause was to imply an obligation on the reinsured not to obstruct the reinsurers.

On appeal the Court of Appeal disagreed. The initial point was that the typed clauses prevailed over the printed clauses, this being a general principle of construction. The Court of Appeal accepted that, but for the claims control clause, the clause which required the reinsurers' consent to any settlement would not have precluded recovery by the reinsured if it had been able to prove its loss: that clause was not a condition precedent and (just as in the *Scor* case) its only effect would have been to prevent reliance on the follow the settlements clause.

Turning to paragraph (b) of the claims control clause, the Court of Appeal analysed its two sentences separately. The Court of Appeal was unanimous that the first sentence—"The Underwriters hereon shall control the negotiations and settlements of any claims under this Policy"—did not impose any obligation on the reinsurers to take over the control of the settlements, but rather conferred upon them the right to do so. There was at this point a dispute as to the time at which the reinsurers were entitled to take control. The reinsured argued the clause was in the nature of an option which had to be exercised on notification of the loss under paragraph (a) (or at least within a reasonable time), and that thereafter the right to control was lost and the reinsurers were obliged to follow the reinsured's settlements. The Court of Appeal preferred the reinsurers' interpretation that the reinsurers were entitled to be informed by the reinsured when negotiations began so that the reinsurers could at that point decide how the negotiations should be conducted, so that the clause was an allocation rather than an option. The reinsured's construction would make it almost impossible for the reinsurers to make an informed choice, as at the date of the notification it was possible that full information would not be available. Longmore L.J.'s only reservation was to express doubt—without deciding the point—that the clause enabled the reinsurers to dictate that negotiations should begin earlier than the reinsured thought to be right or sensible.

The next issue concerned the second sentence of paragraph (b), "In this event the Underwriters hereon will not be liable to pay any claim not controlled as set out above". The Court of Appeal held that, consistently with the first sentence of the paragraph, the words "In this event" did not mean in the event that the reinsurers opted to control the proceedings, but rather in the event that there were negotiations in respect of a claim. Once that meaning was given to the words, the following words—"the Underwriters . . . will not be liable to pay any claim not controlled . . . " inevitably constituted a condition precedent to the reinsurers' liability as that was what the clause said. The absence of the phrase "condition precedent" was not regarded by the Court of Appeal as fatal to this conclusion, as the meaning was otherwise clear. Putting the matter another way, once there were negotiations in respect of a claim, if the reinsurers did not control those negotiations then the reinsured was simply unable to recover: it was not a case of the reinsured being required to notify the reinsurers of settlement negotiations (by means of some implied term) but rather there was an absolute bar to recovery if the reinsurers were not involved.

The Court of Appeal also addressed one further matter, namely, how would a claims co-operation clause expressed in this fashion operate where the reinsurers simply refused to exercise control? If the wording does give rise to a condition precedent, and the reinsurers simply decline to participate, the reinsured is lost because any settlement made by the reinsured will by definition not be binding on the reinsurers. Looked at in this way, if the reinsurers' rights are unlimited, the reinsurers in effect have an absolute discretion to refuse to honour the reinsurance agreement. Rix L.J. suggested two possible ways round this problem. The first was waiver, so that in appropriate circumstances a refusal to participate by reinsurers could be construed as a willingness to follow the reinsured's settlements. The second solution was that there was an implied term, or in the alternative a duty of good faith, whereby reinsurers would not exercise their discretion under a claims provision in bad faith, capriciously or arbitrarily.

***Royal and Sun Alliance Insurance plc* v. *Dornoch Ltd* [2004] Lloyd's Rep. IR 544**

RSA had taken a 21.5% subscription on each of the three layers of a "Master Subscription Policy" issued to the Coca-Cola group of companies. Part of the cover related to D&O liability and general liability of Coca-Cola, and was written on a claims made basis. Notice was to be given under the MSP as soon as practicable after any claim had been made. RSA acted as a front for reinsurers, who reinsured RSA for 100% of its liability. The reinsurance contained a full reinsurance clause and also a claims control clause which provided that:

> *(a) the Reassured shall upon knowledge of any loss or losses which may give rise to claim under this policy, advise the Underwriters thereof by cable within 72 hours,*
> *(b) the Reassured shall furnish the Underwriters with all information available respecting such loss or losses and the Underwriters shall have the right to appoint adjusters, assessors and/or surveyors and to control all negotiations, adjustments and settlements in connection with such loss or losses.*

Claims were made against Coca-Cola and three of its directors and officers in two class actions commenced in Georgia on 27 October 2000 and 13 November 2000. It was alleged that the defendants had overstated the value of Coca-Cola's stock, causing the claimants to purchase stock in the market at inflated prices. The basis of the claims was that Coca-Cola had artificially inflated its sales figures by forcing bottlers to accept unwanted deliveries of concentrate. RSA was informed of the claims on 30 December 2000, notice having earlier been given to the leading underwriter. RSA duly informed the reinsurers on 19 January 2001. The reinsurers asserted that there had been a breach of the claims control clause, as notification was required within 72 hours of RSA obtaining knowledge of losses. The dispute between the parties was as to the meaning of the claims control clause.

Aikens J. held that there had not been any breach of the clause. The word "loss" in the clause referred (as had been argued by the reinsurers) to the loss suffered by those claiming against Coca-Cola, and not (as had been argued by RSA) to the loss suffered by Coca-Cola in the form of a judgment, award or settlement in favour of the claimants. Neither side sought to argue that the loss was that of RSA, as that would have meant that notification would not have been required until after RSA's own liability had been established and quantified. However, Aikens J. went on to hold that, for the purposes of ascertaining the knowledge required of RSA, the word "loss" meant actual loss and not alleged loss. In other words, it was only when RSA obtained actual (and not constructive) knowledge that there had been an actual loss suffered by the claimants that the duty to notify arose. There was no loss until there had been a judgment, award or settlement in favour of the claimants, and accordingly there was no obligation to notify the reinsurers until that point had been reached. This might be regarded as an inherently contradictory interpretation of the clause. The Court of Appeal on appeal upheld the first instance decision of Aikens J. It ruled that the phrase "loss or losses" meant actual loss or losses and not simply alleged loss or losses. It was unnecessary to decide whose loss was being referred to. The Court of Appeal noted that the problem had arisen in the present case because the notification clause was wholly inappropriate to a reinsurance agreement and instead was designed for a property or similar policy where an identifiable loss had occurred. The Court of Appeal rejected the argument that an interpretation deprived the clause of effect, as the parties were to be taken at their word, particularly if they had taken a clause from the precedent book which turned out to be unsuitable for its purpose.

***Insurance Company of Africa* v. *Scor* [1985] 1 Lloyd's Rep. 312**

A facultative reinsurance agreement contained a claims co-operation clause which provided that:

It is a condition precedent to liability under this Insurance that all claims be notified immediately to the Underwriters subscribing to this Policy and the Reassured hereby undertake in arriving at the settlement of any claim, that they will co-operate with the Reassured Underwriters and that no settlement shall be made without the approval of the Underwriters subscribing to this Policy.

The reinsured reached a settlement with the direct policy holder without seeking the approval of the reinsurers, and the reinsurers asserted that the clause was a condition precedent to their liability.

Held (C.A.): that the reinsurers were liable. The clause was divisible. The first part of the clause relating to co-operation with the reinsurers was expressed to be a condition precedent to the reinsurers' liability, whereas the latter part of the clause preventing settlements without the reinsurers' consent was not expressed to be a condition precedent to the reinsurers' liability. Therefore, as long as the reinsured could show that it was liable to the direct assured as a matter of law, then the assured was able to recover irrespective of the breach of the clause.

[*Note*: The *Scor* case is the leading authority on the impact of claims co-operation clauses and on the relationship between the reinsurers' obligation to follow the reinsured's settlements and reinsured's obligations to comply with claims co-operation obligations. See Chapter 7.]

***Gan Insurance Co. Ltd* v. *Tai Ping Insurance Co. Ltd (No. 2)* [2001] Lloyd's Rep. IR 667**

This was a reinsurance of a direct policy on construction of a computer factory in Taiwan. The reinsurance contained a claims co-operation clause in the following terms:

"Notwithstanding anything contained in the reinsurance agreement and/or policy wording to the contrary, it is a condition precedent to any liability under this policy that

(a) the reinsured shall, upon knowledge of any circumstances which may give rise to a claim against them, advise the reinsurers immediately, and in any event not later than 30 days.

(b) The reinsured shall co-operate with reinsurers and/or their appointed representatives subscribing to this policy in the investigation and assessment of any loss and/or circumstances giving rise to a loss.

(c) No settlement and/or compromise shall be made and liability admitted without the prior approval of reinsurers. All other terms and criticisms of this policy remain unchanged."

The reinsurers asserted that there had been a breach of the third condition, in that the reinsured had settled a claim with the third party having admitted liability and without the consent of the reinsurers. A number of questions arose, one of which was whether the obligations in the claims co-operation clause amounted to conditions precedent.

Held (C.A.): that the claims co-operation clause was a condition precedent to the liability of the reinsurers. Any breach of the clause precluded recovery by the reinsured, even if the reinsured was able to prove its loss as a matter of law. The wording was to be distinguished from that in *Scor*, discussed above.

[*Note*: For further issues in this case, and in particular for questions relating to the proper construction of the clause, see Chapter 7.]

***Shinedean Ltd* v. *Alldown Demolition (London) Ltd and Axa Insurance UK plc* [2006] Lloyd's Rep. IR 846**

The assured undertook demolition works at the claimant's premises. The assured excavated a hole which allegedly caused damage to premises belonging to Mr and Mrs P. The claimant settled the claim by Mr and Mrs P, and also incurred the cost of carrying out work to its own premises to stabilise the site and of altering the design of the development. The assured was insured under a public liability policy which required it to give notice of a claim and thereafter to co-operate with the insurers. Compliance with each of the claims conditions was, by a general provision, expressed to be a condition precedent to the insurers' liability. The assured gave due notice of the incident, but thereafter failed to give any information to the insurers despite repeated requests. The information was only provided once proceedings against the assured had started, and took the form of an attachment to a witness statement. The insurers argued that the assured was in breach of the co-operation clause and that because it was a condition precedent the insurers were not liable.

The Court of Appeal, overturning the first instance decision of H.H.J. Richard Seymour QC, held that the insurers were not liable. The co-operation clause was a condition precedent, as it appeared in a list of similar clauses all of which had been deemed to be conditions precedent. The trial judge had ruled that, because the co-operation clause did not impose any time limit for compliance, it was to be implied into the clause that the assured would co-operate within a reasonable time, and what was a reasonable time depended in part upon prejudice to the insurers: on the facts there was no prejudice, so the insurers were liable. The Court of Appeal held that there was no absolute principle that prejudice was a relevant consideration, and that the question was whether the assured had co-operated within a reasonable time: on the facts, this was not the case, as there was no attempt to co-operate until litigation had commenced.

[NOTE: the overturning of the trial judge will be a relief to reinsurers, as under the earlier decision a claims co-operation clause was rendered all but meaningless unless insurers could show that they had suffered prejudice by reason of breach: if the reinsured was liable to the assured, it is difficult to see where the prejudice could come from.]

Bare conditions

Assessment of bare conditions

A bare condition is simply a condition which is not expressed as a condition precedent to the reinsurers' liability. The consequences of a breach of a bare condition are determined in the following fashion. The first step is to consider the term itself, and to ascertain whether it can be classified on its face as either a vital term or a minor term. If it is a vital term then any breach of that term will allow the reinsurers to treat the policy as repudiated as of the date of breach, and the reinsurers have the right to refuse to pay claims arising after the date of repudiation. By contrast, if the term is a minor one, then any breach can give rise only to damages in favour of the reinsurers. In the overwhelming majority of cases, however, it will not be possible to construe a term from the outset as either a vital term or a minor term, as the seriousness of the consequences for the reinsurers will depend upon the seriousness of the breach in any particular case. Such a term is to be regarded as "innominate", and it is almost certainly the case that a reinsurance condition will be construed in this fashion.

If the term is innominate, it is necessary to proceed to the second stage and to examine the seriousness of the breach itself. A breach which has very serious consequences for the insurers is to be treated as repudiatory. In such a case the reinsurers have the right to regard the repudiation as one of the policy as a whole, in which case the policy can be brought to an end as of the date of the breach. By contrast, if the breach is a trivial one, then the reinsurers may only claim damages and remain liable to pay the claim.

In practice, these principles will be of little assistance to reinsurers faced with a reinsured who is in breach of a policy condition. There are relatively few policy conditions which can from the outset be classified as so fundamental that their breach will be repudiatory: the most obvious obligation of the reinsured, to pay the premium, is not regarded as one which, if broken, amounts to a repudiation of the policy (see the discussion of premium, in the section "The Premium" of this chapter). Claims conditions are by their nature impossible to classify as fundamental terms: at best they are innominate. However, even if the condition is an innominate one, this is unlikely to be of any further assistance to the reinsurers. It is difficult to contemplate a condition whose breach is so serious that it amounts to a repudiation of the policy, and in the case of a claims condition it might be thought that such a finding would be all but impossible. After all, the reinsurers' allegation would have to be that the reinsured's failure to make a claim in accordance with the policy's provisions was so serious that it demonstrated an intention on the part of the reinsured to disavow the contract as a whole. The outcome, therefore, is that the reinsurers will have to satisfy themselves with a claim for damages. However, it may be difficult for the reinsurers to establish that they have suffered any loss by reason of a breach of condition, particularly if the condition relates to the claims process and the reinsurers would have faced liability in any event. In *Friends Provident Life and Pensions Ltd* v. *Sirius International Insurance Corporation* [2006] Lloyd's Rep. IR 45 Waller L.J. described the reinsurers' action for damages as "illusory" and Mance L.J. stated that in many cases damages would at best be "highly speculative".

These problems led to the suggestion by Waller L.J. in *Alfred McAlpine plc* v. *BAI (Run-off) Ltd* [2000] Lloyd's Rep. IR 352 that if the breach is a serious one but not sufficiently serious to justify the policy as a whole being treated as repudiated, it would be appropriate to regard the reinsured as having repudiated the claim, so that the reinsurers can refuse to pay the claim while leaving the policy unaffected. That suggestion was assumed to be correct in two subsequent Court of Appeal cases involving direct policies, *K/S Merc-Skandia XXXXII* v. *Certain Lloyd's Underwriters* [2000] Lloyd's Rep. IR 694 and *Glencore AG* v. *Ryan, The Beursgracht* [2002] Lloyd's Rep. IR 335, although in each of these the assured's breach was found not to be repudiatory either of the policy or of the claim. Subsequently, however, in *Friends Provident Life and Pensions Ltd* v. *Sirius International Insurance Corporation* [2005] EWCA Civ 601 the Court of Appeal, by a majority (Waller L.J. dissenting on the point) denied the existence of the concept of the repudiation of a claim. Accordingly, in future cases, if the reinsurers cannot show that the term is a fundamental one, or that the term is innominate but its breach was repudiatory of the policy as a whole, they will have to pay the claim and will be confined to an action for damages (assuming that loss can be proved).

Application of the principles

The operation of the law can be illustrated by the following direct insurance cases. Discussion of the now discredited concept of repudiation of the claim has been omitted.

Alfred McAlpine plc v. _BAI (Run-off) Ltd_ [2000] Lloyd's Rep. IR 352

This case concerned a claim under a contractors' liability policy in respect of liability for personal injury. The policy required the assured to give notice to the insurers as soon as possible after the happening of any occurrence which might give rise to a claim against the assured. The relevant accident occurred on 1 May 1991, but it was never notified by the assured: the insurers became aware of the accident in July 1992. The insurers denied liability, relying on breach of the condition.

Held (C.A.): the insurers were liable.

(1) The term was not a condition precedent.

(2) The term was an innominate term. However, failure to comply with an ancillary claims condition of the present type was not normally to be regarded as a repudiation of the entire policy.

K/S Merc-Skandia XXXXII v. _Certain Lloyd's Underwriters_ [2000] Lloyd's Rep. IR 694

The assured, a ship repairer in Trinidad, was insured against legal liability under policies which required the assured to give prompt written notice to underwriters in the event of an accident which might result in a claim and generally to keep the underwriters fully advised of the progress of the claim. A third party made a claim against the assured on 1 July 1988, and in May 1989 it was agreed between the third party and a senior employee of the assured that the dispute should be resolved in England under English law. Proceedings were commenced by the third party in England. Subsequently the assured came to believe that it would be advantageous for the action to be heard in Trinidad, and the assured produced a document dated 1 July 1988 which had allegedly been sent to the third party and which removed the authority of anyone other than the assured's controllers to negotiate in respect of the claim. The document thus undermined the jurisdiction agreement entered into in May 1989. Underwriters, acting on this document took steps to have the English proceedings stayed. It subsequently transpired that the document was a forgery and that a valid jurisdiction agreement had been entered into. The underwriters claimed that the co-operation clause had been broken and that they were thereby discharged from liability.

Held (C.A.): that the underwriters were liable.

(1) There was a breach of the claims clause, as giving false information did not amount to keeping the underwriters fully advised.

(2) The clause was not a condition precedent to liability. It was a bare condition, but the breach of that condition was not sufficiently serious to give rise to a repudiation of the policy even though fraud had been involved.

(3) In the absence of any repudiation there could be no breach of the continuing duty of utmost good faith. (For this aspect of the decision, see Chapter 3.)

Glencore AG v. _Ryan, The Beursgracht_ [2002] Lloyd's Rep. IR 335

The insurance in this case was a direct policy taken out in respect of the assured's liability arising out of the use of vessels from time to time chartered by the assured. The policy was in the form of an open cover [equivalent to a reinsurance treaty], which provided that the assured was to make a declaration to the insurers by means of monthly bordereaux as and when a vessel falling within the terms of open cover was chartered by the assured. A vessel was chartered by the assured in October 1987, but no declaration was made. An accident on board occurred at the end of that month, and this led to a claim against the assured in June 1991. The claim was notified to the insurers in 1992, and it then became apparent that no declaration of the vessel had been made. Judgment was obtained against the assured in June 1996, and the assured sought indemnification from the insurers. The insurers relied upon breach of the declaration condition as a defence.

Held (C.A.): that the insurers were liable.

(1) The open cover was an automatic one, so that a risk attached automatically on acceptance by the assured. The making of a declaration was not, therefore, a condition precedent to the attachment of the risk. The requirement to make a declaration was an important part of the contractual machinery, but it did not affect the attachment of a risk.

(2) The obligation on the assured to make monthly declarations did not mean that a declaration had to be made at the first possible available declaration date after it had been accepted by the assured: a declaration had to be made within a reasonable time only.

(3) The term was not a condition precedent to the insurers' liability, as the wording did not so specify. It would have been easy for the insurers so to provide.

(4) The term was innominate, and the consequences of the breach depended upon its seriousness. In the present case the breach was not serious: the insurers had been on risk from the acceptance of the risk by the assured, and while there had been no formal rectification until 1992 the insurers were by this time aware that there had been an over-sight. The default could be made good by the assured proffering the unpaid premium with interest.

Friends Provident Life and Pensions Ltd v. _Sirius International Insurance Corporation_ [2006] Lloyd's Rep. IR 45

FPLP was the successor in title of LMA. LMA was engaged in selling pensions, and obtained professional liability insurance cover for the period 1 February 1993 to 31 January 1994. The insurance was in the form of a primary layer in respect of losses up to £1 million, and an excess layer of £4 million in excess of £1 million. Both layers were placed by brokers, Bowrings, and were written on a claims made basis, providing an indemnity against losses arising from claims made against LMA during the period of the policy. General Condition 2 of the primary layer policy stated that LMA was required, as a condition precedent to the right to be indemnified "give to the Underwriters notice as soon as possible during the period of this policy . . . of any circumstance of which [LMA] shall become aware which may give rise to a claim or loss against them or any of them." The clause also provided that once notice was given, LMA was required to give full details in writing to the insurers, and if it did so then "any claim or loss to which that circumstance has given rise which is subsequently made after the expiration of the [policy] shall be deemed for the purposes of this Policy to have been made during the subsistence hereof." The second layer cover consisted of a co-insurance policy which incorporated the wording of the primary layer policy and also a different claims notification clause. Also forming a part of the second layer cover were two other policies which similarly incorporated the terms of the co-insurance policy.

On 28 January 1994 in the context of negotiations for the renewal to take effect on 1 February 1994, LMA wrote to the underwriters at the address of Bowrings in Exeter and confirmed that it knew of no circumstances likely to give rise to a claim under the policy other than in respect of pension misselling. Losses from pensions misselling ultimately reached some £9 million, and claims were made under the 1993–1994 year cover on the ground that the letter of 28 January constituted notice and that in accordance with General Condition 2 the subsequent losses were brought back into that year. Liability was admitted under the first layer and co-insurance policy, but the other second layer insurers denied liability. A number of preliminary issues arose.

Held (C.A.): (1) General Condition 2 had been incorporated into the excess layer policies. It was invariable practice for liability insurers to insure on a claims made basis, with an extension covering liabilities established during later years as long as the claims were notified to underwriters in the policy year, and it was to be assumed that the excess layer policies had been written on the same basis. Incorporation could be effected with only the most minor textual manipulation.

(2) It was sufficient for notice to be given to the primary layer underwriters, and both layers were bound by such notice: the words "the underwriters" in General Condition 2 referred to only the primary layer insurers, so that notice to them was notice to all of the insurers on risk. However, if that was wrong, then the notice to Bowrings was notice to the primary layer underwriters, who had nominated Bowrings for this purpose in the first layer policy, but not to the other underwriters. The relevant clause was not incorporated into the second layer policies, as it was not germane to the risk and was purely a matter of administration.

(3) The letter of 28 January 1994 was sufficient to constitute notice to the underwriters on both the primary layer and on the co-insurance, but not to the other excess layer insurers. Even though the letter was designed to be a declaration for renewal purposes, there was no reason why it could not double up as a notification of losses under General Condition 2. However, as the letter was not addressed to the other insurers, it did not constitute notice to them.

(4) The obligation to notify details of the claim to the underwriters under General Condition 2 was not expressed to be a condition precedent to liability, unlike the earlier part of the clause. Accordingly it was not to be construed as a condition precedent. The provision could be regarded for present purposes as an innominate term. However, if there was a serious breach of the term, the insurers would have the right to refuse the claim only by treating the policy as a whole as repudiated: there was not (Waller L.J. dissenting) any implied term whereby a serious breach of a claims condition could give the insurers the right to reject a claim while the policy remained valid: such a term was not necessary, and might give rise to disproportionate results where the prejudice related to, eg, loss of a subrogation claim worth £50,000 in respect of a loss of £1 million. It was difficult to conceive of a case in which the policy could be regarded as having been repudiated, and it would in any event give rise to conceptual difficulties,

including whether the loss to which the breach related would be affected. The insurers' only remedy in the vast majority (if not all) cases was damages, although it was the case that the calculation of such damages would be difficult (or, *per* Waller L.J., illusory).

REINSURANCE WARRANTIES

Types of warranties

All warranties are described as "promissory" in that they are a promise by the policy holder to the underwriters. The nature of the promise may vary from case to case. Warranties may be of the following types:

- A promise that facts are as stated by the policy holder at the date the policy was taken out.
- A promise by the policy holder that he holds a particular belief at the date the policy was taken out.
- A promise by the policy holder that he intends to act in a particular way after the policy has incepted.
- A promise by the policy holder that certain facts will remain true throughout the currency of the policy or that he will act or refrain from particular acts during the currency of the policy.

The first three of these types of warranty may be referred to as "present" warranties, in that they relate to facts, opinions or intentions at the date of the policy. The last type of warranty may be referred to as a "future" warranty, as it is concerned with matters which may or may not happen while the policy is in force. A warranty is defined more precisely by section 33(1) of the Marine Insurance Act 1906:

> **Marine Insurance Act 1906, s. 33(1)**
> (1).—A warranty . . . means a promissory warranty, that is to say, a warranty by which the assured undertakes that a particular thing shall or shall not be done, or that some condition shall be fulfilled, or whereby he affirms or negatives the existence of a particular state of facts.

Section 33(2) of the 1906 Act states that a warranty may be express or implied. This principle, however, applies only to marine policies: there are no implied warranties in non-marine insurance. This was so held by the Court of Appeal in *Euro-Diam Ltd* v. *Bathurst* [1988] 1 Lloyd's Rep. 228. The marine implied warranties are set out in the 1906 Act, and relate, most importantly, to the neutrality of a vessel (section 36), to the legality of the voyage (section 41) and, in the case of a voyage policy (from place to place), to the seaworthiness of the vessel at the date the risk incepted (section 39(1)). There is no seaworthiness warranty in a time policy (one for a fixed period) although section 39(5) does give a defence to an insurer where the vessel was put to sea when it was known by the assured to be unseaworthy and the loss was attributable to that unseaworthiness.

Creation of reinsurance warranties

Whether a policy term is a warranty is a matter of construction. In direct policies it has long been the tradition to add to the bottom of the proposal form a statement to the effect that the answers on the proposal form the "basis of the contract", and it is settled law that each of the answers on the proposal is thereby converted into a warranty. However, this practice is not adopted in reinsurance, and accordingly it is necessary to consider each term on its merits. A warranty must, however, be contained in or at least incorporated into the policy:

> **Marine Insurance Act 1906, s. 4(1)**
> (2).—An express warranty must be included in, or written upon, the policy, or must be contained in some document incorporated by reference into the policy.

A policy which covers a number of diverse classes of risk, and which is divided into sections, may lay down different warranties for different sections. Thus, in the event that a warranty is contained in one distinct section of a policy, it will be applicable to only that section and breach will not preclude recovery under other sections (as in *Printpak* v. *AGF Insurance* [1999] Lloyd's Rep. IR 542).

Warranties are draconian in their effect, and the courts are reluctant in practice to construe policy terms as warranties unless the intention is clear. Accordingly, a term which is described as a warranty will not necessarily be construed as such: it may, for example, be appropriate to construe the term as one which merely suspends the risk while the term is not being complied with (see below).

However, the fact that a term is not described as a warranty does not preclude a finding that it takes effect as a warranty. This point is emphasised by section 33(1) of the Marine Insurance Act 1906 (set out above), which states that a term, however expressed, may be a warranty. All will depend upon the significance of the term to the risk run by the reinsurers.

***HIH Casualty and General Insurance Co.* v. *New Hampshire Insurance Co.* [2001] Lloyd's Rep. IR 596**

The claimant had issued insurance cover to banks who had invested in film production companies. The insurance was designed to cover any shortfall in the repayments to the banks by the film production companies. The insurance was placed by way of two slips, the "7.23" slip and the "Rojak" slip. The 7.23 slip stated in the interest clause that "7.23 Productions will produce and make six made-for-TV films". The interest clause in the Rojak slip similarly provided that "Rojak Films Inc will produce and make 10 made-for-TV films". The claimant reinsured with the defendants on the basis that the terms of the direct policy were incorporated into the reinsurance. The full number of films was not made, and the issue for the Court of Appeal was whether the statements as to the number of films took effect as warranties.

Held (C.A.): that the statements were warranties. A clause or provision could be a warranty even though it was not specifically described as such. Relevant considerations were: (a) did the term go to the root of the transaction; (b) was the term descriptive of the risk or did it bear materially on the risk of loss; and (c) would damages be an unsatisfactory or inadequate remedy? These conditions were satisfied on the facts.

***GE Reinsurance Corporation* v. *New Hampshire Insurance Co.*, [2004] Lloyd's Rep. IR 404**

The facts of this case were given in Chapter 4, but are summarised here for convenience. US$100 million had been loaned by investors to a film distribution and production company, Destination, secured by the issue of notes to trustees acting for the noteholders. The key employee and creative mind of Destination was Steve Stabler, who was in charge of production for Destination. Insurance brokers acting for the noteholders placed 40% of the risk of non-payment by Destination with Axa, 20% with New Hampshire and 40% with various other insurers. The cover was later varied with Axa taking 40% of the risk and New Hampshire taking the remaining 60%. One-third of New Hampshire's subscription was taken for itself, and the remaining two-thirds was accepted by New Hampshire as a fronting company for the other insurers, who became New Hampshire's reinsurers under a facultative contract for that purpose. The direct policy subscribed to by Axa and New Hampshire was silent on the position of Mr Stabler within Destination, but New Hampshire's outwards reinsurance stated that it was a condition of the reinsurance that a contract in respect of Steve Stabler "to be maintained for the duration of the policy". There was also contained in the reinsurance contract the express statement: "warranted . . . that [the reinsured] retains during the currency of this Policy at least the amount stated in the Schedule as the retention". Soon after the insurance and reinsurance risks incepted, Mr Stabler departed from Destination. New Hampshire had also separately reinsured a part of the one-third of the risk which fell outside the facultative reinsurance policy. In due course Destination became insolvent and defaulted on its payments to the noteholders. In the present action New Hampshire sought to recover its liability to the noteholders from the reinsurers. The defences raised by the reinsurers were that: (1) the reinsurance contained a warranty to the effect that Mr Stabler would continue to be employed by Destination; and (2) there was a warranty by New Hampshire that they were to retain one-third of their 60% subscription for their own account and would not reinsure it elsewhere, and that this had been broken.

Held (Langley J.): that the reinsurers were discharged from liability.

(1) Applying the tests laid down by Rix L.J. in *HIH Casualty and General* v. *New Hampshire Insurance* [2001] Lloyd's Rep. IR 596 that the term relating to Mr Stabler's employment was a warranty. The wording used by the clause was clear, and required Mr Stabler to remain in employment. It was not possible to argue that the wording was simply a statement of existing fact or that it imposed obligations upon Destination but not upon New Hampshire. While the clause was described as a "condition" it was appropriate to construe the clause as a warranty: it went to the root of the transaction, as Mr Stabler was the key figure within Destination; it bore materially on the risk of loss; and its breach could not adequately be compensated by way of damages. That meant that as soon as Mr Stabler's employment ceased, the risk under the reinsurance came to an end by reason of breach of warranty. Langley J. dismissed a further argument that the warranty was overridden by the incorporation of the terms of the direct policy (which was silent on the matter) into the reinsurance agreement: see Module 4 for consideration of this point.

(2) There was no breach of the retention provision, which was not to be construed as a warranty preventing New Hampshire from reinsuring that part of the direct risk which it had accepted for its own account. The reality was that New Hampshire had taken 20% of the direct risk for its own account and had agreed to front 40% of the risk

for the facultative reinsurers, and it was irrelevant to the reinsurers whether New Hampshire chose to retain that 20% for its own account or to reinsure it separately.

***Toomey* v. *Banco Vitalicio de Espana SA de Seguros y Reaseguros*, [2004] Lloyd's Rep. IR 354**

The Spanish football club Atletico de Madrid took out insurance with the defendant insurers, a Spanish company, covering the club against loss of broadcasting rights in the event that the club was to be relegated from the First Division of the Spanish Professional Football League. The policy was valued, paying 2.9 billion pesetas without proof of actual loss. The defendants reinsured with London market reinsurers under a facultative agreement which contained the full reinsurance clause (so that the terms of the reinsurance were "warranted . . . as original"). The reinsured's brokers informed the reinsurers that the direct policy was not valued, thereby leaving the reinsurers with the impression that in the event of relegation the club would be required to prove their loss and that the sum of 2.9 billion pesetas simply represented the maximum amount recoverable. The reinsurers sought to avoid the policy for misrepresentation and breach of warranty.

Held (C.A.): that judgment would be given for the reinsurers.

(1) There had been a material misrepresentation as to the nature and amount of liability faced by the insurers under the direct policy. This was enough to dispose of the case.

(2) The statement as to the nature of the direct policy took effect as an independent warranty. While that statement had not been described as a warranty, it met the requirements for a warranty laid down by Rix L.J. in *HIH* v. *New Hampshire*: the statement had a direct bearing on the risk run by the reinsurers, and went to the root of the transaction.

(3) It was not necessary to decide whether the phrase "warranted same terms and conditions as original" merely had an incorporating effect, or whether the phrase operated to treat the reinsured as having warranted that the terms of the direct policy were as stated by the reinsured.

Contrast *Assicurazioni Generali* v. *Arab Insurance Co.* [2003] Lloyd's Rep. IR 3, where Morison J. held at first instance (the point did not go to the Court of Appeal) that a statement by the reinsured that it would bear a retention was held not to be a warranty as there was no commercial justification for freezing the reinsured's rights and obliging the reinsured to maintain a retention to the stated precise percentage point.

Effect of the full reinsurance clause

As was seen in Chapter 4, the full reinsurance clause, which typically reads something like "warranted same gross rate, terms and conditions as original and to follow the settlements", is designed to incorporate the terms of the direct policy into the reinsurance so that back to back coverage can be achieved. The word "warranted" does not create a warranty that the reinsured's statements as to the content of the direct policy match the actual terms of the direct policy. This interpretation of the full reinsurance clause was put forward by Lord Griffiths in *Forsakrings Vesta* v. *Butcher* [1989] 1 A.C. 852, in an attempt to avoid the conclusion that the full reinsurance clause had an incorporating effect, but his views were rejected by the rest of the House of Lords. The majority view was that the full reinsurance clause had an incorporating effect, bringing the terms of the direct policy into the reinsurance. Subsequently, in *Toomey* v. *Banco Vitalicio de Espana SA de Seguros y Reaseguros*, [2004] Lloyd's Rep. IR 354, the facts of which were given above, Andrew Smith J. held that no warranty was created by the terms of the full reinsurance clause, and that the majority view of the clause in *Vesta* v. *Butcher* was correct. In *Prifti* v. *Musini Sociedad Anonima De Seguros y Reaseguros*, [2004] Lloyd's Rep. IR 528 Andrew Smith J. repeated his conclusion without reference to his judgment in *Toomey*. However, in the appeal in the *Toomey* case, [2004] EWCA Civ 622, the Court of Appeal expressly reserved its position on this point and held that the effect of the full reinsurance clause should be determined only after full argument in a future case which turned on the point.

Consequences of breach of warranty

> **Marine Insurance Act 1906, s. 33(3)**
> (3).—A warranty . . . is a condition which must be exactly complied with, whether it be material to the risk or not. If it be not so complied with, then, subject to any express provision in the policy, the insurer is discharged from liability as from the date of the breach of warranty, but without prejudice to any liability incurred by him before that date.

Exact compliance

Early marine cases on warranties established that a warranty must be exactly complied with, a principle which was codified in section 33(3) of the 1906 Act.

Materiality

It is a feature of English insurance law that a warranty need not be material to the risk. The most important feature of a warranty from the point of view of underwriters is that they are able to deny coverage where a false statement has been made to them even though the statement was not material and thus would not have justified avoidance on the grounds of misrepresentation (see Chapter 3). The leading authority on this point is the decision of the House of Lords in *Yorkshire Insurance Co. Ltd* v. *Campbell* [1917] A.C. 218, where a false statement as to the pedigree of a horse was held to preclude recovery when the horse was lost in a marine casualty while being transported.

Automatic termination

If a warranty is broken then the risk is automatically determined as of the date of breach. The principle of automatic termination was first laid down by the House of Lords in *Bank of Nova Scotia* v. *Hellenic Mutual War Risks Association, The Good Luck* [1991] 2 Lloyd's Rep. 191. This was a marine case, but it is now clear that automatic termination applies to all forms of insurance, including reinsurance.

Thus in the case of a present warranty, where the fact, opinion or intention proffered to the underwriters was false, the risk never attaches. There are many cases in which statements made by the assured or reinsured have been factually incorrect or where the assured has expressed an opinion which he could not possibly have held (see *Gerling-Konzern General Insurance Co.* v. *Polygram Holdings* [1998] 2 Lloyd's Rep. 544—opinion as to health of performer for purposes of a business interruption policy taken out by concert promoters).

In the case of a future warranty the risk will automatically come to an end in the event that the circumstance in respect of which the warranty was given should occur. It is to be emphasised that the policy itself does not come to an end: it is simply the case that reinsurers cannot be liable for any losses which occur after the breach of warranty. The distinction between termination of the risk and termination of the policy is graphically illustrated by the decision in *J A Chapman & Co.* v. *Kadirga Denizcilik Ve Ticaret* [1998] Lloyd's Rep. IR 377, where the warranty broken was a premium warranty whereby instalments of premium were warranted to be paid on given days. An instalment was not paid, and it was held that the breach of warranty terminated the risk but did not relieve the assured from the obligation to tender both the missing instalment and all future instalments, as the premium had been fully earned on the inception of the risk.

A necessary consequence of the automatic termination principle is that the manner in which the loss itself has occurred, or indeed whether there has been a loss at all, is of no account. England is one of the few jurisdictions to maintain this rule: in civil law countries a causal connection between breach of warranty and loss is required, and in the majority of commonwealth jurisdictions the need for a causal connection between the breach of warranty and the loss has been established by legislation. The isolation of English law in this regard, and its consequences for reinsurance, are illustrated by *Forsakrings Vesta* v. *Butcher* [1989] 1 Lloyd's Rep. 331, a case also discussed in Chapter 4 in the context of incorporation of direct insurance terms into reinsurance agreements.

***Forsakrings Vesta* v. *Butcher* [1989] 1 Lloyd's Rep. 331**

A direct policy on a fish farm in Norway was issued by the claimants, Norwegian insurers. The policy was governed by Norwegian law and contained a warranty whereby the assured was required to maintain a 24-hour watch on the fish farm. The claimants were reinsured in London under a facultative contract which was expressed to be "as original" and which was governed by English law. As a result of a storm the barriers of the fish farm were damaged and numerous fish were lost. The bad weather made it impracticable for a watch to be maintained, and accordingly there was a breach of warranty. Under Norwegian law the insurers were nevertheless required to make payment as there was no causal link between the breach of warranty and the loss. The reinsurers argued that the warranty had been incorporated into the reinsurance agreement and that the breach of warranty afforded them a defence under English law.

Held (H.L.): that the reinsurers were liable. The warranty was incorporated into the reinsurance agreement, and although the reinsurance was governed by English law it was appropriate to construe the policy in accordance with the rules laid down by Norwegian law in order to achieve back to back cover. This meant that the reinsurance warranty was effective only if its breach was the proximate cause of the reinsured's loss, which was not the case on the facts. Lord Griffiths commented that the notion of automatic termination, which necessarily denied any need for nexus between the breach of warranty and the loss, was one of the less satisfactory features of the English law of warranties.

***Groupama* v. *Catatumbo* [2000] 2 Lloyd's Rep. 350**

A marine policy governed by the law of Venezuela laid down a classification warranty. The insurers reinsured under a facultative slip policy governed by English law which contained the usual full reinsurance clause and incorporated the terms of the direct policy into the reinsurance. The slip policy contained its own classification warranty which was framed in slightly different terms. The assured failed to obtain classification for the insured vessel, which was subsequently lost. Under Venezuelan law the insurers remained liable for the loss, as Venezuelan law provided a defence to the insurers in the event of breach of warranty only where the loss was causally connected to the breach of warranty. The reinsurers relied upon the English law warranty in the reinsurance agreement.

Held (C.A.): that the reinsurers could not rely upon the breach of warranty. While as a matter of English law breach of warranty would have provided a defence to the reinsurers despite the absence of any causal connection between the breach of warranty and the loss, the reinsurance warranty was—in the interests of back to back cover—to be construed in the same manner as the warranty in the direct policy, and accordingly the reinsurers could not deny liability.

Some policies specify that there has to be a causal link between breach and loss. The clause in a fire policy on a restaurant, in *Bennett* v. *Axa Insurance plc* [2004] Lloyd's Rep. IR 615 provided that "Non-compliance with any such warranty in so far as it increases the risk of loss destruction or damage shall be a bar to any claim in respect of such loss destruction or damage". On the facts the assured's failure to dispose of trade waste was held to be both a breach of warranty and a cause of the ensuing fire, so that there was no recovery despite the more generous wording.

The problem of continuing warranties

As seen above, a continuing warranty is one which imposes an obligation on the assured or reinsured to act, or refrain from acting, in a particular way during the currency of the policy. The automatic termination principle means that as soon as the warranty is broken the risk comes to an end, and anything done by the assured or reinsured to put matters right will be to no avail. The principle is expressed by section 34(2) of the 1906 Act.

Marine Insurance Act 1906, s. 34(2)

(2).—Where a warranty is broken, the assured cannot avail himself of the defencc that the breach of warranty has been remedied, and the warranty complied with, before loss.

In some cases this principle may work harshly, as the breach may be trivial, of very short duration and incapable of contributing to any loss. With these matters in mind, the courts have developed two devices to protect assureds.

First, there is a general presumption that a warranty is not to be regarded as a continuing promise, but rather is to be regarded as a statement of existing fact, intention or opinion at the inception of the risk. See, e.g., *Woolfall & Rimmer* v. *Moyle* [1942] 1 K.B. 66 (statement by employer that machinery was properly fenced did not impose a continuing obligation). That said, it may be that a warranty is of no real purpose unless it is construed as applying to the future as well as to the present: on this point see *Agapitos* v. *Agnew (No. 3)* [2003] Lloyd's Rep. IR 54, where a warranty that a vessel had obtained London Salvage Association certification for its fire-fighting and mooring arrangements was held to amount to a continuing promise that the certificate would be renewed on its expiry.

Secondly, in a number of cases the courts have refused to construe a clause as a warranty and instead have held it to be a term which is "descriptive of the risk" or a "suspensory condition". These are two names for the same concept, which is that at any time that the assured has failed to comply with the term in question the insurers cannot be liable for a loss, although once the assured has resumed compliance then the insurers are back on risk: thus it may be said that the risk is suspended during the period of breach, or that the clause describes the circumstances in which the insurers will face liability. The principle is best illustrated by the leading authority, *Provincial Insurance Co.* v. *Morgan* [1933] A.C. 240, in which a term providing that a lorry was to be used only to carry coal was held not to be a warranty which brought the risk to an end as soon as any other cargo was loaded onto the lorry but instead was one which merely suspended the risk while anything other than coal was being carried. The assured was thus able to recover for a loss occurring shortly after the lorry had unloaded a cargo of wood, as at the time of the loss nothing prohibited was being carried. There is some difficulty in distinguishing the continuing warranty cases from the suspension of the risk cases, and the matter will often be one of impression for the judge as to the effects of finding the term to be a continuing warranty. The point is made by *Kler Knitwear* v. *Lombard General Insurance Co. Ltd* [2000] Lloyd's Rep. IR 47 where attempts by counsel to find distinguishing factors were rejected by Morland J., and the judge specifically refused to hold that a single fixed obligation (in that case to obtain a fire safety inspection of premises within 30 days from the inception of the risk) was a warranty. The court's view was that the clause merely suspended the risk after 30 days and up to the date that the inspection actually took place.

Defences to breach of warranty

> **Marine Insurance Act 1906, s. 34**
> (1).—Non-compliance with a warranty is excused when, by reason of a change of circumstances, the warranty ceases to be applicable to the circumstances of the contract, or when compliance with the warranty is rendered unlawful by any subsequent law.
> . . .
> (3).—A breach of warranty may be waived by the insurer.

A breach of warranty may be waived by the contract itself or by the underwriters' conduct after the breach. Contractual waiver is common in direct professional indemnity policies, as professional rules require insurers to guarantee payment. A waiver which purports to remove the right of insurers to avoid or repudiate the policy for misrepresentation will not, however, be effective to waive breach of warranty, as the remedy for breach of warranty is not avoidance of the policy *ab initio* or treating the policy as repudiated but rather the automatic termination of the risk as from the date of breach (*HIH Casualty and General Insurance Ltd* v. *New Hampshire Insurance Co.* [2001] Lloyd's Rep. IR 596). A different conclusion had been reached in the earlier decision, *Kumar* v. *AGF Insurance Ltd* [1999] Lloyd's Rep. IR 147, but in that case the policy had been drafted at a time when it was believed that breach of warranty did not have an automatic terminating effect and that the appropriate remedy was treating the policy as repudiated. If underwriters have agreed to pay irrespective of breach of warranty, they have a right to recover damages for breach of contract insofar as the breach has contributed to the loss (*Kumar* v. *AGF Insurance Ltd* [1999] Lloyd's Rep. IR 147).

Waiver by post-breach conduct is more problematic, by reason of the concept of automatic termination of risk on breach of warranty. In the usual case of breach of contract, the innocent party has the right either to affirm the contract or to treat it as repudiated and to terminate it for breach. No such option is open to underwriters following breach of warranty, and it follows that the possibility of waiver by affirmation cannot apply to breach of warranty: this was suggested in *J Kirkaldy & Sons* v. *Walker* [1999] Lloyd's Rep. IR 410 and confirmed by Deputy High Court Judge Jules Sher QC in *HIH Casualty and General Insurance Co.* v. *Axa Corporate Solutions*. However, waiver by estoppel —whereby underwriters take positive action to confirm the continuation of the risk—remains a possibility in breach of warranty cases. This was so held by Mr Sher QC in *HIH* v. *Axa*, and on appeal the Court of Appeal set out the circumstances in which waiver by estoppel can arise.

***HIH Casualty and General Insurance Co.* v. *Axa Corporate Solutions* [2003] Lloyd's Rep. IR 1**

This was a sequel to the decision of the Court of Appeal in *HIH Casualty and General Insurance Co.* v. *New Hampshire Insurance Co.* [2001] Lloyd's Rep. IR 596, discussed above. HIH had issued insurance to film financiers in respect of two slates of films, the 7.23 slate and the Rojak slate: under the policies HIH was to indemnify the financiers in the event that the revenues from the films fell short of what was owed to them on a given day. HIH reinsured its liabilities with the defendant reinsurers. It was held in *HIH* v. *New Hampshire* that the direct policy and the reinsurance contained warranties that six films would be made in respect of the 7.23 slate and that ten films would be made in respect of the Rojak slate. Losses were sustained, and payment was made by HIH. However, only five films had been made in respect of the 7.23 slate and only seven films had been made in respect of the Rojak slate. HIH argued that it had waived the breaches of warranty (so that it was liable under the direct policies) and HIH also argued that the reinsurers had waived the breaches of warranty in that they had, before payment by HIH, raised questions about the number of films and had expressed concern, but had not followed the matter up.

Held (at first instance, Deputy High Court Judge Jules Sher QC): that there was no waiver.

(1) The warranties were broken at the latest at the end date in respect of each slate, and as of that date the insurance cover was automatically discharged without the need for any action by the reinsurers.

(2) It was not possible for a breach of warranty to be waived by election. There could be waiver by election only where the innocent party had a choice either to continue with a contract or to terminate it. By contrast, in the case of a warranty, the risk automatically came to an end and the insurers had no such choice. Accordingly, the only form of waiver which was possible in relation to a breach of warranty was waiver by estoppel.

(3) On the facts there was no waiver by estoppel. This form of waiver required a clear and unequivocal representation by the reinsurers that they did not intend to treat the risk as discharged made with knowledge of such right and in circumstances in which it would be inequitable to allow the reinsurers to resile from the representation. It was also necessary for HIH to have appreciated that the reinsurers intended to waive their rights. In the present case HIH had no reason to believe that the reinsurers were waiving their rights and in any event there was no unequivocal representation which had been relied upon by HIH.

HIH appealed to the Court of Appeal. There was no appeal against the ruling that waiver by affirmation was unavailable in breach of warranty cases, and the appeal focused on the requirements for waiver by estoppel.

Held (C.A.): that the appeal would be dismissed.

(1) There had not been a clear and unequivocal representation of the type required to trigger waiver by estoppel. HIH had not shown that the reinsurers had stated that they would not insist upon their right to treat the policy as repudiated.

(2) Any representation by the reinsurers had to carry with it some apparent awareness of the right upon which they had represented they would not be relying on, as it was essential that HIH understood that the reinsurers were aware that they had rights which were not going to be relied upon.

(3) The reinsurers had not adopted a course of conduct which was inconsistent with its right to treat the cover as discharged. They had merely chosen a policy of silence and inactivity, but in the absence of any duty to speak that could not give rise to an estoppel.

(4) There had been no reliance by HIH: no significance had been attached to the reinsurers' request for information.

THE PREMIUM

The amount of the premium

The amount of premium varies as between classes of insurance. The premium for proportional reinsurances is based on a percentage of the premium charged by the reinsured to its policy holders, whereas the premium for non-proportional reinsurances is determined by the reinsurers' own assessment of the risk. Where the insurance is a front for reinsurers, the entire premium will be passed on to reinsurers subject to deduction of commission for the reinsured for its participation.

The general rule is that the premium is fixed at the outset and stays at that level irrespective of later events during the currency of the agreement. Reinsurance contracts may, however, be long-term engagements which are reviewed on an annual or other basis, and such contracts may contain premium review clauses which allow the premium to be increased in response to the amount of claims faced by the reinsured and the reinsurer. A clause of this type was considered in *Charman* v. *New Cap Reinsurance Corporation Ltd* [2003] EWCA Civ 1372, [2004] Lloyd's Rep. IR 373, the issues being the manner in which the clause could be invoked and the consequences of doing so. The clause in *Charman* was regarded as being very poorly drafted, and the Court of Appeal did its best to ascertain what had been intended.

***Charman* v. *New Cap Reinsurance Corporation Ltd* [2004] Lloyd's Rep. IR 373**

The reinsurance agreement in this case ran for the period 1997 to 1999 and contained a premium review clause which provided that "The reinsurer reserves the right to increase the Annual Premium at any Anniversary Date during the Term on a pro rata basis, if prior to the Termination Date, there is a material change in the normal underwriting guidelines, classes of business, volume of business or proportion of business, as described in the submission and/or any extraordinary claims developments. Material change to be deemed to be substantial and as mutually agreed". The reinsurer gave notice of cancellation at the end of the first year and asserted that the contract had come to an end at that point. Morison J., at first instance, held that the notice at the end of the first year was ineffective, but that the notice given in 1997 remained in place and that there was good ground for terminating the policy at the end of the third year as there had been an unusual claims experience.

Held (C.A.): that the contract had not come to an end.

(1) The review clause had no effect unless it was invoked.

(2) There had not been any separate attempt by the reinsurer to invoke the clause at the end of the second year. The original 1997 notice could not be regarded as a continuing one.

(3) The attempt to invoke the clause at the end of the first year was invalid, as no notice had been given to the reinsured stating the policy was to be cancelled and providing the reasons for the giving of notice. There was nothing to indicate that there had been exceptional claims development so as to bring the clause into play.

(4) Even if there had been a formally valid notice at the end of 1997, there were no grounds for invoking it as the reinsurer's intention was to avoid liability for potentially large claims in the following years rather than for exceptional claims development in the first year, as required by the clause.

(5) Although the point did not arise, the correct construction of the premium review clause was that if the parties could not agree a new premium then the contract would come to an end. There was no unilateral right vested in the reinsurer to increase the premium, and at most the reinsurer had the right to nominate a fresh premium which could then be accepted or rejected.

Payment of the premium

The method of payment of the premium is to be agreed between the parties. It is often the case that there is an agreed procedure whereby premiums and losses are accounted for quarterly, with the balance being payable to the party in credit from the transaction. Accounting is frequently managed by brokers, and there may be obligations on them to hold receipts in separate trust accounts.

The effect of late payment of the premium depends upon the policy terms. Some policies use premium warranties, the effect of which is to require payment on a given day: if payment is late the risk automatically comes to an end but the full premium remains outstanding (*J A Chapman & Co.* v. *Kadirga Denizcilik Ve Ticaret* [1998] Lloyd's Rep. IR 377). Non-payment of the premium will generally preclude any recovery under the policy as the obligations of the parties to make payment are not independent of each other: this was so held by the South African Supreme Court in *Lake* v. *Reinsurance Corporation Ltd,* 1967 (3) SA 124 (W). However, in the absence of a warranty or a provision that time is of the essence, late payment does not of itself entitle the reinsurers to treat the policy as repudiated: where the policy is silent there can only be a repudiation if the reinsurers have served notice on the reinsured demanding payment within a reasonable period and have specified in their demand that time is of the essence.

***Fenton Insurance Co. Ltd* v. *Gothaer Versicherungsbank VVag* [1991] 1 Lloyd's Rep. 171**

This case concerned a marine quota share reinsurance treaty entered into in 1976 by the defendant reinsurers with the claimant reinsured. The defendants were represented by underwriting agents, and the risk had been placed with the defendants by brokers acting for the reinsured. Accounts were to be settled quarterly. The claimant sought to recover losses for the period 1976 to 1979. The defendants denied liability, on the basis that no premiums had been paid at any time from inception up to 1985 and that the defendants were entitled either to regard the treaty as abandoned and their liability under it discharged, or as repudiated.

Held (Potter J.): that the reinsurers were liable for the claims even though the evidence showed that premiums had never been paid.

(1) There was no basis for a finding that the treaty had been abandoned, as there had been communications, including quarterly statements, sent to the reinsurers by the reinsured.

(2) Delay in making payment did not amount to repudiation. Potter J. put the matter as follows:

"In cases concerned with insurance, where accounts are rendered and paid through the medium of brokers and/or underwriting agents and delays in payment are not infrequent, it seems to me that one could rarely, if ever, infer a repudiatory intention under a treaty of this kind by reason of non-payment of balances simpliciter (by way of distinction from a failure persisted in despite receipt of demands and/or protests)."

***Figre Ltd* v. *Mander* [1999] Lloyd's Rep. IR 193**

Five per cent of the claimant's liability under an excess of loss reinsurance treaty was retroceded to the defendants by an agreement made in March 1984. The premium under the retrocession was payable by an initial instalment and subsequent adjustments, and although debit notes were sent by the brokers to the retrocedant no payment was made. The premium was adjusted in 1988, but the adjusted sum was again not paid. Losses arose, and a claim was made by the retrocedant in July 1990. The defendants asserted that there had been a repudiation of the policy.

Held (Cresswell J.): that the retrocessionaires were liable for the losses and that the retrocession had not been repudiated by late payment of premium.

(1) Time was not of the essence for the payment of premium, and in the absence of express provision the obligation to pay was to be regarded as an innominate term. The retrocedant had not, by failing to make payment, been guilty of repudiation. The evidence showed that delays were common on the London market.

(2) It would have been open to the retrocessionaires to make time of the essence by a notice so stating and requiring payment within a reasonable period failing which the policy could be regarded as repudiated. However, this had not been done.

See also *Glencore AG* v. *Ryan, The Beursgracht* [2002] Lloyd's Rep. IR 335, discussed above, where it was held that failure by the assured to send the required bordereau to the insurers, so that a risk was not declared and the premium was not collected, did not relieve the insurers from liability even though the premium was not tendered until the claim had been made some years later.

The position is necessarily different if the reinsured has repudiated the policy by making it clear that outstanding and future premiums will not be paid. The liquidation of the reinsured has this effect.

***Pacific and General Insurance Co. Ltd* v. *Hazell* [1997] L.R.L.R. 65**

Reinsurance premiums owing by the reinsured were not paid. The reinsured subsequently went into liquidation. The reinsurers asserted that the liquidation amounted to a repudiation of the reinsurance agreement, as it showed that the reinsured would never be able to pay the premiums.

Held (Moore-Bick J.): that the reinsurance agreement had been repudiated.

Payment of premium by brokers: marine cases

The broker's rights and obligations

Section 53(1) of the Marine Insurance Act 1906, which codifies a long-standing market practice, provides as follows:

> (1).—Unless otherwise agreed, where a marine policy is effected on behalf of the assured by a broker, the broker is directly responsible to the insurer for the premium, and the insurer is directly responsible to the assured for the amount which may be payable in respect of losses, or in respect of returnable premium.

The broker is entitled to be indemnified by the assured for any payment made by him under this section. The broker's security for payment is a lien on the policy, as stated by section 53(2) of the 1906 Act:

> (2).—Unless otherwise agreed, the broker has, as against the assured, a lien upon the policy for the amount of the premium and his charges in respect of effecting the policy; and, where he has dealt with the person who employs him as a principal, he has also a lien on the policy in respect of any balance on any insurance account which may be due to him from such person, unless when the debt was incurred he had reason to believe that such person was only an agent.

The leading authority on this section is *Eide UK Ltd* v. *Lowndes Lambert Group Ltd, The Sun Tender* [1998] 1 Lloyd's Rep. 389, where it was held that the broker's lien extends to a claim against the proceeds of the policy. A broker may also to some extent secure his position by insisting upon the inclusion in the insurance or reinsurance wording of a "broker's cancellation" provision whereby the underwriters agree to cancel the policy in the event that the broker is not indemnified by his client.

There is no market practice requiring the broker to pay the premium in relation to non-marine insurance, and although the point has not been tested in the courts, the generally accepted view is that the position is the same in both the Lloyd's and the companies market. Thus, while there are still occasional suggestions that a Lloyd's broker is liable to pay the premiums for all Lloyd's placements, this is thought not to be the case. In *Goshawk Dedicated Ltd* v. *Tyser & Co. Ltd* [2005] Lloyd's Rep. IR 379 Christopher Clarke J. assumed that the rule was confined to the marine market.

Position of placing broker

It is often the case in reinsurance placements in the London market that the risk has originated from local (producing) brokers appointed by the reinsured, and that the producing brokers have in turned hired London placing brokers to actually place the risk. In this type of case the obligation to pay the premiums rests on the placing broker, but there is doubt as to whether the obligation to reimburse the placing broker is faced by the producing broker, by the reinsured or by each of them. A further issue which may arise where the direct policy originates from some other jurisdiction is whether section 53(1) applies where the law applicable to the insurance or the reinsurance is that of some other jurisdiction. Both of these questions were addressed in the following case, which also considered the further issue of the date on which a broker's obligation to pay the premium accrues (for limitation purposes).

***Heath Lambert Ltd* v. *Sociedad de Corretaje de Seguros*, [2004] Lloyd's Rep. 905**

In 1994 INC, a Venezuelan shipping company, appointed producing brokers in Venezuela, Scort, to place its marine insurance. The risk was placed with a Venezuelan insurer, Banesco, as a front for the London market. Scort appointed HL as its London placing brokers in obtaining reinsurance cover. HL placed cover with underwriters under a facultative contract containing the full reinsurance clause and stating "Subject to Venezuelan Law and/or Venezuelan Jurisdiction if required". There was a premium warranty requiring payment within 90 days' of the attachment of the risk, and the reinsurance cover also incorporated a brokers' cancellation clause entitling HL to cancel the policy in the event of the premium not being paid to them when due and requiring the underwriters to repay that part of the premium representing the unexpired period of the cover.

The initial placement was followed by a number of extensions to the cover, agreed between January and July 1996. Additional premium was payable in respect of each of these. All payments were funded by HL, but HL was never indemnified. HL commenced the present action against Scort and Banesco to recover the premium. Those companies contested service on them outside the jurisdiction. It was common ground that the English court had jurisdiction, as the obligation to indemnify HL was one to be performed in England (creditor must seek out his debtor), but three other issues arose: (1) which of Scort or Banesco was liable to indemnify HL; (2) did section 53 of the Marine Insurance Act 1906 apply to a case with an international dimension; and (3) whether HL's claim for indemnification was time-barred by section 5 of the Limitation Act 1980. Jonathan Hirst QC, Deputy High Court judge, held as follows. The appeal to the Court of Appeal was on point (3) only.

(1) The basic rule was that there was no contractual relationship between the reinsured and the placing broker—the only contract was between the producing broker and the placing broker (*Prentis Donegan & Partners Ltd* v. *Leeds & Leeds Co. Inc* [1998] 2 Lloyd's Rep. 326). It followed that the liability to indemnify HL fell on Scort and not on Banesco. However, the court thought that it would be premature to set aside the proceedings against Banesco until the possibility of the existence of special circumstances giving rise to a contract had been considered.

(2) HL could recover from Scort/Banseco only if HL had paid the premium under a legal liability, as the law did not assist a volunteer. The question was whether HL had been liable to pay. The problem was raised by the fact that the direct policy was governed by Venezuelan law, it was unclear which law governed the relationship between Scort and HL, and the reinsurance agreement contained choice of law provisions allowing Venezuela to be nominated. The court was able to sidestep many of the difficulties by holding that the reinsurance was governed by English law, and accordingly that section 53 applied. This was so because the choice of law clause was a floating one, allowing Banesco to nominate Venezuelan law if it so wished: however, as this had not been done, the default law was English law. [Note that other cases hold that a floating choice of law clause is valid only if the nomination is made as soon as the contract comes into effect—the court in the present case assumed, wrongly, that the nomination could be made at some later date.] What, however, if the reinsurance had been governed by Venezuelan law? The court held that the same result would have followed. The court ruled that there had been an acceptance of responsibility by HL to pay the premium, recognised by the inclusion in the policy of the brokers' cancellation clause. Thus, irrespective of the applicable law, HL was under a duty to the reinsurers to pay the premium and was not a volunteer.

(3) As to limitation, the court ruled that the six year period in section 5 of the Limitation Act 1980 for HL's claim against Scort/Banesco started to run when the premium fell due under the reinsurance. This would normally be on the inception of the risk, although in the present case HL had been given 90 days' credit, so the limitation period started to run 90 days after the inception of the risk under the policy and the extension. As the proceedings had only been commenced in May 2003, all payments but that made in respect of the final extension were time-barred. The appeal

to the Court of Appeal concerned only the premium due for the final extension, and the Court of Appeal agreed with the trial judge that the policy on its proper construction conferred 90 days' credit for the payment of the premium so that time did not begin to run until 90 days after inception.

A final supplementary issue, not raised at first instance, was the effect of the "as original" clause in the reinsurance agreement. There appears to have been a faint attempt to argue that the clause incorporated all of the terms of the direct policy into the reinsurance, including the obligation on INC to pay the premiums when the policy was contracted. That argument would, if upheld, have eliminated the 90 day credit period. However, the Court of Appeal, without deciding whether this type of clause could be incorporated, simply stated that the express terms of the reinsurance dealing with premiums could not be overridden by any incorporated provision.

INSPECTION CLAUSES

Nature of inspection clauses

The primary form of protection for treaty reinsurers is the right to inspect the reinsured's books and records in order to ensure that the risks accepted by the reinsured are prudent and that claims are being settled in an appropriate fashion. The right to inspect is regarded as sufficiently important by the English courts to justify the implication of a term in favour of an obligatory reinsurer (i.e., one who has no power to reject risks ceded by the reinsured) giving the right to inspect when reasonable to do so (see *Phoenix General Insurance Co. of Greece SA* v. *Halvanon Insurance Co. Ltd* [1985] 2 Lloyd's Rep. 599, discussed in Chapter 4).

The right to inspect under an express policy term is in most cases framed generally, and allows inspection at any time on reasonable notice to the reinsured whether or not there have been significant claims by the reinsured. That said, the right to inspect will frequently be exercised where claims have been made by the reinsured: that right may be exercised under a general inspection clause, or under a clause specifically designed to allow the reinsurers to become involved in the claims process (e.g., a claims co-operation clause—see Chapter 6).

As general inspection clauses are not necessarily connected with claims, the willingness of the reinsured to submit to an inspection is not normally expressed to be a condition precedent to the right of the reinsured to recover claims from the reinsurers. In *Baker* v. *Black Sea and Baltic General Insurance Co. Ltd* [1995] L.R.L.R. 261 Potter J. at first instance expressed the view that an inspection clause implied by the courts would similarly not be regarded as a condition precedent to the attachment of the risk and thus the reinsurers' liability for claims. In the same way, it is unlikely that breach of an inspection clause is to be regarded as a repudiatory breach of contract. It follows that breach of an inspection clause by the reinsured will not give the reinsurers the right to treat themselves off risk or to treat the policy as repudiated. It is nevertheless possible for the inspection clause to relate specifically to claims, in which case the position will be different.

***Baker* v. *Black Sea and Baltic General Insurance Co. Ltd* [1995] L.R.L.R. 261**

The claimant represented a Lloyd's syndicate which had reinsured with the defendants under a proportional facultative obligatory cover in respect of US and Canadian fire and casualty business. The treaty operated without any real problem for some 27 years even though no treaty wording was ever produced. After this period the defendants refused to pay claims arising out of liabilities for the use of asbestos and "Agent Orange" which had been settled by the syndicate. A large number of issues arose for determination, one of which concerned inspection clauses. Potter J. commented as follows:

"The obligations, express or implied, upon a reassured to maintain proper records, from which he is able to make available on request information to the reinsurer as and when reasonably required is a matter separate from the question of whether or not a cession becomes binding or effective before notice of it is given. It may well be . . . the case that a re-insurer will be content simply to receive such accounting information as is called for in the Treaty as sufficient information on the position between the parties from time to time, in the absence of some ground for further enquiry."

Exercising the right of inspection

The drafting of inspection clauses is such that the reinsurers have the right to inspect at any time and for any reason, as long as the appropriate reasonable notice has been given to the reinsured. No reason is required for undertaking an inspection, although the courts will exercise vigilance to ensure that the right to inspect is not being exercised in a manner which is oppressive or excessive, or which is designed purely as a fishing expedition to see if something turns up which might provide a defence.

***Re A Company No. 008725 of 1991, Ex parte Pritchard* [1992] B.C.L.C. 633**

The reinsured made claims against reinsurers, and refused to allow inspection until the claims had been paid. The reinsurers refused to pay, and the reinsured sought to pressurise the reinsurers into making payment by presenting a winding up petition against the reinsurers to the court. The reinsurers sought an order preventing the advertising of the winding up petition.

Held (Hoffmann J.): that a winding up petition could not be advertised if the debt was disputed on good and substantial grounds. In the present case, the denial of inspection entitled the court to draw the inference that such grounds existed. The device of presenting a winding up petition was not to be used to force a perfectly solvent company into making payment. On the question of inspection, Hoffmann J. expressed the view that the reinsurers were entitled to exercise their right of inspection unless "the proposed inspection was excessive or otherwise in bad faith".

***SA d'Intermediaires Luxembourgeois* v. *Farex Gie* [1995] L.R.L.R. 116**

Claims were made under a reinsurance agreement. The reinsurers sought permission to amend their pleadings and to raise by way of defence a number of speculative claims of misrepresentation and non-disclosure. The Court of Appeal by a majority rejected the defences and refused permission for the pleadings to be amended. Hoffmann L.J. in the course of his judgment held that there was no procedure whereby a reinsurer could delay judgment by raising speculative defences and then seeking evidence to justify those defences:

"I am not deterred from reaching this conclusion by the thought that it means that whether or not a reinsurer can find the material to raise a prima facie case of non-disclosure in respect of a particular risk may depend on the accident of his access to information such as the first year claims records of the renewed risks in this case. If the need to find better evidence causes difficulties for reinsurers, they are at liberty to stipulate for greater access to information. But I think that the requirements of certainty and the expeditious enforcement of payments in the insurance market requires that courts should not too readily grant leave to defend on the basis of speculative allegations."

In particular, a reinsurer will not be permitted to invoke the right to inspect at the very last moment in order to stave off summary judgment.

***Trinity Insurance Co. Ltd* v. *Overseas Union Insurance Ltd* [1996] L.R.L.R. 156**

The claimant was the reinsured under various quota share reinsurance treaties issued by the defendants. Claims were made under the treaties and a dispute arose as to whether the claimant was in breach of the terms of the treaties. The claimant applied for summary judgment. An application for inspection was made after the proceedings were commenced, and an application was made to the court to stay its proceedings so that the inspection could go ahead.

Held (Longmore J.): that the proceedings should not be stayed. In the present case the application for inspection (unlike that in *Ex parte Pritchard*) had not been refused, but it was merely inconvenient to arrange inspection before the hearing of the action. Longmore J. explained his decision as follows:

"The position is that many years have passed and only at the door of the Court is a request for inspection made. It does not seem to me therefore to be right to say at this very late stage that, because a defence might emerge after the records had been inspected, either there should be a stay of the claims . . . or indeed that there should be no judgment if I am otherwise satisfied, as I am, that there is no defence to these claims."

***Aetna Reinsurance Co. (UK) Ltd* v. *Central Reinsurance Corporation* [1996] L.R.L.R. 165**

Claims were made under a series of reinsurance treaties. Those treaties contained provisions requiring regular statements of account, and also conferred upon the reinsurers the right to undertake inspections. The reinsured commenced proceedings for summary judgment, and the reinsurers applied for permission to defend, arguing that summary judgment should not be given until an inspection had been undertaken. The request for inspection had been made shortly before the proceedings had been commenced.

Held (Longmore J.): that the application would be refused. The court ruled as follows:

"There is no reason why in a proper case [summary judgment] should not be given if at the time of the application there is no defence, even if at some later stage it may become apparent that there could be some arguable defence, in which case no doubt matters would have to be reconsidered for the future. But the idea that proceedings can be held up merely for inspection of documents to take place is not one which any Court can happily countenance."

***Pacific and General Insurance Co. Ltd* v. *Baltica Insurance Co. (UK) Ltd* [1996] L.R.L.R. 8**

The claimant reinsured sought summary judgment against the defendant reinsurers in respect of claims arising under a reinsurance agreement. The agreement stated that settlements were binding on the reinsurers "upon reasonable evidence of the amount paid being given by the reinsured". In the event of a claim, "all papers in connection therewith shall be at the command of the Reinsurers on this reinsurance or parties designated by them for inspection". In addition to these clauses, there was a general inspection clause. The defendants sought an adjournment of the proceedings so that inspection could take place.

Held (Rix J.): that in the circumstances the proceedings should be adjourned for inspection to take place and that summary judgment should not be given. Where a court was faced with a claim under a follow the settlements clause and with reinsurers who wished to inspect, three considerations had to be taken into account:

(1) whether the reinsured had given or refused to the reinsurers their contractual rights of inspection.
(2) the circumstances in which the claim to inspect comes forward—"if a reinsurer passes by his rights of inspection until the very last moment when he is under the lash of a claim for summary judgment pursuant to a follow the settlements clause, the court will be reluctant to refuse summary judgment simply upon the basis that if inspection belatedly takes place something may turn up in a Micawber-like way. Where, however, there have been timely requests for inspection, the matter may well be different".
(3) Whether some substantial reason had been put forward as to why inspection was requested or required and as to what a reinsurer hoped to find upon such inspection.

On the present facts, requests for inspection had been made long before the trial but not been complied with (although this position was later rectified), and there was reasonable evidence of legitimate concern that a defence might exist by reason of non-notification of claims.

Effects of an inspection

A particular problem has arisen in relation to the enforcement of an inspection clause following claims made by the reinsured. If the reinsurers believe that they have a right to avoid the policy for non-disclosure or misrepresentation, and decide to inspect in the hope of discovering evidence sufficient to justify their view, they run the risk of having been taken to have waived the right to avoid. This is because the right to inspect is a contractual right, whereas the right to avoid involves an assertion that there never was a contract in the first place. If, therefore, reinsurers who believe that they have the right to avoid undertake an inspection without reserving their rights while so doing, there is a risk of a finding of waiver, as is demonstrated by the following case:

***Iron Trades Mutual Insurance Co. Ltd* v. *Companhia de Seguros Imperio* [1992] Re L.R. 213**

The reinsurers sought to avoid two quota share reinsurance treaties on the grounds of non-disclosure and misrepresentation. Hobhouse J. held that the right to avoid had been lost by affirmation, as the reinsurers had with knowledge of their possible defences sought to exercise inspection and other contractual rights.

This case was distinguished by Colman J. in *Strive Shipping* v. *Hellenic Mutual War Risks Association, The Grecia Express* [2002] Lloyd's Rep. IR 669. The view was here expressed that a claims condition is ancillary to the policy, and that an insurer's insistence that the assured complies with his contractual claims obligations ought not to be regarded as a waiver of the right to avoid whether or not the insurer has reserved his rights. It is nevertheless doubtful whether this reasoning is applicable to an inspection clause: such a clause is not a claims condition and, in the context of an obligatory reinsurance treaty, can scarcely be described as ancillary.

TEST YOUR UNDERSTANDING

1. Which of the following statements accurately reflect the approach of the courts to the construction of reinsurance agreements?

(a) Any ambiguities in the agreement will be resolved in favour of the reinsured.
(b) Previous negotiations between the parties may be taken into account in ascertaining the meaning of express clauses.
(c) The slip may be taken into account in construing the words of the policy.
(d) The courts must take account of the market background against which the policy was written.

2. Which of the following statements is true?

(a) If the reinsured fails to comply with a condition precedent to the risk, the risk never attaches.
(b) If the reinsured fails to comply with a condition precedent to the risk, the reinsured may recover but may face liability in damages.
(c) If the reinsured fails to comply with a condition precedent to the risk, the policy may be avoided *ab initio.*

3. Which of the following statements is true?

(a) If the reinsured fails to comply with a condition precedent to the reinsurers' liability, the reinsurers are not liable.
(b) If the reinsured fails to comply with a condition precedent to the reinsurers' liability, the reinsured may recover but may face liability in damages.
(c) If the reinsured fails to comply with a condition precedent to the reinsurers' liability, the policy may be avoided *ab initio.*

(d) A condition precedent to liability may be created only by unequivocal wording.

4. Which of the following statements is true?

(a) If the reinsured fails to comply with a bare condition, the insurers are always able to treat the contract as repudiated.
(b) If the reinsured fails to comply with a bare condition, the insurers are able to treat the contract as repudiated if the condition is essential to the policy.
(c) If the reinsured fails to comply with a bare condition, the insurers are able to treat the contract as repudiated if the breach is a serious one.
(d) If the reinsured fails to comply with a bare condition the reinsurers may have the right to refuse to pay the claim but not to treat the policy as repudiated.

5. Which of the following statements are accurate in relation to warranties?

(a) Breach of warranty automatically terminates the policy.
(b) Breach of warranty automatically terminates the risk.
(c) Breach of warranty renders the policy voidable *ab initio.*
(d) Breach of warranty is a repudiation of the policy.

6. Which of the following statements are true in relation to the payment of the premium under a reinsurance agreement?

(a) The premium must always be paid by the broker.
(b) The amount of the premium may be varied during the course of a long-term agreement.
(c) Failure to pay the premium allows the reinsurers to treat the policy as repudiated.
(d) Time is of the essence for the payment of the premium.

7. Which of the following statements are true in relation to inspection clauses?

(a) An inspection clause is generally expressed as a condition precedent to the liability of the reinsurers.
(b) An inspection clause can be exercised at any time and for any reason, subject to reasonable notice to the reinsured.

(c) An inspection clause cannot be relied upon once the reinsured has commenced proceedings against the reinsurers.

(d) An inspection clause cannot be relied upon during proceedings if the reinsurers' purpose is to conduct a fishing expedition for possible defences.

CHAPTER 6

FOLLOW THE SETTLEMENTS AND FOLLOW THE FORTUNES

INTRODUCTION

Insurance as a concept is predicated upon the law of large numbers—the prediction of losses through accurate statistical analysis of many similar risks, and their transfer from one entity to many others. In essence it is the spreading of risk by one party who may not wish or be unable to bear it all himself over the financial ability of many others to do so, each of whom will pay a small proportion of any loss. The spreading of risk is not only economic; a geographical spread of risk of, say, flood damage in different countries will also avoid an accumulation of exposure by any one insurer to any one source or type of risk.

The optimum spreading of risk occurs in reinsurance where a reinsurer can effectively participate either in a specific risk accepted by an insurer or in his portfolio of risks, so that the original risk can fan outwards exponentially ultimately to be borne by many reinsurers and indeed their reinsurers. Of course there are frictional costs, which have to be absorbed by the parties, and excessive frictional costs may give rise to the infamous spiral (e.g., the Personal Accident LMX Spiral). The reinsurer receives proportionately less premium for the same amount of risk than the original insurer and although reinsurers will contribute specific sums towards the cost of acquiring the original business and its maintenance, reinsurance works commercially because reinsurers are able to avoid incurring the huge administrative and other overheads of direct insurance, such as the investigation and adjustment of claims, etc.

A key element in minimising overheads—and therefore maximising profits—is the extent to which control over the activities of the direct insurer is retained by the reinsurer. Where a reinsurer attempts to exercise control over all claims, then the cost of doing so will probably make the reinsurance uneconomic. On the other hand the reinsurer could vest in the direct insurer total authority to select business and deal with claims in any way he sees fit, the reinsurer relying upon his own business judgement in agreeing to reinsure that insurer and on the business judgement and acumen of that insurer to select appropriate risks to insure and reinsure. There is a tension between the desire of the reinsurer not to be bound by what he might consider to be imprudent settlements made by the reinsured and the desire of the reinsurer not to have to reinvestigate every matter.

The sensible solution adopted by reinsurers is to allow the reinsured considerable latitude in selecting risks and dealing with claims but to retain the right to control the activities of their reinsureds in their entirety should they so wish, on top of which sits the ultimate sanction of refusing to pay a claim.

This balancing of profitability through minimising overheads but retaining control is usually found in the wording of the appropriate follow the settlements clause, and any claims co-operation or control clauses that restrain such clauses. Where the parties are intending that reinsurance should operate but either have not concluded a formal contract or have concluded a formal contract which does not contain a specific follow the settlements clause, then it will be implied that the reinsurer will follow the settlements of the reinsured. Most modern reinsurance contracts will contain a follow the settlements clause with or without modifications, in place of the "pay as may be paid thereon" or other provisions more commonly in use before the 1960s. In the absence of any specific provision relating to the liability of the reinsurer, and presumably on the basis of a general intention on the part of both reinsured and reinsurer to agree that the reinsurer will pay something to the reinsured following the latter's loss, then a reinsurer has a far wider scope for challenging any settlements made by the reinsured and the principle in essence is that the reinsured must prove the loss against the reinsurer in the same manner as the original insured should have proved it against him, i.e. the insurer must show that he was under a legal liability to pay the claim to the insured. In effect it places the same burden on the reinsured as that which falls upon the insured making the claim against that reinsured, and reinsurers are clearly entitled to raise all defences which could have been raised by the reinsured against the insured.

THE UNQUALIFIED FOLLOW THE SETTLEMENTS POSITION

At one end of the scale lies the "full" reinsurance clause, which might read "Being a reinsurance of and warranted same gross rate, terms and conditions as and to follow the settlements of the reinsured". Such a clause has been categorised as "unqualified" in the sense that although certain implied terms will operate to restrict its operation, there are no specific qualifications or limitations other than those usually implied by law or custom or by the parties. This was carefully analysed by the Court of Appeal in *Insurance Company of Africa* v. *SCOR*:

***Insurance Company of Africa* v. *SCOR* [1985] 1 Lloyd's Rep. 312**
The Insurance Company of Africa ("ICA") insured a warehouse in Monrovia belonging to the African Trading Company (Liberia) Limited ("ATC") for US$3.5 million, and then reinsured 98.6% of that risk as a quota share in London with SCOR as leading reinsurer. The policy contained a full follow the settlements clause (as above), together with a claims co-operation/control clause. The warehouse burned to the ground, taking its full complement of stock with it into cinders and ashes. The Fire Brigade were unable to take any substantive steps to minimise the fire because the water had been turned off. The Liberian Army then levelled the site within two days and the only loss adjuster in Liberia (who had watched the fire) was appointed by ICA

to adjust the loss. The parent company of ICA sent another adjuster to Liberia to oversee the local adjuster's work and they concluded that the loss of stock and cost of rebuilding would exceed US$3.5 million, and that ATC was not responsible for the fire.

ATC therefore claimed under its policy with ICA, who informed SCOR accordingly. SCOR then received anonymous letters which alleged that the fire had in fact been started deliberately, that certain senior management at ICA had been taking bribes, that the army were involved and that the local loss adjuster had a specific interest in maximising the adjustment of the loss because he would receive 10% of any insurance payout. SCOR therefore refused to authorise the claim but chose not to provide any explanation to ICA, instead sending its own loss adjusters to Monrovia to look into the loss but in reality to investigate whether the anonymous claims were correct. ICA were unaware of the allegations made behind their back and took offence at the manner in which the new adjustment was being conducted, and ended up withdrawing their co-operation. ICA did not feel able to pay the loss and instead were sued by ATC in the Liberian courts, resulting in judgment against ICA for the policy limit—US$3.5 million, together with $600,000 general damages and $58,000 in costs. ICA sued SCOR not only for the US$3.5 million, but also for the additional general damages and costs.

The matter went to the Court of Appeal who agreed that the follow the settlements clause was subject to two implied conditions:

(a) As a matter of *fact*, that in settling the claim the reinsured had acted honestly and taken all proper and businesslike steps in making the settlement;
(b) As a matter of *law*, that the claim paid by the reinsured to the original insured falls within the risks covered by the policy of reinsurance.

The Court of Appeal upheld Leggatt J's interpretation of the "follow the settlements" clause but considered by majority that the "claims co-operation" clause was paramount and emasculated the "follow the settlements" clause, so that SCOR had only to pay for those settlements which had received their approval. However, the claims co-operation clause was not a condition precedent and although breach would entitle SCOR to damages if they could be proven, ICA had properly proved that the loss was payable and were entitled to an indemnity, up to $3,500,000.

The first proviso: the reinsured has acted honestly and has taken all proper and businesslike steps

A settlement made by a reinsured of an original claim will be presumed to be both honest and businesslike and if either element is challenged by the reinsurer, the onus of proof is on that reinsurer to show a lack of honesty or businesslike operations (*Charman* v. *Guardian Royal Exchange Assurance plc* [1992] 2 Lloyd's Rep. 607).

The obligation to act in a businesslike fashion can be discharged by appointing a reputable loss adjuster provided that:

(i) the appointment is made in a businesslike fashion, i.e. that the firm appointed is apparently competent or not known to be incompetent in the area of adjustment required;
(ii) the reinsured must act in a businesslike fashion when settling the claim in the light of any report produced by the loss adjuster, so that where it is obvious or should be obvious to the reinsured that the

report has been prepared inadequately, perhaps because the loss adjuster has assumed something which the reinsured knows to be incorrect, then the reinsured is not acting in a businesslike fashion simply by slavishly following the recommendations of the adjuster. Where the report appears to be defective the reinsured must take appropriate steps to sort it out.

The second proviso: Claims must fall within the terms of the reinsurance contract as a matter of law

It might seem self-evident that for a claim to be payable by the reinsurer it must fall within the reinsurance contract as matter of law, but in reality it is often difficult to make a clear distinction between a matter of fact and a matter of law. Thus, if an insurance policy expires at midnight and a burglary occurs during the night but it is not clear precisely at what time the burglary took place, the reinsured is entitled to allege that the loss is covered by the policy as a matter of fact if he can show that there is any circumstance indicating that the burglary took place before midnight. If, however, there is a term of policy requiring that the premises are protected by a burglar alarm, and that the burglar alarm that had been installed was not functioning properly, there may be a legal dispute arising over the meaning and construction of the word "protected". It could mean simply in existence or alternatively in existence and properly working at all material times. Thus a reinsurer could argue that the burglary was not covered as a matter of law because the premises were not properly "protected".

The provisos set out in *ICA* v. *SCOR* have been analysed and refined by the courts in several cases since, as follows:

***Hiscox* v. *Outhwaite (No. 3)* [1991] 2 Lloyd's Rep. 524**
The reinsurance agreement considered by the court was in excess of loss form, and contained the usual "ultimate net loss" clause whereby the reinsurer agreed to pay the reinsured unlimited sums in excess of the reinsured's ultimate net loss (retention) of $7,500,000. The ultimate net loss was (as is generally the case) defined in terms of sums actually paid by the reinsured, including legal costs. The reinsuring clause provided that the reinsurance agreement was "*subject to the identical periods, terms, clauses, conditions and warranties as contained in the original policies . . . and in all things falling within the scope of this agreement the Reinsurers shall share to the extent of their interest the fortunes of the reinsured*". This provision was supplemented by a further clause which required the reinsured to exercise due diligence in dealing with its liabilities, subject to which all reasonable compromises and settlements (including ex gratia settlements) were to be "*unconditionally binding*" on the reinsurer. It was common ground that the combined effect of these clauses was to produce a "follow the settlements" obligation on the reinsurer. This case concerned the liability of the reinsurer for payments made by the reinsured under the 'Wellington Agreement', which settled coverage disputes between asbestos producers and their insurers by allocating a percentage of the total liability to each producer, irrespective of whether that producer had been named as a defendant by a claimant and irrespective of whether that producer could have been legally liable to that claimant. Its purpose was to reduce the overall cost of asbestos settlements.

The arbitrator found that the reinsurer was not liable for Wellington Agreement payments made by the reinsured which were not based on any legal liability, although the reinsurer was liable for reasonably agreed settlements in respect of claims actually made against the reinsured. In support of this ruling, the reinsured claimed that the reinsurer was liable for all claims which had been settled in a reasonable fashion; the reinsurer, however, argued that he could only be liable for sums paid out under legal liability.

Evans J. considered the *SCOR* ruling, and derived from it three principles applicable to "follow the settlements" clauses:

(a) The reinsurer is only liable for those losses which fall within the reinsurance agreement itself.

(b) If the terms of the reinsurance are identical with those of the original insurance policy, the reinsurer is able to plead by way of defence that claims met by the reinsured *without legal liability* are not binding on the reinsured and thus do not fall within the reinsurance agreement, and this remains so despite the presence of a "follow the settlements" clause and despite the fact the reinsured has acted in a reasonable and business-like fashion.

(c) However, by way of exception to (b), the reinsurer is bound to follow the reinsured's reasonable settlement of a disputed claim, and cannot subsequently seek to establish that the reinsured would not have been found liable for that claim had the matter proceeded to litigation i.e. if reinsured could have been liable, that is enough.

Applying these principles the judge held that the arbitrator had been correct in holding that the reinsurer was not liable for payments made by the reinsured to persons towards whom the reinsured plainly faced no legal liability. However, the reinsurer was liable for payments made by the reinsured where the reinsured was either liable in law to make payment or at least arguably liable to do. The reinsured may settle the claim at a higher level than reinsurers consider appropriate but as long as the adjustment and settlement are conducted in an honest and businesslike manner, the reinsurer will remain liable. (Both *Hiscox* and *Hill* were distinguished in *Sphere Drake* v. *Basler Versicherun-Gesellschaft* [1998] L.R.L.R. 35, 89 because the contract in question was not a contract of reinsurance but a Marine Pool Agreement between pool members to engage in an underwriting business run by one of them with the widest possible power to settle claims and pass them on to the pool members.)

***Commercial Union* v. *NRG Victory* [1998] 2 Lloyd's Rep. 600**

In this case Exxon claimed from its insurers in Texas the costs of clean-up after the *Exxon Valdez* disaster. Insurers repudiated the two claims and finally agreed a substantial settlement of one claim in the expectation that they would lose and on the second claim the matter went to trial and insurers lost. Insurers had purchased excess of loss protections which contained the "follow the settlements" clause in the same form as *Hill* v. *M&G* (see below); that is to say that it was made clear that any settlements to be followed had to fall both within the original policy and the contract of reinsurance. Insurers then sued reinsurers in London for an indemnity in respect of the settlement which they had agreed in Texas. They relied upon evidence from their Texas attorney who admitted in an affidavit that the settlement might have been outside the cover of the original policy but made it clear that the judge and jury in Texas were either unlikely to appreciate the legal arguments or would simply be biased against the insurers, who would probably lose and end up paying a higher figure than the settled claim.

The reinsurers defended the claim on the basis that the insurers must prove that they were liable for the loss under the original policy of insurance, so that even if the Texas court had given judgment against insurers, that judgment would not in itself prove that there had been a loss under the original policy. They also argued that the evidence of the Texas attorney could not amount to proof of insurers' liability under the original policy, however prudent the insurers' decision to settle might have been. The matter went to the House of Lords who accepted the reinsurers' argument that the evidence of the insurers' attorney did not establish liability under the original insurance, and insurers would not be permitted to recover in reliance upon it. However, the Court of Appeal made it clear that a judgment of a court or arbitration panel in favour of the insured was conclusive proof of insurers' liability under the original policy, provided four conditions were met:

(a) the foreign court had jurisdiction;
(b) the original judgment was not obtained in breach of a clause giving exclusive jurisdiction to some other court;
(c) the reinsured took all proper defences;
(d) the judgment was not manifestly perverse.

Thus a judgment on the original insurance policy appears now to be conclusive evidence of the liability of the insurer, which he can rely upon in claiming against his reinsurers. Manifest perversity is a subjective and uncertain concept; the fact that the foreign tribunal may have held a reinsurer liable in circumstances where an English court would not be sufficient perversity to overturn that liability.

Settlements made by the reinsured in the ordinary course of business will discharge the burden of proof that the claim falls within the insurance and reinsurance policies, and the burden of disproving that they do then shifts onto the reinsurer (*Wurttembergische Feuerversicherung AG* v. *Home Insurance Company* [1993] 2 Re L.R. 253.

THE QUALIFIED FOLLOW THE SETTLEMENTS POSITION

Hill and Charman v. *Mercantile & General Reinsurance Company plc* [1996] 1 W.L.R. 1239

The case of *Hill and Charman* v. *Mercantile & General Reinsurance Company plc* arose from the appropriation by Iraqi forces of aircraft belonging to Kuwait Airways and one belonging to British Airways during the Gulf war. The original insurers made a single $300 million payment to Kuwait Airways on the basis that the loss of all the aircraft constituted one event under the terms of the contract. This initial $300 million worked its way up the reinsurance and retrocession ladder. One of the retrocessionaires, Mercantile & General, took the position that they were entitled to reject the claim on the grounds that it fell outside the terms of the underlying reinsurance contract as a matter of law. In particular, Mercantile & General argued that the loss of the Kuwaiti aircraft was a series of events and not one event and further that the losses fell within the following year to that under which the claim was settled.

Instead of arguing about the number of events the insurers' position focused upon the interpretation of the follow the settlements clause commonly found in reinsurance excess of loss contracts:

"All loss settlements by the reassured including compromise settlements and the establishment of funds for the settlement of losses shall be binding upon the reinsurers, providing such settlements are within the terms and conditions of the original policies and/or contracts . . . and within the terms and conditions of this reinsurance."

Technically this is not a follow the settlements clause but its effect is largely the same and the courts have treated such "losses shall be binding" clauses as being synonymous with follow the settlements clauses. Lord Mustill stated that the conflict inherent in reinsurance, namely the need to avoid an investigation of the same issues twice as against the need to ensure that the integrity of the reinsurer's bargain is not eroded by an agreement over which he has no control, is easily managed where the insurance and reinsurance are on the same terms and the parties are essentially co-adventurers. The problems become more acute when the terms of policies are different, so that a claim under the direct policy may not require the determination of an issue crucial to liability under the reinsurance, or the reinsurance is of another reinsurer, at one or more remove from the direct cover.

Lord Mustill stated that there are only two rules, both of which are obvious. The first is that the reinsurer cannot be held liable unless the loss falls both within the cover of the policy reinsured and within the cover created by the reinsurance. The second is that the parties are free to agree on ways of proving whether these requirements are satisfied.

He went on to distinguish this case from *ICA* v. *SCOR* on the grounds that the follow the settlements clause in dispute in this case specifically required claims under the outwards reinsurance to be within the terms and conditions of the original policies and the outwards reinsurance. Although he stated that the numerous variations of these clauses and their differing application under different types of reinsurance contracts make it confusing and fruitless to lay down general principles, so that each contract should be considered separately, the fact is that the clauses are broadly similar and if incapable of being legally distinguishable the principles laid down in previous judgments will obviously be applied. The House of Lords also made it abundantly clear that every wording had to be considered specifically on its terms and merits, and that the approach of the Court of Appeal, which had been to force or follow the settlements clauses into a simpler category for the purposes of interpretation, and its "strenuous efforts . . . to maintain some continuity of principle by applying prior decisions given on one form of clause in one state of facts to another form of clause in a different state of facts" would not be upheld. One obvious result from this perhaps unduly sensitive approach is to provide considerable scope for legal dispute in the future on the basis that the clause in question is worded slightly differently from those previously considered by the courts, and the facts can be as different as any advocate would wish to make them. There will, hopefully, come a day when all possible variations have at least been considered in general terms by the courts, but that day is still, sadly, some way off.

It is also important to realise that the application in question was one for summary judgment under the then Order 14 of the Rules of the Supreme Court, and so all decisions of the courts in this matter were only to the effect that the reinsured was entitled to argue the points raised and could not be found liable without the benefit of a full trial. Indeed, one of the first points raised in this case as a defence was that the losses caused by the invasion of Kuwait were not attributable to one "event", an issue that was later taken up and confirmed by the Court of Appeal in *Scott* v. *Copenhagen Re* [2003] Lloyd's Rep. IR 696.

It is probably correct to say that the second of the provisos in *ICA* v. *SCOR* remains important where insurance and reinsurance agreements are worded differently in any significant respect, or where they are not intended to be back-to-back. On any interpretation the distinction drawn in *ICA* v. *SCOR* between questions of fact and questions of law remains intact, so that any reinsurer is entitled to argue that as a matter of law the claim does not fall within the policy of reinsurance. See paragraph (c) in next section, below.

CAN THE REINSURED DECIDE WHAT WILL BE BINDING ON REINSURERS?

One possibility would be to remove all rights from the reinsurer to query any claim, which would give rise to certainty for the reinsured and initially reflect the trust of the reinsurer in the reinsured's good faith, business acumen and underwriting ability, but perhaps also to bad feeling between the parties in the event of unexpected losses thereby leading to a possible termination of their commercial relationship. Nevertheless, this has been attempted, using clauses which entitle the reinsured to reimbursement in respect of claims which are settled without any strict legal obligation or on an ex gratia basis (see *Hiscox* v. *Outhwaite (No. 3)*, above). Another variation on this theme is simply to state that the reinsurer will follow any settlements whether they are made by the reinsured under any liability or not.

(a) This was attempted in *Charman* v. *GRE* in which Charman reinsured with GRE under a facultative slip policy which provided that GRE would "follow the settlements" of Charman "whether liable or not liable". Charman agreed to settle with the insured on the basis of a loss adjuster's recommendation. GRE disputed liability and although interlocutory, the matter was treated as if at full trial, but without much of the necessary evidence.

Did the additional words "whether liable or not liable" have any impact upon GRE's obligation to follow the settlements of Mr Charman? *ICA* v. *SCOR* determines that the reinsurer will be obliged to indemnify a reinsured who has settled with the assured in a businesslike fashion, even though it subsequently transpires that the reinsured was not liable. *Prima facie*, therefore, the words "whether or not liable" have no real meaning, except perhaps to delete any certainty as to the reinsured's obligations under the contract. It is possible, although hopefully unlikely, that a laundry bill settled by the reinsured as part of the agreed settlement with the insured would fall within this category. To avoid this conclusion, Charman argued that the addition of the phrase "whether liable or not liable" had the effect of removing the reinsured's obligation to act in a businesslike fashion when settling with the assured, in a similar way to (and predating) but not analysed before the court the direction of Evans J. in *Hiscox* v. *Outhwaite (No. 3)*, i.e. that if it arguably could have been paid, then that was sufficient. The logical consequence of this was that under such wording the reinsurer would be liable to indemnify the reinsured for any payment made by him, even though known to be ex gratia. The judge plainly thought that this argument was not tenable, and that a better interpretation of the additional words was that they clarified, without adding anything to or qualifying, the reinsurer's obligation to follow settlements. However, the judge did not need to reach a concluded view on this point, as there was no evidence that Charman had settled other than in a businesslike fashion. In effect, therefore, these words mean nothing. The reinsured will still have to be arguably liable under the insurance, which would not include a laundry bill. Removing one of the key defining parameters to the collection of risks that the reinsured could pass to the reinsurer—that of the liability of the reinsured to the insured—was not and can never be the answer.

(b) In *Brown* v. *GIO* [1998] Lloyd's Rep. IR 201 a clause entitling the reinsured to be the "sole judge" of what constituted one risk or one event was given a literal interpretation. The clause read "*The Reassured shall be the sole judge of what constitutes each and every loss and/or one event*" and was substantiated by a later clause which read "*The Reassured's definition of each and every loss and/or one event shall be final and binding on the Reinsurers*". Mr Brown, the underwriter of the reinsured syndicate, decided that the negligence of an insured equated to one event, a decision which replicated the findings of the Commercial Court in two reported cases. These cases were later overturned by the Court of Appeal (*Caudle* v. *Sharp*, 1995) and House of Lords (*Axa Re* v. *Field*, 1996). The issue was of mixed fact and law and the court accepted that the conferring of the discretion on the reinsured did not fall within the *Glacier Bay* [1998] Lloyd's Rep. IR 201 situation, which the court would not enforce on the basis that its own jurisdiction was ousted. Thus the decision of a market man could only be attacked if it were unreasonable, which would not be shown merely by the fact that the court would take or had taken a different view. The reasonableness is determined as at the time the decision is made, and is applied to the question that is being addressed. The decision can be wrong but if reasonable and made in good faith it will stand; it is only if the wrong question is addressed that it can be attacked.

(c) In *Assicurazioni Generali SpA* v. *CGU International Insurance plc* [2003] EWHC 1073 the phrase in question was deliberately unqualified more than usual because the reinsurer was obliged to "follow without question the settlements of the Reassured except without gratia and/or without prejudice settlements". The Court of Appeal upheld the judgment of the Commercial Court, and as the latter was more detailed, it is useful to consider to two judgments separately. The key element is the back-to-back nature of the insurance and reinsurance.

(i) *Commercial Court*

The effect of the two provisos outlined by Robert Goff L.J. in *ICA* v. *SCOR* is that the reinsured need not establish that the loss claimed by its underlying insured actually falls within the cover of the policy reinsured, but merely that the claim as settled falls within the reinsurance as a matter of law. In *Assicurazioni* the deputy judge accepted as a consequence of the first *SCOR* proviso that it would be necessary to investigate the settlement and its surrounding circumstances in order to determine the true basis on which it was reached. The deputy judge also looked at the question of whether there was a further restriction on the first rule as set out by Lord Mustill in *Hill* v. *Mercantile and General Reinsurance Co. plc*, particularly where the contract of insurance and reinsurance are back-to-back. He looked again at *Hiscox* v. *Outhwaite (No. 3)* [1999] 2 Lloyd's Rep. 524 where the judge had commented that although the reinsurer would not be precluded from raising issues as to the scope of reinsurance contract, he would still be "bound to follow the insurer's settlement of a claim which arguably as a matter of law is within the scope of the original insurance, regardless of whether the court might hold, if the issue was fully argued before it, that as a matter of law the claim would have failed". Thus a reinsurer who has agreed to an unqualified follow the settlements clause may be liable to indemnify the reinsured even though the underlying claim falls outside the scope of the reinsurance contract.

The deputy judge in this case agreed with Evans J. for three reasons. First, an option available to reinsurers of reopening a settlement by arguing coverage issues as matter of law would make any follow the settlements clause qualified in the sense that claims would have to fall within the terms and conditions of both contracts of insurance and reinsurance, which would thereby defeat the purpose of any follow the settlements clause. Secondly, it would be inconsistent for reinsurers to dispute the same question of law in relation to the reinsurance contract which they had agreed they would not dispute in connection with the insurance contract because they were back-to-back. A clear and conscious decision to deal with the reinsured on a back-to-back basis obliged the reinsurer to follow the reinsured's settlements, notwithstanding that the two contracts were independent bargains. Thirdly, if insurers had to prove that they were legally liable to the underlying insured, the unqualified clause would become in effect a fully qualified clause, which would be a "significantly different" proposition and something to which the reinsured had not agreed. The court accepted that this position departed from the first rule of Lord Mustill in *Hill* v. *Mercantile & General*, but was able to reconcile the cases on the basis that the clause in *Hill* v. *Mercantile & General* was not an unqualified follow the settlements clause but in fact fully qualified. The court then said that the disparity between the two types of clause meant that Lord Mustill's "crucial" comments were not strictly binding on anyone seeking to interpret an unqualified clause. Indeed, Lord Mustill recognised that a co-adventure between reinsured and reinsurer, e.g. a quota share, gave rise to their interests being broadly the same and therefore that reinsurers would not be imprudent in placing their interests in the hands of the reinsured, a proposition reinforced where the reinsurance is back-to-back.

The court therefore held that the reinsurer was obliged to indemnify the reinsured for its settlements on the basis that the claim recognised by the reinsured fell within the risks covered by the reinsurance as a matter of law, and that it had acted honestly and taken all proper businesslike steps in making that settlement. The follow the settlements obligation therefore binds the reinsurer not only as to whether the original claim falls properly within the underlying insurance contract but also whether the claim under the reinsurance policy falls properly within the scope of that policy. Using the phrase "without question" takes the matter no further. The words "without question" do not describe or qualify what the reinsurers have agreed to follow, namely [the reinsured's] settlements, but rather how or the manner in which they are required to follow the settlements" (para 54). " . . . where reinsurers have bound themselves to a contract of reinsurance (in particular a facultative or proportional contract of reinsurance, not for example excess of loss) containing an unqualified follow the settlements clause in circumstances where the contract of insurance and reinsurance are consciously back-to-back, the reinsurers have agreed that, if by admission or compromise the insurers accept liability under the contract of insurance on a basis which, if valid, falls within the risks covered by the contract of reinsurance as a matter of law, they will follow that settlement. *A fortiori*, if by admission or compromise of liability the insurers settle an issue concerning the scope and application of the contract of insurance, the reinsurers should not be entitled to raise the same issue on the same terms albeit this time under the contract of reinsurance. Subject as above, the reinsurers have to that extent consciously entrusted their liabilities to the insurers" (para 53). Thus the words "without question" emphasise the fact that it is assumed by both parties that all proper and businesslike steps would be taken and that reinsurers would be bound by any admission of liability under the insurance and imported into the reinsurance.

(ii) *Court of Appeal*

The court upheld the decision and its rationale in the Commercial Court. In essence the issue remained the extent to which the second *SCOR* proviso entitled the reinsurer to dispute its liability in back-to-back reinsurance in respect of issues already determined by the reinsured under the original policy.

One argument put forward by the reinsured related to the philosophy of follow the settlement clauses, namely that they avoided multiple claims enquiries, simplified and accelerated claims procedures, and reduced the possibility of dispute between insurers and reinsurers. The court held that this strand of pragmatic philosophy was countered by an opposing strand, that identified in *Hill* v. *Mercantile & General* as the right of the reinsurer not to pay out for settlements which might not fall within his bargain with the reinsured, and over which he has no control.

The court reviewed the reinsured's submission that a reinsurer effectively could only refuse to indemnify the reinsured in a back-to-back programme if the reinsured had not settled properly and in a bona fide and businesslike manner. The element of congruence between the two contracts meant that the reinsurers could not re-open issues in the direct policy which by definition appeared by "automatic transfer" into the reinsurance, unless there was something in the reinsurance—and therefore not within the insurance—which entitled the reinsurer to do so. The court disagreed with the reinsured's proposition. It upheld *Hiscox* and stated that:

- The reinsurers were bound by reasonable settlements of liability and quantum under the original policy;
- The reinsured did not have to prove that it was objectively actually and incontrovertibly liable under the original policy (because such an obligation would entitle reinsurers to re-open coverage issues and remove the commercial purpose of the follow the settlements clause), merely that it was arguably liable;
- The reinsured does not have to show that the settled claim falls within the risks covered by the reinsurance, merely that it arguably does so; and
- The reinsurer can require the reinsured "to show that the basis on which he settled was one which fell within the terms of the reinsurance as a matter of law or arguably did so".

The case confirms that a reinsured able to show that he was arguably liable on the facts and the law and has acted reasonably and properly in settling will be entitled to payment under the reinsurance, and that the reinsurer can then only query whether the reinsured has actually done so.

The court also looked at the impact of two other phrases within the clause which dealt with exceptions to the follow settlements obligation on the basis that settlements were ex gratia and without prejudice. Many settlements are effected on this basis, either because a deal can be done at a good price for the insurer when viewed against the unrecoverable costs and uncertainty of litigation. There is always a chance that an apparently strong (or weak) case can be reversed by the actual evidence of a witness under cross-examination, or the fact that the court does not believe one witness to be credible, whatever he may have intimated in his written witness statement, or documents may come to light late in the day. Settlements may be agreed at a "nuisance value", either to avoid costs or damage to reputation.

An arguable liability on the part of the reinsured removes it from the category of "ex gratia" into the category of payments for which reinsurers are liable. A true ex gratia payment which has no possible liability would not be covered by either the insurance or the reinsurance, and reinsurers would therefore not be liable. As indicated above, the words "without question" and "ex gratia" emphasise the fact that it is assumed by both parties that all proper and businesslike steps would be taken in ascertaining loss and liability. The fact that it may later turn out that the reinsured was in fact not under any liability to pay will make no difference to the liability or reinsurers; the position is viewed as at the date of the payment by the reinsured.

Another case revolving around the use and meaning of "Without Prejudice" and "Ex Gratia" is *Faraday Capital Ltd* v. *Copenhagen Reinsurance* [2007] Lloyd's Rep. IR 23, in which a follow the settlements clause was in standard terms but expressly excluded "Without Prejudice and Ex-Gratia Settlements made by the Original Underwriters arising out of and in connection with the Original Insurance". After some argument the reinsured settled a substantial claim with a full and final settlement by way of a compromise "without prejudice to or waiver" to the parties' positions, which was not to be construed as an admission of coverage. The reinsurers refused to pay out and the matter went to the Commercial Court as a preliminary issue, where the judge held that the word "Settlement" meant any binding agreement, not just the formal document (ie it could include the underlying basis of the settlement) or anything which could be later reconsidered, and a "Without Prejudice" settlement arose where there was no admission of liability. If the reinsured were not prepared to admit liability to the insured, then the reinsurers were entitled to insist that the reinsured prove that it was under a liability under the insurance policy before they were required to pay. Alternatively the reinsured could investigate the claim in accordance with the SCOR provisos and admit liability to the extent that it could, thereby bringing itself within the follow the settlements clause. In this case the clause was expressed in clear terms which stated that the reinsurers would not be liable for a "Without Prejudice" settlement, which this clearly was. Further, the court could not be persuaded to look outside the four corners of the actual agreement, because it contained what was effectively an entire agreement clause. Reinsureds should try to avoid the inclusion of a clause which excludes without prejudice settlements, particularly given that it will often include this phrase to minimise its own loss with obvious benefits to reinsurers but with potential disbenefits to itself. Ironically, the reinsured might be better off admitting liability in order to maxmise its own recovery.

The reinsurer should also take care to define any circumstances as to which he requires notification, and the definition of "loss". The question of whether the reinsured had complied with its notification requirement as to loss, which appeared to be a condition precedent and upon discharge would enable the reinsurers to control the claim, was considered by the Court of Appeal in *Royal & Sun Alliance Insurance Plc* v. *Dornoch* [2005] Lloyd's Rep. IR 544 in the context of a claim against directors for damages in respect of overvalued stock, and thence an indemnity under a Directors & Officers Liability Insurance policy. The reinsured was required to advise the reinsurer upon knowledge of any loss that may give rise to a claim, and one issue was whether the loss was that of the insured, the claimant against the insured or the reinsured. The court said that "loss" must mean an actual loss, which means either a proven loss or a loss that is obviously a loss (eg because the value of the stock has fallen so much that there must be a loss, and therefore more than simply a claimed or alleged loss), and although a possible conclusion it could be known until established. In this case the share price fall could have been a natural market fluctuation. Once established that the loss had to be actual, the reinsured could not have had knowledge of any loss until there was an agreement or award against the insured.

This case was followed in *AIG Europe (Ireland) Ltd* v. *Faraday Capital Ltd* [2007] Lloyd's Rep. IR 1 which also involved Directors & Officers Liability

Insurance and an allegation that the loss in question was that of the shareholders, which was known considerably earlier than notified to the reinsurers owing to the percentage drop in value and the fact that the reinsured had posted a reserve. The Commercial Court said that posting a reserve did not establish knowledge of a loss, merely the prudent anticipation of one. It confirmed that the loss is that of the claimant, not the insured, is different from an alleged, claimed or potential loss, and will only "occur" once proven. A "loss" is quite different from an "alleged" or "claimed" loss but need not be the subject of a judgment or agreement against the insured; a point in time does exist between an alleged loss and a known loss at which notification must be made—the real issue is determining when that point occurs.

The issue in the form of whether a settlement was a settlement (effectively a loss for the purposes of the reinsurance) floated up in *English and American Insurance Co. Ltd* v. *Axa Re SA* [2007] Lloyd's Rep. IR 14, following an agreement by the reinsured to pay a sum in respect of past, pending and future known or unknown claims—in effect a commutation on a market wide basis. The court found that part of the payment had been for valid claims, which were accordingly properly settled, and for which sum the reinsurer could advance no plausible assertion that it could realistically defend the claim against it. There was clearly a liability that had been discharged by the reinsured. The "Incurred but not reported" portion, however, being contingent and unparticularised, was not payable by the reinsurer. Another plank of the reinsurer's defence in this case was the fact that the settlement had not been categorised in such a way that the payment was allocatable to particular claims but rather on a lump sum basis reflecting an estimate that all claims would exceed that amount. The evidence showed that the settlement figure was below the clear liabililty of the reinsured and the point, colloquially known as the Lumbermen's point after its genesis in *Lumbermen's Mutual Casualty Co* v. *Bovis Lend Lease Ltd* [2005] 1 Lloyd's Rep. 494 in which an insured could not recover by relying on a settlement of insured and uninsured losses without evidence of clear allocation between the two, is effectively of limited value in the light of its trenchant judicial criticism. In this case the court held that such an argument could not apply to a reinsurance claim involving a follow the settlements clause. It also said that if necessary extrinsic evidence could be used by the reinsured to explain the attribution between insured and uninsured claims, which would seem to end the life of this type of argument.

It will be clear from the above, and from other recent judgments, that clauses authorising one party to the reinsurance contract to make decisions binding the other, however clear or well-drafted they may appear to be, are rarely free from disputes as to interpretation. Giving an insurer carte blanche to decide all issues relevant to its contracts of insurance and reinsurance and thereby removing any ability of the reinsurer to raise any issue about the reinsured's settlements seems well nigh impossible, despite the suggestion of Lord Mustill that the methods of proving loss—and therefore that ability of the reinsurers to question any aspect of that loss—are capable of being agreed by the parties, in a way that makes the rights of each party sufficiently clear to preclude any need to go to the courts for clarification. The reality behind all of these clauses is that they were attempts to vest more discretion in the reinsured and remove the reinsurer's right to question, and yet resulted in more trips to court following the refusal of the reinsurers to pay. The courts have so far resiled from vesting in the reinsured the discretion which the parties clearly intended but perhaps through the difficulties inherent in finding wording acceptable to the courts were unable to effect. This perhaps reflects the conflict inherent in reinsurance: the need to minimise costs and disputes by giving latitude to the reinsured but somehow still retaining a power for the reinsurer to have some control over what the reinsured can do. But a full back-to-back deal means that the second *ICA* v. *SCOR* proviso is largely neutered.

Full reinsurance clause: a clause incorporating the original terms into the reinsurance or a warranty?

In *Toomey* v. *Banco Italico de Espana SA* [2004] EWCA Civ 622 a term in the reinsurance slip as to the description of the risk was held by the Court of Appeal to be a warranty because it went to the root of the transaction and was descriptive of and materially bore on the reinsured risk, and all the more so because the reinsurers had not seen the underlying policy wording. A second argument was put forward to the effect that the Full Reinsurance Clause—"Being a reinsurance of and warranted same gross rate, terms and conditions as and to follow the settlements of the [reinsured] . . . ." —was an express warranty that the terms of the insurance and reinsurance were identical. The Commercial Court had rejected the reinsurers' contention to this effect, and the Court of Appeal specifically expressed no view on this "difficult issue", which had previously arisen as a minority/dissenting view in the form of Lord Griffiths' speech in the House of Lords' decision in *Vesta* v. *Butcher* [1989] A.C. 852. Whilst failing to grasp the nettle and take the matter further, the express reservation of the position may be a signal that the perception of the incorporating effect of the full reinsurance position is incorrect and open to review and change.

(In *Eagle Star* v. *Cresswell* [2003] EWHC 2224 (Comm) a bespoke claims cooperation clause was considered by the courts on four separate occasions.)

FOLLOW THE FORTUNES

More commonly used in the United States of America, the "follow the fortunes" clause often reads as follows:

"It is agreed that in all things coming within the scope of this agreement the reinsurer shall follow, to the extent of its interest, the fortunes of the reinsured."

The courts of the United States have tended to equate "follow the fortunes" with "follow the settlements" and the usual problems arise, particularly in relation to ex gratia payments and also to those payments where there may be some concern over the liability of the reinsured to indemnify the insured. In

American Insurance Co v. *North American Company for Property and Casualty Insurance*, 697 F 2d 79 (1982) the court held that the liability of the reinsurer was effectively similar to the obligations in *ICA* v. *SCOR*, so that a payment in respect of which the reinsured has no liability to pay the insured, will not result in an indemnity under the reinsurance. A reinsured must act honestly and arrive at any settlement in a proper and businesslike manner for the claim to be passed on to the reinsurer.

WHY NOT CHARACTERISE THE OBLIGATION AS A DEBT RATHER THAN A CONTRACTUAL OBLIGATION?

One other way of attempting to enforce payment from a reinsurer was argued before the Supreme Court of New South Wales in *Odyssey Re (Bermuda) Ltd* v. *Reinsurance Australia Corp Ltd* (12 April 2001) to the effect that an amount payable to it under a reinsurance policy placed with ReAC was a debt. There are considerable advantages in having a claim characterised as a debt. First, a claimant can normally obtain judgment for a debt with a minimum of supporting evidence. Secondly, once the claimant proves the existence of the debt, the onus of proof shifts to the defendant, who must prove that the debt has been paid or is not payable. Thirdly, a person claiming for debt does not normally need to comply with the rules requiring mitigation of loss. These rules apply to a breach of contract. Finally, the claimant of a debt is able to take advantage of the statutory demand procedure available in most jurisdictions.

In *Odyssey Re* the reinsured sought to take advantage of the last of these factors by issuing a statutory demand for payment by ReAC. The effect of such a demand is that if the recipient is unable to prove there is a genuine dispute regarding the amount payable, the recipient must either pay or face the prospect of being wound up. Not surprisingly, ReAC opposed the statutory demand on a number of grounds. One of its arguments was that the amount claimed by the reinsured was not a debt, so the statutory demand procedure was not available. ReAC had to contend with the fact that the reinsurance agreement contained a form of follow the settlements clause which provided that the reinsured's loss settlements shall be binding upon the reinsurers and . . . payable by them upon reasonable evidence of the amount paid being given by the reinsured, which according to Odyssey resulted in ReAC's obligations under the agreement taking the form of a debt. It has long been settled that a claim under a contract of insurance is not a debt, but instead is a claim for damages for breach of contract. The one exception to this rule is in the case of valued policies, where the amount payable is a specific liquidated sum. Justice Windeyer of the New South Wales Supreme Court accepted this position, but noted that this raised the question whether the same principle applied to a contract of reinsurance. He found that the same approach did apply to the reinsurance in this case, his principal reason being that payment by the reinsured does not trigger an automatic obligation on the reinsurer to pay. The existence of an agreement to arbitrate in the reinsurance agreement also indicated that the reinsurance obligation was not a debt.

EXTRA-CONTRACTUAL LIABILITY

It is possible that a reinsured could be liable to the insured in excess of its specified limit of contractual liability. For example, a reinsured may fail to settle the loss promptly in breach of an express term to do so, such as the 60-day time for payment within *ICA* v. *SCOR* (see above). Equally there may be a breach of the duty of utmost good faith owed by the reinsured to the insured, and this would apply to the position prior to the formation of the contract as well as to the limited duty of good faith applicable once the contract has been concluded. There could also be liability on the grounds of a wilful failure to reach agreement with the insured, or in respect of a voluntary assumption of responsibility which gives rise to liability upon breach. It is certainly the case that in the absence of any specific clause covering such additional liability, the reinsurer would not be liable. Thus in *ICA* v. *SCOR* (see above) there was effectively a punitive element of US$600,000 payable by the reinsured to the insured, as "general damages". This sum was not payable by the reinsurer because it fell in excess of the reinsurance policy limit, and an open-ended liability was not what either party had intended upon entering into the contract of reinsurance. The Court of Appeal also said that to imply such a term would be inconsistent with the claims co-operation clause, although it is of course uncertain as to what the position would be where no such overriding claims co-operation clause existed. Further, *ICA* v. *SCOR* does not determine whether a follow the settlements clause which is unaffected by any claims co-operation requirement obliges the reinsurer to make such excess liabilities, provided that its total liability remains within the limits fixed by the reinsurance contract. There is no English authority on any aspect of the extra-contractual obligations clause, although it is thought that a follow the fortunes clause may impose a higher degree of liability upon the reinsurer, particularly in respect of the reinsured's extra-contractual payments, than a standard follow the settlements clause. See, however, *Gan Insurance Co. Ltd* v. *Tai Ping Insurance Company Ltd* below.

It is certainly the case that, following *Lancashire County Council* v. *Municipal Mutual Insurance Limited* [1995] L.R.L.R. 293, it is not contrary to public policy for insurance to cover both compensatory awards and awards of exemplary damages against the insured, and such liabilities can be passed by the reinsured to the reinsurer provided there is a sufficiently clear contractual obligation to do so. Only where there is an element of moral culpability—deceit, fraud, dishonesty or recklessness—could the insurer refuse to pay, or the reinsurer to indemnify.

One other aspect that has yet to be judicially explored is the liability of the reinsurer to indemnify the reinsured in situations where the reinsured has been required by the court to pay more to the insured under section 51 of the Supreme Court Act 1981, where the losing party to legal proceedings has been the reinsured in all but name, and five criteria have been satisfied, e.g. the reinsured funded and conducted the litigation, and the defence failed in its entirety. In the absence of any implied term post-*Baker* v. *Black Sea* (see below) it is unlikely that reinsurers would be liable for extra-contractual third party legal costs.

COSTS

In the absence of clear provision for the reinsured's costs in the contract of reinsurance, the position used to be capable of division into two parts. These are as follows.

Where the costs and claim together do not exceed the policy limit

In *British Dominions General Insurance Co* v. *Duder* [1915] 2 K.B. 394 the Court of Appeal held that the cost of reaching a settlement could be recovered from the reinsurer, who had to pay 66% of the reinsured's costs, the reinsured having settled with the insured for 66% of its liability. The original cover was for £20,500, and the reinsurance was only for £2,500. The reinsurer therefore paid £1,000, i.e. 66% of £2,500, equivalent to its proportion of liability under the reinsurance.

In contrast the court refused to award the costs of the reinsured in proving that he was not liable to the insured in *Scottish Metropolitan Assurance Co* v. *Groom* (1924) 20 Lloyd's Rep. 44. The reinsured incurred costs in establishing that it was not liable at all to the insured but had it merely paid the claim, there was a likelihood that it would not have been able to establish that it was under any legal liability to do so, which would have precluded a valid claim being made on the reinsurance. Thus if the reinsured were unable to recover from the reinsurer the claim paid to the insured, why should it be entitled to claim the costs of establishing that the claim should not be paid? The reinsured in both cases reduced the reinsurer's potential liability, but in *Duder* the reinsured was clearly liable to the insured. Today the issue to some extent revolves around the construction of "settlement" in the relevant clause of the reinsurance contract; it seems reasonable that the reinsured should recover his costs where the aggregate does not exceed the policy limit, a possibility reviewed by Stephenson L.J. in *ICA* v. *SCOR* in construing "settlements" as including "all sums reasonably paid in the normal course of disposing of the assured's claim" (*ibid.*, p. 53), provided these costs relate to the original claim and not to a dispute involving the reinsurance policy.

Where the costs and claim together exceed the policy limit

The initial problem is that a reinsurer who specifies his maximum liability should not be forced to pay any greater sum. This was the position in *ICA* v. *SCOR*. Leggatt J. at first instance implied a term into the contract that the reinsurer would reimburse all expenses incurred by its refusal to authorise payment to the reinsured. In the Court of Appeal Stephenson L.J. agreed, pushing the term to include all costs voluntarily incurred in establishing liability. Robert Goff and Fox L.JJ. disagreed, on the basis that the maximum liability had been agreed and was inviolate, the implied term was inconsistent with the original agreement, and the claims co-operation clause enabled the reinsurer to refuse to authorise a settlement without becoming liable for the consequences of such refusal. Such an implied term was not necessary to provide business efficacy to the contract, and the reinsured therefore did not recover his costs of $58,000, although the final result seems to be more one of public policy than pure legal analysis. Although *ICA* v. *SCOR* confirms the sanctity of the limit of cover, in fact its other main effect does no more than establish the rule that a reinsurer who is entitled to refuse its consent to a settlement will not be liable for the consequences of so doing.

***Colin Baker* v. *Black Sea and Baltic General Insurance Co. Limited* [1998] Lloyd's Rep. IR 327**

A short answer to some of the problems posed by these cases was given in *Colin Baker* v. *Black Sea and Baltic General Insurance Co. Limited*, in which a Lloyd's syndicate ceded risks under a proportional reinsurance treaty and went to the House of Lords on an issue as to whether or not the cedant was entitled to recover a proportion of the costs incurred in investigating, settling or defending claims made by their insured on the basis that proportional reinsurance requires the reinsurer to share the same underwriting fortunes as the reinsured as to risk and premium, and therefore it was unreasonable and not intended that the cedant would bear all the costs having effectively received only a portion of the premium, paying the balance over to the reinsurer. The cedant's case was made on three grounds. First, that the reinsurer was liable under the follow the settlements clause in the reinsurance policy, an allegation rejected by Millett L.J. on the basis that "A 'follow the settlements' clause does not extend cover but operates to prevent the reinsurer from reopening a settlement or other disposal of a claim which is within the cover". The argument was that the presence of a follow the settlements clause required the reinsured to defend claims in which liability was disputed with a consequential indemnity from the reinsurer for the costs of so doing, but on the majority judgments of the Court of Appeal in *ICA* v. *SCOR* it was clear that the clause was not to be construed as a request to defend. The follow the settlements argument which was validated by the dissenting judgment of Stephenson L.J. in *ICA* v. *SCOR* now would appear to have run out of steam, subject to any extension to which it may judicially be granted folowing the comments of Mance L.J. in *Gan* (below).

The second argument put forward by the cedant was that the reinsurer was effectively a partner or joint venturer and the costs incurred by the reinsured were for their mutual benefit. A term as to its proportionate payment was therefore required to give the contract business efficacy or to give effect to the presumed intention of the parties. This view was disposed of on the grounds that a proportional reinsurance treaty does not have the character of a partnership; further, any costs incurred by the reinsured are as principal in its own right and not as agent for the reinsurer.

The third ground that a term could be implied by way of custom or usage was held by the House of Lords to have incomplete evidence in the lower courts and this aspect was remitted to the Commercial Court for fresh determination, but the matter settled after the decision of the House of Lords.

It is still open to a cedant to show that there is a custom to the effect that the costs should be shared, but it will be a custom that is difficult to prove.

The reinsured did not seek to recover any part of their overheads or fixed costs, and the only costs in issue were the variable costs specific to the particular claim, e.g. legal expenses in defending the claim, but not the cost of the salaries of the claims manager who would be employed anyway, even though they were dealing with the claim in question. The syndicate also confined its application for costs to proportional reinsurance and it was never suggested that the reinsurer should be liable for costs in non-proportional reinsurance in the absence of any express provision to that effect.

Can the actions of the reinsurer give rise to liability where they not only prevent the reinsured from reaching an agreement with the insured, but also give rise to a liability of the reinsured which is in excess of the reinsurance limit of indemnity? In *ICA* v. *SCOR* additional damages of $600,000 were payable by the reinsured because the reinsurer would not approve any settlement and would not divulge the information which may have assisted the reinsured to refute the claim or reach a compromise.

Robert Goff L.J. said that the effect of the claims co-operation clause was that "if a settlement is made without the approval of the reinsurer, it cannot be relied upon as a settlement authorised by the policy, and so cannot constitute a settlement which the reinsurers are bound to follow under the follow the settlements clause" (*ibid.*, p. 332). It is therefore clear that the presence of the claims co-operation clause was an overriding consideration in respect of extra-contractual payments. This clause has been refined since *SCOR*, in *Gan Insurance Co. Ltd* v. *Tai Ping Insurance Co. Ltd (No. 2)* [2001] 2 All E.R. (Comm) 299 (see also Chapter 7) where the Court of Appeal held that a provision in a reinsurance treaty that the reinsurers were to approve any settlement was subject to qualification. Mance L.J. explained that such qualification does not "arise from any principles or considerations special to the law of insurance. It arises from the nature and purpose of the relevant contractual provision". He went on: " . . . it is possible to envisage circumstances in which reinsurers' refusal or approval could take place for reasons extraneous to the claim and prejudice insurers".

However, whether the courts will imply such a term will depend on the facts. Although it may be easier to imply such a term than one whereby consent is not to be unreasonably withheld (despite the finding of Longmore J. of an implied term that the reinsurer would not unreasonably withhold consent) the Court of Appeal thought the term to be implied was that the withholding of approval should take place in good faith after consideration of and on the basis of the facts giving rise to the particular claim, and not with reference to considerations wholly extraneous to the subject matter of the particular reinsurance or arbitrarily.

Mance L.J. went on to add that if any further implication were to be made it would be "along the lines that the reinsurer will not withhold approval arbitrarily, or . . . will not do so in circumstances so extreme that no reasonable company in its position could possibly withhold approval. This will not ordinarily add materially to the requirement that the reinsurer should form a genuine view as to the appropriateness of settlement or compromise without taking into account considerations extraneous to the subject matter of the reinsurance".

GAN Insurance Co. Ltd v. *Tai Ping Insurance Co. Ltd (No. 2)*

In *GAN Insurance Co. Ltd* v. *Tai Ping Insurance Co. Ltd (No. 2)* the Court of Appeal looked at the claims control clause (which had been revised after *ICA* v. *SCOR* to make each aspect a condition precedent). The Commercial Court had been asked to consider whether a term should be implied into the reinsurance contract to the effect that reinsurers would not withhold their approval to a settlement unless it had reasonable grounds for doing so, even where the claims control clause was a condition precedent. It said that the right of a reinsurer to refuse to approve a settlement without reasonable grounds for so doing would defeat the purpose of the reinsurance, and that such a term that the reinsurers would not unreasonably withhold its consent would be implied. To force the reinsured to litigate his liability with the insured in every case is uncommercial and unbusinesslike, and unlikely to have been the intention of the parties.

The Court of Appeal started from the premise that the parties are free to contract on whatever basis they wished and applied the traditional tests of implication—necessity for business efficacy, and the obvious but unexpressed intention of the parties. Mance L.J. pointed out that the necessity for the reinsured to obtain a judgment against itself in order to claim against its reinsurer provided stringent protection to the reinsurer, which could not have been intended by the parties without some qualification, which in his view was that the reinsurers' right to withhold approval to a settlement should be exercised in good faith after consideration of the facts giving rise to the claim and without consideration of matters wholly extraneous to the subject matter of the reinsurance. The reinsurer must not withhold approval arbitrarily or in circumstances so extreme that no reasonable reinsurer could possibly withhold approval. It must consider the underlying claim as a whole without regard to its own sectional exposure as a reinsurer, and would therefore have to disregard its ability to influence the reinsured's approach to another claim, particularly because a reinsurance contract creates a community of interest between insurer and reinsurer, namely that of determining how best to deal with the original claim. Thus, a reinsurer must not use its right to refuse approval as an attempt to influence the reinsured in relation to a matter arising under another quite separate reinsurance; as an attempt to harm the reinsured as a competitor or in the eyes of a local regulator; simply to delay payment for as long as possible despite it being clear that the claim will have to be paid; or to force the reinsured to litigate in the hope that some defence to the underlying claim might emerge during the action. The decision was not unanimous and was one which sought to give guidance rather than order the declaration in the terms sought by the reinsured, who lost the case.

The Court of Appeal in *Paragon Finance plc* v. *Nash* [2001] EWCA Civ 1466 considered that "a lender will not exercise his discretion in a way that no reasonable lender acting reasonably would do". However, it added that "it is unlikely that a lender who was acting in that way would not also be acting either dishonestly, for an improper purpose, capriciously or arbitrarily".

The courts are increasingly willing to imply terms limiting a party's contractual discretion, formulated in terms either that any relevant approval or consent is not to be unreasonably withheld, or, more likely, that any such approval or consent is to be exercised in good faith after consideration of and on the basis of the facts giving rise to the particular claim and not with reference to considerations wholly extraneous to the subject matter of the particular contract or arbitrarily.

Thus it still seems to be arguable, subject to the impact which the courts may still give to the limit of indemnity set out in the reinsurance contract (which would mean overturning the majority decision in *ICA* v. *SCOR*), that if the reinsurer breaks its obligation not to act capriciously or unreasonably or act in accordance with its sectional interests, then arguably it should be liable in damages for the consequences of such breach. If the insurer has to incur additional costs in proving that the underlying claim should be paid, which are directly attributable to the consequences of the unreasonable attitude of the reinsurer, then there would appear to be no good reason why reinsurers should not pay.

There is one other method by which a reinsurer could technically be liable for costs incurred by the reinsured in unsuccessfully defending a claim by the insured. This arises out of section 51 of the Supreme Court Act 1981 which enables a court to award costs against any person, whether or not that person is party to the litigation or a third party. Such a situation would only arise in the event that the reinsured had become insolvent but had incurred liability to the insured for the insured's legal costs in establishing the liability of the reinsured to it. Since 1996 there has been a spate of cases on this point, most notably *Murphy* v. *Young's Brewery* [1996] L.R.L.R. 60, *TGA Chapman Limited* v. *Christopher* [1998] 1 All E.R. 873, *Pendennis Shipyard Limited* v. *Magrathea (Pendennis) Limited* [1998] 1 Lloyd's Rep. 315, *Gloucester Health Authority* v. *Torpy* [1999] Lloyd's Rep. IR 203, *Citibank NA* v. *Excess Insurance Co. Limited* [1999] Lloyd's Rep. IR 122, *Cormack & Cormack* v. *Excess Insurance Co. Limited* [2002] Lloyd's Rep. IR 938, *Bristol & West Plc* v. *Bahdresa* [1999] Lloyd's Rep. IR 138 and *Monkton Court Limited* v. *Perry Prowse (Insurance Services) Limited* [2002] Lloyd's Rep. IR 408. The issue has not yet arisen in a reinsurance context but no doubt will do so upon the insolvency of a reinsured with liabilities to the insured for the insured's costs.

COMMUTATIONS: IS A REINSURER LEGALLY OBLIGED TO PAY THE COMMUTED SUM TO THE REINSURED?

The main issue to be considered in connection with this question is whether the "claims" proposed to be commuted between insurer and reinsurer constitute "loss settlements" for the purposes of the reinsurer's retrocession.

The provisions of the retrocession are obviously relevant to the question under discussion and these should contain an Ultimate Net Loss Clause, Notice of Loss Clause and a Reinsurance Clause.

Notwithstanding the retrocessionaire's burden of proving that the settlement was *not* made honestly and in a businesslike fashion, a commutation arrangement is inherently likely to be more exposed to objection by a retrocessionaire than is the compromise of a single quantified claim. This will be particularly the case when outstanding and IBNR claims are a substantial element of any commutation. It will be important for a reinsured (or retrocedant) to be able, if required, to justify why he has agreed to a particular commutation figure and how this was calculated. The fact that a retrocedant did not obtain expert actuarial advice will probably be evidence of an unbusinesslike settlement.

The argument likely to be made by the retrocessionaire is that such claims are not recoverable because they are not "losses". It would be suggested that the IBNR claims have been artificially crystallised as "losses" and quantified only for the purposes of the commutation. The retrocessionaire could contend that the outstanding and IBNR reserves may never in fact become claims at all and even if they do they may not be properly recoverable under the outwards treaties.

Although there has, to date, been no English court decision which gives authoritative guidance about the question whether quantified IBNR claims are recoverable under an excess of loss treaty, some limited assistance may be gleaned from *In Re A Company No. 0013734 of 1991* [1992] 2 Lloyd's Rep. 415. The case arose from an application by an unidentified insurance/reinsurance company to strike out a winding-up petition which was presented by Cambridge Re (not in liquidation, although ordered to be wound up in Bermuda in May 1985). One of the principal difficulties faced by liquidators of reinsurance companies is that the winding-up of such companies can take many years because the need to run-off the portfolio of business written by the insolvent company. In a novel and imaginative response to this problem, the liquidators of Cambridge Re applied to the Bermudian court to obtain its approval to actuarial valuations of contingent claims and claims of uncertain value. These actuarial valuations were approved by the court. The reinsurance company submitted, however, that the order of the Bermudian court was not binding on it as the valuations were not "loss settlements" under the reinsurance agreement concerned.

This case was heard by a deputy judge, Mr Roger Kaye QC, who made the following interesting observations about the question under discussion:

> "It seems to me that there is a serious and complex argument of construction as to whether, in the particular circumstance of the case, the valuation pursuant to the Bermudian court order could be a loss settlement as suggested. As I have explained above, the reference in Article 15 to loss settlements seems at first blush to presuppose that an actual loss has arisen and been settled by agreement between the assured and the insurer and not to relate to an actuarial valuation of contingent claims or claims of uncertain value, still less in the context of an order permitting a valuation which was principally made and expressly made binding for the purposes of the litigation only and which fixed the liabilities of the Petitioner primarily with a view to dividend and the timing of proofs. On the other hand, I have considerable sympathy with the liquidators. Their argument has the undoubted merit of good common sense and is in keeping with the views [expressed in the previous cases]. It may well be that the consequential effect is that it also serves to fix the underlying liability for the purposes of claims by the Petitioner against reinsurers. It may well be that many reinsurers did not challenge the order. It may be that the company would not be able to or would not wish to challenge the actuarial methodology . . . In my judgement, however, the hearing of an interlocutory application to strike out a Winding-Up Petition and the hearing of the Winding-Up Petition itself is not the appropriate forum for resolving what could be an important and serious matter of fact and law affecting the insurance and reinsurance market as a whole."

There are certainly indications in the above observations that English courts would be sympathetic to argument that valuations of IBNR claims approved by a court should be considered to be "loss settlements" under excess of loss treaties. However, these observations should be viewed with considerable caution in connection with this particular case because:

(a) The deputy judge expressly declined to express any concluded view about the application of the "loss settlement" provision to the actuarial valuation of the IBNR reserves. *In Re a Company* is, therefore, *not* authority for the proposition that IBNR claims, even if they are quantified, are "loss settlements" under excess of loss treaties.

(b) The English courts have generally been sympathetic to arguments that reinsurers should not be allowed to evade their legal liabilities because their reinsureds are insolvent.
(c) The fact that actuarial valuations had been approved by the Bermudian court was a further special factor favouring a broad interpretation of "loss settlement" in the above decision.

CAN THE INSURED CLAIM AGAINST THE REINSURER IF THE REINSURED FAILS TO PAY HIS CLAIM, OR BECOMES INSOLVENT?

The insured has no contractual link with the reinsurer and the contract between the reinsurer and reinsured is of no concern of his, unless it contains a cut-through clause.

A cut-through clause can often be found either as an indorsement on the insurance policy or more formally contained as a clause in the body of the contract of reinsurance. Such clauses are usually agreed for the purposes of marketing by the insurer to the insured of the fact that there should be sufficient security behind the insurer should any insolvency occur, or alternatively where the insured is anxious about the continuing ability of its insurer to meet claims. A third party, i.e. the insured, will have the right to enforce a contractual term either:

(a) if the contract expressly provides for this to happen; or
(b) if the term in question confers a benefit on the third party, unless it is clear, on a true construction of the contract, that this was not intended.

The insured third party then has the same rights to enforce the contract as if he were one of the original signatories. This means that such a right is subject to the reinsurance contract's terms and conditions, so, for example, if it provides that rights arising under it will only be enforceable within a certain time limit, the insured will be bound by this. A third party seeking to enforce its rights can take advantage of all the remedies available to a person bringing a claim for breach of contract, but the normal rules of law, including those relating to causation, remoteness and mitigation, apply equally to the third party's claim. It constitutes either a priority payment arrangement in circumstances where it is intended that the insured can have the benefit of any reinsurance receivables due to the reinsurer and in priority to other creditors, or a direct payment arrangement in circumstances where the insured is entitled to hold the reinsurer secondarily responsible to meet its claims. Unfortunately in situations where the insurer becomes insolvent, such expectations are false. Although a cut-through clause would clearly satisfy both limbs of the test under the Contracts (Rights of Third Parties) Act 1999, it is a cardinal principle of English insurance law that all creditors of an insolvent company should receive equal treatment of the limited funds available to the liquidator of that company on a pro rata basis.

The House of Lords made this clear in *British Eagle International Airlines Limited* v. *Compagnie Nationale Air France* [1985] 1 W.L.R. 758, in which a clearing agreement provided for multi-lateral netting off but was held void in respect of the provision for payment of debts which conflicted with the *pari passu* insolvency principle. All claims stand alone and cannot be affected by any agreement to net off. Thus the liquidator was able to recover sums which had not been netted off prior to the presentation of a winding-up petition against the broker, even though the [insured] had authorised the operation for the movement of funds through the central accounting system which utilised netting off.

Cut-through clauses are intended to ensure that the insured is paid in priority to other creditors. Unfortunately, however, this principle is subject also to an overriding objective of public policy to achieve equitable treatment of creditors of insolvent companies, and it simply was not acceptable that an insolvent debtor (the reinsured) could contract out of this principle to the benefit of one of its creditors.

Further, the problems outlined above in relation to attempts by the insured to allege that a trust has been set up in its favour will also apply. English courts look at attempts to allege that trusts exist in favour of one creditor very carefully in situations involving insolvency. One other option would be for the contract of insurance to provide for an assignment by the insurer to the insured of the right to be paid any reinsurance monies payable to the reinsured, but such an assignment may give rise to the need to register the security. If the appropriate registration formalities are not fully complied with, the security would be unenforceable against other creditors of the insurer in the event of its insolvency.

More recently in *Nemgia v. AGF Holdings* [1997] 2 B.C.L.C. 191, Nemgia, an insurer, sold parts of its business to AGF who also reinsured other business (which Nemgia retained). AGF acquired the goodwill of Nemgia's policyholders and negotiated and agreed claims direct with the policyholders, although AGF actually paid the claims on behalf of Nemgia. Nemgia went into liquidation and it was feared that the liquidator would require AGF to pay to Nemgia all sums due after the commencement of the liquidation, payable under the reinsurance agreement, which would then have been available to meet the claims of other creditors. Further, Nemgia policyholders might not renew with AGF and so AGF agreed to pay the Nemgia policyholders direct in return for an assignment from them of their claim against Nemgia. AGF thereby prevented claims being filed against Nemgia and Nemgia, having suffered no loss, was unable to claim on the reinsurance policy against AGF.

The court held that this Direct Payment Arrangement did not cause Nemgia any actionable loss and was neutral to its insolvent state. The decision (although decided on narrow contract issues) therefore reveals how the indemnity nature of the contract between an insurer and reinsurer may bolster the insured's ability to obtain an effective cut-through by this means. The insolvent estate is relieved simultaneously of both the benefit of the reinsurance receivable and the burden of the relevant insurance liability. No privity of contract arises although this and other cut-through mechanisms may give rise to other legal and regulatory issues, particularly as regards solvency margins and insolvency.

Such direct payment arrangements may be relatively straightforward to engineer in facultative transactions but will be much more difficult to negotiate in the context of excess or non-proportional treaty reinsurance.

The Contracts (Rights of Third Parties) Act 1999 is unlikely to be enforced by the courts in favour of those creditors of an insolvent insurer (despite their foresight in attempting to protect their position) because to do so would be to destroy the *pari passu* rule, a primary tenet of insolvency law and itself the product of public policy: fairness to and equality to all. It will be for the courts to reconcile the interaction of the third party rights made enforceable by the Act and the principle of *pari passu* distribution in insolvency. Cut-through clauses would appear to be unobjectionable in situations that do not involve insolvency, but they become of limited value in these circumstances.

CAN THE REINSURED OBTAIN INTEREST FROM THE REINSURER?

In many cases the contract of reinsurance will specify that interest is to be paid by the reinsurer in the event of any late payment. Nevertheless, the courts are empowered to award interest under section 35A of the Supreme Court Act 1981 which states that:

> "Subject to the rules of court, in proceedings (whenever instituted) before the High Court for the recovery of a debt or damages there may be included in any sum for which judgment is given simple interest, at such rate as the court thinks fit or as rules of court may provide, on all or any part of the debt or damages in respect of which judgment is given, or payment is made before judgment, for all or any part of the period between the date when the cause of action arose and:
>
> (a) in the case of any sum paid before judgment, the date of payment; and
> (b) in the case of the sum for which judgment is given, the date of the judgment."

Section 17 of the Judgments Act 1838 provides that a judgment debt shall carry interest from the date of judgment until the date of actual payment; Section 49 of the Arbitration Act 1996 authorises arbitrators to award simple or compound interest at any rate they consider just unless the parties have agreed otherwise.

The rate of interest will usually be 1% above base rate or the nearest equivalent appropriate index such as the US Prime Rate. The fact that the reinsured would have been able to borrow money, owing to its business status or contacts or for whatever reason, is not relevant and although the rationale for the payment of interest is to restore the reinsured to the position in which it would have been had it borrowed the equivalent amount on the money markets, generally the rate would be base rate plus 1% (which is in effect the US Prime Rate), save in exceptional circumstances. Thus a rate will not be awarded which is only applicable to term or secured borrowing. Interest is payable from the date on which the cause of action accrued, although it will only be payable once it has become clear to insurers or reinsurers that a claim is being pursued and they have had some time to appreciate its effect and consider their courses of action. Thus in *Kuwait Airways Corporation* v. *Kuwait Insurance Co. SAK* [2001] 1 All E.R. (Comm) 972, the Court of Appeal held that interest should generally be payable from the date on which the cause of action for the relevant payment arose, which in this case would have been on the invasion of Kuwait on 2 August 1990, but it was not apparent until November 1990 that a claim would be made, following which the insurers were entitled to consider their response to the claim. The claim was in fact rejected on 5 December 1990 and interest was awarded from this date.

WHEN DOES THE REINSURED'S CAUSE OF ACTION ACCRUE?

The general rule is that time for the purposes of limitation under a reinsurance agreement begins to run when the reinsured's own underlying liability is established by judgment, award or settlement against it in favour of its own assured. The leading authority is *Versicherungs und Transport Aktiengesellschaft Daugava* v. *Henderson* (1934) All E.R. Rep. 626.

In this case, the assured owned a building in Riga, Latvia, insured against fire. It was reinsured by the Latvian insurer with a London underwriter. In April 1930 a fire occurred which damaged the building and after some dispute, the insurer and assured agreed to a settlement figure and the loss was paid in January 1932 in Latvian lats.

The insurer then brought an action against the reinsurer under the contract of reinsurance. The question arose as to whether the sum in Latvian lats for which the reinsurer had been liable (659,292.43 lats) was to be converted into sterling—the currency of the reinsurance agreement:

at the date of the fire (April 1930)

or

at the date of the settlement and payment (January 1932).

In the meantime the pound had been devalued and the reinsurer argued that his liability arose at the date of the fire when the pound was worth more and his liability in sterling would have been £26,038 rather than at the time of settlement when his liability for the same number of lats was £38,353.

The Court of Appeal held that the relevant date for conversion was the date of settlement of liability in 1932, so the reinsurer was liable for the larger sterling sum. Scrutton L.J. said:

> "I do not understand how the reinsurer can be liable to pay an account till it has been fixed between insurer and assured. It is then that the insurer pays and it is then that the reinsurer is bound to indemnify him. If the rate of exchange is fixed as at a date before the insurer's liability to pay is quantified and satisfied, the insurer may, as in the present case, recover more than an indemnity, which is contrary to all principles of insurance."

Maugham L.J. also said:

> "A policy of reinsurance is an agreement by way of complete or partial indemnity to the insurer. That has long been settled, and has been stated in more than one case. Like every contract of indemnity, it can only operate if the liability of the debtor, the insurer, is established, and it is necessarily contingent on that liability being established. It follows that the insurer has no cause of action against the reinsurer until the loss for which the former is liable (if any) has been ascertained."

So the general rule is that under a reinsurance contract the limitation period starts to run when the reinsured's underlying liability is established by judgment, award or settlement.

However, this general rule may be altered by an express agreement in the contract between reinsured and reinsurer. If the reinsurance provides that, as a condition precedent to the reinsurer's liability, certain steps must be taken—e.g. an arbitration award must be obtained against the reinsurer, or particular claim documents have to be submitted to the reinsurer—time will only run from the date on which that specified event occurs. In the absence of any express condition precedent the general rule remains valid. It is not ousted by a bare condition that the reinsured must submit accounts to the reinsurer.

This was emphasised by the Court of Appeal in *Halvanon* v. *Cia de Seguros* [1995] L.R.L.R. 303 where Steyn L.J. in answer to an application to adduce further evidence in a case concerning contracts of reinsurance between an Israeli reinsured and four Brazilian reinsurers said:

> "The (application) is based on the proposition that a cause of action in this field arises when an account is rendered. In my judgment that proposition is contrary to well-established principles. In the absence of special clauses that is not the case. The cause of action arises when the underlying liability is ascertained by agreement, by an award or by judgment. It is not postponed until the rendering of an account."

Another reason for the court to delay the date for the commencement of interest is the position of an excessive delay in the making or pursuing of a claim, or indeed its complexity, the ability to investigate it adequately but comprehensively and the way in which the claim has been presented (*Quorum A/S* v. *Schramm (No. 2)* [2002] Lloyd's Rep. IR 315).

TEST YOUR UNDERSTANDING

1. Which of the following best describes the tension of reinsurance?

(a) The uncertainty felt by a reinsurer as to the extent of the claims that he will have to pay.
(b) The uncertainty felt by a reinsured as to what he may validly cede to the reinsurer.
(c) The problem of ensuring that the reinsurer's agreement with the reinsured is not undermined by the actions of the reinsured and insured in an agreement over which the reinsurer may have no control.
(d) The fact that nothing is wholly predictable and that catastrophes can occur at any time.

2. Can a reinsurer refuse to pay a claim on the basis of breach of the following by the reinsured?

(a) The reinsured will underwrite sensibly.
(b) The reinsured will take all proper and businesslike steps in settling a claim.
(c) The reinsured has made a payment designated as "without prejudice".
(d) The claim does not fall within the reinsurance as a matter of law.
(e) The reinsured has failed to comply with a standard claims control clause which is not a condition precedent.
(f) The original claim is arguably not covered by the insurance.

3. Which of the following are true?

(a) The parties are free to agree whatever they want in order to ascertain which losses will fall within the insurance and reinsurance, and this can include the insured's laundry bill.
(b) Each Follow the Settlements wording must always be considered independently by the courts, in the context of its factual background.
(c) Allowing the reinsured to determine what will be final and binding on the reinsurer is void because it ousts the jurisdiction of the courts.
(d) A decision made by a reinsured on what is covered as a matter of law can be reconsidered and overturned if there is a subsequent court decision to the contrary.
(e) It is easier for a reinsurer to argue about claims under a back-to-back reinsurance than any other type.

(f) In certain circumstances an obligation of a reinsurer to follow a specific claim that has been properly adjusted can be a debt and therefore easier to collect by the reinsured.
(g) The reinsured can never obtain payment for costs which with the claim exceed the limit of the reinsurance contract.
(h) A standard claims control clause can be exercised by the reinsurer in any way he sees fit.
(i) A commutation by a reinsurer of all his liabilities and potential liabilities must be followed by his retrocessionaire if the commutation is reasonable.
(j) Interest is payable by the reinsurer from the date on which the reinsured pays the original claim.
(k) A cut-through clause is perfectly enforceable under English law at all times, so that an insured can bypass the insurer and obtain payment from the reinsurer.
(l) A judgment of a foreign court against the reinsured is an unimpeachable adjustment of the loss which the reinsurer must follow.
(m) A reinsured must be paid in full for any loss substantiated by a report of a well-known loss adjuster.
(n) The parties can agree any rate of interest applicable to claims paid late by the reinsurer.

CHAPTER 7

CLAIMS

INTRODUCTION

The speed at which a reinsurer handles and pays claims is one of the most important factors for a reinsured since taking some of the burden of the payment of losses when they occur is the reason for entering into a reinsurance contract in the first place. Apart from the initial contact which insurers have with the reinsurance underwriters (assuming that they do since many reinsurance inceptions and renewals are simply handled by the brokers) the most contact that an insured will have with its reinsured will be when a large claim occurs which he is contractually required to report to reinsurers or for which he is seeking reimbursement, and it is therefore of paramount importance that the reinsurer has an efficient claims service.

This chapter covers:

- The nature and status of various claims conditions such as claims cooperation and claims control clauses;
- The rights and duties of the reinsurer;
- How certain key words such as "occurrence", "event" and "cause" may be interpreted by the courts;
- How reinsurers may deny liability;
- Limitation periods and how they operate in the reinsurance context;
- Issues relating to runoff, such as commutation.

THE NOTIFICATION AND PAYMENT OF CLAIMS

For the reinsurer it is important that claims are reported to it in a timely manner in order that the claims may be reserved in its books. Normally the reinsurer will input the reserve into its computer systems recommended by the insurer. However, sometimes the reinsurer will feel that the reserve recommended is inadequate, perhaps because the Insurer has adopted too optimistic an approach in relation to liability or quantum on the case. In this situation the reinsurer will discuss the matter with the claims manager at the insurer and suggest that the reserve be increased; if the insurer disagrees then the reinsurer may decide to input an additional case reserve (ACR) on the matter so that the figure in the reinsurer's books is adequate to pay what the reinsurer believes that the claim will settle for.

Notification

***Australia and New Zealand Bank* v. *Colonial Eagle Wharves Limited* [1922] 2 Lloyd's Rep. 241**

This case involved all-risks insurance in relation to the misdelivery of goods. McNair J. considered the meaning of "each and every claim", and concluded that " . . . in this clause, 'claim' means the occurrence of a state of facts which justifies a claim on underwriters" (at p. 255).

The amount payable, when the amount is payable and what supporting documentation will be required will depend upon the actual wording of the contract. The reinsurance contract may contain wordings such as claims to be notified "immediately" or "as soon as reasonably practicable" or it may even say nothing at all on the subject, which is common in the case of slip policies.

Notification to reinsurers in the case of quota share reinsurance is easy because reinsurers simply pay a fixed proportion of the reinsured's liability.

In excess of loss treaties the reinsurer's liability is activated when the loss exceeds the reinsured's retention and it is therefore usual for the reinsurer to insist that the reinsured notifies him of a claim which is likely to exceed 50% or 75% of the retention.

If the notification clause is a condition precedent to the reinsurer's liability then the reinsurer may repudiate the claim, but if it is not then the reinsurer is obliged to pay the claim and the reinsurer's only recourse will be to recover nominal damages in relation to the prejudice caused to him by the delay in notification. The reinsurer would have to prove that it is more difficult for him to investigate the claim because of the delay, but in practice this will be difficult to prove and any damages awarded will therefore be nominal. If there is a strict notice clause in the contract and it is a condition precedent then the reinsured must notify the loss within that time period or the reinsurer may refuse to deal.

It is common for reinsurance contracts to require notification to be given to the broker or to a responsible person at the reinsurer's Head Office Claims department. It is not clear if the reinsured is obliged to notify his reinsurers of a loss of which the reinsurer already has knowledge and there is unfortunately no reinsurance authority on this topic. However, in the insurance context, *Barratt Brothers (Taxis)* v. *Davies (Lickliss* v. *Milestone Motor Policies at Lloyd's, Third Parties)* [1966] 2 All E.R. 972 establishes that provided the insurer is notified of the loss within the requisite time by another source then that is sufficient and the insured is not obliged to inform his insurers. In this case a motorcyclist was involved in an accident with a taxi. The insured never informed his insurers of the accident but the court held that he had not breached the policy conditions because the insurers had received all of the information from the police. Presumably, the same rules would apply to reinsurance cases. The case of *CNA International Reinsurance Company Limited*

v. *Companhia de Seguros Tranquilidade SA* [1999] Lloyd's Rep. IR 289 illustrates how important it is that notification clauses are properly contained in the relevant documentation. In this case the notice provisions were supposed to be included in the schedule with the wording, but instead it had become common to include it in the slip and on this occasion this information had not been included. This case involved a concert to be given by Placido Domingo in Lisbon. The concert promoters, Fundacao das Descobertas (FDD), insured themselves against cancellation of the concert. The insurers, Tranquilidade (T), reinsured 90% of the risk with London market reinsurers and the reinsurance was placed before the direct insurance was. Several days before the concert was due to take place it was cancelled because Placido Domingo's mother was very ill. FDD made a claim under its policy with T who settled the claim in full and then T sought indemnity under its reinsurance contract. The reinsurers refused to pay. The court had to decide if the Lloyd's standard contingency wording had been incorporated into the reinsurance contract. The Lloyd's wording was clearly intended for direct insurance since it mentioned "insureds" and not "reinsureds". It contained a claims procedure clause requiring insurers to be notified promptly of claims and prohibiting insureds from admitting liability without the insurers' approval. It also contained a condition precedent that the insured must make all necessary enquiries regarding any matters, which could increase the possibility of a loss. Clarke J. held that the question of incorporation was a matter of construction and that although all of the terms of the Lloyd's contingency wording were terms of the reinsurance contract, each term had to be looked at individually to see if it was actually applicable in the reinsurance context.

Usually, proper notification of a claim will mean receipt of the notification of the claim by the reinsurer.

Normally reinsurance contracts do not specify a particular time period in which to notify a claim to reinsurers and rely simply on as soon as possible, which can cause problems of interpretation, and what is reasonable will depend on the facts of the particular case. The effect of late notification was considered in the insurance context in the case of *George Cranes Limited* v. *Scottish Boiler and General Insurance Company* [2002] 1 All E.R. (Comm) 366, where under indemnity insurance the insured was obliged to:

> "within 30 days after (any) loss . . . or such further time as the company may in writing allow at the expense of the insured, deliver it to the company a claim in writing . . . No claim under this policy shall be payable unless the terms of this condition have been complied with."

The insured failed to give notice of the claim in the required time. The Court of Appeal held unanimously that the clause constituted a condition precedent to liability. The purpose behind a notification clause is to ensure that the insurer has a reasonable time in which to make a reasoned decision regarding the claim.

Payment of the claims

If the contract does not contain clear language obliging the reinsurer to settle the reinsured's claim then according to *Re London County Commercial Reinsurance Office Limited* [1922] 2 Ch. 67 the onus lies upon the reinsured to prove that the reinsurer is legally liable to indemnify him and that the quantum figure is correct.

"Follow the settlements"

This phrase has basically been taken to mean that if it is included in a reinsurance contract that the reinsurer will be bound to follow claims settlements agreed by the reinsured.

***Insurance Company of Africa* v. *Scor (UK) Reinsurance Company Limited* [1985] 1 Lloyd's Rep. 312**

This is the leading case on this subject. ICA insured warehouses and their contents in Liberia and Monrovia against fire. The buildings were owned by the government of Liberia but were leased to the Africa Trading Company. Facultative reinsurance cover was obtained in London with Scor (UK) being the lead reinsurer. In February 1982 the warehouses caught fire and the warehouses were burned to the ground. The water supply had been cut off overnight and within a few days the whole site had been flattened by the Liberian army. There were allegations of fraud, corruption and collusion. There was only one loss adjuster in Monrovia at the time who was instructed to investigate the loss and was subsequently joined by another loss adjuster from Athens. In view of the allegations of fraud Scor appointed its own loss adjuster to investigate the loss.

ATC commenced proceedings in Liberia against ICA, arguing that ICA had no real defence to the claim. The Liberian court ordered ICA to pay ATC for their loss plus additional damages and legal costs. ICA commenced proceedings in the Commercial Court in London for the amount of the Liberian judgment.

Scor argued that ICA had failed to comply with the obligations under the claims cooperation clause by refusing to cooperate with Scor's loss adjusters. The court held that such a refusal was acceptable and understandable in the circumstances.

Scor appealed and applied for a new trial both of which were denied. The appeal was based upon the fact that there was a "follow the settlement" clause in the reinsurance agreement and the effect which the claims cooperation clause would have upon it. The two clauses were contradictory because the "follow the settlement clause" meant that the reinsurer simply follows the settlements reached by the reinsured whereas the "claims cooperation clause" requires the approval of reinsurers before settlement is agreed.

The Court of Appeal held that ICA's settlement had been made without Scor's approval but nevertheless Scor were obliged to pay the judgment of the Liberian Court. Following *Scor*, if there is a "follow the settlements" clause in the contract, provided the reinsured can show that the claim is covered under the reinsurance policy as a matter of law, that the reinsured acted in good faith and was not fraudulent and that in investigating and settling the claim they acted in a "proper and businesslike manner", then the reinsurer is obliged to settle any payments made by the reinsured and they cannot re-open the question of whether or not the reinsured was actually liable to its insured.

Hill v. *Mercantile and General Reinsurance Company Limited* [1996] L.R.L.R. 841

The "follow the settlements" issue was also considered in *Hill* v. *Mercantile and General Reinsurance Company Limited* [1996] L.R.L.R. 841. The plaintiffs in this case were Lloyd's syndicates and companies who wrote excess of loss reinsurance of the primary Insurers which covered 15 aircraft owned by the Kuwait Airways Corporation and one aircraft belonging to British Airways. On different days in August and September 1990 the 15 Kuwaiti aircraft were removed from Kuwait, seven of the aircraft were later destroyed in Iraq during the "Desert Storm" campaign in early 1991 and eight were recovered. The British Airways aircraft was destroyed at Kuwait airport in February 1991. Claims were made against the insurers who passed it up the chain to the outwards reinsurers (retrocessionaires).

The retrocession reinsurance contract provided that "the settlement of losses shall be binding upon the reinsurers, providing such settlements are within the terms and conditions of the original policies and/or contracts (or as provided for in the Extra Contractual Obligations clause hereof) and within the terms and conditions of this reinsurance", and the settlements included compromised settlements and the setting up of funds for the settlement of losses.

At first instance Rix J. held that the reinsurers had raised arguable defences on the coverage issue, they argued that the losses arose out of one "event" which meant that the excess had not been breached.

The Court of Appeal reversed the first instance decision and gave judgment on liability in favour of the plaintiff. The Court of Appeal followed *Scor* and stated that reinsurers cannot re-open the liability issue.

The House of Lords found that summary judgment was not available to the plaintiff in this case. The House of Lords was not convinced that the payments made by the original insurer were actually "settlements". Kuwait Airlines made a claim for each of its aircraft and spares under the confiscation and detention section of the policy. The London Market paid for one event under the war wording section which was accepted, and the claims were paid on the assumption that there was only one event, which occurred in 1990, but this was said to only be a provisional agreement.

There was disagreement regarding the coverage periods. If the loss date was August 1990 then all of the insurance and reinsurance covers would be in force but if the loss date was January/February 1991 when the aircraft were physically destroyed then not all of the covers would run.

Mustill L.J. made it clear that the reinsured must check that a claim is covered under his policy and, if it is, settle it in a professional manner and then prove that it is covered under the reinsurance contract. The decision encourages reinsured's to be more careful and vigilant in the way they deal with claims.

Assicurazioni Generali Spa v. *CGU International Insurance plc and others* [2004] Lloyd's Rep. IR 457

In *Assicurazioni* the Court of Appeal endorsed earlier decisions on "follow the settlement clauses". The cover was back-to-back. The reinsurance contract contained the wording that the reinsurer "would follow without question the settlements of the reassured . . . " At first instance Deputy Judge Kealey found in favour of the reinsurer regarding the interpretation of this clause. Generali appealed on two grounds:

1. To what extent is the reinsurer precluded from raising coverage issues where there is "back-to-back" cover?

Generali argued that the reinsurer should not be able to raise any coverage issues where the cover it provides is co-extensive with the insurance coverage.

Tuckey L.J. endorsed Deputy Judge Kealey's view that: "the insurers do not have to show that the claim they have settled in fact fell within the risks covered by the reinsurance, but that the claim which they have recognised did or arguably did".

Therefore, the insurer is obliged to show that the claim arguably falls within the scope of the reinsurance coverage, which where the coverage is back to back will be the same as the insurance coverage, so that there is a legal basis for the settlement.

2. Does the inclusion of the words "without question" to the "follow the settlements" clause actually add anything to the clause?

Deputy Judge Kealey held that the addition of the words "without question" had no real meaning in the context of the clause. Tuckey L.J. agreed, that the words "without question" were not sufficiently clear to change the meaning of the "follow the settlements" clause. It therefore appears that courts will interpret "follow the settlement" clauses in the usual way unless the parties are able to demonstrate by using clear words their intention to widen or narrow the reinsurer's right to challenge the underlying settlement.

CLAIMS COOPERATION AND CLAIMS CONTROL CLAUSES

Claims cooperation clauses

A typical claims cooperation clause would read something like this:

"Notwithstanding anything herein contained to the contrary, it is a condition precedent to any liability under this policy that

1. the Reinsured shall upon knowledge of any loss(es) and occurrence(s) which may give rise to a claim recoverable hereunder advise the Reinsurers thereof as soon as reasonably practicable.
2. the Reinsured shall furnish the Reinsurers with all information available respecting such loss(es) or occurrence(s) and shall cooperate with the Reinsurers in the adjustment and settlement thereof."

Claims cooperation clauses mostly use the "as soon as reasonably practicable" language; occasionally the word "promptly" is used instead. Both wordings cause problems of interpretation as both sides argue what is reasonable. It is difficult for such clauses to be more specific and inevitably interpretation will depend upon the specific circumstances of the case. There are also problems concerning whether or not the reinsured has cooperated sufficiently with the reinsurer, especially since any ambiguities in the clause will be construed against the reinsurer. It is increasingly common for reinsureds to delay reporting claims to reinsurers until a crucial moment such as a settlement conference, trial or judgment and then present the reinsurers with a "*fait accompli*" but appearing to provide reinsurers with just enough information to suggest "cooperation". It is therefore vitally important for reinsurers to ensure that their claims cooperation clauses are as tight and clear as possible. Ideally they should also be backed up with a detailed claims handling procedure, which should also be stated to be a condition precedent to liability. The claims procedure should specify the loss adjusting firm to be used, ideally a specifically named one (which should be reputable and international), the law firms to be used, the regularity and the format of the reporting to reinsurers (by fax/mail or email).

According to Webster J. in *Charman* v. *Guardian Royal Exchange Assurance plc* [1992] 2 Lloyd's Rep. 607 (at p. 614) if there is not a claims cooperation clause in the reinsurance contract then the reinsurers "are not entitled at all to be actually involved in or consulted about the steps taken to settle the claim or the amount at which it should be settled". Even in the absence of a claims cooperation clause or other obligation in the contract to keep reinsurers advised it is still good practice to keep reinsurers informed of developments, especially where large losses are involved, because the reinsurers could delay in reimbursing the reinsured.

The courts may also punish reinsureds in respect of their costs for failing to keep reinsurers informed, such as in *The National Fire and Marine Insurance Company of New Zealand* v. *The Australian Mercantile Union Insurance Company* (1887) 6 N.Z.L.R. 144. In that case Richmond J. held that the reinsured was not entitled to his costs because the litigation could have been avoided if he had consulted his reinsurers.

In *Eagle Star Insurance Company Limited* v. *J N Cresswell and others* [2004] EWCA Civ 602 the central issue related to the construction of a modified claims cooperation clause in a reinsurance policy issued by Lloyd's and London Market Companies. In its original form the clause was expressed in terms, which made it a condition precedent to the liability of the reinsurers under the reinsurance policy:

1. that the reinsured should advise the reinsurers within seven days of acquiring knowledge of any losses which might give rise to a claim, and
2. that the reinsured should furnish the reinsurers with available information and cooperate with them in the adjustment and settlement of claims.

However, the parties decided to cancel this clause by stamping "This clause void" across it and substituting the following:

"CLAIMS COOPERATION CLAUSE

The company agree

(a) To notify all claims or occurrences likely to involve the Underwriters within seven days from the time that such claims or occurrences become known to them.
(b) The Underwriters hereon shall control the negotiations and settlements of any claims under this Policy. In this event the Underwriters hereon will not be liable to pay any claim not controlled as set out above."

In fact it was a claims control clause.

The claimant (Eagle Star) paid US$1million to Varian pursuant to the Settlement Agreement and Release and incurred costs and expenses totalling US$615,177.36 in defending and/or investigating the claim against it by

Varian. The defendant argued that they had not been given control of the negotiations or settlement of the claim and that the claim was settled without their knowledge or consent and that as a result of breach of sub-clause (b) of the claims cooperation clause they were not liable to pay the claim.

The Court of Appeal held that reinsurers were not bound to follow the Varian settlement because they had not consented to it and they did not control its negotiation or agreement.

Interestingly, the duty of bad faith was also considered in this case with Rix L.J. commenting:

> "A reassured such as Eagle Star is not an inexperienced consumer, but well able to negotiate its own contract. He can take care to ensure that his reinsurers are kept in the picture of any negotiations or settlement activities. Moreover, if reinsurers simply refuse to exercise control, the reinsurer acts in bad faith, capriciously or arbitrarily, then there is the implied term found by Mance L.J. and Latham L.J. in *Tai Ping* to protect the reinsured (see paras 66 and 81)."

Claims control clauses

A typical claims control clause would read like this:

> "Notwithstanding anything herein contained to the contrary it is a condition precedent to any liability under this policy that
>
> 1. the reinsured shall immediately advise the reinsurers of any loss(es) or occurrence(s) which may give rise to a claim recoverable hereunder.
> 2. the reinsured shall furnish the reinsurers with all available information regarding such loss(es) or occurrence(s) and the reinsurers shall have the right to appoint adjusters, assessors, and/or surveyors and to control all negotiations adjustments and settlements in connection with such loss(es) or occurrence(s)."

The claims control clause goes much further than the claims cooperation clause. For example, the claims control clause requires "immediate" notice to reinsurers rather than "as soon as reasonably practicable". It also gives the reinsurer the right to appoint experts such as lawyers and adjusters and for the reinsurers to effectively direct and take over the handling of the claim.

Claims control clauses are most common in facultative reinsurance, especially in developing markets. In these situations the reinsured only retains a very small portion of the risk and the rest is passed to reinsurers, normally because the reinsured does not have the financial capacity to write these risks alone, it may also be because the reinsured is relying upon the technical expertise of the reinsurer. It is effectively like a "fronting" arrangement with the local insurer fronting the risk while the reinsurer actually assumes the risk and is common in countries where local law prohibits foreign reinsurers from underwriting such risks directly.

Claims control clauses also make sense where the business reinsured is new and risky or where the reinsurer does not yet have much confidence in the cedant's claims handling capabilities. It makes sense for the reinsurer to have more control over claims handling in certain situations especially where there could potentially be a large number of significant claims since in such cases it will largely be the reinsurer's money which is being paid out as the claim exceeds the cedant's retention.

Worryingly for reinsurers though, it appears the courts are not always happy to uphold a claims control clause even in cases where the clause is clearly worded, for example, in *Forsikringsaktieselskapet Vesta* v. *Butcher* [1989] 1 Lloyd's Rep. 331, which concerned a remote Norwegian fish farm which was destroyed by a storm. The fish farm was reinsured with Forskringsaktiels Kapet Vesta who reinsured 90% of the risk through Lloyd's on a J1 Form with "as original" wording and a claims control clause and condition requiring the site to be watched 24 hours a day. The condition was breached and there was no watch when the storm occurred. The original insurance contract was governed by Norwegian law, which only provided the Insurer with a defence if the breach had caused the loss, which clearly in this case it had not. The claims control clause stated:

> "In the event of loss hereunder, no payment, offer or compromise shall be made without the consent of underwriters who shall have sole control of all negotiations.
>
> Failure to comply with any of the warranties outlined hereunder will render this policy null and void. All warranties to be completed at the assured's expense."

Nevertheless, the House of Lords refused to accept that the failure to comply with the clause prevented the reinsured from enforcing the policy.

The case of *Royal and Sun Alliance Insurance plc* v. *Dornoch Ltd and others* [2004] EWHC 803 (Comm) involved the application of a "notice of loss" provision in a standard claims control clause in a slip reinsurance of liability risks.

RSA (the reinsured) insured Coca-Cola for a wide range of risks including Directors and Officers (D&O) liability which it then ceded 100% to the defendant Lloyd's syndicates (the reinsurers) by way of identical slip policies each containing a standard claims control clause (CCC) stating:

> "Notwithstanding anything herein contained to the contrary it is a condition precedent to any liability under this policy that:
>
> a. the reassured shall upon knowledge of any loss or losses which may give rise to a claim under this policy, advise the underwriters thereof by cable within 72 hours."

The slips also contained a standard "full reinsurance clause".

Coca-Cola and three of its directors were sued in the US in two class actions alleging that they had artificially inflated the company's stock value.

Allianz, who was the leader of the insurance was notified of the suits in November 2000. It notified co-insurers (including the reinsured) of the suits in December 2000. On 30 December 2000 the reinsured's brokers forwarded copies of the suits to the reinsured. The reinsured informed reinsurers of the suits on 19 January 2001, which was more than 72 hours after RSA had been informed of the claims in the two class actions.

The reinsurer raised the argument that the reinsured failed to give notice of the "loss or losses" within the agreed time and that if the clause was indeed broken that this would be a procedural bar to a claim that would ordinarily be covered.

The court had to determine:

1. Whether the words "loss or losses" meant loss of the claimant's shareholders against Coca-Cola and its directors or the actual loss of Coca-Cola and its directors itself.

Looking at the actual wording of the CCC the judge stated: "If and when [the reinsured] does obtain actual knowledge that the third-party claimant against Coca-Cola has suffered an actual loss, then RSA will have actual knowledge of a loss which may give rise to a claim under the reinsurance . . . (i) such losses by third-party claimants may give rise to a claim against [the insured] which (ii) may give rise to a claim by [the insured] on [the insurance], which (iii) may then give rise to a claim on the reinsurance. Therefore the actual losses of a third-party claimant against Coca-Cola may 'give rise to' a claim on the reinsurance contracts."

Thus, the relevant losses were those of the claimant shareholders suing Coca-Cola and not the losses of the insured or reinsured.

2. What constitutes knowledge of actual "loss or losses"?

The judge held that since the underlying facts of the case against the insured were still in issue because no judgment, award or settlement had occurred in the action it could not be said that the third-party claimants had suffered an actual loss. The pleadings in the underlying dispute were merely allegations of loss. Therefore the reinsured was not obliged to give notice to the reinsurer under the CCC before it in fact did so and the reinsured was not in breach of the condition precedent to notify reinsurers.

The case illustrates the inappropriateness of using the words "loss or losses" in liability coverage because it is very difficult to objectively determine if a loss has occurred. It is much better to use the word "claim or claims" instead.

Loss settlements of the reinsured

The leading case on this topic is *Commercial Union Assurance Company* v. *NRG Victory Reinsurance Company Limited* [1998] 2 Lloyd's Rep. 600 (C.A.).

***Commercial Union Assurance Company* v. *NRG Victory Reinsurance Company Limited* [1998] 2 Lloyd's Rep. 600 (C.A.)**

The plaintiff reinsured in this case had issued an excess of loss reinsurance contract to Exxon. When the *Exxon Valdez* oil spillage occurred Exxon sued its insurers in the Texan state court claiming for the clean-up costs of the spillage and punitive damages for breaches of the Texan Insurance Code (under sections 1 and 3 of the policy).

In respect of the section 1 claim, settlement between the insurers and reinsurers was agreed at US$300 million. The section 3 claim went to trial in Texas where the jury awarded Exxon US$250 million. The insurers initially appealed the section 3 decision but later a compromise was reached between the parties.

The plaintiffs brought an action against the reinsurers in respect of the first settlement. The plaintiffs had relied upon advice given to them by a Texan lawyer, Mr Reasoner, who was of the opinion that the plaintiffs would be found liable for the claim if it proceeded to trial and Clarke J. agreed with these arguments.

The Court of Appeal took a different view and said that the Texan court may have taken a completely different view in a section 1 trial!

***King* v. *Brandywine Reinsurance Co. (UK) Ltd* [2004] EWHC 1033 (Comm), Commercial Court, 10 May 2004**

After the oil spill, Exxon, which owned the oil cargo paid clean-up costs of US$1.2billion while its subsidiary, Exxon Shipping, which owned the *Exxon Valdez*, paid US$800million.

The *Exxon Valdez* was insured under a "Global Corporate Excess" (GCE) policy, which provided coverage of US$850 million. Exxon made claims under three sections of that policy. Exxon sued its insurers in the US. In 1996/1997 the insurers settled the GCE claim (removal of debris costs) for US$300 million. They settled the section IIIA and IIIB claims (marine liability and third party liability) together for US$480 million. However, some XL reinsurers refused to indemnify the insurers on the basis that payments to Exxon under sections I and IIIB were not covered by the GCE policy. The reinsurers who did settle faced similar problems when they sought to recover from their retrocessionaires.

A number of the XL contracts were on the Joint Excess Loss Committee (JELC) terms, which did not include "follow the settlements" language. The reinsurers therefore required their cedants to prove that the GCE insurers actually had a legal liability to Exxon.

In view of the fact that Exxon failed to exercise an option in the service of suit clause to choose New York/US law and since all other factors pointed to English law the court decided that English law would apply to the GCE policy.

The court held that Exxon could not recover the oil pollution clean-up costs under section I because "debris" did not usually include liquids such as oil sludge, and even if there was apparent coverage the "notwithstanding" clause prevented any possible coverage overlap between sections I and III. There was also no liability under section IIIB because of restrictions in relation to ocean carriage of oil on board a tanker.

Even if the insurers had been liable to Exxon the court held that a seepage and pollution exclusion in the JELC terms prevented recovery from reinsurers for pollution on land. Most of Exxon's claim was for cleaning up of the shoreline as opposed to offshore pollution. The court held that Exxon Shipping could not claim against reinsurers for its clean-up costs. Exxon Shipping had not made a claim against its insurers under section I of the GCE policy and was not a party to the Exxon settlement. Any claims made by Exxon Shipping would now be time-barred.

The case makes it very clear that in the absence of a strong "follow the settlements" clause in the reinsurance contract, insurers should only settle inwards claims with the full consent of reinsurers, or at least only when they have received legal advice that legal liability exists.

THE COSTS OF LITIGATION

Litigation costs can form a substantial part of any claim (and in some cases they can exceed the damages award) and whether or not these costs will be recoverable will very much depend upon the wording of the reinsurance contract.

The Court of Appeal in *Insurance Company of Africa* v. *Scor (UK) Reinsurance Company Limited* [1985] 1 Lloyd's Rep. 312 made it clear that unless the claims cooperation clause or another clause in the reinsurance contract actually states that the reinsurers shall be liable for the costs of defending coverage litigation between the reinsured and the insured, the reinsurers shall not be responsible for the costs.

In *British Dominion General Insurance Company* v. *Duder* [1915] 2 K.B. 394 the plaintiff insurers compromised the claim from its original insured at 66% of the loss and was forced to sue its reinsurers to prove that it had been liable under the original insurance contract. The reinsurers were not only obliged to reimburse the 66% figure but were obliged to share the reinsured's defence costs, which was fair in the circumstances since the reinsurers had done everything possible to avoid indemnifying their reinsured.

Baker v. _Black Sea and Baltic Insurance Company Limited_ [1995] L.R.L.R. 261

In *Baker* the plaintiff reinsured (Syndicate 947) sought to recover two types of legal and investigative costs. The syndicate insured various liability risks in the United States which produced massive losses, including asbestos disease related claims and injuries suffered by American marines in Vietnam as a result of the use of Agent Orange. Initially there were difficulties concerning the geographical scope of the reinsurance cover but these were resolved in the Court of Appeal. On the issue of defence costs, the first type of costs were costs incurred by the original insured and claimed against the syndicate. The second type were legal costs that the Lloyd's syndicate had incurred in investigating, settling and defending the claims. The syndicate relied upon a clause in the reinsurance contract which said that the reinsurer would "follow the settlements and agreements" of the syndicate. At first instance, Potter J. held that if the costs of the original insured were covered under the insurance policy and the syndicate had paid them then the reinsurer would be obliged to pay. With regard to the syndicate's costs he held that these were not recoverable from the reinsurer since there was no universal practice that reinsurers paid these costs. This decision was upheld by the Court of Appeal. The House of Lords took the view that there was possibly a market practice for sharing defence costs but that this had not been properly considered in the lower courts. Accordingly, the House of Lords decided that the case should be referred to the Commercial Court for a hearing of expert evidence on this point. Therefore, it is not possible to imply a term that the reinsurer will share the reinsured's defence costs on a pro rata basis by way of business efficacy, but it is not clear if you can imply a term that costs should be shared by way of trade practice—which makes the law in this area very unclear.

National Insurance Company for Co-operative Reinsurance v. _St Paul Reinsurance Company Limited_ (April 1998, unreported)

In this case St Paul were one of the 13 reinsurers of National Company for Co-operative Reinsurance (NCCR). A facsimile containing four dishonest statements was sent by the brokers to the leading reinsurers and an offer to settle the claim against the reinsurers (which had not been authorised by NCCR) and, on the basis of this fax, the reinsurers settled the claim with NCCR. The original insured refused to settle the claim and sought full payment of the claim. St Paul sought the recovery of its legal costs (which amounted to £1.5 million) on an indemnity basis. Although there was no evidence of fraud on the part of NCCR, Thomas M.J. held that it was appropriate to award indemnity costs on this occasion since the broker was an agent of the reinsured and the reinsured was obliged to accept responsibility for the broker's fraud. However, the court only allowed costs of two Counsel because the case was not sufficiently complex to warrant use of the three Counsel (which St Paul had engaged).

Problems can arise for the reinsured in settling a claim where there are different reinsurers on the programme over different years. For example, in *Municipal Mutual Insurance Company Limited* v. *Sea Insurance Company Limited* [1996] L.R.L.R. 265, Municipal Mutual Insurance (MMI) insured the Port of Sunderland Authority as harbour authority for Sunderland. In 1985 the Port Authority took custody of and responsibility for two partly-dismantled dragline excavators belonging to Concorde which were sent to the port for storage and were subjected to theft and vandalism. The acts of vandalism occurred over an 18-month period. The wording in the insurance and reinsurance contracts included a term that the excess and limit would apply to "occurrences or series of occurrences arising out of one source or original cause". The problem was that there were different excess limits for different policy years. For some years there were two layers and for other years just one. Waller J. combated the problem of apportioning the losses over the three policy years by deciding that the losses arose out of one event—the lack of supervision—and that since most of the stealing occurred in 1987/1988 the losses fell to be dealt with by that underwriting year. The Court of Appeal took a slightly different view holding that the loss fell into two periods of cover and that two thirds of the theft and vandalism occurred in the 1987/1988 year, so that is what the reinsurers would be required to pay for that period. The Court of Appeal pointed out that reinsurers would have had a powerful argument for multiple losses if they had adopted a one-event terminology.

EX-GRATIA PAYMENTS

Often insurers will settle claims on an ex-gratia payment basis where technically the claim is not covered under the insurance policy but the insurer makes a payment to the insured simply as a goodwill gesture to maintain good relations with the insured.

Most reinsurance contracts specifically state that ex-gratia payments are excluded under the terms of the reinsurance contract. In the event that it is not specified in the contract the case law in this area states that ex-gratia payments cannot be recovered from the reinsurer. For example, in *Fireman's Fund Insurance Company Limited* v. *Western Australia Company Limited* [1927] 28 Ll. L. Rep. 243, the original insurance policy contained an exclusion that insurers were not liable to pay a cargo claim if the ship was unseaworthy. The ship was not in fact seaworthy but the insurer paid the claim without investigating whether or not the ship was seaworthy. The court held that the reinsurers could refuse to pay the reinsured's claim because the reinsured had not handled the claim in a businesslike manner by failing to investigate it properly.

Reinsurers themselves often make ex-gratia payments to their reinsureds in respect of claims, which are strictly speaking not covered in order to maintain or develop good relations with the reinsured. In this situation the reinsurer may also encounter problems recovering these payments from their retrocessionaires (the reinsurer's reinsurers).

THE LIABILITY OF THE REINSURER

Probably one of the widest reinsurance policy wordings is that of *Toomey* v. *Eagle Star Insurance Company Limited* [1993] 1 Lloyd's Rep. 429 where the reinsurer agreed to pay "all claims returns, reinsurance premiums and other outgoings . . . payable by the reinsured . . . in respect of the 1965 Underwriting Account" which does not require the syndicate to prove to Eagle Star that they were legally liable to pay the claims under the terms of their insurance policy. However, in practice, reinsurance contracts are much narrower than this.

When does the reinsured become liable to pay the insured?

Obviously the reinsured is keen to recover monies as soon as possible from the reinsurer since this will help with the reinsured's solvency and cash flow. Naturally, reinsurers will wish to delay making any payments for as long as possible since they will be earning investment income on that money.

Some reinsurance contracts provide for simultaneous payment so that the reinsurer pays the reinsured at the same time as the reinsured pays its insured but these are not very common.

***Versicherungs und Transport A/G Daugava* v. *Henderson* [1934] 49 Ll. L. Rep. 252**

In this case, involving a proportional contract, the court held that provided the reinsured can prove to his reinsurers that he is liable for a specific amount to his insured and the loss is covered under the policy the reinsurer is obliged to reimburse the reinsured even though the reinsured has not actually paid the loss. The case involved fire insurance and reinsurance in Latvia. On 11 April 1930 a fire occurred at the factory which was seriously damaged. The Dougava company paid their original insured and made a claim against their reinsurers and the point to be decided was, when was the loss payable? The insurance and reinsurance policies were in the Latvian currency (Lats). At the date of the fire there were 25.22 Lats to the pound. Dougava paid their original insured in January 1932, which was after Britain had gone off the gold standard and there were 17.19 Lats to the pound. The Court of Appeal held that the date of settlement and payment by the insurer in January 1932 is the correct date at which the rate of exchange is to be applied. The Court of Appeal were keen to ensure that the reinsured was not over-compensated with Scrutton L.J. commenting: "If the rate of exchange is fixed at a date before the insurer's liability to pay is quantified and satisfied, the insurer may, as in the present case, recover more than an indemnity, which is contrary to all principles of insurance indemnity" (at p. 253).

The leading case on the subject is:

***Charter Re* v. *Fagan* [1997] A.C. 313**

The plaintiff reinsured in this case was insolvent and was reinsured with Lloyd's Syndicates 540 and 542. Under two excess of loss treaties the reinsurers undertook to indemnify the insurers against "all losses howsoever and wheresoever arising" during the period of reinsurance on any interest under policies and contracts of insurance or reinsurance underwritten by the reinsured in their whole account. The third policy was an aviation risks policy. All policies provided that the reinsurer was to be liable for the losses of the insurers in excess of an ultimate net loss of a specified amount. The term "net loss" was defined as "the sum actually paid by the reinsured in settlement of losses or liability after making deductions for all recoveries, all salvages and all claims upon other reinsurances whether collected or not and shall include all adjustment expenses arising from the settlement of claims". The insurers were in provisional liquidation and sought determination of the issue of whether or not it was necessary for the insurers to have made payments in respect of the claims before the reinsurers became liable. The focus of the case was on the meaning of "actually paid". At first instance Mance J. held that "actually paid" was not enough to impose a condition precedent of payment. The Court of Appeal upheld the view of Mance J. with the exception of Staughton L.J., who insisted that the words should be given their literal meaning. He said: "The literal meaning of the words in the contract requires that the insurers shall have paid before the reinsurers are liable" (at p. 368). The House of Lords endorsed Mance's decision and gave the words a technical meaning, which was considered appropriate for this specialised form of reinsurance.

INTERPRETATION—EVENTS, CAUSES AND OCCURRENCES

Often the reinsurance contract contains the words "event", "loss" or "occurrence" which can be very vague and which can cause difficulties when claims arise. It is not surprising that there has been a great deal of litigation in this area as reinsureds try to maximise their recoveries and reinsurers attempt to minimise the payments they have to make.

"Event"

As mentioned earlier in *Municipal Mutual* v. *Sea Insurance Company Limited* [1996] L.R.L.R. 265, acts of vandalism over an 18-month time period were regarded as one event, with the event being the lack of supervision.

***Caudle* v. *Sharp* [1995] L.R.L.R. 433**

This case illustrates the difficulty of interpreting the word "event". The reinsured was the Sharp Syndicate at Lloyd's, which was the Employee and Officer's insurers of Outhwaite. Outhwaite, who was a Lloyd's underwriter, wrote 32 run-off reinsurance contracts which were subject to huge losses because of environmental pollution and asbestos claims. As a result the Lloyd's Names on the Outhwaite syndicate suffered enormous losses and sued Outhwaite for negligence. Settlement with the Names was agreed at £116 million. The Sharp syndicate as insurers of Outhwaite paid a large proportion of the settlement and sought a recovery from their reinsurers, Caudle. Sharp argued that its contribution in respect of the Outhwaite action amounted to one loss and since the excess had been breached the reinsurers should reimburse them. The reinsurers argued that each of the 32 run-off reinsurance contracts constituted a separate loss, which meant that the excess had not been breached and reinsurers were not required to make any payments. They also contended that the member's agents' claims did not fall within the cover period of the reinsurance contract.

The excess of loss reinsurance contract contained an arbitration clause. The arbitrators held that the payments made by Sharp to the Outhwaite syndicate related to a series of losses arising out of one event. The event being Outhwaite's failure to appreciate or investigate the asbestos problem. The court of first instance agreed with the arbitrator's decision.

The Court of Appeal reversed the first instance decision and decided that there were 32 events. Evans L.J. said that "There were 32 separate occasions when Mr Outhwaite's 'failure' manifested itself and his ignorance gave rise to an occurrence of negligence, whether an act or omission, which itself gave rise to a claim and a loss under the original policy" ((1995) L.R.L.R. 433 at p. 439).

***Axa Re* v. *Field* [1996] 1 Lloyd's Rep. 26**

In this case the defendant Lloyd's syndicate was liable to pay claims for the negligence of the underwriters following the *Cox* v. *Bankside* decision. The syndicate then sought reimbursement from its reinsurers. The reinsurance policy was an excess of loss contract with "one event" language. The original insurance policy contained the wording "series of events or occurrences attributable to one originating cause" and the reinsured argued that this was the same as "series of occurrences arising out of one occurrence" in the reinsurance contract and that therefore the reinsurers should accept that the losses arose out of just three events.

At first instance Phillips J. thought "event" and "cause" were the same thing. The Court of Appeal held that the reinsurers were bound as to the result in the *Cox* v. *Bankside* decision and that in this case it was sensible to conclude that there were three causes.

The House of Lords came to a completely different decision. It decided that "originating cause" and "event" meant totally completely different things. Lord Mustill commented that " . . . an event is something which happens at a particular time, at a particular place, in a particular way. A cause is to my mind something altogether less constricted. It can be a continuing state of affairs, it can be in the absence of something happening" (at p. 239). He also made it clear that if the reinsured planned his reinsurance cover to be the same as his cover for his insured then he would have used the same words in each contract. Therefore, it will be prudent for reinsureds to check that the wording of their reinsurance contracts is compatible with the wording used in their own policies.

"Cause"

In *Cox* v. *Bankside* [1995] 2 Lloyd's Rep. 437 there were hundreds of LMX contracts, which were negligently underwritten by three underwriters. The court held that this amounted to three originating "causes".

"Occurrence"

Kuwait Airways Corporation v. _Kuwait Insurance Company Limited_ [1996] 1 Lloyd's Rep. 664

In *Kuwait Airways Corporation* v. *Kuwait Insurance Company Limited* [1996] 1 Lloyd's Rep. 664 (which involved the seizure of aircraft from Kuwait by Iraqi forces), the Kuwait Airways Authority had cover in respect of war risks which carried a $300 million limit in respect of "any one occurrence, any one location" for ground risks. According to Rix J. there was only one "occurrence", and that was the invasion of Kuwait and the capture of the aircraft. He said that the question of whether or not there was one occurrence must be scrutinised from the point of view of an informed observer placed in the position of the insured, and there must be a degree of unity in relation to cause, locality and the intentions of the human agents concerned. In this case the human agent was Saddam Hussein and his intention was to remove all assets from Kuwait. He also decided that the entire airport constituted one location in the context of war risks insurance. The House of Lords gave "seizure" its normal meaning in an insurance and reinsurance policy so that it included forcible seizure as in this case. In relation to the spares extension the House of Lords found that the words used—"it is noted and agreed that the indemnity provided by this policy other than paragraph (a) of section one is extended to include loss of or damage to aircraft spares . . . "—made it clear that it was an extension clause. Since the war perils were not excluded under the clause this meant that under the usual principles Kuwait Airways could recover. Lord Hobhouse emphasised that the courts will not correct badly worded clauses and said "if, as here the parties have used plain language to express their intention then that should be an end to it; the courts should enforce the contract in accordance with its terms".

REINSURANCE CONTRACTS—GOVERNING LAW AND JURISDICTION

Which law governs the reinsurance contract?

It is very important from the claims perspective which law governs the reinsurance contract since this will assist the claims handler in determining whether he should run the risk of letting the dispute between the reinsurer and insurer being litigated.

Normally the governing law is specified in the reinsurance contract. If it is not specified then you have a situation where reinsurance is placed in different countries and a different law may govern the relationship between the reinsurer and the reinsured in each jurisdiction. Where reinsureds do not believe that their own law will apply to the contract it is very common for them to "forum shop" by commencing proceedings in their home court for a negative declaration, which gives them the benefit of their own law applying to the contract and the benefit of litigating in their home court where they know the judges and can use their home lawyers.

Governing law is determined by Article 3 of the Rome Convention which was given effect in the United Kingdom by the Contracts (Applicable Law) Act 1990, which says that contracts are governed by the law chosen by the parties either expressly or as "demonstrated with reasonable certainty by the terms of the contract or the circumstances of the case".

If there is no specific choice of law in the contract then Article 4 states that the law of the contract shall be "the law of the country with which it is most closely connected", which is presumed to be the country where the party "who is to effect the performance which is characteristic of the contract" resides.

The issues of governing law were discussed in the following two cases:

***Gan Insurance Company Limited* v. *Tai Ping Insurance Company Limited* [1999] Lloyd's Rep. IR 229; *Royal Insurance Company* v. *Central Insurance Company* [1999] Lloyd's Rep. IR 229**

The plaintiffs in both of these cases were facultative reinsurers of Taiwanese insurers who had written all-risks cover for a factory in Taiwan. A fire occurred at the factory causing extensive damage. Tai Ping Insurance coordinated the actual handling of the claim. The direct insurers rescinded the contracts arguing that the policy terms in respect of fire protection had been breached, and in addition Article 68 of the Taiwanese Insurance Law had been breached with regard to disclosure requirements.

The reinsurers refused to pay the claims and commenced proceedings in England seeking declarations that they were not liable to the reinsureds because the reinsureds had breached the claims cooperation clauses which were conditions precedent to liability and they could avoid the contracts because of misrepresentation. The contracts did not state which governing law should apply.

The reinsureds argued that Taiwanese law governed the contract because the risks were Taiwanese, they were in respect of a Taiwanese factory owned by a Taiwanese company and insured by Taiwanese insurers under a policy governed by Taiwanese law. They argued that the reinsurance contract was governed by Taiwanese law because it contained "as original" wording and the insurance policy was governed by Taiwanese law.

The reinsurers argued that the contracts were governed by English law because the facultative slips contained several standard London market clauses, including claims cooperation wording. They argued that the "as original" wording only related to the nature of the risk, the period of cover and the geographical limits. They said that the use of London market clauses indicated an implied choice of English law as the governing law. Furthermore, the contracts were more closely connected with England since the reinsurance was placed in London using London market forms and with reinsurers operating in the London market.

Cresswell M.J. held that there was an implied choice of English law and that English law would apply because the contracts were more closely connected with England and he completely agreed with the arguments of the reinsurers. The Court of Appeal supported this view.

It appears from these cases that if a reinsurance contract is made by English reinsurers operating in the London market that the English courts will decide that English law is the governing law. The only way to rebut this presumption is for the reinsured to check the reinsurance contract very closely before agreeing to it and ensure that the governing law he wishes to apply is expressly stated in the contract.

Underwriters are often sloppy when writing a risk about the issues of governing law and dispute resolution, assuming that problems will not arise.

Nevertheless, it is important that the governing law and seat of arbitration are stated in the reinsurance contract since, if issues do arise at a later stage over a claim or a series of claims, then both parties know exactly the procedure and law which will apply.

Which jurisdiction governs the reinsurance contract?

Normally the parties to a reinsurance contract would have agreed in advance which jurisdiction should hear a dispute between them and this will usually be stipulated in the jurisdiction clause of the reinsurance contract. A typical jurisdiction clause would read like this:

> "Jurisdiction Clause
>
> This agreement shall in all respects be governed by and construed in accordance with English law and the parties hereby irrevocably agree to submit to the exclusive jurisdiction of the English courts."

There have been a number of recent cases involving the appropriate jurisdiction for hearing disputes between parties to a reinsurance contract. In these cases the courts appear to have adopted a pragmatic and commercial approach to the issue.

In *King* v. *Brandywine Reinsurance Co. (UK) Ltd* [2004] 2 All E.R. (Comm) 443 arising out of the 1989 *Exxon Valdez* oil spill in Alaska, King relied on a service of suit clause in the policy which provided that the insured had an option to select the jurisdiction of New York, arguing that New York was the proper law of the contract. The court dismissed this argument—the risks covered by the policy were worldwide, as was a significant portion of the following market, and London market wordings were incorporated or referred to in the policy. These factors all pointed to English law being the proper law of the policy.

In *Travelers Casualty and Surety* v. *Sun Life Assurance Company of Canada (UK) Ltd* [2004] EWHC 1704 (Comm) the court decided that it would be cheaper and easier for the trial to take place in England. In *Markel International Insurance Company Ltd* v. *La Republica Compania Argentina de Seguros Generales SA* [2004] EWHC 1826 the court decided that although the underlying risk and the defendant insurers were based in Argentina, the fact that most of the witnesses were English-speaking, that most correspondence was in English and that the reinsurance contracts were governed by English law was sufficient for the court to decide that the appropriate forum for the dispute was England.

In *Tonicstar Ltd (t/a Lloyd's Syndicate 1861)* v. *American Home Assurance Co.* [2004] EWHC 1234 (Comm) it was held that the natural forum for disputes concerning insurance contracts made in London, placed through Lloyd's Brokers and incorporating standard Lloyd's terms was England.

THE LIMITATION ISSUE

In the UK the limitation period relating to reinsurance contracts is stated in section 5 of the Limitation Act 1980 as "an action founded on simple contract shall not be brought after the expiration of 6 years from the date on which the cause of action accrued". For the purposes of reinsurance the time period starts to run from the date that the reinsured's liability is established by agreement, judgment or award.

The leading case on this subject is *Dougava* v. *Henderson* (1934) 49 Ll. L. Rep. 252 (discussed earlier), where the Court of Appeal held in relation to a fire policy that the cause of action of the reinsured did not start running until the reinsured's liability was an ascertained sum. Scrutton L.J. put it succinctly as "I do not understand how the reinsurer can be liable to pay an amount until it has been fixed between insurer and insured" (at p. 253). In *Halvanon Insurance Company* v. *Companhia de Seguros do Estado de Sao Paolo* (1995) L.R.L.R. 303 the plaintiff reinsured argued that a cause of action did not arise until an account was rendered to the reinsurer under the reinsurance contract. This was rejected by the Court of Appeal.

Therefore usually the reinsured has six years from the date upon which the claim has been quantified in which to make a recovery from his reinsurers. This is reasonable since sometimes it takes a long time for the quantum of the claim to be established and if the time for limitation purposes began when the loss occurred then time would start running against the reinsured before he knew the amount of his liability and the extent of the recovery he needs to make from reinsurers.

There are, however, certain situations in which the time period may be altered. The most common of these is by agreement between the parties in the reinsurance contract. For example, the parties could state in their reinsurance contract that for limitation purposes time will not begin to run until the reinsured presents an account to the reinsurers for payment. Using an example from the insurance context, in *Walker* v. *Pennine Insurance Company* [1980] 2 Lloyd's Rep. 156 the court held that a clause stating that the insured had just one year in which to enforce the policy against the insurer was reasonable.

The limitation period will stop running if proceedings are commenced, or an arbitrator is appointed in respect of the matter between the reinsured and reinsurer.

If the reinsurer admits liability under the contract in a very clear way then he will not be able to rely upon the limitation point to dispute the quantum of the claim.

Similarly, a signed written acknowledgement or part payment of the claim will start the limitation period running from the beginning again.

Sometimes the reinsured and reinsurer may be involved in long, protracted negotiations regarding the claim and the limitation period may be rapidly approaching. In this situation the parties may enter into a standstill agreement which will serve to stop the limitation period on that date while the negotiations continue.

The problem of limitation can be especially acute in the case of reinsurance underwriting pools, which was highlighted in the following case:

***Companhia de Seguros Imperio* v. *Heath (REBX) Ltd* [1999] Lloyd's Rep. IR 571 (Q.B. Com. Ct.); [2001] Lloyd's Rep. IR 109 (C.A.)**

Imperio participated in a pool, which was run by Heath between 1977 and 1979. In 1995 Imperio issued a writ against Heath claiming for breach of contract, negligence and breach of fiduciary duty. Imperio argued that the pool had been unlawfully operated by Heath because Heath had chosen Imperio to "front" for the pool, thereby exposing it to 100% of the risk when it was unnecessary to do so. A number of pool members had become insolvent and Imperio insisted that it would only pay its net line. Since the causes of action in contract and tort accrued when Imperio were committed to front a particular risk the claims were statute-barred. Although deliberate concealment by Heath served to suspend the commencement of the limitation period as a result of four years of investigation, there was no good reason for Heath to use Imperio as a front in 1988 and the claim was statute-barred because all of the facts were known to Imperio from the outset. In respect of the fiduciary duty, the limitation period would not apply if, in addition to acting as an agent for Imperio, Heath acted as a trustee of the pool's money under a trust. The Commercial Court held that the six-year limitation period applied to the fiduciary claim on this occasion and thus it was time-barred.

Some people believe that an "honourable engagement clause", which permits arbitrators to opt out of the strict rules of law, allows them to disapply the limitation period. However, this appears to be incorrect. For example, in *Orion Compagnia Espanola de Seguros* v. *Belfort Maatschppij Voor Versekgringeen* [1962] 2 Lloyd's Rep. 257 a Belgian Insurance company applied to set aside an award made by an umpire in favour of the Spanish Insurance Company (Orion). The arbitration arose from a dispute about a quota share non-marine reinsurance treaty. Megaw J. argued that arbitrators are bound by the usual rules on limitation.

The new limitation regime

The Law Commission has recommended that the different limitation periods, which currently apply to different causes of action, be abolished and replaced by a new core regime. Under this core regime, any claimant who wishes to commence an action must do so within three years of the date upon which they knew or ought reasonably to have known that they had a significant cause of action and knew the identity of the defendant. In the reinsurance field reinsureds are presumed to know when the action against their reinsurers accrues and the date when they have a claim against their reinsurers will be the same. This effectively means that for reinsureds the period in which they have to bring a claim against their reinsurer would be reduced from six years to three years. In addition there will be a 10-year long stop limitation period, which would begin to run from the date of the act or omission which gave rise to the claim. The Law Commission proposes that the new regime should have retrospective effect, so that it will apply to all causes of action which accrue before it commences, except where the action is already time-barred or where the action has already been commenced. For the reinsurance industry this will mean that all claims, which are currently older than three years will immediately become time-barred unless the claimant commences proceedings or a standstill clause is agreed between the parties. The new proposals will be particularly problematic where there are chains of reinsurance in operation because it can take a long period of time for claims to filter their way through the market to the end of the reinsurance chain. This would mean that if the original insured's claim was settled or determined 10 years ago and the reinsurer has not yet made a recovery under his own reinsurance cover then he will be unable to do so.

THE RIGHTS OF THE REINSURER

Payment of premium

The case of *Fenton Insurance Company* v. *Gothaer Versicherung* [1991] 2 Lloyd's Rep. 172 establishes that the fact that the reinsured does not pay the reinsurer the premium does not mean that the contract has been abandoned, and the reinsured may therefore still present claims to the reinsurer for reimbursement unless the contract specifically provides that the contract can be cancelled if the premium is not paid. Otherwise, the only option available to the reinsurer is to sue the reinsured or pay the claims less the premium amount. It is common for reinsureds to delay paying the reinsurance premium until they have received the insurance premium from their insured. Nevertheless, at law the reinsured is obliged to pay the reinsurance premium regardless of whether or not he has received the insurance premium from its original insured.

There are a number of ways in which reinsurers can protect themselves from reinsureds who fail to pay the premium. These mostly involve the inclusion of appropriately worded premium payment warranties some of which are discussed below:

"Late Payment Clause

In the event that the Insured fails to pay any premium due hereunder within 6 months together with any interest due thereon in accordance with the provisions of this agreement, then the Insurer has the option by written notice served within 90 days of expiry of the said six months to reduce the limit to 125% of the premium actually paid."

Another option is for the reinsurer to charge interest on the unpaid premium.

"Late Payment Clause

In the event that the Insured fails to pay any premium due hereunder on the day that it falls due then interest shall accrue on the amount outstanding at the rate of . . . % per month."

Sometimes the payment of additional interest is simply not enough since the reinsured may have no intention of paying the reinsurance premium. If this is the case then a clause such as the two outlined below will be more appropriate which will enable the reinsurer to terminate the reinsurance contract *ab initio* if the reinsured has not paid the premium within a specified time period.

"Non Payment of Premium Clause

In the event that the Insured fails to pay any premium due hereunder together with interest thereon as appropriate within . . . months/days of the inception date of this agreement then this agreement shall be automatically terminated and the Reinsurer shall be released from all liabilities, past, present and future, with regard to this agreement."

"Premium Warranty

The Reinsured warrants that it shall pay the premium due hereunder within . . . months/days of the inception date of this agreement. In the event that the Reinsured fails to so pay then this agreement shall be automatically terminated *ab initio* and the Reinsurer shall be released from all liabilities, past, present and future, with regard to this agreement."

The type of clause which the reinsurer considers appropriate to include in the reinsurance contract will depend upon the market practice in the jurisdiction and the business relationship that the reinsurer has with the reinsured.

It is important to remember that reinsurers should be clear of their intentions before demanding payment of the premium since by doing so they may prejudice their position. For example, in *Compagnia Tirrena Di Assicurazioni Spa* v. *Grand Union Insurance Company* [1991] 2 Lloyd's Rep. 143 there was a premium warranty, which stated "premium and claims to be settled in account. Premium warranty on due dates". The reinsured did not render an account or pay the premium and therefore breached the warranty. However, the court held that by demanding payment of the premium the reinsurers had succeeded in affirming the contract.

The inspection of records

Generally, it is common for reinsurers to inspect the records of their reinsured although this practice is more widespread in the USA and the UK than in continental Europe. During an inspection the reinsurer will be checking to ensure that the reinsured is settling claims properly and is not making payments which he should not be making. An inspection is a good opportunity for the inspectors (usually experienced claims professionals) to feed back information to underwriting on claims handling procedures and loss developments, which can prove invaluable on renewal.

Reinsurance contracts normally expressly provide that the reinsurer has the right to inspect the reinsured's records and if it is not explicit then it will be implied into the contract. In *Phoenix* v. *Halvanon* [1985] 2 Lloyd's Rep. 552 Hobhouse J. held that the reinsurer had an implied right to inspect the reinsured's records, but this was not a problem in this case because both parties agreed that there existed an implied right to inspect anyway.

However, sometimes the courts may not be prepared to infer a right of inspection as in *Société Anonyme Intermediaries Luxembourgeois* v. *Farex Gia and others* [1995] L.R.L.R. 116, where Hoffmann L.J. said that the right to inspect depends upon the terms of the contract and since the contract in this dispute contained no inspection clause the reinsurers had no access to the reinsured's books. It is therefore much better for reinsurers to include an inspection clause in the contract to make sure that they have the right to inspect the reinsured's records if they need to.

Clearly there is little value in inspecting documents if you are unable to photocopy or use the documents. This issue was discussed in *Mutter* v. *Eastern and Midlands Railway Company* (1888) 38 Ch.D. 92 when the Court of Appeal said that a person having a right to inspect a document had a consequential right to take a copy of it or of so much of it as he requires "for some legitimate purpose". This is very vague and may lead to abuse of the information. It is therefore very important that a confidentiality agreement is signed by the parties prior to granting the reinsurer access to information so that the information is not abused.

In the Irish case of *Winterthur Swiss Insurance* v. *The Insurance Corporation of Ireland plc* [1989] I.L.R.M. 13 the first instance court decided that the inspections clause in the reinsurance contract authorised the reinsurer to copy documents "legitimately required for the purposes of inspection".

The reinsurer must be careful not to prejudice its legal position by inspecting the cedant's records. In *Iron Trades Insurance Company Limited* v. *Companhia de Seguros Imperio* [1991] 1 Re L.R. 213 claims were made by Iron Trades and others against their reinsurers for payments made in respect of two marine quota share treaties. In 1982 the reinsurers were aware that there had been misrepresentations by the reinsured but they waited until late 1983 before exercising their right to inspect the reinsured's records. Hobhouse J. held that because the reinsurers had not reserved their rights under the contract and had delayed before carrying out the inspection it had affirmed the contract. Therefore, if the reinsurer has evidence of misrepresentation it should reserve its rights under the contract immediately, but if it only has suspicions then it should carry out an inspection immediately to obtain further information.

Often the inspection of records by the reinsurer can lead to tension between the reinsurer and the reinsured. It is therefore imperative that the inspection is carried out in an efficient and professional manner. Some reinsurers choose to use their own in-house inspection team, whereas others prefer to use an external consultancy. The difficulties of inspections of records were highlighted in:

***Yasuda Fire and Marine Insurance Company of Europe Limited* v. *Orion Marine Insurance Underwriting Agency Limited* [1995] 1 Lloyd's Rep. 525**

This case, although it actually involved agency agreements, has equal application to reinsurance matters. The plaintiffs were involved in a number of run-off reinsurance pools, which were managed by the defendants. The underwriting agency agreements, which were similar to reinsurance contracts, contained detailed express clauses permitting the inspection of records. Representatives of the plaintiffs carried out a very detailed inspection of the defendant's files, which included the reviewing of 16,000 risk files. However, problems arose when the plaintiffs wanted access to the defendant's computer records because the defendants kept confidential records on the computer about other pool members to which the plaintiffs should not be granted access. In Coleman J.'s view the computer database represented part of the records, which should be made available to the plaintiff for inspection purposes. He said: "If they (the defendants) are to perform their obligations to provide inspection of all such records as are relevant, but object to disclosure of that which is irrelevant, it is for them to find some means of either concealing the irrelevant . . . or of extracting that which is relevant from the mass of the material" (at p. 527).

The case warns companies that they should be careful about how and where they store information which they may be required to make available for inspection. The result could be harsh on small companies, since it may require a great deal of work to separate the relevant from the irrelevant and the confidential from the not confidential. However, if inspection does not mean a full inspection, then material could easily be concealed in computers by unscrupulous reinsureds to prevent their reinsurers accessing it.

In addition to the reinsurance inspections it is becoming increasingly popular for reinsurers to perform audits of their reinsureds. The audits fall into three categories:

- The first kind of audit is the pre-contract audit. In such an audit the reinsurer will examine the underwriting standards and claims handling procedures of its prospective reinsured to check that it is satisfied that the standards are acceptable and that the premium quoted by the reinsurer is correct for the risk.
- The second type of audit is the underwriting audit, which involves an examination of the reinsured's underwriting philosophy.
- The final type of audit is the claim's audit. The reinsurers will check that adequate reserves are being held in respect of claims, there is no "step reserving" and that the reinsured is taking a realistic and pro-active stance in the claims handling. The reinsurers will also look at the claims which have not been notified to the reinsurers because they have not breached the retention figure, to see if these claims should be reported to reinsurers because there is a likelihood that the claims will have a serious potential. It ensures that the reinsurer has a realistic view of his likely liabilities and the profitability of the business; it is also

marketed by the reinsurer as an advantage to the reinsured since it gives the reinsured feedback on their claims handling and offers them the opportunity of a fresh review of the files by new personnel.

GROUNDS FOR DENYING LIABILITY

Good faith

In reinsurance law there is a strict duty of disclosure imposed upon the parties by virtue of the duty of utmost good faith.

The duty of utmost good faith was established in the common law in the case of *Carter* v. *Boehm* (1776) 3 Burr 1905. This case involved insurance in respect of Fort Marlborough in Sumatra for property loss that would occur if the Fort was attacked and taken by a foreign country. During the cover period the fort was attacked and taken by the French. Liability was denied by the underwriter on the grounds that the fort was poorly defended and was sure to fall if it was attacked by a European power and that the insured was aware that the fort may be attacked. Lord Mansfield made it clear that the underwriter depended upon what the insured told him and therefore it is imperative that the insured holds nothing back and supplies the underwriter with all of the information he should know about the risk and the holding back of information will be a fraud and will render the policy void. The general principle was stated thus, "Good faith forbids either party by concealing what he privately knows, to draw the other into a bargain, from his ignorance of that fact, and his believing the contrary" (at p. 1910) but Lord Mansfield took the view that the principle applies to all contracts.

The Marine Insurance Act 1906, s. 17, also deals with the duty of utmost good faith and says that "a contract of marine insurance is a contract based upon the utmost good faith, and, if the utmost good faith is not observed by either party, the contract may be avoided by the other party".

Container Transport International Inc and Reliance Group* v. *Oceanus Mutual Underwriting Association (Bermuda) Limited
[1984] 1 Lloyd's Rep. 476

Oceanus argued that CTI had put forward an inaccurate and misleading claims record and that they had failed to disclose the refusal by Lloyd's underwriters to renew the cover, and also that they had failed to make a full disclosure when obtaining the insurance with Lloyd's. The Court of Appeal held that an insurer could avoid a contract under section 18(1) of the Marine Insurance Act 1906 if there was a failure to disclose any circumstance which a prudent insurer would take into account when deciding whether or not to accept the risk before the contract was finalised. Furthermore, there would be no waiver of material information unless it should have been disclosed by an inquiry by the underwriter, which common prudence demanded, and the contract would not be affirmed unless the underwriter had full knowledge of the information before he entered into the contract. According to Kerr L.J., the reinsured is required to make a fair presentation of the risk but above that there is a threshold limit at which the emphasis shifts to the reinsurer, and it is up to the reinsurer to ask for more information if he so wishes.

The insured is under a duty of good faith not to misrepresent material facts before the underwriter actually accepts the risk, and the case of *Orakpo* v. *Barclays Insurance Services* [1995] L.R.L.R. 443 makes it clear that this duty continues when the claim is put forward so that the insured must forward the claim honestly. In *Orakpo* the insured stated on his proposal form that the property was in a good state of repair, which it was not, the claims for lost rent of the bedsitting rooms was grossly exaggerated by Mr Orakpo. The first instance judge held that Mr Orakpo's claim was clearly fraudulent and must therefore fail. The Court of Appeal agreed with the first instance decision but the judges had different interpretations of the duty of utmost good faith. Hoffmann L.J. believed that the policy was broken from the date of breach of the contract. Sir Roger Parker took the view that Mr Orakpo's fraud rendered the policy void *ab initio*, while Staughton L.J. was of the opinion that the insured could only recover the amount of his genuine loss and nothing more.

***Direct Line Insurance Plc* v. *Khan and Others* [2002] Lloyd's Rep. IR 634**

A husband and wife made a claim on a policy in joint names in respect of damage to a property, which they jointly owned, including a claim for the rental of alternative accommodation. The claim proved to be fraudulently exaggerated. The claim form had been filed by Mr Khan. His wife, Mrs Khan, subsequently alleged that she was not tainted by her husband's fraudulent exaggeration of the claim and she had no knowledge of it. A separate issue also arose as to whether or not the fact that there had been exaggeration of a substantial part of the claim was sufficient to make the entire claim void. The Court of Appeal held that the exaggeration of a substantial part of the claim entitled the insurer to avoid the whole claim. The Court of Appeal also found that Mrs Khan had granted actual or apparent authority to Mr Khan to pursue her claim on her behalf and accordingly she was bound by his fraud, as she could not demonstrate that it was outside the scope of his agency.

***Konstantinos Agapitos and Another* v. *Ian Charles Agnew and Others* [2002] 3 W.L.R. 616**

In this case, the insured had not been fraudulent in making the claim, in that he had not made up the loss or exaggerated it, but he had lied about the surrounding circumstances in order to bolster the strength of his claim for the purpose of recovery in litigation. The Court of Appeal held that if a claim is made up or deliberately exaggerated, then it is irrelevant as to whether insurers are actually misled or not, if part of the claim is not itself immaterial or unsubstantial.

***Svenska Kreditfursakrings AB* v. *Munchener Ruckversicherungs-Gesselschaft, Schweizeriche Ruckversicherungs-Gesellschaft and other Reinsurers* (Swedish Arbitration, Stockholm, 11 November 1998)**

In this case the duty of utmost good faith and misrepresentation were considered closely. Svenska Kredit was a Swedish Insurance and reinsurance company, which embarked upon an ambitious plan to increase its market share in the financial guarantee business. From late 1989 to the end of 1991 Svenska Kredit suffered heavy losses, by 1992 it was in crisis and in October 1992 bankruptcy proceedings were adjudicated on Svenska Kredit. In December 1992 and January 1993 several reinsurers tried to avoid the reinsurance treaties and refused to make payments under the treaties. The estate of Svenska Kredit filed claims for payment against the reinsurers under the treaties and the reinsurers filed claims for a declaration that they could avoid the treaties and that they could avoid liability for certain individual risks for the underwriting years 1988 to 1991. With regard to applicable law, the Tribunal decided that the treaties were governed by Swedish substantive law and that although the Swedish Contracts Act 1927 did not specifically apply to reinsurance it would apply by analogy. The "honourable engagement" clause in the reinsurance treaties enabled the Tribunal to decide the disputes in a way that they considered fair and equitable having regard to the customs and practices of the insurance industry. The Tribunal was chaired by Kenneth Rokison, a former UK judge, together with a well-known Danish attorney and a Swedish University professor.

The Tribunal decided that insurance and reinsurance contracts are ruled by the principle of utmost good faith which carries with it the duty of disclosure of material facts by the insured or the reinsured.

For treaty reinsurance and especially obligatory proportional reinsurance treaties where the reinsured effectively underwrites on behalf of the reinsurer the reinsured has a duty to disclose to reinsurers facts which may influence the reinsurer's decision as to whether or not to continue with the business relationship with the reinsured. The Tribunal had to decide if there was a duty on the reinsured to disclose the increase in its financial guarantee business. There is no such duty in Swedish law or in international reinsurance market practice. The tribunal decided that the reinsured is under a duty to disclose all facts and circumstances which would be material for any decision to be taken by the reinsurer in relation to the formation and continuing existence of the treaty and its terms. Since the reinsurer and reinsured decided whether or not they wished to continue the business relationship on 30 September each year, Svenska Kredit were required to disclose all material facts and circumstances to the reinsurer on 30 September each year. There was a non-disclosure by Svenska Kredit in relation to the increased volume of financial guarantee business and Svenska Kredit also failed to report a large loss to reinsurers but these did not allow the reinsurers to avoid the treaties.

The Tribunal looked at the attitude of the reinsurers and since all reinsurers were keen to develop good relations with Svenska Kredit and obtain their business they were prepared to rely upon Svenska Kredit's reputation and business sense. The Tribunal believed that even if the material facts had been disclosed to reinsurers they would still have continued to participate in the treaties but would have insisted that guidelines were imposed and followed in relation to the borrower's creditworthiness.

Svenska Kredit was found guilty of failing to comply with reasonable underwriting standards but under Swedish law the termination of a contract for breach did not operate with retroactive effect and the reinsurers only gave notice of supposed termination after the bankruptcy proceedings had begun, which was too late.

The Tribunal made it clear that the reinsured owes a duty to the reinsurer not to write business to be ceded to the treaties recklessly or irresponsibly and not to cede risks which exceed treaty limits. There was evidence that Svenska Kredit had accepted some very poor risks where the borrower's ability to pay the loans was doubtful, such risks were not underwritten in strict adherence to accepted insurance and reinsurance market underwriting practice, and were not in accordance with Svenska Kredit's own underwriting guidelines. Accordingly, the Tribunal held that the reinsurers were able to avoid liability in respect of these risks and were not liable to Svenska Kredit for these risks.

Since the reinsurer is far removed from the original insured it depends heavily on the insurer to make detailed investigations of the original claim to ensure that it is legitimate and covered under the terms of the original insurance policy. The Court of Appeal in the recent case of *Brotherton and Others* v.

Aseguradora Colseguros SA and Another (2003) EWCA Civ 705 held that where a reinsured has knowledge of allegations of misconduct on the part of the original insured, and of official investigations into such misconduct, the question of whether such allegations are well founded is irrelevant to the reinsurer's determination of the reinsurer's case of non-disclosure of such allegations and investigations.

When does the duty of good faith come to an end?

It appears that the duty of good faith terminates when the insurer rejects the claim. This was established in *Manifest Shipping Company Limited* v. *Uni-Polaris Insurance Company Limited* (*The Star Sea*) [1995] 1 Lloyd's Rep. 65. This involved a ship which had caught fire. The Court of Appeal held that once the claim has been rejected the parties are adversaries, which makes sense, since otherwise the insured would be obliged to disclose information to assist his opponents.

DISCHARGING THE REINSURANCE CONTRACT

Non-performance

If one of the parties clearly refuses to perform his obligations under the contract then this will amount to a repudiation of the contract. Sometimes, the party will not perform his duties under the contract without expressly stating his intention in this regard and in this situation it will be up to the court to determine the intentions of that party by examining its conduct to see if it really does not wish to be bound by the contract. The case of *Universal Cargo Carriers* v. *Citati* [1957] 1 Lloyd's Rep. 174 involved a voyage by ship of 6,000 tons of scrap iron from Basrah to Buenos Aires. Delays occurred by the charterer in nominating the shipper, nominating the berth, and in providing the cargo. The owners claimed for damages and argued that they were entitled to rescind the contract because the charter party had breached fundamental terms of the contract. Devlin MJ held that the charterers had breached the warranty but that such breaches did not *ipso facto* entitle the owners to rescind the contract. He pointed out that the aggrieved party could rescind the contract if the delay was so long as to go to the root of the contract, and what constituted a "reasonable time" would very much depend upon the facts of each particular case. In order to rely upon an anticipatory breach the owners had to show that the charterer had renounced his liabilities, which they were unable to do in this case. The matter was referred back to the arbitrator to see if performance of the contract was in fact impossible.

If one of the parties behaves in such a way as to make it impossible for the other party to perform his obligations under the contract then that party may regard itself as being discharged from the contract.

If one of the parties fails to perform a major part of the contract then the other party will be discharged from the contract.

The innocent party will normally be awarded damages for breach of contract. However, to be successful in this regard, there must be a causal link between the breach of contract and the loss, the damages suffered must not be too remote and the innocent party will be expected to mitigate his losses. In practice it will be very rare for courts to insist upon specific performance of the contract.

***Fenton Insurance Company Limited* v. *Gothaer Versicherungsbank WaG* [1991] 1 Lloyd's Rep. 172**

The reinsured did not provide quarterly statement accounts to the reinsurer or statements of premiums or claims or any other documentation concerning balances. The question for the court to consider was whether this failure on the part of the reinsured amounted to a discharge of the reinsurance contract, breach of the contract or abandonment. Potter J. explained in some detail how reinsurance and insurance works in practice and he emphasised that communication between the two parties is often poor and delays in payment are frequent. He concluded that the non-payment was not an agreement to abandon, there being no evidence that the statements had not been sent to the reinsurer nor was the contract discharged. In his view it would be very rare for the courts to regard a delay in payment in a reinsurance case to be a repudiatory breach and for it to consider doing so there would have to be formal written demands from the reinsurer and then the reinsured would have to fail to pay for a reasonable time afterwards. He examined what the likely remedy would be for such a breach and believed that it would only enable the reinsurer to terminate the contract from the date of the non-payment but the reinsurer would still be liable to pay all of the claims covered by the contract until that point.

Misrepresentation

If a party makes a misrepresentation or non-disclosure to the other party in relation to the contract then the other party will be able to terminate the contract *ab initio*. This requirement is especially strong in the insurance and reinsurance fields because of the application of the duty of utmost good faith.

***Black Sea Shipping Corporation* v. *Massie (The Litsion Pride)* [1985] 1 Lloyd's Rep. 437**

The plaintiffs were owners of the ship which was insured against war risks with the defendant underwriters. The policy contained a condition that if the ship sailed into hazardous waters, an additional premium should be paid to the underwriters. During the Iran/Iraq war the ship entered the danger zone and was destroyed by missile fire. The court held that the shipowners and the brokers acted fraudulently and that the duty imposed upon the insured to disclose circumstances which will affect the premium charged does continue after the risk has been accepted on cover.

***Continental Illinois Bank Trust Company of Chicago* v. *Alliance Assurance Company Limited (The Captain Panagos)* [1986] 2 Lloyd's Rep. 470**

In *Continental Illinois Bank Trust Company of Chicago* v. *Alliance Assurance Company Limited (The Captain Panagos)* [1986] 2 Lloyd's Rep. 470 the insured made a fraudulent claim. The insured who owned the ship grounded the ship and set it alight and then sought to recover the cost of a constructive total loss under the terms of the insurance policy. The court held that the insured had been fraudulent and by virtue of section 17 of the Marine Insurance Act 1906 the insurers were able to terminate the contract *ab initio.*

***Orakpo* v. *Barclays Insurance Services and Another* [1995] L.R.L.R. 443**

The plaintiff made misrepresentations to Commercial Union regarding the condition of his property in London. He was aware that there had been dry rot problems with the property for some time and he exaggerated the claims for loss of rent from the bedsitting rooms in the property. The Commercial Union insurance policy had recently been revised to make it conform to "plain English", and as a result the section (relating to the fact that the submission of a fraudulent claim would remove all benefits under the insurance policy) had been removed. Nevertheless, the Court of Appeal held that this made no difference. The fact of the matter was that as part of the duty of utmost good faith the insured is obliged to put forward honest claims, and if a fraudulent claim is made then this will mean that the insurer can be discharged from liability.

***Insurance Corporation of the Channel Islands and Royal Insurance Company Limited* v. *McHugh and Royal Hotel Limited* [1997] L.R.L.R. 94**

In *Insurance Corporation of the Channel Islands and Royal Insurance Company Limited* v. *McHugh and Royal Hotel Limited* [1997] L.R.L.R. 94 the insured inflated the claim by exaggerating the room occupancy at the hotel. This case was unusual in that the contract contained special conditions regarding the options available to the insurer in the event that the insured presented a fraudulent claim, and the case very much focused upon the interpretation of the terms. However, the court still mentioned the continuing duty of utmost good faith.

In *Direct Line Insurance plc* v. *Khan and Others* [2002] Lloyd's Rep. IR 634 (see earlier in the chapter for details) the Court of Appeal held that exaggeration of a substantial part of the claim was sufficient for the Insurer to avoid the whole claim.

Instead of making a fraudulent claim the insured or reinsured may misrepresent the facts of the claim. For example, in *Manifest Shipping Company Limited* v. *Uni-Polaris Insurance Company Limited (The Star Sea)* [1997] 1 Lloyd's Rep. 360 (see earlier) a ship was lost at sea by fire. The insured did not disclose relevant experts' reports to the insurer. The Court of Appeal held that this was "culpable" conduct and the duty not to make fraudulent claims included this "culpability".

***Toomey* v. *Banco Vitalicio de Espana SA de Seguros y Reaseguros* [2003] EWHC 1102 (Comm)**

In this case a Spanish insurer issued a policy, which provided for payment of Pts 2.9 billion in the event that the insured, a Spanish football club suffered relegation from the Spanish first division. The policy was reinsured facultatively on the basis of a slip policy containing the terms "as original" and "full reinsurance clause". The judge held that the reinsurers were entitled to reject the reinsured's claim because on the proper construction of the reinsurance contract the reinsured had given an undertaking by way of a warranty that the original insurance was properly described in the statement of interest. The statement actually contained a fundamental misdescription of the reinsured interest. It stated that the policy was one of indemnity against actual loss, subject to a maximum of Pts 2.9 billion when in reality it was a valued policy, which meant that the insured sum became payable upon relegation of the club whether or not it could show that it had actually suffered measurable financial loss.

In the recent case of *Wise* v. *Grupo Nacional Provincial SA* [2004] 2 Lloyd's Rep. 483 the Court of Appeal heard an appeal by the respondent insurer against a decision that the reinsurer of the cargo cover could avoid the reinsurance on the grounds of non-disclosure. The non-disclosure in this case was that a certain cargo included Rolex and other expensive watches. As a result of a mistranslation the slip referred to the cargo as "clocks". The Court of Appeal agreed with the first instance judge that the mis-description was material and had not alerted the reinsurer of the high value of the watches. When the reinsurer became aware of the non-disclosure they gave notice of cancellation of the policy instead of immediately seeking to avoid the policy. The Court of Appeal held that that was an affirmation of the contract and as a result the reinsurer had waived its right to avoid the policy.

The case makes it very clear that insurers and reinsurers should seek to avoid the contract as soon as they are made aware of misrepresentation or non-disclosure and not risk affirming the contract and thereby waiving their rights.

Remedies available

In the event of a non-disclosure by the insured the insurer will rescind the contract.

This will be a satisfactory result for the reinsurer but it will not be sufficient for the reinsured because if the claim is not covered then all he will receive will be the return of his premium, which in most circumstances will not cover the loss.

***Banque Keyser Ullman SA* v. *Skandia (UK) Insurance Company Limited* [1987] 1 Lloyd's Rep. 69**

In the Commercial Court, Steyn J. in *Banque Keyser Ullman SA* v. *Skandia (UK) Insurance Company Limited* emphasised that the contract of insurance is reciprocal and it requires both sides to disclose material circumstances which may influence the insurance, and he expressed the fact that avoidance of the policy will be an ineffective remedy for the insured in such a situation. Nevertheless, the House of Lords ([1990] 2 Lloyd's Rep. 377) decided that the only remedy available to the insured in the event of breach of the duty of utmost good faith is avoidance of the policy and the recovery of the premium. The circumstances of this case were that Mr Ballestero persuaded syndicates of banks to enter into separate loan agreements with four companies which he owned and the securities offered in support were a pledge of gemstones and a credit insurance policy. The value of the pledges of gemstones were confirmed by the Gemmologisch Instituut Antwerpen and verified by a Zurich jeweller. Each policy contained a fraud exclusion clause. The banks advanced the monies. The borrowing companies defaulted on the loans and it was discovered that the value of the gemstones was negligible and that Mr Ballestero had executed a large fraud on the banks. The banks sought reimbursement under the insurance policies but the insurers denied liability because the loss was caused by Mr Ballestero's fraud and the fraud exclusion clause applied. The House of Lords made it clear that the money advanced would have been lost whether it had been insured or not because the banks had accepted and paid a premium for insurance which contained a fraud exclusion clause.

According to section 2(1) of the Misrepresentation Act 1967, if a person makes a misrepresentation to another party in respect of a contract then he will be liable in damages, unless he can prove that he believed until the point when the contract was made that the facts were true. This point was considered in *Banque Financiere De La Cite* v. *Westgate Insurance Company Limited* [1989] 2 All E.R. 952, and the Court of Appeal decided that for damages to be payable the misrepresentation had to be fraudulent, with the party making the misrepresentation aware that it would be acted upon by the other party, and the party who received the misrepresentation must have acted upon it to his detriment and suffered a loss.

***Morrison* v. *Universal Insurance Company* (1873) L.R. 8 Ex. 197**
Before executing the insurance policy Universal became aware of information which had not been disclosed to it by the brokers. They proceeded to issue the policy until a loss was reported four days after the policy was issued and then Universal sought to avoid the policy. The court held that Universal had not elected to abide by the insurance contract by not raising the non-disclosure when it became aware of it. The court did, however, make it clear that the decision may have been different if Universal had induced Morrison to believe that they would not raise the non-disclosure point and in doing so prevent Morrison from obtaining alternative insurance.

CTI v. *Oceanus* [1984] 1 Lloyd's Rep. 476 makes it clear that the contract would not be deemed to be affirmed by the underwriter unless the underwriter had full knowledge of the information and then entered into the contract.

It seems obvious that in order for an underwriter to affirm the contract he must have "knowledge" of the issue. The matter of "knowledge" was discussed in the following case:

***Mahli* v. *Abbey Life Assurance Company Limited* [1996] L.R.L.R. 237**
Abbey Life tried to avoid a joint life policy upon the death of Mr Mahli. The insurers argued that there had been a non-disclosure of Mr Mahli's alcoholism and malaria. Mrs Mahli argued that Abbey Life were aware of these medical conditions because they had been disclosed in a joint application they had made in 1986. The problem was that the application for a further policy had not been cross-referred with the original proposal and reinstatement request. The Court of Appeal held that the insurance company could not have imputed knowledge of all documents in its records, the information would have been forwarded to different departments. The Court of Appeal recognised that communication within insurance and reinsurance companies is often poor, and it outlined the circumstances in which providing information would be sufficient for the company to have knowledge and concluded that the information must be given to an "authorised person" within the company who appreciates the significance of the information in order for knowledge to be passed to the insurance company, and on this occasion knowledge had not passed to the insurer and presumably the same would apply in the reinsurance context.

***Pan Atlantic Insurance Company* v. *Pine Top Insurance* [1992] 1 Lloyd's Rep. 101**

Pine Top reinsured Pan Atlantic under an excess of loss treaty for casualty risks for 1982. At renewal in 1982 the brokers only showed the reinsurer's underwriter a short report of the risks which did not show all of the losses, yet a longer report was available. The reinsurer argued that there had been non-disclosure and misrepresentation in failing to produce the longer report. Walker J. held that the losses missed off the short report did amount to non-disclosure, but the failure to advise the underwriter of the existence of the longer report did not amount to a non-disclosure. He also set down some guidelines on affirmation of contracts. The contract would be affirmed if the reinsurer being aware of the misrepresentation and non-disclosure treated the contract as continuing. Simple delay would not in itself amount to affirmation of the contract.

***Sirius International Insurance Corporation* v. *Oriental* [1999] Lloyd's Rep. 343**

Oriental insured a number of warehouses in the Philippines. Sirius, who were one of Oriental's three reinsurers, claimed to be able to avoid the reinsurance when a fire occurred at one of the warehouses in 1995 because of misrepresentation.

Sirius requested further details regarding fire-extinguishing equipment at each of the warehouses. On 23 February 1995 the producing broker sent a fax confirming that there were portable fire extinguishers, security guards, fire alarms and hydrants at each of the locations. The placing broker took the slip around the market and it was subscribed by the Sirius underwriter who also signed and scratched the fax.

Sirius argued that they could avoid the reinsurance since there were no hydrants at the warehouse, only dry risers, and that the sprinkler system did not work because the pump had never been supplied. The court considered the meaning of "hydrants" and decided that a hydrant had to be connected to a mains water supply, so clearly there were no hydrants within this definition at the warehouse.

Longmore MJ concluded that a misrepresentation in relation to the hydrants had been made to Sirius because they had signed and scratched the fax, but there was no evidence that a misrepresentation had been made to the other two reinsurers. However, the problem for the reinsurers was that by the time they had seen the fax they were already on risk and could not have relied upon the misrepresentation to reinsure the risk.

As discussed earlier, *Iron Trades Insurance* v. *Companhia de Seguros Imperio* [1991] 1 Re L.R. 213 confirms that if the reinsurer is aware of misrepresentation but inspects the reinsured's records without a reservation of rights then that contract will be treated as affirmed.

THE LEADING UNDERWRITER AND THE FOLLOW MARKET

The leading underwriter has a powerful role. He can agree policy wordings and agree amendments to cover and settle claims on behalf of the follow market. The extent of the lead's authority is determined by the wording of the leading underwriter clause.

You would think that if the following reinsurers are prepared to be bound by the lead reinsurer's decision that the reinsurer should be clearly identified. Normally the lead reinsurer will be clearly identified in the slip and in the case of claims processed on the London Processing Centre's claims system

CLASS, the lead reinsurer is normally clearly identified since the lead's response needs to be given before the follow market can view the claims detail and respond to it. However, the identity of the leading underwriter is not always clear.

***ROAR Marine Limited* v. *Bimeh Iran Insurance Company* [1998] 1 Lloyd's Rep. 423**

In this case, the following market agreed to follow the leading underwriter in relation to the settlement of claims. The leading underwriter settled a claim and one of the defences raised was to dispute the identity of the leading underwriter. The judge decided that since the purported leading underwriter:

- appeared first in the list of market participants
- appeared first in the broker's list of underwriters
- scratched an endorsement in the box reserved for the leading underwriter, and
- scratched the claims endorsement in its capacity as leading underwriter

that he was the leading underwriter. Therefore, if the leading underwriter looks and behaves like the leading underwriter then he will be the leading underwriter. The court stressed that it did not matter that the leading underwriter did not have the largest participation in the risk because when the leader first scratched the risk he did not know if subsequent underwriters would take more of a share than he himself took.

It was argued in *ROAR* that the follow the leader clause was subject to a condition that the settlement must have been concluded in a proper and businesslike manner. This was rejected by the court since it would undermine the purpose and operation of the clause, and that following underwriters have to accept the advantages and risks of the leading underwriter's handling of settlements.

It should be borne in mind when agreeing to giving the leading underwriter authority to settle claims that the leading underwriter has very wide powers to bind the following market to settlements.

In order for there to be certainty in the disposal of claims the courts have consistently favoured following the leader, regardless of whether or not he actually intended to bind the market and whether or not he acted in accordance with market practice.

Unfortunately, the actual scope of the responsibilities of the leading underwriter to the following market is unclear. In *Barlee Marine Corporation* v. *Trevor Rex Mountain (The Leegas)* [1987] 1 Lloyd's Rep. 471 the judge expressed the opinion that underlying the entire relationship between the leading underwriter and the following underwriters was the leading underwriter's "manifest duty of care".

In *Mander* v. *Commercial Union* [1998] Lloyd's Rep. IR 93 the court rejected the idea that the leading underwriter was the agent of the following market. Instead the court construed the agreement as a trigger to bind the following market and refused to impose the unrealistic fiduciary duties of an agent. However, the judge did say that if a leading underwriter does owe a duty of care then it is to the following market rather than to the insured.

From a practice perspective there seems to be an increase in the leader's authority to bind the following market. This is especially so in relation to the wide use of the LMP slip wording, which effectively means that the follow market give claims handling authority to the lead reinsurer on their behalf to such an extent that requests for information by the follow reinsurers cannot delay settlement of the claim once it has been agreed by the lead reinsurer. This can create problems where the following reinsurers have little faith in the decisions taken by the lead. In this situation of course the following market can still examine the claims documentation and form their own view on the matter but it is likely that the wording of the leading underwriter clause will prevent the follow market from taking a different view to that of the lead, although naturally they can air their views with the leading reinsurer. The actual rights of the following market are currently underdeveloped and it is not clear what recourse might be available to the followers against the lead for abuse by the leader. It is therefore very important that the leaders and followers pay close attention to the wording of the leading underwriter clause to avoid problems at a later stage.

ISSUES RELATING TO RUN-OFF

The expression run-off has become very fashionable in recent years but it can actually have a number of different meanings. It may mean that a particular contract is in run-off because the cover period has expired and the contract has not been renewed. It may relate to a number of old contracts, which are no longer current but the account is still active. It may also relate to the entire business of a reinsurance company, which has stopped underwriting new business. For example, when Mercantile and General was acquired by the Swiss Re its general business went into run-off while its life business continued under the Swiss Re banner.

In view of the fact that run-off companies will not receive new income they will be paying claims out of an ever-decreasing pool of money. It is therefore very common for run-off companies to take a more bullish stance in relation to claims handling, to exercise legal rights to raise coverage issues and to delay paying claims for as long as possible.

One of the most expensive costs in relation to run-off will be the claims handling fees and these can be reduced by commuting as much of the business as possible.

Commutation

A commutation agreement is an understanding between the reinsurer and the reinsured whereby in consideration of a payment by the reinsurer to the reinsured the reinsured releases the reinsurer from future liabilities under the reinsurance contract.

It is difficult to determine the correct price for a commutation but in considering the value the reinsurer will look at the claims history of the contract or contracts and project into the future what claims are likely to be made and the likely cost of those claims, and what payments are likely to be made in the future in respect of existing claims. The reinsurer will normally carry out a without-prejudice inspection of the reinsured's records prior to a commutation to give it a better understanding of the reinsured's claims statistics and to assist with calculating the incurred but not reported (IBNR) figures. The reinsurer will project the claims figures into the future and then make a deduction to take account of the fact that the reinsured is in receipt of the payment earlier than he would have been if the claims had been paid when they were presented in the future and will thus be able to invest this money. Reinsurers should liaise closely with their retrocessionaires when they are considering commuting business in order to avoid any difficulties which may arise when the reinsurer tries to recover the "commutation deal" payment from its own reinsurers.

When the commutation terms have been agreed between the parties they will be confirmed in a release agreement. The release agreement will clearly identify the contracts which have been commuted, specify the payment details and outline where and when the payment should be made. It will contain a confidentiality clause preventing the parties from disclosing the details of their agreement to other parties, a clause stating which law will govern the agreement and the jurisdiction within which any disputes regarding the agreement will be determined. It is also common for the agreement to contain an arbitration clause to ensure that any disputes regarding the parties' agreement are determined by the arbitration process rather than by litigation.

A typical commutation agreement would look like this:

COMMUTATION AND RELEASE AGREEMENT
(hereinafter referred to as the "Agreement")

THIS Agreement *is entered into by and between [insert name of Reinsurer], domiciled in . . . (hereinafter referred to as the "REINSURER") and [insert name of the Company], domiciled in . . . (hereinafter referred to as the "COMPANY"), and made effective [insert effective date].*

WHEREAS, *the REINSURER and the COMPANY entered into a reinsurance contract, Number [insert policy number], effective [insert date], and executed by the REINSURER on [insert date], and by the COMPANY on [insert date] (the "Contract"). The term Contract shall include all other arrangements, representations and agreements (whether written or not), which the REINSURER and the COMPANY may have made with respect to the reinsurance obligations which are the subject of the Contract;*

WHEREAS, *the REINSURER and the COMPANY desire fully and finally to settle and commute all past, present and future obligations and liabilities known and unknown of the REINSURER and the COMPANY arising under or in any way connected with the Contract;*

NOW, THEREFORE, *for good and valuable consideration the receipt of which is hereby acknowledged,* ***IT IS AGREED BY AND BETWEEN THE REINSURER AND THE COMPANY THAT:***

1. *The REINSURER shall pay to the COMPANY the sum of . . . , detailed in Schedule A, attached hereto/ within . . . days after the signing the Agreement by both parties.*
2. *Subject to the receipt of the sum of . . . described in Paragraph 1. above herein the COMPANY hereby releases and fully discharges the REINSURER, its predecessors, parents, affiliates, subsidiaries, agents, officers, directors and shareholders and assigns from any and all past, present and future payment obligations, adjustments, executions, offsets, actions, causes of action, suits, debts, sums of money, accounts, reckonings, bonds, bills, covenants, contracts, controversies, agreements, promises, damages, judgments, claims, demands, liabilities and/or losses whatsoever, all whether known or unknown, which the COMPANY, and their successors and assigns ever had, now have, or hereinafter may have, whether grounded in law or equity, in contract or in tort, against the REINSURER or any of them by reason of any matter whatsoever arising out of or under or relating, directly or indirectly, to the terms and conditions of the Contract, it being the intention of the parties that this release operate as a full and final settlement of the REINSURER's past, present and future liabilities to the COMPANY under said Contract.*
3. *Subject to the release by the COMPANY of the REINSURER as provided for in Paragraph 2, herein above, the REINSURER hereby releases and fully discharges the COMPANY, its predecessors, parents, affiliates, subsidiaries, agents, officers, directors and shareholders and assigns from any and all past, present and future payment obligations, adjustments, executions, offsets, actions, causes of action, suits, debts, sums of money, accounts, reckonings, bonds, bills, covenants, contracts, controversies, agreements, promises, damages, judgments, claims, demands, liabilities and/or losses whatsoever, all whether known or unknown, which the REINSURER, and their successors and assigns ever had, now have, or hereinafter may have, whether grounded in law or equity, in contract or in tort, against the COMPANY or any of them by reason of any matter whatsoever arising out of or under or relating, directly or indirectly, to the terms and conditions of the Contract, it being the intention of the parties that this release operate as a full and final settlement of the COMPANY's past, present and future liabilities to the REINSURER under said Contract.*
4. *The rights, duties and obligations set forth herein shall inure to the benefit of and be binding upon any and all predecessors, successors, affiliates, officers, directors, employees, parents, subsidiaries, stockholders, liquidators, receivers and assigns of the parties hereto.*
5. *The parties hereto expressly warrant and represent that they are entities in*

good standing in their respective places of domicile; that the conclusion and the execution of this Agreement is fully authorized by each of them; that the person or persons concluding and executing this Agreement have the necessary and appropriate authority to do so; that there are no pending agreements, transactions, or negotiations to which any of them are a party that would render this Agreement or any part thereof void, voidable, or unenforceable; and that no authorization, consent or approval of any government entity is required to make this Agreement valid and binding upon them.

6. *This Agreement contains the entire agreement between the parties as respects its subject matter. All discussions and agreements previously entertained between the parties concerning the subject matter of the commutation are merged into this Agreement. This Agreement may not be modified or amended, nor any of its provisions waived, except by an instrument in writing, signed by the parties hereunder.*
7. *The parties hereto and each of them do hereby covenant and agree to do such things and execute such further documents, agreements and assurances as may be necessary or advisable from time to time in order to carry out the terms and conditions of this Agreement in accordance with their true intent.*
8. *This Agreement shall be governed by and construed in accordance with the laws of . . . and the parties hereto hereby irrevocably submit to the non-exclusive jurisdiction of the Courts in . . . , . . . and to the extent permitted by law expressly waive all rights to challenge or otherwise limit such jurisdiction.*
9. *This Agreement shall be read and be considered as an integral part of the Contract and in the case of any conflict with any part of said Contract the provisions of this Agreement shall prevail.*
10. *This Agreement may be executed and delivered in one or more counterparts, each of which shall together constitute one and the same instrument.*
11. *Neither party shall disclose the details of this Agreement to any third party other than with the prior consent of the other party except where otherwise required by law or authority of a court or arbitration panels in which event disclosure shall, insofar as is practicable, be made only after consultation with the party taking into account the reasonable requirements of the other party.*

IN WITNESS WHEREOF, this Agreement has been executed this —— day of —— by

For and on Behalf of

—————————————— [insert name of Company]

Name: *Title:* *Date:*

For and on Behalf of

—————————————— [insert name of Reinsurer]

Name: *Title:* *Date:*

Schedule A

Contract description	*Contract number*	*Reinsurer's reference*	*Cedant's reference*	*Underwriting year*

The tendency is for the industry to think of commutation as a way to dispose of "dead" business but commutations can also be attractive to the reinsurer to get them off risk on a line of business, which is no longer profitable with an existing client so that they can focus on more profitable business lines going forward.

The commutation protocol

On 25 June 2003 the Association of Run-Off Companies launched a Commutations Protocol aimed at making it easier for reinsureds to conclude commutations. It was issued initially as a consultation document with a target effective date of 1 October 2003. Unfortunately the plan of having a commutation protocol which all companies would sign up to has proved to be too ambitious. However, the Protocol may be used by any parties if both parties agree to it. (Further information about the Protocol may be found at *www.arcrunoff.com*)

The Protocol addresses a longstanding difficulty over recognition of outstanding loss reserves and Incurred But Not Reported claims (IBNR). This arises when a reinsured commutes a book of business and then seeks to make a recovery from its reinsurers. If reinsurers have not previously agreed to recognise the commutation, they may refuse to indemnify the reinsured for anything other than accounted balances (i.e., paid claims). This is a disincentive to reinsureds wishing to commute. It makes it more difficult for companies no longer trading to run-off their business.

The aim of the Protocol is to provide, on a reciprocal basis, predetermined limits for recognition of reserves and IBNR in commutations.

Four classes of business have been identified—Life and Health, Liability, Property, and Pecuniary Loss—and for each class different percentages are recoverable from reinsurers for loss reserves or IBNR. The percentages vary according to the underwriting year in which the business being commuted falls: current and up to two years old, 3–5 years, 6–9 years, 10–20 years, 20 years plus. The maximum recoverable amounts for each period are set out in a schedule to the Protocol. There is nothing to prevent separate arrangements being agreed with reinsured for higher amounts but in the absence of any separate agreement these proportions of loss reserves and IBNR are binding.

DISPUTE RESOLUTION

Arbitration and dispute resolution are dealt with in greater detail in Chapter 10. However, dispute resolution is very relevant to claims since often any difficult issues and tensions between the reinsurer and cedant will arise in relation to non-disclosures, misrepresentations or the non-payment of claims.

The parties will normally incorporate an honourable engagement clause or an arbitration clause into their reinsurance contract to ensure that disputes between the parties in relation to the contract will be determined by arbitration rather than litigation.

An honourable engagement clause indicates the parties' wish not to fetter the decision-making process of the arbitrators with the application of strict legal principles if they consider that the dispute should be resolved on an equitable basis.

A standard *Honourable Engagement Clause* would read like this:

> " . . . shall interpret this treaty as an honourable engagement, and shall determine any reference in accordance with current reinsurance market practice pertaining during the currency of this Agreement, with a view to effecting the general purpose of this reinsurance in a reasonable manner rather than in accordance with the strict rules of law and literal interpretation of the language."

The parties often prefer to have their dispute decided by arbitration because it is perceived to be quicker, cheaper and less public than court proceedings. They also are keen to have their dispute resolved by someone who is familiar with insurance and reinsurance market practice and who will be familiar with their problems. Arbitration is seen to be more informal than court proceedings, certainly arbitrators are less restricted by the doctrines of precedent and the law but the style of the arbitration is very much dependent upon the view of the arbitrators appointed by the parties and in some situations the arbitration can mirror court proceedings in relation to evidence, disclosure and exchange of documents. In relation to speed, arbitrations can be quicker but the speed depends upon the attitudes of the parties and the issues in dispute. In many respects, arbitration may not be a cheaper alternative to litigation because the cost of expert arbitrators can be substantial and the parties will also be required to pay the cost of the venue where the arbitration is held.

The ARIAS (The Reinsurance and Insurance Arbitration Society of the International Association For Insurance Law (AIDA)) arbitration clause and rules are frequently used in reinsurance contracts and the rules can be added to a contract by simply including the words "ARIAS Arbitration Clause". The rules lay down guidelines regarding the appointment of arbitrators, the composition of the Tribunal, the communication of the decision, the position in relation to fees and so on. The general rule is that there will be three arbitrators, one appointed by each of the parties and the third to be appointed by the two arbitrators. With regard to the qualification of the arbitrators, according to ARIAS they should be people with at least 10 years' experience in the insurance or reinsurance industries or have 10 years' experience as a lawyer or "other professional adviser" of serving the industry. (The ARIAS Rules are dealt with more specifically in Chapter 10.)

The case of *Orion Compagnia Espanola de Seguros* v. *Belfort Maatschappij voor Algemene Verzekgringeen* [1962] 2 Lloyd's Rep. 257 makes it clear that arbitration clauses will not be permitted where they seek to oust the jurisdiction of the courts.

***Home Insurance Company Limited* v. *Administratia Asigurailor de Stat* [1983] 2 Lloyd's Rep. 674**

A dispute arose regarding the validity of the reinsurance contract. The honourable engagement clause said "This treaty shall be interpreted as an honourable engagement rather than a legal obligation and the award shall be made with a view to effecting the general purpose of this treaty rather than in accordance with a literal interpretation of its language". The reinsurers argued that the agreement was not binding in law only in honour. The court disagreed and decided that the parties had a clear intention to arbitrate and to abide by that award.

***Home and Overseas Insurance Company Limited* v. *Mentor Insurance Company (UK) Limited* [1989] 1 Lloyd's Rep. 473**

In *Home and Overseas Insurance Company Limited* v. *Mentor Insurance Company (UK) Limited* [1989] 1 Lloyd's Rep. 473 the arbitration clause said "The arbitrators and the umpire shall interpret this reinsurance as an honourable engagement and they shall make their award with a view to effecting the general purpose of this reinsurance in a reasonable manner rather than in accordance with a literal interpretation of the language". At first instance Hirst J. held that the arbitration clause was valid, and this was endorsed by the Court of Appeal with the proviso that the arbitrators should have regard to the law and the clause must not try to oust the applicability of general law.

The case law makes it plain that the courts are not prepared to incorporate an arbitration clause from the original insurance contract into the reinsurance contract simply because the reinsurance contract contains the words "as original".

***Trygg Hansa Insurance Company Limited* v. *Equitas and Butcher* [1998] 2 Lloyd's Rep. 439 (Comm)**

Trygg Hansa reinsured certain Lloyd's syndicates in respect of professional indemnity excess of loss contracts. Trygg Hansa attempted to avoid the reinsurance contracts on the basis of misrepresentation and non-disclosure. Equitas as the assignee of the Lloyd's syndicates commenced proceedings against Trygg Hansa to recover the reinsurance monies owed. Trygg Hansa argued that since the original policy contained an arbitration clause and the reinsurance was "as original" that the dispute between the reinsurer and reinsured should be determined by arbitration and that accordingly the court proceedings should be stayed in accordance with section 9 of the Arbitration Act 1996. Judge Jack QC held that since an arbitration clause is a special clause, which does not relate to the actual performance of the contract, in the absence of "special circumstances" something more than general words of incorporation would be required to incorporate the arbitration clause into the reinsurance contract. Unfortunately, it is not specified in the judgment what is meant by "special circumstances", but it appears that for an arbitration clause to be successfully incorporated into a reinsurance agreement the slip must either contain a specific arbitration clause or state something like "as original", including any arbitration clause contained or incorporated into the "original contract".

There will be certain situations in which the parties will wish to dispense with the arbitration clause and instead have the dispute determined by the litigation process. This will be common for example where there has been negligence on the part of the brokers and the parties wish to join the brokers to the action in order to make a recovery from them.

In order for a matter to be referred to arbitration it is necessary for there to be a "dispute" between the parties. In *Hayter* v. *Nelson* [1990] 2 Lloyd's Rep. 265 Saville J. said that the words "dispute" and "difference" should be given their usual meaning according to the English language. He made it clear that just because one party was clearly correct and the other party was obviously wrong and that this could easily be proven did not mean that there was not a dispute.

CONCLUSIONS

Reinsurers used to try and cultivate long-lasting business relationships with their clients and they would participate in the ceding company's reinsurance programme for many years. In the current economic climate original insureds are happy to shop around for the best cover for their properties and cars at the lowest price and this attitude has moved up the insurance chain to the insurance companies who also have to be competitive and are content to move from reinsurer to reinsurer to negotiate the best possible terms. The reinsurers too have become more commercially astute and are keen to axe unprofitable business and to fight claims where cover is not strictly afforded under the reinsurance contract. This is also illustrated by the reinsurer's keenness to carry out inspections and audits of its clients' business to ensure that claims which ought to be reported have been reported and to check that the reinsured is applying appropriate reserves to the claims that have been reported.

Where there is a reinsurance contract the courts will look very closely at the substance of the contract and although they are happy to look at the background circumstances of the contract the courts will only look at the parties' negotiations prior to the contract formation in very exceptional circumstances. The courts have made it clear in a number of decisions that the words in a reinsurance contract are to be given their "ordinary and everyday" meaning. For example, in *Charter Re* v. *Fagan* [1997] A.C. 313 Staughton L.J. in the Court of Appeal believed that the term "actually paid" should be given a literal meaning. In certain circumstances though the courts have been content to adopt a technical interpretation of the terms as did the House of Lords in *Charter Re*. The courts have also indicated a growing willingness to call expert evidence, especially to confirm what the common reinsurance market practice or custom is, such as in *Baker* v. *Black Sea and Baltic Insurance Company* [1995] L.R.L.R. 261.

Many of the words used in reinsurance contracts have unclear meanings and this has presented the courts with difficulties. In *Caudle* v. *Sharp* [1995] L.R.L.R. 433 the Court of Appeal construed the disastrous underwriting of 32 run-off reinsurance contracts to amount to 32 "events". Whereas in *Municipal Mutual Insurance Company Limited* v. *Sea Insurance Company Limited* [1996] L.R.L.R. 265 numerous acts of vandalism were treated as one "event". In the *Kuwait Airways Corporation* v. *Kuwait Insurance Company Limited* [1996] 1 Lloyd's Rep. 664 the "occurrence" was the invasion of Kuwait.

The reinsurance contract normally states the procedure for reporting claims and the reinsured has six years from the date when the claim has been quantified in which to make a recovery from his reinsurers. The position in relation to the reinsured's litigation costs is unclear. In *Insurance Company of Africa* v. *SCOR* [1985] 1 Lloyd's Rep. 312 the Court of Appeal emphasised that the reinsurer will only be responsible for the cost of defending coverage litigation if the reinsurance contract specifically says so. In *Baker* v. *Black Sea and Baltic Insurance Company* [1995] L.R.L.R. 261 the possibility of sharing defence costs was raised but was not satisfactorily resolved by the courts.

The reinsurance contract may be discharged if one of the parties fails to perform his obligations under the contract or if a party makes it impossible for the other party to perform his side of the contract. Normally if the contract cannot be performed then the innocent party will be awarded damages as compensation.

With regard to the termination of the reinsurance contract the law seems to be weighted in the reinsured's favour. For example, the reinsurer cannot terminate the contract simply because the reinsured has not paid the premium unless the contract specifically allows the reinsurer to do so. Furthermore, the reinsurer must be very careful in the way it behaves since otherwise it may affirm the contract, such as by demanding premium or by inspecting the reinsured's records without reserving its rights.

The duty of utmost good faith applies to insurance and reinsurance contracts and if it is breached then the other party will be able to end the contract, although the remedy available will depend upon the circumstances of the case. The authorities make it clear that the reinsured is under a duty not to misrepresent the facts before the underwriter accepts the risk and this duty continues as claims are presented for payment, but terminates when the claim has been rejected by the reinsurer. With regard to misrepresentation, the underwriter must have actually acted upon that misrepresentation to his detriment such as by accepting a risk which he would have not accepted had he known all of the true facts. Where there has been a non-disclosure by the reinsured the reinsurer will be entitled to rescind the contract, which means that the reinsurer simply returns the premium to the reinsured. This is a good result for the reinsurer since he will lose nothing, but the reinsured may be left with a large number of losses for which there is no reinsurance cover in place.

There is much evidence in the case law of the fact that reinsurers must make decisions promptly and must act in a professional and business-like manner or they will be penalised by the courts. For example in *Svenska Kreditfursakrings AB* v. *Munchener Ruckversicherungs-Gesellschaft, Schweizeriche Ruckversicherungs-Gesellschaft and other Reinsurers* (Swedish Arbitration, Stockholm, 11 November 1998) the Arbitration Tribunal recognised that the reinsurers were content to rely upon Svenska Kredit's reputation and follow them blindly simply to acquire and retain the business. The Tribunal pointed out that reinsurers must react swiftly and unambiguously when they detect failures on the part of their reinsureds or they run the risk of waiving any legal remedies. In relation to inspections and audits the balance is very much in the reinsurers' favour since most contracts contain an express inspection clause, and even if it does not the courts will usually imply a right of inspection. The whole concept of inspections suggests that reinsurers do not trust their clients. The case law shows that the reinsurer can copy what information it requires and it is the obligation of the reinsured to ensure that he provides the reinsurer with all of the information, which the reinsurer requires for inspection purposes. Furthermore, in recent years there has been a trend towards audits where the information gathered by the reinsurer is very detailed. However, as Gerathewohl points out in *Reinsurance Principles and Practice* it is only reasonable that the reinsured allows the reinsurer to review the business and check that everything is in order since the reinsurer does after all allow the reinsured to underwrite, cede business and adjust claims which the reinsurer will be obliged to contribute towards.

On the limitation issue, the contract may specify a shorter period of time than the statutory six years, but most contracts rely upon the six years period. The proposed changes to the limitation periods will mean that both reinsureds and reinsurers must act quickly to recover monies under their reinsurance contracts.

As companies merge or business is no longer profitable companies move into run-off. Run-off is a growth area and can be profitable business and the large number of run-off management agencies bears testimony to this fact.

A thorny issue between reinsurers and reinsureds is the jurisdictional issue. Reinsurers usually make sure that the law they wish to apply is contained in the reinsurance contract and it is up to the reinsured to bargain before agreeing to the contract terms and if the reinsurers do not get their favoured applicable law then they are keen to forum shop if a dispute does arise.

It is very clear that so much in reinsurance law depends upon the actual wording of the reinsurance contract. The huge number of cases bear testimony to the fact that reinsurance contracts are often poorly drafted, ambiguous words are very often used, conflicting clauses are included, and when disputes arise the courts frequently adopt conflicting approaches—sometimes they give words their "natural and everyday" meaning and on other occasions a technical meaning. The golden rule is for the parties to agree upon a clear and precise reinsurance wording when underwriting the business since the clearer the reinsurance contract is the less likely there will be problems at a later stage. For example, the terms, inspection rights, position regarding premiums, or the non-payment of premium, claims cooperation/claims control and claims payment, applicable jurisdiction and governing law and dispute resolution methods should be made as clear as possible and then the courts can simply give effect to the parties' agreement. However, the reality is that reinsurance underwriters are often under time pressure to accept new business and combined with internal new business (bonus driven) targets leads to underwriters accepting risks without fully understanding the terms as well as they should. Often it is weeks or even months after the business has been incepted that the reinsurer receives the contract wording, sometimes after a claim has been submitted by the reinsured for payment, and frequently the wording is unsigned with neither party really knowing what they have actually agreed to. If the parties do not actually know what they have agreed to then how is it possible for a court to interpret their intentions years later when a dispute has arisen between the parties?

It is important not to forget that reinsurers can add real value to the reinsured's claims handling. In view of the international nature of reinsurance business reinsurers regularly see losses from a wide range of jurisdictions, so if a small European reinsured has a claim in the USA/Asia or Latin America then he can look to his reinsurers for guidance on reserving, claims handling, and which loss adjusters or lawyers he should appoint. Reinsurers are also in a good position to provide reinsureds with advice on which experts to use on large claims since they may have experienced these experts "in action" in other cases. Reinsurers can also provide reinsureds with advice on rehabilitation and fraud screening since many reinsurers have specific units dealing with these topics.

Reinsurers have experience of seeing many reinsureds' claims operations in practice so can provide good advice on workflow, processes and claims handling practices. The claims review/audit by a reinsurer can provide the reinsured with peace of mind if all is well, and if it is not the reinsurer can provide constructive feedback to the reinsured which is external but not hostile.

TEST YOUR UNDERSTANDING

1. Fill in the blanks to state how a typical claims cooperation clause might read:

"Notwithstanding anything contained herein to the contrary, it is a ——— ——— to any liability under this policy that

(1) the Reinsured shall upon ——— of any loss(es) and occurrence(s) which may give rise to a claim recoverable hereunder advise the Reinsurers thereof as soon as reasonably practicable.

(2) the Reinsured shall furnish the Reinsurers with all information available respecting such loss(es) or occurrence(s) and shall co-operate with the Reinsurers in the ——— and ——— thereof."

2. In a claims control clause notification of a loss or an occurrence, which may give rise to a claim, should be advised:

(a) promptly,
(b) without delay,
(c) as soon as reasonably practicable,
(d) immediately.

3. Which of the following will not stop the limitation period from running?

(a) the commencement of court proceedings,
(b) the appointment of an arbitrator,
(c) the entering into a standstill agreement by the parties,
(d) an honourable engagement clause.

4. According to the Law Commission's proposed changes to limitation periods, how long would the Reinsured have in which to bring a claim against his reinsurers?

(a) 1 year,
(b) 3 years,
(c) 6 years,
(d) 10 years.

5. If an insured grossly exaggerates a "substantial part" of the claim, this would appear to permit the insurer to:

(a) do nothing and still pay the entire claim,
(b) refuse to pay only that part of the claim which was grossly exaggerated,
(c) to avoid the entire claim.

6. When does the duty of utmost good faith come to an end?

(a) when the proposal form has been signed and returned to the Insurer,
(b) on submission of a claim,
(c) when the Insurer rejects the claim,
(d) on commencement of court proceedings.

7. If a reinsurer suspects that there has been misrepresentation on the part of the reinsured, what should the reinsurer do first in order to protect his legal position?

(a) request further information and documentation from the reinsured,
(b) express a full, written reservation of rights to the reinsured,
(c) perform a detailed inspection of the reinsured's records,
(d) instruct outside counsel to investigate.

8. The purpose of an honourable engagement clause is to:

(a) permit any disputes between the parties to be determined by arbitrators whose decision will not be in accordance with the strict rules of law,
(b) permit any dispute to be determined by litigation applying the strict rules of law,
(c) permit any disputes to be determined by litigation applying market principles.

9. According to the ARIAS Rules, the general rule for the Tribunal is that there should be:

(a) 1 arbitrator with 5+ years' professional experience,
(b) 3 arbitrators, each with 5+ years' professional experience,
(c) 3 arbitrators, each with 10+ years' professional experience,
(d) 5 arbitrators, each with 10+ years' professional experience.

CHAPTER 8

INTERMEDIARIES

INTERMEDIARY, BROKER OR AGENT?

The description "intermediary" is usually synonymous with the concept of a third party whose role is to ensure that the parties to a contract both obtain what they want, the third party working for both parties for their joint benefit (underwriting agents are fully dealt with in Chapter 2). This explanation reflects the European or American approaches, but under English law an intermediary in its purest form is very difficult to find, because the intermediary is usually held to be the agent of one party. English reinsurance uses the words "agents" or "brokers" to reflect the rather more one-sided position. Agency is the legal relationship between two parties in which one is invested with power by the other to affect the other's legal relationship with third parties. Agency is consensual since the principal and agent must agree (by words or conduct) that the agent should act for the principal, and to all intents and purposes effectively as the principal. The relationship is almost invariably contractual, and usually the agent is intended to be paid for his services by commission, which forms part of and is usually taken out of the premium.

Agents can materialise in many forms. Until July 2001 the phrase "insurance broker" was a term of art, defined in the Insurance Brokers (Registration) Act 1977. Anyone using the term in breach of the Act committed a criminal offence. Consequently, any intermediary who chose not to register as a broker with the Insurance Brokers Registration Council would style himself a financial consultant, financial management consultant, insurance consultant, insurance adviser, tax mitigation consultant or any combination thereof. The categories of intermediary were then limited only by the ability of insurance salesmen to invent new job descriptions. The Act was repealed in July 2001 and it is currently the case that anyone can call himself an insurance broker.

Nevertheless, it is still the case that someone styling himself as a broker is (in the absence of evidence to the contrary) considered to be the agent of the party seeking the insurance and reinsurance.

The role of the reinsurance broker

The role of the reinsurance broker is dictated by the type of reinsurance in question. In facultative reinsurance he does little more than he would during "normal" insurance; in treaty reinsurance he continues to play an active part throughout the subsistence of the contract and maintains a regular dialogue with the parties. He is much more the intermediary as defined in European terms than the English broker, although he continues to act primarily on behalf of the reinsured, in whose success the reinsurance broker may be a key factor. He must understand the essential character and business of the reinsured company and assist it in preparing an effective reinsurance programme to protect it from bad underwriting or bad fortune. His relationship with the parties effectively governs their relationship, and he should be well versed in "public relations", knowing when to advise the parties to insist upon or concede an issue. The parties' best interests in treaty reinsurance lie in a long-term relationship, out of which the reinsured obtains security for the future and the reinsurer hopes to achieve a modest profit. Such a relationship depends on trust, gained through good faith and fair play. The broker can assist the business expansion of the reinsured by providing reinsurance to complement increased underwriting, or to test new areas. He must therefore obtain the best match between the parties to their mutual advantage.

In legal terms his role is substantially similar to that of an insurance broker but the fact that reinsurance broking is a separate business, carried out by a specialist department or company, indicates that it has a distinctive nature, the skills and tools of which can only be acquired by experience. Thus he must prepare a fair and substantially accurate picture of the reinsured so that the reinsurer can assess the risk properly by disclosing all material facts within his knowledge, consider the financial position of the reinsurer, and often arrange the preparation of the wording. In facultative reinsurance a policy usually remains a "slip policy", and actual policies are only issued where a foreign reinsured is required by local legislation to obtain insurance from a state owned insurer, who then reinsures in the London Market. Usually these follow the terms of the original insurance. In treaty reinsurance the broker may provide his own policy wording for adaptation, or use wordings prepared by either of the parties. As treaty reinsurance is a continuing process, the regular accounting as to the state of the reinsured is conducted by itemising claims or details of the policies allocated to the treaty on bordereaux, the extent of which are determined by the policy. In reality accounting problems occupy most of the broker's time because each party's view of the position differs, owing to delay in processing, differences in exchange rates at the relevant dates, different interpretations of accounting methods, and problems caused by other parties involved in the transaction. Into these the broker must fit suitable operating systems to ensure that all terms of trade and credit between the parties themselves and the broker are observed, whilst developing suitable management information to enable him to continue assessing the financial position of the parties for the purposes of security and claims recovery, and to apply internal policies such as a rule not to fund either party's obligations.

The reinsurance broker must maintain a thorough knowledge of markets throughout the world, based upon his dealings and perceptions of leading companies in each country, and in particular their suitability for and compatibility with the reinsured's requirements. He should know the main aspects of each country's laws, and in particular the local requirements concerning the carrying on of insurance and reinsurance. His knowledge is specialised and requires constant updating, with a view to advising reinsureds on reinsurers in any jurisdiction, and in practice reinsurers upon contracts with reinsureds similarly.

In summary, his functions are to advise the reinsured as to a suitable reinsurance programme and ways of improving its current programme, to obtain suitable reinsurers for a long term relationship on the best terms, to negotiate the terms of the reinsurance and to prepare the contract wording, or to ensure that any wording prepared by the reinsurers conforms to the agreed terms, to arrange the collection of claims and payment of premiums, to prepare any records or documentation for use by the reinsured for his accounting requirements or for renewal, and to assist the reinsured generally by using his relationship between the parties to fulfil their agreement to their mutual advantage.

One feature peculiar to reinsurance is the fact that a primary insurer may ask the broker, who has placed the risk with him, to obtain reinsurance for that risk if it cannot be fitted into his existing reinsurance arrangements. The broker therefore will act as the agent of the insured in placing the insurance, and the agent of the insurer in placing the reinsurance. This is acceptable provided that the broker's duties to his principal, the insured, do not give rise to any potential conflicts of interest. Providing the placement of the reinsurance is separate and required for proper purposes the broker need not disclose its presence to the insured.

Another anomaly which may arise is that the broker may approach a reinsurer before the primary insurance has been broked, so as to prepare a complete "package" which should make the placement of the direct insurance easier. However, the reinsured is not identified on the reinsurance slip at this stage. Of course the reinsured cannot be so identified, because it is not known whether the primary insurance will be written, or by whom, or whether the primary insurers will require reinsurance, and, if they do, whether they will accept the reinsurance terms offered by the broker, or whether the participating reinsurers will be acceptable security to the reinsureds (*Wace* v. *Pan Atlantic Group Inc* [1981] 2 Lloyd's Rep. 339, 349). The reinsurance contract is therefore created by the offer of the reinsurer and the acceptance by the reinsured/insurer falling within the category of persons anticipated by the reinsurer as offerees, who requests reinsurance after he has initialled the slip. This gives effect to the commercial intention of the transaction, the general requirement of notification of acceptance being waived by the parties (*General Accident Fire & Life Assurance Corporation* v. *Tanter, The "Zephyr"* [1984] 1 Lloyd's Rep. 58).

Whilst the above section may be a short exposition of the broker's customary role, his status and therefore his duties and obligations will depend on the authority with which he is clothed, and the capacity of the agent to bind his principal to contracts of reinsurance will depend upon the authority granted to that agent by the principal.

There are three types of authority: actual authority, which is generally a question of fact; apparent or ostensible authority, which is a matter of perception; and usual authority, which is a matter of market practice.

Actual authority

Actual authority is the authority actually given by the principal to the agent, so that where the reinsured instructs his broker to obtain reinsurance, that broker has express authority to enter into a contract of reinsurance. If that authority is circumscribed by the reinsured specifically telling the broker to obtain a particular type of reinsurance with a specified reinsurer, then the broker will have actual authority to agree with that reinsurer and nobody else. If, however, the authority is provided in general terms to the broker, then he will have both express and implied actual authority to obtain what in his opinion is the appropriate reinsurance, and will also be entitled to agree the form and content of the policy, to disclose all matters material to the risk and to provide all relevant information, and generally to do all related or incidental acts necessary to obtain a contract of reinsurance.

Apparent authority

Apparent authority will often shadow actual authority but can on occasion be considerably wider. In essence, it is the authority with which a broker is clothed when he is requested by the reinsured to take a certain course of action, such as obtaining reinsurance, and the reinsured holds the broker out as possessing the necessary authority to do so. The essence is the representation of the broker by the reinsured as having the appropriate authority to third parties such as the reinsurer.

Usual authority

Ascertaining such authority requires discussion of current practices with insurance brokers operating in the market, and considering the case law over the last two centuries. In essence it is simply the authority that an agent would usually possess, such as agreeing the terms of a policy. A broker acting as an agent of the reinsurer:

(a) cannot give credit when employed to receive premiums;
(b) cannot waive compliance with a condition where the policy makes it clear that such dispensation can only be authorised by the reinsurer;
(c) can waive a breach of condition if authorised to receive premiums and negotiate the terms of cover, provided a new contract is not formed and the reinsured is not on notice of any lack of authority;

(d) can receive notice of termination, loss or bordereaux from the reinsured;

(e) cannot terminate the contract of insurance on behalf of the reinsured, because (i) he does not act for him (*Hoffmann* v. *Economic Insurance Co.* (1956) 4 SA 380(W) and (ii) the reinsured's broker has no authority to request termination anyway (*Pacific & General Insurance Co.* v. *Hazell* [1997] L.R.L.R. 65).

Dual capacity of brokers

In some circumstances a broker may act in a dual capacity as agent for both the reinsured and the reinsurer, e.g. where the policy provides for notice of the claim to be given to the broker, who would owe a duty of care to the reinsurer to inform him of the claim, or in relation to documents engendered by the reinsurer but held by the broker. The broker may also owe other duties to the reinsurer, e.g. if an insurer relies upon the broker to introduce and monitor the activities of a coverholder in the context of a binding authority, or the broker agrees to sign down the participation of a reinsurer. However, the cardinal rule is that the broker is the agent of the party seeking insurance or reinsurance and he must not allow any other possible duty to conflict with his obligations to his primary principal. If such a conflict is perceived to exist, the broker must obtain the principal's fully informed consent to the broker acting in a dual capacity. It was suggested in *Prentis Donegan* v. *Leeds & Leeds* [1998] 2 Lloyd's Rep. 326 that brokers are "common agents". It is undoubtedly the case as a matter of general legal principle that a broker can owe duties of care to the reinsurer, and it was recognised by the Court of Appeal in *Chapman* v. *Kadirga Denizcilik ve Ticaret* [1998] L.R.L.R. 377 that some functions carried out by the broker do not sit easily within the general principle that the broker is the agent of the party seeking the insurance or reinsurance, and that a more plausible explanation in some circumstances might be that the broker is acting either in a dual capacity or as a principal in his own right, i.e. as a pure, truly independent intermediary (a possibility enunciated in print by Professor Merkin and endorsed by the court). The courts' view has traditionally been one of polarisation to prevent disputes arising where the broker is wearing two hats.

***Anglo African Merchants Ltd* v. *Bayley* [1970] 1 QB 311**
In this case the court stated that:

"In the absence of such express and fully informed consent . . . it would be a breach of duty on the part of the insurance broker so to act . . . Such a relationship with the insurer, inevitably, even if wrongly, invites the suspicion that the broker is hunting with the hounds whilst running with the hare . . . a custom will not be upheld . . . if it contradicts the vital principle that an agent may not at the same time serve two masters—two principals—in actual or potential opposition to one another: unless, indeed, he has the explicit, informed consent of both principals."

***North & South Trust Co.* v. *Berkeley* [1971] 1 W.L.R. 470**
However, in *North & South Trust Co.* the court held that such a breach of duty did not entitle the insured to insist that the brokers were bound to disclose any information obtained in breach of duty, including information which had been obtained by the brokers on terms that it be kept confidential from the insured. The insured had a legitimate complaint and could claim damages from the broker for loss caused by the conflict of interest, but could not see the documentation held by the brokers.

The upshot of these cases is that a court continues to take a very dim view of a broker who acts for two parties *where their interests may conflict* (without their explicit and fully informed consent to do so) and usually will prefer to find that the broker acts for one party only. The issue often arises in the context of information given to the broker as agent for one party, and as to whether that information can also be attributed to a party for whom that broker also acts (see below).

Why it matters to the broker

The actions of a broker will be circumscribed by the type and extent of the authority under which they fall and disputes often arise as to the nature and extent of his authority, for example because the boundaries of his actual authority may not have been clearly identified by the reinsured, or the usual debate about what is sufficiently certain to be a feature of market practice (and therefore the broker's usual authority) rears its head.

The nature or indeed absence of authority defines or limits the nature and extent of their dealings. Where the agent has no authority or it is deficient in a material way there may be a claim against him by the reinsurer—i.e. not the party for whom the broker is acting—for failing to place valid reinsurance and for which the reinsurer would have been paid premium, known as an action for breach of warranty of authority.

***Collen* v. *Wright* (1857) E.L. & B.L. 622**
This case established the principle that an agent acting without deceit or fraud who purported to incur liability on behalf of his principal, but actually failed to do so, was liable on an implied but separate warranty of authority. Thus an agent who attempted to bind his "principal", the reinsured, to a contract of reinsurance but does not have the appropriate authority to do so may be liable to the reinsurer for the premium. An agent acting fraudulently can be sued in tort for deceit or in contract for breach of warranty of authority (*Lewis* v. *Nicholson* (1852) 18 Q.B. 503, 511). The latter course is usually more certain since the burden of proof is lower, and is therefore to be preferred, although an action founded in deceit may be better rewarded, since a finding in deceit may carry with it some moral obloquy and censure in the form of higher damages.

The liability for breach of warranty of authority is strict and does not depend on deceit or negligence. In the absence of another's negligence, deceit or fraud, it is only right that the liability should fall on the party who represents his authority as being complete, and that he is capable of rendering his principal liable to the third party, if such representation is incapable of being sustained and therefore occasions a loss on the part of the third party. It may not be his fault, but then neither is it the fault of the third party, who may be worse placed to confirm such authority and is under no duty to enquire as to the extent of the authority. The fact that it is warranted is sufficient. The immutability of strict liability may give rise to legal decisions which appear to be harsh, in that the broker may not be negligent, but then neither is the third party. Thus, a broker who warrants that he is capable of negotiating an agreement on behalf of his principal to give rise to a binding contract must warrant that the principal is competent to contract. In the absence of such capacity on the principal's part, e.g. for insanity (*Yonge* v. *Toynbee* [1910] 1 K.B. 215), death (*Smout* v. *Ilbery* (1842) 10 M. & W.), lack of juristic capacity (e.g. after dissolution of a company—*Salton* v. *New Beeston* [1900] 1 Ch. 43, or appointment of a receiver or provisional receiver—*Pacific & General Insurance Co.* v. *Hazell* [1997] L.R.L.R. 65), the broker breaks his warranty of authority. Negligence is, however, not required to found an action against the agent (*Yonge* v. *Toynbee* [1910] 1 K.B. 215).

Ways around the warranty

(a) A disclaimer by the broker or sufficient action by words or conduct by the broker or another should negative the warranty, although one wonders why a reinsurer should attempt to agree a contract with a broker who is acting without authority, unless the broker agrees to obtain authority (*Halbot* v. *Lens* [1901] 1 Ch. 344).

(b) Ratification by the reinsured—the process whereby the reinsured agrees by words or conduct that the contract will be binding upon him, despite the broker's lack of authority—will usually mean that the reinsurer suffers no loss because the premium is payable and therefore that no claim for breach of warranty can be made by the reinsurer against the broker. Similarly, one might think that the reinsured cannot make any substantive claim against the broker, having ratified his action.

However, in some instances the reinsured's ratification may not be fully voluntary, and may have been effected for commercial convenience or to protect his reputation, in which case the reinsured may be able to argue that he has not waived his broker's breach to the extent that not only should the commission not be paid to the broker, but he may also have a claim in damages against the broker for the full amount of the premium. The former possibility is rendered tortuous by virtue of the fact that the broker is usually paid by the reinsurer (see below), and the reinsured (theoretically) pays nothing in any event; no legal authority is known which enables the reinsured to obtain the broker's commission in such circumstances. The matter was touched on in *Great Atlantic Insurance Co.* v. *Home Insurance Co.* [1981] 2 Lloyd's Rep. 219 where Lloyd J. commented that: "If the principal has held out his agent as having a certain authority, it hardly lies in his mouth to blame the agent for acting in breach of a secret limitation placed on that authority." The inference is that a ratification which must be made by the reinsured must also negate any claim by the principal against the broker, even though it may have been involuntary owing to commercial pressure. However, in principle there seems to be no reason why an agent with apparent power to bind the reinsured should not be liable to the reinsured if the reinsured had forbidden him to use his apparent authority, i.e. restricting his actual authority, and the same must be true of ratification out of commercial necessity, a proposition endorsed by Waller J. in *Suncorp* v. *Milano* (at p. 235).

***Suncorp Insurance* v. *Milano Assicurazioni SpA* [1993] 2 Lloyd's Rep. 225**

In *Suncorp* v. *Milano* Milano took a 20% actual participation in a pool but did not sign a fronting agreement. The underwriting agent of the pool used Milano as a fronting insurer for 32.5%, to disguise the somewhat less satisfactory nature of certain pool members, whose security probably would not have been acceptable. Suncorp sued Milano for their 32.5% fronted line, rather than their 20% actual line. Waller J. took the view that *Great Atlantic* does not assist in a situation where commercial pressures impact upon the principal's decision to ratify but that in *Great Atlantic* the principal had not preserved its position against the broker. He suggested that the test fell into two parts: *has the principal ratified and has he waived the agent's breach of duty?* He accepted, however, that "Often the facts will lead to both ratification and exoneration, but not always".

***National Insurance and Guarantee Corporation plc* v. *Imperio Reinsurance Company (UK) Ltd and Russell Tudor-Price & Company Limited* [1999] Lloyd's Rep. IR 249**

Colman J. was more stringent in this case, where he commented that Waller's analysis was "strictly obiter, but . . . persuasive . . . I would only add that . . . investigation of whether the principal has ratified the contract so as to cause it to be binding as between him and a third party would not be directly relevant because the essential enquiry is not whether the conduct had that effect but whether it amounted to a waiver of the agent's breach of duty". "There will no doubt be many cases where the conduct by which the contract is ratified evidences not merely an intention to be bound by it but also a representation that 'the principal' releases the agent from claims in respect of the contract . . . *There may, however, be more complex cases where, although 'the principal' is prepared to treat the contract as binding on him, the agent would not be entitled to assume from such conduct that the principal was thereby releasing him from all claims. Were the position otherwise, ratification would operate as a shield for professional agents which could be justified neither conceptually nor as a matter of justice.*" Given the courts' ability to apportion the loss it will rarely be the case that the reinsured should bear all of the loss arising from the defect in cover, although conceptually there may be no difference between a contract formed through a valid and proper agency and one made valid and proper through the medium of ratification. The reinsured, after all, in the absence of other commercial pressure does not actually have to commit himself to the contract of reinsurance, and if he does so then arguably any problems that may arise that would not in the absence of ratification be attributable to the broker should not be so attributed merely through the insured's ratification. This area is still capable of judicial refinement.

Imputation

When and how does information known by the broker effectively become that of the reinsured, and what obligations is he under to the parties? (see Chapter 2).

Section 19 of the Marine Insurance Act states that the agent must disclose:

(a) Every material circumstance which is known to himself, and an agent to insure is deemed to know every circumstance which in the ordinary course of business ought to be known by, or to have been communicated to, him; and
(b) Every material circumstance which the insured is bound to disclose, unless it come to his knowledge too late to communicate it to the agent.

Section 19 was designed to oblige an agent to disclose any facts to an insurer or reinsurer which the agent knew but which might not be known by the insured or reinsured. It did not necessarily place a liability upon the agent *to the reinsurer* for any failure to do so. It simply meant that the reinsured could not state that he had disclosed every aspect simply by pointing to the fact that he was not aware of a material fact but that his agent was. A breach by the broker of section 19 which results in avoidance will mean that he will usually be liable to the reinsured, not the reinsurer. However, it is clear from *Pryke* v. *Gibbs Hartley Cooper* [1991] 1 Lloyd's Rep. 602 that the broker may well fall under a personal responsibility to reinsurers where he misrepresents the position effectively on his own behalf and clearly without any authority from the reinsured, as distinct from a misrepresentation emanating from the reinsured. Waller J. said "it seems to me that section 19 of the Marine Insurance Act certainly supports the view that a broker has a personal responsibility in the insurance market. Furthermore, there is no reason why on the principles of *Hedley Byrne* v. *Heller* why the broker should not be personally liable in relation to any negligent misrepresentation . . . Thus the practice in the market . . . for brokers to disclose material facts . . . would seem to me to be one that almost certainly would follow naturally and properly from the way in which negotiations take place; and furthermore, brokers might themselves be personally liable in damages for any failure in that regard".

It may be the case, therefore, that the non-disclosure, or more likely the misrepresentation, will need to have emanated from the brokers "off their own bat" before giving rise to liability to the reinsurer, i.e. it is something that they have mentioned independently and on their own behalf to the reinsurer, amounting to an assumption of responsibility. Thus a clear endorsement of the reinsured, such as his solvency and excellent risk management techniques, which the reinsured would not himself rate in such glowing terms, amounting to an active misrepresentation, could lead to the broker being liable to the reinsurer. The possibility that the broker would be liable for a simple non-disclosure is, following *HIH Casualty and General Insurance Ltd* v. *Chase Manhattan Bank* [2003] Lloyd's Rep. IR 230, no longer likely. The problem with this analysis is that if the representation falls within the broker's ostensible or usual authority, then it is effectively made on behalf of the reinsured; where it does not and the reinsurer knows this, then the broker can simply state that the knowledge of the reinsurer means that he is not entitled to rely on it.

Given that the only remedy is avoidance a broker cannot, however, be liable to the reinsurer for pure non-disclosure (i.e. in the absence of allegations of deceit or misrepresentation), following *HIH Casualty and General Insurance Ltd* v. *Chase Manhattan Bank*, so that the last suggestion of Waller J. is unlikely to be upheld.

Where the agent effects the reinsurance, his knowledge in so doing in most cases is imputed to his principal, the reinsured, and vice versa, whether or not the knowledge was actually passed from one to the other. The reinsured will therefore be estopped from denying that he was aware of the information, provided that the broker obtains the information in his capacity as broker for that reinsured during the relevant transaction.

***Blackburn, Low & Co.* v. *Haslam* (1888) 21 Q.B.D. 144**
In this case the claimant underwriters in Glasgow employed a local firm of insurance brokers to reinsure a ship which was overdue. The Glasgow brokers received information that the ship had been lost. This information, however, was given in confidence, and so was not communicated by the Glasgow brokers to their client underwriters. The Glasgow brokers telegraphed instructions (in the name of the claimant underwriters and with no mention of the loss) to their London agents to insure the vessel, who replied with the relevant premium rates to the claimant underwriters, who then carried on the telegraphic discussion. The London agents then placed the reinsurance. It was held that there had been merely a handing over of the negotiations by the Glasgow brokers to their London agents, and therefore the non-disclosure by the Glasgow brokers of the loss of the ship was non-disclosure by the claimant underwriters, and the reinsurance was voidable at the instance of the reinsurers.

***Blackburn Low & Co.* v. *Vigors* (1887) 12 App. Cas. 531**
The above case should be contrasted with the earlier case of *Blackburn Low & Co.* v. *Vigors* (1887) 12 App. Cas. 531, arising out of the same facts save that the claimant underwriters instructed another broker to insure the same overdue ship, which (without either the new agent or the claimant underwriters being aware of the loss) he effected with different reinsurers. Both the claimants and the actual placing broker acted in good faith, and the question was whether the knowledge of the first broker would be imputed to the claimants, thereby enabling the defendants to avoid the policy on the ground of non-disclosure of material information. The House of Lords decided that the policy could not be avoided because the authority of the first broker had ended before the reinsurance in question had been effected, and thus only the knowledge of the broker who actually effected the reinsurance could be imputed to the claimants; and he was unaware of the information material to the risk. The distinction drawn between the two cases is that the transaction was seamless in *Haslam* but separate in *Vigors*. These cases provide the rationale for section 19 of the Marine

Insurance Act 1906. If the broker obtains information material to the risk whilst acting as agent for the reinsured, and prior to the conclusion of a contract of reinsurance, it is his duty under section 19 to disclose it to the reinsurer. Any failure to do so will enable the reinsurer to avoid, and the broker's reason for not disclosing it is irrelevant.

***SAIL* v. *Farex* [1995] L.R.L.R. 116**

SAIL had acted as agents for an insurer seeking reinsurance and engaged London brokers to arrange a facultative reinsurance facility. The brokers approached a reinsurance company which initially declined but whose manager of its international facultative department agreed in principle to share in retrocession cover if another reputable reinsurer could be found and interposed as reinsurer between the insurer and itself as retrocessionnaire. The brokers then placed this package using an appropriate reinsurer. The retrocessionnaire later claimed that it was entitled to repudiate liability on the grounds that its manager had no authority to bind it, and that this had been known to the brokers.

One contention made by the reinsurer was that if the retrocessionaire's allegations were true, the brokers had known that there was no effective retrocession agreement and should, as agent for SAIL, have disclosed this fact to the reinsurer in relation to the reinsurance contracts. SAIL contended, however, that any knowledge that there was no effective retrocession agreement had been acquired by the brokers in the capacity of the reinsurer's agents to obtain the retrocession cover, and not as agents for SAIL.

One of the issues, therefore, which the court had to determine was whether there had been non-disclosure as to the invalidity of the retrocession. The Court of Appeal held that in placing the retrocession the broker was acting as agent for the reinsurer and not for SAIL. Even if the broker had been aware that the retrocession was invalid, this knowledge would not be imputed to SAIL and SAIL had therefore not failed to make full disclosure. Thus, information acquired by a broker acting for a reinsurer is not acquired also in its capacity as agent for the insurer, despite the clear relationship between the two contracts and the fact that reinsurance cover is often sold at the same time as request for the original cover. Knowledge can only be imputed where the agent is under a duty to its principal either to disclose it to that principal, or where the relationship between principal and agent is so close that it can only be concluded that the agent's knowledge is also that of the principal.

Is the broker's knowledge imputed to the reinsured?

One central argument of *Deutsche Ruck* v. *Walbrook Insurance Co. Limited* [1994] 4 All E.R. 181 (and its associated litigation) concerned the juristic basis for the attribution of knowledge from the broker to the reinsured, namely whether the agent owes an obligation to disclose all material facts within his knowledge or because the knowledge of the agent is imputed to his principal. It may seem to be an issue of little significance but its resolution affects the application of an exception to the rule whereby the agent's knowledge is imputed to his principal: the rule in *In Re Hampshire Land* [1894] 2 Ch. 632, which obviously would not apply as an exception if the juristic rationale were the obligation to disclose all material facts. The argument occupied the minds and time of two Commercial Court judges and three lords justice, the primary issue concerning the nature and extent of the speech of Lord Macnaghten in

Blackburn Low & Co. v. *Vigors*, and in particular whether it was a minority view. Lord Macnaghten railed against the imputation argument in favour of the obligation to disclose, an analysis of the law rejected by Phillips J. in *Deutsche Ruck* v. *Walbrook*—which analysis was itself rejected by Dillon and Hoffmann L.JJ. in *SAIL* (pp. 142 and 150 respectively) where the latter said:

"... I think that Lord Macnaghten was right. His analysis is supported by the structure of the Marine Insurance Act 1906, which distinguishes between the duty of the insured in s18 to disclose matters within his knowledge and the duty of the agent in s19 to disclose matters within his. The latter section would not have been necessary if the knowledge of the agent was imputed to the insured. It is also supported by the actual decision in *Blackburn* in which the knowledge of an agent was *not* imputed to the insured because, although he had acted on behalf of the insured, he had not actually concluded the contract ... it makes much more sense to adopt Lord Macnaghten's analysis."

Further endorsement was supplied by Staughton L.J. in *PCW Syndicates* v. *PCW Reinsurance* [1996] 1 W.L.R. 1136 where he pithily commented that "What in my judgment is clear is that section 19 enacted Lord Macnaghten's view. Since in the present case it is agreed that the Act has the same effect as the common law, we are presumably entitled to conclude that Lord Macnaghten's view was the common law".

***Simner* v. *New India Assurance Co. Limited* [1995] L.R.L.R. 240**

The subject of imputed knowledge was considered in *Simner*, in which the reinsured, a Lloyd's syndicate, instituted proceedings against the reinsurer, New India, under a stop loss reinsurance agreement. The original policy underwritten by the Lloyd's syndicate was a participation in a binding authority. Prior to agreeing in June 1990 to participate in the binding authority, the syndicate was informed that there were no loss statistics available as the scheme was a new one. The Syndicate did not request further information before signing the slip in July 1990 and was not informed that an ominous level of claims had become apparent by this date. Instructions were given to its broker by the syndicate to place the stop loss reinsurance soon after its acceptance of the share of the original policy, who were told that there were no claims figures. The reinsurer signed the reinsurance slip in August 1990 although various amendments were made and initialled by the reinsurer during the following month.

By early September 1990 it became clear that substantial claims had been submitted under the binding authority. The [different] broker who had placed the binding authority had become aware in early June that a larger than anticipated number of claims had been received, but this fact had been disclosed neither to the syndicate nor, given the syndicate's lack of knowledge, to the reinsurer New India. By March 1991 the syndicate's losses were considerable. Shortly afterwards, the reinsurer purported to avoid the stop loss reinsurance on the basis of misrepresentation and non-disclosure.

The deputy judge held that there had not been any misrepresentation by the Lloyd's syndicate. The allegations of non-disclosure related primarily to the up-to-date claims figures and the amount of premium received. It was common ground that these matters were material. The facts were not actually known to the syndicate or to its brokers when the reinsurance slip was presented to and signed by the reinsurer, but were in the possession of the broker of the original insurance binding authority. The reinsurer, nonetheless, claimed that knowledge of these facts should be imputed to the syndicate.

Two alternative arguments were advanced with regard to the alleged imputed knowledge of the syndicate:

(a) the broker of the original insurance binding authority was the agent of the syndicate to receive information on these matters, and his knowledge was to be imputed to the syndicate; or
(b) the syndicate had delegated the entire management of the binding authority to the broker of the original insurance binding authority, so that his knowledge was to be imputed to the syndicate.

The deputy judge held that there were three situations in which the knowledge of an agent is deemed to be the knowledge of the insured:

(a) Where the insured relies upon a particular agent for information as to the risk, the insured is deemed to know any information which ought to have been communicated to him by the agent in the ordinary course of business (approved in *Blackburn Low & Co.* v. *Vigors* subject to the proviso that it applies only to a category of agent described as an "agent to know", and not to all agents without restriction). The court commented that: "It should be noted that the principle, as . . . explained by Lord Watson [in *Blackburn Low* v. *Vigors*], is not strictly a case where the knowledge of the agent is imputed to the assured. The principle is rather different, namely that both parties contract on the basis that the assured has disclosed both material facts within his knowledge and also material facts that would have been within his knowledge if the agents whom he employed to provide knowledge of the subject matter of the insurance, or in the ordinary course of his business ought to have employed, had communicated to the assured in ordinary course such facts as the agents knew or ought to have known in the ordinary course of business."
(b) Where the agent can be regarded as being in such a predominant position in relation to the insured that his knowledge can be regarded as being that of the insured. One illustration of this possibility is the situation where the agent is a director of the insured company.
(c) Where the agent places insurance on behalf of the insured, the agent is required to disclose to the insurer all information in his possession including "every circumstance which ought to be known by, or communicated to him under section 19 of the Marine Insurance Act 1906".

On the facts, the reinsurer had to argue that the broker of the original insurance binding authority was the agent of the syndicate in the sense described in (a) above, i.e. that the syndicate had relied upon the original broker for information and was accordingly deemed to know the information in that broker's possession. The deputy judge held that the administration of the binding authority was set out in the binding authority and placed in the hands of the original broker, whose obligation was to report to the leading underwriter and not to the syndicate itself as part of the following market: this claims reporting procedure was typical in the Lloyd's market. There was no evidence that either the loss adjuster who handled the claims or the leading underwriter had any duty to forward information to the syndicate and the *Blackburn Low* principle was, therefore, inapplicable.

The reinsurer further submitted that the original broker was a general agent of the syndicate because the syndicate had delegated the whole management of the business connected with the binding authority so that the claims reporting provisions were not definitive as to the facts which the syndicate was deemed to know in the ordinary course of business, but the deputy judge held that the syndicate had not delegated any general underwriting or other decisions to the original broker, so that the limited nature of the agency meant that the original broker was not in a predominant position as regards the syndicate. The knowledge of the original broker could not, therefore, be imputed to the syndicate.

The impact of fraud by an agent

The effect of fraud on the insured's contracts was considered in *Deutsche Ruck* v. *Walbrook Insurance Co. Ltd* [1994] 4 All E.R. 181 and associated litigation (*PCW Syndicates* v. *PCW Reinsurers* [1996] 1 Lloyd's Law Rep. 241; *Group Josi Re* v. *Walbrook* [1996] 1 Lloyd's Law Rep. 345). The reinsurers purported to avoid certain reinsurance contracts on the grounds of misrepresentation and/or non-disclosure based upon a report of inspectors appointed by the Department of Trade and Industry to investigate the reinsured's holding company. The material sections of the report found that three directors of the holding company, who were also directors of the reinsured and related companies which had underwritten the original business on behalf of the reinsured and had arranged the reinsurance of that business with the reinsurer, had improperly diverted overriding commissions from the reinsured to other companies controlled by those directors. The reinsurers' case was that the three directors had acted fraudulently in misappropriating the overriding commissions which should have been credited to the reinsured; that this fraudulent conduct was a material fact, that knowledge of this conduct was to be imputed to each of the reinsured companies because the directors concerned were the directing minds of those companies in relation to reinsurance and that, accordingly, those companies were obliged to disclose such conduct to the reinsurers; and that the directors themselves, as the agents placing the reinsurances on behalf of the reinsured, were obliged to disclose all material facts within their knowledge, including the fact of their own fraudulent conduct.

Phillips J. had two options. He could apply the rule in *Fitzherbert* v. *Mather* (1785) 14 East 494 that where an agent's fraud, default or wrongdoing caused loss or prejudice to two parties, the loss or prejudice should fall on the party by whom the agent was trusted or employed or who took the risk of the agent's wrongdoing, or the rule in *In Re Hampshire Land* [1896] 2 Ch. 743 whereby the knowledge of any fraud of an agent against his principal will not be imputed to the principal. The judge, although incorrectly deciding that the method of transferring knowledge was through imputation from agent to principal, considered that any fraud having a direct impact on an insured risk should be subject to the rule in *Fitzherbert*, but that the knowledge of the directors was *not* to be imputed to the reinsured in circumstances where the fraud is indicative of the moral hazard. It was "an affront to common sense that the cover of the insured or reinsured should be at risk because of failure to disclose a fraud committed on itself of which only the fraudster was aware", i.e. the rule in *In Re Hampshire Land*.

The Court of Appeal subsequently made it clear that the rule in *In Re Hampshire Land* would be applied, to the effect that *any imputation of information from an agent to his principal is negated when that agent has acted fraudulently against his principal*; an agent was acting on his own behalf when he effected a fraud on his principal (*PCW Syndicates* v. *PCW Insurers* [1996] 1 All E.R. 774). Further, where the agent has not carried out any fraud but rather the lower sin of misconduct directed against the reinsured, there will again not be any imputation of the knowledge of that misconduct to the reinsured (*Kingscroft Insurance Co. Ltd* v. *Nissan Fire & Marine Insurance Co. Ltd* [1999] Lloyd's Rep. IR 371). Equally any attempt by the agent to defraud reinsurers will not taint the reinsured by imputation, and the rule will apply to normal principles of attribution, so that the failure of the managing director of the insured to disclose previous fraud to insurers would not affect the rights of the insured company (*Arab Bank plc* v. *Zurich Insurance Co.* [1999] 1 Lloyd's Rep. 262).

The other contribution made by the PCW trilogy of cases, *Sail* v. *Farex* and *Simner* v. *New India* is the further categorisation by capacity of agents acting for the insured. Section 19(a) clearly refers to an "agent to insure", which would not include an underwriting agency responsible for obtaining insurance but not for actually placing it, or where the part played by the agent was so small that its role limited the transfer of its knowledge to the insured. "Agents to insure" are clearly caught by section 19, but intermediate agents or "agents to inform" are not. The obligations *vis-à-vis* the reinsurer and reinsured are not affected by this distinction because "The agents will either be agents to insure under that section [19], and thus will have to disclose material circumstances within their knowledge, or will be intermediaries, in which event the agent to insure will be deemed to know material circumstances which ought in the ordinary course of business to be communicated to them" (*Group Josi* v. *Walbrook*) so that a producing broker would be obliged to pass on material information to the placing broker and the insurer could avoid if it were not disclosed to him.

If the broker is acting for the reinsurer, any knowledge acquired by him within his authority to acquire such knowledge will be imputed to the reinsurer. Knowledge acquired prior to his employment by the reinsurer or in another capacity is irrelevant. In *Wilkinson* v. *General Accident Fire & Life Assurance Corp Ltd* [1967] Lloyd's Rep. 182 the agent acquired knowledge of the sale of a car as a car dealer and not as agent for the insurer, and therefore the knowledge could not be imputed to him as agent of the insurer when he also effected the insurance. However, an exception was outlined in *Taylor* v. *Yorkshire Insurance Co. Ltd* (1913) 2 I.R. 1, 21 where the agent's position and relationship with his principal enabled previously obtained information to be imputed where the agent was "an agent to know". It will be relatively rare, however, for the broker to act as the agent of the reinsurer when it is being placed, unless perhaps the broker has a binding authority from the reinsurer to effect the reinsurance.

OBLIGATIONS

Duties of brokers

(a) A duty to exercise reasonable skill and care and to act honestly

Whatever the nature of the authority conferred upon the broker (however derived from the instructions from the reinsured), the broker is always under a duty to use reasonable skill and care in the execution of the contract and agency to a standard ordinarily exercised by reasonably competent insurance brokers. This obligation, if not expressed, is implied at common law and by section 13 of the Supply of Goods and Services Act 1982. The question that is immediately raised is whether or not the standard of care owed by a broker differs according to the apparent quality of its operation, i.e. is a reinsured entitled to expect a higher quality of service from a mega-broker in the London market than a small broker in Doncaster? The short answer is that the English courts have taken a realistic approach and have generally applied a lower standard of care to, for example, a provincial broker than to a London specialist, but there has to be some standard and that still remains at least that of the broker practising in the relevant area. In *NRG* v. *Bacon & Woodrow* [1997] L.R.L.R. 744 the court held that any professional person undertaking professional responsibility effectively represents that he has the necessary professional ability to carry that out—"the standard of care to be expected is to be measured by a reference to the quality of work reasonably to be expected from a professional firm or organisation possessed of the skills which by undertaking the work in question that firm or organisation has warranted that it has. If the skill that is warranted is a specialist skill, that client is entitled to the standard of work reasonably to be expected of a specialist professionally possessed of that skill." Thus a reinsured is entitled to a higher standard of care from a London market broker specialising in the relevant area than to another entity in the provinces which does not profess to have the appropriate professional skills.

An interesting side effect of this proposition that will work to the detriment of the reinsured is that the position of the reinsured as a professional working in the same market as the broker may give rise to a form of duty to the broker in the sense that where the broker is professionally negligent, the reinsured may not recover the full amount of any gross sum awarded in principle by a court on the basis that the reinsured may have negligently contributed to his own loss. In the *Superhulls* case ([1990] 2 Lloyd's Rep. 431) the judge allowed the brokers' claim of contributory negligence, holding that the reinsured would have queried the clause with the brokers had the reinsured exercised reasonable skill and care in conducting their business. The liability was apportioned between them, but substantially in the insurer's favour, with the brokers being liable for 80% of the damage.

(b) Duty not to disclose confidential information

The broker is under a clear duty not to disclose any information confidential to his principal to any other party save at Lloyd's where he is under a requirement to report misconduct to the Head of the Regulatory Department under Byelaws No. 5 of 1983 and No. 11 of 1989. Where the broker believes that his client is effecting or involved in a fraud, such as inflating stock figures in relation to a fire policy, then he is not obliged to report the suspected fraud but should take all necessary steps to disassociate himself from that fraud. If he suspects fraud and remains involved, then he may be subject to civil and criminal liability under the Theft Act 1968 and the Prevention of Corruption Act 1986. Where he takes steps to expose fraud, he will be protected from any action for breach of confidence by the reinsured where exposing such misconduct is in the public interest. The broker, in exposing any suspected fraud, should have good grounds for so doing in order to avoid any claim for defamation or malicious falsehood.

(c) A duty to account

This obligation on the broker as a fiduciary falls into two sub-divisions: an obligation to declare all monies received and to account for monies spent or disposed of, and a duty not to make secret profit.

(d) Documentation

The rights of the reinsurer to documents held by the broker

It is often the case that the broker holds documentation which may be of assistance to one party, and detrimental to the other, particularly since the reinsurer rarely retains a detailed file. Upon notification of a claim the reinsurer may wish to re-evaluate the information provided by the broker on behalf of the reinsured when the risk was accepted, the drafts of the slip or policy wording as evidence of the parties' intentions and expectations, and any inconsistencies with the reinsured's current stance, and evidence as to any admission by the reinsured. However, the only documents to which the reinsurer may have unrestricted access in the placing file are the initialled slip and policy wording, and as a matter of market practice those documents used by the broker in his presentation to that reinsurer at placing. The reinsurer has no right to see other documentation in the file where it clearly relates to work done by the broker as agent for the reinsured, and if the broker hands it over without authority to do so from the reinsured, he will be in breach of his duty of confidentiality. In *Goshawk Dedicated Ltd* v. *Tyser & Co. Ltd* [2006] 2 All E.R. (Comm) 115 the court held that (in the absence of express authority to the contrary) the broker should not hand over documents retained by the broker; the insurer does not own the document or the information it contains, the action of handing the documents back to the broker does not constitute the broker as trustee or place him in any fiduciary relationship with the insurer, and no contact can be inferred from the circumstances because neither party would "naturally regard themselves as entering into a contract". It also found that the practice, despite all its habitual adherence by the market, was not sufficiently clear, invariable, well known and reasonable to found a custom; the last aspect having more credibility than the others on the basis that a custom which is inconsistent with the instructions or best interests of the broker's clients is unreasonable and unenforceable. The matter was appealed and the Court of Appeal reversed the decision. Insurers' arguments were put on a different basis, namely that there was an implied term in the contract of insurance which entitled insurers to call from the brokers and reinspect those documents which they had seen on placing and which had been retained by the brokers, and the court agreed that the insurers could not safely operate the policy otherwise. There is no obligation to provide documents which the insurer has retained, and the broker is not obliged to hand back any documents that it has not retained. Bizarrely, the insurers do not appear to have any rights in respect of the documents which the broker has given back to the insured. The only obligation on the insured is an implied term that he will authorise the broker to release those documents which the broker has retained. In the absence of the reinsured's consent the reinsurer will have to wait until litigation and disclosure before seeing other documentation. The obvious exception to this rule will occur where the broker has acted for the reinsurer in any capacity, e.g. where he holds a binding authority from the reinsurer, in which case some documents may be the property of the reinsurer, or in respect of information obtained by the broker on behalf of the reinsurer which is the property of the reinsurer, such as loss adjusters' or solicitors' reports. If such documents exist, the broker is placed in an invidious position largely of his own making, and he must minimise any conflict of interest, either by ceasing to assist the reinsurer in the handling of the claim or removing himself altogether where he has obtained confidential information as agent for the reinsurer which should be disclosed to the reinsured but cannot, since to do so would be to break the duty of confidentiality which he has assumed to the reinsurer. Such documents should not be sent to the reinsurer via the broker where the information contained is detrimental to the reinsured, particularly at Lloyd's.

The rights of the reinsured to documents held by the broker

The reinsured will have a strong *prima facie* case to the production of all documents held by the broker on the basis that the broker is his agent and that the documents therefore belong to the reinsured. The reinsured is entitled to see the placing file of his broker, although he does not have a right to see its entire contents; attendance notes of conversations or meetings, internal memoranda, draft slips and wordings, and internal accounting documents are deemed to be the broker's own documents, made for the benefit of the broker "in carrying out his expert work" (*Leicestershire CC* v. *Michael Faraday & Partners Ltd* [1941] 2 K.B. 205, 216); the relationship being not just that of principal and agent but more particularly that of a client and his professional adviser. They need not be handed over (unless they formed part of the broker's presentation to the reinsurer—*Formica Limited* v. *ECGD* [1995] 1 Lloyd's Rep. 692, 703), although they may be subjected to a witness summons (previously a *subpoena duces tecum*) for production at trial. Documents provided to the broker by the reinsured, and carbon copies of letters to third parties or the reinsured belong to the reinsured. In particular the broker is obliged to hand over records of transactions into which he has entered on behalf of the reinsured.

***Yasuda Limited* v. *Orion Underwriting Limited* [1995] 1 Lloyd's Rep. 525**

In *Yasuda* the defendants acted as underwriting agents for the claimant under various underwriting agency agreements. For practical reasons these agreements provided that although all records were to be the property of the underwriting agent, the claimant was entitled to inspect and take copies of "all necessary books, accounts, records and other documentation". Following termination of the contract the underwriting agent refused the claimant access to any documents. Having held that there existed an agency at common law, and that contract merely supplemented this, Colman J. stated (at p. 530):

"The nature of the defendant's mandate was such that, subject to express qualification by the terms of any agency agreement, they were in the course that the agency clearly had a general duty to keep and provide records of all the transactions into which they had entered on behalf of the claimant including those which were in the process of being run-off . . . The nature of the duty to keep and provide records in such a case would, by necessary implication, involve full disclosure of records of all transactions and the current state of premium, outstanding claims and reinsurance protection in relation to each.

That obligation to provide an accurate account in the fullest sense arises by reason of the fact that the agent has been entrusted with the authority to bind the principal to transactions with third parties and the principal is entitled to know what his personal contractual rights and duties are in relation to those third parties as well as what he is entitled to receive by way of payment from the agent. He is entitled to be provided with those records because they have been created for preserving information as the two very transactions which the agent was authorised by him to enter into. Being the participant in the transactions, the principal is entitled to the records of them . . .

. . . the agent's duty to provide records of transactions to the principal is founded on the entitlement of the principal to the records of what has been done in his name . . . ."

Reinsurers' rights to documents generated by the reinsured

Although the interests of insurer and reinsurer potentially conflict, and reinsurers' interests differ amongst themselves, for practical purposes an insurer in handling the original claim is acting for himself and his reinsurer where the latter is obliged to follow his settlements. There is therefore a common interest in the investigation and defence of the original claim. This community of interest means that insurers cannot withhold from reinsurers documents brought into existence for the purposes of handling the original claim. This right is contractual; if the reinsurer avoids the contract he will retain the common interest but will have no contractual platform for his claim to the documents (which itself may dispose of the commonality of interest) and his application for their disclosure will fail (*Commercial Union* v. *Mander* [1996] 2 Lloyd's Rep. 640). Reinsurers would not be so blighted had they obtained the documents prior to their election to avoid having first reserved their rights, or alternatively they could run the risk that obtaining the documents constitutes an affirmation of the reinsurance and rely upon *Strive Shipping Corporation* v. *Hellenic, The "Grecia Express"* [2002] Lloyd's Rep. IR 669, to the effect that the right to see such documents is an ancillary term of the contract and that its implementation should not constitute an affirmation.

However, in *GRE* v. *Charman* [1992] 2 Lloyd's Rep. 607 there was no express claims cooperation or control obligation and the court could find no authority for the reinsurer's argument that it was entitled to receive from the reinsured sufficient information and documents to demonstrate that the reinsured was entitled to seek an indemnity. However, the court was prepared to assume that a reinsurer would be entitled to information and documents showing the claim by the assured, how the claim was dealt with, and answers to other relevant questions which might enable the reinsurers to contend that the claim was not settled in a business-like fashion. Curiously, reinsurers were not entitled to answers to questions necessary to satisfy them that the claim had been properly adjusted and settled. This finding was made without the benefit of tested evidence at full trial and is therefore capable of refinement.

A reinsurer or retrocessionnaire would be entitled to see documentation in one of three ways:

(a) First, through the enforcement of a contractual term giving him such rights. In the absence of an express inspection provision one will be implied, but generally it would exist to provide the reinsurer with protection against "dumping" or anti-selection, and against what would otherwise be an unilateral assertion by the reinsured as to the reinsurer's obligation to indemnify. In *Phoenix General Insurance Co. of Greece SA* v. *Halvanon Insurance Co. Ltd* [1988] Q.B. 216 the court held that a facultative/obligatory treaty contained various implied terms, including to:

> *keep full and proper records and accounts* of all risks accepted or premiums received and receivable and all claims made or notified; *keep full and proper accurate accounts* showing at all times the amounts due and payable by the claimants to the defendants and by the defendants to the claimants under the contracts; *obtain, file or otherwise keep in a proper manner, all accounting, claims and other documents and records and make these [reasonably] available to the defendants.*

(b) Secondly, through the reinsurer's attempts to confirm that the loss had been settled in a proper and businesslike way (see Chapter 7). This aspect was considered in 1992 in *GRE* v. *Charman*, in which the court could find no authority for GRE's argument that, *in the absence of an express claims cooperation or control obligation*, a reinsurer is entitled to receive from the reinsured sufficient information and documents to demonstrate that the reinsured was entitled to seek an indemnity. The court held that a reinsurer would be entitled to information and documents showing the claim by the assured, how the claim was dealt with, and answers to other relevant questions which might enable the reinsurers to see that the claim was settled in a businesslike fashion. These documents are often held by the broker, although they should not be released without the consent of the reinsured.

(c) Thirdly, through Disclosure under CPR if the matter is litigated, or arbitrated.

(e) Claims

At first blush it may seem odd even to question whether a broker is obliged to handle all claims for a reinsured, because "everyone knows that that is what they do", but the issue has been thrown into relief in recent times by the claims for asbestos-related problems, whereby the brokerage may be paid decades before a claim need be pursued, so that the broker actually pursuing the claim might feel that he is not being paid for his efforts (particularly where the original broker has been merged into his organisation). The *Rowland Report on Lloyd's* commented that brokers' incentives were distorted by the mismatch between their costs and revenues on long-tail business, owing to the cost of handling claims years after the commission had been generated, thereby providing poor recompense to those brokers concentrating on long-term continuity and service. One solution would have been to agree at the outset that claims would only be handled for a limited period, after which a claims collection commission or a fee would be payable. The alternative of course would have been to accept a lower commission when placing the business, and obtain a specified claims collection commission thereafter, but these are either not within the long-term radar of the brokers at the time of placement or, if they are, the brokers may not wish to introduce such a negative element into their relationship with the reinsured, particularly where other brokers would seize the opportunity to obtain the business using as a carrot the fact that they will handle all claims collections at no extra cost.

For all practical purposes the issue was laid to rest in *Johnston* v. *Leslie & Godwin* [1995] L.R.L.R. 472 which stated that a Lloyd's broker was obliged to collect claims, and that he was paid to do so as part of his brokerage:

"it is and was the universal practice of Lloyd's brokers to collect claims when called upon to do so . . . In the non-marine market brokers have never been paid additional commission for collecting claims in the absence of a special arrangement . . . it is and has always been an ordinary incident of the duty of a Lloyd's broker to collect claims on behalf of his principal."

The court went on to say that it was also one of the incidents of the duty of a broker to take all reasonable care and skill to collect claims when asked to do so, from which it must follow that the broker must exercise all reasonable care and skill in order to be in a position to collect such claims. This means that a reinsurance broker must be able to ascertain the names of the relevant (re)insurers so that he will be able to advance a claim on behalf of the reinsured when called upon to do so, which means in practice that he must also retain the slip.

However, the broker's obligation in respect of claims appears to have been conceded and was therefore not argued. It may still be open for further judicial discussion, although as a reasonable proposition it has generally been accepted. It would certainly appear odd if a broker felt that he was obliged to pursue claims through Lloyd's but not for any balance of participation in the London companies market.

Nevertheless, it is apparently the case that outside Lloyd's the broker's obligation to assist without payment is arguably harder to prove, particularly as additional fees may sometimes be charged for claims processing. However, it seems reasonable that the broker who holds himself out as able and prepared to obtain insurance also holds himself out as able to effect all ancillary aspects of that insurance, and the inclusion of Lloyd's syndicates or non-Lloyd's companies as reinsurers should make no difference at all. The position will, of course, always depend on the contract between the parties, and whether it contains any express or implied term dealing with claims. Where the broker charges a fee for placement in or outside Lloyd's, it is by no means clear that this fee also includes the cost of his servicing any claims, and it would be advisable to clarify the position prior to formation of the contract of agency.

(f) The broker's other obligations post-placement

HIH Casualty & General Insurance Ltd v. *JLT Risk Solutions Ltd* [2006] EWHC 485 (Comm) recently stated that the scope of any duty owed by the broker post-placement would always depend on the circumstances of the case, and this would of course include whether the broker is obliged to advise his principle that the reinsurance is expiring, and as to other aspects as well. The brokers, JLT, had simply forwarded risk management reports (which revealed that there was a reduction in the number of films to be made) to HIH but had not alerted them to the potential coverage issues that this might cause HIH. HIH alleged that JLT (in its capacity as HIH's reinsurance broker) should have specifically drawn HIH's attention to the reductions in numbers of the insured/reinsured films and their significance to the contracts.

Langley J. held that in simply forwarding the Risk Management Reports the brokers had failed in their duty of care. He refused to accept that JLT were obliged only to act as a post box and held that JLT should not only have read the Risk Management Reports carefully, but also that if any of the information ought to have been thought to be a matter of any concern on coverage issues to their client then they should have alerted their client to it. Merely forwarding the information was not enough to discharge any duty, particularly as the brokers had played an important role in disseminating information and were aware of the importance of the contracts being back to back. In the absence of instructions from HIH to notify reinsurers, JLT had a duty to seek instructions from HIH or at least to ensure that HIH were sufficiently aware of potential concern to assess what, if any, instructions to give. As it turned out HIH failed on causation, but the cat is now out of the bag and it remains to be seen how far the courts will go. The matter was argued in the Court of Appeal in March 2007 and a decision is awaited, which should also deal with the potential conflict faced by a broker when he acts for insurer and reinsurer.

LIABILITIES OF BROKERS

A broker may be concurrently liable in contract and also in tort for effectively the same breach to comply with the implied terms of the contract (to use reasonable skill and care) and not to cause loss negligently in tort. More worrying for the broker is that as a professional he can be liable personally, particularly in small broking houses where it may be easier to show that the broker had assumed a personal responsibility to the insured.

(a) Failing to obtain any reinsurance

Failure to obtain any reinsurance at all will give rise to liability on the part of the broker unless he can show that he took all reasonable steps to effect the reinsurance but that it was unobtainable in any of the appropriate markets, and that he informed the reinsured or took all reasonable steps to do so. The obligation to inform the reinsured that the reinsurance cannot be obtained is designed to enable the reinsured to make alternative arrangements, such as utilising the services of another broker or proceeding to reinsurance markets considered to be inferior.

(b) Failing to obtain the requisite or enforceable reinsurance

Unless the broker specified in clear terms that he *will* obtain the required reinsurance, his duty is only to use reasonable skill and care in attempting to obtain the reinsurance requested. He is not usually under an absolute obligation because the hallmark of any professional is that the service that he provides cannot be guaranteed, and so it is usually inadvisable to specify to any client that the course of action or service which he requires will be obtained or satisfied. Nothing is certain and a broker would be ill-advised to guarantee that insurance will be available on the terms specified.

Generally speaking the reinsured will specify the scope of the reinsurance required in general terms and leave it to the broker to obtain in his discretion, leaving the broker to weigh up all the proposed terms of various reinsurers and decide which is the best for his client, the reinsured. The fact that a broker may have placed reinsurance on more expensive terms does not of itself prove that he has been negligent, because it may be that the terms are better, or simply that either the broker or the reinsured has a good working relationship and on balance this will result in, say, an easier claims process or one more likely to result consistently in payment without the reinsurer querying every settlement.

There are two other areas in which a broker may face liability, which are that specific instructions may have been given by the reinsured which are either ambiguous or which the broker believes to be defective in some way. Where the instructions are ambiguous the broker is under a duty to resolve the ambiguity because if he fails to do so he will in effect be making a judgment on his own account which may result in liability if he is incorrect. The liability would depend on the circumstances, so that a broker may not be liable if the insurance must be concluded before a certain date and the instructions cannot be obtained from the reinsured to clarify the position before the date in question.

The courts used to lean towards the broker in cases of ambiguity.

***Waterkeyn* v. *Eagle Star & British Dominions Insurance Co. Ltd/ Price Forbes & Co.* [1920] 4 Lloyd's Rep. 178 and [1920] 5 Lloyd's Rep. 42**

In this case the insured requested his broker to insure against the collapse of the Russian Bank for Foreign Trade in the light of the Russian Revolution in 1917, since he rightly feared the expropriation of the bank's funds, which included his own. The broker obtained insurance for loss "directly due to damage or destruction of the premises and contents of the said banks through riots, civil commotion, war, civil war [etc]", which was worthless. Upon its construction of the wording the court held that the broker was not liable since he had only "acted prudently in carrying out his activities". This case is interesting not only because the Belgian insured pointed out to the broker that the subject matter of the risk for which cover was required was not tangible, but was that of credits owed to them by the bank being rendered worthless by the vicissitudes of revolution, but also because the court held that the risk could have been covered by the addition of an "extremely simple clause" so that the policy provided for "insolvency caused by rioters, civil commissions, war, civil war [etc]". A more obvious reason to hold the broker liable would be difficult to find. Nevertheless, the court held that this was the only insurance that the broker could have obtained in the circumstances. It is thought that a court would struggle to uphold the "only insurance available" reason for this decision today, unless the insurance obtained broadly reflected the insurance requested but contained "unavoidable" clauses which the insured would prefer not to have. This rationale is also subject to the probable extension of a broker's duties that a broker must not blithely place the insurance or reinsurance requested by his principal, but must attempt to ensure that the insurance properly meets the principal's real requirements. The broker should inform the reinsured so that he can reiterate his instructions, or has an opportunity to obtain the reinsurance elsewhere, and so that he can decide whether he wishes to pay premiums for inferior reinsurance. A broker today may be unable to refute liability by adhering rigidly to specifications made by the insured, which are clearly wrong and would be seen to be wrong by a reasonable broker, without initially questioning his instructions. It will, however, always depend on the facts at the time. A broker was more successful in *O'Brien & Others* v. *Hughes-Gibb & Co. Limited* [1995] L.R.L.R. 90.

***O'Brien & Others* v. *Hughes-Gibb & Co. Limited* [1995] L.R.L.R. 90**

In *O'Brien & Others* the theft of Shergar in 1983 caused some concern to the owners of £280,000 worth of shares in the top racehorse purchased two years earlier by the insureds. The insurance obtained included all risks of mortality but did not include cover against the theft of the horse, because it was always thought that the theft of a racehorse was very unlikely to occur. Nevertheless, cover against theft as an extension of mortality cover was readily available for no additional premium. The insureds failed to prove that there was any settled practice during the relevant period that theft cover was usually obtained, and therefore alternatively argued that they had no expertise in insurance and relied upon the brokers to ensure that they were covered against all foreseeable insurable risks. However, the insureds had in this case given specific instructions as to the cover they required and the brokers were only under a duty to use reasonable skill and care to procure that cover, which they did.

***National Insurance and Guarantee Corporation plc* v. *Imperio Reinsurance Co. UK Limited and Russell Tudor-Price Jones & Co.* [1999] Lloyd's Rep. IR 249**

More recently, in *National Insurance and Guarantee Corporation plc* the court held the broker to be negligent for failing to query whether or not NIGC required insurance in respect of loss of interest on its own funds used in its property purchase scheme as well as protection in respect of loss of interest on borrowed monies. The broker prepared and agreed the endorsement with the reinsurers and sent a copy to the reinsured, who replied that it "seemed to do what we wanted it to do". The reinsured then sent details of losses falling within the endorsement to the broker for payment by the reinsurer, until they validly denied liability. The brokers were held negligent but only up to 70%, the remaining 30% remaining for the account of the reinsured to reflect its failure to read the wording properly. Three defences of the broker were rejected.

The first was that the reinsured had waived the broker's breach by responding in these terms but the court considered that the reinsured could not have had the requisite knowledge of the breach at the time of its alleged waiver. The second was that the reinsured's statement that the broker had appeared to fulfil his obligations was neither an estoppel by representation nor an estoppel by convention, because it simply was a representation that the reinsured believed what he had been told by the broker. The third was that the reinsured had ratified the defective contract. This argument still seems attractive but the judge here, and another in *Suncorp* v. *Milano*, held that the effect of ratification depended upon its context and did not automatically relieve the broker from liability.

***First National Commercial Bank* v. *Barnet Devanney & Co.* [1999] 2 All E.R. (Comm) 233**

In this case the Court of Appeal found the broker liable because he did not include a mortgagee protection or non-invalidation clause in the policy, which was readily available at no extra premium to protect lenders interested in the insurance. The insurer avoided the policy, following non-disclosure etc. by the mortgagor, who settled its claim against the insurer for a small amount following advice from six leading counsel that the claim was no better than arguable, owing to the lack of clarity surrounding the issue at that time as to whether an innocent insured under a composite policy was entitled to be paid following innocent non-disclosure by the other composite party. The court considered that the broker was not entitled to take a view on undetermined points of law—the expert evidence showing that there was considerable doubt and confusion in the minds of brokers at the relevant time, despite the broker's view ultimately being proved correct in *New Hampshire Insurance Co.* v. *MGN* [1997] L.R.L.R. 24—partly because he might have been wrong as to the law, but in any event because the protection obtained should be such that the insured need not become involved in legal disputes at all, and the presence of the relevant clauses would have avoided this problem.

What is the position where the broker has a clearly worded letter of engagement or set of instructions (e.g. in a letter) which is narrow in scope and which he strictly fulfills, but there is an aspect which falls outside the retainer which he should have noticed whilst discharging the retainer and which is of considerable significance to the insured? It is certainly the case that an insured cannot expect a broker to undertake work which he has not requested and for which the insured will not pay, but a broker will be liable if, whilst acting within the scope of his retainer, he notices or should have noticed a risk or information which is not confidential and clearly of potential significance to the insured and fails to draw it to his attention (*Credit Lyonnais* v. *Russell Jones & Walker* [2002] Lloyd's Rep. PN 7). It is the same professional obligation that a dentist would have to a patient if whilst treating one tooth he were to notice another which needed attention; a slavish following of instructions may not necessarily amount to a discharge of any professional's duties. Although Oliver J. commented in *Midland Bank* v. *Hett Stubbs and Kemp* [1979] Ch. 384 that " . . . the court must be aware of imposing on . . . professional men . . . duties which go beyond the scope of what they are requested and undertake to do", and "[a professional] is under no duty whether before or after accepting those instructions to go beyond those instructions by proffering unsought advice on the wisdom of the transaction. To hold otherwise would be to place an intolerable burden on the [professional]" (*Clark Boyce* v. *Moyatt* [1994] 1 A.C. 428), it remains the case that "An inexperienced client will need and will be entitled to expect the [professional] to take a much broader view of the scope of his retainer and of his duties than will be the case with an experienced client" (*Carradine Properties Ltd* v. *DJ Freeman* [1999] Lloyd's Rep. PN 483). Whatever obligation can be deduced from these and other cases, the broker usually has the fallback defence that he was acting for a professional reinsured who could be expected to act professionally, although the reality is that a broker cannot simply hive off his responsibility on this basis; the best that he can achieve is a reduction in any damages payable, and so far the courts have not reduced such liability by more than 30%.

It is also axiomatic that the insurance must be enforceable, because if it is not enforceable it is worthless. Where the reinsurance is placed with an English reinsurer the position should not present any problems, because even if the reinsurer is not properly authorised by the Financial Services Authority, sections 26, 27 and 28 of the Financial Services and Markets Act 2000 will in most cases entitle the reinsured to enforce payment from the reinsurer. Where, however, the broker places the reinsurance with a foreign reinsurer who is not properly registered or authorised to conduct for insurance business within the property law or jurisdiction of the contract, then the broker may well be liable for failing to take reasonable steps to ensure that the reinsurer is properly authorised and the contract fully enforceable.

(c) Failing to ensure disclosure of all material facts and failing to inform the reinsured of all relevant matters

This obligation falls more appropriately upon a broker advising a direct insured, because every reinsured should be fully aware of his obligation to disclose all material facts to the reinsurer. Nevertheless, a broker should ensure that a reinsured is made aware as to whether or not a fact is material, particularly where it is linked specifically to the reinsured's business or *modus operandi*.

(d) Security

There is very little English case law defining the extent of brokers' duties regarding their selection of insurance or reinsurance security. From what little there is can be distilled the principle that the broker is under a duty to select a reinsurer which it reasonably believes to be solvent, which effectively means that it must be capable of meeting claims as they fall due. English courts have not yet provided any guidance to the extent of the investigations which the broker must carry out to satisfy this test.

***Osman* v. *J. Ralph Moss Ltd* [1970] 1 Lloyd's Rep. 313**

The leading English authority concerning brokers and their obligations as to security is *Osman* v. *J. Ralph Moss Ltd* in which insurance brokers placed a contract of motor insurance with Belvedere Motor Policies Limited, a company whose shaky financial foundation was well known in insurance circles at that time. The Court of Appeal held that the brokers were guilty of negligence in recommending Mr Osman to insure with a company known to be in financial difficulties. In fact shortly after the contract had been concluded, a winding up order was made against Belvedere and the brokers wrote in ambiguous terms to Mr Osman, suggesting that he insure with another company. However, he was a cabinet maker of Turkish origin; his ability to read and understand English was limited, and he did not understand that he did not have insurance. A few months later, he was involved in an accident with another car, and was only then informed that he was uninsured. He was fined £25 for driving without an insurance policy, and the Court of Appeal held not only that the letter sent by the brokers was grossly negligent and would not have aroused the suspicion that all was not well, but also that Mr Osman was entitled to recover the premium he had paid, the £25 fine which had been imposed, and various other costs, on the basis that these were reasonably foreseeable consequences of the broker's breach of duty to inform Mr Osman that he was uninsured.

The Court of Appeal commented that:

"It was the broker's duty in the circumstances to give Mr Osman a plain warning in the strongest terms and to tell him that they were ready to account to him for the premium that he had paid. If they had been concerned to do their duty by him, they would have taken further and urgent steps to ensure that he realised the position; but they did not."

but this obligation can be qualified by the fact in this case that the brokers were aware that the insurer was financially unsound when the insurance was placed. The Australian case of *Lewis* v. *Tressider Andrews Associates* [1987] 2 Qd. R. 533 considered various English authorities and concluded that the broker is obliged to inform the insured of any information which he receives which indicates that the insurer may not remain financially sound, even if the broker is personally satisfied that no real problem exists. The court stated that "so long as the relationship of broker and client subsists there is a continuing duty of care". This aspect has not yet been the subject of a substantive legal decision in the UK, although there have been cases where the broker has assumed such a duty (e.g. *HIH* v. *JLT* above).

Where a reinsured selects the security which he requires and asks the broker to place the reinsurance with that market, the broker may be able to avoid any liability for any later insolvencies within that market by stating that he acted as a mere agent to carry out his principal's request. Certainly this defence used to succeed, but today there is a growing awareness in the courts that brokers are not just agents. They are professional men, i.e. they use specific mental skills within a specialised market; they have usually undergone a period of theoretical and practical training; they are regulated by GISC and from 2005 by the FSA; broking is recognised by the public as an occupation with professional status; and—the hallmarks of any profession—they are unable to guarantee absolute success, either in placing the insurance or processing claims, and they have an overriding duty to the public. It may therefore be the case that the broker is obliged to evaluate the security requested by his client because he is no longer just an agent, and advise if he feels that it is inadequate. In *The "Zephyr"* [1984] 1 Lloyd's Rep. 58, Hobhouse J. said:

"The broker's skill and expertise extends beyond merely giving his client advice and complying with his client's instructions. He must make use of his knowledge of the market and use appropriate skills."

This may come as a shock to some brokers in the face of specific instructions from their client, but the client's knowledge of the market may be based on invalid or obsolete information, and the broker should be better placed to evaluate the market in any event, particularly as that is one of the prime reasons for his existence. Another good example for enforcing this obligation of the broker is that the broker may have picked up market knowledge which would not be available to the client, such as the fact that the reinsurer requested has recently become unwilling to pay claims, or is delaying them unreasonably. The broker may, however, be able to avoid liability by informing his client that he has not evaluated the proposed security and is acting as agent only.

The broker may also be able to rely upon *O'Brien* v. *Donoghue* [1995] L.R.L.R. 90 (see also p. 337 of this chapter) in which the claimants had purchased £280,000 worth of shares in 1981 in the racehorse Shergar, which was stolen in 1983. The insurance obtained included all risks of mortality but did not include cover against the theft of the horse, because it was always thought that the theft of a racehorse was very unlikely to occur. Nevertheless, cover against theft as an extension of mortality cover was readily available for no additional premium. In this case, the claimants failed to prove that there was any settled practice during the relevant period that theft cover was usually obtained. The claimants alternatively argued that they had no expertise in insurance and relied upon the brokers to ensure that they were covered against all foreseeable insurance risks. However, the claimants had in this case given specific instructions as to the cover they required and the brokers were only under a duty to use reasonable skill and care to procure that cover, which they did. The question would then be whether or not a broker can simply comply with these clients' instructions as to the market required or whether he must apply reasonable skill and care to the discharge of his contract of agency. The insured's claim failed because the broker was able to show that the insured had given specific instructions as to the cover required and the court held that the brokers were only under a duty to use reasonable skill and care to procure that cover, which they had done. Kidnap was not considered to be a significant risk and had not been sought, even impliedly.

The reinsured is, however, a professional operating in the same generic area of insurance as the broker, and is expected to have some expertise such that the obligations of the broker may to some extent be tempered. The principle that a reinsured must take some responsibility for the reinsurance security either selected or specifically endorsed by him is also apparent from *Berriman* v. *Rose Thomson Young (Underwriting) Ltd.*

***Berriman* v. *Rose Thomson Young (Underwriting) Ltd* [1996] I.R.L.R. 426**

In this case the judge asked

"what, if any, is the duty of a Lloyd's underwriter to satisfy himself as to the adequacy of the security offered to him by the broker who acts on his behalf in placing his outwards reinsurance arrangements?

On this issue I had the benefit of expert evidence from a Lloyd's broker . . . who accepts that it is the duty of a broker to satisfy himself that the security put before an underwriter was reasonably appropriate to the type of business written; for example, he would have regard to whether it contained a high proportion of long-tail business. But the broker would not be concerned with the finer details of such a book of business. Brokers . . . would have a security committee and would maintain a list of approved securities. That list would be prepared from information which the brokers had acquired over the years from various sources, including Standard and Poors and ISI rating information. He accepted that a broker owed a duty to the client, whether he be a professional underwriter . . . or someone with no such expertise.

In many ways, [the broker's] evidence convinced me that the defendants were right in this case to accept, also, that [the reinsured underwriter] was under a duty to satisfy himself that the security offered was appropriate for the purposes he had in mind. The broker could not be expected to know the details of the underwriter's book of business. The list of approved companies prepared by the broker was compiled for general use, although some would be more appropriate than others in some instances. But all the companies on the list would have been approved as sound, in principle. It would be quite inappropriate for a broker to maintain within that list different tiers or levels of soundness. The underwriter, on the other hand, knows better than the broker the nature of the risks which he is writing and the length of the tail, if any. He will know how much risk he intends to cede, and he will have been able to evaluate the nature of those risks and the likely impact on them of foreseeable events. The roles of broker and underwriter neatly complement one another: in normal circumstances, an underwriter would be entitled to assume that the broker would only have presented him with a prospective reinsurer which the broker considered to be generally sound, and the broker can assume that a competent underwriter will make a judgement as to the appropriateness of that security having regard to his particular needs. However, there may be circumstances which alter the general position: if, for example, a broker made it clear that he was giving no 'comfort' to the underwriter about the reinsurer he was putting forward. When satisfying himself that the security is suitable for the particular purpose he has in mind the underwriter will wish to pay particular attention to those aspects of 'soundness' which will be most challenged if foreseeably disastrous catastrophes were to impact his book. Thus, the underwriter will look carefully at the 'size' of the reinsurer, having regard to the amount of business he intends to cede, and to the reinsurers' 'expectation of life', having regard to his knowledge of the likely length of the tail. The names on the brokers' list are 'off the peg'; whereas the underwriter must tailor the material to meet his own special needs."

Upon renewal the broker must reassess the quality of each reinsurer, particularly where it has been originally selected by the reinsured.

Where the security is clearly inadequate, so that it should have been obvious to any professional reinsurer reading the cover note from the broker which sets out the identity of the reinsurers, then arguably the broker will not be liable for the selection of the inadequate security. In *General Accident Fire & Life Assurance Corporation Ltd* v. *Minet* (1942) 72 Ll. L. Rep. 48, Atkinson J. stated:

"It may very well be that if the defect is so obvious that it springs to the eye and had been indeed observed by the insured, use might be made of the point."

In the *Superhulls* case, the judge commented that:

"The client who signs a letter such as the order letter thereby exposes himself to the risk of an estoppel . . . if there is an obvious defect in the cover, as Atkinson J. observed, a waiver or an estoppel may result."

It is not absolutely clear whether or not the insured *must* actually notice the defect and appreciate it fully, or whether the defect simply has to be *so obvious* that the allegation of the insured that he had not noticed it is not believable.

Where the broker can show that given the quality of information that he would have been able to obtain had he properly researched the position, at least to the extent of exercising reasonable diligence, which would not have shown that the reinsurer was either insolvent, close to insolvency or likely to be incapable of meeting future claims as they fell due, then the broker will not be liable to the reinsured.

Two other arguments are occasionally utilised by a broker in defence to any claim for his selection of inadequate security. The first is that the quality of the reinsured's business is not sufficiently high to make it capable of being accepted by a reinsurer of good quality, which resulted in the broker placing the business with reinsurers of lower quality. A broker might still be liable to the reinsured if he failed to inform the reinsured that the reinsurance was of dubious value, to enable the reinsured to attempt to place the business with a reinsurer who might be more secure, or alternatively not place it at all and save himself the premium.

Secondly, a broker might allege that had the reinsurance been properly placed with a better quality reinsurer, the claims would not have been paid in any event. Occasionally this succeeds where it is clear that there has been a material non-disclosure which on anyone's view would have induced the underwriter of the reinsurer not to accept the risk. Nevertheless, the courts tend to take the view that the relationships between contracting parties are usually intended to be fulfilled and that reinsurers will pay out in most cases, although sometimes courts will reduce the damages payable by the broker to the reinsured, on occasion to reflect the additional premium that would have been payable by the reinsured with a better quality reinsurer.

(e) Advising on matters outside his expertise

Where a broker advises a reinsured on a matter falling outside the ambit of the duties owed as a broker, then he is subject to the same duty to exercise reasonable skill and care not of a broker who considers himself capable of giving advice in that area but of a practitioner in that field. A broker giving legal advice to a reinsured or advice on the effect of a clause or on claims adjustment may lead him into liability to the reinsured if that advice is incorrect. A broker is nevertheless expected to understand the general principles of insurance and reinsurance law and its application to both his own and to the reinsured's business, and in particular to any contracts, including their drafting. Thus a broker may be liable if he obtains reinsurance which does not attach properly or contains clauses making it unworkable in practice or of limited value because the broker failed to consider the relevant law, provided that it was not difficult to ascertain or would reasonably have been ascertained by a competent practitioner.

(f) Measure of damages

The highest figure for the liability faced by a broker who had negligently failed in its obligations to the reinsured used to be considered as being capped at the limit of the cover forming the subject of the claim. The rationale for this peak was that the reinsured would have received no more than the reinsurer should have paid had all been well with the contract of reinsurance, i.e. the limit of indemnity. However, it is well established that a voluntary assumption of responsibility by a party can give rise to full liability should, say, the piece of advice given or the (mis)representation made prove to be incorrect and the cause of loss. There have been two recent cases which have taken this proposition to new heights.

***South Australia Asset Management Co.* v. *York Montague Ltd* [1997] A.C. 191**

The House of Lords held valuers liable for negligent overvaluations but not for the further loss resulting from the 1991 UK property crash and the principles enunciated extend in appropriate circumstances to any breach of professional duty. The nature of the duty breached by the professional must be analysed in order to identify the type of damages recoverable, to reflect the distinction between a professional's duty to provide information and a duty to advise (where he will be liable for all the consequences of any wrong advice, which would include all the losses flowing from any contract entered into in reliance on that advice). Thus where a professional has a duty that is confined to providing information, he is only liable for such losses as fall within the ambit of that particular duty and his potential liability does not extend to all losses incurred.

The SAAMCO principles therefore apply where a professional is engaged to provide information for a specific transaction or project; the client is to decide whether or not to proceed with that transaction or project; the information to be supplied is to be relied on by the client as part of the information to be used in that decision-making process; and the relevant decision as to whether to proceed with that project or transaction is neither to be participated in by the professional nor is dependent on the advice of that professional.

What is less clear is the nature and extent of the broker's duty. Does he provide information about the availability and cost of insurance or does he advise his clients? It will be a question of fact in each case.

***Aneco Re Underwriting* v. *Johnson & Higgins Ltd* [2002] Lloyd's Rep. IR 91**

The claimant reinsurers agreed to provide treaty reinsurance cover for a scheme on condition that the defendant brokers put in place retrocessional cover in respect of liabilities arising under the treaty. The defendants had acted as the reinsured's brokers when placing the underlying reinsurance.

The defendant brokers obtained fully subscribed slips for the reinsurance for the claimants which, if binding, would have provided an indemnity in respect of losses aggregating to $11,000,000. The defendants duly informed the claimants, who then underwrote the underlying reinsurance.

The reinsurances were avoided for misrepresentation/non-disclosure by the brokers when placing the retrocession in the claimants' favour. The claimants sued the defendants for recovery of all losses which they had incurred as a result of entering into the underlying reinsurance ($35,000,000).

The reinsurer was successful in its claim against its broker because the reinsurer could show (and it was common ground) that it would not have entered into the underlying treaties of insurance if the broker had properly advised it that retrocession cover was not available (which meant at commercially sensible rates) to enable the reinsurer to lay off its risk. The retrocessionaires avoided cover because they had been informed that the treaties were obligatory quota share, when in fact they were facultative/obligatory (which are more open to abuse). The brokers took the view that any negligence on their part could not give rise to a claim in damages in excess of what the reinsurer would have received had the retrocession been validly placed ($11,000,000). The House of Lords held that the broker owed a duty to the reinsurer to advise on the state of the market and was accordingly liable for all of the foreseeable consequences of their negligence ($35,000,000).

The majority of the House effectively categorised the provision of information as the provision of advice, on the basis that the brokers' obligation to explain that the market would not provide the retrocession cover was the equivalent of explaining that the market took an adverse view of the risk, and that this was supported by the commercial relationship and inherent probabilities in the broker/principal relationship.

The potential conflict of the broker between the two roles (of acting for the reinsured and the reinsurer) was not a problem; not only was it not unusual, but if actually problematic the broker could simply have dropped out (but this issue may be subject to comment by the Court of Appeal in the awaited decision of *HIH* v. *JLT* above). The case was largely dismissed at the time by market practitioners as being "fact specific" and of limited wider significance, but it is likely that reinsureds will attempt to establish that if the broker had disclosed or represented the true state of affairs the market would have refused to reinsure, a factual situation which the broker should then have reported to the client, thus widening the scope of the broker's duty and increasing the quantum of damage.

Following *Aneco* the quantum of damages payable by a broker may increase to reflect a commensurate increase in his duties of care. A broker should at all times be able to recognise precisely for whom he is acting, and consequently the duties which he owes to each client. Even with an engagement letter clearly setting out the broker's role, the fact is that he may well amend these duties or accept new ones, often without realising that he is doing so. Commenting on even one aspect of the placement may well widen the scope of any duty.

The case has recently formed the premise for a successful claim at first instance against a broker, arising out of its negligent advice as to the method of calculating insured gross profit in a business interruption insurance, which differed from the normal accounting method. The subsequent underinsurance following disruption by fire led the insured to sue its broker for loss of profits in *Arbory Group Ltd* v. *West Craven Insurance Services Ltd* (QBD 13/3/2007) on the basis that the smaller sum paid out by the insurer was insufficient to maintain the business as a profitable "going concern", a state of affairs that had been foreseeable when the insurance had been placed. The court considered three SAMCO principles:

1. Did the broker owe a duty in respect of the loss of profit?
2. Was the loss foreseeable if the business was underinsured?
3. Could the cause of the loss of profitability be attributed to the broker's breach of duty?

The court distinguished business interruption insurance from other types of insurance, the point of the former being to inject additional funds into a profitable concern in order to maintain it as such. The loss was therefore reasonably foreseeable and the claim was not for damages for the late payment of damages because the insurer had paid promptly and a full payment would have been made if the business had not been underinsured. The broker was therefore liable. The sticking point in this decision would appear to be the fact that usually the courts refuse to take the claimant's impecuniosity into account but effectively did so here, because the insurance was intended to counter any such impecuniosity and was therefore of a nature that fell outside the usual rules and indeed by its very nature involved a foreseeable loss.

RIGHTS OF BROKERS

(a) A right to remuneration

A reinsurance broker will be paid when what appears to be a valid contract of reinsurance has been placed, which in legal terms means an offer and acceptance between the reinsured and reinsurer which constitutes a binding contract. Thus although a broker may put a great deal of effort into placing a contract of reinsurance, if the contract is not "closed" the broker will usually be entitled to nothing.

More interestingly, perhaps, is the concept that the broker is not paid by the party to who he owes almost all of his duties, the reinsured, but rather by the reinsurer for introducing the reinsurance business to him. The matter has never been fully argued in court but the proposition has been repeated, most recently in *Pryke* v. *Gibbs Hartley Cooper* [1991] 1 Lloyd's Rep. 602.

The liability of the reinsurer to pay brokerage to the broker comes into existence at the precise moment of formation of the contract of reinsurance. The fact that the parties may agree to pay the premium in instalments does not alter the fact that there is a legal liability upon the reinsurer to pay the broker at the date of formation of contract, although in reality he will usually only be able to obtain his commission when the premium actually passes through his accounts from the reinsured to the reinsurer.

These arrangements (whereby the reinsurer pays brokerage to the broker for the introduction of the business) can be circumvented by agreement between the insured, the broker and the insurer that the insured will instead pay a fee to the broker for his services, in return for a lower gross premium to reflect the fact that the insurer need not pay brokerage to the broker.

The issue of who is liable to the broker for his remuneration is not entirely free from doubt. Clarke J. in *Johnston* v. *Leslie and Godwin* [1995] L.R.L.R. 472 commented that "In consideration of the insured (or reinsured as the case may be) agreeing to pay the broker's commission the broker agrees inter alia to collect the claims", but this was not argued and did not matter to the decision; all that was needed was that the broker was paid. It can probably be ignored in the absence of appellate authority, even if it reflects a more reasonable and modern approach to the effect that the broker really acts (and should only act) for the insured.

In *Carvill America Inc* v. *Camperdown UK Ltd* [2005] the Court of Appeal refused an application by XL Specialty Co. Ltd to set aside service of a claim under English law upon them in the USA, probably Connecticut. The issues concerned the liability of the reinsurer or reinsured to pay brokerage to the broker, and whether it was earned on placement or when the premium was paid, given the continuing servicing obligations of the broker after placement. The court felt unable to accept that there was no "serious issue to be tried" because one assumption was that the contract of agency was subject to US law, which might not be identical to UK law, and which applied to a clause in the contract which stated that the brokers' remuneration was to be received from the reinsurers "as is customary in the industry". There was a letter from a firm of US attorneys to the effect that a Connecticut court might consider this ambiguous. The judge felt that the English court should be cautious in determining a question of foreign law, and that he did not know whether a Connecticut court would remain within the four corners of the contract or more widely at the factual background. Another point was that the broker deducts his brokerage from the gross premium paid by the reinsured, before remitting the balance to the reinsurer. On the reinsured's termination of the agency the court felt that it was arguable that the liability to pay brokerage reverted to the reinsured. Their Lordships also thought that the cases did not clearly establish that the underwriter's promise to pay brokerage for the introduction of the business is a promise that is legally enforceable. All the cases relied on were insurance, not reinsurance.

It will be interesting to see whether any of these conclusions in this case will be upheld. There is a commonsense argument that as payment by the insurer is anomalous (because technically it is a bribe, being paid by a third party to the contract of agency, albeit one sanctioned by the courts), the insured should be liable. However, the consensus is that the insurer is liable, although the broker rarely enforces his right because the commercial repercussions generally militate strongly against the broker pursuing the insurer. The most telling point is that it is the insurer who actually fixes the brokerage, in the absence of a fee arrangement. In fact the case was due to be heard in November 2005 but it is likely that it has settled, so the matter remains in limbo.

Lloyd's take the view that the insurer or reinsurer is liable for brokerage. A draft decision paper headed Grossing Up and Net Equivalent 24b was put to the Lloyd's Regulatory Board for consideration on 25 July 1994. At paragraph 2.6(a) the paper stated that generally the underwriter pays brokerage to the broker where the two agree a gross premium, and that any commission above what is usual should be endorsed by the insured. Where, however, the underwriter provides a net quote for the premium, then this arrangement is changed so that the insured becomes the party paying the broker, who must therefore agree the amount of that brokerage with the broker (paragraph 2.6(b)).

The Lloyd's Market Bulletin dated 6 September 1996 also stated (in the context of net rating by underwriters) that in discharging his primary function to the insured as his agent, it would be contrary to the broker's obligations as agent to place his interests above those of the insured and in particular to make a secret profit in the absence of informed consent from the insured.

Where this leaves us is with the principle that the insurer or reinsurer is responsible to the broker for the payment of his brokerage in the absence of agreement to the contrary. The only caveat is that the Commercial Court could decide to make new law and hold the insured/reinsured liable for brokerage if this case were to reach trial.

An issue that often arises is the position in which the reinsurer validly avoids the reinsurance contract and returns the premium net of brokerage to the broker for transmission to the reinsured, with the broker making up the balance of the premium by refunding brokerage to the reinsured. The reinsurer may have some grounds for arguing that the broker should not retain his brokerage because his function was to obtain a binding contract of reinsurance, which has not happened, and therefore all monies should be returned from whence they effectively came. For years the brokers simply returned their brokerage because to do otherwise would possibly mean facing legal proceedings, or at least a very irritated client, and potentially an ex-client who would not be instructing them again.

In fact the legal analysis is simply that the reinsurer has paid the broker under a mistake of fact or law, namely that the contract is valid and binding, although voidable for non-disclosure at his option. On avoidance the reinsurer will therefore have a cause of action against the broker either on the basis of money had and received or as a claim for restitution on the basis that had the reinsurer known the true state of affairs he would not have paid brokerage to the broker. The reinsurer would have to show that he acted under a mistake, that he would not have made the payment had he known of the mistake, and that the broker cannot show that he was entitled to the brokerage on some other ground. Avoidance *ab initio* is a state of affairs whereby the contract simply never existed. In most cases a reinsurer should be entitled to a return of all brokerage, or at least to insist that the broker returns the brokerage to the reinsured (as the balance of the gross premium).

There are, however, three defences available to the broker. The first is known as change of position, whereby the broker can show that he has spent the money in good faith (unless he has spent it on items that he would have bought anyway), he could argue that he has changed his position and should therefore not return any brokerage to anyone. The second possibility is that the broker could argue that he should at least be paid for the time and effort that he has put into placing the reinsurance. There is some very limited judicial authority for this possibility but it is somewhat fact specific, and the key concept of brokerage is not related to the amount of time and effort spent but simply to the fact that a valid contract has been obtained. The third hole through which any party can slip in claims in contract is the Limitation Act 1980, so that if brokerage has been paid more than six years prior to the institution of proceedings for its reclamation, the broker need not pay it. The position may be different where the broker has agreed a fee-based deal, where hopefully the contract of agency would contain the relevant terms relating to the potential return of brokerage.

(b) An indemnity from the reinsured

The reinsured is liable to the broker for all sums validly spent by the broker in the proper discharge of his duties for that reinsured, and in particular in respect of any liabilities which the broker might incur on behalf of the reinsured which fall within the brokers' apparent authority. Thus any act which a broker does resulting in his liability which falls outside his actual authority cannot form the subject of a claim for indemnity from the reinsured, such as paying a premium when he is not obliged so to do. Obviously those expenses incurred by the broker in the normal course of his business, such as salaries or other overheads, cannot be passed on to the reinsured as a specific item.

(c) Lien

Section 53(2) of the Marine Insurance Act 1906 states:

> "Unless otherwise agreed, the broker has, as against the assured, a lien upon the policy for the amount of the premium and his charges in respect of effecting the policy; and, where he has dealt with the person who employs him as a principal, he has also a lien on the policy in respect of any balance on any insurance account which may be due to him from such person, unless when the debt was incurred he had reason to believe that such person was only an agent."

The lien of the marine insurance broker was recognised prior to 1906 and probably extends to the non-marine broker on the basis of custom and trade usage, and the words "on any insurance account" in section 53(2). The lien entitles the broker to retain any policy document until all his expenses have been paid and may also provide him with sufficient proprietary interest in the insured's claim to establish the necessary mutuality to enable him to set off claims monies received from insurers against premiums owed to him by the insured.

In *Eide UK Ltd* v. *Lowndes Lambert Group, The "Sun Tender"* [1998] 1 Lloyd's Rep. 389 the Court of Appeal extended the operation of the lien beyond the policy document into the proceeds of a claim, but held that the lien did not extend to a co-insurance where the rights of the insureds were composite. Section 53(2) can only apply where there is one principal as a matter of construction, and as a matter of law an insured could not create rights over an interest that did not belong to him, such as his co-insured's rights. It would appear that a lien can exist in a co-insurance, the broker being able to exercise it against each party in respect of proceeds owed to that party who is also indebted to the broker, but not in such a case against the policy document.

LIMITATION ISSUES

Usually, claims must be brought against brokers within six years of any loss occurring. If this general limitation period has expired, however, claims can still be brought within three years of a claimant discovering his loss if he was unaware of the loss at the time it was caused (the "latent damage" period). No claims can be brought at all 15 years after the loss has occurred (the "long stop" limitation period).

In *Iron Trades Mutual Insurance Co. Ltd* v. *JK Buckenham Ltd* [1989] 2 Lloyd's Rep. 85 the reinsured was uninsured as a result of their broker's non-disclosure, the date of the broker's breach of contract being the date of such non-disclosure. The reinsured tried to claim in tort after the limitation period had expired on the basis that the limitation period for torts was extended by the Latent Damage Act 1986 which introduced section 14A of the Limitation Act 1980 to apply a starting date for limitation purposes to the date when the necessary knowledge to bring an action accrued, i.e. when the avoidance occurred. The important date in claims in tort is the date of damage; in contract the breach occurs when the defective service is rendered or completed. The court found that as a matter of construction the time-barred claim was not assisted by the Latent Damage Act. The court confirmed that the Limitation Act expressly preserved the distinction between actions based in tort and contract, so that the claim remained time-barred.

In *Knapp and Another* v. *Ecclesiastical Insurance Group plc and Another* [1997] All E.R. 44 the Court of Appeal accepted that a cause of action accrued against a broker in respect of his alleged breach of duty in failing to advise his client as to how to comply with his obligations of disclosure and looked at the date upon which this accrued. In applying the principles laid down by early decisions of the Court of Appeal, together with two leading first instance decisions (*Iron Trades* v. *Buckenham* [1990] 1 All E.R. 808 and *Islander Trucking* v. *Hogg Robinson* [1990] 1 All E.R. 826), the court confirmed that a cause of action in tort can accrue once the claimant has acted upon relevant advice "*to his detriment*" and failed to obtain a valid policy of insurance.

At this point there exists a factual situation in which the "insured" has suffered real (as opposed to purely minimal) damage, which would entitle the "insured" to obtain a judgment against his broker. The insured has failed to receive that to which he was entitled and is less well off than he would have been had the broker not been negligent. The court would have been able to place a monetary value upon that loss at that time, even though the policy was only *voidable*: the fact that any damage would have had to have been estimated is only relevant to its quantification, not to its accrual as a cause of action. Accordingly, the broker's negligence was actionable at the inception of the renewal of the policy and the claim against the broker was therefore time barred.

Section 32(1)(b) of the Limitation Act 1980, however, postpones the start of the limitation period where "*any fact relevant to the [claimant's] right of action has been deliberately concealed from him by the defendant*". Section 32(2) states that "*Deliberate commission of a breach of duty in circumstances in which it is unlikely to be discovered for some time amounts to deliberate concealment of the facts involved in that breach of duty*".

Another way of circumventing the limitation defence was attempted in *Companhia de Seguros Imperio* v. *Heath REBX Ltd* [2001] Lloyd's Rep. IR 109, where the reinsured was obliged (in the face of a clear limitation defence) to allege that the brokers owed and had broken a fiduciary duty to the reinsured, although largely in their capacity as the reinsured's underwriting agent in respect of the management and operation of a reinsurance pool. The Court of Appeal stated that it should apply the usual six-year limit applicable to claims in tort and contract by analogy to the claim for fiduciary duty because the claim for breach of fiduciary duty was based on the same facts as the identical claims in tort and contract against the broker and should therefore be subject to the same limitation period.

REGULATION

On 15 January 2005 the Financial Services Authority became the regulatory entity overseeing the activities of insurance agents, as a result of the Financial Services & Markets Act 2000.

The FSA has four statutory objectives:

(a) to maintain market confidence in the financial system;
(b) to increase public awareness;
(c) to ensure consumer protection; and
(d) to prevent and reduce financial crime.

The FSA has eleven Core Principles for Business with which authorised entities should comply:

1. A *firm* must conduct its business with integrity.
2. A *firm* must conduct its business with due skill, care and diligence.
3. A *firm* must take reasonable care to organise and control its affairs responsibly and effectively, with adequate risk management systems.
4. A *firm* must maintain adequate financial resources.
5. A *firm* must observe proper standards of market conduct.
6. A *firm* must pay due regard to the interests of its customers and treat them fairly.
7. A *firm* must pay due regard to the information needs of its clients, and communicate information to them in a way which is clear, fair and not misleading.
8. A *firm* must manage conflicts of interest fairly, both between itself and its customers and between a customer and another client.
9. A *firm* must take reasonable care to ensure the suitability of its advice and discretionary decisions for any customer who is entitled to rely upon its judgment.
10. A *firm* must arrange adequate protection for clients' assets when it is responsible for them.

11. A *firm* must deal with its regulators in an open and cooperative way, and must disclose to the FSA appropriately anything relating to the firm of which the FSA would reasonably expect notice.

The FSA also has certain Threshold Conditions which must be met by an agent, as follows:

Threshold Condition 1—Legal Status

If the regulated activity is effecting or carrying out contracts of insurance, the firm must be an incorporated firm (but not a limited liability partnership), a registered friendly society or a member of Lloyd's.

Threshold Condition 2—Location of offices

A regulated UK firm must have its head office and registered office in the UK or (if not a body corporate) carry on business in the UK.

Threshold Condition 3—Close links

The FSA must be satisfied that it can effectively supervise a firm, taking into account the structure of the group to which it belongs or the other firms to which it has close links.

Threshold Condition 4—Adequate resources

The FSA must be satisfied that the firm has adequate resources. Adequacy of resources is not just about financial resources. The FSA also looks at whether the firm has adequate management and staff, both in terms of quantity and quality.

Threshold Condition 5—Suitability

The FSA must be satisfied that the firm is "fit and proper" to be authorised. In assessing this, the FSA looks at the competence and ability of management, as well as its commitment to carrying on the business with integrity and in compliance with the regulatory regime.

The Act is intended to coordinate and modernise financial regulatory arrangements which were established under a number of different enactments including the Insurance Companies Act 1982, Insurance Brokers (Registration) Act 1977 and the Financial Services Act 1986. These Acts are generally supplemented by secondary legislation and rules but have now been repealed and replaced by the FSMA. The FSMA is in essence a framework to enable appropriate legislation to come into force after detailed consultation with the appropriate markets.

In December 2001 it was decided that the FSA would regulate the sale and administration of general insurance contracts. The FSA subsequently produced several Consultation Papers as part of its due process, with the intention of liaising with the relevant markets in order to produce a set of rules that reflected not only the standards and practices of those markets but also to provide either a better deal or greater certainty for the consumer of insurance and reinsurance products. Following receipt and consideration of all responses the FSA has produced an appropriate set of rules. The predominant rule book for matters of insurance is entitled "Insurance: Conduct of Business" Source Book (abbreviated to ICOB), set out in seven sections and directing the user to the appropriate sections of other rule books where appropriate. ICOB implements various provisions contained in the IMD, the Distance Mediation Directive, the Consolidated Life Directive, the Third Non-Life Directive and the Fourth Motor Insurance Directive. ICOB applies to any insurance intermediary, which is defined as a firm carrying on an insurance mediation activity, i.e. one which deals with the regulated activities specified in the Regulated Activities Order and includes those parties assisting in the administration and performance of a contract of insurance. ICOB does not apply to reinsurance contracts but it does apply to agents carrying out reinsurance mediation activities.

In addition other requirements may need to be discharged, including, for example, those in the Training and Competence Sourcebook, to the effect that its employees are competent; that its employees remain competent for the work they do; that its employees are appropriately supervised; that its employees' competence is regularly reviewed; and that the level of competence is appropriate to the nature of the business.

The beauty of the system from the FSA's point of view is that if it considers that a broker is doing something which the FSA feels it should not be doing, but that activity does not fall squarely as a breach of a specific regulation, it may be able to call upon the Core Principles to discipline the broker.

Intermediation: broking harmony throughout Europe

The Insurance Mediation Directive replaces a 1977 Directive and on implementation in January 2005 became the only binding EU law covering individuals or companies selling insurance products on behalf of others. On compliance with the Directive intermediaries are free to sell their services anywhere in the EU. The Directive applies to all brokers and tied agents carrying on "insurance mediation" which is defined as "the activities of introducing, proposing or carrying out other work preparatory to the conclusion of contracts of insurance and reinsurance, or of concluding such contracts, or of assisting in the administration and performance of such contracts, in particular in the event of a claim". The Directive therefore applies to the activities of both producing and placing brokers carrying on either insurance or reinsurance business. Each Member State has to take all necessary action to ensure that insurers only use the insurance mediation services of registered brokers. The Directive requires that all individuals or companies who carry out insurance or reinsurance mediation must be registered with the competent authority in their home Member State (in England the FSA) on the basis of the following minimum requirements:

- possession of "appropriate general, commercial and professional knowledge and ability, as determined by the home member state of the intermediary";
- being of good repute;
- possession of professional indemnity insurance or any other comparable guarantee against liability arising out of professional negligence;
- sufficient financial capacity to protect customers against any failure by the intermediary to transfer customers' premiums to insurance companies or to pass on to customers money received for claims under the policies they hold.

Once registered with the FSA, the broker will then be entitled to operate anywhere in the EU by notifying the FSA of the other Member States in which it intends to carry on business. The FSA will then notify the competent authorities of those other Member States and one month after the FSA has told the broker that such notice has been provided, the broker can operate in those Member States.

TEST YOUR UNDERSTANDING

(1) Does it matter to the enforceability of a contract by the reinsurer that the reinsured limited the actual authority of his broker in a material way?

(2) Is the broker usually the agent of both reinsured and reinsurer?

(3) What is the effect of the liquidation of the reinsured on a reinsurance contract concluded after that liquidation, and are there any remedies available to the reinsurer against the reinsured or its broker?

(4) Does the ratification by the reinsured of the contract placed by the broker in excess of his authority automatically exonerate the broker from acting unlawfully?

(5) What is an "agent to insure"?

(6) Can a broker ever be liable for non-disclosure or misrepresentation to the reinsurer?

(7) Would a material fact of the reinsured known by the postboy of the broker be attributed to the reinsured and therefore be disclosable to the reinsurer?

(8) Does the fraud of the broker upon the reinsured, which impacts on the reinsurance, have any effect on the validity of the reinsurance?

(9) What steps should a broker take to ensure that he is not responsible for the collection of claims many years after placement?

(10) What should a broker do when faced with an ambiguity in his instructions?

(11) Should a broker accept his instructions at face value or should he check that they reflect the actual needs of the reinsured?

(12) Should a broker convey to the reinsured every doubt that he may have about the intended security of the reinsurer, or should he make an overall decision as to its solvency?

(13) How much reinsurance law should a broker know?

(14) For what purpose does a broker receive payment, and from whom?

(15) What is the maximum period within which legal proceedings should be commenced for a broker who has failed to pass on all material information, which has resulted in avoidance of the contract by the reinsurer?

CHAPTER 9

JURISDICTION AND APPLICABLE LAW

INTRODUCTION

The first half of this chapter considers *jurisdiction*.

When a dispute arises, the court which is competent to adjudicate the dispute is said to have jurisdiction. Reinsurance contracts tend to be international by their nature, and often there is more than one court which might be willing to accept jurisdiction over the dispute. There is a complex (and rather dry) body of rules which the English court applies to determine whether or not it has jurisdiction. We give an overview of these rules.

The second half of this chapter considers *applicable law*.

Once the dispute comes before a court, the court has to consider which law applies to the contract. In other words, what set of legal rules should it apply when interpreting and giving effect to the contract's terms? It may have a significant effect on the parties' rights and obligations if a contract is governed by, say, French law rather than English law.

It is important not to confuse the jurisdiction in which disputes relating to a contract are to be heard with the law applicable to the contract (although it is surprising how often even highly experienced lawyers make this slip). It is perfectly possible for an English court to have jurisdiction over a dispute even if the contract is governed by, for example, Texan law: in this situation, the court may hear evidence as to the relevant principles of Texan law (or, if the parties do not raise the point, the court will proceed on the pragmatic assumption that Texan law is materially the same as English law).

JURISDICTION

The following sections consider why jurisdiction is an important issue, outline the four sources of rules which the English courts apply when deciding whether they have jurisdiction, and then consider the rules themselves.

Significance of jurisdiction

The place where the dispute is heard (sometimes called the "forum") can be important for several reasons. In the context of reinsurance, the most significant differences include the following:

(i) *Enforcement of judgments*. There is no point in a party going to court and obtaining a judgment against a defendant unless that judgment can be enforced. So each party should consider, at the outset, where is it likely to wish to enforce any judgment? This will usually be a place where the other side (the potential defendant) has substantial assets, perhaps its country of incorporation. The potential claimant will want any disputes to be heard in a court whose judgments will be recognised and applied in that country of enforcement. There is a large number of bilateral and multilateral treaties between countries which determine which countries recognise which other countries' judgments. The detail of these is outside this chapter, except to note that EU and European Free Trade Area ("EFTA") Member States recognise and enforce each other's judgments.

(ii) *The judiciary.* If a reinsurance dispute is adjudicated by judges who are familiar with the complexities of the reinsurance industry and the relevant legal principles, then less time needs to be spent bringing the judge up to speed on this area, and the judge's decision is likely to be more predictable than that of someone without relevant experience. The Commercial Court in London is very experienced in dealing with reinsurance matters. By contrast, in many jurisdictions reinsurance cases are assigned to non-specialist judges who are likely to have little or no experience in this area. In virtually all US states, claims for damages (even in the context of reinsurance) may be decided by juries, which could increase the uncertainty of the outcome.

(iii) *The speed and cost of bringing proceedings.*

(iv) *The location of factual witnesses, experts and documents.* If a transaction is concluded in one place, and most of the parties and the documents are in that place, then for reasons of convenience and economics it may make sense for any disputes to be heard there.

(v) *Procedural rules.* Procedural rules differ from country to country. Examples are: who bears the burden of proving particular matters, what disclosure of documents is required, and rules of evidence. Although in practice these factors are likely to have a considerable effect on how the action proceeds, they tend to carry less weight in the parties' minds than the factors previously mentioned when they are considering which court they would like to have jurisdiction in the event of a dispute.

(vi) *The availability of appropriate counsel.* There are a limited number of places worldwide which have specialist reinsurance counsel.

So it is crucial to know which court has jurisdiction to hear any dispute, and it is (or should be) the first point which lawyers will check if a dispute arises (together with the law applicable to the contract).

Sources of rules on jurisdiction

In working out whether to accept jurisdiction, the English court will follow rules laid down in four sources:

(a) The original rules on jurisdiction developed as part of the English common law. These rules remain relevant today whenever the legislation described below does not apply.

(b) In 1968 the members of the European Community signed a Convention on Jurisdiction and the Enforcement of Judgments in Civil and Commercial Matters (known as the "Brussels Convention", after the place where it was signed). The purpose of this convention was to make judgments given by the courts of any Member State enforceable in any other Member State. To help to make this arrangement workable, the various Member States included in the convention a standardised set of rules which all of the national courts would follow when deciding whether to assume jurisdiction over a dispute. The Brussels Convention differed significantly from the approach of the common law, in that it laid down several strict, binding tests, whereas the common law approach involved considerable subjectivity and flexibility. The Brussels Convention was implemented into law in the United Kingdom on 1 January 1987 by the Civil Jurisdiction and Judgments Act 1982.

(c) In 1988 another international convention was opened for signature by the European Community Member States and those of the EFTA namely, Iceland, Norway and Switzerland (the "Lugano Convention"). It has now also been signed by Poland. The Lugano Convention was implemented into law in the United Kingdom on 1 May 1992 by the Civil Jurisdiction and Judgments Act 1991. Its provisions are very similar to those of the Brussels Convention.

(d) In 2002 the Council of the European Union adopted a Regulation, Council Regulation (EC) No. 44/2001 of 22 December 2000, which largely replaces the Brussels and Lugano Conventions. The Regulation applies in all of the EU member states apart from Denmark (which opted out of it). It is very similar to the Brussels and Lugano Conventions.

Figure 1 is a (slightly simplified) summary of whether the rules of the Brussels Convention, the Lugano Convention, the Brussels Regulation or the common law apply to any particular dispute. Although it is important to be aware of the existence of the Brussels Convention, the Lugano Convention and the Brussels Regulation, the provisions which are relevant to reinsurance are largely identical and, for the most part, we are able to treat them together for the purpose of this chapter.

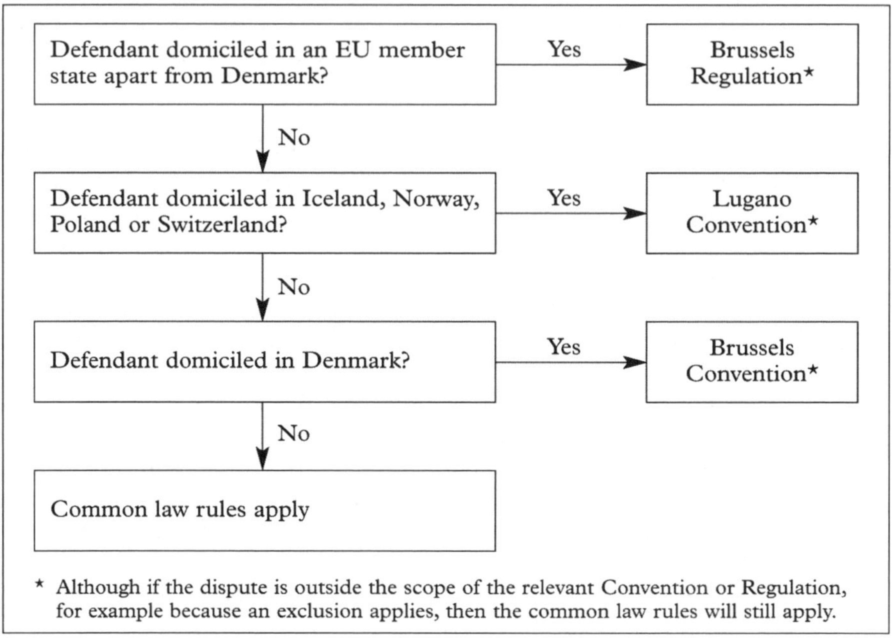

Figure 1. Which rules apply?

How to interpret the Conventions and the Regulation

The Conventions were drawn up in several different language versions, and where these differ each version is to be given equal weight. In addition, the courts may have regard to the official reports which accompanied each Convention as an aid to its interpretation.

In interpreting the Conventions, the courts adopt a "teleological", or purposive, rather than a pedantically literal approach to interpretation. For example, where this is consistent with the objectives of the Convention they may interpret the expression "contract" as encompassing agreements which do not fulfil the strict English law requirements as to offer, acceptance and consideration.

To ensure consistency of interpretation across the EU, a Protocol to the Brussels Convention provided for national courts to be able to refer questions of interpretation to the European Court of Justice ("ECJ"). The ECJ's judgments on these questions bind all national courts. The ECJ's judgments are also likely to be relevant when interpreting the Brussels Regulation, the terms of which are very similar to the Brussels Convention.

The Lugano Convention was not limited to EU Member States, and there is no mechanism for questions to be referred to the ECJ. However, the national courts are required to give such weight as is appropriate to the judgments of other Member States' courts, and the official report on the Lugano Convention (which, as mentioned above, is to be used as an aid to interpretation) states that the Lugano Convention should be construed in accordance with the decisions of the ECJ.

Scope of the Conventions and the Regulation

There are a number of limitations on the scope of the Conventions and the Regulation. For the most part these limitations are unlikely to be relevant to reinsurance disputes, and are therefore covered very briefly:

(i) *Civil and commercial matters.* The Conventions and the Regulation apply only to "civil and commercial matters".

(ii) *International element.* The Conventions and the Regulation apply only where the dispute contains an international element. Even if the parties to a contract are situated in the same country, if they choose a different jurisdiction to hear their disputes this creates a sufficient international element for the Conventions and the Regulation to apply.

(iii) *Relationship with other more specialised conventions.* The Conventions and the Regulation are not intended to override other more specialised international conventions.

(iv) *Insolvency.* The Conventions and the Regulation do not apply to insolvency proceedings.

(v) *Arbitration.* The Conventions and the Regulation do not apply to "arbitration". In the context of reinsurance, this is the most significant exclusion.

It is clear that the Convention does not determine where an arbitration should be held. In *The Atlantic Emperor* (*Marc Rich & Co* v. *Società Italiana Impianti PA*, Case C-190/89, [1991] E.C.R. I-3855) the ECJ considered whether the arbitration exclusion meant that the rules of the Brussels Convention were not applicable to court proceedings relating to an arbitration. In that case, a seller sued a buyer in Italy on a contract of sale. The buyer applied to the English court for an order appointing an arbitrator under a purported arbitration agreement. The English courts queried whether they should determine their jurisdiction under the Brussels Convention (in which case they probably would have had to decline jurisdiction) or the rules of common law, and referred this question to the ECJ. The ECJ held that the related proceedings were excluded from the scope of the Convention: in other words, faced with proceedings relating to an arbitration, an English court would apply common law to determine whether or not it had jurisdiction. The ECJ's judgment was drawn in narrow terms, however, and there remains some uncertainty in this area.

(vi) *Defendant not domiciled in a Member State.* Most of the rules in the Conventions and the Regulation apply only where the defendant in a dispute is domiciled in one of the relevant Member States. For example, an English court would apply the Regulation when determining whether a New York cedant could start proceedings in England against its French-domiciled reinsurer (because the defendant would be domiciled in a Member State); but it would apply the common law when determining whether the French-domiciled reinsurer could sue the New York cedant (because the defendant would not be domiciled in a Member State).

Relevance of special "insurance" rules in the Conventions and the Regulation

The Conventions and the Regulation contain sections which lay down special rules covering jurisdiction in matters relating to "insurance". The effect of these rules is to protect insureds by, in essence, preventing their insurer from being able to sue them anywhere but in their home courts; agreements ("jurisdiction clauses") in insurance contracts which give the insurer the right to sue the insured in any other jurisdiction are usually ineffective (unless the insured risk is a marine, aviation or transport risk).

The common-sense view was that these special rules applied only to direct insurance, and had no application to reinsurance. The argument was that in this context the word "insurance" should be construed narrowly, because the provisions in question were of a consumer-protection nature and were not relevant to the world of reinsurance.

Until recently, the absence of an ECJ decision on the point meant that it was not entirely safe to assume that this view was correct. Lloyd L.J. expressly made this point in *New Hampshire Insurance Co.* v. *Strabag Bau AG* [1992] 1 Lloyd's Rep. 369. Indeed, in submissions before the ECJ the European Commission argued the contrary interpretation: " . . . any exclusion of such a substantial nature would need to be expressly stated in the text of the Convention, and not merely inferred" (*Overseas Union Insurance Ltd* v. *New Hampshire Insurance Company* [1991] E.C.R. I-3317). On that occasion the ECJ made no findings on this point, disposing of the case on other grounds.

Fortunately for reinsurers, in *Group Josi Reinsurance Company SA* v. *Universal General Insurance Company* [2000] 2 All E.R. (Comm) 467, the ECJ has now confirmed that the insurance section of the Brussels Convention does not apply to a dispute between a cedant and a reinsurer in connection with a reinsurance contract. This was because the cedant was not in a position of weakness such that it required special protection under the Convention. This removes the concern that jurisdiction clauses in reinsurance contracts could have been struck down wholesale.

However, the *Group Josi* judgment is not *entirely* good news for reinsurers. The ECJ commented that the special insurance rules *would* be applicable where, under the law of a Member State, a policy holder, insured or beneficiary was entitled to make a direct approach to its insurer's reinsurer and to assert rights under the reinsurance contract, for example where the insurer had become insolvent. The ECJ considered that in this situation the insured would be in a weak position, and would be entitled to benefit from the special protections in the Convention. This is relevant to the issue of cut-through clauses: when considering whether to agree to "cut through" clauses, reinsurers should now bear in mind the possibility that if they end up in a dispute with the original insured, they may have to fight that dispute in the insured's home country regardless of the provisions of any jurisdiction clause in the reinsurance contract.

Jurisdiction clauses

A contract can stipulate which courts are to have jurisdiction to hear any dispute, and such a stipulation is called a "jurisdiction clause". We discuss below the rules which the English courts follow when a contract contains a jurisdiction clause, and those which they follow when the contract is silent.

As will be seen, in most cases a jurisdiction clause will be upheld, whether the court is following the rules of the common law or the Conventions/Regulation. Where the contract is silent as to jurisdiction, the position becomes much more complicated and the scope of uncertainty increases greatly. It is therefore good practice to include a jurisdiction clause in any reinsurance contract. However, it is surprisingly common for contracts to be silent as to jurisdiction, and as a result much time and money is spent arguing over which courts have jurisdiction to hear the substance of the dispute.

A jurisdiction clause need not be complicated. The following is a fairly typical example:

> "The courts of England and Wales shall have exclusive jurisdiction to hear any dispute arising out of or in connection with this agreement."

Where a reinsurance slip incorporates the terms of the underlying policy by means of the words "As original", this may be insufficient to incorporate the underlying jurisdiction clause. For example, in *AIG Group (UK) Ltd* v. *The Ethniki* [2000] Lloyd's Rep. 343, the Court of Appeal held that these words were intended to incorporate the substantive underlying terms of the original policy, but refused to assume that the jurisdiction clause was intended to be carried over in the absence of an absolutely clear intention to that effect. As a result, it is desirable for reinsurance contracts to contain their own jurisdiction clause and not merely rely on "As original" wording.

Exclusive and non-exclusive jurisdiction clauses

An "exclusive" jurisdiction clause is one whereby the parties agree that they shall submit all disputes to a particular country's courts.

A "non-exclusive" jurisdiction clause is one where the parties give themselves the right, but do not bind themselves, to bring claims in a particular court: in other words, a claimant has the option of starting proceedings in that court, but may sue elsewhere if it prefers.

Common law rules on jurisdiction

General jurisdiction

The English courts may accept jurisdiction over a dispute where the defendant is present in England. Companies are present for this purpose if they are incorporated in England, or have a registered office, or a place of business, or if they appoint agents in England to accept service of suit or to carry out transactions on their behalf.

Special jurisdiction

Where the defendant is not present in the UK, the English courts may still accept jurisdiction. The claimant must obtain the leave of the court, and will have to satisfy the court of three matters:

First, that there is a good arguable case that the situation falls within one or more of a number of defined categories. The most relevant of these to reinsurance are as follows:

(a) A claim has been made against someone in England and the potential additional defendant outside England is a necessary or proper party to that claim.
(b) The contract in question was made in England.
(c) The contract was made by or through an agent trading or residing in England. This would allow a claimant to sue a foreign reinsurer where the reinsurer had used a London broker to negotiate the contract, even though the contract was actually executed elsewhere: *Alfia Worldwide Insurance Co* v. *Deutsche Rückversicherungs AG* (1983) N.L.J. 621.
(d) The contract is governed by English law.
(e) The contract contains a choice of English jurisdiction.
(f) The claim is made in respect of a breach of contract committed in England.
(g) The claim is in tort and (i) damage was sustained in England or (ii) damage was sustained from an act committed in England.

These categories are fairly similar to the grounds of special jurisdiction under the Conventions and the Regulation, which are discussed below.

The second matter which the claimant must establish is that there is a "reasonable prospect" of the claim succeeding. In other words, that there is a serious issue to be tried.

Thirdly, the claimant must persuade the court that England is the most appropriate forum for the dispute to be heard in ("*forum conveniens*"). The claimant must establish that substantial justice would not be done if the case were tried in another forum (*Spiliada Maritime Corporation* v. *Cansulex Ltd* [1987] 1 Lloyd's Rep. 1 (H.L.)).

The test of "*forum conveniens*" is a flexible one, and the key point to note is that it is a matter for the court's discretion. The court is entitled to take all of the circumstances into account, for example the convenience of the forum for the parties and witnesses, the time and cost involved in obtaining evidence, and the speed of obtaining judgment. The court may also take account of the law applicable to the contract: for example, if the applicable law of the contract is English law and the dispute relates to English market practice, the court may well consider that it would be appropriate and helpful for the dispute to be resolved in an English court by judges who are familiar with English law and market practice.

In *Trade Indemnity plc* v. *Forsakringsaktiebolaget Njord* [1995] L.R.L.R. 367, reinsurers sought to avoid a Swedish cedant's reinsurance. The judge found that the focus of the dispute was how the cedant had conducted its business in Sweden, that local witnesses would be required, and that the fact that the cover was governed by English law was not sufficient to make England the appropriate forum.

Where the parties to a contract have made a choice of jurisdiction, then the courts will generally uphold that choice.

In *Ace Insurance SA-NV* v. *Zurich Insurance Company* [2000] 2 Lloyd's Rep. 423, a Swiss reinsured provided cover to a Texan company in respect of an oil well. Reinsurers brought proceedings in England against the reinsured. The reinsurance was to "follow the original [insurance] in all respects", and the original policy contained an exclusive jurisdiction clause for Texan law. The reinsured subsequently brought competing proceedings in Texas pursuant to a clause (Non-Marine Association 1998) which provided that "Underwriters hereon . . . will submit to the Jurisdiction of a Court of competent jurisdiction within the United States", and sought to have the English proceedings stayed. The English court stayed its proceedings, and this decision was upheld unanimously by the Court of Appeal ([2001] 1 Lloyd's Rep. 618). Rix L.J. observed that whilst the service of suit clause contained in the reinsurance policy is not an exclusive jurisdiction clause if "a party agrees to submit to the jurisdiction of the courts of a state, it does not easily lie in its mouth to complain that it is inconvenient to conduct its litigation there".

In *BAS Capital Funding Corporation Ltd et al.* v. *Medfinco Ltd et al.* [2003] EWCH (Ch), Lawrence Collins J. stated that there was a very strong presumption in favour of upholding the parties' choice of jurisdiction. Where the parties had chosen English jurisdiction, a party asserting that the English courts should decline jurisdiction would face a "heavy burden", and there would have to be "exceptional circumstances" to justify this. In this situation, the other factors which are usually weighed up in considering jurisdiction had very little, if any, role to play. However, the presumption might be somewhat easier to displace if the jurisdiction clause provided for non-exclusive jurisdiction, and one factor which might be relevant was the existence of parallel proceedings in another jurisdiction (parallel proceedings are considered later in this chapter).

The English court retains discretion not to enforce a jurisdiction clause, even though it will rarely do so. *Citi-March Limited et al.* v. *Neptune Oriental Lines Ltd et al.* [1997] 1 Lloyd's Rep. 72 is an example of a situation where the courts did not uphold a jurisdiction clause. The claimant sued three defendants who were located in England and one in Singapore. The Singaporean defendant asked the English court to stay the proceedings against it on the basis of a Singaporean exclusive jurisdiction clause. The claimant would not have been in a position to pursue its claim in Singapore, because the claim was already time-barred. Colman J. considered that there was strong cause not to stay the English proceedings, on the grounds that if the jurisdiction clause were applied it could have led to proceedings in both Singapore and London with the risk of inconsistent judgments over the same subject matter.

We now consider the Conventions'/Regulation's rules on jurisdiction. It will be seen that the main difference is that the common law approach described above is a flexible one, which involves the courts in exercising their discretion and weighing up the relevant factors to determine whether it is appropriate for them to accept jurisdiction. The Conventions'/Regulation's approach does not involve such discretion. It lays down fixed tests under which the court is obliged to accept or decline jurisdiction.

Conventions'/Regulation's rules where there is a jurisdiction clause

The Conventions and the Regulation provide that where the parties to a contract are domiciled in a Member State (see the section on "Domicile", below), and the jurisdiction clause gives jurisdiction to the courts of a Member State, then those nominated courts shall have exclusive jurisdiction.

In three circumstances the nominated courts' jurisdiction will not be exclusive, so a claimant will have the option (but not the obligation) to bring any proceedings in the nominated forum:

(a) *If the clause states that the jurisdiction is non-exclusive*. The Conventions stated that nominated courts "shall" have exclusive jurisdiction, which caused some uncertainty. Does it mean that courts are to have exclusive jurisdiction even where the parties' jurisdiction clause states that it was non-exclusive? In one case, *Kurz* v. *Stella Musical Veranstaltungs GmbH* [1992] Ch. 196, the English courts gave effect to a non-exclusive jurisdiction clause, but in *Continental Bank NA* v. *Aeakos Compania Naviera SA* [1994] 1 Lloyd's Rep. 505 (C.A.) Steyn L.J. declined to express a view on whether this decision was correct. This uncertainty does not arise under the Regulation, which provides that the nominated courts shall have exclusive jurisdiction unless the parties provide otherwise.

(b) *If the clause was concluded for the benefit of only one of the parties, then that party is not restricted by the jurisdiction agreement and is free to bring proceedings elsewhere if it chooses to do so.* This rule applies only to the Conventions, and was abandoned in the Regulation because of uncertainty as to what it meant. In *Anterist* v. *Crédit Lyonnais* [1986] E.C.R. 1951, the ECJ stated that the fact that one party's home courts are nominated does not of itself mean that the jurisdiction clause was concluded for that party's benefit. Given that the rule does not apply under the Regulation, it is likely to be of relatively little importance in practice.

(c) *If the clause nominates courts which are not in a Member State.* In this case, it is unlikely that the Conventions and the Regulation would apply to the agreement, and an English court should therefore decide whether to uphold the agreement by applying common law principles.

The Conventions and the Regulation also refer to the situation where none of the parties to the contract is in a Member State but the jurisdiction clause nominates the courts of a Member State. In practice, it is quite common for international commercial contracts to provide for English jurisdiction even where none of the parties is domiciled in England or indeed any other EU or EFTA member state.

In this case, the Conventions and the Regulation do not actually specify which courts have jurisdiction (and the English courts would therefore apply common law principles to determine whether they should take jurisdiction). However, to avoid the risk of irreconcilable judgments being handed down by the courts of different Member States, the Conventions lay down a rule of priority which provides that unless and until the nominated court declines jurisdiction no other Member State's courts may hear the dispute.

> **Example**: A New York cedant and a Bermudian reinsurer choose English jurisdiction. The English courts would apply common law rules to determine whether to accept jurisdiction. Other EU and EFTA courts must decline to hear the dispute unless and until the English court has declined jurisdiction.

Conventions'/Regulation's rules where there is no jurisdiction clause

General jurisdiction

The main rule of the Conventions and the Regulation is that a claimant may sue a defendant in the courts of the defendant's domicile, regardless of the defendant's nationality. So if a French-domiciled cedant has a dispute with its English-domiciled reinsurer, the cedant may bring proceedings in England against the reinsurer, and the reinsurer may bring proceedings against the cedant in France (although, as we will see later, the Conventions and the

Regulation have rules which prevent there being two sets of parallel proceedings in different courts regarding the same subject matter).

Domicile

The Conventions and the Regulation both use the concept of "domicile", but it has different meanings in each.

Under the Regulation, a company is domiciled where it has its registered office; or if there is no registered office, in the place where it is incorporated; or if there is no such place, in the place under whose laws the company was formed.

Under the Conventions, domicile is determined by national law. Under English law, a company is domiciled where (i) it was incorporated or formed under that state's law and it has its registered office or some other official address, or (ii) its central management and control is exercised.

So under the Conventions, a company may have more than one domicile at the same time, and this could give claimants against the company a wider choice of forum than under the Regulation.

Special jurisdiction

The Conventions and the Regulation provide certain grounds of special jurisdiction, which may give claimants a further choice of forum in which to bring proceedings against the defendant. The relevant four grounds of special jurisdiction are considered below.

(i) Matters relating to a contract

In "matters relating to a contract", the claimant may sue the defendant in the courts for "the place of performance of the obligation in question". The ECJ has held that "the place of performance of the obligation in question" means (except in employment cases) the obligation which forms the basis of the claim. So where a cedant sues its reinsurer for non-payment of a reinsurance claim, the obligation in question is the obligation to make payment.

> **Example**: An English cedant makes a claim under a reinsurance contract. The German reinsurer refuses to pay the claim. Under the terms of the contract, claims must be paid in England. Under this ground of special jurisdiction, the cedant could sue the reinsurer in England. (Of course, if it preferred, the cedant could instead sue in Germany, under the general ground of jurisdiction.)

Under English law there is a rebuttable presumption that payments are due at the address of the payee. In practice, therefore, where the contract is governed by English law and the claim is for non-payment, the claimant will have the option of suing in his own country or that of the defendant.

Fisher and Others v. *Unione Italiana di Riassicurazione SpA* [1999] Lloyd's Rep. IR 215 illustrates this ground of special jurisdiction. An Italian retrocedant agreed to a retention requirement. Its English retrocessionaire sued, in England, for a declaration that it was not liable to pay because the retrocedant had breached the retention requirement. The claimant argued that the "obligation in question" was its obligation to pay claims in England. Colman J. disagreed. Reviewing the way in which the claim was formulated, he said that the obligation in question was the retention requirement. This was to be performed in Italy, not England, and so the English courts did not have special jurisdiction.

If payments are made to a broker, does the broker's address become "the place of performance of the obligation in question"? This is likely to depend on whether there was a binding obligation to make payment to the broker, rather than a mere voluntary practice. If a binding obligation is established, then "the place of performance of the obligation in question" should be the country in which the broker is located.

There has been disagreement about whether this ground of special jurisdiction would apply where the claim is for repayment of premiums under a reinsurance contract which has been avoided for misrepresentation or non-disclosure, or indeed where the claimant is seeking a declaration that a contract is void.

In *Ian Charles Agnew* v. *Lansforsakringsbolagens AB* [1996] L.R.L.R. 392, reinsurers in the London market sued in England for declarations that they were entitled to avoid because of alleged misrepresentations in England by the cedant which had induced them to enter into the reinsurance. Accepting earlier authority on the point, the defendant cedant conceded that the dispute was a "matter relating to a contract", and the judge (Mance J.) stated that this concession was well-founded because the claims were "on any objective appreciation intimately concerned with and closely related to the contracts". However, the defendant argued that pre-contractual misrepresentations or non-disclosures could not be breaches of an "obligation in question", since they did not arise under the contract. Mance J. disagreed. He took the view that once it is established that the matter relates to a contract, it is not appropriate to distinguish between pre- and post-contractual obligations. The duty to make a fair presentation of the risk was one which was capable of being "the obligation in question", and one which provided a "sensible and convenient" basis of jurisdiction. That judgment was upheld by the Court of Appeal.

The cedants appealed to the House of Lords, but their appeal failed (despite an intervening House of Lords decision in a non-insurance case, *Kleinwort Benson* v. *Glasgow City Council* [1997] 4 All E.R. 641, which appeared to be very helpful to them). Their Lordships agreed that the claim to avoid the reinsurance was a "matter relating to a contract". Although their Lordships had differing views as to the precise nature of the obligation which founded special jurisdiction, it is clear from the speeches that the English courts do have special jurisdiction over reinsurance disputes where it is alleged that non-disclosure or misrepresentation occurred in England.

(ii) Matters relating to tort

In matters relating to tort, the claimant may sue in the courts for "the place where the harmful event occurred". This expression was considered by the ECJ in *Handelskwekerij G.J. Bier BV* v. *Mines de Potasse d'Alsace SA*, Case 21/76 E.C.R. 1735. Waste water was released in the Rhine in France and caused damage to seed beds in the Netherlands. Was the place where the harmful event occurred France or the Netherlands? The ECJ held that it was both: the claimant could sue (at its option) in either (a) the place where the harmful act was committed or (b) the place where the damage was suffered.

(a) PLACE WHERE THE HARMFUL ACT WAS COMMITTED

Where a reinsured negligently or intentionally breaches its duty to make a fair presentation of the risk, the reinsurer should in principle be able to found special jurisdiction in the place where the misrepresentation or non-disclosure was committed.

Under English law, a representation is usually considered to be made at the place where it is received. However, in *Domicrest Ltd* v. *Swiss Bank Corporation* [1998] 3 All E.R. 577, Rix J. held that for the purpose of the Conventions the location of the harmful event should be given an "autonomous meaning" rather than being determined by particular national laws. On that basis, he held that for the purpose of the Conventions a negligent misstatement occurs where it is made, and not where it is received.

> **Example**: A German reinsurer sues an English cedant for a declaration of avoidance, alleging misrepresentation. The misrepresentations were made in telephone conversations between the cedant and the reinsurer. The harmful event occurred in England, and the English courts would have special jurisdiction.

(b) PLACE WHERE THE DAMAGE WAS SUFFERED

The *Bier* case concerned physical damage, but in most reinsurance cases the "damage" incurred will be purely financial.

In *The ERAS EIL Actions* [1992] 1 Lloyd's Rep. 570, the Court of Appeal held that where the manager of a reinsurance pool suffered economic loss at its head office, it could not invoke special jurisdiction under this head. However, the manager could obtain leave to sue the pool's underwriting agents because the agents had exposed it to claims by the pool participants which did constitute "damage" of the kind required.

This is consistent with ECJ decisions which have held that if the initial damage occurs in one country, the claimant cannot sue in another country merely because it indirectly suffers financial loss elsewhere: to hold otherwise would almost invariably entitle a claimant to sue in its home country, which the ECJ stated was inconsistent with the primary jurisdictional rule of the Convention, namely that defendants should generally be sued in their home countries.

(iii) Disputes arising out of a branch, agency or other establishment

As regards a dispute arising out of the operations of a branch, agency or other establishment, a claimant may sue in the courts for the place in which the branch, agency or other establishment is situated.

The ECJ has interpreted the expression "branch, agency or other establishment" so that it has a very narrow meaning. It exists only where the entity in question is under the direction or control of a parent body, has a management, and is materially equipped to negotiate business with third parties on behalf of the parent (which must be domiciled in a Member State). In addition, it must have the appearance of permanence.

Insurance brokers are not within this provision. This was confirmed by the English courts in *New Hampshire Insurance Co* v. *Strabag Bau AG* [1990] 2 Lloyd's Rep. 61. A German cedant failed, via its broker, to disclose material facts to its reinsurer. The judge (Potter J.) held that the reinsurer could not rely on the fact that the broker was situated in England to bring proceedings there against the cedant because the broker was not a "branch, agency or other establishment": this expression was intended "to connote an organ or business presence which is itself an extension or emanation of the defendant's own business and subject to its general control, rather than an independent entity whose business it is to act as agent or broker for others".

(iv) Other defendants

The claimant may sue the defendant in a court where related proceedings are brought. Where the defendant is one of a number of defendants it may be sued in the courts of the place where any one of them is domiciled. So for example, where a lead reinsurer is domiciled in Germany and the following reinsurers are domiciled in England, the reinsured could sue all of the reinsurers in Germany or England.

It might be thought that a claimant could abuse this provision by joining a second defendant solely for the sole purpose of dragging the "true" defendant into a court which is more suitable to the claimant. However, the ECJ has ruled that this provision may be used only where the claim against the additional defendant is "related", in the sense that it would be expedient to hear the claims together to avoid the risk of irreconcilable judgments: and where the claim against one of the defendants is clearly untenable, there is little or no risk of an irreconcilable judgment being given.

CONCURRENT PROCEEDINGS

Introduction

This section addresses the complexities which can arise when disputes relating to the same matter are litigated in separate proceedings in different jurisdictions.

Such multiple proceedings are common in reinsurance disputes, where parties often "forum shop" for a jurisdiction which holds some advantage to them (often, but not always, their home country). As we mentioned at the start of the chapter, the place where a dispute is heard can have a significant effect on the conduct of the proceedings, for example it will impact on the speed and cost of the proceedings and the ease of obtaining evidence.

It is obviously undesirable for the same issue to be litigated in more than one forum for reasons of costs and inconvenience, but perhaps the greatest concern is the possibility of the different courts giving conflicting judgments.

The rules relating to concurrent proceedings

The Conventions/Regulation contain rules which deal with concurrent proceedings in the courts of Member States, and which proceedings must yield (or be "stayed"). Where the English court is considering proceedings which are not in a Member State, it will apply principles of common law (see *Re Harrods (Buenos Aires) Ltd* [1992] Ch. 72 (C.A.)—but it has been argued that the Conventions/Regulation must be given a wider role than this, and this question has been referred to the ECJ for decision: *Owusu* v. *Jackson* [2002] EWCA Civ 877).

Stays and injunctions

The two tools which the English courts use to deal with concurrent proceedings are stays (i.e., stopping actions from proceeding within England) and anti-suit injunctions (i.e., injunctions to restrain a party from pursuing proceedings elsewhere).

In the following sections consideration is given to the position under the common law (cases involving a conflict of jurisdiction between the English courts and the courts of a non-contracting state) and the procedural tools which are applied, as well as the rules which the Conventions/Regulation apply in relation to concurrent proceedings.

When should proceedings be stayed?

English courts have the power to order a stay of proceedings which are concurrent with proceedings pending in a foreign court. In the context of disputes involving a conflict of jurisdiction between the English courts and the courts of a non-contracting state, this power is exercised where it can be shown that England is an inappropriate forum (*forum non conveniens*). This test can be summarised as follows (*Spiliada Maritime Corp* v. *Cansulex Ltd* [1987] A.C. 460):

(a) the defendant must show that there is another competent court with jurisdiction which is clearly more appropriate than English courts for determining the dispute; and
(b) there is no injustice to the claimant in not having the dispute determined in England.

The following are two examples of the English courts' approach to applications by parties to stay English proceedings in favour of concurrent proceedings in foreign jurisdictions:

***New Hampshire Insurance Company* v. *Philips Electronics North America Corporation* [1999] Lloyd's Rep. IR 58 (C.A.)**

An insured, based in Illinois, presented claims to its English insurer, who issued proceedings in England seeking a declaration that losses claimed by the insured were excluded under the policy terms, which were governed by English law. The insured subsequently commenced proceedings in Illinois in respect of its claim and sought to stay the English action. At first instance the stay application was refused and this decision was upheld by the Court of Appeal. In the Court of Appeal's view, as the policy was governed by English law, the English courts were the more appropriate forum in which to resolve issues relating to policy construction. Of particular relevance was the fact that a determination on the construction of the policy was likely to obviate the need for a full trial.

This case should not however be seen as representing a hard and fast rule in terms of these types of stay applications, as it was determined very much upon its own facts, particularly that the construction issues were complex and that the determination of these construction issues was likely to resolve the dispute. A further point of relevance was that the insured had been tardy in commencing its proceedings in Illinois. Indeed the Court of Appeal commented that it was undesirable for matters of fact and matters of construction to be determined in different jurisdictions. But see *Royal & Sun Alliance Ins Plc* v. *Retail Brand Alliance Inc* [2004] EWHC 2139 (proceedings in England would be stayed in favour of proceedings in New York, despite a master policy being governed byEnglish law, as that was the only factor favouring English law).

***HIB Limited* v. *Guardian Insurance Company* [1997] 1 Lloyd's Rep. 412 (Q.C. Com. Ct.)**

This case involved a dispute between a reinsured based in the US Virgin Islands, an English reinsurer, and an English broker. The reinsured entered into communications with the reinsurer and the broker, alleging that the broker had been negligent and had breached his duties to the reinsured. The broker issued proceedings in England seeking a declaration that he was not in breach of his broking duties. In response, the reinsured commenced an action in the US Virgin Islands. Following from this both parties sought stays of the proceedings commenced by the other. The reinsured's application to have the English proceedings stayed was unsuccessful. Longmore J. concluded that as the broking agreement was governed by English law, and the negligent acts were alleged to have taken place in England, England was the appropriate forum.

When should anti-suit injunctions be granted?

Another tool which can be deployed by an English court in respect of concurrent proceedings is the anti-suit injunction. Anti-suit injunctions prohibit a party from either filing or continuing proceedings in a foreign jurisdiction, the rationale being that disputes should be litigated and determined only once and in the appropriate forum. Importantly anti-suit injunctions will be granted against a party only if they will be effective. This means that it will be possible for an anti-suit injunction to be granted only against a party which is present in England or is already a party to English proceedings.

In the context of disputes involving a conflict of jurisdiction between the English courts and the courts of a non-contracting state, the English courts will invoke anti-suit injunctions where the applying party can show that the English courts are the natural forum for the determination of the dispute, and that the foreign proceedings are vexatious or oppressive in nature.

To determine whether an anti-suit injunction should be granted, a determination needs to be made as to:

(a) which is the appropriate forum; and
(b) whether the foreign proceedings are indeed vexatious or oppressive.

The following case demonstrates the English courts' application of this test.

***Donohue* v. *Armco Inc & Others* [2000] 1 Lloyd's Rep. 579 (C.A.), [2002] 1 Lloyd's Rep. 425 (H.L.)**

An anti-suit injunction was applied for, arising from proceedings commenced in New York relating to management buy-out contracts, which contained English exclusive jurisdiction clauses. At first instance an anti-suit injunction was refused on the basis that not all of the issues present in the New York proceedings fell within the ambit of the exclusive jurisdiction clauses in the relevant contracts. Further, not all of the parties to the New York proceedings were signatories to the contracts, and indeed only some of the claims fell within the ambit of those contracts. In these circumstances it was held that England was not the appropriate forum and that the New York proceedings were not vexatious and oppressive.

The Court of Appeal overruled the first instance decision and granted an anti-suit injunction, placing more emphasis on the existence of the exclusive jurisdiction clause. In the Court of Appeal's view it was vexatious and oppressive to pursue proceedings other than in the agreed forum. The Court of Appeal also appears to have considered it relevant that the instigating of the issues in New York exposed certain of the parties to treble damages and higher litigation costs.

The House of Lords overturned the Court of Appeal's decision and discharged the anti-suit injunction. The House of Lords held that the English court should decline to grant an anti-suit injunction even where an exclusive English law jurisdiction clause existed, where parallel proceedings would take place in any event: here, as there were parties who were not subject to the relevant contractual provisions but were nevertheless party to the New York proceedings, the New York proceedings would proceed regardless of any anti-suit injunction, leading to the risk of inconsistent decisions.

The position under the Conventions/Regulation

The common law doctrine of *forum conveniens* involves a high degree of judicial discretion. There is no such judicial discretion under the Conventions/ Regulation. Instead fixed rules apply. We now give an overview of the key rules of the Conventions/Regulation and briefly discuss the interpretation of some of the more important terms.

The court first seised of the dispute

Under the Conventions/Regulation, where proceedings involving the same cause of action between the same parties are brought in the courts of different Member States, the court which is first seised of the dispute is deemed to have jurisdiction, and any subsequent courts where proceedings are brought must decline of jurisdiction. This encourages a "race to the court house" as parties to disputes aim to bring proceedings in their preferred forum before their opponents, thus gaining the upper hand in terms of jurisdiction. This in turn places considerable importance on exactly when a court becomes seised of a dispute.

The Conventions

Article 21
Where proceedings involving the same cause of action between the same parties are brought in the courts of different contracting States, any court other than the court first seised shall of its own motion stay its proceedings until such time as the jurisdiction of the court first seised is established.

Article 23
Where actions come within the exclusive jurisdiction of several courts, any court other than the court first seised shall decline jurisdiction in favour of that court.

The Regulation

Article 27

1. *Where proceedings involving the same cause of action and between the same parties are brought in the courts of different Member States, any court other than the court first seised shall of its own motion stay its proceedings until such time as the jurisdiction of the court first seised is established.*

2. *Where the jurisdiction of the court first seised is established, any court other than the court first seised shall decline jurisdiction in favour of that court.*

Article 29

Where actions come within the exclusive jurisdiction of several courts, any court other than the court first seised shall decline jurisdiction in favour of that court.

We consider below some of the expressions used in these provisions.

"Seised"

The Conventions did not contain any definition of the term "seised", and it was left to the courts of individual Member States to determine, in accordance with their national laws, exactly when they were first seised. In *Zelger* v. *Salinitri* [1983] C.M.L.R. 366, the ECJ held that a court is first seised of an action when "the requirements for proceedings to become definitively pending are first fulfilled". In most cases it would seem that the English court is first seised only when the claim form is served on the defendant, and not merely upon issue of the claim form (*Dresser UK Ltd* v. *Falcongate Freight Management Ltd* [1991] 2 Lloyd's Rep. 557 (C.A.), *SDL International Ltd* v. *Centre de Co-operation International*, 2000, unreported).

By contrast, the Regulation contains a provision which lays down when a court becomes seised of a dispute.

Article 30

For the purposes of this Section, a court shall be deemed to be seised:

1. *at the time when the document instituting the proceedings or an equivalent document is lodged with the court, provided that the plaintiff has not subsequently failed to take the steps he was required to take to have service effected on the defendant, or*
2. *if the document has to be served before being lodged with the court, at the time when it is received by the authority responsible for service, provided that the plaintiff has not subsequently failed to take the steps he was required to take to have the document lodged with the court.*

The effect of this provision is that, under the Regulation, the English court is first seised when a claim form is issued. As a result, a party which wishes to seise the English court would be able to do so more quickly in cases to which the Regulation applies than in Convention cases.

"The same cause of action"

The Conventions and the Regulation do not define "same cause of action". One important question is whether a claim for a declaration constitutes the "same cause of action" as a claim for payment under a contract. Proceedings seeking declaratory relief on the construction of a policy, and proceedings seeking damages under the same policy, have been held to share the same cause of action: *The Maciej Rataj* [1991] 2 Lloyd's Rep. 458 (Q.B.), [1992] 2 Lloyd's Rep. 552 (C.A.). A practical consequence of this is that a party which fears being sued for non-payment in an unfavourable jurisdiction will often be able to start a pre-emptive action in a more favourable forum, seeking a declaration of non-liability. That court having been seised, proceedings subsequently started elsewhere would be stayed.

"The same parties"

The interpretation of the expression "the same parties" is important to reinsurance disputes, which can often involve multiple parties who, while being signatories to the same policy or treaty, may not have the same involvement in proceedings issued in separate jurisdictions. For tactical or substantive reasons, one particular party may not be named in proceedings seeking declaratory relief relating to a policy interpretation point, but may be party to proceedings claiming damages under that policy.

The ECJ has concluded that the parties to the competing actions must be identical for the first seised rule to apply: *The Maciej Rataj* [1995] 1 I.L.Pr. 81. So if the second proceedings involve some but not all of the parties in the first action, the second court need only decline jurisdiction in respect of the parties common with the first proceeding.

Both the Conventions and the Regulation make provision for the consolidation of "related proceedings", which would be relevant in such a situation.

Article 22 (Conventions)

Where related actions are brought in the courts of different Contracting States, any court other than the court first seised may, while the actions are pending at first instance, stay its proceedings.

A court other than the court first seised may also, on the application of one of the parties, decline jurisdiction if the law of that court permits the consolidation of related actions and the court first seised has jurisdiction over both actions.

For the purposes of this Article, actions are deemed to be related where they are so closely connected that it is expedient to hear and determine them together to avoid the risk of irreconcilable judgments resulting from separate proceedings.

Article 28 (Regulation)

1. *Where related actions are pending in the courts of different Member States, any court other than the court first seised may stay its proceedings.*
2. *Where these actions are pending at first instance, any court other than the court first seised may also, on the application of one of the parties, decline jurisdiction if the court first seised has jurisdiction over the actions in question and its law permits the consolidation thereof.*

3. *For the purposes of this Article, actions are deemed to be related where they are so closely connected that it is expedient to hear and determine them together to avoid the risk of irreconcilable judgments resulting from separate proceedings.*

APPLICABLE LAW

Reinsurance is a particularly international industry. The contracts are often entered into by parties in different countries with different legal systems, covering risks around the world (or, indeed, in space). The question arises, which law applies to the contract? This may make a huge difference to the way in which the contract works, and to the parties' rights and obligations: for example, if there is a breach of warranty this may entitle the reinsurer to avoid the contract (if the applicable law is English law) or merely to some lesser remedy such as damages (if another law applies).

How do the English courts determine the applicable law? Originally, rules were developed as part of the common law. These rules have been largely superseded by the Convention on the Law Applicable to Contractual Obligations of 1980 (the "Rome Convention"), although the common law rules continue to apply where the contract in question was effected before 1 April 1991 or the contract falls outside the scope of the Convention (see *Figure 2*, below). The rest of this chapter outlines the common law and Convention rules for determining the law applicable to a contract.

In the remainder of this chapter, references to the "Convention" are to the Rome Convention—not to be confused with references to the "Conventions" (the Brussels and Lugano Conventions) in the jurisdiction part of Chapter 8.

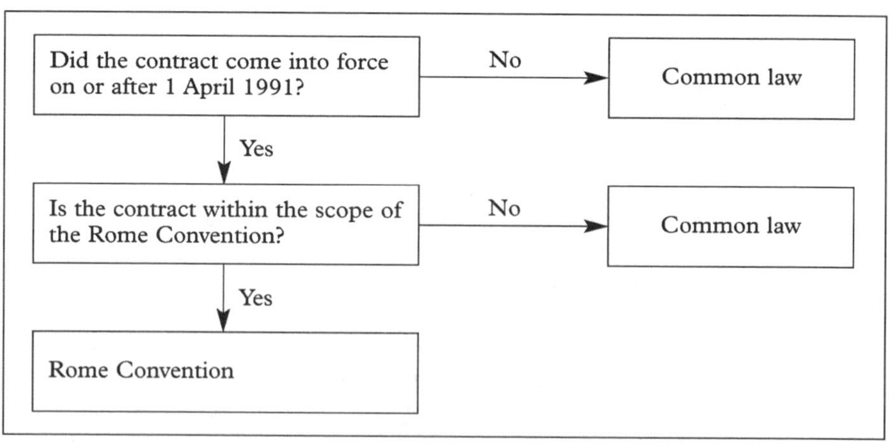

Figure 2. How to determine the applicable law of contract

Choice of law clauses

The English courts have long recognised that parties may select the law which they wish to apply to their contracts. Where a contract includes a statement of the law which is to apply to the contract (a "choice of law clause"), both the common law and the Convention will uphold such a choice.

A typical choice of law clause is as follows:

"This contract is governed by and shall be construed in accordance with English law."

The clause should nominate a clearly defined system of law. For example, reference should be made to "English law" (or, more accurately, "the laws of England and Wales") rather than "the laws of Great Britain" or "the laws of the United Kingdom" as the latter expressions are ambiguous (England and Wales have one law and Scotland and Northern Ireland have their own). Similarly, reference should be made to (for example) "the laws of New York" rather than "the laws of the United States".

As with jurisdiction, the rules are more complicated where the contract does not explicitly make any choice. In this situation there is greater uncertainty, which often ends in litigation. Given this fact, it is surprising how often contracts omit to choose the applicable law: perhaps the parties, in their enthusiasm to conclude the deal, simply overlook the point. Good practice is to make sure that every contract includes a choice of law clause.

Where a reinsurance contract provides coverage on terms "As original", this may not be sufficient to incorporate any choice of law clause from the underlying contract. As a result, the insurance and reinsurance contracts could turn out to be governed by different applicable laws, and this could create a mismatch in coverage. Therefore, a choice of law should be inserted even in "As original" wordings.

The Rome Convention

The English courts will usually determine the applicable law by following the rules laid down in the Rome Convention. This was adopted into English law by the Contracts (Applicable Law) Act 1990. The Convention largely supersedes the old common law in this area, although the common law is still relevant where the contract is outside the scope of the Convention, and the old common law authorities are also sometimes considered by the English courts when they are determining how the Convention rules should be applied.

The Convention has also been adopted by the other EU Member States, so in theory any court in the EU should reach the same conclusion as to which law governs the contract. The Convention regulates all choice of law matters heard in the courts of signatory States, regardless of whether or not the domicile of the parties to the contract or the applicable law in question is that of a Convention State.

Example: A Californian cedant and a Bermudian reinsurer agree to a choice of New York law. An English court hearing the dispute would determine the applicable law by following the rules in the Convention (the Convention would uphold the parties' express choice of law).

Exclusions from the Convention

Article 1 of the Convention sets out various exclusions from its scope. The exclusions which are most relevant are as follows:

(a) Contracts of direct insurance relating to risks located in the EU. Special rules apply to these risks (in essence, the contracts will often be governed by the law of the insured's country, regardless of any agreement to contrary): these rules are laid down in the second life and non-life insurance directives.
(b) Arbitration/jurisdiction clauses. When looking at arbitration/jurisdiction clauses, courts will not apply the Convention's rules to determine which law governs the arbitration/jurisdiction clause.
(c) The question whether an agent is able to bind a principal.
(d) Procedural issues are to be determined by reference to the law of the forum. In other words, an English court will continue to apply English procedure regardless of the law which applies to the contract.

As mentioned above, where the obligation is outside the scope of the Convention, the English courts will apply the old common law rules to determine the law applicable to the obligation.

Express choice of law

Where the parties have made an express choice of law, that choice will be upheld, both under the Convention and common law. This is subject to certain qualifications which are discussed later in the chapter.

Example: A German cedant and a French reinsurer enter into a contract which makes an express choice of New York law. An English court hearing a dispute relating to the contract would apply New York law to the contract.

No express choice of law

The common law

Where no choice of law clause exists, a court applying the common law will consider the contract and the factual background to ascertain whether the parties have made any choice of law by implication.

In the following two examples the use of Lloyd's forms was considered to be demonstrative of the parties' intention that the underlying contracts be governed by English law.

***Amin Rasheed Shipping Corporation* v. *Kuwait Insurance Co.* [1983] 2 Lloyd's Rep. 365**

The House of Lords found that the use of a Lloyd's marine form was a factor which suggested that English law was the governing law, even where the other relevant circumstances surrounding the contract pointed to the law of Kuwait.

***Tiernan* v. *Magen Insurance Co. Ltd* [2000] I.L. Pr. 5178 (Q.B. Com. Ct.), Longmore J.**

Where a contract was in Lloyd's form and contained London market clauses and bore all of the hallmarks of clauses framed in London, English law was implied as the parties' choice of law.

Arbitration clauses are weighty but not conclusive evidence of an intention to have the jurisdiction's substantive law govern. In *Mitsubishi Corporation* v. *Castletown Navigation Ltd* [1989] 2 Lloyd's Rep. 383, the inference usually drawn from the presence of a London arbitration clause was displaced because all other relevant factors suggested that the parties intended that Japanese law should determine their rights under a bill of lading.

If no implied choice of law can be ascertained, the courts will determine the applicable law by weighing up all the circumstances surrounding the conclusion of the contract and determining, on balance, the system of law with which the contract is most closely connected. Factors to be taken into account include the place of residence of the parties, the place of conclusion of the contract, the place of performance, and the currency of the transaction. In this exercise, the court is attempting not to identify the subjective intentions of the parties but rather to "determine for the parties what is the proper law which, as just and reasonable persons, they ought to have intended if they had thought about the question when they made the contract" (*The Assunzione* [1953] 2 Lloyd's Rep. 716, *per* Singelton L.J.).

In *Cantieri Navali Riuniti SpA* v. *NV Omne Justitia ("The Stolt Marmaro")* [1985] 2 Lloyd's Rep. 428, the Court of Appeal decided that an insurance contract was governed by English law because of the role which the English marketplace had played in the transaction: the contract was made in London, with English leading underwriters, through brokers working in the London market, under a policy introduced by the London brokers who were accustomed to working in accordance with English law and practice. So although the insured was Italian, the relevant insurer was Italian and other insurers were situated elsewhere, the court held that the "centre of gravity" of the contract was England.

A similar approach was taken in *Citadel Insurance Co* v. *Atlantic Union Insurance Co. SA* [1982] 2 Lloyd's Rep. 543 (C.A.). Canadian cedants were reinsured by a Greek reinsurer under a facility operated by London brokers. The Court of Appeal held that the "centre of gravity" was London.

The Convention

Where there is no express choice of law, the Convention also provides for two alternatives, which may be described as "implied" choice of law and no choice of law.

Implied choice of law

Under the Convention (Article 2) an implied choice of law exists where the parties to a contract made a choice of law which is not expressed but is:

"demonstrated with reasonable certainty by the terms of the contract or the circumstances of the case".

The official report on the Convention (the *Giuliano and Lagarde Report*) states that an implied choice should be found only if the parties have made a "real" choice of law: it "does not permit the court to infer a choice of law that the parties might have made where they had no clear intention of making a choice": in other words, the parties must have addressed their minds to the question.

By way of illustration of terms and circumstances which may lead the court to conclude that the parties had made a "real" choice of law the *Report* cites the following: (i) that the contract is in a standard form which is known to be governed by a particular system of law even though there is no express statement to this effect, such as a Lloyd's policy of marine insurance; (ii) that there has been a previous course of dealing between the same parties under contracts containing an express choice of law and the choice of law clause has been omitted in circumstances which do not indicate a deliberate change of policy; (iii) that the parties have chosen a particular forum (but any presumption that they intended the law of the forum to apply must always be subject to the other terms of the contract and all the circumstances of the case); (iv) that the contract refers to the provisions of a particular law such as specific Articles of the French Civil Code; (v) that there is an express choice of law in related transactions between the same parties; and (vi) that there is a choice of the place of arbitration in circumstances which indicate that the arbitrator should apply the law of that place.

Some of these examples seem to confuse situations where the parties have made a real choice with situations where they have not. For example, the fact that the parties have used a Lloyd's marine policy does not in reality show that they have given any thought to the question of the applicable law. Moreover, the suggestion that the law applicable to Lloyd's marine policies or any other contract should be determined, in effect, by custom appears to conflict with the Convention's aim of providing a consistent framework of rules by which to determine the applicable law.

The English courts have not shown reluctance to find an implied choice of law. One example is:

***Gan Insurance Co. Ltd & Another* v. *Tai Ping Insurance Co. Ltd* [1999] Lloyd's Rep. IR 229**

Taiwanese risks were insured by a Taiwanese insurer and reinsured in a London placement which was part of an international programme. The slip policies contained standard London market terms. The reinsurers claimed that the reinsurances were governed by English law because the contracts were in standard London market form using English legal terminology, the placement was through London brokers to London market reinsurers, and the slip policies contained "as original" language which was intended to ensure that the scope of the cover underwritten by reinsurers was identical to that of the original policy. The cedant argued that the reinsurance should be governed by Taiwanese law, so that its international programme would have a consistent applicable law. Cresswell J. accepted the reinsurers' arguments and held that there was an implied choice of English law.

Applicable law in the absence of any express or implied choice

Where the parties have not made a choice of law which is expressed or demonstrated with reasonable certainty by the terms of the contract or the circumstances of the case, the Convention provides that the contract is governed by the law of the country with which the contract is most closely connected. This differs from the common law approach, which looked to the legal system with which the contract is most closely connected.

The Convention provides a rebuttable presumption as to the country with which the contract is most closely connected. The presumption involves two stages. First, the court must determine which of the parties to the contract is required to give the "performance which is characteristic of the contract" (see below). Secondly, the court must then identify the country in which (at the time of conclusion of the contract) that party's principal place of business was situated (or if under the terms of the contract the performance is to be effected through a place of business other than the principal place of business, the country in which that other place of business is situated). The presumption is that the contract is most closely connected with the law of this country.

The concept of "characteristic performance" is not defined in the Convention. The *Report* explains that contractual obligations typically fall into two types, the first being an obligation to pay money, the second (the characteristic performance) being the performance for which the payment is due. Although it might be thought that a contract of reinsurance involves no characteristic performance, as both parties' obligations involve the payment (or potential payment) of money, the *Report* cites the provision of insurance as an example of characteristic performance. The usual presumption will therefore be that a contract of reinsurance is most closely connected with the law of the country in which the reinsurer has its principal place of business.

> **Example:** An English cedant purchases reinsurance cover from a reinsurer which has its principal place of business in Bermuda. The contract would, in the absence of an express or implied choice of law, be rebuttably presumed to be governed by Bermudian law.

Where the same risk is covered by reinsurers with their head offices in several countries, this approach would have the consequence that different laws may apply in respect of the same risk. This would be disadvantageous to the cedant, because its reinsurance programme could end up being governed by a variety of different laws. This could be contrary to the Convention's aim of encouraging legal certainty. It also fails to give effect to the purpose for which the concept of "characteristic performance" was devised, which (according to the official report) was to "link . . . the contract to the social and economic environment of which it will form part".

In *Lincoln National Life Insurance Co.* v. *Employers Reinsurance Corporation* [2002] Lloyd's Rep. IR 853, Moore-Bick J. held that it was necessary to find a single country with which various contracts were most closely connected. He found that, contrary to the presumption, the contracts were most closely connected with England on the basis that they were negotiated there by London market brokers using London market documentation. Similarly, in *CGU International Insurance plc* v. *Szabo* [2002] Lloyd's Rep. IR 196, Toulson J. held that a global policy was governed by a single applicable law, and that the law could not vary depending on the place in which the relevant claim was made. He found that English law governed the contract on the grounds that the policy was negotiated, concluded and issued in England, the premium was in sterling, and various terms of the policy were consistent with the application of English law principles. This approach is similar to the "centre of gravity" approach adopted in the common law cases.

Circumstances where choice of law clauses may be overruled by the courts

Although the courts are reluctant to interfere with a choice of applicable law, the common law and the Convention provide some limited circumstances in which such a choice will not be upheld.

Contravention of public policy

English law recognises the freedom of parties to choose a law which is not connected to their transaction. The courts may, however, refuse to uphold a choice in exceptional circumstances. In *Vita Food Products Inc* v. *Unus Shipping Co. Ltd* [1939] A.C. 277, Lord Wright upheld a choice of English law by two overseas companies, stating that "connection with English law is not as a matter of principle essential". However, he left open the possibility of the courts overriding a choice of law clause by stating that the choice must be "bona fide and legal" and that there must be no reason for "avoiding the choice on the ground of public policy". There is no reported case of this principle having been applied to strike down a choice of law clause, and it would seem to be relevant only in the unusual situation where the applicable law is chosen merely to evade some prohibition in the law of the place where the contract was made or was to be performed.

The Convention mirrors the common law to some extent on the question of public policy.

> **Article 16**
> *The application of a rule of the law of any country specified by this Convention may be refused only if such application is manifestly incompatible with the public policy ("ordre public") of the forum.*

The *Report* makes it clear that this Article is intended to be of very narrow application.

In *Akai Pty Ltd* v. *People's Insurance Co. Ltd* [1998] 1 Lloyd's Rep. 90, the court enforced an express choice of law clause notwithstanding that the clause in question was invalid in the domicile of one of the parties (the Australian Insurance Companies Act 1984, which provided that choice of law clauses are void insofar as they provide for non-Australian law to apply in circumstances where the proper law of the contract would otherwise be the law of an Australian state).

The Convention provides that, regardless of the law generally applicable to the contract, the court may sometimes apply certain rules (known as "mandatory rules") of a different law. "Mandatory rules" are those legal rules which cannot be derogated from by contract. They are typically found in the fields of consumer and employment law. For example, an English court might find that a consumer contract is governed by French law, but nevertheless apply a specific "mandatory rule" of English law which strikes down unreasonable exclusion clauses. This is unlikely to be of great relevance in the context of reinsurance contracts.

TEST YOUR UNDERSTANDING

Jurisdiction

1. Why is the forum in which a dispute is heard important?

(a) It may affect whether any judgment is enforceable against the defendant.
(b) The judiciary may be more experienced in one forum than another.
(c) The rules of contract law vary from forum to forum.
(d) It may have practical consequences for the attendance of witnesses and the gathering of evidence.
(e) It may affect the speed at which the proceedings can be pursued.

2. Which of the following is not concerned with determining the courts which have jurisdiction to hear a dispute?

(a) Common law.
(b) Brussels Convention.
(c) Lugano Convention.
(d) Hague Convention.
(e) Brussels Regulation.

3. A jurisdiction clause provides: "The Reinsurer may bring proceedings against the Cedant in any forum including, without limitation, the courts of England and Wales." This clause is:

(a) An exclusive jurisdiction clause.
(b) A non-exclusive jurisdiction clause.

4. Under the common law rules, which one of the following is not a ground for the English courts to accept jurisdiction against a defendant?

(a) The defendant is present in England.
(b) The contract was made in England.
(c) The contract was made through a London broker.
(d) The contract is governed by English law.
(e) The claimant is present in England.
(f) The contract chooses English jurisdiction.

5. In addition to establishing that one or more of the above criteria applies, what else does a claimant have to demonstrate in order to persuade the English court to accept jurisdiction under the common law rules?

(a) There is a reasonable prospect of the claim proceeding (a serious issue to be tried).
(b) The claimant is situated in the EU.
(c) The claim exceeds £100,000.
(d) England is the most appropriate forum for the dispute to be heard in (*forum conveniens*).

6. Under the common law rules, what approach do the English courts take where a contract contains a jurisdiction clause in favour of the English courts?

(a) The English court must accept jurisdiction. It has no discretion.
(b) The English court may accept jurisdiction. It will weigh up all the

factors. The jurisdiction clause will be a very strong factor in favour of accepting jurisdiction.

(c) The English court may accept jurisdiction. It will weigh up all the factors, but the jurisdiction clause has no more weight than any other factor.

7. Under the Conventions/Regulation, where can a claimant sue a defendant?

(a) The defendant's country of domicile.
(b) The place where the contractual obligation in question was due to be performed.
(c) The place where the tort was committed (where the dispute relates to a tort).
(d) In the most convenient forum having regard to matters such as the availability of evidence and convenience for witnesses.
(e) The place where the defendant has a branch or agency (if the dispute arises out of the branch or agency).
(f) The place where the broker is situated.
(g) Where related proceedings have been brought against another defendant.

Applicable Law

8. Which of the following sources are used by the English court to determine the law which governs a reinsurance contract made in 2004?

(a) Common law rules.
(b) Brussels Convention.
(c) Lugano Convention.
(d) Rome Convention.
(e) Brussels Regulation.

9. When may the English court refuse to uphold a choice of law?

(a) Where the parties to the dispute have no connection with England but have nevertheless chosen English law to govern the contract.
(b) Where the English court considers that it would be inconvenient to apply English law.
(c) Where it would be contrary to English public policy to uphold the choice of law, because the choice is made to evade a rule of law.

10. Where the parties to a contract have made no express or implied choice of law, the courts seek to ascertain either the system of law (common law rules) or the country (Convention) with which the contract is most closely connected. How do the courts do this?

(a) The common law weighs up all the factors and looks to the "centre of gravity" of the transaction. The Rome Convention rebuttably presumes that the applicable law is the law of the reinsurer's head office.

(b) The common law weighs up all the factors and looks to the "centre of gravity" of the transaction. The Rome Convention rebuttably presumes that the applicable law is the law of the reinsured's head office.

(c) The common law rebuttably presumes that the applicable law is the law of the reinsurer's head office. The Rome Convention looks to the "centre of gravity" of the transaction.

(d) The common law rebuttably presumes that the applicable law is the law of the reinsured's head office. The Rome Convention looks to the "centre of gravity" of the transaction.

CHAPTER 10

ARBITRATION

INTRODUCTION

What is arbitration?

Arbitration is an agreement between two or more parties to resolve a dispute or difference between them. The dispute or difference is resolved by a tribunal whose award is final and binding on the parties and enforceable in law. Appeals from the tribunal's award are permitted, but only in certain circumstances. The arbitration process is private and consensual and is usually derived from contract. It provides an alternative to litigation but not to ADR which may still be used in conjunction with the arbitration process. An arbitration agreement may specify in some detail how a dispute is to be referred to arbitration although a simple statement in writing as to an agreement to arbitrate will also be sufficient.

The Arbitration Act 1996

The relevant national legislation that one must consider when agreeing upon arbitration with a seat in England, Wales or Northern Ireland (referred to in this paper as England for convenience) is the Arbitration Act 1996 (the Act).[1] In addition to providing the framework for judicial control of arbitration, the Act sets out certain minimum requirements relating to the conduct of arbitral proceedings in England. It is intended to provide a "non-interventionist" regime for commercial arbitration in England and is designed to be accessible.

The 1996 Act repeals virtually all the 1950, 1975 and 1979 Arbitration Acts and the Consumer Arbitration Agreements Act 1988 and is a comprehensive restatement and modernisation of the law of arbitration. The 1996 Act also codifies important principles established by recent case law, although the body of case law which has grown up over the years remains relevant insofar as it is not inconsistent with the 1996 Act.

1. Section 3 of the 1996 Act defines the "seat of the arbitration" as the juridical seat of the arbitration, designated by the parties to the arbitration agreement, or by any arbitral or other institution or person vested by the parties with the power to determine the seat, or by the arbitral tribunal, (if authorised by the parties), or otherwise determined having regard to the parties' agreement and all the relevant circumstances. A copy of the 1996 Act is available at *http://www.hmso.gov.uk*.

The three general principles of the 1996 Act

Section 1 of the 1996 Act recites three general principles on which it is founded. These principles are essentially three key features of English arbitration law as it stood at the time of the drafting and publication of the 1996 Act:

- The object of arbitration is to obtain the fair resolution of disputes by an impartial tribunal without unnecessary delay or expense;
- The parties should be free to agree how their disputes are resolved, subject only to public policy safeguards;
- The Court should not intervene in the conduct of arbitrations except in the limited circumstances set out in the 1996 Act.

The impact of the 1996 Act on arbitration in England is discussed further throughout this chapter.

International arbitration

Where one or more of the parties is situated outside of England, the parties may choose to have their dispute resolved in a jurisdiction neutral to both parties and in accordance with international arbitration rules administered by institutions such as the London Court of International Arbitration (LCIA) or according to ad hoc rules.

The impact of the most commonly used international arbitration rules are discussed further throughout this chapter.

THE USE OF ARBITRATION IN REINSURANCE DISPUTES

Most reinsurance treaties (but not usually facultative agreements) contain clauses requiring the parties to submit their disputes to resolution by arbitration rather than by court proceedings. Traditionally, insurers and reinsurers have favoured arbitration (often ad hoc—this is discussed further below) for a variety of reasons. For example, arbitration is perceived as enabling experts to hear a dispute on a confidential basis and then give a non-binding decision. Arbitration is also thought to be quicker and cheaper than court proceedings and can provide a neutral forum. In addition, enforcement of an arbitration award may be easier than enforcement of a judgment of a foreign court. In the past reinsurance agreements have also frequently contained "engagement" clauses along the following lines:

> "The arbitrators should interpret the reinsurance as an honourable engagement and should make their award with a view to effecting the general purpose of the contract in a reasonable manner, rather than in accordance with a literal interpretation of the language, the true intention of the parties being that the reinsurers should follow the fortunes of the reinsured."

Under English Law, the Court of Appeal's decision in *Home & Overseas Insurance Co. Ltd* v. *Mentor Insurance Co. (UK) Ltd* [1990] 1 W.L.R. 153 expressly recognised that the effect of the "honourable engagement" provisions within the arbitration clause of excess of loss reinsurance contracts was to enable the arbitrators to consider the general purpose of the contracts and to depart if necessary from the literal and ordinary meaning of the words so that the contracts could be construed as far as possible to achieve the purposes of the transactions. This approach was reinforced by section 46(1)(b) of the 1996 Act by providing for arbitrators to decide the dispute "*if the parties so agree, in accordance with such other considerations as are agreed by them or determined by the tribunal*". The use of this provision by the parties will, however, usually exclude appeals on the law as, pursuant to section 69 of the 1996 Act, a court can hear an appeal on a point of English law only. This is discussed later in this chapter.

In practice, however, it is unclear what the "honourable engagement" clause means. For example does the clause allow arbitrators to avoid laws of limitation? Does it allow arbitrators to apply different rules of construction when construing contracts? Whatever the meaning and effect of honourable engagement clauses, they are perceived as being of benefit, whether rightly or wrongly.

Many of the other reasons given above for traditionally using arbitration to resolve reinsurance disputes have now also become diluted and this is discussed in more detail in this chapter.

Other methods of dispute resolution available—a brief outline

Court proceedings

Over the last 20 years the Commercial Court in England has developed tremendous expertise in determining reinsurance disputes and many of its judges have been drawn from the pool of barristers who practise insurance and reinsurance law. The judges are therefore genuine experts in this field. In light of the implementation of the Civil Procedure Rules in 1999 (the "CPR"), the Commercial Court has actively embraced proactive case management and often sets fairly tight timetables for taking disputes through to trial, sometimes making Commercial Court proceedings quicker than arbitration proceedings. Proactive case management by the Commercial Court will also sometimes involve limitations on the amount of disclosure to be given by the parties and restrictions on the amount of witness and expert evidence (all issues which often prompt parties to arbitrate rather than litigate). As a result, Commercial Court proceedings are now usually comparable to arbitration proceedings from a cost perspective (and the cost of court fees are substantially less than the fees and expenses of arbitration). In addition, parties to a reinsurance dispute may find it positively advantageous to have their dispute resolved by the Commercial Court where the dispute involves multiple parties (including intermediaries), where interim remedies are likely to be sought (such as injunctive relief) or where the matter is suitable for disposal by summary judgment or where the parties are looking for a precedent. These issues are discussed further in the next section.

However, notwithstanding the fact that the number of reinsurance related disputes resolved through the Commercial Court has increased substantially in recent years, the majority of disputes are still resolved by arbitration.

A hybrid?

In some circumstances parties may agree to arbitrate disputes of a certain type or value with other disputes being determined by litigation or ADR.

ADR

ADR is used increasingly by parties in reinsurance disputes in advance of arbitration or litigation. It may take the form of either negotiation, mediation, conciliation, mini-trial, non-binding arbitration, expert determination or early neutral evaluation.

Negotiation—parties may enter into negotiations once a dispute has arisen. Alternatively, they may, in advance of any dispute arising, include a clause in their agreement which provides that the parties enter into "good faith" negotiations in relation to any dispute before resorting to litigation or arbitration. This effectively provides the parties with a cooling-off period, enabling them to focus on the benefits of settlement rather than rushing into litigation or arbitration. It is usual for the parties to agree a time period within which the parties will try to negotiate a settlement to their dispute and if there is no successful outcome within this period, either party is then able to commence litigation or arbitration proceedings as appropriate.

Mediation—an impartial third party will facilitate discussions between the parties with a view to the parties negotiating their own solution to the dispute.

Conciliation—usually appointed by agreement between the parties, a conciliator usually takes an active role in negotiations, including possibly making recommendations as to what would be a fair resolution of the dispute.

Mini-trial—both parties present their legal cases to a panel consisting of a senior executive from each party and a neutral chairman (usually a retired judge or senior lawyer). A non-binding decision will be given by the panel, which the parties may use as a basis for settlement discussions.

Non-binding arbitration—An appointed arbitrator may make a finding on a particular part of the case or based on a limited review of the documents and evidence. The parties are not bound by the arbitrator's decision but they can later agree to accept it.

Expert opinion—An independent expert's opinion may be obtained on any aspect or aspects of the case at any stage in the dispute. The parties are not bound by it but they may agree to accept it.

Early neutral evaluation—An independent opinion of the parties' legal, factual and/or technical cases may be obtained with a view to encouraging settlement between the parties. It may be done on an ad hoc basis or by using an ADR organisation (for example, the City Disputes Panel, based in London).

In January 2007 the London Market adopted the CPR International Reinsurance Industry Dispute Resolution Protocol, a statement of "best practices" aiming to encourage the early and efficient resolution of disputes between reinsurers and reinsureds. Reinsurers are free to refer to it or incorporate it in their treaties and agreements or adopt it on a unilateral basis, as a statement of their own policies and procedures. Parties to particular disputes may also adopt the protocol as a means of managing information exchange and the protocol may also be modified by parties to meet the challenges of a specific matter.

The protocol provides a four step method for identifying and giving early notice of a dispute relating to a reinsurance contract, exchanging information and documents to permit a commercially reasonable assessment of the issues in dispute, directly negotiating with the parties to resolve the dispute and if required, introducing a neutral third party to facilitate negotiations through a mediation procedure. Although the protocol is not legally binding it is anticipated that the reinsurance industry will use it and will gain substantial economic benefits by doing so.

The protocol is available at *www.InsuranceMediation.org*

Mode of arbitration: ad hoc v. institutional

Reinsurance arbitrations may be conducted under the auspices of an international arbitral institution such as the LCIA. There are other international arbitral institutions such as the International Court of Arbitration (the ICC) or the American Arbitration Association (the AAA) but these are rarely used in reinsurance arbitrations. An arbitral institution provides rules pursuant to which the arbitration is conducted and assistance with the general administration of the arbitration, such as initiation of the arbitral proceedings, formation of the tribunal and appointment of arbitrators.

Alternatively, reinsurance arbitrations may be conducted on an ad hoc basis whereby the parties conduct the arbitration without the assistance of an arbitral institution. If the parties opt for a pure ad hoc arbitration, rules will also be tailor-made to the specific requirements of the parties and to the circumstances of a likely dispute under the reinsurance contract. However, if this approach is adopted there will usually be a heavy administrative burden on the parties (sometimes once the dispute has already arisen) in terms of agreeing the framework for the arbitration process and a risk of delay through non-cooperation between the parties. For example, if a party chooses to be uncooperative, applications may need to be made to the appropriate national court to appoint arbitrators or to resolve questions of jurisdiction. Both of these issues are likely to be dealt with more effectively and quickly using an institutional structure. In addition, many institutional rules have short time frames for complying with the early stages of the arbitration, with the result that an institutional arbitration is likely to be up and running much more quickly than an ad hoc arbitration. Notwithstanding the initial advantage for the parties of not having to pay the administration costs of an institutional arbitration, they may therefore find that the ad hoc arbitration process is in fact more expensive and time consuming.

A further alternative available is for the parties to choose ad hoc arbitration but with ARIAS Rules (see further below). This is usually considered preferable to pure ad hoc arbitration as it enables the parties to avoid involving an arbitral institution if they wish to do so but have the benefit of having their arbitration determined in accordance with a set of generally accepted rules. The options available to parties are discussed further below.

Pure ad hoc arbitration

Where parties choose a pure ad hoc arbitration, they should agree in advance the framework of the arbitral procedure but they should avoid setting out every detail. These aspects are best dealt with once a dispute has arisen. Within the arbitration clause in a contract, the key area that needs to be covered is the procedure to be followed, at least until the arbitral tribunal is created. This will include:

- How the arbitration is to be commenced;
- The appointment procedure for arbitrators;
- The timetable for an initial exchange of pleadings (this enables the parties and the arbitrators to understand the nature of the dispute);
- The finality of the award.

ARIAS

London Market insurers and reinsurers adopted the ARIAS rules with effect from January 1994. These rules have since been revised and the revised rules took effect from 1 June 1997. They are specific to insurance and reinsurance disputes and may be used in any venue in the world, although in the absence of the parties stating otherwise the venue of the arbitration will be London. ARIAS provides a panel of independent arbitrators and mediators (many of whom have occupied senior positions as underwriters, brokers or claims executives in the reinsurance sector) who provide assistance in the resolution of insurance and reinsurance disputes, primarily through arbitration in London but also ADR. Most of the arbitrators and mediators are UK based, however some are based in Europe and the USA. Most reinsurance disputes involving London Market insurers and reinsurers will be determined under ARIAS.

Institutional

Institutional arbitration is often known as "administered" or "supervised" arbitration. The main institution that tends to be used for reinsurance arbitrations is the LCIA. An arbitral institution provides trained staff and a governing body to administer the arbitration and advise users. In particular, the governing body will ensure that the arbitral tribunal is appointed, the arbitrators' fees and expenses and mode of payment are agreed and that time limits prior to the formation of the tribunal are complied with.

LCIA

The LCIA is London-based and was founded in 1892. It selects arbitrators to determine disputes. Its membership is extremely international, with no more than one quarter of its members being allowed to be British nationals. Arbitrations under LCIA rules may be held anywhere in the world, although in the absence of a contractual choice the place of arbitration will usually be London. It operates according to revised rules which took effect from 1 January 1998. Strict confidentiality is maintained in arbitrations under the LCIA as it does not publish any awards made under its rules. LCIA disputes typically relate to a diverse range of industries and in 2002 insurance-related disputes accounted for 6%. Despite the LCIA being London based, almost 80% of the parties involved in disputes are not of UK nationality. It has an excellent reputation for administration and its fees (both for administration and arbitrators) are broadly based on time spent, calculated using hourly or daily rates.

Appendix 4 sets out the key features of arbitration under the LCIA and ARIAS rules.

WHAT ARE THE ADVANTAGES AND DISADVANTAGES OF USING ARBITRATION TO RESOLVE REINSURANCE DISPUTES?

The advantages?

Speed

Arbitration is historically perceived as being swifter and more efficient than litigation. However, in England, since the advent of the 1999 Civil Justice reforms and the implementation of the CPR (which have their overriding objective of enabling the courts to deals with cases justly, including so far as practicable—saving expense, dealing with a case in ways which are proportionate and ensuring that a case is dealt with expeditiously and fairly), this perception may well now be misconceived. One reason for this is the reduction in the Commercial Court waiting times for trial and the use of tight timetables mentioned above, often imposed as a result of active case management by the court. Conversely, in arbitration proceedings, it can often take months even to constitute a panel. One of the main reasons for this is that in the reinsurance field there is a relatively small pool of suitably qualified arbitrators. Furthermore, panel members tend to have very full diaries and it is by no means a foregone conclusion that the parties will be able to fix a two-week hearing within a year of the commencement of arbitral proceedings.

Another important factor in reducing the speed and efficiency with which arbitrations are conducted is that arbitrators have less power to sanction deliberate delaying tactics by parties. In England, the 1996 Act (ss. 41 and 42) deals with the situation where a party defaults on his obligations (such as employing deliberate delaying tactics). Section 41 allows the parties themselves to agree on the powers of the tribunal in case of a party's failure to do something necessary for the proper and expeditious conduct of the arbitration although arbitrators are sometimes reluctant to use the powers given to them. However, in the event that the parties do not agree on such powers various default powers apply. These default powers are more limited in scope than those available to a court. In the context of international arbitration, the rules of some institutions give powers to the tribunal to deal with a party's delaying tactics in certain circumstances but these powers will vary according to the rules chosen by the parties.

Because arbitration is essentially a cooperative process, there is always a risk that the parties will allow their disputes to spill over into the procedural conduct of the arbitration thereby nullifying some of the advantages which might otherwise be obtained.

Cost

Arbitration is perceived as the cheaper alternative to litigation, but it should be noted that this tends to be borne out where the process is swift and where the parties cooperate with each other in the arbitral process.

Another additional cost factor to be considered in arbitration is that arbitrators are paid by the parties, whereas judges are not. The cost will obviously depend on a number of case-specific factors, but a full multi-jurisdictional arbitration involving a panel constituted of three members could well turn out to be much more expensive than a Commercial Court trial.

Furthermore, it is also necessary for the parties to an arbitration to pay for the arbitration venue. This may amount to considerable costs in long running international disputes—for example if, as is often the case in international arbitration, the parties are from two different jurisdictions and the arbitration venue is in a neutral jurisdiction.

Flexibility

A major advantage of arbitration over litigation is that, if conducted properly, arbitration can be a more flexible forum in terms of resolving disputes. Litigation, in English court proceedings, is governed by the CPR and active case management by the courts. In contrast, section 1(b) of the 1996 Act states that:

> "(b) the parties should be free to agree how their disputes are resolved, subject only to such safeguards as are necessary in the public interest."

This flexibility can be particularly useful in documentary matters such as disclosure and evidence where the parties may agree to limit disclosure or witness evidence (in English court proceedings the courts may make these decisions). The advantage of flexibility in litigation in relation to disclosure and evidence does, of course, depend upon the nature of the claim being pursued. If, for example, a party has few documents, arbitration may not necessarily provide any real advantage over litigation.

Sadly, recent experience suggests that the disclosure process in reinsurance arbitrations all too often follows the costly and time-consuming format of disclosure in litigation, where parties not only have to disclose a wide ranging variety of documents (in short, documents that support both parties' cases) but they also have to list each and every one of these documents. Also the parties may have to apply to the court (the Commercial Court deals with applications arising out of arbitrations in England) to obtain disclosure of documents from third parties, such as brokers.

A further example of the way in which arbitrations can be more flexible is the use of "honourable engagement" clauses (also known as "equity clauses") which were discussed in the previous section. As mentioned above, there is some uncertainty as to what these clauses actually mean in practical terms.

Finality

Arbitration decisions are notoriously hard to appeal and therefore the parties are less likely to be subjected to the long-running and costly appeals process sometimes experienced by parties who have their disputes heard by the English courts. The 1996 Act provides that a party can appeal the decision of a tribunal in only very limited circumstances:

- under section 67 to challenge the substantive jurisdiction of the arbitral tribunal;

- under section 68 if there is serious irregularity affecting the tribunal; and
- under section 69 on a point of law.

Appeals are considered in more detail in the section on "Judicial Control of Arbitration", below. In each case, permission must be sought from the courts in order to appeal the decision of the arbitral tribunal.

Furthermore, as discussed above, no appeal on a point of law is available where an "honourable engagement" clause is used. In addition, the right to appeal on a point of law can also be excluded by the agreement of both parties.

Whilst the relative finality of arbitrations may be seen as attractive to parties when considering whether or not to include an arbitration clause in their reinsurance contract, such limited rights of appeal will be, of course, unsatisfactory for a party who feels he has been the victim of a poor decision.

Expertise of arbitral tribunal

In arbitration proceedings the parties usually choose either a sole arbitrator or a panel comprising three members. In reinsurance cases the arbitration panel will usually consist of a mixture of lawyers and market men. There are undoubted advantages of having market men on the panel. Many clauses require the arbitrators to be drawn from the market. The wealth of their experience in the reinsurance market inevitably assists with the understanding and smooth running of often complex and technical disputes. Furthermore, the existence of market men on the arbitration panel may obviate the need for the parties to appoint experts.

However, as stated in the previous section above, Commercial Court judges assigned to hear reinsurance disputes are invariably highly experienced in insurance/reinsurance matters and so the advantage of having market men, who are experienced in the reinsurance field, appointed as arbitrators to the panel may not be as great as may at first seem.

Enforcement of arbitral awards

The ease with which arbitration awards can be enforced is discussed in detail in the final section of this chapter. In summary, an arbitration award made in England has the benefit of being enforceable in any of the countries that have signed up to the 1958 New York Convention on the Recognition and Enforcement of Foreign Arbitral Awards (the "New York Convention") (currently over 140 signatory states including the US, France, Japan, China, Germany, Japan, New Zealand, South Africa). This is a possible advantage to any multi-jurisdictional dispute, as enforcing an English court decision abroad can be a complex, costly and uncertain process. However, the enforcement of court decisions in EU and EFTA countries (under the Brussels and Lugano Conventions) is also extremely straightforward and so the ease with which arbitral awards can be enforced is unlikely to be a factor where enforcement is required in one of these countries.

Confidentiality

Confidentiality is generally perceived as being one of the principal benefits of arbitration as opposed to litigation and it is assumed that parties to the arbitration, as well as the tribunal, are bound to keep even the existence of the arbitration confidential. However, whether an implied obligation of confidentiality arises out of the nature of arbitration is controversial and there are discrepancies between the laws of different countries and the rules of different arbitral institutions on the subject. In the absence of any express provision in the arbitration agreement to keep the proceedings, documents, evidence, etc, confidential, it is necessary to look to the national law which governs the proceedings, or to any relevant institutional rules, for guidance.

Looking therefore at the position under English law, although the 1996 Act is an extensive arbitration code, there are a small number of areas which are not covered by the 1996 Act, including the issue of confidentiality. Until 1995 it had always been assumed that the nature of the arbitration agreement between the parties implicitly required the proceedings to be kept confidential between the parties and between themselves and the tribunal. This approach had been consistently followed by the English courts. However, in 1995, the High Court in Australia (*Esso/BHP* v. *Plowman* [1995] 128 A.L.R. 391) rejected the prevailing English view that a general duty of confidentiality exists. The result of this controversial decision was that one of the parties could use information obtained from the arbitral proceedings in court proceedings outside the scope of that arbitration.

Following on from this, attempts were made to formulate the principles of confidentiality in the draft Arbitration Bill, but it was concluded that this would be too difficult and controversial.

Accordingly, under English law, one must fall back on the common law in order to determine the scope and extent of the duty of confidentiality in arbitration. Under English law, a party to an arbitration agreement is subject to an implied obligation of confidence not to make use of material generated in the course of the arbitration outside that arbitration (*Ali Shipping Corp* v. *Shipyard Trogir* [1998] 2 All E.R. 136). This was earlier established in *Dolling-Baker* v. *Merrett and Another* [1990] 1 W.L.R. 1205, where it was held that there exists an implied obligation of non-disclosure by the parties due to the very nature of arbitration. As a result under English law, documents prepared for the purposes of the arbitration are confidential and are protected from disclosure in any subsequent proceedings. The same applies to the award/judgment. However, the principle is subject to exceptions and qualifications:

information regarding an arbitration may be disclosed with the consent of the parties, where there is a legal requirement to do so or an order of the Court, with the leave of the Court, where disclosure is necessary to protect the legitimate interests of an arbitrating party (*Hassneh Insurance Co.* v. *Mew* [1993] 2 Lloyd's Rep. 243), or where disclosure is required in the public interest/interests of justice (*London and Leeds Estates Ltd* v. *Paribas Ltd (No. 2)* [1995] 1 E.G.L.R. 102). The position is different, however, in certain other jurisdictions.

The issue of confidentiality under English law was considered again in *The Department of Economic Policy & Development, City of Moscow* v. *(1) Bankers Trust Company & (2) International Industrial Bank* [2003] EWHC 1377 (Comm) Q.B.D., 5 June 2003. Here, the Commercial Court held that an application to the court made in respect of an arbitration, whilst being a form of disclosure, could not be a breach of any duty of confidentiality. The Commercial Court also held that there can be no breach of the duty of confidentiality in disclosing the fact of the commencement of arbitral proceedings, the existence of an arbitration or the result of that arbitration where there is any legitimate reason to do so. Equally, disclosure of the existence of any challenge to an award, the existence of consequent litigation and the result of that litigation does not amount to a breach. In the *Moscow* case, the Commercial Court also held that disclosure to the investors of the result of an arbitral award was necessary, the situation being analogous to disclosure to shareholders in a company if an arbitration dispute had a material impact upon its accounts. However, the Commercial Court found that where the issues raised were not questions of law, the parties' desire for privacy (implicit in their agreement to arbitrate) should be respected in the context of any proceedings arising out of the award. The Commercial Court found that the underlying arbitration itself and everything raised in relation to the underlying arbitration was confidential. This issue was considered further by the Court of Appeal ([2004] EWCA Civ 314). Upholding the Commercial Court's decision in part, the Court of Appeal commented that there could not properly be a blanket protection of non-publication in all cases that fell initially to be heard in private and when preparing and giving judgment the court had to bear in mind that any judgment should be given in public where that could be done without disclosing significant confidential information. The public interest in ensuring appropriate standards of fairness in the conduct of arbitrations militated in favour of a public judgment in the context of judgments given on applications under section 68 of the 1996 Act and the factors militating in favour of publicity have to be weighed together with the desirability of preserving the confidentiality of the original arbitration and its subject-matter.

In *Hassneh* (*Hassneh Insurance Co.* v. *Mew* [1993] 2 Lloyd's Rep. 243) the court had held that an arbitrating party could properly disclose an award and the reasons behind that award to a third party against whom it had a claim on the grounds that such disclosure was necessary for the establishment or assertion of the arbitrating party's rights. The exception was not extended to the evidence and pleadings in the arbitration proceedings which remained confidential. The Court of Appeal in *Ali Shipping Corp* v. *Shipyard Trogir* [1998] 2 All E.R. 136, however, extended the exception in *Hassneh* to "pleadings, written submissions, and the proofs of witnesses as well as transcripts and notes of the evidence given in the arbitration".

Other exceptions have also traditionally been recognised by arbitration practitioners in England, including the fact that non-parties, such as a parent company or an insurer, can have legitimate interests in being informed as to the contents of a pending arbitration. Furthermore, it is recognised that a company might also have statutory and other duties to make disclosure of arbitration proceedings or awards which have an effect on its financial position.

However, there may be disadvantages relating to having confidentiality in arbitration proceedings. In *Insurance Company* v. *Lloyd's Syndicate* [1995] 2 Lloyd's Rep. 272 the court considered a similar situation to that in *Hassneh* but found on the facts that the party wishing to make disclosure of an award to another was not able to demonstrate that it was necessary (as opposed to merely helpful or persuasive) to disclose the award in order for that party to enforce or protect its rights. The *Insurance Company* case is a prime example of one undesirable consequence that can arise out of the confidential nature of arbitration. In this case, the defendant reinsured wished to disclose the interim arbitral award that had been made in its favour as against the lead reinsurers (the claimants) to various other reinsurers who were part of the same syndicate as the claimants. The claimants applied for an injunction restraining the defendants from disclosing the award to the other reinsurers. The court granted the injunction, thereby preventing the defendant reinsured from disclosing the award that it had obtained against the reinsurer claimants in arbitral proceedings with other reinsurers, even though the issues against the other reinsurers were virtually identical to those in respect of which the award had been made.

Clearly, from a reinsured's point of view, this is a very unsatisfactory situation. Had the dispute in respect of which the award been made been litigated in the English courts, the judgment would have been in the public domain, and the legal principles, insofar as they related to the same issues, would then have been binding on a court hearing the parallel proceedings between the reinsured and its other reinsurers. Instead, the reinsured was forced to go through the time and expense of prosecuting a virtually identical claim for a second time. Had the reinsured been able to disclose the earlier award to the other reinsurers with whom it was in dispute, it is likely that this would have encouraged the other reinsurers to settle the claim against them. Furthermore, if a party has an arbitration award made in its favour, it may find that, due to confidentiality, it is unable to disclose it to other organisations such as brokers and rating agencies.

On the other hand, the decision of the Privy Council in *Associated Electric Gas Insurance Services Limited* v. *European Reinsurance Company of Zurich* [2003] UKPC 11 provides some comfort to a party who succeeds in an arbitration. In this case, the Privy Council was asked to decide whether a reinsurer (European Re) who had succeeded in an earlier arbitration against a reinsured (Aegis) should be allowed to place the award before a later tribunal where the same principles that had been decided in the earlier arbitration were in issue between the same parties in the later arbitration.

Aegis' principal argument was that disclosure of the earlier award to the new tribunal would breach European Re's obligation of confidentiality in relation to the original arbitration and the terms of an express agreement that had been reached during the course of the original arbitration. The parties had expressly stipulated that: "*The parties, their lawyers, and the Court of Arbitration agree as a general principle to maintain the privacy and confidentiality of the arbitration. In particular they agree that . . . the arbitration result will not be disclosed at any time to any individual or entity, in whole or in part, which is not a party to the arbitration between Aegis and European Re.*"

In finding against Aegis, the Privy Council stated that: "*The otherwise legitimate use of an earlier award in a later, also private, arbitration between the same two parties would not raise the mischief against which the confidentiality agreement is directed . . . the essential purpose of arbitration is to determine disputes between the parties to the arbitration . . . as Section 58 of the UK Arbitration Act 1996 says, '. . . an award made by the Tribunal pursuant to an arbitration agreement is final and binding . . . on the parties'. It is an implied term of an arbitration agreement that the parties agree to perform the award.*"

The Privy Council went on to say:

> "Taking these factors into account and construing this confidentiality agreement, that is to say, the mischief at which the clause is directed and the fundamental purpose of an arbitration agreement, it becomes clear that it should not be construed so as to prevent one party from relying upon an award as having given him rights against the other. But that is what the application for an injunction sought to achieve . . . It will be appreciated that, if the prohibition *[against disclosure of any aspect of the arbitration]* was to be given an unrestricted construction, it would mean that any award would be unenforceable . . . This would be fundamentally inconsistent with and frustrate the purpose of arbitration."

From a practical perspective therefore, it may be worth considering making express provision for confidentiality in the arbitration agreement where appropriate. Alternatively, where there is no express provision in the arbitration agreement, the parties may consider making a request to the tribunal to make appropriate provisions in a procedural order or the Terms of Reference. For completeness, it is worth noting that the only international institutional rules that deal with the issue of confidentiality are those of WIPO (reflecting the importance of confidentiality in the field of intellectual property disputes) and the LCIA.

The disadvantages?

Inability to compel joinder of third parties and consolidate proceedings

As discussed above, an agreement to arbitrate is contractual which means that the decision to proceed and the rules adopted for the arbitral proceedings are matters of agreement as between the parties to the contract.

It is therefore not usually possible for a tribunal to hear the underlying dispute between the original assured and the insurer/reinsured at the same time as the dispute between reinsured and reinsurer unless all parties have the same arbitration clause in their contracts and they agree to consolidate all the arbitration proceedings. Under English law, section 35 of the 1996 Act allows parties to agree to consolidate arbitration proceedings with other arbitration proceedings; however, the agreement of all parties is needed. If agreement is not reached then under section 35(2) of the 1996 Act the tribunal has no power to order consolidation of proceedings or concurrent hearings. In practice, this means that section 35 can be of limited value.

However, as policies between insurers and assureds often contain dispute resolution clauses that refer disputes to the courts, a further complication arises as it is not possible to consolidate arbitration proceedings with court proceedings. This may create difficulties in a reinsurance context where coverage disputes arise. The court hearing the dispute between the insurer and original assured will be unable to hear the dispute between the insurer/reinsured and his reinsurer, unless the latter both consent to dispense with the arbitral proceedings. This inability to consolidate proceedings will often lead to multiple actions, with one dispute being heard by the courts and the other dispute being heard in arbitration. This is likely to be extremely expensive and can, from time to time result in inconsistent decisions.

In addition, due to the fact that not all of the parties in a reinsurance dispute can necessarily be joined to an arbitration, the arbitration between reinsured and reinsurer will often not be the end of the story. Where an arbitral tribunal finds in favour of a reinsurer, a Commercial Court action will often follow dealing with the liability (or otherwise) of the placing broker with the reinsured often arguing that but for the broker's breach of contract and/or negligence, he would have had cover under the reinsurance contract. Again, this will often involve the reinsured having to go to the time and expense of fighting a further case, the underlying facts of which have already been dealt with and considered at length in the original arbitration with reinsurers. Arbitration should therefore not necessarily be seen as a "one-stop-shop" for reinsurance dispute resolution.

Limited scope for summary judgment/other interlocutory procedures available in the courts

The powers given to a tribunal are either decided by agreement between the parties, or where the arbitration clause is silent and the arbitration is governed by the 1996 Act, section 41 of the Act will apply. Section 41, however, does not contain any provisions for making interim applications such as applications for a summary judgment. Consequently, where the parties have agreed to arbitrate and it subsequently transpires that the claim lacks merit, the claim may continue to be heard at arbitration without granting the tribunal the power to dispose of the claim summarily. The absence of any ability to award interim payments of any kind is particularly important in the run-off market where reinsurers regularly take unmeritorious positions and can take the case to the end of the arbitration process, at great cost and inconvenience to the reinsured without being ordered to pay any sums up front.

Lack of precedent in the market

As stated above, the majority of reinsurance disputes are arbitrated. Furthermore, as discussed above, the award and the reasons behind the award are, in general, confidential. As a consequence, interesting/important points decided by an arbitral tribunal will not, in theory, come into the public domain and will not create precedent. This can lead to uncertainty and to the same, or similar, points being arbitrated/litigated over and over again. The advantage of course for a party who receives an unfavourable award is that this will not bind him in other disputes relating to the same issue. This is in contrast to court proceedings which establish precedents and thereby create, on the whole, more certainty in relation to particular areas of the law. Lord Justice Mance's comments in the Court of Appeal's decision in *Sun Life Assurance Co. of Canada, American Phoenix Life and Phoenix Home Life* v. *Lincoln National Life Insurance Co.* [2004] EWCA Civ 1660 sum up the problems that arbitration can give rise to:

> "The resulting inability to enforce the solutions of joinder of parties or proceedings in arbitration, or to try connected arbitrations together other than by consent, is well recognised . . . Different arbitrations on closely interlinked issues may as a result lead to different results, even where . . . the evidence before one tribunal is very largely the same as that before the other. The arbitrators in each arbitration are appointed to decide the disputes in that arbitration between the particular parties to that arbitration. The privacy and confidentiality attaching to arbitration underline this; and, even if they do not lead to non-parties remaining ignorant of an earlier arbitration award, they are calculated to lead to difficulties in obtaining access, and about the scope of any access, to material relating to that award."

THE ARBITRATION AGREEMENT

Arbitration clause v. submission agreement

Under English law, section 6 of the 1996 Act defines an arbitration agreement as:

> (1) . . . an agreement to submit to arbitration present or future disputes (whether they are contractual or not).

(2) The reference in an agreement to a written form of arbitration clause or to a document containing an arbitration clause constitutes an arbitration agreement if the reference is such as to make that clause part of the agreement.

Although section 6(1) of the 1996 Act covers arbitration agreements in relation to present and future disputes, in practice, an agreement to submit to arbitration any "future" disputes will generally take the form of an arbitration clause. However, any existing or "present" disputes will be the subject of a submission agreement.

What is an arbitration clause?

An arbitration clause is usually a short clause in a commercial contract. Since it relates to future disputes, it does not usually provide any detail regarding the nature of the dispute or the mechanism of arbitration.

What is a submission agreement?

A submission agreement is an agreement to submit existing disputes to arbitration. Unlike the arbitration clause, the submission agreement is usually a relatively long document and, since the dispute has already arisen, it is drafted to cover the specifics of the dispute and the procedure for its determination.

Elements of an effective arbitration agreement

Irrespective of the form it may take, and whether it is domestic or international, an arbitration agreement should comply with certain requirements.

"in writing"

The 1996 Act only applies to written arbitration agreements. Section 5(1) of the 1996 Act provides that an arbitration agreement must be "in writing", made by an exchange of communications in writing or be "evidenced in writing" (for example, recorded in a memorandum by one party or a third party provided it has the authority of the parties to the agreement) (s. 5(4) of the 1996 Act). Although oral agreements are enforceable at common law (see section 81 of the 1996 Act) they are not governed by the 1996 Act.

Clarity and certainty

An arbitration agreement must be clear and certain for it to be valid and the wording used must adequately reflect the parties' intentions and be unambiguous.

SCOPE OF THE ARBITRATION CLAUSE

The scope of an arbitration clause and the matters that will be referred to arbitration are determined by agreement reached between the parties as set out in the contract. An arbitration clause should therefore be drafted in clear unequivocal terms (see above) and contain a number of elements in order to be effective. In particular, as a matter of good practice, an arbitration clause should expressly state that the parties submit their disputes to arbitration and that the submission shall be binding and final. Furthermore, if the parties would like subsequent disputes that arise to be determined by the arbitral tribunal this should also be stated. However, this is strictly speaking not necessary, as the courts have held for example that a QC clause contained within an insurance policy to the effect that:

Any dispute or difference arising hereunder between the Assured and the Insurers shall be referred to a Queen's Counsel of the English Bar to be mutually agreed between the Insurers and the Assured or in the event of disagreement by the Chairman of the Bar Council

will be treated as an arbitration clause (see the Court of Appeal's decision in *Walkinshaw* v. *Diniz* [2000] 2 All E.R. (Comm) 237).

However, in order to avoid issues arising as to what disputes are covered by the arbitration clause it is prudent for the parties to clearly set out its scope; that is, the range of disputes and claims that will be subject to the arbitration agreement. Three categories of claim potentially fall within the scope of an arbitration agreement: contractual, tortious and statutory. It is advisable to draft the arbitration clause as widely as possible to demonstrate the parties' intent to submit the widest possible range of issues to arbitration. The wording set out below is commonly used in arbitration clauses:

" . . . *all claims, disputes and controversies arising out of or in connection with the contract*".

The wording "*all claims, disputes and controversies*" encompasses the widest possible range of disputes. The wording " . . . *arising out of or in connection with this Agreement* . . . " will encompass all quasi-contractual and tortious claims, including misrepresentation and fraud.[2]

Although the wording set out above is wide, it is also advisable to specifically include issues relating to the existence, validity and termination of a contract within the scope of the arbitration clause. This will prevent a party who is claiming that the underlying contract is void or invalid from alleging that the

2. See also the recent case of *Fiona Trust & Holding Corporation &20 Ors* v. *Yuri Privalov &17 Ors* [2007] EWCA Civ 20 in which the Court of Appeal held that any arbitration clause in an international commercial contract should be liberally construed. The words "arising out of" should cover every dispute except a dispute as to whether there was ever a contract at all. Although the words "arising under the contract" had sometimes been given a narrower meaning, that should no longer be so.

arbitration clause is also invalid and that the claim relating to the existence, or termination of the contract cannot be determined by the arbitral tribunal. For example, in *Harbour Assurance Co. (UK) Ltd* v. *Kansa General International Insurance Co. Ltd* [1993] 1 Lloyd's Rep. 455, a retrocession agreement contained an arbitration clause that included the words "*all differences or disputes arising from the agreement*". The claimant argued, inter alia, that the arbitration clause was not wide enough to cover disputes about the alleged illegality of the underlying contract. The Court of Appeal held that the arbitration clause could survive if the underlying contract was void for initial illegality. Although the "doctrine of separability", which provides for an arbitration agreement to survive any alleged termination or nullity of the contract (this is discussed further below) is widely recognised, it is prudent to provide for this issue in the arbitration clause. The wording set out above will not, however, enable the arbitrators to insert terms left unsettled by the parties (*May and Butcher* v. *R* [1934] 2 K.B. 17).

A widely drawn arbitration clause also determines the scope of the arbitral tribunal's mandate or jurisdiction. This is discussed further in the section on "Jurisdiction of Arbitrators" below. As an arbitral tribunal may not exceed its jurisdiction by deciding issues which are not covered by the wording of the arbitration agreement, any matter not specifically dealt with in the arbitration clause will fall to be resolved by litigation.

There have been a number of decisions in the reinsurance context which illustrate the importance of keeping the scope of an arbitration clause as wide as possible. For example, in *New Hampshire Insurance Co.* v. *Strabag Bau* [1990] 1 Lloyd's Rep. 61, affirmed by the Court of Appeal at [1992] 1 Lloyd's Rep. 361, the arbitration clause in a contract of insurance covered "any differences as to the amount to be paid under the policy, liability otherwise being admitted". The court held that the arbitration clause did not apply to a claim in respect of which the insurer had not admitted liability. In another case, *Overseas Union Insurance Ltd* v. *AA Mutual and International Insurance Ltd* [1988] 2 Lloyd's Rep. 63 the court found that an arbitration clause which provided for "*all disputes or differences . . . in respect of this reinsurance . . . .*" was wide enough to allow a dispute as to the existence of a collateral contract and a claim for rectification to be referred to arbitration.

Effect of institutional rules on scope of arbitration clause

As discussed in the section on "The Use of Arbitration in Reinsurance Disputes" above, given that the parties have a choice between institutional and ad hoc arbitration they should expressly specify their choice in the arbitration clause. Each arbitral institution has a model arbitration clause that provides for the adoption and use of its rules. Absent any special circumstances, the parties should adopt one of the model clauses to avoid confusion and uncertainty. Parties are also advised not to alter institutional clauses substantially since altered clauses will be subjected to increased scrutiny and may lead to disputes over the jurisdiction of the arbitral tribunal.

It is prudent, however, to supplement the institutional model clause with terms covering the seat of arbitration ("arbitral *situs*"), number of arbitrators and their selection process, the language of arbitration and the choice of applicable law. These issues are discussed further below.

Seat of arbitration

In a purely national arbitration the problem of identifying the seat of arbitration (that is, the arbitral *situs*) does not arise as the seat will simply be the relevant country, unless the parties agree otherwise. The situation is less straightforward in the context of international arbitration when it becomes essential to determine the arbitral *situs* in the arbitration agreement. In choosing the seat of arbitration, parties should consider matters such as:

- a favourable legal environment (since a number of issues relating to judicial supervision of the arbitration will be subject to the law and the courts of the arbitral *situs*, independent of the parties' choice of substantive law);
- whether the relevant *situs* is a New York Convention country (since only countries who are signatories to the New York Convention will offer the arbitral award the protection of the New York Convention's enforcement regime). This is discussed further in the final section of this chapter.

If parties fail to specify the seat of arbitration then the arbitral tribunal or the court will have to determine the seat, usually by applying the proper law of the arbitration clause (*Sumitomo Heavy Industries* v. *Oil & Natural Gas Commission* [1994] 1 Lloyd's Rep. 45).

Number of arbitrators

Parties are free to choose the constitution of the arbitral tribunal. The arbitration agreement will usually provide for the arbitral tribunal to consist of one or more (usually three) arbitrators. If the arbitration is governed by the 1996 Act, section 15(3) of the Act provides that if there is no agreement between the parties on the number of arbitrators, the tribunal shall consist of a sole arbitrator. If parties are not content with the appointment of a sole arbitrator and fail to agree on a procedure to resolve the appointment issue either party can apply to the court under section 18 of the 1996 Act to ask it to exercise its powers set out in section 18(3)(a) to (d), including the power to make any necessary appointments (s. 18(3)(d)).

In the context of international arbitration, the LCIA rules provide that if the arbitration clause is silent, then the relevant institution will designate a sole arbitrator unless the circumstances justify a three-member tribunal. It is preferable to deal with this expressly in the arbitration agreement and, generally speaking, the preference in international arbitration is three arbitrators, unless the amount in dispute is small.

As regards selection of arbitrators the LCIA rules provide for each party to select an arbitrator and for the LCIA Court to appoint a chairman. The rules also make provision for the selection process where the parties fail to nominate their arbitrator. The relevant procedure for the LCIA is discussed further in Appendix 4.

The difficult issue is how to deal with the selection of arbitrators where there are more than two parties in the arbitration. Possible solutions may be as follows:

- make provision for an appointing authority to appoint all three (or sole) arbitrators; or
- attempt to align the parties on two "sides" each of which may appoint a single arbitrator by joint action.

The powers of the arbitral tribunal

As the arbitrator controls the procedure of the arbitration (see further section on "Judicial Control of Arbitration"), it is important to give the arbitrator a wide range of powers in order to enable him to "customise" the procedure to the particular dispute.

If the arbitration is governed by the 1996 Act, parties are generally free to agree on particular powers "exercisable by the arbitral tribunal for the purposes of and in relation to the proceedings" (s. 38(1) of the Act). However, if parties cannot agree on those powers, sections 38(3) to (6) will apply to give the arbitrators extensive powers under the 1996 Act (subject to the parties' right to contract out of these provisions), that is, powers relating to security for costs, preservation of property and preservation of evidence.

It is also prudent to include within the arbitrator's powers the right to grant interim relief. Generally provisional measures can be sought from both the arbitrators (section 39 of the 1996 Act) and the court (subject to the rules chosen by the parties and the governing arbitration law—that is, the law of the seat).

An arbitral tribunal may not, however, be able to act as quickly as a court. Furthermore, courts have more extensive powers than arbitral tribunals. For example, a court is usually the only forum competent to issue an order *ex parte* (i.e., before giving notice to or hearing from the affected party) and, generally speaking, the tribunal will not be able to order summary judgment. Moreover, courts, unlike consensual tribunals, can deploy coercive measures to enforce an order. However, most parties do comply with tribunal orders for interim measures. If a party does not do so, his opponent must then take the added step of seeking court enforcement.

It is advisable to expressly address the issue of interim measures within the arbitration clause and specify that:

- notwithstanding the arbitration agreement, the parties retain the right to ask the courts for interim relief;
- the arbitrators can issue interim measures, but only to maintain the status quo, e.g. to preserve evidence; and
- the parties can seek interim measures from the courts but only before the tribunal is in place and not afterwards.

Language of arbitration

Parties are also advised to expressly stipulate the language of the arbitration. In the absence of any agreement the tribunal will most probably apply the language of the contract.

Choice of applicable law

In an international dispute the parties should specifically choose and clearly state in the contract the applicable law, that is, the law governing the parties' substantive rights and obligations under the underlying contract. If no choice is made the courts will look at the agreement as a whole to determine whether a choice of law can be implied. The law governing the arbitration clause (and its interpretation) will generally be that of the underlying contract and in the absence of an express choice to this effect, there will be a presumption that the law of the underlying contract will apply. This may differ from the law governing the arbitration itself (that is, the procedural law governing the conduct of the arbitration proceedings). This is determined by the parties subject to any institutional rules they have chosen. The law of the arbitral *situs* also impacts on the arbitration procedure because the national courts of that jurisdiction may have a supportive and supervisory role, for example, in relation to the appointment (as in s. 18(3) of the 1996 Act) and removal of arbitrators (as in s. 24 of the 1996 Act).

It is therefore common and in fact preferable to have a "governing law clause" separate from the arbitration clause in a contract to avoid confusion.

Multi-party arbitration

In the reinsurance context there will often be a web of related or interdependent contracts either between the same parties or between different parties. In this situation difficulties arise relating to the question of whether it is possible to consolidate different arbitration claims into one multi-party arbitration, and/or allow the joinder of a third party or third parties. These issues in turn relate back to the issue of whether the parties in question have consented to that type of arbitration (for example, if one agreement provides for ad hoc arbitration in Switzerland and the other for LCIA arbitration in London, then in the absence of agreement between the parties, there will be no scope to consolidate those arbitrations, even if they relate to the same parties and the same issues). These issues are discussed in more detail on p. 402 of this chapter.

Joinder

As discussed earlier, there is very limited scope for joining a third party to an arbitration without its consent. This is because the principle of party autonomy is so important that it will generally outweigh the benefits of joinder or intervention, even if that would be in the interests of justice.

Parties may, however, consider using the LCIA rules which give the tribunal power to allow a third person to be joined to the proceedings provided the third person and the contracting party wishing to join the third person agree in writing.

Consolidation

In England as discussed on p. 402, section 35 of the 1996 Act provides that parties may agree to consolidation of disputes, or may agree to confer on a tribunal a power to order consolidation. Consolidation can only take place where the arbitration proceedings arise from the same transaction or relate to the same subject matter and all the parties agree.

It is important therefore to ensure that related contracts contain arbitration agreements in the same (and preferably identical) terms, such as in the case of institutional arbitration, referring to the same institution, same seat, same governing law, etc. In addition, it is advisable to incorporate express consent to consolidation in the related contracts and to check whether the proposed consolidation provisions are effective under the applicable law that has been chosen and any institutional rules.

Doctrine of separability

The doctrine of separability provides that an arbitration clause contained within an underlying commercial contract is nevertheless separate and independent from it and generally survives the termination of the underlying contract. Alternatively, the arbitration clause and the underlying contract incorporating it can be viewed as two separate contracts. The arbitration clause forms a collateral contract which contains an obligation to submit a dispute to arbitration and if a dispute arises and the arbitration clause comes into operation, it will constitute the contractual basis for the resolution of that dispute (Redfern and Hunter, *Law and Practice of International Commercial Arbitration*, 3rd edn, 1999, p. 154).

At common law the doctrine of separability was first considered in *Heyman* v. *Darwins Ltd* [1942] A.C. 356, in which the House of Lords held that an arbitration agreement is not terminated by a breach of the underlying contract. This was considered more recently in a reinsurance context in the *Harbour Assurance* case (discussed above)[3] and, in an insurance context, in *XL Insurance Ltd* v. *Owens Corning* [2001] 1 All E.R. (Comm) 530.

In the *XL* case the insurance policy with Owens Corning contained an arbitration clause as follows:

> "any dispute, controversy or claim arising out of or relating to the Policy or the breach, termination or invalidity thereof shall be finally and fully determined in London, England under the provisions of the Arbitration Act 1996 . . . "

However, the governing law clause in the insurance policy stated that the policy had to be "*construed in accordance with the internal laws of the State of New York, United States except insofar as such laws . . . are inconsistent with any provision of this policy*". XL applied to the English court for an order to restrain Owens from pursuing the claim against XL in Delaware or in any forum other than arbitration in London, relying on the arbitration clause set out above. One of the issues in the case was whether the arbitration clause could be "severed" from the policy and be governed by different law, namely English law. Further, if so, could English law be applied, not just to interpret the arbitration clause but to decide the very question of whether or not it was valid? Based on the presumption that an arbitration clause is "an agreement within an agreement", the court concluded that the parties had chosen English law as the law governing the arbitration clause. The concept of separability has been enacted in section 7 of the 1996 Act. (For the international rules on the doctrine of separability see UNCITRAL Arbitration Rules, Article 21.2.)

INCORPORATION OF ARBITRATION CLAUSES

Under English law, pursuant to section 6(2) of the 1996 Act, reference may be made in a contract to a written form of arbitration clause or to a document containing an arbitration clause and this will have the result of incorporating the arbitration clause into the contract.

However, if this approach is adopted, the parties should check not only the clarity of the reference to the arbitration clause or document which contains it, but also the sufficiency of the arbitration clause contained in that document. The courts of many countries, including England, are suspicious of an incorporation-by-reference mechanism and are more likely to decline to give effect to an arbitration clause incorporated by reference than to an express provision in the contract.

3. See also *Fiona Trust & Holding Corporation &20 Ors* v. *Yuri Privalov &17 Ors* [2007] EWCA Civ 20 discussed above.

In the reinsurance context there have been a number of authorities on the question of what requirements need to be satisfied in order for an arbitration clause in an underlying insurance policy to be effectively incorporated into a reinsurance contract. Many have decided that the general words of incorporation which were used were insufficient to incorporate an arbitration clause into the reinsurance or retrocession contract.

In *Pine Top Insurance Co.* v. *Unione Italiana Anglo Saxon Reinsurance Co.* [1987] 1 Lloyd's Rep. 476 third party insurers underwrote holiday insurance which was reinsured with excess of loss reinsurers. The reinsurance contract provided that all terms and conditions of the reinsurance were to be as per the original cover. The original cover contained a limited arbitration clause. Excess of loss reinsurers subsequently retroceded their risk to Pine Top, on similar terms to those in the excess of loss reinsurance contract. When disputes arose between Pine Top and Unione Italiana over the scope of the cover, Pine Top sought a declaration that the arbitration clause in the original insurance was not incorporated into the retrocession agreement which was in the form of a retrocession slip. The Court agreed with Pine Top's contention and held that there was no express reference to arbitration in the slip and on its true construction, the arbitration clause was not incorporated into it.

This issue also arose in *Excess Insurance Ltd* v. *Mander* [1997] 2 Lloyd's Rep. 119 where the court held that general words of incorporation which made no reference to the arbitration clause could not amount to any intention to incorporate the arbitration clause. This decision was also followed in *Trygg Hansa Insurance Co. Ltd* v. *Equitas Ltd* [1998] 2 Lloyd's Rep. 439,[4] where the court held that in the absence of special circumstances, general words of incorporation were not effective to incorporate an arbitration clause under s. 6(2) of the 1996 Act.

This has recently been confirmed in *Cigna Life Insurance Co. of Europe SA NV* v. *Intercaser SA de Seguros y Reaseguros* [2002] 1 All E.R. (Comm) 235 in which the court again held that general words of incorporation were insufficient to incorporate an arbitration clause as such clauses were personal to the parties to the agreement and collateral to their main obligations. The court's decision again emphasises the severable nature of the arbitration clause.

These cases reinforce the point that if parties wish a reinsurance dispute to be determined by arbitration, they should make sure that there is an arbitration clause in the slip as well as in the policy or treaty wording. As the arbitration is a separate contract a court will not automatically assume that the parties intended to be bound by it. Furthermore, following the decision in *Unum Life Insurance Co. of America* v. *Israel Phoenix Assurance Co. Ltd* [2002]

4. Trygg Hansa (as reinsurer) sought to stay proceedings against it, in favour of arbitration pursuant to s. 9 of the 1996 Act. The contract of primary insurance provided for arbitration and the reinsurance agreements entered into by Trygg Hansa included the provision that the reinsurance "follow the same terms . . . as the policy of the primary insurers". Trygg had sought to rely on s. 6(2) of the 1996 Act to incorporate the arbitration clause contained in the primary insurance by reference.

Lloyd's Rep. I.R. 374 even where the wording, including an arbitration clause, was agreed by the lead underwriter, it may not bind the following market if it has not been provided for on the slip and provisions such as "wording underlying" will not necessarily import the arbitration clause.

JURISDICTION OF ARBITRATORS

As previously stated, the scope of an arbitration clause determines the extent of the arbitral tribunal's jurisdiction. Therefore, the wider the scope of the clause the more extensive the arbitral tribunal's jurisdiction to consider and rule on disputes covered by the clause (including, as in *Harbour Assurance*, disputes regarding initial illegality of the underlying contract). For example, in a reinsurance context the jurisdiction of arbitrators can be widened considerably if the parties include an "honourable engagement" clause in their reinsurance contract (as discussed in the section on "The Use of Arbitration in Reinsurance Disputes", above) as this will enable arbitrators to apply market principles in deciding the issue in dispute.

The arbitral tribunal should not exceed the jurisdiction conferred on it by the arbitration clause which the parties have negotiated and agreed. However, an issue arises if one of the parties believes that the arbitrators exceeded their jurisdiction and seeks to challenge it. The arbitration clause gives the arbitral tribunal powers to resolve disputes but does not identify who should decide on whether the arbitral tribunal has jurisdiction to rule on a particular matter if its jurisdiction is challenged. The general position is that the arbitral tribunal can decide on its own jurisdiction. This concept is known as the doctrine of Kompetenz-Kompetenz (that is, jurisdiction ruling upon jurisdictional matters) and has been enacted in England in section 30 of the 1996 Act.

Section 30(1) provides that, unless parties agree otherwise, the arbitral tribunal may rule on its own substantive jurisdiction as to:

- whether there is a valid arbitration agreement;
- whether the tribunal is properly constituted; and
- what matters have been submitted to arbitration in accordance with the arbitration agreement.

Section 31 of the 1996 Act sets out the provisions regulating objections to the substantive jurisdiction of arbitral tribunals. If a party seeks to challenge the arbitral tribunal's substantive jurisdiction it must do so "at the outset of the proceeding" pursuant to section 31(1) of the 1996 Act. Further, if a party wishes to challenge the arbitral tribunal's jurisdiction to rule on a particular matter in relation to an existing dispute, it must do so as soon as possible after the matter has arisen (s. 31(2) of the 1996 Act). A challenge of this type may target the arbitral tribunal's jurisdiction to rule on matters outside the scope of the arbitration clause. However, in practice, this situation may be easily resolved by the parties expressly agreeing to the arbitrators' having jurisdiction on the additional matters previously outside the scope of the arbitration agreement.

If a challenging party complies with all of the relevant provisions contained within the 1996 Act and puts forward an objection to the tribunal's jurisdiction, the tribunal is entitled under section 31(4) of the 1996 Act to follow either of the following courses subject to the parties agreeing otherwise:

- issue a ruling on a particular matter of jurisdiction; or
- deal with the challenge in its award on the merits.

Two main elements arise out of section 31(4) of the 1996 Act. First, the arbitral tribunal can only rule on its own jurisdiction if section 30 of the 1996 Act has not been excluded by the parties. Where the arbitrator does not have the power to determine his own jurisdiction, it is relatively simple for a party wishing to play for time to plead want of jurisdiction before the arbitrator, thereby rendering him incompetent to take the matter further. It will then be necessary for the other party to apply to the court for a declaration as to jurisdiction, and only then can the arbitration proceed. This may be the only mechanism available where the Kompetenz-Kompetenz principle has been excluded (comment on *Road Management Services (A13) plc* v. *Power Networks plc* [2003] B.L.R. 303, in "Jurisdiction of Arbitrators, Determining Jurisdiction", in *Arbitration Law Monthly*, September 2003).

Second, the arbitral tribunal can only deal with the challenge in its award on the merits if it concluded it had jurisdiction in a particular dispute. An arbitrator has no power to proceed to an award on the merits if the arbitration clause does not authorise him to do so (*LG Caltex Gaz Ltd & Conti Group Inc* v. *China National Petroleum and China Petroleum Technology and Development Corporation* [2001] EWCA Civ 788).

In England, the arbitral tribunal's decision on jurisdiction may be challenged in court in two ways. First, a party can apply to the court to determine the issue whether the arbitral tribunal has substantive jurisdiction under section 32(1) of the 1996 Act. Second, a party may, under section 67(1)(a) of the 1996 Act, seek to challenge an arbitrator's award on the basis that the arbitrator had no substantive jurisdiction to make such an award. See further Appendix 5 for the resolution of jurisdictional disputes under the 1996 Act.

CONDUCT OF ARBITRATION

What determines the conduct and procedure of the arbitration?

As mentioned in the section on the "Scope of the Arbitration Clause", above, the procedure for the conduct of an arbitration is generally determined by agreement between the parties, and failing that, by the arbitral tribunal. Party autonomy is one of the guiding principles of arbitration, and is endorsed in most national laws and institutional rules. It allows the parties to adopt either an adversarial/common law approach (as followed in the English courts) or an inquisitorial/civil law approach, or alternatively a blend of the two, regardless of the procedure that is followed in the courts of the state where the arbitration is being held. In international arbitration, experience indicates that the procedure adopted depends not so much on the place where the arbitration takes place but more on the background and experience of the tribunal and the parties' legal advisers ("The 'Americanization' of International Arbitration?", Lucy Reed and Jonathan Sutcliffe (Freshfields Bruckhaus Deringer), *Mealey's International Arbitration Report*, Vol. 16, No. 4).

Arbitration can be conducted in many different ways and there are no fixed rules of procedure that will apply. Whilst party autonomy is, of course, fundamental in determining the procedure, there are a number of considerations that determine and impact on the conduct of the proceedings, namely any national legislation (in particular any mandatory rules) and public policy requirements of the place of the arbitration, any institutional rules (where the parties have opted for institutional arbitration) and any international conventions that may apply. (In England, the Arbitration Act 1996 addresses certain aspects of the conduct of the arbitration; see in particular sections 33 to 41, which set out the tribunal's powers and duties with regard to the conduct of the proceedings. This is discussed further below.)

It is generally thought that control of the arbitral procedure shifts as the arbitration progresses. (See for example *The Law and Practice of International Commercial Arbitration*, Alan Redfern and Martin Hunter, 3rd edn, 1999, at paragraph 6–02; also Thomas Webster, "Party Control in International Arbitration", in *Arbitration International*, 2003, Vol. 19, No. 2.) When the parties are agreeing upon arbitration and negotiating the arbitration agreement, the parties have complete control over the question of how their dispute will be resolved, and are free to choose the type of arbitration (institutional or *ad hoc*), the governing law and the seat. At the point when the dispute arises, the parties still have substantial control over key matters, such as the selection of the tribunal, the formulation of statements of case, etc. However, once a tribunal has been appointed, their role becomes much more significant, so that whilst the parties will maintain a significant degree of control over the procedure, for example by providing input on procedural orders and on the Terms of Reference, the tribunal will exercise a degree of control. During the conduct of the arbitration itself, the parties may need to seek assistance from national courts, either at the seat of the arbitration, or in the country where an interim remedy is required (for example, the preservation of evidence) and so certain parts of the arbitration may fall within the control of the state courts. By the time the award is issued, assuming it is not complied with voluntarily, then the tribunal will often have become *functus officio* and the successful party will be dependent upon the national courts of the country where the losing party's assets are located in order to seek enforcement of its award. This is discussed in detail in the final section of this chapter.

Effect of institutional rules on conduct of arbitration

The degree of control exercised by the tribunal will vary depending upon the institutional rules that have been chosen and any applicable national legislation. For example the LCIA Arbitration Rules provide in Article 14 (Conduct of Proceedings):

"14.1 The parties may agree on the conduct of their arbitral proceedings and they are encouraged to do so, consistent with the Arbitral Tribunal's general duties at all times:

(i) to act fairly and impartially as between all parties giving each a reasonable opportunity of putting its case and dealing with that of its opponent; and
(ii) to adopt procedures suitable to the circumstances of the arbitration, avoiding unnecessary delay or expense, so as to provide a fair and efficient means for the final resolution of the parties' dispute.

Such agreements shall be made by the parties in writing or recorded in writing by the Arbitral Tribunal at the request of and with the authority of the parties.

14.2 Unless otherwise agreed by the parties under Article 14.1, the Arbitral Tribunal shall have the widest discretion to discharge its duties . . . "

This Article categorically sets out the importance of party autonomy in determining the conduct of the proceedings, and subsequent provisions concerning the procedure to be followed are stated to apply "*unless the parties agree otherwise*".

Conduct of international arbitration

The consequence of the procedural flexibility of arbitration is that there is no set arbitral procedure, but there are, nevertheless, established ways of conducting arbitration and the procedures that are often adopted at different key stages of the arbitration are considered further below.

It is usually the case in international arbitration that a preliminary meeting will take place after the constitution of the tribunal at which the procedure for the arbitration will be determined. Further procedural orders are often issued during the course of the arbitration as the need arises. The parties may chose to adopt the IBA Rules on the Taking of Evidence in International Commercial Arbitration 1999 ("IBA Rules"), or, if they do not formally adopt the IBA Rules, they will often rely on them as a guide for determining what procedure should be followed.[5] The parties may also rely on the checklist of procedural points set out in the UNCITRAL Notes on Organizing Arbitral Proceedings.

5. The IBA Rules (first issued in 1983, and then revised and re-issued in 1999) were drafted by eminent members of the International Bar Association from both common and civil law backgrounds and are a useful harmonisation of the procedures commonly used in international arbitration. See also the "Commentary on the New IBA Rules of Evidence in International Commercial Arbitration", IBA Working Party, BLI, Issue 2 (2000).

In international arbitration, the tribunal will generally adopt elements of both common and civil law procedure, often with a bias towards one or the other depending on the legal background of the tribunal and, in particular, of the chairman, and also influenced, to some extent, by the background of the parties and their legal advisers. The blending of common and civil law techniques is important in enabling the tribunal to address the differing expectations of the parties and to fulfil its obligation to treat the parties equally and fairly.

In practice, most arbitrations are a variation on a common procedural theme. Provision is often made in the procedural order for the parties to submit written memorials or submissions on fact and law. Such submissions may contain very full arguments and be accompanied by documentary evidence and the written testimony of witnesses; this is usually the case where a relatively short hearing is anticipated at which the parties will clarify legal and factual arguments. Alternatively, the written submissions may take a more concise form, which is generally appropriate where a more substantial hearing is contemplated.

The procedural order will usually make provision for the parties to disclose those documents which support their case. Document production tends to encompass documents, or categories of documents, that can be identified with reasonable specificity and that are relevant to the dispute. The IBA rules, for example, allow disclosure but require a party to limit its request to named documents or categories and to state why they are relevant.

The parties generally rely on witnesses to support their case. The scope and extent of examination of witnesses is usually a matter for the tribunal to determine in its discretion, and it is often the case that the parties will be permitted to cross-examine all witnesses called by the opposing party, in addition to the tribunal itself being free to put questions to witnesses. The common and civil law approach to the use of party affiliated witnesses and to the issue of preliminary contact between a party and a witness differ, but the IBA Rules do in fact consider that a party's officers, employees and other representatives are acceptable witnesses, and that it is not improper for a party or its lawyers to interview its own witnesses. The use of party-appointed and/or tribunal-appointed experts is also accepted practice in international arbitration; in the case of tribunal-appointed experts the parties are generally involved in the briefing, choice and interrogation of the expert. Some arbitrators use more innovative procedures, such as witness conferencing, whereby all witnesses are heard simultaneously rather than one by one.

There is usually an oral hearing for short opening and closing statements from the lawyers and examination and cross-examination of witnesses, and these hearings tend to be shorter than one would encounter in common law jurisdictions for a comparable dispute. The hearing is usually adversarial rather than inquisitorial in nature, although the tribunal frequently takes a more active role than the judge in a common law court.

Appendix 4 sets out a summary of how arbitration proceedings will be conducted under the LCIA and ARIAS rules. The 1996 Act contains provisions relating to the conduct of arbitration proceedings in England. These are discussed further below.

Conduct of arbitration under the 1996 Act

Sections 33 to 41 set out the tribunal's powers and duties with regard to the conduct of the proceedings. The Act imposes a mandatory duty on the tribunal to conduct the proceedings fairly and impartially, giving the parties a reasonable opportunity to present their respective case and to adopt suitable procedures tailored to the dispute in question.

Section 34 provides that it is for the tribunal to decide all procedural and evidential matters, subject to the right of the parties to agree any matter. The Act sets out a non-exhaustive list of procedural and evidential matters for the tribunal to decide, subject to the parties' agreement, including:

- whether, and in what form, written statements of claim and defence are to be used;
- whether, and to what extent, disclosure of documents is necessary;
- whether, and to what extent, there should be oral or written evidence or submissions; and
- whether strict rules of evidence will apply.

Section 38 sets out certain general powers exercisable by the tribunal in the conduct of the arbitration and reflects a significant change in the relationship between the tribunal and the court. The aim is to reduce the need for applications to the court whilst arbitral proceedings are pending by giving the tribunal the widest possible powers, subject to contrary agreement of the parties. For example, the tribunal may:

- give directions relating to the preservation, custody, detention, inspection and photographing of property;
- direct that a party or witness shall be examined on oath; and
- give directions as to the preservation of evidence in the custody or control of a party.

There may potentially be a conflict between the tribunal's mandatory duty to conduct the proceedings fairly and the principle of party autonomy and this is addressed by section 40 which provides that the parties themselves are under a duty to do all things necessary for the proper and expeditious conduct of the arbitral proceedings, including complying without delay with any order or direction of the tribunal as to procedural or evidential matters.

Arbitrators may make awards on different issues during the course of the arbitration. Each award is treated as a full award for the purposes of the 1996 Act. When making their award, in default of agreement between the parties, the arbitrators may make any order which may have been made by the court under section 48 of the 1996 Act. However, the parties are free, for example, to agree that there should be proportionate recovery in an utmost good faith case—a remedy which the court is not able to give. The award should be in writing (under s. 52 of the 1996 Act) and contain reasons, although the parties can agree to dispense with the latter requirement, in which case it will also be assumed that they have contracted out of any right to appeal on a point of law. An award is deemed to be made at the place of the seat of arbitration and is dated. The date then fixes the period for enforcement of the award for limitation purposes (under s. 54 of the 1996 Act).

JUDICIAL CONTROL OF ARBITRATION

Introduction

Although the parties' agreement as to the conduct of the arbitration, together with any applicable institutional rules will substantially determine the arbitral procedure, the place of the arbitration will have a significant impact on the conduct of the arbitration for two reasons. First, the law of the place of arbitration sets the minimum procedural requirements for the arbitration and second, the courts of the place of the arbitration have jurisdiction ultimately to decide procedural issues such as challenges to arbitrators and annulment of awards.

Arbitrations in England: The 1996 Act

Mandatory and non-mandatory provisions

Mandatory provisions: The Act clearly indicates which of its provisions are mandatory and which are not. The mandatory provisions are listed in Schedule 1 and, consistent with the principle of party autonomy, only four of the 26 mandatory provisions can be regarded as restrictions on the will of the parties. The rest are intended to protect the arbitrators, the arbitral institutions and other third parties and to entrench certain legal remedies for an aggrieved party.

Non-mandatory provisions: The non-mandatory provisions are "fall-back" provisions which will apply if the parties do not otherwise agree. Indeed, almost all of the non-mandatory provisions are prefaced by the words "*unless otherwise agreed by the parties . . .* ". Accordingly, the parties can contract out of them, either by agreement or by adopting institutional rules which conflict with the Act (indeed, s. 4(3) of the Act specifically provides for the parties to agree to the application of institutional rules or to provide for "*any other means*" by which a matter may be decided). Where the parties have agreed upon institutional rules and those rules apply to the matter in issue, then the English court has either no power to intervene at all, or, in the case of certain "mandatory" provisions, such as the removal of an arbitrator (s. 24) no power to intervene unless the aggrieved party has first exhausted its remedy under the institutional rules.

The seat of the arbitration (s. 2 of the 1996 Act)

The 1996 Act applies where the seat of the arbitration is in England, Wales or Northern Ireland.

A limited number of the provisions of the Act apply where the seat is outside England, for example the provisions relating to stay of English court proceedings brought by a party who is party to an arbitration agreement, and provisions relating to taking witness evidence, preserving evidence and granting interim injunctions in support of arbitration proceedings elsewhere.

Stay of legal proceedings (s. 9 of the 1996 Act)

The courts have a very limited discretion to refuse to stay court proceedings in favour of arbitration, usually if it is satisfied that the arbitration agreement is null and void, inoperative or incapable of being performed.

Application of Limitation Acts (s. 13 of the 1996 Act)

The Limitation Acts apply to arbitration proceedings. Arbitration proceedings are deemed commenced for limitation purposes when one party writes to the other party requesting a submission to the jurisdiction of a named arbitrator. If parties are required to appoint arbitrators, arbitration proceedings will be deemed to commence when one party serves written notice on the other party requiring them to appoint arbitrators. Alternatively, if the appointment of arbitrators is to be made by a third party, the arbitration is deemed to commence when one party serves written notice on a third party asking the third party to make an appointment.

The arbitral tribunal (ss. 15 to 29 of the 1996 Act)

Sections 15 to 18 give the parties complete control over the appointment of the tribunal. The parties can agree on the number and qualification of the arbitrators and the procedure for their appointment. In the absence of agreement, the tribunal will consist of a sole arbitrator and the Act sets out the mechanism for his appointment. Provision is also made for the situation where a party refuses or fails to appoint an arbitrator within the specified time and for circumstances where the appointment procedure fails.

Section 24 enables a party to apply to the court to remove an arbitrator in certain circumstances, including where there are justifiable doubts about his partiality. However, before considering this provision, it is useful to look at the question of independence and impartiality generally.

Generally speaking, arbitrators are under a duty to disclose to the parties all facts which may be relevant in ensuring compliance with the requirements of independence and impartiality.

Impartiality: requires that an arbitrator neither favours one party nor is predisposed as to the question in dispute.

Independence: requires that there should be no such actual or past dependant relationship between the parties and the arbitrator which may, or at least may appear, to affect the arbitrator's freedom of judgment.

The duty of disclosure is expressly provided for in most arbitration rules and laws. Although no disclosure obligations are contained within the Act, such a duty would generally follow from an implied term of the agreement between the parties and the arbitrator. (Note also that the Act provides (in s. 1) that one of the three key principles on which the Act is founded is the fair resolution of disputes "*by an impartial tribunal.*") One of the most significant decisions is that of *R* v. *Gough* [1993] A.C. 646 which identified a marked preference for the test of "real danger" of bias over the test of whether there is a reasonable apprehension that justice might not be seen to have been done.[6]

Some institutions describe in detail what type of information must be disclosed and extensive guidelines can be found in Article 4.2 of the IBA Rules of Ethics for International Arbitrators.[7]

In addition, the IBA published *Guidelines on Conflicts of Interest in International Arbitration* in May 2004 that deal with the issues of impartiality, independence and disclosure. (A copy of the publication can be seen on the IBA's website at *http://www.ibanet.org/pdf/InternationalArbitrationGuidelines.pdf*)

Under section 24 of the 1996 Act other grounds for an application to remove an arbitrator include where he does not have the physical or mental capacity to conduct the proceedings or where he has failed or refused properly to conduct the proceedings.

6. Other significant decisions include *Locabail (UK) Ltd* v. *Bayfield Properties Ltd* [2000] Q.B. 451 and *AT&T Corporation and Lucent Technologies Inc* v. *Saudi Cable Co.* [2000] Lloyd's Rep. 127, although the latter case, whilst of interest, is based on the Arbitration Act 1950 and the 1988 version of the ICC Rules.

7. This provides that a prospective arbitrator should disclose:

"(a) any past or present business relationship, whether direct or indirect including prior appointment as an arbitrator, with any party to the dispute, or any representative of a party, or any person known to be a potentially important witness in the arbitration. With regard to present relationships, the duty of disclosure applies irrespective of their magnitude, but with regard to the past relationship only if they were of more than a trivial nature in relation to the arbitrator's professional or business affairs. Non-disclosure of an indirect relationship unknown to a prospective arbitrator will not be a ground for disqualification unless it could have been ascertained by making reasonable enquiries;

(b) the nature and duration of any substantial social relationship with any person likely to be an important witness in the arbitration;

(c) the nature of any previous relationship with any fellow arbitrator (including joint prior service as an arbitrator);

(d) the extent of any prior knowledge that he may have of the dispute;

(e) the extent of any commitments which may affect his availability to perform duties as arbitrator as may reasonably be anticipated."

Under section 29 of the 1996 Act, arbitrators now have immunity in the performance of their functions as arbitrators unless they have acted in bad faith. This is no doubt directed at ensuring finality by discouraging secondary litigation designed to undermine the arbitral process.

Jurisdiction of the tribunal (ss. 30 to 32 of the 1996 Act)

The tribunal has power to make an award on its own jurisdiction as to:

- whether there is a valid arbitration agreement;
- whether the tribunal is properly constituted; and
- what matters have been submitted to arbitration in accordance with the arbitration agreement.

Evidence (s. 43 of the 1996 Act)

Arbitrators do not have the power to enforce the attendance of a witness (essentially because of the absence of any substantive sanction, such as a fine). However, a party may seek the assistance of the English courts in securing the attendance of a witness who is unwilling to testify. Accordingly, the English court on application by a party, with the tribunal's permission or with written agreement of the other parties, will give assistance to compel the attendance of witnesses in the United Kingdom and to ensure the production of documents. This power is reinforced by the court's powers to impose sanctions for contempt of court.

Determination of a preliminary point of law (s. 45 of the 1996 Act)

The power to decide questions of law lies with the tribunal, but occasionally it may be advantageous for a question of law arising in the course of the proceedings to be decided there and then by the court, for example a point of law which is of great general interest and affects a large number of arbitrations.

This subsection requires the consent of all the parties to the agreement and the permission of the tribunal, and in the latter case, the court must be satisfied that the determination is likely to produce substantial savings in costs. This section is not mandatory.

Costs (ss. 59 to 65 of the 1996 Act)

Sections 59 to 65 of the Act set out a code on how the costs of the arbitration are to be allocated. Only s. 60 is mandatory, invalidating any agreement before the dispute has arisen that one party is to pay the whole or part of the costs of the arbitration even if that party loses. Otherwise the parties are free to agree between themselves the allocation of recoverable costs.

The Act is based on the assumption that costs should "follow the event", i.e. be awarded against the losing party and unless otherwise agreed, and that the successful party should be allowed a "*reasonable amount in respect of all costs reasonably incurred*", with any doubt to be resolved in favour of the paying party. This is in similar terms to the process that would apply to an assessment of costs awarded to a successful party in English High Court litigation. If the tribunal does not determine the recoverable costs, either party may apply to the court to determine the recoverable costs.

Under section 38(3), the tribunal has the power to order a claimant or counterclaimant (but not a respondent to a claim or counterclaim) to provide security for the costs of the arbitration so as to ensure that the losing claimant or counterclaimant cannot simply walk away from its obligations under an adverse costs award. However, it seems that the tribunal's discretion will rarely, if ever, be exercised unless there is good reason to believe that the claimant will be unable to pay any order for costs which may be made against him or that there will be serious difficulties in enforcing an order for costs (other than difficulties arising from the fact that the claimant is resident abroad).

Interest (s. 49 of the 1996 Act)

The power of an arbitral tribunal is greater than that of the English courts (which is restricted to the power to award *simple* interest) as it may award *compound* interest and (subject to any agreement of the parties) it may award interest up to the date of payment. This is quite a striking development and is a factor to be carefully considered by the respondent party.

Interest may be awarded "at such rates and with such interests as [the court] considers meets the justice of the case".

Challenging the award (ss. 67 to 69 of the 1996 Act)

The arbitration laws of many countries reflect the "pro-enforcement" tendencies of the Model Law and the New York Convention, and mean that the available options for challenge are relatively limited.

As a preliminary point, it is worth noting that any "internal" appeal procedure must be followed before resorting to the national courts. Some institutional rules provide a mechanism for the correction of minor errors, and certain industry-specific arbitral systems (for example maritime) contain a review procedure.

Under English law, there are three grounds on which an award may be challenged:

- challenge on the ground of lack of jurisdiction (s. 67);
- challenge on the ground of serious irregularity (s. 68); and
- appeal on a point of law (s. 69).

Sections 67 and 68 are mandatory and cannot be contracted out of, whereas section 69 is non-mandatory and arbitration agreements may contain an "*exclusion agreement*" expressly providing for section 69 not to apply. This may be more appropriate in the case of institutional arbitration with a three-member panel, so that there are likely to be adequate checks and balances in the arbitral process therefore reducing the desirability of an appeal on a point of law. In fact, some institutional rules expressly provide that such recourse is excluded by agreeing to arbitrate under that institution's rules. (For example, by agreeing to the LCIA rules, the parties irrevocably waive their right to any form of appeal, review or recourse to any national court, insofar as such waiver may validly be made.)

Under section 67 the time for making an objection will usually be the time the party took part in, or continued to take part in, the arbitration proceedings, unless he can show he could not have discovered the grounds for objection with reasonable diligence at the time. Any application to the court must be made within 28 days of the date of the award.

The three areas of substantive jurisdiction that may be challenged are:

- lack of a valid arbitration agreement;
- improper constitution of the tribunal; and
- matters not submitted to arbitration in accordance with the parties' arbitration agreement.

The remedies available to the court here are to confirm or vary the award or to set aside the award in whole or in part.

Section 68 only applies to *awards* and not decisions or orders of the tribunal, and therefore does not permit intervention during the course of the arbitration.

Section 68 sets out an exhaustive list of circumstances in which a party may make an application (most of which relate broadly to failure of due process or failure by the tribunal to act properly or in accordance with the agreed procedure). The court may only intervene if one of the stated grounds applies and even if a "serious irregularity" is shown, the court will only intervene if that irregularity has caused or will cause substantial injustice (this represents a real and significant shift towards finality and non-intervention, as compared with the previous legislation under which the court would intervene if there was a mere possibility that the misconduct might affect the result).

The available remedies are to remit all or part of the award to the tribunal for reconsideration, to set aside all or part of the award and to declare all or part of the award to be of no effect. Remission is the primary remedy. Similar restrictions and time limits apply as per challenges under section 67.

Under section 69 a limited right of appeal on a point of law is available in restricted circumstances. The rationale for this is that the parties had implicitly agreed that the tribunal should apply the law properly and if it failed to do so, it was not reaching the result contemplated by the parties.

An appeal may only be brought with the agreement of all the other parties to the arbitration or with the leave of the court, and the circumstances in which the court may give leave are restricted (for example that the determination of the question of law *will* rather than *could* substantially affect the rights of the parties). The guidelines for granting leave are that:

- the decision of the tribunal was obviously wrong; or
- the question is one of general public importance and the decision of the tribunal is at least open to serious doubt; and
- it is just and proper in all the circumstances for the court to determine the question.

The right of appeal is expressly limited to a question of law and section 82(1) of the Act defines questions of law for an application to the English Court as a question of English law. Accordingly there can never be an appeal on a question of fact or a question of foreign law.

Enforcement

Part III of the Act (ss. 99 to 104) deals with the recognition and enforcement of arbitral awards and this is discussed below.

ENFORCEMENT OF ARBITRATION AWARDS

Generally speaking, enforcement will take place in the country where the losing party has its principal place of business or where it has money or other assets against which the award can be enforced. Arbitration awards may be enforced more readily and more widely around the world than judgments of national courts due to the existence of a simplified international enforcement regime.

Any arbitration award will be enforceable by the English courts as long as the party to the arbitration agreement and against whom the award is made is within the jurisdiction of the English courts. Enforcement may take the form of an action on the award by the successful party, alternatively the procedure under section 66 of the 1996 Act may be used.

Enforcement of domestic awards

Pursuant to section 66 of the 1996 Act a successful party may obtain the leave of the court to enforce the award and, where this is given, judgment will be entered in the terms of the award. An application is then made to commence enforcement proceedings. Leave to enforce the award will not, however, be given where the person against whom the award is to be enforced shows that the tribunal lacked substantive jurisdiction to make the award. It is therefore unnecessary to commence an action on the award as the simple enforcement mechanism set out in the 1996 Act can be used instead.

Enforcement of foreign awards

Under English law, foreign awards may be enforced under Part III of the 1996 Act. Pursuant to section 99 of the 1996 Act, Part II of the Arbitration Act 1950 (ss. 35 to 42) continues to apply to foreign awards as defined within that Act which are not also New York Convention awards. (The procedure for the enforcement of New York Convention awards is discussed further below). Section 35 of the Arbitration Act 1950 requires that the award has been made under an arbitration agreement subject to the 1923 Protocol on Arbitration Clauses, as supplemented by the 1927 Geneva Convention on the Execution of Foreign Arbitral Awards (the Geneva Convention). The award must also have been made within a jurisdiction that is a party to the Geneva Convention and reciprocal enforcement arrangements must exist with that jurisdiction. Once these requirements have been satisfied, a foreign award will be enforceable as long as the conditions set out in section 37 of the Arbitration Act 1950 have been satisfied. These include that:

- the award was made pursuant to an agreement for arbitration which was valid under the law which governed it;
- the award was made by the tribunal provided for in the agreement or that the tribunal was constituted in a manner agreed upon by the parties;
- the award was made in conformity with the law governing the arbitration procedure;
- the award is final in the country in which it was made;
- the award relates to a matter which could lawfully be referred to arbitration under English law; and
- enforcement of the award would not be contrary to public policy.

Furthermore, pursuant to section 37(2) of the Arbitration Act 1950, the award will not be enforced by the English courts if the award has been annulled in the jurisdiction in which it was made; the party against whom the award is to be enforced has not been given notice of the arbitration proceedings in sufficient time to enable him to present his case, or if he was under some legal incapacity and was not properly represented; or the award does not deal with all the questions referred or contains decisions on matters beyond the scope of the arbitration agreement.

Procedure

Section 38 of the Arbitration Act 1950 requires the party seeking to enforce the award to produce the original award or an authenticated copy, evidence that the award has become final, that the award is a foreign award and that the conditions set out in section 37(1) are satisfied.

New York Convention awards

More than 140 states have ratified or acceded to the New York Convention and in particular, have adopted the "reciprocity reservation" within the New York Convention. Pursuant to the "reciprocity reservation", the courts of a state that has adopted the New York Convention will enforce an award under the New York Convention only if it has been made within the territory of another state that has also ratified or acceded to the New York Convention. Accordingly, the nationality of the parties is immaterial: it is the nationality of the award that counts. This is determined according to the place where the award is made, i.e. where the arbitration has its seat.

Where a foreign award is made in a state that is a party to the New York Convention, the English courts have no power to review the validity of that award. As long as the requirements of the 1996 Act are complied with, the award must be enforced by the English courts (this is discussed further below). Similarly, as the United Kingdom is a party to the New York Convention, an award made in England will be a New York Convention award and capable of enforcement in other New York Convention states. The procedure for enforcement of awards does, however, vary from state to state. For example, Switzerland requires that an award be deposited or registered with a court or other authority but can then be enforced as if it were a judgment of the court. In France a prior application must be made to the court for recognition of the award before it will be enforced.

In England, section 101 of the 1996 Act provides that a New York Convention award may, by leave of the court, be enforced in the same manner as a judgment or order of the court and that where leave is given, judgment may be entered in the terms of the award. Normally, an order giving leave to enforce the award in the same manner as a judgment is sufficient to give the successful party the benefit of the court's powers of execution. But it may sometimes be advantageous to have a formal judgment, for example where a judgment is necessary in order to enforce the award abroad, or in order to serve a bankruptcy notice.

An order or judgment enforcing an award may include the costs awarded by the arbitrator and the arbitrators' fees. The tribunal has power to award interest from the date of the award until payment (as discussed above, now either simple or compound interest) and the order or judgment enforcing the award will be in similar terms.

Procedure

The procedure for enforcing a Convention award under section 102 of the 1996 Act simply requires the enforcing party to produce a duly authenticated original award or a certified copy of it and the original arbitration agreement or a certified copy of it.

As the award can be enforced in the same manner as a judgment or order, the usual means of enforcing English judgments and orders will be available, for example, charging orders on land, stop notices on securities, etc.

The only grounds on which the English courts may refuse enforcement of a Convention award are the grounds set out in the New York Convention and re-enacted in the 1996 Act under section 103, including that the arbitration agreement was not valid under the law governing the arbitration agreement; that the award deals with differences not contemplated by the arbitration agreement or goes beyond the scope of the arbitration agreement; that the composition of the tribunal or the arbitral procedure was not in accordance with the parties' agreement; that the award has been set aside under another system of law or has not yet become binding on the parties. The English courts are under a positive obligation to enforce a foreign award unless one of the grounds set in section 103 of the 1996 Act are satisfied and the party resisting the enforcement must prove the grounds for challenge not the enforcing party (*Yukos Oil Co.* v. *Dardana Ltd* [2002] EWCA CIV 543). Therefore, even if the defendant against whom the award is made has no assets in the UK (as in the case of *Rosseel NV* v. *Oriental Commercial Shipping (UK) Ltd* [1991] 2 Lloyd's Rep. 625) the court will still be required to enforce the award.

Most of the national courts of other countries party to the New York Convention have interpreted narrowly the grounds on which enforcement of Convention awards can be resisted. In many cases they have retained discretion when grounds for refusal do exist as to whether or not to enforce the award and have usually adopted a pro-enforcement approach.

The Brussels and Lugano Conventions

While the Brussels and Lugano Conventions provide a framework for the enforcement of foreign judgments (the Brussels Convention covers EU states and the Lugano Convention covers EFTA states), neither Convention provides an enforcement mechanism for arbitral awards as they are specifically excluded from the Conventions' remit (see Articles 1 and 25 of the Brussels and Lugano Conventions).

TEST YOUR UNDERSTANDING

1. **Which of the following arbitral institutions tends to be used in reinsurance arbitrations?**

   (a) ICC;
   (b) AAA;
   (c) LCIA.

2. **Which of the following are not considered to be an advantage when using arbitration?**

   (a) Speed;
   (b) Enforcement;
   (c) Finality;
   (d) Limited availability of summary judgment.

3. **Which of the following statements is incorrect?**

   (a) The Arbitration Act 1996 applies to written arbitration agreements;
   (b) The Arbitration Act 1996 applies to oral agreements to arbitrate;
   (c) An arbitration agreement must be in writing or evidenced in writing;
   (d) An arbitration agreement must be clear and certain for it to be valid.

4. **An arbitration clause containing the wording "all claims, disputes and controversies arising out of or in connection with the contract" will not necessarily include disputes relating to which type of claim?**

   (a) Quasi-contractual claims;
   (b) Tortious claims;
   (c) Statutory claims;
   (d) The legality of the underlying contract.

5. **Which of the following areas is not regulated by the Arbitration Act 1996?**

   (a) Confidentiality in arbitrations;
   (b) The number of arbitrators that can be appointed to a tribunal;
   (c) The circumstances in which an arbitrator can be removed from the panel of arbitrators;
   (d) The power of the arbitral tribunal to award interest on an arbitral award.

6. **Which of the following statements is correct?**

   (a) Arbitration proceedings between the original assured, the insurer and the reinsurer can be consolidated without the consent of all the parties;
   (b) Brokers or other intermediaries can be joined to arbitration proceedings between the original assured and the insurer;
   (c) Arbitration proceedings between insurers and reinsurers which relate to different facts but the same legal issues can be consolidated;

(d) Arbitration proceedings between the original assured, insurer and reinsurer can be consolidated with the consent of all the parties.

7. Which of the following are arbitrators empowered to order?

(a) Compound interest;
(b) Interim payments;
(c) Third party disclosure;
(d) Summary judgment.

8. Which of the following statements is incorrect in relation to arbitration proceedings subject to the Arbitration Act 1996?

(a) A party can appeal the decision of an arbitral tribunal to challenge its substantive jurisdiction;
(b) A party can appeal the decision of an arbitral tribunal if there is a serious irregularity affecting the tribunal;
(c) A party can appeal the decision of an arbitral tribunal on a finding of fact;
(d) A party can appeal the decision of an arbitral tribunal on a point of law.

9. Arbitration awards can be enforced under which of the following Convention procedures?

(a) The Brussels Convention;
(b) The Lugano Convention;
(c) The Hague Convention;
(d) The New York Convention.

APPENDIX 1

A MARKET REFORM—SLIP STRUCTURE

Fields likely to be in the core MR Slip are shown in bold.

UMR	The unique market reference.
TYPE	The nature of the risk.
FORM	The NMA reference or other identification of the policy jacket. The wording or clauses should not be shown here, these should be included in the "Conditions" heading.
INSURED/REINSURED	The (Re)insured's name, address and/or business as applicable.
PERIOD	Period of risk, including reference to time and time zone, bdi (both days inclusive) is acceptable where appropriate but time zone must be shown.
INTEREST	Interest or subject matter insured or nature of liability.
SUM INSURED	Sum insured or reinsured or indemnity or monetary limits.
ORDER HEREON	100% of 100%
SITUATION	Situation, territorial limits or location.
CONDITIONS	Identification, qualification or variation in perils including the wording, clauses, conditions and amendments to any clauses in basic form. All standard wordings and clauses should be clearly identified by name and reference. Any non-standard wording or clauses should be referred to here and attached to the slip. If there are no Conditions, field need not be shown.
EXPRESS WARRANTIES	Any express warranties that apply to the contract (in addition to those that are specified in the wording if already indicated), including when specified the penalties for non-compliance. If there are no express warranties this heading would not be included.
CONDITIONS PRECEDENT	Details of any conditions precedent that apply to the contract (in addition to those that are specified in the wording if already indicated), including when specified the consequences of non-compliance. If there are no conditions precedent this heading would not be included.
SUBJECTIVITIES	For subjectivities that do not have specific "homes".
SEVERAL LIABILITY	The several liability clause that applies, and the text of the clause (LSW 1001).
CHOICE OF LAW & JURISDICTION	The court that will have jurisdiction in the event of a dispute between (Re)insured and (Re)insurers and the law that will apply.

PREMIUM	The Premium to be paid by the Insured.
PAYMENT TERMS	The "specific" Premium Payment Terms applied to the contract by the Slip Leader, including Premium Payment Clauses, Warranties and Conditions.
FEE PAYABLE BY CLIENT	Yes/No.
TOTAL BROKERAGE	The brokerage allowance.
OTHER DEDUCTIONS FROM PREMIUM	e.g. Commission.
TAXES PAYABLE BY INSURED AND ADMINISTERED BY UNDERWRITERS	Any premium taxes and charges payable by the Insured in addition to the premium stated above, which are collected and/or administered by underwriters, e.g. UKIPT. Any premium taxes and charges payable by underwriters should be shown in the Fiscal & Regulatory section.
RECORDING, TRANSMITTING & STORING INFORMATION	Details of procedures for storage of data, documents and other information. This heading is optional.
SIGNING PROVISIONS	These must be shown. Model words have been provided.

SUBSCRIPTION AGREEMENT

NB: Last Sections are very much to do with London Market systems.

SLIP LEADER	State who is the Slip Leader.
SETTLEMENT DUE DATE	To be entered as appropriate.
BASIS OF WRITTEN LINES	To be entered as appropriate.
OTHER AGREEMENT PARTIES FOR CONTRACT CHANGES, IF ANY	State those underwriters, other than the Slip Leader, who will agree contract changes on behalf of the subscribing underwriters in accordance with the terms agreed below **under the GUA**. This should not include those underwriters who wish to agree contract changes on their own behalf. NB: Care should be taken to avoid conflict with current leading underwriter agreements. **This field should only be shown where there is a GUA mentioned in the next field.**
BASIS OF AGREEMENT TO CONTRACT CHANGES	Specify any leading underwriter agreement that applies, e.g. NMA, LUAMC, GUA and applicable class of business schedule(s) etc. To include the method of advising agreed endorsements to the following market e.g. use of email and/or access to repositories.
DOCUMENT PRODUCTION	The type of insuring documentation to be produced, who produces it, who agrees it and any particular requirements, e.g. specific language.
CLAIMS AGREEMENT PARTIES	Identity of the claims agreement parties, e.g. Slip Leader, plus the first IUA company and LCO.

BASIS OF CLAIMS AGREEMENT	Specify the basis of the claims procedure such as the Lloyd's 2006 claims scheme including the parties for the agreement of claims and/or IUA claims agreement practices.
CLAIMS ADMINISTRATION	All claims related information with the exception of identification of agreement parties and the basis of claims agreement should be included here. Clarification is required as to which underwriters will use CLASS and the use of email and/or access to repositories.
RULES AND EXTENT OF ANY OTHER DELEGATED AUTHORITY	If any of the claims agreement parties specified above have delegated their claims processing and agreement to any other party this should be specified here including any limits that may apply, e.g. all claims less than GBP xxxx.
EXPERT(S) FEES	The party(ies) responsible for the collection of experts fees. There are eight options available under the experts fees collection arrangements. One of these options MUST be used.
BUREAUX ARRANGEMENTS	Any specific arrangements relating to the bureaux including administrative arrangements for premium settlement, delinked accounting, and policy signing or basis of policy agreement clauses.

INFORMATION

Details of any information provided to underwriters to support the assessment of the risk at the time of placement. Where the information is appropriate for inclusion in the slip it should be shown here. Where the size or format of the information is not suitable for inclusion the location of the information should be clearly referenced from this section but should be made available to all underwriters during placing.

FISCAL AND REGULATORY

TAX PAYABLE BY UNDERWRITER(S)	Any premium taxes and charges payable by underwriters from the premium paid to them e.g. US Federal Excise Tax. Any premium taxes and charges payable by the Insured in addition to the premium which are collected or administered by underwriters should be shown in the Taxes Payable by Insured heading of the Risk Details.
COUNTRY OF ORIGIN	To be entered as appropriate.
US CLASSIFICATION	To be entered as appropriate.
NAIC CODES	To be included when applicable.
ALLOCATION OF PREMIUM TO CODING	Any allocation of premium where multiple risk codes exist.
FSA CLIENT CLASSIFICATION	To be entered as appropriate.

APPENDIX 2

GUIDANCE ON CONVERTING A SUBJECTIVITY INTO A FULLY CLAUSED CONDITION OF THE INSURANCE

Introduction

1.1 There is a need in the Market to address the challenges associated with the imposition of subjectivities in (re)insurance contracts. In the past, these have given rise to considerable uncertainty in relation to the contract of (re)insurance since the precise terms of the relevant requirement, and the consequences if the requirement was not met, were rarely specified at the time the risk was placed.

1.2 Subjectivities are conditions of the contract, and must be expressed as such, to avoid unnecessary ambiguity. Principle 2 of the Contract Certainty ("CC") Code of Practice requires that:

> *"Each insurer will be satisfied that the submission meets the contract certainty definition and checklist before formally committing to the contract, ensuring that any conditions or subjectivities are clearly expressed."*

The guidance to Principle 2 states:

> *"Issues may remain outstanding after inception, for example an outstanding survey requirement.*
> *Subjectivities should be imposed within the placing document. The responsibilities and timescales for resolution, and the consequences of failure, must also be clearly specified. Where subjectivity is outstanding at inception then it must be stated as a fully-claused condition of the cover given."*

1.3 The Market Reform Slip (issued in June 2006) contains a "Subjectivities" heading within the Risk Details section under which these conditions are to be set out or referred to as being attached.

Purpose

2.1 This guidance aims to help ensure that a subjectivity takes the form of a clearly expressed condition (specifying the responsibilities and timescales for resolution, and any consequences of failure), thereby fulfilling the CC requirements in this area as defined in the Code of Practice and the CC Checklist.

2.2 The guidance comprises a common subjectivity example with its shortcomings highlighted by explanatory guidance, followed by an illustrative example drafted on the basis of this guidance.

Guidance

3.1 There are subjectivities that:

- must be complied with or resolved before the contract becomes binding;

- apply both before and after inception, compliance with which is a condition of all or part of the coverage; and
- apply after the formation of the contract as conditions of continued coverage.

3.2 A subjectivity should set out:

(i) the condition/action that needs to occur, by whom and to what standard;
(ii) the timescale, if any, within which the condition is to be met;
(iii) the terms which are to apply until the condition is met; and
(iv) the consequences which are to follow if the condition is not met.

3.3 A subjectivity that simply states "subject to survey" clearly falls short of the standards expressed at paragraph 3.2 above. In order to satisfy the CC Code of Practice the following key requirements need to be considered:

(i) the condition/action that needs to occur, by whom and to what standard;

This involves consideration of:

- what type of condition/action is necessary;
- by whom it is to be undertaken; and
- what will be deemed to be satisfactory compliance.

The expression of the standard of compliance with the subjectivity may need to involve two factors:

- the standard of quality of the necessary documentation to be provided, or action to be undertaken
  (e.g. the particulars which may be required to be included in documentation and/or the form it should take); and
- the standard(s) by which the outcome/result of the action taken or documentation will be assessed and by whom it will be approved (e.g. that it must be satisfactory to (re)insurers).

For example:

> *"The insured shall provide to the insurers a survey report on [insert property address] prepared by [insert name of firm of surveyors] which is satisfactory to the insurers."*

(ii) The timescale, if any, for the condition to be met;

The timescale for completion of the condition involves a consideration of what is the intended timeframe for the subjectivity to be applicable. Is it to be complied with before or after the formation of the contract? If after formation, is it to be complied with before or after inception?

A timescale may be inappropriate in certain circumstances, for example, where the relevant condition provides for a continuing obligation. However, where a timescale is imposed, it is best expressed either as a specific date or by setting out a method of calculation of the deadline date.

For example:

> *"The required survey report shall be provided by the insured to insurers by [insert time and time zone] on [insert date]."*

(iii) The terms which are to apply until the condition is met;

Possible terms may affect:

- the commencement of all or part of the coverage;
- the premium;
- recourse to the full limit(s) of indemnity; and/or

- recovery of any loss.

For example:

> *"Until the insured has provided to the insurers a survey report and such report is confirmed in writing by the insurers to be satisfactory to them, coverage in respect of the specified property shall be limited to [ ]% of the sum insured set out in [insert reference to the relevant section of the contract]."*

(iv) The consequences if the condition is not met.

Possible consequences may include:

- any of the possible terms referred to in (iii) above;
- imposition of additional terms;
- termination of the contract, with (re)insurers ceasing to be under any liability whatsoever, including in the period before the deadline for compliance with the condition;
- insurers coming off risk and ceasing to be under any further liability as from the date of non-compliance with the condition;
- insurers not being under any liability prospectively and/or retrospectively in respect of a particular aspect or aspects of coverage;
- additional premium chargeable; and/or
- that the terms of the contract of (re)insurance are open to re-negotiation by the (re)insurers.

The condition may also need to incorporate specific provisions dealing with the service and timing of any notice on the insured particularly as regards cancellation. For example:

> *"In the event that the insured fails to provide a survey report by the date specified, the insurers shall be entitled to terminate this contract by giving not less than fourteen days' notice in writing to the insured at their address shown in the contract. In the event of such termination, the insured shall be entitled to pro rata return of premium for the unexpired period of the contract."*

Subjectivity Example

4.1 Below is an illustrative example of a survey subjectivity that contemplates the four key requirements of a fully-claused condition. This example is intended for illustrative purposes only, as the particular wording of such a condition will depend entirely on the intentions of the insurers on any given contract.

Some conditions may need to be more comprehensive than the illustrative example below.

> *"Survey Condition*
> *The Insured shall provide to the Insurer a survey report on [insert property address] such report to be prepared by [insert name of surveyor(s)] ("the Survey"). The Survey shall be so provided by [insert time and time zone] on [insert date] ("the Survey Deadline").*
>
> *Between inception and the Survey Deadline, cover is provided by the Insurer on the terms and conditions specified in the contract to which this condition is attached ("the Contract Terms").*
>
> *Where the Survey is not submitted to the Insurer by the Survey Deadline cover shall terminate at the Survey Deadline.*
>
> *Where the Survey is submitted to the Insurer by the Survey Deadline, cover shall continue from the Survey Deadline on the Contract Terms until expiry of the period of the contract unless and until terminated in accordance with the following paragraph.*

In the event that the Survey is unsatisfactory to the Insurer, the Insurer shall have the right, within [ ] days of its receipt, to terminate the contract by serving not less than [ ] days' notice in writing to the Insured at the Insured's address as shown in the contract, such notice expiring no earlier than the Survey Deadline.

In the event of termination under this survey condition, the Insured shall be entitled to pro rata return of premium for the unexpired period of the contract unless a loss has arisen for which the Insured seeks indemnity under this contract in which case the Insurers shall remain entitled to the full premium specified in the Contract Terms.

To the extent that this survey condition conflicts with any other cancellation, notice and premium provision in the Contract Terms, this survey condition shall prevail."

www.marketreform.co.uk

This note is provided for information purposes only and is not intended to be binding. The Market Reform Programme Office, Society of Lloyd's, IUA, LMA and LMBC accept no responsibility whatsoever for liability as a result of any reliance placed on it. Furthermore, non-compliance with any matter contained in the note shall not invalidate or call into question any contract or agreement nor shall failure to comply with the standards or guidelines create any right of action or claims in any third party. This note does not affect the legal relationships between the parties to insurance/reinsurance contracts.

APPENDIX 3

THE PROVISIONS OF THE MARINE INSURANCE ACT 1906

Insurance is a contract uberrimae fidei

17.—A contract of marine insurance is a contract based upon the utmost good faith, and, if the utmost good faith be not observed by either party, the contract may be avoided by the other party.

Disclosure by the assured

18.—(1) Subject to the provisions of this section, the assured must disclose to the insurer, before the contract is concluded, every material circumstance which is known to the assured, and the assured is deemed to know every circumstances which, in the ordinary course of business, ought to be known to him. If the assured fails to make such disclosure, the insurer may avoid the contract.

(2) Every circumstance is material which would influence the judgment of a prudent insurer in fixing the premium, or determining whether he will take the risk.

(3) In the absence of inquiry the following circumstances need not be disclosed, namely:

(a) any circumstance which diminishes the risk;
(b) any circumstance which is known or presumed to be known to the insurer. The insurer is presumed to know matters of common notoriety or knowledge, and matters which an insurer in the ordinary course of his business as such, ought to know;
(c) any circumstance as to which information is waived by the insurer;
(d) any circumstance which it is superfluous to disclose by reason of any express or implied warranty.

(4) Whether any particular circumstance, which is not disclosed, be material or not is, in each case, a question of fact.

(5) The term "circumstance" includes any communication made to, or information received by, the assured.

Disclosure by agent effecting insurance

19.—Subject to the provisions of the preceding section as to circumstances which need not be disclosed, where an insurance is effected for the assured by an agent, the agent must disclose to the insurer—

(a) every material circumstance which is known to himself, and an agent to insure is deemed to know every circumstance which in the ordinary course of business ought to be known by, or to have been communicated to, him; and
(b) every material circumstance which the assured is bound to disclose, unless it came to his knowledge too late to communicate it to the agent.

Representations pending negotiation of contract

20.—(1) Every material representation made by the assured or his agent to the insurer during the negotiations for the contract, and before the contract is concluded, must be true. If it be untrue the insurer may avoid the contract.

(2) A representation is material which would influence the judgment of a prudent insurer in fixing the premium, or determining whether he will take the risk.

(3) A representation may be either a representation as to a matter of fact, or as to a matter of expectation or belief.

(4) A representation as to a matter of fact is true, if it be substantially correct, that is to say, if the difference between what is represented and what is actually correct would not be considered material by a prudent insurer.

(5) A representation as to a matter of expectation of belief is true if it be made in good faith.

(6) A representation may be withdrawn or corrected before the contract is concluded.

(7) Whether a particular representation be material or not is, in each case, a question of fact.

APPENDIX 4

COMPARISON OF LCIA AND ARIAS ARBITRATION RULES

LCIA Rules (London Court of International Arbitration) (effective from 1 January 1998)	**ARIAS (effective from 1 June 1997)**
Nature of the Institution/Rules	
Rules for Institutional Arbitration: References to the Court are the LCIA Court and not a court of law. Low level of supervision by the institution itself.	Ad-Hoc Arbitration: The parties to a contract agree to follow the ARIAS rules in a dispute in relation to the contract (r.1.1). ARIAS is not an institution and does not exercise any supervisory jurisdiction over the arbitration. If advisory or administrative assistance is required application may be made to the Registrar of the LCIA in accordance with r.20.
Commencement of Arbitration	
Requesting party sends written request for arbitration (containing/accompanied by information listed in A.1.1). Date of receipt by the Registrar is treated as the commencement date (A.1.2). Response required within 30 days of the service of the Request on the Respondent (A.2.1). Failure to do so within that time shall not preclude the Respondent from denying any claim or from advancing a counterclaim in the arbitration (A.2.3).	Notice is to be given by the Claimant containing information set out in r.4.1. Arbitral proceedings are deemed to commence on the date the Respondent receives the Notice or as determined by the arbitral tribunal (r.4.2, 15.1).
Appointment of Arbitrators	
Sole arbitrator to be appointed unless agreed otherwise in writing between parties or unless LCIA Court feels three-member tribunal preferable (A.5.4). (Three-member tribunals will have the Chairman appointed by the LCIA Court (A.5.6)). LCIA Court alone empowered to appoint but will give due regard to selection criteria agreed in writing by the parties (A.5.5). Where parties agree to nominate arbitrators the Court will appoint those nominees unless it determines they are not suitable, independent or impartial (A.7.1).	Parties to agree number of arbitrators within a certain period of time otherwise three shall be appointed (r.6.1, 6.2). Appointment of sole arbitrators: arbitrator to be determined by agreement. If no agreement as to arbitrator, ARIAS will appoint sole arbitrator upon application of either party (r.6.4). Appointment of three arbitrators: each party to appoint one (although if no appointment made by the Respondent, ARIAS will appoint). The two arbitrators (failing that ARIAS) to appoint the third arbitrator (r.6.5, 6.6, 6.8).

Appointment of Arbitrators—*continued*	
The LCIA Court will appoint if no party-appointment is made in time (or at all) or if the Request for arbitration is made without a nomination (A.7.2). If arbitration agreement requires party nomination of arbitrators failure to respond or nominate waives the Respondent's rights to nominate (A.2.3). Three or more parties (see A.8).	Third member of Tribunal to sit as third arbitrator and not as umpire unless parties agree otherwise (r.6.9). Procedure for appointment of umpire (r.6.10).
Obligations on the Arbitrators	
Required to sign a declaration of impartiality and independence (A.5.3). Continuing duty to disclose to the Tribunal and all parties such circumstances relevant to the declaration made (A.5.3). The duty lasts until the arbitration is concluded. None shall act as advocates for any party (A.5.2). No arbitrator shall advise on the merits or outcome of the dispute before or after their appointment (A.5.2). Power to continue as a two-member Tribunal where the third refuses or fails to act (A.12). But there is also the ability to discontinue the arbitration without the third arbitrator (reasons to be given by the two arbitrators if so determined (A.12.2)) leading to referral to the LCIA Court for revocation of the third arbitrator's appointment (A.12.3). General duty to act fairly and impartially, allowing cases to be put forward, adopting suitable procedures avoiding delay and unnecessary expense (A.14.1).	No specific provisions.
Removal of Arbitrators	
In the event that the LCIA Court determines that any appointed arbitrator is to be replaced for any reason, it shall have complete discretion to decide whether or not to follow the original nominating process (A.11.1).	No specified procedure for challenges to appointees. A substitute arbitrator or umpire will be appointed (upon death, resignation or if unable to act or otherwise removed from

Removal of Arbitrators—*continued*	
A nominating party may nominate again. If not done within a certain period the LCIA Court will appoint a replacement arbitrator (A.11.2). Challenge of arbitrators may also be made by any party in accordance with A.10.	the reference), ARIAS will in default of re-appointment by parties or remaining member of Tribunal, make appointment (r.6.12).
Determining the Arbitration Procedure	
The parties may and are encouraged to agree the conduct of the proceedings consistent with the Tribunal's general duties (A.14.1). A.15 sets out an alternative if no procedure has been specifically determined (A.15). Unless agreed otherwise by the parties the Tribunal shall have the widest discretion allowed under such law(s) or rules of law as the Tribunal may determine to be applicable (A.14.2). The parties agree the place of arbitration (otherwise London until the LCIA deems otherwise) (A.16).	The parties can agree any procedure for the conduct of the arbitration and in the absence of agreement as to how the proceedings are to be conducted, the Tribunal may determine procedure by making orders and directions as it considers necessary for the final determination of the matters in dispute (r.9). Unless agreement by the parties, the chairman of the Tribunal may make procedural rulings above (r.9.3). The Tribunal must give parties reasonable notice of the place and date of meetings/ hearings which are private and confidential to the parties. The parties may be represented by lawyers or other appointed representatives (r.11.1, 11.2 and 11.3). The Tribunal may decide whether or to what extent these should be oral or written evidence submissions (r.12). The parties may agree in writing that the Tribunal makes an award on basis of documents alone (r.11.3). Seat of arbitration is London unless agreed otherwise by the parties (r.10.1).
Rules on Discovery	
Unless the parties (at any time) agree otherwise the Tribunal shall have the power to order any party to make any property etc. subject to inspection, and to produce documents for inspection, custody or power which they consider to be relevant (A.22.1)—only after giving the parties a reasonable opportunity to state their views.	The Tribunal may order the disclosure of documents relevant to the dispute and determine when the documents are to be disclosed (r.13.1.2). The Tribunal may also order the inspection by either party of the books and records of the other party in partial substitution for or in addition to documentary disclosure (r.13.1.3).

Right of Appeal	
The parties irrevocably waive their right to any form of appeal, review, recourse to any state court or judicial authority, insofar as any such waiver may be validly made (A.26.9). Decisions of the LCIA Court are conclusive and binding on the Tribunal and the parties (A.29.1). The parties shall be taken to have waived their right of appeal or review in respect of any LCIA Court decisions—to the extent permitted by the law of the seat of arbitration (A.29.2). If such appeals are possible (due to mandatory provisions of any applicable law), the LCIA Court subject to the applicable law will decide whether the proceedings are to continue, notwithstanding an appeal/review (A.29.2).	Clerical errors or mistakes or clarification or removal of ambiguity in the award may be made by the Tribunal on its own initiative or upon application by either party within a certain period (r.16.11.1). Additional awards in respect of any matters which were presented to the Tribunal but which were omitted from the award may be made by the Tribunal on its own initiative or upon application by either party within a certain period of time (r.16.11.2).
Nature of the Award	
Awards are final and binding. Shall be in writing unless agreed otherwise and shall state reasons (A.26). Decisions shall be by majority in three-member Tribunals, failing a majority the Chairman shall decide (A.26.3).	Awards are final and binding and in writing (including reasons unless otherwise agreed) (r.16.2). Award is valid if signed by a sole arbitrator, an umpire or majority of arbitrators where there are three (r.16.3). The Tribunal may make a partial award (r.16.7).
Fees	
Costs shall be determined by the LCIA Court in accordance with the Schedule of Costs (A.28). The Tribunal will then specify those costs in the award as determined by the LCIA Court (A.28.2). Unless agreed otherwise the Tribunal determines the proportion each party will pay of the costs (A.28).	Amount and apportionment of Tribunal's fees and expenses fixed in the award (r.17.5). The Tribunal may tax and fix reasonable fees and expenses of a party prior to the publication of the final award (r.18.2). Fees and expenses of the arbitrators shall be reasonable in amount, determined taking into account time spent by arbitrators. The Tribunal may request a claimant to provide security for the costs of the arbitration (r.13.1.8). Deposits for fees and expenses of the Tribunal can be requested during the proceedings (r.17.4) unless agreed in writing by the parties on some other basis (r.17.2).

APPENDIX 5

RESOLUTION OF JURISDICTIONAL DISPUTES UNDER THE ARBITRATION ACT 1996

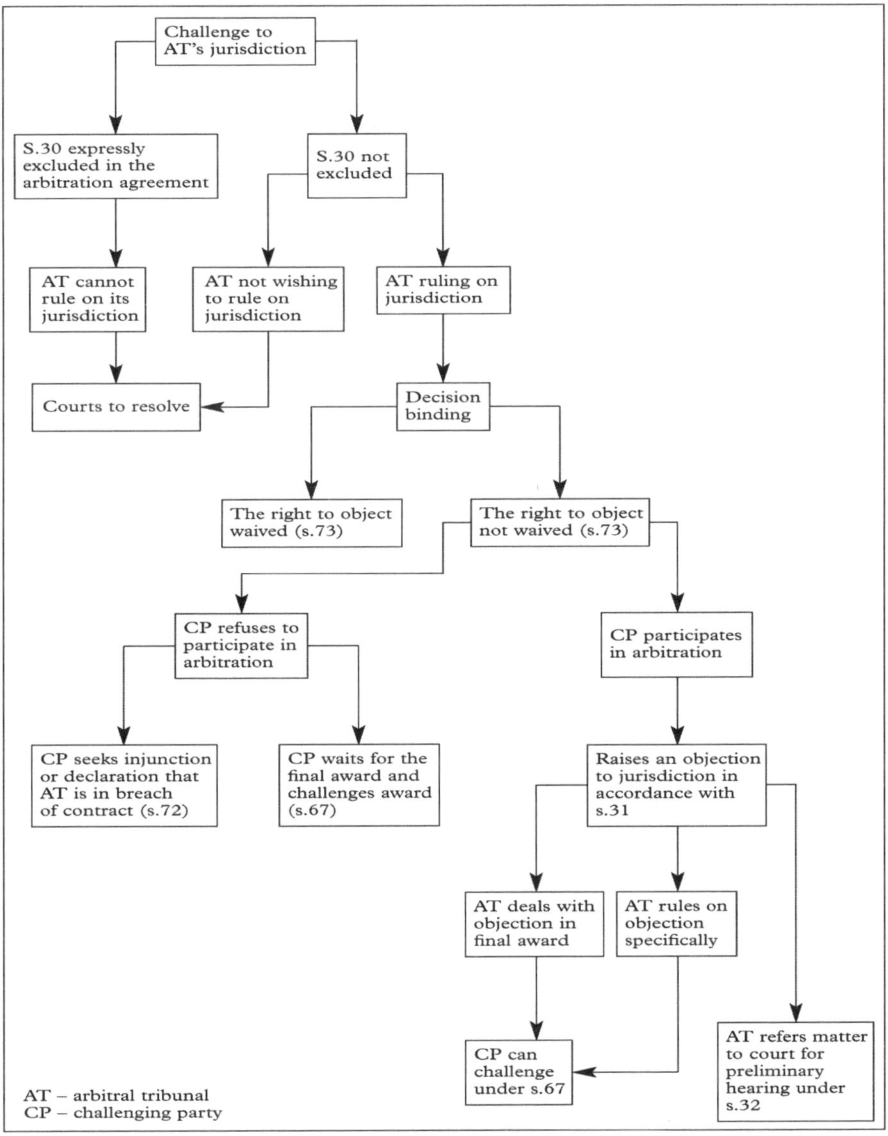

BIBLIOGRAPHY

The ARIAS Arbitration Rules, 2nd edn, 1997.
Barlow, Lyde & Gilbert International Risk Team, *Reinsurance Practice and the Law*, Informa, 2007.
Birds, John, *Modern Insurance Law*, 6th edn, Sweet & Maxwell, 2000.
Clarke, Malcolm, *Policies and Perceptions of Insurance: An Introduction to Insurance Law*, Clarendon Press (Oxford, 1997).
Clarke, Malcolm, *The Law of Insurance Contracts*, 3rd edn, LLP Ltd.
Gerathewohl, Klaus, *Reinsurance Principles and Practice*, Underwriter Printing & Pub Co., 1980.
Golding, C.E., *The Law and Practice of Reinsurance*, 5th edn, Witherby and Co., 1987.
Grossman, M., *Reinsurance—An Introduction*, The Institute of Insurance, University of St Gallen, 3rd edn, 1990.
Hansell, D.S., *Elements of Insurance*, 4th edn, Longman Publishing, 1985.
Kluwer's Insurance Contract Law, Kluwer (Kingston upon Thames, 2000).
Kluwer's Reinsurance Law, edited by John S. Butler and Robert Merkin, 1999 edn.
Legh-Jones, Nicholas (Gen. Ed.), *MacGillivray on Insurance Law*, 9th edn, Sweet and Maxwell (London, 1997).
Merkin, Robert, *Colinvaux's Law of Insurance*, 7th edn, Sweet & Maxwell (London, 1997).
Merkin, Robert, *Tolley's Insurance Handbook*, 2nd edn, Tolley Publishing Company Limited, 2004.
O'Neill, P.T. and Woloniecki, J.W., *The Law of Reinsurance*, 2nd edn, Sweet and Maxwell (London, 2004).
Park, Semin, *The Duty of Disclosure in Insurance Contract Law*, Dartmouth Publishing Company Limited, 1996.
Redfern & Hunter, *Law and Practice of International Commercial Arbitration*, 3rd edn, Sweet and Maxwell, 1999.

ANSWERS TO TEST YOUR UNDERSTANDING QUESTIONS

Chapter 1—The Nature of Reinsurance

1. Is the following statement true or false? "Insurance and reinsurance are fundamentally different in legal terms."
Answer: False. In "Common Law" countries around the world, reinsurance is generally seen as legally akin to insurance.

2. Which of the following most accurately describes Facultative Reinsurance?
Answer: (c) Facultative reinsurance is reinsurance that the reinsured can offer to reinsurers and reinsurers can accept.

3. Which of the following could be described as Proportional RI and which Non-Proportional?
Answer:
(a) Quota Share—Proportional
(b) Facultative Obligatory—Proportional
(c) Stop Loss—Non-Proportional
(d) Facultative—Could be both.

4. Which of the following is likely to be described as Obligatory Reinsurance?
Answer: (a) Surplus. Reinsured (normally) must cede, Reinsurer must accept.
Whereas (b) Risk X/L—Granting cover for a period for a price; (c) Stop Loss—Granting cover for a period for a price; (d) Facultative Obligatory—Reinsured does not have to cede, Reinsurer must accept.

5. Under Proportional Reinsurance which reflects the correct method of calculating a loss?
Answer: (d) Allocation of losses between reinsured and reinsurers is based on the allocation of the original risk—the percentage of any loss (and any premium) is calculated based on the allocation of the original risk. SI 100,000, Retain 40,000, Cede 60,000—Allocation 40%–60%.
Whereas (c) Allocation of losses between reinsured and reinsurers depends if the loss is large or small—more likely to reflect Non-Proportional.

6. Which of the following explains the correct workings of a 2nd Surplus Treaty?
Answer: (d) Reinsurers will receive a share of risks that are larger than the retention and cession to 1st Surplus. If the programme is based on

Surplus Treaties, all smaller risks which fall within the retention will be retained 100%—if the risk is larger than the retention the "surplus" will be ceded to the 1st Surplus until that is full, only then will a share of the risk (premium and any losses) be ceded to the 2nd Surplus.

7. Reinstatements—which of the following are true?
Answer: None of them.
(a) Reinstatements are common in all types of reinsurance—No. Normally only applies to Excess of Loss "Treaty"
(b) The term "1 reinstatement at 100%" means:
   (i) The reinsured can put in 1 claim in the year—No. The reinsured can reinstate up to 100% of the overall limit given (1 x the limit)
   (ii) The Reinstatement Premium will be 100% of what the reinsured paid for 12 months cover—No. 100% means that the date of loss will NOT be taken into account when calculating the premium due.

8. Which is the true explanation of the extended expiration clause?
Answer: (d) If a peril covered has started causing damage at the end of the contract period this clause confirms that the whole loss falls on the year the loss started in—subject to no loss from the same "happening" being claimed of any subsequent year as well.

9. Based on "market terminology" which of the following best reflects the term "Stop Loss"?
Answer: (c) A reinsurance protecting a portfolio of business that will pay if a loss in the year for all risks covered a loss ratio of X%—"Stop Loss" is normally used to describe this form of reinsurance where the Cover and Deductible are expressed as a % of retained premium—its more accurate name perhaps—"Excess of Loss Ratio Cover".
Whereas (a) A Facultative Reinsurance that will pay if an individual loss is larger than $?—This term normally would apply over a portfolio of business for a period of time.

10. Do the words "Terms; As original, and to follow settlements in all respects" mean that the following terms are likely to be automatically incorporated into a Reinsurance?
Answer:
(a) Original Premium—Yes
(b) Original deductions—Yes
(c) Arbitration—No
(d) Local Law—No
(e) Local Jurisdiction—No.
A wide range of court cases continue to insist that if the parties intend items such as (c), (d) and (e) to be reflected in the Reinsurance, this should be made specifically clear in the Reinsurance.

Chapter 2—Formation of Reinsurance Agreements

1. Which of the following elements determine whether a reinsurance company is carrying on business in the United Kingdom?
Answer:
(a) the place where the agreement is negotiated and made
(b) the place where the underwriting decision is taken
(d) the place where losses are paid.

2. Which of the following statements are true in relation to the authorisation requirement?
Answer:
(a) a reinsurer must be authorised to carry on insurance business in the U.K.
(b) a reinsurer must be authorised to carry on reinsurance business in the U.K.
(d) U.K. authorisation confers the right of direct sales elsewhere in the EEA.

3. Which of the following statements are correct?
Answer:
(a) an unauthorised insurer is always liable to its policy holders
(d) an unauthorised insurer who has to pay its policy holders is able to recover from its reinsurers in all circumstances.

4. Which of the following statements are correct?
Answer: (b) a subscription to a reinsurance slip is a contract of reinsurance.

5. Which of the following statements are correct?
Answer: (d) the broker can vary the subscribed percentages to an oversubscribed slip.

6. Which of the following statements are correct?
Answer:
(b) a contract of reinsurance made in advance of a contract of insurance is a unilateral contract
(d) a broker can face personal liability to reinsurers when placing reinsurance in advance of insurance.

7. Which of the following statements are correct?
Answer:
(b) policy wording is subject to the wording in the slip
(c) the following market can always avoid a subscription where false statements have been made to the leading underwriter
(d) the following market can always avoid a subscription for material non-disclosure to the leading underwriter.

8. Which of the following statements are correct?
Answer:
(a) a line slip constitutes an agency agreement between underwriters
(d) a leading underwriter clause is irrevocable.

9. In the *Sphere Drake* case, which of the following head of liability were faced by the underwriting agent?
Answer: All of them.
(a) breach of contract
(b) breach of duty of care
(c) breach of fiduciary duty
(d) conspiracy to injure.

10. Which of the following risks does the external reinsurance of the members of a reinsurance pool cover?
Answer:
(a) underwriting losses incurred by the pool's members
(b) extended liability in the event of the insolvency of a pool member
(c) breach of duty on the part of the underwriting agent.

11. Which of the following statements concerning the insurable interest of a reinsurer are true?
Answer:
(a) the reinsured's insurable interest is always in its liability
(c) the rules relating to insurable interest under the direct policy apply to reinsurance.

Chapter 3—Utmost Good Faith

1. Which of the following statements are correct?
Answer: (c) the reinsured must disclose all material facts which he knew or which he turned a blind eye to.

2. Which of the following statements are correct?
Answer: (a) any material false statement made by the reinsured is a breach of the duty of utmost good faith.

3. In which of the following circumstances is a fact material?
Answer: (a) it was regarded as material by the reinsurers involved.

4. Which of the following must be shown to give rise to inducement?
Answer:
(b) the reinsurers must show that the risk would on the balance of probabilities been written on different terms, or not at all, had full disclosure been made

(d) the reinsurers can rely upon the presumption of inducement only if they are unable to give their own evidence on inducement.

5. Which of the following facts are material for reinsurance purposes?
Answer:
(b) the reinsured's claims experience
(c) rumours that events giving rise to possible losses have occurred
(d) the dishonesty of the assured.

6. Which of the following statements are true?
Answer:
(a) a fact need not be disclosed if it was known to the reinsurers
(b) a fact need not be disclosed if it ought to have been known to the reinsurers in the ordinary course of their business.

7. Which of the following statements describes the reinsured's post-contractual duty of utmost good faith?
Answer:
(b) the reinsured is required to disclose facts after the contract has been entered into only if there is a contractual obligation to provide information
(c) the reinsurers may avoid the policy if there is a breach of the continuing duty.

8. Which of the following statements concerning the reinsurers' remedies for breach of the duty of utmost good faith are correct?
Answer: (a) the reinsurers can avoid the policy.

9. The reinsurers are entitled to avoid the contract for non-disclosure by the reinsured's brokers in which of the following circumstances?
Answer:
(a) the facts were not known to the broker but were known to the reinsured
(c) the facts were known to the reinsured's placing broker and were derived from his relationship with the reinsured
(d) the facts were known to the reinsured's placing broker but were derived from general market knowledge.

10. The reinsurers are free by contract term to waive their rights under the duty of utmost good faith in which of the following circumstances?
Answer:
(a) innocent or negligent failure by the reinsured to disclose material facts
(b) innocent or negligent failure by the reinsured's broker to disclose material facts.

Chapter 4—Terms of Reinsurance Agreements

1. Which of the following statements is true?
Answer:
(a) A term may be implied into a reinsurance agreement if the term is necessary to give business efficacy to the agreement
(c) A term may be implied into a reinsurance agreement if there is market evidence of a custom.

2. Which of the following statements is true in relation to the "full reinsurance clause"?
Answer: (c) The clause incorporates those terms of the direct policy which are germane to reinsurance.

3. Which of the following terms will generally be incorporated by a full reinsurance clause?
Answer:
(a) coverage clauses
(b) claims provisions
(c) warranties.

4. Where a term has been incorporated by a full reinsurance clause, which of the following effects may the term have in the reinsurance agreement?
Answer: Both.
(a) The incorporated term may operate as a provision which governs the contractual relationship between reinsured and reinsurer
(b) The incorporated term may operate as a statement of the contractual position as between the reinsured and the direct assured.

5. Which of the following conditions are necessary for the incorporation of an arbitration (or exclusive jurisdiction) clause into a reinsurance agreement?
Answer:
(b) The arbitration clause must be capable of "manipulation" so that it can be extended to reinsurance disputes.
(c) There must be an express reference to the arbitration clause in the incorporating words in the reinsurance agreement.

6. Where a warranty has been incorporated from a direct policy governed by a foreign law into a reinsurance agreement governed by English law, which of the following statements is true?
Answer: (b) The construction of the warranty is to be regarded as governed by the foreign law.

7. Which of the following statements relating to the principle of back to back cover are correct?
Answer:
(b) The principle of back to back cover applies only to proportional reinsurances

(d) The principle of back to back cover is a rebuttable rule of construction only.

Chapter 5—Rights and Obligations of the Parties

1. Which of the following statements accurately reflect the approach of the courts to the construction of reinsurance agreements?
Answer:
(c) The slip may be taken into account in construing the words of the policy
(d) The courts must take account of the market background against which the policy was written.

2. Which of the following statements is true?
Answer: (a) If the reinsured fails to comply with a condition precedent to the risk, the risk never attaches.

3. Which of the following statements is true?
Answer:
(a) If the reinsured fails to comply with a condition precedent to the reinsurers' liability, the reinsurers are not liable
(d) A condition precedent to liability may be created only by unequivocal wording.

4. Which of the following statements is true?
Answer:
(b) If the reinsured fails to comply with a bare condition, the insurers are able to treat the contract as repudiated if the condition is essential to the policy
(c) If the reinsured fails to comply with a bare condition, the insurers are able to treat the contract as repudiated if the breach is a serious one
(d) If the reinsured fails to comply with a bare condition the reinsurers may have the right to refuse to pay the claim but not to treat the policy as repudiated.

5. Which of the following statements are accurate in relation to warranties?
Answer: (b) Breach of warranty automatically terminates the risk.

6. Which of the following statements are true in relation to the payment of the premium under a reinsurance agreement?
Answer: (b) The amount of the premium may be varied during the course of a long-term agreement.

7. Which of the following statements are true in relation to inspection clauses:
Answer:

(b) An inspection clause can be exercised at any time and for any reason, subject to reasonable notice to the reinsured
(d) An inspection clause cannot be relied upon during proceedings if the reinsurers' purpose is to conduct a fishing expedition for possible defences.

Chapter 6—Follow the Settlements and Follow the Fortunes

1. Which of the following best describes the tension of reinsurance?
Answer: (c) The problem of ensuring that the reinsurer's agreement with the reinsured is not undermined by the actions of the reinsured and insured in an agreement over which the reinsurer may have no control.

2. Can a reinsurer refuse to pay a claim on the basis of breach of the following by the reinsured?
(a) The reinsured will underwrite sensibly—No
(b) The reinsured will take all proper and businesslike steps in settling a claim—Yes
(c) The reinsured has made a payment designated as "without prejudice"—No
(d) The claim does not fall within the reinsurance as a matter of law—Yes
(e) The reinsured has failed to comply with a standard claims control clause which is not a condition precedent—No
(f) The original claim is arguably not covered by the insurance—Yes.

3. Which of the following are true?
Answer:
(a) The parties are free to agree whatever they want in order to ascertain which losses will fall within the insurance and reinsurance, and this can include the insured's laundry bill—True.
See Lord Mustill in *Hill* v. *M & G*. But the wording must be sufficiently clear, and the courts have resiled from giving effect to the exercise of excessive discretion by one party.
(b) Each Follow the Settlements wording must always be considered independently by the courts, in the context of its factual background —True.
Lord Mustill again.
(c) Allowing the reinsured to determine what will be final and binding on the reinsurer is void because it ousts the jurisdiction of the courts—Untrue.
The courts still have jurisdiction over what is final and binding on the reinsurer because it will be determining the effect of clauses within the reinsurance contract.

(d) A decision made by a reinsured on what is covered as a matter of law can be reconsidered and overturned if it there is a subsequent court decision to the contrary—Untrue.

See *Caudle* v. *Sharp*.

(e) It is easier for a reinsurer to argue about claims under a back-to-back reinsurance than any other type—Untrue.

If the reinsured has acted honestly and in a businesslike manner and is arguably liable for the claim, the reinsurer must pay.

(f) In certain circumstances an obligation of a reinsurer to follow a specific claim that has been properly adjusted can be a debt and therefore easier to collect by the reinsured—Untrue.

A claim under a contract of reinsurance is technically a claim for damages in breach of the contract, which is one of indemnity. Even though the underlying settlement or award may have been properly quantified, it is not a debt.

(g) The reinsured can never obtain payment for costs which with the claim exceed the limit of the reinsurance contract—Untrue.

The caselaw is incomplete. In the absence of an express term the reinsured is not entitled to costs of the original claim, and certainly not if the claim with the costs exceeds the limit of indemnity. See *ICA* v. *SCOR*. But it is still open to a reinsured to prove that there is a custom enabling him to recover his costs. He may also try to use s. 51 of the Supreme Court Act 1981, or *Gan* v. *Tai Ping* where the reinsurer has acted in bad faith.

(h) A standard claims control clause can be exercised by the reinsurer in any way he sees fit—Untrue.

A claims control clause may be of little effect if it is not expressed to be a condition precedent. Where it is a condition precedent the reinsurer is in a strong position but must nevertheless abide by some standard of reasonableness, at least not to act in bad faith, following *Gan* v. *Tai Ping*.

(i) A commutation by a reinsurer of all his liabilities and potential liabilities must be followed by his retrocessionaire if the commutation is reasonable—Untrue.

A commutation by a reinsured or reinsurer of its liabilities does not necessary fall within the definition of loss settlement and although reasonable may enable the reinsurer or retrocessionnaire not to pay.

(j) Interest is payable by the reinsure from the date on which the reinsured pays the original claim—Untrue.

Interest is not payable unless there is an operative contractual provision or legal proceedings are instituted before the principal sum is paid to the reinsured, following which interest can be awarded by the court or tribunal in its discretion.

(k) A cut though clause is perfectly enforceable under English law at all times, so that an insured can bypass the insurer and obtain payment from the reinsurer—Untrue.

A cut through clause is enforceable against a reinsurer by an insured under the Contracts (Rights of Third Parties) Act 1999 unless an insolvency has occurred, so that the pari passu rule will apply to give all creditors equal rights.

(l) A judgment of a foreign court against the reinsured is an unimpeachable adjustment of the loss which the reinsurer must follow—Untrue.

A judgement of the foreign court is not unimpeachable because it may be perverse, the court may not have had jurisdiction, another court may have had jurisdiction, or the reinsured may not have taken all proper defences. See *Commercial Union* v. *NRG Victory*.

(m) A reinsured must be paid in full for any loss substantiated by a report of a well-known loss adjuster—True.

Provided there are no obvious discrepancies on the face of the report, in which case the reinsured will not be able to an indemnity for the settlement from the reinsurer.

(n) The parties can agree any rate of interest applicable to claims paid late by the reinsurer—True.

The parties can agree anything they want.

Chapter 7—Claims

1. Fill in the blanks to state how a typical claims cooperation clause might read:

"Notwithstanding anything contained herein to the contrary, it is a **condition precedent** to any liability under this policy that:

(1) the Reinsured shall upon **knowledge** of any loss(es) and occurrence(s) which may give rise to a claim recoverable hereunder advise the Reinsurers thereof as soon as reasonably practicable.

(2) the Reinsured shall furnish the Reinsurers with all information available respecting such loss(es) or occurrence(s) and shall co-operate with the Reinsurers in the **adjustment** and **settlement** thereof."

2. In a claims control clause notification of a loss or an occurrence, which may give rise to a claim, should be advised:

Answer: (d) Immediately.

3. Which of the following will not stop the limitation period from running?

Answer: (d) An honourable engagement clause.

(See page 20. *Orion Compagnia Espanola de Seguros* v. *Belfort Maatschppij Voor Versekgringeen* [1962] 2 Lloyd's Rep. 257.)

4. According to the Law Commission's proposed changes to limitation periods, how long would the Reinsured have in which to bring a claim against his Reinsurers?

Answer: (b) Three years.

5. If an insured grossly exaggerates a "substantial part" of the claim, this would appear to permit the Insurer to:
Answer: (c) to avoid the entire claim.
(See page 25. *Direct Line Insurance Plc* v. *Khan* [2002] Lloyd's Rep. IR 634.)

6. When does the duty of utmost good faith come to an end?
Answer: (c) when the Insurer rejects the claim.
(See page 26. *Manifest Shipping Company Ltd* v. *Uni-Polaris Insurance Company Ltd (The Star Sea)* (1995) 1 Lloyd's Rep. 65.)

7. If a Reinsurer suspects that there has been misrepresentation on the part of the Reinsured, what should the Reinsurer do first in order to protect his legal position?
Answer: (b) express a full, written reservation of rights to the Reinsured.
(See page 31. It is important that if the Reinsurer suspects misrepresentation or fraud that he immediately reserves his rights under the contract (before obtaining more information, before instructing outside counsel, and certainly before inspecting the Reinsured's records (*Iron Trades Insurance* v. *Compagnhia de Seguros Imperio* [1991] 1 Re. L.R. 213) since otherwise the contract may be treated as affirmed and the Reinsurer may be stopped from raising the misrepresentation issue.)

8. The purpose of an honourable engagement clause is to:
Answer: (a) permit any disputes between the parties to be determined by arbitrators whose decision will not be in accordance with the strict rules of law.

9. According to the ARIAS Rules, the general rule for the Tribunal is that there should be:
Answer: (c) Three arbitrators, each with 10—years professional experience.

Chapter 8—Intermediaries

1. Does it matter to the enforceability of a contract by the reinsurer that the reinsured limited the actual authority of his broker in a material way?
Answer: No, unless the reinsurer is aware of the limitation placed on the actual authority of the broker. The key element is the apparent authority of the broker, namely what the reinsurer properly understands the broker's authority to be as a result of representations made by the reinsured.

2. Is the broker usually the agent of both reinsured and reinsurer?

Answer: No. The broker is usually the agent of the reinsured.

3. What is the effect of the liquidation of the reinsured on a reinsurance contract concluded after that liquidation, and are there any remedies available to the reinsurer against the reinsured or its broker?
Answer: The principal for whom the broker is trying to place reinsurance can only act through its liquidator, so that the broker will in the absence of instructions from the liquidator be in breach of his warranty of authority. The broker will be liable for any loss caused, which will probably be limited to the premium that the reinsurer would have been paid had the broker been properly authorised by the reinsured.

4. Does the ratification by the reinsured of the contract placed by the broker in excess of hisauthority automatically exonerate the broker from acting unlawfully?
Answer: No. It will always depend on the circumstances.
(See *Suncorp* v. *Milano* and *NIGC* v. *Imperio.*)

5. What is an "agent to insure"?
Answer: An agent to insure is the party placing the insurance, rather than an agent to inform or an agent to know or an agent with no substantive role to play. An agent to insure is subject to s. 19 of the Marine Insurance Act.

6. Can a broker ever be liable for non-disclosure or misrepresentation to the reinsurer?
Answer: Perhaps. It is unlikely but could occur where the broker has assumed a responsibility or liability to the reinsurer such that the non-disclosure or misrepresentation is not made or not made on behalf of the reinsured but rather exclusively by the broker, and for which he alone is responsible.

7. Would a material fact of the reinsured known by the postboy of the broker be attributed to the reinsured and therefore be disclosable to the reinsurer?
Answer: No. A postboy is not an agent to insure and his knowledge is not sufficiently substantive to make it the same as the reinsured.

8. Does the fraud of the broker upon the reinsured, which impacts on the reinsurance, have any effect on the validity of the reinsurance?
Answer: No. Where the fraud is that of the broker against the reinsured.

9. What steps should a broker take to ensure that he is not responsible for the collection of claims many years after placement?
Answer: A broker is responsible for the collection of claims unless he has been paid on a fee basis only for placement. A broker should

ensure that the position is clear as a matter of contract at the outset, and if it is not clear then he will generally be responsible for claims.

10. What should a broker do when faced with an ambiguity in his instructions?
Answer: He should take instructions from the reinsured.

11. Should a broker accept his instructions at face value or should he check that they reflect the actual needs of the reinsured?
Answer: He should act professionally to ensure that the instructions received accurately reflect the needs of the reinsured where there is the slightest doubt that they may be wrong.

12. Should a broker convey to the reinsured every doubt that he may have about the intended security of the reinsurer, or should he make an overall decision as to its solvency?
Answer: A broker should only convey substantive doubts about any aspect of the security of a reinsurer, rather than every item, however small. In essence his security committee should make an overall judgement as to the security of a reinsurer; if there is any aspect of which it is doubtful, and that aspect is relevant or substantive such that it constitutes a genuine doubt about that security, then the security should not be used and if the reinsured wishes to use it the broker should make its doubts very clear.

13. How much reinsurance law should a broker know?
Answer: Enough! The broker should understand the general principles of the law relevant to the contract of reinsurance which he is placing, including those principles relevant to the underlying insurance which might impact on the reinsurance. He should also understand the relevant principles of drafting and interpreting the wording.

14. For what purpose does a broker receive payment, and by whom?
Answer: The broker in placing insurance is actually paid by the reinsurer for the introduction of the business. Nevertheless, he owes more duties to the reinsured than the reinsurer, and he is only allowed to accept the payment from the reinsurer because the reinsured has impliedly consented to his remuneration being taken out of the premium.

15. What is the maximum period within which legal proceedings should be comenced for a broker who has failed to pass on all material information, which has resulted in avoidance of the contract by the reinsurer?
Answer: The Latent Damage Act has a long-stop of 15 years from the date of the actual negligence of the broker. In the absence of concealment, however, the usual limit is six years.

Chapter 9—Jurisdiction

1. Why is the forum in which a dispute is heard important?

Answer:

(a) It may affect whether any judgment is enforceable against the defendant

(b) The judiciary may be more experienced in one forum than another

(d) It may have practical consequences for the attendance of witnesses and the gathering of evidence

(e) It may affect the speed at which the proceedings can be pursued.

2. Which of the following lay down rules on jurisdiction which may be applied by the English courts?

Answer:

(a) Common law

(b) Brussels Convention

(c) Lugano Convention

(e) Brussels Regulation.

3. A jurisdiction clause provides "The Reinsurer may bring proceedings against the Cedant in any forum including, without limitation, the courts of England and Wales." This clause is:

Answer: (b) A non-exclusive jurisdiction clause.

4. Under the common law rules, which one of the following is not a ground for the English courts to accept jurisdiction against a defendant?

Answer: (e) The claimant is present in England.

5. In addition to establishing that one or more of the above criteria applies, what else does a claimant have to demonstrate in order to persuade the English court to accept jurisdiction under the common law rules?

Answer:

(a) There is a reasonable prospect of the claim proceeding (a serious issue to be tried)

(d) England is the most appropriate forum for the dispute to be heard in (*forum conveniens*).

6. Under the common law rules, what approach do the English courts take where a contract contains a jurisdiction clause in favour of the English courts?

Answer: (b) The English court may accept jurisdiction. It will weigh up all the factors. The jurisdiction clause will be a very strong factor in favour of accepting jurisdiction.

7. Under the Conventions/Regulation, where can a claimant sue a defendant?
Answer:
(a) The defendant's country of domicile
(b) The place where the contractual obligation in question was due to be performed
(c) The place where the tort was committed (where the dispute relates to a tort)
(e) The place where the defendant has a branch or agency (if the dispute arises out of the branch or agency)
(g) Where related proceedings have been brought against another defendant.

8. Which of the following sources are used by the English court to determine the law which governs a reinsurance contract made in 2004?
Answer: (d) Rome Convention.

9. When may the English court refuse to uphold a choice of law?
Answer: (c) Where it would be contrary to English public policy to uphold the choice of law, because the choice is made to evade a rule of law.

10. Where the parties to a contract have made no express or implied choice of law, the courts seek to ascertain either the system of law (common law rules) or the country (Convention) with which the contract is most closely connected. How do the courts do this?
Answer: (a) The common law weighs up all the factors and looks to the "centre of gravity" of the transaction. The Rome Convention rebuttably presumes that the applicable law is the law of the reinsurer's head office.

Chapter 10—Arbitration

1. Which of the following arbitral institutions tends to be used in reinsurance arbitrations?
Answer: (c) LCIA.

2. Which of the following are not considered to be an advantage when using arbitration?
Answer: (d) Limited availability of summary judgment.

3. Which of the following statements is incorrect?
Answer: (b) The Arbitration Act 1996 applies to oral agreements to arbitrate.

4. An arbitration clause containing the wording "all claims, disputes and controversies arising out of or in connection with the contract" will not necessarily include disputes relating to which type of claim?

Answer: (d) The legality of the underlying contract.

5. Which of the following areas is not regulated by the Arbitration Act 1996?
Answer: (a) Confidentiality in arbitrations.

6. Which of the following statements is correct?
Answer: (d) Arbitration proceedings between the original assured, insurer and reinsurer can be consolidated with the consent of all the parties.

7. Which of the following are arbitrators empowered to order?
Answer: (a) Compound interest.

8. Which of the following statements is incorrect in relation to arbitration proceedings subject to the Arbitration Act 1996?
Answer: (c) A party can appeal the decision of an arbitral tribunal on a finding of fact.

9. Arbitration awards can be enforced under which of the following Convention procedures?
Answer: (d) The New York Convention.